The Federal Future of Europe

To David Calleo, with the expression of my gratitude for his warm welcome and my hopes concerning

The Federal Future of Europe

From the European Community to the European Union

Warmest wishes, Dusan S.

Dusan Sidjanski

Geneva, 21 May 2008.

Ann Arbor

THE UNIVERSITY OF MICHIGAN PRESS

English translation copyright © by the University of Michigan 2000
Originally published in French as *L'avenir féderaliste de l'Europe*
© by Presses Universitaires de France, 1992.
All rights reserved
Published in the United States of America by
The University of Michigan Press
Manufactured in the United States of America
⊚ Printed on acid-free paper

2003 2002 2001 2000   4 3 2

The author is grateful to the Latsis Foundation for its constant
support and to the University of Michigan Press, who together
have made the publication of this book possible.

A CIP catalog record for this book is available from the British Library.

Library of Congress Cataloging-in-Publication Data

Sidjanski, Dusan.
    [Avenir fédéraliste de l'Europe. English]
    The federal future of Europe : from the European Community to the
European Union / Dusan Sidjanski.
        p.   cm.
    Includes bibliographical references and index.
    ISBN 0-472-11075-6 (cloth : alk. paper)
    1. European federation — History.   2. Federal government — Europe —
History.   3. Europe — Economic integration — History.   4. European Union.

JN15 .S456 2000
320.94 — dc21   00-033801

To the memory of my mother, Masha
To Clarina
and to Sacha, Antoine, and Patrick

Contents

Jacques Delors

Introductory Note

It is with great pleasure that I pay tribute to the English edition of Professor Dusan Sidjanski's *The Federal Future of Europe*. As Professor Harold Jacobson rightly says in his foreword, this work fills a gap in the literature, since Anglo-Saxon studies tend to underplay the federal approach to European integration. Furthermore, this English edition is the most up-to-date publication of a book that during the past decade has become a classic in European analysis.

Federal thinking has been implicit throughout the history of European integration. Overtly present at the outset, sometimes muted or even running underground at times, the logic of federalism has in fact been present at all the main stages of European integration. One can trace it all the way from the Spinelli Report, which relaunched the integration process in the early 1980s, to a great many of the political programs put forward during the elections to the European Parliament in 1999.

This federal thinking has a singular relationship with the neofunctionalist approaches, which are more familiar to the Anglo-Saxon reader. It is a kind of historical and dialectical process during which the failures of each of them contributed in turn to the successes of the other, a process which is probably far from over. Thus the original failure to achieve political integration outright in the early 1950s led to the Monnet-Schuman functional approach epitomized in the Treaty of Rome. Similarly, the relative failure of this approach — integration "spillovers" occurred at an economic level but went nowhere on a political level — led, ultimately, to the political developments of the Single Act and the Treaties of Maastricht and Amsterdam.

Today the European Union must grapple with the conceptual problems of enlargement, a challenge that surpasses all previous experience. Our only certainty is that Europe, in its perpetual evolution, cannot rely on a preexisting road map or on some historical model to guide us in this new adventure. We are breaking new ground. Dusan Sidjanski's particularly opportune analysis in the framework of European federalism casts a clear light on one of the deepest and most permanent mainsprings of European action.

This work is all the more welcome in that it does not just retrace the history of European integration in light of the theory of federalism but also provides a critical assessment of what the author calls "European federalsm." I would not go so far as to say that every episode, every twist and turn in the story of Europe could be explained exclusively by this theory. However, if this analysis is not the only possible interpretation, it is certainly one of the most illuminating and enriching analyses of the future of Europe, a future which will doubtless be both difficult and exciting.

I wish English-speaking readers of this new edition, which is now at last at their disposal, the pleasure of discovering this major work in European integration.

Harold K. Jacobson

Foreword

T*he Federal Future of Europe: From the European Community to the European Union* is a marvelous addition to the English literature on the European Union. This insightful and powerful book has been available in its original French and in other languages since the early 1990s but not in English. Here finally is an English edition. This English edition, however, is more than a translation of a previously published book. This version brings the story up to date and adds new evaluations and recommendations. It is in many ways a new book.

The Federal Future of Europe is a book of profound scholarship. It is an unparalleled history and analysis of the evolution of the European Union. It analyzes changes in civil society as well as in state behavior and institutional structures. It is informed by, but not beholden to, American scholarship on international relations and comparative politics broadly and on the European Union in particular. It introduces European scholarship, particularly the work of Denis de Rougemont, that is seldom considered by English-speaking scholars.

The Federal Future of Europe is also — perhaps even more so — a book of advocacy. Dusan Sidjanski is a deeply committed federalist. His book makes a powerful case for a federal future for Europe. He believes that only through the creation of a federation can Europe overcome the national and ethnic divisions that have caused such great catastrophes in the twentieth century. The blending of scholarship and advocacy makes this a very special book. Since May 1950, when Robert Schuman proposed that Germany and France merge their coal and steel industries, English speakers have followed the process of European integration closely. Americans particularly have sought theoretical constructs to provide a framework for analyzing the process.

Ernst B. Haas, drawing from the tactics employed by Jean Monnet, developed the theory of neofunctionalsim in his masterful *The Uniting of Europe* (1958). According to Haas the key to the process of European integration was the expansive logic of sectoral integration: technology and the expanding size of economic activity would lead to integration in one sector; integration in one sector would create pressures that would "spill over" and force integration in other sectors; the process would be led and shaped by supranational actors. For many years, neofunctionalism was the favored American explanation for the process of European integration. Federalism was the eventual outcome envisaged by Monnet and by many neofunctionalists, but in neofunctionalism federalism was achieved almost by stealth. Moreover, not all neofunctionalists have been explicit about the eventual outcome that they envisioned for European integration.

More recently American analysts of European integration have been divided between those who continue in the tradition of neofunctionalism to emphasize the role of supranational actors and those who argue that the governments of major states are principally responsible for driving and shaping the process. Andrew Moravcsik argues the latter case forcefully in his *The Choice for Europe* (1998). For Moravcsik the driving forces are commercial advantage, the relative bargaining power of governments, and interstate bargaining. Moravcsik and others of his persuasion note the transfer of sovereign power from the member states to European institutions and argue that this will endure, but they draw back from predicting a federal future for Europe.

The federalist position has generally been left out of analyses of European integration written by English-speaking authors. Curiously, given the United States' own proud history of federalism, Americans have particularly ignored the federalist position. The English version of *The Federal Future of Europe* fills a major gap in the literature. It will stand with Haas's and Moravcsik's works as a seminal statement about Europe. Sidjanski clearly articulates the federalist position. He makes clear how deep the historical roots of European federalism are and he shows how strongly committed contemporary leaders are to the concept and how much it has affected European civil society.

American social scientists will be intrigued by *The Federal Future of Europe*. We are not used to reading books that are both profound works of scholarship and powerful statements of advocacy. *The Federalist* was in this tradition, as was Woodrow Wilson's *Congressional Government,* but in the second half of the twentieth century social scientists have rarely written such books. Because the effective linking of advocacy and scholarship is so rare, *The Federal Future of Europe* is a treat to be savored.

Its message must be pondered. The future of Europe is one of the great questions of contemporary life. Is European integration a process that will resemble in historical retrospect the unification of Germany and Italy in the nineteenth century? Or will it create new forms of political authority, as in the seventeenth century when, through the Peace of Westphalia and subsequent developments, the sovereign territorially defined state emerged as the dominant form? Sidjanski makes a powerful case for a federated Europe as both the most desirable and the most likely outcome. Whether or not one agrees, his argument must be considered and addressed. The publication of the English version of Sidjanski's book will help make this argument a vital part of the academic and popular debate about the future of Europe.

Sidjanski's book reflects his life. Born in Yugoslavia, he emigrated and eventually settled in Switzerland and became a Swiss citizen. His professional career was spent in Switzerland, where he became a professor of political science and founder of the department of political science at the University of Geneva. He was one of the first Swiss political scientists to employ modern analytical techniques, and he modernized and strengthened the University of Geneva's political science department. As a Yugoslav, he knows the terrible consequences of ethnic conflict. As a Swiss citizen, he knows the benefits and operating principles and practices of federalism.

The Federal Future of Europe was written with insight, knowledge, and passion. Readers will be informed and moved. I strongly commend it to everyone interested in Europe and to those more broadly interested in contemporary international affairs.

Preface

The path toward a European Union has been mainly guided by two models. Jean Monnet's functional approach, aimed at building the United States of Europe, was inspired by the United States of America. Denis de Rougemont's global federalist approach was based on European culture and its diversity, bearing the stamp of Swiss experience. Both models, however, aimed at creating a European federation, albeit by different means.

For centuries, the concept of a united Europe was outlined in various utopian ideas and projects before taking shape in concrete political action, starting with the creation of the Pan-European Movement by Coudenhove-Kalergi in 1924. After this, the first official project was proposed by Aristide Briand, a free trade approach. Today the argument still seems to be valid despite the United Kingdom's full membership in the European Union (EU) since 1973.

After World War II, the United States fully supported reconstruction in Europe as well as the movement in favor of European integration. The Marshall Plan was an extraordinary initiative, which provided massive aid to Western European countries through the Organization for European Economic Cooperation (OEEC). It implied multinational cooperation, the elimination of quantitative restrictions, and the establishment of the European Payments Union. In this way, the American government built the basis for European integration, the creation of the European Coal and Steel Community, and the European Economic Community. At the same time, Americans, many of whom were friends of Jean Monnet, supported the European Movement, which vigorously promoted the idea of a United Europe from below. The origins of European citizenship and identity that today constitute one of the aims of the European Union are to be found here.

Two testimonies reflect the ambivalence of American policy toward the European Union. On the one hand, in January 1956 John Foster Dulles summed up the essential problems in Europe from the American point of view:

The problem of tying Germany organically into the Western Community to diminish the danger that over time a resurgent German nationalism might trade neutrality for reunification with a view to seizing a controlling position between East and West.

The weakness of France and the need to provide it with a positive alternative to neutralism and defeatism.

The consolidation of a new relationship between France and Germany, which has been developing since 1950 through the movement toward integration.[1]

The continuously supportive policy of successive U.S. presidents and administrations corresponds to a global political vision and is still in force notwithstanding sectoral conflicts of interest or opinions. Many examples illustrate this ambiguity: the chicken and soya wars, the contrasting positions during the Uruguay Round and in the World Trade Organization regarding public subventions, civil aviation, services, and culture, in particular, as well as the question of the extraterritorial enforcement of American law.

Slightly differing convergent policies were enforced during the Gulf War under American leadership. Later, the Yugoslavia crisis compelled the Western allies to act together and also revealed divergences, mainly due to national constraints and political and economic contingencies.

In short, it could be argued that there are two main dimensions in the pattern of U.S.-EU relations. The economic dimension includes not only the benefit of having a solid and dynamic partner with a large and open market but also the fear of having to face a powerful competitor or even a challenger in the political and security fields represented mainly by NATO and American leadership. The United States and the EU are facing the dilemma of American domination versus American-European partnership with a greater or lesser degree of EU autonomy. In 1962, President Kennedy proposed an Atlantic partnership between the new European and the old American Unions. This plan, designed by the young visionary president and based on a concept of Atlantic economic interdependence and common values, was partially applied to economic relations.

In contrast, dependency is still the prevailing relationship in the security field. It has become even more apparent since the communist threat vanished, leaving the United States as the only superpower. Faced today with the threat of new nationalism, civil war, and intra-European conflicts, the EU, with U.S. support, is trying to build a strong European pillar within NATO. This involves attributing an effective autonomous and operational capacity to the Western European Union (WEU), which represents the military arm of the EU. This means both increased autonomy and a greater burden and responsibility for the European partner. It is the precondition for effective common foreign and security policy in the EU and for more evenly balanced relations between the United States and the EU. It could also open a perspective for a new security system in Europe with the participation of Russia and the Central and Eastern European countries.

This is one of the problems underlining the complexity of interrelated issues facing Europeans: how to strengthen the Union, achieve economic and monetary union, stimulate growth and employment, establish an effective common foreign and security policy, create a system of common defense, and at the same time enlarge the Union. There are also questions of how to respond to the challenge of democratization in the EU, reinforce European citizenship and solidarity between states and regions, promote high technology, and support common research programs in order to restore competitive capacity and the influence of the EU in world politics. The demands and needs of these different fields, in combination with ideas and projects as they are perceived and conveyed by political elites and socioeconomic factors, are contributing to new and continuous creativity in the European Community and Union. This original organization, sui generis, includes diverse institutions and practices belonging to federal, confederate, and intergovernmental experiences and structures. It also augurs the concept of neofederalism, which transcends purely process and organizational approaches to combine basic democratic and federalist values with high technology in communications and management. This will make it possible to manage the complexity of Europe as well as preserving a rich diversity inside the Union.

At this point, I would like to yield the floor to Professor Lester Thurow, dean of the Sloan School at MIT. In the conclusion of his book *Head to Head,* he provided the following forecast.

While having been the slowest mover in the 1980s, Europe starts the 1990s with the strongest strategic position on the world economic chess board. If it makes the right moves, it can become the dominant economic power in the twenty-first century, regardless of what Japan and the United States do. In this case the right moves are easy to see but very difficult to make. If Europe can truly integrate the EEC (337 million people) into one economy and gradually move to absorb the rest of Europe (more than 500 million people) into the House of Europe, it can put together an economy that no one else can match. If the high science of the former Soviet Union and the production technologies of the German speaking world are added to the design flair of Italy and France and a world class London capital market efficiency directing funds to Europe's most productive areas, something unmatchable will have been created. The House of Europe could become a relatively self-contained, rapidly growing region that could sprint away from the rest of the pack.

Since European countries represent both the communitarian and the individualistic strains in capitalism, the compromises necessary for the integration of Europe could lead to a mix and match of the best strains of both. The Europeans don't have to adopt foreign — American or Japanese — ideologies.

The Europeans also have the advantage of getting to write the trading rules for the twenty-first century. Those who write the rules will not surprisingly write rules that favor those who play the game the European way.

The right moves involve two major problems. The economies of Western Europe really have to integrate, and that integration has to be quickly extended to Middle and Eastern Europe. The former communist economies of Middle and Eastern Europe have to become successful market economies. Neither is an easy task. Western Europe will have to be willing to give large amounts of economic aid to Middle and Eastern Europe in order to get capitalism started. Ancient border and ethnic rivalries in both Eastern and Western Europe will have to be put aside. The English and the Germans will both have to become Europeans.[2]

This statement coincides with my personal view and could have been perfectly placed as the conclusion of this book. Nevertheless, the main difference concerns the role of economic and political variables. While Lester Thurow focuses his analysis principally on economic factors, my approach is more global and political. In the first case, political variables are among the preconditions for Europe's economic capacity and competitiveness, while from the political perspective ideologies, basic culture and values, and normative functioning through institutional frameworks and decision-making processes are the principal components of political power, which interacts with economic and social power. In both cases, the general environment, the major official and unofficial actors, and mainstream events play a central role.

This book presents an extraordinary case of traditional enemies becoming close friends and forming the dynamic core of the European Community and the European Union, the Franco-German alliance. This emergent system, based on a voluntary association of democratic states, has made an exceptional contribution to peace in Western Europe for the first time in history.

This fresh experience not only conveys a strong message to the people and countries of Central and Eastern Europe, but it also affects regional integration elsewhere. It is a particularly concrete response to explosive nationalist and ethnic movements, promoting a model that conciliates opposing trends: globalization as well as the quest for national, ethnic, regional, and local identity. Based on principles of democracy and federalism, the European Union aims to create synergy between those two powerful streams in a huge, pluralistic Europe. At the same time, the reemergence of a dynamic Europe signals its return to the world scene in close collaboration with the United States, in partnership with Russia, and in negotiations with Japan and China. In realizing its aims, the European Union will be capable of reassuming its role in world affairs.

This English translation is in some respects a new book. While initially based on the original work in French, first published by Presses Universitaires de France in 1992 and 1993, this new edition not only has been revised but contains three supplementary chapters. All in all, it aims to take account of the many changes that, at the regional or global level, have had an impact on Europe's future.

NOTES

1. FRUS, *Western European Security and Integration,* vol. 4 (1955–57), 399–400.
2. Lester Thurow, *Head to Head: The Coming Economic Battles among Japan, Europe, and America* (London: Nicholas Brealy Publishing), 251–53.

Acknowledgments

I would like to thank Dr. Cyprian Blamires, who made the first translation into English, as well as Malcolm and Thomas Bain who completed it with Richard A. Dunkley. I am indebted to Maximos Alighisakis, Tilla Kohler, and particularly to Thérèse Rolle, my personal assistant, who helped me to prepare this new edition. Special thanks are due to Jeffrey Sacks in Geneva, who cheerfully and bravely undertook a complete and thorough revision and edited the entire text. Without his contribution, the English edition would not have been ready for publication. Claus Hässig compiled the index and Chamouni Stone helped me in reading the proofs.

I am also indebed to my students and colleagues who motivated me and particularly to the late Professor Karl W. Deutsch as well as to Professors Victoria Curzon Price and Charles Méla with whom we strived to reactivate the Graduate Institute of European Studies originally created by Denis de Rougemont.

I am especially grateful to my friends at the University of Michigan: Professors Harold Jacobson, Roland Inglehart, and Kenneth Organski, with whom I have enjoyed a long, fruitful, and friendly collaboration since 1970. During my first stay in Ann Arbor, I was introduced to quantitative methods while doing research at the prestigious Center for Political Studies of the Institute for Social Research. Since then our collaboration has resulted in several joint works and publications and has now led to the publication of this book by the University of Michigan Press. It is my pleasure to thank its director, Colin Day, his assistant Heather Lengyel, and copyediting coordinators Alja Kooistra and Jennifer Wisinski for their efficient cooperation.

Once more, I seize the opportunity to express my gratitude to the LATSIS Foundation for its constant support.

Abbreviations

ACP African, Caribbean, and Pacific countries, parties to the Lomé Convention

BCC Business Cooperation Center

BEUC European Bureau of Consumers' Unions

CAP Common Agricultural Policy

CCEE Countries of Central and Eastern Europe

CEEP European Center of Public Enterprises (also ECPE)

CFSP Common Foreign and Security Policy

CGT Confédération générale du travail (General Trade Union Confederation); has close ties to the French Communist Party

CNPF French National Council of Employers

CIS Commonwealth of Independent States

COCCEE Committee of Commercial Organizations in the EC

COGECA General Committee for Agricultural Cooperation

Comett Community Action Programme in Education and Training for Technology

COPA Committee of Professional Agricultural Organizations in the EC

Coreper Committee of Permanent Representatives

CSF community support framework (Structural Funds)

CR Committee of the Regions

EAGGF European Agricultural Guidance and Guarantee Fund

EBRD European Bank for Reconstruction and Development

EC European Communities or European Community

ECB European Central Bank

ECE United Nations Economic Commission for Europe

ECU European currency unit

EDC European Defence Community

EDF European Development Fund

EEA European Economic Area

EEA European Environmental Agency

EEB European Environmental Bureau

EEIG European Economic Interest Grouping

EFTA European Free Trade Association

EIB European Investment Bank

EIF European Investment Fund

EMI European Monetary Institute

EMS European Monetary System

EMU Economic and Monetary Union

Erasmus European Community Action Scheme for the Mobility of University Students

ERDF European Regional Development Fund

ESA European Space Agency

ESC Economic and Social Committee

ESF European Social Fund

ETUC European Trade Union Confederation

EU European Union

EUR-OP Office for Official Publications of the European Communities

Europol European Police Office

Eurostat Statistical Office of the European Communities

Eurotecnet Community Action Programme in the Field of Training and Technological Change

FAO Food and Agriculture Organization of the United Nations

FNSEA French National Federation of Farmers

FRY Federal Republic of Yugoslavia

FYROM Former Yugoslav Republic of Macedonia

GATT General Agreement on Tariffs and Trade

GDP gross domestic product

GNP gross national product

IBRD International Bank for Reconstruction and Development (World Bank/UN)

ICCTU International Confederation of Christian Trade Unions

ICFTU International Confederation of Free Trade Unions

IFOR Implementation Force (NATO, Dayton Agreement)

IGC Intergovernmental Conference

ILO International Labor Organization

IMF International Monetary Fund

INTAS International Association for the Promotion of Cooperation with Scientists from the

Newly Independent
States of the Former
Soviet Union

KFOR Implementation Force
in Kosovo

Mercosur Southern Cone
Common Market

NATO North Atlantic Treaty
Organization

NGO nongovernmental
organization

NIS Newly Independent
States (of the former
Soviet Union)

NPA New Partnership
Approach

OECD Organization for
Economic
Cooperation and
Development

OSCE Organization for
Security and
Cooperation in
Europe

PHARE Programme of
Community Aid for
Central and Eastern
European Countries

PLO Palestine Liberation
Organization

RTD Research and
Technological
Development

SEA Single European Act

SMEs small and medium-
sized enterprises

Stabex system for the
stabilization of export
earnings

Sysmin system for the
stablization of export
earnings from mining
products

TACIS Programme for

Technical Assistance
to the Independent
States of the Former
Soviet Union and
Mongolia

TEDIS Trade Electronic Data
Interchange Systems

Tempus trans-European
mobility scheme for
university studies

TENs trans-European
networks

UN United Nations

UNCED United Nations
Conference on
Environment and
Development

UNCTAD United Nations
Conference on Trade
and Development

UNESCO United Nations
Educational,
Scientific, and Cultural
Organization

UNHCR/HCR United Nations High
Commissioner for
Refugees

UNICE Union of Industries of
the EC (today, the
Union of Industries
and Employers of the
EC)

UNPROFOR United Nations
Protection Force in
Bosnia

WEU Western European
Union

WHO World Health
Organization

WIPO World Intellectual
Property Organization

WTO World Trade
Organization

European Federalism:
An Introduction

Federalism is our future. That is the conclusion of this examination of current European projects and their implementation from the birth of the European Community (EC), a conclusion that marks the beginning of a new era for European federalism. Long considered by governments to be a threat to the unity of the "nation," federalism today appears to be the only form of social and political organization capable of keeping national and regional identities safe in the context of growing interdependence and globalization. In the networks of today's information-based society, it becomes the antidote to the strong revival of the nation-state built upon virulent nationalism. Once more Europeans are faced with a choice between a united Europe and its balkanization.

Having regained their independence, several former or new Eastern European states are being sorely tempted to build the homogeneous nation-state, despite the attraction of the European Union. As they emerge from communism, these countries are finding it impossible to make *state* coincide with *nation* because the people, cultures, and religions in their region are so severely mingled and even antagonistic. Against this background, reconstituting the nation-state involves imposing the culture of a dominant majority, if necessary by force, an act of assimilation that often leads to discrimination and in the worst cases conflict, as in the case of Yugoslavia. In contrast to the process of creating a union in Europe, this causes disintegration and violent confrontation. The fall of the Berlin Wall not only revealed the gaps in economic development between East and West but, worse, it exposed differences in values, attitudes, and behavior. Learning how to apply democracy and federalism is a long, slow process.

In view of this revival of nationalism, I thought it urgent to trace the steps taken by the European Union and go back to the origins of European federalism before turning to the Maastricht and Amsterdam Treaties and their consequences. The history of Europe is full of ideas and projects for a union of European countries. Even during the darkest hours of the resistance and the occupation, projects for a European federation emerged.

Based on utopian values of the free association of men and states in the framework of a democratic community, these ideas were spread following the issue of the federalist *Ventotène Manifesto*. War was declared between democratic Europe and unified Europe under Hitler's hegemony. Taken up after the war by hundreds of pro-European movements, federalist ideals were developed at the Congress of Montreux before coming to fruition in the *European Manifesto,* announced at the Hague Congress in 1948. From then on, the *European Manifesto* became a counterproject to the Marxist manifesto.

The convergence of Jean Monnet's and Robert Schuman's initiatives and action by members of the militant European Movement led, with the blessing of the United States, to the creation of the European Community. Barely five years after World War II, therefore, two deadly enemies were to become principal political and trading partners in the Franco-German alliance, which is now the dynamic core of European integration. The Community has delivered peace and prosperity to Europe as well as encouraging the development of its nations and regions. We have seen the fulfillment of Churchill's premonition, voiced at the Hague Congress, that mergers and the sharing of sovereignty were the only guarantees safeguarding the diversity of peoples, customs, and traditions. This conclusion regarding today's reality is the culmination of a line of thinking that led from Proudhon's "federal principle" to Denis de Rougemont's announcement of the "principles of federalism" at the Montreux Congress a century later.

According to de Rougemont, federalism means renouncing hegemony because federating means uniting different elements in a dynamic equilibrium. It means safeguarding the individuality of each nation, region, and minority; opposing the totalitarian simplification and uniformity imposed by a centralizing nation-state; and living in a space of freedom, democracy, and participation with different cultures, beliefs, political parties, businesses, and interest groups coexisting within a complex and varied social fabric. Based on the recognition of the dignity of man, his right to freedom, and his responsibilities and on a spirit of tolerance, political federalism evolves according to the principles of subsidiarity, autonomy, and participation, going both above and below the "state" through the European federation and the communes and regions, respectively.

By virtue of its principles and its flexible approach, federalism achieves a synergy between two opposing poles of globalization driven by new technologies and cultural individuality at both the national and local levels. On the one hand lies solidarity caused by the division of labor and interdependence, leading to internalization and the creation of continental groupings; on the other lies solidarity based on cultural identity (ethnic or national), which is itself based on history or legends. This contradiction is resolved in a "union in diversity," which permits an alignment of large economic forces and the wealth of individuals and their countries, a union based on a web of solidarity, memberships, and multiple loyalties. Paradoxically, the convergence of the two opposing trends has been achieved through the development of new information technology and the creation of new networks in both business and sociopolitical relations. The future of federalism lies in the microchip, programmed into the proliferation of horizontal networks, transforming the notion and use of power, and reversing the traditional pyramid.

Despite this, in the dynamics of integration nothing is certain. A warning came from the East, reminding us: the collapse of the Soviet empire, the dissolution of the communist bloc, and the implosion of Yugoslavia. The Soviet Union blew apart, sowing nation-, micro-, and ethnic states. The European Union itself is not shielded from the "childhood illnesses" that have spread across the East: national rivalries and ethnic, religious, and cultural intolerance. Although they may be marginal in Western Europe, they could rise again under the banner of national "greatness." Facing this nationalist virus, Western Europe, and indeed the Community, is vulnerable. The Yugoslav crisis serves as a brutal reminder to a Community too proud of its economic power and exposes its gaps and weak political clout. The Treaty on Union, followed by the Treaty of Amsterdam, aims to fill these gaps and build coherence and solidarity via cooperation in internal matters and coherence in joint external actions.

This is a great step forward, but I believe it is insufficient to repel such threats. More than ever I am convinced that, as much for Eastern as for Central and Southern Europe, a strong federated community is needed, a European Union that is capable of assuming its European and international responsibilities and can serve as a reference for Eastern Europe.

Four perspectives have been examined in studying European integration:

Federal

Neofunctional

Systemic

Communication

The federal perspective sets the guidelines for this work, complemented by the others. It has the advantage of being global and political. It reveals autonomy and participation, how states, regions, or citizens are represented, and the division of powers according to the principle of subsidiarity. However, by focusing on the institutional aspects of political power it tends to ignore the real processes and actors. Therefore, neofunctionalist and other approaches have been taken to enrich the global and institutional analysis.

The neofunctionalism of Ernest B. Haas has brought to the fore the agents and actors involved (and their changing loyalties) in the analysis of decision-making processes. These actors, leaders, interest groups, political parties, and public sentiments contribute to the dynamics of the integration process by means of their interaction.

Neofunctionalism is often set in a framework based on a systemic analysis that establishes the concept of retroaction in the processes of demands and responses. In this perspective, the political system is a processor of demands made on it, selecting and transforming them into decisions and actions. Studying this process from a global point of view and at the expense of content and substantive issues, D. Easton helps us to understand these political systems and interpret them in context. The internal view is thereby complemented by this view from the outside.

Similarly, Karl W. Deutsch's communicative approach outlines the importance of informal integration through an analysis of exchanges and transactions. In this perspective, the nation, or a community of nations such as the European Union, is a privileged area of exchanges and communication. Although initiated in the 1940s and adjusted in later years, this approach has acquired a second life with the development of modern means of communication and information technology.

The basis of this book is a practical and coherent approach, based on these four perspectives, leading to a new federalism.

PART 1

From the First Steps to the Single European Act

Chapter 1

The Roots of the European Union

The Long Maturation of Projects for Europe

The Birth of the Idea of Europe
(thirteenth to the twentieth century)

Different European movements are at the root of a united Europe and its dynamic core, the European Union. This is the key difference between the European union process and other attempts at regional integration, which have always been based on the initiatives of governments or other official institutions. Of course, official initiatives are not totally absent from the European union process, but the first steps down the road to unification, which began with the creation of the Council of Europe and continued in the European Community, were taken as a result of several different European movements.

Looking back, one can trace the origins of the idea to the Middle Ages, in particular to Dante's *De Monarchia,* which called for a supranational power showing respect for the diversity between different peoples and their traditions, or to Pierre du Bois's idea of a Christian Republic. Ever since, one project has followed another, proposing confederations with common institutions, parliaments, and even armies. These grandiose schemes made no impression on the nobility of the time and subsequently never left the drawing board. Nonetheless, their contribution is fundamental, as they initiated and disseminated the idea of a united Europe.[1]

Political in conception, the ideology underlying these projects reflected the problems of the time, the nature of political power, and aspirations to harmony and peace. It was reinforced by the doctrine of human rights and the progress of democracy and enriched, for example, by Kant's *Perpetual Peace,* which affirmed the need for a regrouping of republican states. The idea of a European federation or a United States of Europe was subsequently developed by intellectuals and men of action alike, men such as Hugo, Proudhon, Lamartine, and Mazzini. Their projects were based on human rights and the active participation of the people, *freely* united. They opposed a union imposed by force in the manner of Napoleon and Hitler, advocating a union based on consent. Thus, they created the ideas and language that inspired thinkers such as Denis de Rougemont and the federalist movements of today. The federalist ideology led to the Congress of European Federalists, held in Montreux in 1947, and, one year later, the Congress of Europe at the Hague.

To this political concept of a federation, Saint-Simon added an *economic and technical* aspect bearing the stamp of the nineteenth century. Basing his plan on economics while foreseeing a global organization of European society, he saw the issue as a question of concrete common interests and solid commitments. He concluded that "that which is common to European society may be considered as falling within the categories of the sciences, the arts, government, commerce, administration and industry." At the heart of his organization lies a European parliament. All nations "governed by a parliament" were also to

> recognize the sovereignty of one single general parliament placed above all national governments and invested with the power of judging their differences. . . . [F]or every million men able to read and write in Europe, representatives should be chosen to sit in the house of commons of the great parliament—a businessman, a man of letters, an administrator and a magistrate. In each case the member will be chosen by the corporations to which they belong.[2]

Even if one interpretation of this procedure can lead to confusion, because of the double criteria for deputies to be elected both by constituencies and by the corporations to which they belong, what is noteworthy is Saint-Simon's concern for the representation of both the people and the professions in a European parliament over and above individual nations.

To a certain extent Saint-Simon's ideas foreshadow the *functionalist* approach that led Jean Monnet to create the European Steel and Coal Agreements (CECA) in 1952 and the Economic Community (EEC) in 1957. The 1987 Single European Act (SEA) rather timidly reflected both a federalist and a functionalist approach to European integration. Thus, over the years numerous projects paved the way for the advent of a united Europe. It was only after World War I, then, in the fascist movements of the second European civil war, that these ideas crystallized into action and political movements.

The Pan-European Movement and Briand's Project (1924–30)

The transition from ideas to action was marked by the publication of Richard Coudenhove-Kalergi's *Pan-Europe,* the creation of the Pan-European

Union, and the diffusion of the Pan-European Manifesto in 1924. This first contemporary movement in favor of a European union was reminiscent of the movement of militant Europeans launched by Guiseppe Mazzini after the adoption of his charter in 1834 in Berne. It held its first congress in Vienna in 1926 under the honorary presidency of Seipel, Benes, Loebe, Caillaux, Sforza, and Politis and in the presence of more than two thousand participants from twenty-four states. The Vienna Congress approved the Pan-European Manifesto and established the outline of a European confederation: guarantees of equality, security, and confederal sovereignty; of a military alliance and the progressive creation of a customs union; of the common development of colonies, a common currency, respect for national cultures, and protection of national minorities; and of collaboration between Europe and other states in the League of Nations.

The strategy of this movement was to disseminate its ideas among members of Parliament (MPs) and intellectuals and above all to attempt to obtain the approval of government officials. In 1927, Aristide Briand, minister of foreign affairs and honorary president of the Pan-European Union, convened its Central Committee in Paris to formulate an outline for political action. Two years later, as president of the French government, he gave a powerful speech to the League of Nations Assembly, in the name of France, calling for the peoples of Europe to create some form of "federal bond." To my knowledge, this was the first official proposal from a government inspired by a European movement.

Having been asked to clarify its proposal, the French government published a *Mémorandum sur l'organisation d'un régime d'union fédérale européenne* in May 1930, just as Hitler was celebrating his first electoral victory. Streseman's death, the rise of Hitler, and the 1929–30 crises were bad omens for any hopes of implementing such a federal union. Even though it was stillborn, this project is of definite interest to historians and was influential because of the ideas it put forward and its invention of a European "language." There is nothing surprising in this when you know that the author of the project was Alexis Léger, a close colleague of Briand, general secretary of the Quai d'Orsay (the French foreign office), and a well-known poet who wrote as Saint-John Perse. A few of his expressions have become common in the Euro-specialist jargon: supranational federative organization (first mentioned in the preface of an official document); common market; customs union; movement of goods, capital, and people; assistance to lesser developed regions; de facto solidarity; community of European peoples; and everlasting momentum.

The Briand project belongs to a long tradition of European initiatives that run from Dante to Saint-John Perse, embodying from the start the dreams and inventions of visionaries and poets past and present. It may have failed, but its ideas inspired the way people thought and talked about Europe.

A Europe United in Resistance (1939–45)

The resistance movements fought against Hitler's drive to unite Europe by force and for the ideal of a federal Europe based on free and democratic assent. The resistance showed that the idea of a united Europe was still very much alive in the thick of war and occupation. In 1939, at the start of the war, Léon Blum argued for a federal Europe in *Le Populaire*.[3] "The solutions we socialists have in mind are those that would bring about *the integration of Germany into a European organisation,* thereby providing solid guarantees against a renewal of military adventures and laying the foundations for real security and a durable peace. *Our constant theme is this very same formula and this conclusion: the independence of nations within a disarmed federal Europe.* Those are our 'war aims' . . . in our eyes they are the conditions for peace." In England during the war, the association called the Federal Union carried out studies on the need and conditions for establishing a federal organization of democratic countries.

As early as 1941, two prisoners of war on the island of Ventotène, Altiero Spinelli (a communist converted to federalism) and Ernesto Rossi, wrote and secretly circulated the "Ventotène Manifesto," thus founding the European Federalist Movement (EFM). At its first meeting in Milan in 1943, the EFM established a structure and strategy for action. Its program suggested a European federation as the only means of avoiding international anarchy and regaining a sense of freedom in Europe: "the creation of a European federation to which all sovereign powers relating to common interests of all Europeans are transferred." It also proposed that "the inhabitants of the different states should have European citizenship and must therefore have the right both to choose and control the federal government and to be directly subject to federal laws."[4]

In France, the review *Combat,* created in 1941, attracted many writers who made their mark on European history. Henri Frenay, Georges Bidault, Albert Camus, Henri Teitgen, Edmond Michelet, François de Menthon, and many others worked together in the Resistance and fought the same battle for a United Europe. "European resistance will be the cement of tomorrow's unions," Frenay wrote in a December 1943 editorial entitled "Resistance, a Hope for Europe."[5]

During the same year, Jean Moulin, as a delegate of General de Gaulle, formed a "General Studies Committee" whose members included, in addition to several of those already mentioned, Paul Bastid, Robert Lacoste, Alexandre Parodi, Professor René Courtin, and later Michel Debré. The first edition of their *Cahiers Politiques,* published in 1943, was devoted to "France and the European ideal." In the same vein, in the January 1944 edition they declared that "politics will have to stop being imprisoned by the narrow borders of separate states . . . [and] one of the first things to do is to create a United States of Europe. This is no utopia, the United States of Europe is on its way."[6] These appeals were echoed by the Belgian, Dutch, German, and Polish resistance movements.

In January 1943, Thomas Mann addressed Europeans in a radio broadcast from New York.

> The great European ideal has been appallingly perverted and corrupted; it has fallen into the hands of nazism which conquered Germany ten years ago and thanks to lack of unity on the continent, it has managed to conquer the continent as a whole. This conquest is presented as if it were a unification of Europe, a "new order," conforming to the laws of history. Of all Hitler's lies, the most insolent is his concept of "Europe," a perversion of the idea of Europe. You should know, European listeners, that the real Europe will be created by yourselves, with the help of the free world.[7]

In Nazi Germany, Carl Friedrich Goerdeler, architect of a conspiracy against Hitler, put his idea of Europe on paper in a secret memoir in March 1943: "[U]nification of Europe on the basis of independent European states, unified in stages! An economic union, with an economic council that sits in permanence, will be immediately created. Political unification will not precede economic integration, but will follow it."[8] A few months later he was to complete his project with the idea of a European ministry for the economy, a European army, and a European ministry for foreign affairs. The idea grew in the Resistance that a democratic Germany should join in the integration process, particularly in France. After all, the struggle was against Nazi Germany and the German resistance was on the side of the Allies; once liberated from Hitler, the German people would be free to take part in building a free, democratic Europe. It was clear that integrating Germany into a democratic community would be the best guarantee against another military adventure.

In the thick of battle, therefore, the different resistance movements, through their converging publications and actions, endorsed the idea of a united Europe. The first meeting of nine resistance movements in Geneva on 31 March 1944 included one representative of the German anti-Nazi movement. This was followed by four more meetings, which led to the drafting of a common declaration. This was the first political action of the European federalists and the first attempt to coordinate resistance movements. It led to the creation of an office to coordinate the liberation efforts of the Resistance, to organize a *federal union of European peoples,* and to establish and maintain peace and justice in the world.

In this declaration, the resistance movements "committed themselves to consider these particular national problems as particular aspects of a larger European problem." The federal union should be based on a declaration of civil, political, and economic rights, guaranteeing the free development of individuals and the normal operation of democratic institutions. Additionally, states must irrevocably cede to the federation their sovereign rights in the areas of defense and security, foreign policy with third countries, and international trade and communications.

The federal union should possess above all:

    1. A government responsible to the people rather than the governments of the member states with whose mandate it will be able to exercise direct jurisdiction subject to the limits of its attributions;

    2. An army under the orders of this government to the exclusion of any other national army;

    3. A supreme court that will decide all questions relating to the interpretation of the federal constitution and any disputes between member states.

Germany and its satellites would take part in the economic reconstruction of the regions they had destroyed, but Germany would be helped, or forced if necessary, to change its political and economic structure. In view of this, Germany would be disarmed and subjected temporarily to federal control. This would:

Ensure that power would remain in the hands of sincerely democratic people who had fought against nazism,

Reconstruct a democratic and decentralized state without Germany's typical Prussian bureaucratic and military aspects,

Break down the feudal agricultural and industrial structure,

Integrate German heavy and chemical industries into a European industrial organization that would prevent them from being turned to German nationalist uses,

Prevent the German educational system from promoting Nazi, militarist, or totalitarian doctrines.[9]

The European Federalist Movement was not the only political movement within the Resistance, but, unlike nationalist and communist trends, it played a crucial role in the governments emerging from the war and in formulating European policy. Many leaders who later joined national governments were able to benefit from European contacts and solidarity with other resistance networks. Coming out of hiding, they and their movements would play a key role in the union process.

The Crucial Role of the European Movements

The Emergence of the European Movements (1946–47)

The main militant European movements were established in 1946 and 1947. The reconstituted *Pan-European Union* and its sister organization, the *European Parliamentary Union,* organized congresses and generally agitated for European union. These two unions were typical examples of *promotional groups* for the European idea, drawing their inspiration from a *supranational ideology,* that is, transcending national or partisan ideologies. Such movements attracted elites and militants of all parties and nationalities with their programs. The *Union of European Federalists* (UEF), established in Paris in December 1946, was another such "purely" European organization. Together with the bodies favoring this supranational multiparty approach there were promotional groups of partisan inspiration, each attracting an international following from adherents of particular political creeds: the *Socialist Movement for a United States of Europe* (SMUSE) and the *Nouvelles équipes internationales* (NEI), which were linked to the Christian Democrat parties or founded by personalities close to them.[10]

The two dominant supranationalist movements had the same objective: the direct election of a *European constituent assembly.*[11] There were only very minor differences of emphasis between them, but the means they proposed to achieve their ends were very different. Both planned to draw up a federal European constitution, but the *Pan-European Union* argued that a draft constitution must be submitted to the different peoples for ratification, either by the parliaments of participating nations or via national referenda. Forty years later these objectives are no closer to being achieved. Their authors wanted the draft European Union Treaty, adopted by the European Parliament in 1984 at the instigation of Altiero Spinelli, to be ratified by the parliaments of European Community member countries. But those indispensable intermediaries, the governments, were not cooperative, preferring to draw up their own draft Single European Act, which, though less ambitious, owed a great deal to certain ideas in the European Parliament draft. At the same time, the federalist group promoting a European union continued to call for a mandate to be given to the European Parliament to prepare a draft constitution. This proposal was supported by public opinion within the European Community, with 60 percent in favor, 13 percent against, and 27 percent undecided. Public opinion was favorable in all countries other than the United Kingdom, where there were 38 percent in favor, 27 percent against, and 35 percent undecided, and in Denmark, where 29 percent said yes, 45 percent no, and

25 percent did not reply. Most enthusiastic were the Italians with 78 percent in favor, the Belgians with 73 percent, and the French with 72 percent.

The suggestion made by the Pan-European Union and the UEF gained increasing support from the public, but the governments remained unconvinced. The Pan-European Union set to work lobbying governments and parliaments while continuing to nurture public opinion. The UEF employed various tactics to mobilize forces active within the European nations. It canvassed among different social milieus, published bulletins and pamphlets, organized courses (a tactic also followed by the Centre international de formation européenne [CIFE], founded by the UEF in 1955), and conducted a *campaign for signatures.* According to its statutes, the UEF, with more than 100,000 members and around ten federated movements or sections, was to aim to create a European federation, an essential element in a world confederation to which would be transferred the sovereign powers necessary to safeguard the common interests of the European states and their citizens. This federation was to guarantee fundamental liberties, including the freedom to organize opposition, and possess effective power over international exchange, currency, foreign policy, and defense.

Partisan-based European movements emerged from the Resistance in the same period. Thus, the Christian Democrats organized themselves at a European level into the *Nouvelles équipes internationales* based on national teams in ten or so countries and especially in the six founding countries of the European Community. The NEI set up a network whose leading members, the heads of Christian Democrat parties or personalities allied with them, played an important role in the promotion of European ideas and the creation of European institutions. At the same time, SMUSE, under the presidency of Paul-Henri Spaak, was actively working for a socialist United States of Europe. In 1948, this idea of a socialist Europe gave way to that of a democratic pluralist Europe whose political hue was to be determined by the electors' choice. SMUSE's aim was to promote the creation of a United States of Europe through socialist parties and trade unions and to pursue socialist policies in the context of an integrated Europe by uniting the forces of the European Left. SMUSE strongly influenced the course of European integration through its Executive Bureau under André Philip, a former minister in the French government, and its national sections in ten countries. These two partisan movements were later joined by the *Liberal Movement for a United Europe.* Together they constituted embryonic federations of parties belonging to the three traditional political families. These parties form the dynamic core of the European Parliament, where they hold a parliamentary majority. The three political families are well established in most of the countries of the European Community, and as of the June 1989 elections they represented two-thirds of the European electorate and even more in 1998. They form the dynamic hard core on which Spinelli's Union Plan was based.

The various ideological and political activities of the European movements are supported by committees having more specific aims, particularly economic and social ones. The *European League for Economic Cooperation* (ELEC), set up in 1947 on the initiative of Paul van Zeeland, was run by a council composed of the presidents of ten national committees together with thinkers on economics. Its object was to encourage cultural and economic rapprochement and cooperation between European states, and to this end it sponsored numerous studies and suggested solutions in the areas of capital movements, cartels and monopolies, and currencies. Its specialized study groups and its network of contacts with official authorities and private sector economists gave it access to exclusive channels of influence.

Such is the picture of the principal European movements on the eve of the Hague Congress, and these are its chief features:

1. Although employing different means, these movements had one and the same objective: a political union of Europe along federal lines.

2. The socioeconomic dimension (which was to become the foundation and principal element of the European Community), with ELEC as its mouthpiece, represented an element in the global political project.

3. Another essential element was still virtually absent: cultural and educative action at the European level.

4. These movements, each representing a different approach to political union, existed and acted in isolation. The task of the Hague Congress was to fill the gaps and make up for the lack of coordination at the European level, as a follow-up to the Montreux Congress, where the principles of European federalism had been formulated.

The Montreux Congress: Denis de Rougemont and Maurice Allais (1947)

Organized by the UEF, the Montreux Congress of 27–31 August 1947 represented the European federalists' contribution to the concept of a federal Europe and also, therefore, their contribution to preparations for the Hague Congress. Among the reports and papers presented at the Montreux Congress, two are particularly worthy of note on account of their scope and relevance today: *L'attitude fédéraliste* by Denis de Rougement and *Aspects économiques du fédéralisme* by Maurice Allais, Nobel Prize winner for economics.[12] While acknowledging the importance of federalist institutions, Denis de Rougemont put forward six principles for consideration. Montesquieu would have called them "virtues," and they form the basis of any federation:

First principle. A federation presupposes the abandonment of any notion of organizational hegemony. The failure of Napoleon and then of Hitler in their attempts to create a unity for Europe are salutary warnings.

Second principle. Federalism presupposes the *abandonment of an obsession with systems.* To federate means quite simply to *organize together,* to set up together as well as possible the concrete heterogeneous realities constituted by nations, economic regions, and political traditions.

Third principle. Federalism does not recognize a minorities problem. In Switzerland, respect for the special qualities of each and every individual is expressed not simply in the system of election to the *Conseil des Etats* but above all and much more effectively in the customs of our political and cultural life, where we see *French-* and *Italian-speaking cantons* playing a role out of all proportion to the number of their inhabitants or the geographical size of their territories. This observation applies today to small states in the European Community and in particular to Belgium and Luxembourg.

Fourth principle. The aim of federation is not to erase diversities and fuse every nation into a single bloc but to safeguard their *individual qualities.* Each of the nations that make up Europe represents a particular function that is irreplaceable, like each organ in a body.

Fifth principle. Federalism is based on a *love of complexity,* in contrast with the brutal oversimplification typical of the totalitarian mind. Switzerland is made up of a multitude of political, administrative, cultural, linguistic, and religious groups and bodies *that do not share the same frontiers;* in fact, they belong to countless separate overlapping blocs.

Sixth principle. A federation is the product of a chain of people. It develops out of *individuals and groups,* not out of decisions taken at the center or government *diktat.* The need for a European federation is evident: it has long been maturing, and its structures already exist in outline. All that is still required are a federal charter, representative organs, and the final move: a mass movement to force the hand of the governments. This is what Denis de Rougemont saw in 1947. But fifty years later the birth of the European federation is proving to be a slow process, for the member states are too strong to be troubled by a movement that for all its popularity is still weak, in spite of increasingly favorable European public opinion. This resistance by nations is what made Denis de Rougemont adopt what many considered an excessively hostile attitude toward the nation-state. His aggressive stance was modified later as a consequence of the principle that requires a federation to be built on concrete realities, including nations, which have to be "organized in accordance with their particular characteristics; their individual features must be respected and fitted together to build the whole."[13]

Dealing with the economic aspects of a federal union, Maurice Allais points out that the powers necessary for regulating all the economic questions that may divide federated states must be attributed to the federal union. As examples of federal powers, he lists the regulation of monetary conditions (a common accounting unit), commercial legislation, capital movements, population movements, and so on. These powers should be allocated on the basis of the following principles: (1) each federated state should be given maximum freedom; and (2) there should be no federal intervention except when decisions may cause difficulties between federated states, since the ultimate aim of economic federation is (a) to achieve the federal economic optimum and (b) to achieve the most equitable division without compromising the maximization of real revenue. As a final objective, this presupposes the free movement of goods (with markets organized on the basis of open competition), capital, and people in the framework of the free circulation of information.

In conclusion, Maurice Allais stressed three essential points as he outlined the prospects for a federal Europe: (1) there cannot be durable political federation without economic federation; (2) economic federation cannot be applicable where no political federation exists; and (3) economic federation reinforces political federation and vice versa. Economic federation and political federation thus appear to be inseparable, and any attempt at federal union must begin by creating the conditions for their simultaneous accomplishment. But however desirable this latter requirement may be, the reality is that it has not worked that way in Europe. Since the failure of the European Defence Community (EDC) in 1954 and the Fouchet Project in 1960, and in spite of the Single European Act, political cooperation has consistently lagged behind economic integration. The forward march of European union shows scant respect for "its preconditions."

The economic advantages of federalism for Europe cannot be overestimated. Federation would considerably reduce military expenditures and would make possible a real increase in national revenues on the order of 50 percent. Likewise, the free movement of goods and means of production would make possible an increase of at least 100 percent in national revenues. All in all, Maurice Allais calculated that within ten years a coefficient of between 2.5 and 3.0 would represent the rise in living standards.

By virtue of its huge economic potential, European federalism would provide an infusion of new vitality, enormously intensify the spirit of invention and enterprise, and ensure that Europe's inexhaustible store of intelligence would be exploited to the full. "Europe still has a card to play, which is her last but also her best. . . . This unexpected opportunity is federalism. It is up to Europe to take advantage of it in our time. Let us hope that Europe becomes aware of the opportunity before it is too late!"[14]

These two papers delivered at the Montreux Congress set out the main lines of the positions that were defended by federalists nine months later at the Hague Congress.

The Hague Congress and the Foundations of the European Movement (1948)

Given the diversity and multiplicity of the union movements, the problem was to ensure that they worked together to make their promotional activities on behalf of a united Europe more effective. Early in 1947, the UEF decided to convene the first congress of European federalists at Montreux in August. It was in the course of this congress that federalists adopted the idea of an estates general of Europe to give a broader basis to their activity. Around the same time Winston Churchill, following up his Zurich speech, with its call for a *union* of European states (with the United Kingdom as just one of the guarantor powers), proposed to call a congress to lay the foundations of a united Europe. These independent initiatives, one federalist and the other *unionist,* led to the Hague Congress, on which they both left their mark. Preparations for it were undertaken by a Coordinating Committee of European unity movements, which relied on three commissions — political, economic, and cultural — and national committees responsible for selecting delegates from all active bodies that were prepared to collaborate: parliaments, political parties, trade unions, professional organizations, churches, women's associations, universities, and intellectual and artistic centers. The Coordinating Committee brought together the UEF (Brugmans), the United Europe Committee (Churchill), ELEC (van Zeeland), Conseil français pour l'Europe Unie (Dautry), the NEI (Bichet, secretary general of the Mouvement républicain populaire [MRP]), and the European Parliamentary Union (Coudenhove-Kalergi).

Coming from a great variety of political and geographical backgrounds, one thousand delegates attended the European conference from 7 to 10 May 1948. Among them were twelve former presidents of the Council of Ministers, twenty current ministers, and one hundred MPs of diverse political affiliation — Christian Democrats like Adenauer, liberals, socialists, and conservatives. All of them attended as private individuals. Famous writers included Jules Romains, Etienne Gilson, Raymond Silva, Raymond Aron, Salvador de Madariaga, and Denis de Rougement. Also in attendance were numerous personalities from the academic world, the trade unions, and the churches. The European elite was there in strength.

A notable feature of the debates was the struggle between *unionist* and *federalist* tendencies. Overall, the Congress was not dominated by party or national considerations, with one exception: the British, conservative and labor alike (apart from Mackay), unanimously defended *unionism* and rejected the notion of federation. They believed in a loose kind of union, based on an idea of international cooperation that would fully respect the sovereignty of individual states. To this day, despite membership in the European Community and a slow transformation of attitudes, the British have not been able to rid themselves of a certain amount of suspicion toward European integration. The attitude of the former prime minister, Margaret Thatcher, is in fact reminiscent of the cautious and pragmatic unionist approach. This British hostility toward federal types of institutions was confirmed by several witnesses. In this connection, Denis de Rougemont wrote: "The participants, all too aware of the seriousness of what was at stake, were clearly very anxious to come to an agreement and much more progress would certainly have been made had it not been for the British. Before the Hague, many people expected the main struggle to be between Labor and the Conservatives but this showed little understanding of the British. The only real internal division within the Congress was that between the Islanders' common front and the (tactically) fragmented initiatives of the Continentals."[15]

The nature of the dispute may be summed up by an exchange that occurred during the Political Commission debates.

Harold MacMillan: "Remember your French proverb — Make haste slowly."
Paul Reynaud: "What a strange thing to say to a drowning man."[16]

Continental federalists were agreed as to their objective but divided on the methods to be employed to achieve it. Some advocated establishing a federal link and an economic grouping that would involve a partial transfer of national sovereignties. As Denis de Rougemont put it, they wanted "a union of diversities." Others, who were allied to the integral federalists, supported the latter's idea of a European assembly, but they had different ideas about how delegates were to be selected. They called for the assembly to be chosen directly by the type of community, which (as Robert Aron pointed out) represents nations' deeper life much better than parliamentary assemblies; the idea was that the assembly would be chosen directly from natural, professional, and spiritual communities such as families, trade unions, and churches.[17]

Although the principle of a European assembly was not questioned as such, participants were divided over the form it should take. Paul Reynaud's proposal for elections under *universal suffrage* (with each deputy representing one million inhabitants) to a *European constituent assembly* caused a stir but won only nine votes and aroused virtually unanimous opposition. Some considered it to be premature and impracticable, while others held that it was at odds with the federalist principle, which favors participation by small nations and minorities. Still others opposed it for reasons of prudence or on principle. Denis de Rougemont summed the situation up thus: "The British made common cause against the idea itself, while the Congress voted against the project in the particular form proposed."[18] More than forty years later, this idea of a constituent assembly finds support in some sectors of opinion, but it is no nearer fulfillment.

Despite these divergences and differences of opinion, the Hague Congress gave a crucial impetus to the actualization of the European idea. Thanks to the men who inspired it and managed to synthesize its conclusions, the congress marked a vital turning point.

1. Its often very lively debates produced a European manifesto inspired by a long tradition of projects for a united Europe, which set out a *global plan of action* for a united Europe in the teeth of the harsh realities of the postwar years.

2. It gave birth to the *European Movement* and was at the origins of the *Centre européen de la Culture,* the *Collège d'Europe,* the Council of Europe, and its Court of Human Rights.

3. It contributed to the creation of the European Communities.

The congress program may be summed up in three resolutions: political, socioeconomic, and cultural.[19] The substance of these resolutions is to be found in the *message to Europeans,* which its author, Denis de Rougemont, persuaded the congress to approve.

Although it argued for the necessity of creating an Economic and Political Union, the resolution fell short of the demands of both the former Resistance and the federalists. The compromise between the two leading tendencies is evident in the use of a dual terminology, *union* or *federation.* The Hague Congress did call for the transfer of certain sovereign rights, the independence of Europe from any other power, and a guarantee of security for its people. It assigned to a united Europe the mission of progressively building social democracy and proclaimed that union or federation was the only viable solution to German problems. However, it made no mention of the need for a European authority or government. This federalist demand, which seems implicit in the term *federation,* was not to be made by the European Movement until 1950 and then only hesitantly. On the other hand, the congress laid down two lines of development with its proposal for a European assembly in addition to a charter and a court of human rights.

Faced with the threat of right- and left-wing totalitarianism, the Hague Congress reaffirmed the essential values of European democracy. It substituted a more prudent and moderate proposal for the "revolutionary" idea put forward by Paul Reynaud.

It demanded the urgent convening of a European Assembly to be elected by the Parliaments of the participating nations — either from among their own number or from outside — an Assembly that would

1. contribute to the creation and expression of a European public opinion;

2. recommend the immediate measures required to establish progressively the needful unity of Europe both on the economic and on the political levels;

3. examine the judicial and constitutional problems posed by the creation of a union or federation and the economic and social consequences; and

4. prepare appropriate plans to achieve these goals.

It opened the way and formulated the goals but did not settle the means.

It was in the sphere of human rights that the Hague Congress came up with a very bold and precise proposal. It set up a commission with a dual role — to draw up a charter and put forward criteria to which democratic regimes would have to conform, criteria defining freedom of thought, assembly, and expression as well as the freedom of political opposition. In order to defend human rights and the principles of liberty, the assembly was to propose the creation of a court of justice for the recourse of citizens of associated countries, a court that would be empowered to impose sanctions. Out of these initiatives were to emerge the Council of Europe, the European Convention on Human Rights, and the European Court of Justice. In fact, it was as a result of initiatives taken by a delegation of the Coordinating Committee, led by André Philip, and on the basis of his memorandum suggesting the creation of a Council of Europe with a European assembly and a committee of ministers, that the governments set up the Council of Europe in 1949. This once more reflects a compromise between the British position and what was proposed by the French and Belgian governments.

Instead of a European assembly or some other organization having powers that were limited but real, the Council of Europe included a consultative Assembly and a Committee of Ministers whose resolutions depended on unanimous voting. In spite of the rapid success of the European Movement and the remarkable developments in the sphere of human rights, the imbalance that existed between the consultative powers of the

Assembly and the deliberative powers of the intergovernmental committee could not but result in an impasse as far as progress toward a united Europe was concerned. However, the Council of Europe took on board the basic principles of a European union: respect for human rights and democratic rules and the representation of peoples. The idea of a European assembly put forward by the Hague Congress was to evolve through the first representative institution and then the European Parliamentary Assembly of the European Communities before it ended up as the *European Parliament,* elected by direct universal suffrage but having powers that are inadequate even today. So it is that the utopian ideas of earlier days have gradually become today's reality.

With a view to establishing *economic union,* the congress put forward some measures for immediate implementation and at the same time formulated long-term objectives. The latter covered the free circulation of capital and workers, monetary unification, the concerted adoption of healthier budgetary and credit policies, complete customs union with a moderate external tariff (so as not to block normal movements or the development of world trade), harmonization of social legislation, and coordination of economic policies with a view to encouraging full employment throughout Europe. The congress sought to achieve a synthesis between personal aspirations and the new economic necessities. In order to avoid drift toward totalitarianism and to secure economic independence for everyone, the congress thought it necessary for workers and their representative organizations to be closely associated with creating and developing the economy of a united Europe. More than one of those proposals have been implemented or are being implemented in the European Community.

In its *cultural resolution,* drawn up by Denis de Rougemont, the Hague Congress stated that European union was no longer a utopia but had become a necessity based on the deep unity of Europe's culture. In order to give a voice to European consciousness, the *Centre européen de la Culture* set itself a series of goals: to encourage a sense of European community through information, projects, and education; to offer a meeting place; to encourage the free circulation of ideas and the coordination of research; and to support work on creating a federation of European universities and developing collaboration between teachers, in particular with a view toward revising history manuals. The *Conférence européenne de la Culture,* meeting in Lausanne in December 1949, set out a program for the European center that was established in Geneva in October 1950.

Following the Hague Conference, the International Coordinating Committee of the European unity movements was transformed into the *European Movement* under the honorary presidencies of Churchill, De Gasperi, Coudenhove-Kalergi, Spaak, Adenauer, and Robert Schuman. A vast organization that brought together and coordinated all the various pro-European-unification groups, the European Movement played the role of a pressure group, lobbying national governments, parliaments, and European institutions. For this activity, it was able to draw on a complex network of member organizations and *personalities* at different levels in their respective organizations. The European Movement held congresses and had an international council made up mainly of seventy-five representatives of the national councils, which brought together various national and local movements, and of fifty members of the Executive Committee, which comprised representatives of European movements. This complex federative structure enabled it to exercise a crucial influence on the initial phase of the integration process. It was the European Movement that prepared and supported the Monnet-Schuman initiative, the starting point for the European Communities. This represented the culmination of a long succession of ideas and projects for union. In the course of this process, there was always a certain lack of synchronization between projects and declarations containing ideas for union, on the one hand, and action programs and their implementation on the other. The program of action that came out of the Hague Congress seemed considerably less ambitious than the grandiose utopian projects that had prepared the way for union in earlier centuries.

A fresh look at the resolutions in the light of progress currently being made toward integration forces us to acknowledge that, on the whole, most of the 1948 proposals seem to have been implemented. There is nothing in the European manifesto that remains to be addressed.

The Fortieth Anniversary Congress (1988)

The Fortieth Anniversary Congress of 1988 confirmed this assessment but lacked the inspiration and courage to formulate a program for the next stage. It was really just a large commemorative celebration that did not take up the proposal for a *European referendum* or other means of increasing *popular participation*. It gave no consideration to the forms that could or should be adopted by the developing European federation nor to the way national, regional, and communal structures and powers should be organized in European institutions. It ignored initiatives that might have aroused the suspicion of governments, even when public opinion seemed favorable to them. Thus, for example, in April of the same year the idea of a referendum on European Union was favored by 76 percent of Community residents — 82 percent in Denmark and 77 percent in the United Kingdom![20] This raises the question whether the European Movement has lost driving force by handing over the initiative to governments, the Commission of the European Community, and the European Parliament. Can it hope to recover its vitality and the creativity it demonstrated at the Hague Congress? There will be no place for it in the future if it fails to do so.

In 1988, forty years had elapsed since the first Hague Congress. Gathered in the same Ridderzaal Hall in Binnenhof, we listened excitedly to speeches by West German president Richard von Weizsäcker and Jacques Delors, president of the Commission of the European Community, on the issue of basic cultural unity and the evolution from union to federation.

By pure good fortune, I was sitting in the middle of the second row in a place left vacant by Mme. Simone Veil, who had been invited to sit beside President Mitterrand of France. In front of me was a row of famous heads and necks. There was the solid profile of President Mitterrand. Further down the line, I could see the bowed head of G. Andreotti, the Italian minister for foreign affairs, the profile of Simone Veil, and the still young outline of Henri Brugmans, a veteran of European affairs who had been involved in every European initiative. Farther away, there was a fighter's neck, that of Cheysson, then the bearded profile of Pisani, the noble outline of R. von Weizsäcker, and the wavy hair of R. Lubbers, the Dutch prime minister. With Jacques Delors in front of me, it was like a film of the history of European union from the Churchillian congress to the European Community.

Those famous heads took me back to the vision described by Denis de Rougemont in his book *L'Europe en jeu* on the 1948 Congress at the Hague.

> I am sitting behind two rows of fascinating heads and necks. The broad red back is that of Ramadier; the placid blond head is that of Van Zeeland, the one without a neck is Paul Reynaud . . . [and] the huge white head above a black coat is Winston Churchill's.

The decor was the same but the actors and the climate had changed. Those first figures were opening the way to the Union by codifying sources and goals in a "European manifesto" and by promoting the objectives of union. This second set of actors was grappling with reality.

The French president's speech evoked his memories of the 1948 congress and the European profession of faith. When he returned to his seat, there was an opportunity to ask him what he thought about the possibility of a referendum on European union. Despite his fatigue (the result of the presidential campaign that had ended the previous day), he gave a subtly worded reply, which, though approving the idea in principle, drew my attention to the risks involved in such an undertaking. This led me to wonder whether, with all the progress made toward European integration and the implementation of so many of its plans, the European Movement had not lost some of its creativity and driving force along the way.

Chapter 2

Political Initiatives and Missed Opportunities

A Union Project Ahead of Its Time (1949)

A Federalist and Presidential Model

More than forty years ago Michel Debré was a convinced European, not just ahead of his own time but even ahead of today's thinking. In his *Projet de Pacte pour une Union d'Etats européens,*[1] he put forward a *federalist and presidential model* involving "a president elected for five years by universal male and female suffrage," a senate composed of ministers of the European states and commissions chosen by the president, and "an assembly of European nations with one deputy for each million inhabitants."[2] This revolutionary proposal dates from 1949.

Since the publication of his book in 1950, Michel Debré's conception of a united Europe has undergone substantial changes. Of course, politicians, like anyone else, have the right to change their minds. But it is particularly interesting to reflect on the way this top politician, once a passionate defender of a European union but now an equally fervent opponent of it, has changed his mind. Having clearly expressed his European convictions,[3] Debré stated in his book that action on the basis of such principles was long overdue.

But such action could not be undertaken without the willing assent of the citizens: "Isolated nations lack the power to hold on to their own territory or even their allies; isolation of nations must give way to union. New doors are open before us. First of all it is possible to formulate a common policy that will be a welcome improvement on the internal divisions and quarrels that still weaken the position of the West both in the East and in the Far East. And then such an association will reestablish nations' powers of mutual attraction, powers that no individual nation can exercise alone and unaided."[4]

Like Paul Reynaud, Michel Debré was convinced that "we must act swiftly. Apparently Churchill recently said 'Europe must be built step by step.' If the great statesmen did say this, then he's making a very bad mistake indeed. We need to build Europe with lightning speed; it's only one stage on a long journey, and we are already behind schedule."[5]

Impatient with the European states' reluctance to unite, Debré gave a visionary account of the changes undergone by the world in the twentieth century.

> I am not just talking bout the revolutions in science and technology. Look at the human revolution. Historically dominant powers are now in a precarious situation; a white race once dominant and mistress of the economic and political arena is now being eclipsed by the astonishing development of the Asiatic peoples; the Japanese eruption, the revolt of a new China carrying the third World along with it, Islam on the move and maybe tomorrow black Africa too; each civilization with its own ethos and religion, each one struggling upwards. It is as though our globe is pregnant with a new world quite unlike the old. And what are we doing about it, we who are imprisoned within our proud little nations?

He ended with this appeal: "It is time to leave behind our provinces—I mean our nations."[6]

Debré proposed a *Fundamental Pact between the European States:* four articles with a commentary, plus an organic law containing five headings and thirty-one articles with a commentary by the author. At the present time, with debates under way about the appropriate form and substance for European union, it seems entirely appropriate to bring this bold project of December 1949 (predating Robert Schuman's 9 May 1950 declaration by a few months) to the attention of European political leaders and citizens.

The Mission of the Union

According to its mission and by delegation from each participating state, a European union would have powers to secure the defense of its citizens, the improvement of their living conditions, economic development and freedom of trade, and the unification of judicial institutions. In addition to areas currently covered by the European Community, Michel Debré thought it essential to include defense as a primary concern of the union.

He assigned a more modest role to external policy, which "although handled in a way that would make it seem secondary" was also to be within the competence and power of the union. Members' policies in this area were to be "unified by coordination." This ambiguous terminology was explicable on account of the anxieties aroused by the prospect of a unified external policy. Each state would be allowed to preserve "the right to organize its foreign policy on its own, the indisputable mark on an international personality. The authorities of the union would be responsible for coordinating policies so that no state could refuse such coordination without withdrawing its signature."[7]

However, according to the author of the project, relations between member states would lose their usual diplomatic character. Michel Debré concluded that "nations do not want to abandon their sovereignty, for they confuse it with the liberty of their citizens. This is a delusion, but we have to be content to accept it and simply make good its harmful consequences."

In this area Debré's approach was not fundamentally different from that prescribed in the Report on a European Union by Leo Tindemans, with its proposal that member states should pledge themselves to pursue a common external policy in a certain number of precisely defined areas chosen according to their importance and the existence of practical means of achieving results.

The Organization of the Union

The organization of the union would reflect the *federalist and presidential* model. Leadership would be conferred on a *president* elected by universal suffrage and assisted by a senate. Inspired by federal ideas, the senate would include one minister from each member state, constituting a committee of ministers, presided over by the president and responsible for coordinating the union's external policy, and commissioners chosen by the president to see to the proper functioning of the union's services.

The proposed senate could give rise to confusion, since its composition and presidency could make it look more like an executive than a legislature. The senate would be presided over by the president, that is, by the head of the executive, elected by universal suffrage. Its membership would include commissioners, who, like the secretaries of the American executive branch, would be chosen by the president to run the services and administration of the union. The principal executive function of the committee of ministers, composed of one minister of state appointed by the government of each state, would be to coordinate external policy. Ministers would meet in a committee of ministers under the president.

Ultimately, "the coordination of the external affairs of the union's member states comes under the personal competence of the president." Accordingly, the senate's role would be to assist the president. In relation to this, the senate "is competent a) to study recommendations for joint action put forward by the president or presented by a member state; b) mandatorily to give an opinion on projects involving matters of principle or needing to be submitted to the assembly; c) to settle the draft budget and all the organic provisions relating to union services."[8] Thus, the union senate is, in reality, a part of the executive under the supervision of the president of the union.

Political control of the chief organs of the union would be in the hands of an *assembly* of European nations *elected by direct universal suffrage.* According to Michel Debré, there could be no election in Europe other than by universal suffrage, since universal suffrage alone (whether direct or in two stages) guarantees the legitimacy of an authority — hence, the election of both the president and delegates to the assembly of European nations. Composed of "deputies each representing a million inhabitants," this assembly would have excluded Luxembourg and put small and medium-sized states at a disadvantage in that it failed to apply the federalist principle, which resides precisely in favoring the representation of small and medium-sized member states (as the European Parliament does). The assembly would not be "competent to take action"; European society being varied and divided, in the nature of things the assembly would reflect the variety and divisions within that society. In this system, the assembly would not govern but would exercise supervision, making its presence felt before any important decision was taken.[9]

Thus, the European assembly of the union would carry out functions comparable to those of national parliamentary assemblies. It would exercise democratic control over government action, examine the budget and vote on it, and debate draft laws or programs drawn up by government. All measures that would impose obligations on member states of the union or deal with issues relating to the rights of persons must be referred to it. "The union assembly hears the report on presidential activities and replies with an address." It would be empowered to put questions to the president.[10]

The decisions of the assembly would be promulgated by the president, who nonetheless would have a suspensive veto. The president could also lawfully veto an assembly decision to revise a project after the committee of ministers had deliberated. If the assembly maintained its amendment, the conflict would be decided by a *referendum* in all the union territories.[11]

These three principal institutions would be assisted by a *union council* with a consultative function. Comprising four sections, this council would ensure that the following categories were represented: (1) production and labor, (2) the education and university sector, (3) towns and urban areas, and (4) public or private undertakings involved in social solidarity. This would be a broad form of an economic and social council. The Economic and Social Committee of the European Community is only a feeble reflection of it. Finally, a union court would be responsible for enforcing the joint obligations and decisions binding both for the union and its member states.

The union court would comprise eight to twenty magistrates, a quarter of them chosen by the president, a quarter by the committee of ministers, a quarter elected by the assembly, and the final quarter chosen by the education section of the union council. Any member state, or indeed the president himself, could apply to the court, but unlike the Community procedure other union institutions or moral or physical persons might not apply to it. Court decisions would be binding, and the president would have the job of overseeing their enforcement.[12]

This organization, as suggested by Michel Debré, is distinguished by two original features: the president and the union assembly, both elected by universal suffrage. The presidency constitutes the active central power. Debré thought it necessary to place at the summit of his edifice "someone whose moral and political prestige are beyond doubt in view of the manner in which they are chosen."[13] Around the president stand the political leaders of the member states, corresponding to the Council of Ministers of the European Community, and the commissioners, who are comparable to the members of the executive branch in a presidential regime. The originality of Debré's project resides principally in the fact that these two institutions, joined together under the title of "senate," are presided over and headed by someone "elected for five years by an absolute majority of votes given by men and women able to read and write and holding the nationality of a member state of the union."[14] The election of the president by universal suffrage was, in Debré's eyes, the only way to guarantee the legitimacy of this kind of new authority.

Similarly, the legitimate authority of the assembly is also based on election by universal suffrage. Having proposed these European elections in 1950, Michel Debré rejected them in 1976. This change of attitude on his part is all the more difficult to understand in that the Assembly he had envisaged would have been endowed with much more extensive powers than those available to the European Parliament. Such an assembly would have represented the citizens of the union and possessed initiative as well as budgetary and supervisory powers.

Although written as long ago as 1949, this proposal has unfortunately not lost any of its relevance, since Europe is being built step by step as recommended by Churchill rather than with lightning speed as Debré once hoped. Looking back over his proposal, I am still impressed by the force and logic of his arguments, and I continue to puzzle over the reasons for the profound change in outlook that has taken him into the camp of the bitterest and most intransigent opponents of the election of a European Parliament.

In rejecting this *direct legitimacy*, Debré in fact is rejecting the very idea of a European union in the name of an outdated nationalism. He was swimming against the tide in 1950 when he asked in the name of Europe that a government be imposed and citizens forced to assent,[15] and he is doing so again when he tries to slow down the prudent efforts of governments by opposing public opinion, which is actually favorable to union. Nonetheless, in spite of himself, Debré has continued to stimulate reflection on the future of European democracy thanks to his 1949 project. In spite of those few of its recommendations that have been implemented or have become outdated, it was well in advance of current projects and proposals. That is why in many ways this youthful "peccadillo" is an important landmark in the theoretical background of the European Union and in the long slow development of its projects.

An Abortive European Political Community

From the Schuman Declaration to the Ad Hoc Assembly Project (1950–53)

From the earliest days of European integration immediately after the war, European politicians and leaders sought to encourage political union in Western Europe. The impetus given by the 1948 Hague Congress was maintained by the Schuman Plan but was blocked by the failure of the EDC in 1954, which dragged down with it the whole project of a political community. This project, which has long been gathering dust in the archives, now seems to merit renewed attention. The truth is that fifty years on it is more timely than ever, for this original concept was a much bolder project than the timid ideas that seem to have inspired the negotiators entrusted with the task of drawing up a political union treaty by the European Council in Rome in December 1990.

In accordance with the principle requiring the parallel development of economic integration and political union, the European Political Community of 1953 aimed to assemble all the elements of a European structure under one political roof. The EDC project and the European Political Community were expressions and confirmation of the political will that provided the principal driving force toward union and the catalyst for efforts toward a united Europe. In 1950, the Schuman Declaration gave expression to the numerous isolated activities that were converging on the same objective — the creation of a European federation. Taking up a stand at a point where federalist and functionalist movements as well as the main political currents of the day converged, Jean Monnet and Robert Schuman laid down the foundations for reconstructing Europe. These foundations — incomplete but solid — were those of a future European federation.

This federalist aim was embodied in Robert Schuman's declaration of 9 May 1950:

The pooling of coal and steel production will immediately establish common foundations for economic development, which represent the first stage on the way to a European federation and will transform the future for those areas that have long been concerned with the manufacture of weapons of war — of which they themselves have been the most frequent victims. . . . By pooling basic production and establishing a new high authority whose decisions will be binding on France, Germany, and such countries as are willing to join them, this proposal will lay the first concrete foundations for the kind of European federation that is indispensable for the preservation of peace.[16]

Jean Monnet took a similar line and demonstrated his determination to see a European federation achieved via a pragmatic sectoral approach: the European Coal and Steel Community (ECSC) "points the way to a future Europe in the form of a pacific *federal community* that will be much larger and more prosperous; within it, the European nations, pooling their capacities and resources, will be able to live according to the rhythm of the modern world in *liberty and diversity.*" This text gives clear expression to one of the fundamental principles of federalism — not as a concept but in practical form. The federal community ensures both an adaptation to the conditions of the modern world through the pooling of resources and the preservation of national diversities. This central idea reappears further on:

Ultimately, it is vital that the states retain their rights while participating in a common market that is the main geographic area of their production and exchanges. This will be an issue for any European structure that *is not the constitution of a unitary centralized state:* if Europe succeeds in creating the federation for which the Coal and Steel Community (according to the French government declaration of 9 May 1950) is to be the first stage, the experiment we have set in motion will provide the answers to the most difficult problems that would arise from a *federal* structure.[17]

The two movements — the federalists, represented by Denis de Rougemont, Alexandre Marc, and Henri Brugmans, and the functionalists, Robert Schuman and Jean Monnet — were both moving toward the same objective — a European federation.

On 24 October 1950, six months after the Schuman Declaration and four months after the outbreak of the Korean War, René Pleven proposed the creation of a defense community, in order to fulfill the requirement of the Schuman Plan and respond to the pressing need for a common defense of Western Europe, including the participation of West Germany. In September 1951, the three Western Allies approved the creation of a continental

European community. In December of the same year, the Consultative Assembly tried to shake the Council of Europe out of its complacency and recommended to the Committee of Ministers that they

> do everything in their power to encourage favorably disposed member states to come to a rapid agreement on the creation of *a political authority subjected to the democratic control of a parliamentary assembly,* with powers limited to defense and external affairs, areas in which the exercise of shared sovereignty would be necessary for the organization of a European army and its use within the Atlantic framework.[18]

At a time when the political circumstances were favorable, a number of factors combined to encourage efforts to construct a union on the model of the Schuman Plan: the spirit of the times; pressure from the European Movement; the simultaneous arrival in power of the Christian Democrats in France, Germany, and Italy, with Schuman, Adenauer, and De Gasperi as their respective leaders; and the support of socialist leaders like Paul-Henri Spaak and Guy Mollet.

Article 38 of the EDC Treaty, signed in Paris on 30 May 1952, sets out the basic structures of a future federal or confederate community and entrusts the EDC Assembly with the task of studying the constitution of an assembly to be elected on a democratic basis with the mission of formulating definitive guidelines for a defense community. At this moment, the *promotional activity* of the Consultative Assembly played a decisive role. Faithful to its earlier recommendation, it viewed the definition of the constitutional foundations of the Community as a priority.

The proposals of the Consultative Assembly were accepted by the six governments, which, under the terms of the Luxembourg Resolution of 10 September 1952, invited the members of the ECSC Assembly to co-opt nine new representatives and draw up a draft treaty establishing a European political community. This was the mandate given to the *Ad Hoc Assembly,* presided over by Paul-Henri Spaak, a much broader mandate than that which article 38 conferred on the EDC Assembly. This resolution also set guidelines on the nature and limits of community powers in the areas of human rights, defense, external policy, and social and economic integration. Thus, for all the impotence resulting from the institutional straitjacket of the Council of Europe, the Consultative Assembly's initiatives, expressing the wishes of the Six, were instrumental in the creation of the Ad Hoc Assembly. In his speech to the Ad Hoc Assembly on 9 March 1953, Georges Bidault, president of the Special Council of Ministers, set out Europe's situation and prospects very succinctly: "We have undertaken to build one Europe. We had wanted its frontiers to be geographical. Here at Strasbourg we have accepted that its frontiers will be those of liberty.

Whether or not such borders are lasting, the one Europe we are now building will have frontiers limited only by our own determination."[19]

Thus, with the war barely over this short period between the 1948 Hague Congress, the 1950 Schuman Declaration, and the Draft Ad Hoc Assembly Treaty in 1953 saw six European countries, including West Germany, move with surprising speed toward union, with France leading the way. In six months, the Ad Hoc Assembly drew up and adopted a European Community policy draft, which was delivered to the six governments on 9 March 1953. But the French Assembly decision of 1954 not to proceed, even though the treaty had been ratified by the parliaments of its partners, sounded the death knell for political union.

According to Raymond Aron, there were three developments during this period: a progressive strengthening of forces hostile to the EDC in the French Assembly and French public opinion; international détente, which made German rearmament difficult; and the increased strength in the government majority of those hostile to the EDC.[20] In this atmosphere of hostility, "domestic politics," according to Jacques Fauvet, "killed off European politics."[21] Following this unceremonious halt in the process of political integration, a long period began that was to be marked by gradual but continuing progress in economic integration and by the enlargement and deepening of the existing communities, in stark contrast to the fate of various abortive initiatives for the creation of a political union.

The failure of the EDC and its natural political accompaniment induced deep political trauma. A series of subsequent initiatives came to nothing. Eight years later, the much less ambitious Fouchet Project, inspired by General de Gaulle (1960–62), was rejected. Twenty-one years on, the Tindemans Report, commissioned by the European Council (1975–76), was equally fruitless. Twenty-five years were to pass before the European Parliament of a then nine-strong European Community was elected by universal suffrage. It took another five years for the European Parliament to come up with a draft treaty on European union (1984) and five more years, just before the 1989 elections, for there to be renewed but unsuccessful discussions on commissioning the European Parliament to draw up a constitution for the European Community. Over forty-five years have passed since 1954, and during that time the good intentions inspired by old dreams of a European constituent assembly, as proposed by Altiero Spinelli, are not yet reality.

The Originality of the Draft: A Two-Chamber Parliament and Majority Voting

Today this astonishing 1953 project for a political community, original both in its content and in its structure, seems strikingly relevant. It falls somewhere between individual or private group projects and official government drafts. Despite the fact that it had gone through all the official channels and been solemnly handed over to the six governments, the crisis that engulfed the EDC prevented it from being adopted. Nonetheless, it constitutes a very significant stage in the process leading up to the Union and in the development of ideas on European institutions. Its preamble opens with "*We, the peoples* of the Federal Republic of Germany, the Kingdom of Belgium, the French Republic . . .' and ends with "have decided to create a European Community. Consequently our respective governments . . . have adopted the present treaty."[22]

Apart from this reference to its popular basis, the preamble contains well-known themes and aims: peace, civilization, and the common heritage; economic expansion and the improvement of living standards; and freedom and human rights. Abandoning their centuries-old rivalries, the people of the six countries were determined to merge their essential interests by establishing institutions capable of directing a destiny that would henceforth be shared. To this end, "the present Treaty establishes a EUROPEAN COMMUNITY having a supranational character," which, as Paul-Henri Spaak and H. von Brentano noted, was "neither a federation nor a confederation." This Community drew on certain rules whose value had been proved by the experience of others but that also contained innovative and original ideas adapted to the circumstances of the day. The project required a complete institutional structure endowed with limited powers in the areas of defense, external relations, and economic and social integration. Its institutions would make up the core of a federal union: Parliament, the European Executive Council, the Council of National Ministers, the Court of Justice, and the Economic and Social Council.

The basic idea behind the proposals, according to spokesman F. Dehousse, was the election of a popular assembly by universal suffrage, that is, involving the people themselves in creating and governing a united Europe. The *Parliament,* made up of two chambers, the *Chamber of the Peoples* and the *Senate,* would constitute the legislature of the European Community. It would vote on *laws, recommendations* (a term used at the time for what we now know as directives), and the budget, and it would exercise democratic supervision. The three largest states would each have sixty-three deputies (with a further seven representing France's overseas colonies); medium-sized states would have thirty each and Luxembourg twelve. This allocation would have greatly favored the small and medium-sized member states since it would not have applied a system of weighted proportional allocation of seats like that of the Swiss National Council. Thus, while drawing on the ideas of various European movements and on Paul Reynaud's proposal (rejected by the Hague Congress), the draft treaty assigned twelve seats to Luxembourg, which would have had one at most on the basis of a more rigorous proportional allocation.

There were to be 268 deputies in the lower house, while the Senate would contain eighty-seven senators elected by the national parliaments. Unlike the American Senate or the Swiss Council of States, it was to be based on egalitarian representation but would involve the same proportionality as the Chamber of the Peoples: twenty-one senators for the larger states and four for Luxembourg. The ratio was the same as for the Chamber of the Peoples but involved a total one-third its size. This formula for the Senate is similar to that of the German Bundesrat, where the states have between three and five votes depending on their population. The two chambers would have the same powers; laws would be voted on by the two chambers in succession and would require simple majorities to pass.

The Parliament would exercise *democratic control* over the European Executive Council. The Senate could pass a motion against the Executive Council by electing a new president, while the Chamber of the Peoples could pass a similar motion by a three-fifths majority. In both cases, the European ministers would resign collectively. One feature of this structure is original: the Executive Council would in turn be entitled to dissolve the Chamber of the Peoples if a vote of censure or a no-confidence motion failed to attract the required majority. In that case, the Executive Council would have the right to decide whether it must resign or dissolve the Chamber. The treaty is modeled on a parliamentary system. It makes the executive responsible to Parliament but saddles it with a majority requirement that is difficult to obtain, as Community experience since 1958 has demonstrated, and it balances this parliamentary power over the executive against the executive's power of dissolution. This type of parliament is as distant from the Swiss model — where the executive cannot be overturned by Parliament and the latter cannot be dissolved by the executive — as it is from the American model, which uses the principle of strict separation of powers. The project's structure established an institutional equilibrium that seems eminently capable of keeping a European executive stable. Finally, the project proposed that each chamber have a right of inquiry, a means of control that has been much developed by the American Congress. This right has been called upon increasingly in the European and national parliaments, including that of the Swiss.[23]

The second original feature of the project for a political community is to be found in its *European Executive Council.* Made up of European ministers, *"The European Executive Council oversees the government of the Community."* The Council may not include more than two members of the same nationality, a formula that was to be repeated in the EEC Treaty and then applied in the case of the present Commission, belonging to the three European Communities. In practice, this leads to the attribution of two commissioners for each of the big states, including Spain, and one commissioner for each of the small and medium-sized states. The Executive Council foreshadowed a European Commission that would take on the tasks of government in the political union.

The *selection process* for the Executive Council was as original as it was audacious. The *Senate would elect the president* of the Executive Council by secret ballot and the majority vote of its members, but the *president would have the responsibility for nominating the members of his Council.* The Executive Council would be invested by Parliament, with the approval of each chamber by majority vote. This procedure guaranteed a certain homogeneity in the collegial executive and strengthened the role of the president, leaving him to choose his ministers freely while subjecting his choice to *parliamentary approval.* The importance of the function of the president was emphasized by his or her power to dismiss or replace any Council member, a decision that must be approved, however, by the Chamber of Peoples and the Senate. By attributing representation of the Community in international relations to the president, the project further reinforced the central position of the presidency. In the European Community in its current form, this function falls either to the president of the European Council, the president of the Council of Ministers, or the president of the Commission. Thus, for example, it is the president of the Commission who represents the Community at meetings of the seven leading Western nations.

The Executive Council would have significant powers, enabling it to carry out the tasks entrusted to it by the treaty. It would have the right of initiative to enable it to achieve the general goals defined by the treaty, and this would be exercised either independently or on the basis of a motion of Parliament or one of its chambers. It would take decisions that would be binding in all their parts, it would formulate recommendations that — like the directives in the Treaty of Rome — would be binding as to the purposes they specify while leaving open the choice of means suitable for the achievement of these purposes, and it would issue nonbinding opinions.

These various provisions relating to the European Parliament and the European Executive Council embodied in the draft treaty are significant on more than one score. The nature of the instruments available to the Executive Council was taken up later by the Treaty of Rome and has long formed part of Community law. Other aspects relating to the nomination of the Executive Council, the role of its president, and the power of the *two-chamber Parliament* were not included in the Treaty of Rome but continue to encourage reflection on the future of the European Community and to stimulate European ambitions and projects. The Court of Justice, conceived as a sort of federal or appeals court, and the Economic and Social Council, with its consultative function representative of the active forces in the Community, complete the picture of the proposed institutional system of the Community. Were it not for the ambiguous role of the proposed *Council of National Ministers,* this system would have laid the ground rules for a federal union. Like the special Council of Ministers of the ECSC, this Council would have had the role of harmonizing the activity of the European Executive Council with that of the governments of member states. Its role would have become central in the process of establishing the Common Market since the Executive Council would have settled projects on the strength of a *favorable opinion* of the Council of National Ministers, requiring unanimity in the course of the first five years and *a simple majority* thereafter. Projects adopted like this would have taken the form of Community laws, but unlike today's European Community decision-making process Parliament, not the Council of Ministers, would have had the last word in the European Political Community. The Council of Ministers also would have had an important role in coordinating external policies, the admission of new members, and Community taxation. On top of this, the experience of the ECSC served as a warning as to the growth of the effective powers of the Council despite the seemingly modest role attributed to it by the treaty. Things developed in this way because essential economic and social powers and *a fortiori* budgetary and political powers remain the prerogative of national states, even when they have lost part of their capacity to exercise these powers effectively. This reality—or perception of reality—is still reflected in the key role played by the Council in the European Community, despite improvements brought about by the Single European Act; it makes ultimate decisions in legislative matters and, together with the Commission, exercises executive powers in relation to various common policies and external relations.

From more than one point of view, the project for a political community produced by the *ad hoc Assembly* was a precursor, a model to be followed and a goal to be attained by the European Community, which is still a long way from home in this respect. At the institutional level, it was well in advance of its time and the Community only partially caught up with it by creating the European Council in 1974, electing a European Parliament in 1979, and passing the Single European Act of 1986 (which went into effect in 1987).

This last step represented significant progress and brought a fresh impetus to Community development, thanks to the potential contained in the 1992 project, with a whole range of measures designed to complete an internal market without borders as well as a wider spectrum of common policies. Although the European Parliament cannot be compared with the proposed two-chamber parliament of the 1953 European Political Community project, its greater involvement in the Community decision-making process underscores the strengthening of the Union. Likewise, the present system has not attained the level of institutional integration that was outlined in the ad hoc Assembly's project. Despite an evident intention to bring together and coordinate the activities of the European Economic Community and despite the efforts made in the sphere of political cooperation — such intention and efforts expressly shown by the use of the title Single European Act — the gap between integration and cooperation has not been reduced. The draft treaty, however, proposed integrating the ECSC and EDC in an institutional framework involving the creation of a common market based on the free circulation of goods, capital, and people together with the coordination of member states' monetary, financial, and credit policies (art. 82) as well as an agreement on common powers in the area of external relations.

The Powers of the Political Community

Among its powers, the Community would be able to set up public services or *autonomous bodies* to carry out various functions under its control (art. 88). The community *budget* would be drawn up by the Executive Council and voted on by Parliament (art. 76). However, the community tax regime and the conditions for the collection of *community taxes* would be contained in bills proposed by the Executive Council with the assent of the Council of National Ministers on a unanimous vote; these bills would then be put before Parliament for approval. Thus, the axis of the legislative process would consist of *community laws* proposed by the Executive Council, on the basis of a favorable opinion in certain areas of substantive political importance, and put to a *simple majority vote* in each of the two chambers (art. 52). Promulgated by the president of the Executive Council and published in the official journal, they would immediately enter into force in the member states. Although adopted via a different procedure, the general rulings of the present-day European Community have the same material value and the same significance as those in the draft project would have had.

Community laws, Executive Council decisions, and Court of Justice decrees would be mandatorily enforced by the member states, as is the case with the Swiss cantons which guarantee and enforce the laws and decisions of the federal authority (art. 106). The same federal procedure operates in the present European Community. The draft treaty also contained an original clause that is found in both the Helvetic Confederation and in the Federal Republic of Germany; member states could ask the Executive

Council to assist them in ensuring respect for constitutional order and democratic institutions within their territory. The conditions under which the Community is empowered to intervene on its own initiative would be established by the Executive Council with the unanimous approval of the Council of Ministers and submitted for parliamentary approval (art. 104). These provisions were inspired by the desire to defend the democratic regimes of the member states against the totalitarian menace of communism. The defense of, respect for, and practice of democratic principles and human rights are both the foundation and the goal of the European construction. In accord with this democratic logic, the political community was to be open to the admission of the member states of the Council of Europe and of any European state guaranteeing the exercise of human rights and fundamental liberties. The act of admission was to be established by the Executive Council with the agreement of the Council of Ministers and submitted to Parliament for its approval (art. 116).

The project was equally innovative in the domain of the Community's external relations. It proposed that the Community should be able to make *international treaties* or *association agreements* within the limits of the powers attributed to it. To this end, the Executive Council would negotiate and approve treaties binding on the Community (arts. 67–68). In order to fulfill its mission, the Community was to be endowed with an active and passive *right of representation* within the limits of its powers (art. 74). This faculty of representation was expressly taken up in the draft European Union Treaty, which was adopted by the European Parliament in 1984 and put into practice in a significant (though sectoral) way by the European Community in the areas of its competence. Although the Single European Act does not refer to it expressly, it aims to establish this practice to the extent that it proposes the coordination of member states' external policies. However, both Europe's participation in the creation of the new international order and the Gulf crisis made abundantly obvious the urgent need for a common external policy, a sine qua non for any effective European presence — or at least for any effective presence of its Community core — on the global stage.

One of the tests of a federal community is its power to revise its constitution autonomously. The draft treaty provided for two cases with different conditions. Any modification of the powers of the Community with respect of the member states or modification of the definition of human rights and the fundamental liberties guaranteed by the Community is subject to stringent conditions. If the Executive Council's proposal were to gain the unanimous approval of the Council of National Ministers, it must then be approved by both the European Parliament and the parliaments of member states. This more or less confederate revision procedure is more flexible with respect to a modification relating to the relations between Community institutions or affecting the guarantees accorded to member states by the composition or the operating rules of the institutions. Here, the approval of national parliaments would not be required.

In a third hypothetical situation, which differs from these two types of modification, the procedure becomes autonomous. The Executive Council's draft amendment would then be subject to the approval of the European Parliament. In all three cases, the amendments would be promulgated by the European Executive Council (arts. 111–13).

A Federal Project

The proposal for a European political community drawn up by the ad hoc Assembly has all the hallmarks of federalism. It falls within the concept of a European union based on the parallel development of economic and political union and indeed on the necessity for integrating various union initiatives into a political structure and articulating them around a European political authority. This project gave formal expression to the powerful impetus imparted by the Hague Congress to union initiatives. Like the present union, this ambitious project brought together not just the *Common Market* and the *coal* and *steel* sectors but also *defense*, a *European army*, and *external relations*. It aimed to combine and organize, to a varying extent, those areas where the powers of a federal community are most appropriately exercised. The breadth and federalist approach of this project indicate what remains to be done and expose the deficiencies and inadequacies of the current integration process. They also provide some indication of the extent of the disappointment aroused by the failure of the EDC, which brought about the collapse of the European political community project. At the same time, they enable us to understand how just over nine months after progress toward union was so crudely blocked the movement could be revitalized at Messina — albeit in a rather more modest and prudent form.

Two years later, in 1957, two new communities came into being — the European Economic Community and the European Atomic Energy Community — but the defense and external relations aspects had disappeared along with the federalist ambitions. Thus, by an accident of history the union process followed the path of economics and technology and stayed on the margins of politics. Hence, the global approach advocated by federalists gave way over quite a long period to a pragmatic/functionalist approach. In fact, for all its sectoral nature the path to economic union nonetheless encroached on politics. Thanks to the continuity of the integration process, the support of informal networks, and interpenetration between the economies, numerous links of various kinds have developed into the foundation of the structure of Europe. Integration and interaction between individuals, businesses, and socioeconomic groups have contributed to changes in values, attitudes, and social structures within a common institutional and normative framework.

Economic interpenetration and high-level commercial exchanges have gone hand in hand with attitudes and behavior favorable to European union. Moreover the activity of the European Parliament, especially in direct elections, has created a role for political groups and federations of political parties, a role that will evolve to reinforce the European Parliament with real powers. The basic conditions all seem to be currently in place, but the European Community and its member states have only just managed to give themselves shared — that is, global — political institutions and powers embracing external and security policies as well as socioeconomic issues. From this point of view, however, the present Community still lags behind the 1953 project despite the substantial progress that has been made since then.

This raises a final question: can the forgotten European political community serve as a model for the political union that the Intergovernmental Conference of 1996 had the task of reforming? On the one hand, the bicameral Parliament in the proposal seems to me to be an example unquestionably worth following if there is a desire to take the federalist path to union.[24] On the other hand, what must be avoided at all costs is paralysis of the entire system by the requirement for unanimous approval by the Council of Ministers. That is why my sketch of a federal European Community proposes a two-tier executive, one composed of the European Council, assisted by the Council of Ministers, and the other formed by the European Commission. Taking its cue from the French system, the European Council would fulfill the function of a collegial presidency while the Commission would take on the role of a European government.[25]

This new structure needs to integrate all the functions and activities of the existing Communities, including economic and monetary aspects as well as European external policy and security, into a single political community. By so doing, the political community project can be resurrected from the oblivion in which it has languished to be embodied in a living community with a federal vocation.

De Gaulle's Initiative: The Fouchet Project (1960–62)

A Europe of States versus a Supranational Europe

The initial success of the European Communities laid the basis for a political community, but, for all the political importance of economics, economic integration does not lead automatically to political integration. To carry out their tasks, the Communities needed political drive and a political structure. In the long term, any failure or delay in the construction of political union threatened to bring an end to the young Community and sap confidence in the economic future of Europe. Lack of political progress created a certain imbalance between European political forces and socioeconomic agents while a new Europe was being created. The Six were certainly obliged by historical circumstances to follow the economic and technological path after the rejection of the EDC in 1954. But this accident of history ought not to have been allowed to accentuate the excessive growth of "economic and technological power" by perpetuating the *political vacuum.*

Moreover, the problems facing Europe do not relate to production and consumption alone. Far from masking reality, the miracle of the community experience actually throws a harsh light on the crucial issues yet to be resolved. From the early 1960s, European leaders have been faced with difficulties that are still very much with us. How is Europe to tackle the problem of a common defense policy, the dilemma of nuclear weapons and their use, and the challenge of the conquest of space? Bread and butter questions that are just as pressing involve the issues of a common external policy and a European strategy in relation to the old Eastern bloc countries and developing nations. And, if progress is made (as it must be) in certain of these sectors, how will the Community bring about better management of shared resources and policies? The pieces of this puzzle will fall into place only in a global, that is, political, framework.

Alert to such concerns and questions, the governments of the Six made a great effort after 1960 to come to an agreement on the French project for a union of European states.[26] But, despite all their efforts, they had to admit defeat at a conference of foreign ministers held in Rome in April 1962. In the name of a union of European peoples and a supranational Europe, Paul-Henri Spaak and his Dutch colleague Mr. Luns resolutely opposed a Europe of states. Two years before, Paul-Henri Spaak had accepted Luns's argument that "if we wish to go forward on the basis of integration and supranationality, we should retain our current dimensions, as London will not go along with us. But nothing in the proposals on the table is going to make it impossible for the British to join." The two men pointed out that on this basis there were no grounds to build a political Europe without the United Kingdom. They suggested either waiting until Great Britain was admitted to the Economic Community or "bringing her into the negotiations right away." Waiting for the United Kingdom meant risking three negative consequences:

1. A feeling of political insecurity among the members and citizens of the Economic Community;

2. A weakening of the negotiating position of the Six;

3. The reluctant acceptance of a union that would clearly be no more integrated and in fact probably even looser than the first Fouchet Project, for the reality was that Britain would certainly strengthen the "minimalist" faction.

But the interests of Europe surely required that the road be taken toward the firmest possible kind of political union — with or without the United Kingdom. If the foundations of a political union were not laid as rapidly as possible, the construction of the new Europe would be undermined. Any pause to enable the British to join would almost inevitably lead to the formation of some kind of classic alliance. It was highly probable and predictable that once the United Kingdom was a member of the Common Market any government, of whatever political complexion or preference, would tolerate few limitations on its "political sovereignty." To construct a political union on the basis of the Six meant to facilitate the future task of a British government and thereby to serve the interests of Europe more securely. Moreover, a first step of this kind — and a timid one at that — did not present the United Kingdom with a fait accompli, since the embryonic political collaboration suggested in the Fouchet Project did not prescribe a particular form for the political organization of Europe. It left a door open for the future; after three years' experience, member states were to revise their pact in light of that experience and in the direction of greater integration. Thus, the United Kingdom would have the chance to participate in fundamental decision making that would fix the form and content of the political union at the end of the pretransitional stage.

Under such conditions, could the European Community of the Six create an integrated supranational union in a short space of time even without the United Kingdom? The major obstacle may well have been General de Gaulle, as some believed, for he certainly was not enamored of supranationalism. But was it desirable to wait for his departure before getting down to the real business at hand? Quite independently of the disadvantages already mentioned, this meant waiting till 1969. Was it wise to sacrifice the possible to the hypothetical, that is, to sacrifice a loose but achievable union to a distant vision of a supranational Europe?

Differences of opinion among the Six were not simply a matter of a Europe of states versus a supranational Europe — though this polarity became something of a leitmotiv. None of the governments gave the impression that it was ready to accept true federation like those of the United States and Switzerland. None seemed ready to cross the Rubicon that divides confederal links from a real federation. Most seemed to regard such an integrated form as a more or less remote objective. This at any rate was the impression given by their negotiating positions — as distinct from their expressions of European faith and intention. Leaving aside ideological questions, straightforward analysis of certain government declarations confirms this view. Thus, for example, when Paul-Henri Spaak spoke of a supranational Europe he almost invariably had in mind substituting majority voting for the requirement of unanimity. The truth is that he dealt with only one aspect of the problem and completely ignored two essential features of supranationality; the independence of a European executive having decision-making powers vis-à-vis national governments and the immediate effect of such power exercised directly over citizens without national intermediaries. This supranationality embodied in the High Authority in its original form was made subordinate to a Council of National Ministers in the Common Market and Euratom. Nobody, not even the intransigent European Spaak, expected to make up lost ground in an area where national sovereignties are so sensitive. Overall, divergences among the Six had less to do with the nature of the union to be created than with the issue of the relative strength of this loose confederal bond.

Later, the positions of the Six tended to grow closer with regard to a handful of practical problems. Spaak revised his views — with the probable agreement of his Dutch colleague — thus harking back to a time when together with Jean Monnet he used to exhort the German government to accept French proposals. His U-turn was partly precipitated by the excessively rigid and anti-European attitude of Gaitskell at the European Conference of Socialist Parties in Brussels but also by discussions with the founding fathers of Europe, including Jean Monnet. In the meantime, the question of waiting for a change of heart by Great Britain became less important. The way seemed to be wide open for a summit of the Six.

What Kind of European Union?

Given agreement on the need for political union, what kind of Europe were the Six proposing to build? What form of government did they have in mind? All in all, their proposals and counterproposals were more or less consciously inspired by the federalist experience. All rejected the centralized model, in which member states would be reduced to the role of mere provinces, and opted for a formula that would guarantee the active participation of autonomous nations in the common enterprise. Their motto was "union of diversities." The union superstructure they envisaged seemed to have fairly modest proportions.

History certainly teaches us that there are dangers in wanting to do too much too quickly, and trying to create a federal state without adequate social foundations implies a high risk for the survival of the new federal structure. There was also a risk in wanting to do too little. Building an overly fragile and ineffective structure might have put a dangerous brake on union or definitively compromised it. Disappointment and discouragement are as threatening as excessive idealism. Was the Fouchet Project a guarantee against these two extremes?

In the absence of any powerful popular movement, two ways were open to forge a political union: European elections and the will of governments. Elections, as set out by the Treaty of Rome, had two limitations. European voting by universal direct suffrage would merely lead to the election of members of a European Parliament with very limited powers. Moreover, even if some kind of parliamentary revolution were to hold out prospects of it being transformed into a real parliament, the accomplishment of such a project would depend on the prior agreement of the six governments and ratification by their parliaments. In other words, neither European elections nor a European union would be possible unless governments desired them and parliaments accepted them.

Once again it was France, in the person of President de Gaulle, who put forward the idea of a confederation of European states in September 1960. His proposal produced various reactions. Some accused the general of hidden intentions, of wishing to put the Communities under the control of a council of national ministers, to weaken the Atlantic Alliance by setting up a common defense policy for the Six, and to impose French "leadership" on the others. Others gave less importance to intentions than to possible results and acknowledged that this proposal had the merit of officially relaunching a political Europe. After a year of difficult negotiations, a Summit of the Six produced a declaration of good intentions on 18 July 1961 in Bonn. In this text, the Six declared their resolution to give statutory form to a political intention that was already implicit in the European Communities, to cooperate in creating the conditions for a common policy, to continue with and encourage the work of the Communities, and to reinforce political alliance through political union. To this end, they planned to widen the sphere of discussions in the Parliament of the Six and gave a commission under the leadership of Ambassador Fouchet the task of drawing up a union project. With a few small modifications, the Fouchet Commission project constituted the basis for discussions among the Six.

The Main Features of the Fouchet Project [27]

The title of the text drawn up by the Fouchet Commission is a reminder of the "peace project for a union of European states" published by Senator Michel Debré in 1950, but its content is far less adventurous than Debré's revolutionary proposals. The *preamble* reaffirms the principles of freedom and democracy that (following the example of the Council of Europe) could constitute a sine qua non for the admission of new members.[28] Furthermore, member states declared themselves resolved to work toward harmonizing their essential interests — something that was already an objective of the existing Communities — "so as to plan for a future that would henceforth be irrevocably shared." The first article stipulates that the union would be *indissoluble*. It does not allow any right of secession, a right generally acknowledged by confederations but forbidden in principle by federal states.

1. *Objectives.*   The aim of the union would be to work for the adoption of common foreign and defense policies in areas of common interest, to secure close cooperation in the domains of science and culture, and to contribute to the defense of human rights and democracy in member states. This last principle confirms my interpretation that all members had to be states that actually operated on democratic principles. There is another point worthy of attention: the text does not just refer to the coordination of member states' foreign policies but more audaciously lays down as a goal "the adoption of a common foreign policy."

2. *Institutions.*   It is not so much in the project's objectives as in the anatomy of institutions and powers that we find the real significance of the proposed union. It was to have three institutions: a council, a parliament, and a political commission. The Council would have a monopoly over decision-making power. It would meet every four months at the level of heads of state or government and in the intervening periods at least once at the level of foreign ministers. A president was to be appointed for each of the summit meetings, but his mandate would last only for four months.

This four-month term obviously was too brief. The Debré project suggested that an "arbiter" be elected by universal suffrage to hold office for five years. The experience of the Councils of the Communities suggests that six months would be the minimum necessary term. But a more crucial question was raised by the voting procedure for the Council of the Union. Apparently in accord with the will of the Six, the Council "is to adopt by unanimous vote the decisions necessary for accomplishing the aims of the Union." Under the system proposed, any state that did not judge a decision "necessary" would have the option of veto or abstention. But according to article 6 the absence or abstention of one or two members would not present an obstacle to the formulation of a decision. Thus, the paralyzing aspect of unanimity, which in its original form requires a favorable vote by all, was attenuated; in this system, unanimity was assimilated to the *veto* in its original meaning, which requires a negative intention to be expressed. Nevertheless, a limit was set to absences and abstentions; at least four members would have to be present and voting in favor. The authors of the proposal hoped to reduce the paralyzing effects of a requirement for unanimity, which are more threatening at the level of heads of state or government than in a community grouping where majorities and unanimity balance. Once a decision has been taken, what is its scope? In principle, it is binding but only for those members who cast their vote in favor of it. In other words, absence or abstention is a means of liberating oneself from the obligatory effect of common decisions.

Such a procedure might conceivably be acceptable in cases of abstention but is quite unacceptable in cases of absence, since it would offer an open door to members wanting to avoid both explanation and obligation. A member who at least is present but abstains participates in the discussion, defends his point of view, and debates with the others. But absence is a means of evading shared responsibility. Another question is that of knowing whether we should accept the use of partial agreements that are not binding on abstainers. In the opinion of some specialists in public law, this would actually result in a more efficient mechanism by reducing the temptation to block measures. Such a practice might be allowed exceptionally, provided that the exception does not become the rule. Of course, solidarity on the part of the Six would seem to offer security against abuses. But would it have been sufficient in this political domain — so primordial and delicate?

The *European Parliament* of the Communities debates matters connected with the aims of the Union, but its powers are to be strictly limited. The European Executive reports on its activities to Parliament and is under its democratic control. In a union, the Council would not be responsible to Parliament (as is the Council of the European Communities) and would hold all the powers. Parliament may address questions and recommendations to it and ask to know what action has been taken by the Council on its recommendations. But Parliament has none of the functions that normally belong to a true assembly — budgetary control and legislative functions. Moreover, this embryo of popular representation is not authorized to give its opinion on the revision of the Union Treaty unless it is invited to do so by the Council. Thus, the Council gradually would extend its domination to the whole structure of the union.

To compound this confusion, the *European Political Commission* is made up of senior officials belonging to foreign ministries. This is a contradiction in terms and a radical change from the community conception, which guarantees the autonomy of an executive composed of independent persons not subject to the instructions of national governments (even though they may still be subject to their influence). But the political union abandons exactly what makes the Communities original and dynamic. In this backward step, the Political Commission is relegated to the rank of a mere collective secretariat exposed to the caprices of national governments.

Accordingly, the project proposed by France, whose president was quick to describe the UN system as ineffective, proposed (in the framework of a narrow community solidarity) a mechanism that is much less advanced than the autonomous international secretariats, protected in principle against state intervention. This was a return to Briand's ideas, outmoded by the way in which the structures of international organizations had developed. In this manner, the authors of the project did not just concentrate all the power in the Council, where the national governments had seats, but, instead of the international secretariats that have now become classic, they proposed an intergovernmental secretariat with the misleading title of the European Political Commission. This is definitely the most negative aspect of the Fouchet Commission's plan.

3. *Revision.* Revision was to take place in light of the progress achieved. According to the draft, revisions would be made with the principle objective of establishing a unified foreign policy and progressively constituting an organization involving the European Communities as central to the union. Nothing, however, would be sufficient to counterbalance the consequences of this original sin, even though, in the opinion of many Europeans involved in the debate, this *obligatory progressiveness* was an extremely positive aspect of the plan.

Presidential Amendments

The Political Union Project produced by the Fouchet Commission was discussed at a meeting of foreign ministers early in 1962, when President de Gaulle made some amendments to it that upset France's partners. These were not just stylistic but signaled a return to the initial ideas that had already aroused lively criticism. Among the functions of the Council, harmonization, coordination, and unification of economic policies reappeared after having been suppressed on the insistence of the Five. This meant that the union would tend to take precedence over the activities of the three Communities, which would be subordinated to it. Instead of lost time being made up in the political construction, there was actually a danger that further delay would occur in the Community sector. A mechanism that was more likely to induce paralysis than guarantee efficiency was to be imposed on institutions that had proved their worth. Moreover, in the absence of the assurances given by the French government in the first version, European defense policy in its relations with the North Atlantic Treaty Organization (NATO) would again be shrouded in a somewhat enigmatic silence. Finally, the union was no longer to be indissoluble.

President de Gaulle's concept was explicitly reiterated in a 15 May 1962 press conference at which he declared that Western Europe must constitute itself politically. Any failure, he alleged, would threaten the long-term future of the Economic Community.

> What is France proposing to her five partners? I repeat: to organize ourselves politically, we must begin at the beginning. Let us organize our cooperation. Let us bring together our heads of state or government at intervals so that they can take decisions that will be Europe's decisions. Let us create a political commission, a defense commission, and a cultural commission, just as we already have an Economic Commission in Brussels studying issues of common concern and preparing for decisions to be taken by the six governments. These commissions will of course each be operating under very different conditions. In addition, the competent ministers will meet whenever necessary to implement council decisions jointly. Moreover, we already have a European Parliamentary Assembly sitting in Strasbourg composed of delegations from our six national parliaments. Let us allow this Assembly to discuss political questions of common interest as well as the economic questions with which it already deals. In three years, with some experience behind us, we shall see what we must do to draw closer together. But at the very least we shall have formed the habit of living and acting together. This is France's proposal, and she believes that this will be the most practical approach.[29]

This fundamental text sums up General de Gaulle's ideas on political union and provides clarification on the nature of the commissions. He abandoned any desire to create institutions built on top of existing executives. He acknowledged that the Six were already involved in politics insofar as they were establishing tariffs and agricultural policies together or undertaking joint negotiations with the United Kingdom. In his opinion, it was arbitrary to want to exclude the economic domain from meetings of heads of state or government when it was such a crucial everyday issue for all of them. But he recognized the Brussels Commission's role and proposed the establishment of three new commissions whose main task would be to pave the way for Council decisions. He then stressed that each commission would be unique, with different procedures and means depending on the conditions peculiar to its sphere.

In this press conference, President de Gaulle in fact was broadly confirming French positions (with a few variations) and the concepts contained in the second French project submitted to the Fouchet Commission on 18 January 1962. Following this meeting, the five delegations drew up their own counterproject for a treaty, which included a provision for the addition of a court of justice and a general secretary as well as guarantees for the European Communities and the Atlantic Alliance. In addition, the

counterproject, while proposing revisions that would enhance the autonomous development of Union institutions and increase their powers, suggested the following objectives: elections to the European Parliament and
a strengthening of its powers, the introduction of majority rule in the
Council, the creation of an independent executive, and the extension of
the powers of the proposed court of justice.[30]

The Breakdown of the Political Union

Disagreement persisted between France and its five partners at the meetings
of 20 February and 15 March 1962. It arose in particular from a fear that the
Council of heads of state or government might gradually deplete the European Communities of their substance (cf. the inclusion of the economy in the
powers of the union) and from anxiety about the reference to the Atlantic
Alliance and the revision clause. Against this background, the Fouchet
Commission adopted a draft treaty with alternative texts for certain articles.
This draft made abundantly clear the points of convergence and divergence
between France and its partners.

    If differences persisted regarding institutions (the Court of Justice and
the General Secretariat), agreement was reached on the creation of three
committees of ministers: a Committee of Foreign Ministers, a Committee
of Defense and Army Ministers, and a Committee of Ministers of Education (or ministers responsible for international cultural relations). On this
subject, it is worth noting that while foreign ministers met regularly in the
context of political cooperation, as did ministers of education, thirty years
later there is no Committee of Defense Ministers. Recourse to the unanimity rule was the subject of a significant addition by the five member states:
for particular questions, the Council could agree by a unanimous decision
to decide by a majority vote. Otherwise, the differences remained the same
as those mentioned above. Suspicion of President de Gaulle and problems
posed by Great Britain's candidacy were further factors that helped bring
about the collapse of this second attempt to give the European Communities political structure.

    Valiant efforts were made by the Italian government and Ambassa-
dor Cattani, the new president of the negotiating commission, but it was
de Gaulle himself who was ultimately responsible for ending the negotiations on the Fouchet Project in his 15 May 1962 speech. Here he recalled
the main lines of the French proposal and noted that France would not
remain satisfied with the Europe of the Common Market.

> Western Europe—whether we are talking about its actions with re-
> spect to other peoples, about its own defense, about its contribution to

developing the regions, or about its capacity for producing international equilibrium and détente — must constitute itself politically.

He concluded further:

The truth is that we cannot guarantee Europe's economic development without it being politically united, and on this issue I must observe how arbitrary is *the idea,* expressed recently in discussions in Paris, *that the economic sphere must be excluded from meetings of heads of state or government — for the simple fact is that for each one of them in his own country economics is the crucial bread and butter issue (my italics).*[31]

As so often happened in the union process, the opposition of certain members of the Community delayed the most modest of steps toward political union because of fears or prejudice with regard to supranationality.[32] Ten years after this first defeat, meetings of heads of state or government have made it possible not merely to agree on the entry into the Community of the United Kingdom, Denmark, and Ireland but also to set up the European Council in 1974. History has proved de Gaulle to be right regarding the undeniable role of the European Council.

Now, fifty years on, the debate has begun again with the Franco-German proposal for political union based on the European Council. This time Holland fears less French than Franco-German hegemony. Dutch fears seem not to be borne out by the experience of the European Council, which has often helped to unblock apparent stalemates such as the budget disputes with Mrs. Thatcher's United Kingdom, to give an impetus to several new policies (research, regions), and to relaunch initiatives — witness the Single European Act and the double negotiations of 1990–91 on the Economic and Monetary Union and the Political Union.

The refusal of both Holland and Belgium in 1962 suggests two observations. As with the failure of the EDC, it is noticeable that a rigid maximalist attitude often has the perverse effect of slowing down progress toward union; in certain cases it may do a disservice to the European cause (despite the intentions of the authors — unless the invocation of an objective that is certainly desirable but hard to achieve is just a pretext or a sign of political myopia). The lesson of the EDC does not seem to have been learned: the objective of the EDC was to set up a kind of European army in which the reemerging German army was to be integrated. According to Raymond Aron, the debate on the question of a European army and its German units provoked the biggest ideological quarrel in France since the

Dreyfus affair. It was a conflict that drove a wedge between leaders and within political parties and groups. Defenders of the EDC and its political embodiment saw in it the best way to prevent the rebirth of a German national army, which seemed inevitable in the face of the Soviet threat and pressure from the United States. Under these conditions, the EDC and the European Political Community seemed to them to offer the best guarantee against a rebirth of German power through the anchoring of Germany in a solid Community.

It hardly seems necessary to remark that the unification of the two Germanies raised the German question all over again and in similar terms. Against this European vision, opponents of the EDC—nationalist, communist, anti-European, and anti-German, a mixture of all sorts of tendencies—worked together, in spite of different motives, for one and the same objective: preventing the reemergence of a German army. By a paradox of history, their victory brought about the result they had mobilized to prevent, the rebirth of an independent German army.

As with the failure of the EDC, which produced the effect feared by its opponents—the rebirth of the German army—the rejection of de Gaulle's project by the most European of the leaders, Spaak and Luns, did a disservice to the European cause they wanted to defend by delaying, and indeed enfeebling, the integration process.

Regrets and posthumous initiatives had no effect. The 1964 German and Italian initiatives were in fact preceded by the Spaak Plan, which broadly resembled the Fouchet Plan with the addition of a Community-type political commission. I heard Paul-Henri Spaak express regret in several speeches about the delay caused by the rejection of the Fouchet Plan. The delay was all the more regrettable in that the plan included a provision for the revision of the initial treaty after an experimental three-year period. Ultimately, the rejection of organized political cooperation between the Six resulted in (in accord with de Gaulle's logic) the drafting of a Franco-German treaty in September 1962 and its signing on 22 January 1963. Thus, maximalist preconditions and persistent refusals led to initiatives that were part of a process that was reductionist in terms of the questions and the number of countries involved.

This reductive effect is sometimes even more pronounced when we compare the progression of ideas and projects with government plans and proposals, the exception being the European Political Community Project drawn up by the *ad hoc Assembly.* Interaction between ideas, official projects, and achievements is largely a part of the reductionist process visible to the observer of the evolution of Europe. The rejection of the Fouchet Plan caused the first of a series of European crises.

The Tindemans Report

A European Identity

In carrying out his mandate from the European Council, Léo Tindemans, then prime minister of Belgium, took extensive soundings from a range of political, socioeconomic, and scientific experts in member states as he sought the widest possible consensus on the main lines of a European union.[33]

The report contained several recommendations, some of which were implemented later while others were simply ignored, but it met the same fate as that of the EDC at the hands of the French National Assembly more than twenty years earlier, ending up in the archives of the European Council and member governments without ever having been studied. However, some of the ideas contained in this report did permeate slowly into people's consciousness and were subsequently taken up by political leaders, finding their way eventually into European programs.[34]

From the start, Tindemans noted that most of the people he talked to had stressed the importance of a *European identity*, a concept that has since become a commonplace in European discourse. At the same time, his report called for a deepening of economic integration in the form of an economic and monetary union, a program that fitted in with the Treaty of Rome and the logic of the Werner Plan. The latter proposed the creation of a monetary zone, involving (among other things) a fixed parity for intra-European currencies. It also suggested that these currencies should float together in relation to currencies outside the area and proposed a shared Community balance of payments. In this conception, the European Fund for Monetary Cooperation was to become the equivalent of a "World Bank" on the European level.

The Tindemans Report was particularly innovative in the areas of external policy and security and in the institutional sphere. It was a logical step to emphasize the external dimension of the Community, which looked like a stunted branch of the Community tree since the failure of the EDC and the Fouchet Project. With respect to external relations, there was a very limited sense of a European economic identity. According to those approached by Tindemans, there was a need for a Community Europe spokesman. On this, he commented:

> I have made concrete proposals; I have suggested that we choose areas where we could agree to speak with one voice. In these areas, therefore, we should also accept the fact that unanimity would no

longer be essential for the formulation of common positions. Of course, differences of opinion could arise in respect to particular problems; in these cases, the minority would, in principle, have to accept the opinion of the majority. As far as I am concerned, we are not talking here about a voting procedure in which the majority overrules the minority. The way of doing things should be closer to government practice in our countries; differences often arise in Cabinet but they do not prevent governments from adopting a position that has unanimous backing. This problem of Europe speaking with a *single voice* becomes particularly clear in relation to the United States. President Kennedy called for an Atlantic partnership in which the United States would have discussions with a single European partner. For me, too, American and European partners should negotiate on the same footing.

I also feel that it is premature to try to tackle *defense* issues, even though one day defense certainly ought to have a place among the main issues in a European union. For the time being, it seems to me that discussion and debate in this area is much too risky on account of the prevailing differences of opinion between member states: France is not part of NATO, although it remains in the Alliance, Ireland is neutral and remains outside that organization, while the other countries have committed themselves to NATO. Under these circumstances, I thought it better to leave this area out of the discussion. Nonetheless, I did feel that we could not completely ignore another fundamental issue that is closely related to it, namely, that of *security.* In this area, there are precedents; at the Helsinki Conference on security and cooperation in Europe, the Nine managed to formulate common positions and speak with one voice through Mr. Moro, president of the Council of Ministers. In my view, these security issues, which need to be distinguished from real defense matters, must now be brought into our discussion and our shared reflection within the Community. Likewise, it seems impossible to me for the Community countries to ignore possible conflicts in the Middle East or other parts of the world.[35]

The report contains a number of proposals aimed at achieving greater coherence. It distinguishes between ministerial meetings that deal with political cooperation and those that handle subjects covered by the treaties. This is the notion of a *single decision-making center.* It implies that the institutions of the Union should discuss any problems that have to do with the interests of Europe and come within the competence of the Union. Mechanisms of political cooperation and Community mechanisms must evolve in a single institutional framework. Economic, social, and political interdependence require this kind of unity.

In the context of a single decision-making center, different procedures can be used, depending on the type of issue under consideration. Here, a threefold distinction is essential:

1. Concerning external relations covered by the European treaties and also (according to the Accord européen des transports routiers [AETR] judgment) with regard to the external elements of new common policies, Community procedures will have to be used outside the limits of the Community treaties.

2. In particular areas, there must be a commitment to agree on a *common policy.* This means that the Council must adopt joint decisions, and that of course assumes that minorities are prepared to accept the conclusions of majorities once debating is over. These special areas are:

    a. the new world economic order;

    b. relations between Europe and the United States;

    c. security; and

    d. crises arising in Europe's immediate geographical environment.

3. In other spheres, the system of *political cooperation,* as set out in the context of the Davignon Procedure (at the time, Davignon was political director in the Belgian foreign ministry), will continue to operate for the time being; it will have to be borne in mind, however, that this procedure fits into a unique institutional framework.

Community methods and means of cooperation coexist and evolve within this single decision-making center. With the aim of making the institutional apparatus more efficient, the report recommends more frequent recourse to the *technique of delegation,* which must make it possible to simplify decision-making mechanisms and facilitate negotiations without damaging the institutional equilibrium. That is why the enforcement and management of common policies ought to lead to wider recourse to article 155 of the treaty, which enables powers to be conferred on the Commission — whose standing will thus be improved.

Again for the purpose of achieving greater efficiency, it is emphasized that recourse to *majority voting* in the Council must become current practice in the Community domain — following the guidelines agreed at the 1974 Paris Summit.[36]

From this point of view, the European Council that was created in 1974 — an innovation in the overall Community system — strengthened the elements of a European authority. Jean Monnet and his Action Committee observed that what was most lacking in Europe was some form of authority and consequently that if heads of state or government had decided to take on such a role together this would have been to Europe's advantage.

*Institutional Equilibrium and the Strengthening
of the Commission*

Although the European Council strengthens the intergovernmental factor in the Community system, it has at least the merit of existing and the capacity to encourage integration with its initiatives — whose execution it hands over to Community institutions — and the added drive they impart. In order to avoid disturbing Community structures, Léo Tindemans based his work on the Rome Treaties and sought to supplement and strengthen them, adding to them the spheres of external policies and security, proposing to confer more importance on the Commission with a new procedure for nominating its president, and attributing a power to initiate legislation to a European Parliament elected by direct suffrage. While avoiding the creation of a confederal entity, Tindemans planned to preserve, and indeed develop, the Community experience by working on the principle of *institutional equilibrium* between, on the one hand, institutions like the European Council, the Council of Ministers, and the Committee of Permanent Representatives (Coreper) — which at different levels have the task of *giving collective expression to national interests* — and, on the other, truly Community institutions. These are the Commission, the European Parliament, and the Court of Justice, which have the function of expressing, embodying, and protecting the *common interest.* This institutional equilibrium, the distinctive and primordial mark of any federative system, is based on the dynamics of autonomous Community institutions and participation by representatives of different interests in the process of shared decision making. With the aim of maintaining this equilibrium, so indispensable for the good functioning of the Community, Tindemans proposed that in addition to the powers it already possessed (especially in the area of the budget) the European Parliament be endowed with a power of initiation that would subsequently become a right, so that it would be in a position to make a positive contribution to the formulation of common policies.

In the second place, his proposal aimed to reinforce the authority of the Commission, which was showing signs of weakness in a time of crisis and frequently seemed unable to make use of the right of initiative attributed to it by the treaty. The president, nominated by the European Council, was to be invested by a vote of the European Parliament. Thus confirmed in his functions, the president had the power to choose the other members of the Commission in consultation with the Council and having due regard for national equilibria.

The Tindemans Report came in for some criticism, especially from D. P. Spierenburg, who complained that Tindemans had prematurely encouraged the international dimension of integration by proposing a global concept of foreign policy instead of working on developing outside the Community the powers exercised inside.[37] The fact is that insofar as the Community has shown itself capable of coherent and effective action it has been on the basis of its internal powers. The Kennedy Round of negotiations, the Lomé Agreement, and the dialogue with the American administration were to be proof of this. On the other hand, without monetary union the Community seems uncertain and even divided in its interventions in the area of reform of the international monetary system. It is true that internal integration and cohesion make possible an increase in available means and therefore in the effectiveness of a common external policy.

But external policy is not a simple projection of internal policy. The United States' withdrawal from Vietnam and Soviet expansion in Africa gave rise to anxieties about the absence of Europe. The need for Europe to return to "high politics" is not to be explained by, or traced back to, the demands of internal politics. The dimension of external policy based on the elements of internal policy is in interaction with them but maintains its own field, involving relations between the players in the international system. Can we then justify the absence of Europe from the search for solutions to international conflicts by an absence of internal powers in the domains that form the arena for such conflicts? External policy, sometimes called "pure politics" or "politics par excellence," is in fact a particular dimension of the life of states and communities of states whose effectiveness depends on an ability to both handle international situations and instruments and make optimal use of available resources.

Even supposing that Europe manages to speak with one voice in international affairs and increases its international presence by pooling its human and material resources, the question remains as to whether its potential for exercising pressure and influence and its political weight will allow it to play a crucial role at the global level after the fall of the Berlin Wall. In the past, Stanley Hoffmann's analysis led him to a conclusion not far distant from that of Henry Kissinger: the European Community is only a regional power, a secondary player limited to a complementary role, and in no way is it a key actor in international affairs.

Hoffman's conclusion was pessimistic: "A fragmented, disorganized Europe is not master of its destiny. And yet the tentative character of its attempts at unification can in part perhaps be explained by a painful awareness that a Union of Europe would not make very much difference."[38] Hoffmann was very much under the spell of American economic might and did not take account of the signs of its gradual weakening in the face of an emerging Japan. Nor did he credit the renaissance of the European Community's economic strength. As Paul Kennedy remarked, a great military and political power cannot enjoy long-term prospects without the support of a solid economy. Criticism based on the mere externalization of internal functions pays too much attention to economic integration, while criticism based on temporary assessments limited by the conditions of the time underestimates the dynamics of European integration and overestimates the (admittedly impressive) power of the United States, even though the latter was in relative decline following the Vietnam debacle. The Tindemans Report may not have had any real impact on the governments of the day, but the ideas and initiatives it embodied have left their mark on the present state of the European debate.

Chapter 3

The Dynamics of
Community Institutions

The Birth and Growth of the European Communities

From Drawing Board to Prototype

In all the initiatives proposed by movements and individual thinkers and in all the various government organizations that paved the way toward European union at the close of World War II, two major streams of thought may be distinguished. The first inspired projects and embodiments of *union* from two points of view — the *federalist* and the *functionalist*. The second came from *governmental organizations,* which emerged in the 1950s and were subdivided into *Atlantic or Euro-American Organizations* on the one hand and *European organizations* on the other. There were numerous examples of these two families of organizations functioning on two levels, the Atlantic and the European. The Marshall Plan, with its provision of American aid for the reconstruction of Western Europe, inspired the collaboration between free European countries within the Organization for European Economic Cooperation (OEEC). It was this "forced" cooperation that led to the first steps toward liberalizing quotas and promoting intra-European trade. This invaluable gift from the Americans, along with the support given to the European Movement, greatly contributed to promoting and encouraging the union of Europe.

If, in the area of economic cooperation, this first push generated a trend toward autonomy for Europe, the same was not the case in the area of security. The Atlantic Alliance (and its organization, NATO) continued to exercise the essential functions required for the defense of Western Europe. In its advance toward union, Europe has yet to acquire autonomy in this crucial political arena. In spite of the collapse of the Eastern bloc and the dissolution of the Warsaw Pact, which coincided with the relative diminution of American economic power and America's reiterated intention to withdraw its armed forces (at least partially) from Europe, European security has remained a shared Euro-American affair, with the leading responsibility for it falling to NATO. Hence, the ongoing debate on the organization of a *European pillar* in NATO—an idea put forward by John Kennedy—and on a greater autonomy for Europe in security matters. This is one of those fundamental questions that periodically haunts those negotiating for political union. Unlike the autonomy gained in the economic and technological areas, security is tied to interdependence, which is like an umbilical cord tying Western Europe to the United States. This "dependency" relationship often has been at the heart of debates on political union and has served as a motive or pretext for delaying its advent. As these links begin to be transformed into a real partnership involving a dialogue between two large powers, Europe and America, the European current is tending to deepen and broaden around the dynamic core formed by the European Union.

At the same time, the real European current has two aspects, two concepts that represent the same quest for union. There is convergence between these two methods, one related to the global-political approach inspired by federalist principles and experience and the other related to the functionalist approach. Conceived by Mitrani and Scelle for specialized international organizations, this approach was put to the test by cooperation between the parties involved in the first French Plan under the direction of Jean Monnet. The first aspect spread throughout the European movements and left a strong impression; resulting European initiatives were the work of propaganda groups and publicists and came out of the Resistance. They were subsequently taken up by transfrontier networks with a common objective, the creation of a European democratic federation. These projects and initiatives, molded by personalities with a variety of viewpoints, were "codified" at the time of the Hague Congress before being taken up again by government authorities at the instigation of the European Movement. The Hague Congress led to the creation of the Council of Europe, the European Center for Culture, and the Collège d'Europe in Bruges.

This impetus, which launched the union process and emanated from European elites and a whole variety of movements, still constitutes one of the original features of the European Community. Initiatives of various pressure groups were subsequently taken up in the activities of numerous political and socioeconomic forces. These activities and structures form one of the social foundations of the Community.

The transition away from the private sector and interest groups toward the public sector took place at the time the Council of Europe was established. Based on principles of democracy and respect for human rights, the Council of Europe expressed the hopes of European federalists, even though from the start it fell victim to a crippling type of unionist compromise, mainly inspired by the British government. The Committee of Ministers, an intergovernmental institution, had weak powers compared to a Consultative Assembly, which, although representing the parliaments of member states, had only consultative powers. This predominantly intergovernmental structure soon found itself blocked. Only the Convention on Human Rights, with such institutions as a commission and a court, escaped the paralysis that afflicted the Council of Europe. Thanks to the fundamental principles relating to human rights, the Council did find its second wind after the fall of the Berlin Wall and the transition to democracy in the Eastern European ex-communist countries. However, while it offers a general framework, the Council of Europe lacks the dynamic economic and social forces that are the flesh and blood of the European Community. From the start of the integration process, the Council of Europe looked like an artificial dissociation of politics from economics, a dissociation in the service of general political principles meant to be applied by a weak international structure.

There were few signs of the coming of the rapid creation of the European Communities at the beginning of the 1950s. The disappointment resulting from the inability of the Council of Europe to achieve European union coincided with an economic crisis marked by a shortage of energy and the overproduction of steel. Only a strong political will supporting a proposal that reflected real needs could possibly bind together the separated threads of the frequently contradictory national interests of the European nations. The crucial spark came in a meeting between the pragmatic political visionary Robert Schuman and Jean Monnet, a creator of synergies with a technological imagination. Thanks to their collaboration, political will found its embodiment in a concrete proposal that led to the creation of the first European Community.

Throughout the process of European integration, we can perceive the outline of a political will of various, more or less explicit colors depending on the period. This will was directed toward a global political union, a federation, or a federal type of community. Whatever its form, the Union aims to establish a dynamic equilibrium between institutions having common powers and the institutions of member states and of their regions. This political will, though clearly expressed in the writings of Robert Schuman and Jean Monnet, took on a more sectoral and less emphatic form in the 9 May 1950 declaration. Inspired by the political and personal experience of Robert Schuman and by the experience of Jean Monnet's first French Plan, this declaration proposed a common organization of two basic sectors, the coal and the steel industries, and common management by a High Authority. The main idea was that these two sectors, which had been at the heart of the Franco-German wars, would be the foundation of the power of nations and might therefore be used to create deep solidarity in a Community based on the unity of a great industrial basin. By forging a de facto solidarity that would spread gradually to other sectors, the new Community would bring about a reorientation of external policies and guarantee peace and prosperity to all its members. At the present time, we cannot but admire this visionary project, which succeeded in translating the idea of union into fact.

In the course of the negotiations under Jean Monnet's presidency, political will found an institutional formulation thanks to a Benelux initiative. In fact, the resulting Community system went beyond the management needs of the coal and steel sectors. It proposed not merely a High Authority having supranational powers and assisted by a consultative committee representing the principal parties involved but also a special council of ministers liaising with national governments and a common assembly and court of justice. Thus, in some respects this ECSC structure echoes the idea of a *political system,* even though it is incomplete and distorted.

Political intent was confirmed by a proposal put forward barely three months after the Schuman Declaration by René Pleven for the creation of a European Defense Community. The failure of the EDC and its natural extension in the European political community provoked the first great European crisis by blocking the drive to union and weakening the powers of the ECSC. Moreover, this failure halted the quest for political union and destroyed the indispensable parallelism or complementarity between the economic and political union. In addition, it made the attitude of the United Kingdom clear, as well as revealing particular difficulties raised by political union because of European dependence on the United States in matters of defense and because of U.S. dominance in NATO and the wider world. Although it is now less of a problem, this dilemma still influences government attitudes and affects current negotiations on political union.

The shock of the EDC's failure aroused distrust of supranationality among political leaders and made them more prudent in their approach to Europe. This revival of nationalism did not prevent the governments of the Six, however, from relaunching the idea of an economic and atomic community just nine months later in Messina. At the time, this historic event received only minimal attention in the media. The Messina Conference of 1 and 2 June 1955 resolved to create an intergovernmental committee, presided over by Paul-Henri Spaak, which proceeded to draw up a report proposing that a general common market be established and atomic energy industries be combined.[1] The report, which was submitted in April 1956, served as a basis for the negotiations that were to lead to the Treaty of Rome. This was signed on 25 March 1957 and came into force at the beginning of 1958. Thus, three years after the EDC shock, the EEC and Euratom confirmed the necessity and vitality of the European integration process set in motion by the creation of the ECSC.

This revival of the movement toward union after a period of stalemate deserves some thought. Depending on how it is read, integration seems to move with either astonishing speed or exasperating slowness. From the perspective of history, this revolutionary process seems remarkably rapid, for only three years after the close of hostilities Europeans, friends and former enemies alike, gathered at the Hague in 1948 to formulate their plan. Two years later, the idea of the ECSC was officially declared, giving birth to the first European Community, with limited but real powers. Though everything seemed to have been wrecked in 1954, continuity was assured by the creation of the Economic and Atomic Communities in 1958. Thirty years later, the Single European Act gave new impetus to the union movement, leading to political cooperation. During the intervening period, the field of action was enlarged, the process being reinforced by the direct election of a European Parliament. The drive was provided by the European Council, while the European Community grew larger with the incorporation of England, Denmark, and Ireland in 1973; Greece in 1981; Spain and Portugal in 1986; and Austria, Finland, and Sweden in 1995. An immense amount of progress was made with astonishing speed in light of the history of the development of nations and federations such as that of Switzerland, which celebrated its seven hundredth anniversary in 1991.

But in the eyes of militant Europeanists progress toward union looks desperately slow in the context of changes in the world. Rapidly changing world events, the speed of technological evolution, and the upheavals in Eastern Europe are factors that require integration. From this point of view, the integration process should not be considered in light of the past but in the context of the present, with rapid, interactive communications making events occur virtually simultaneously when previously they would have taken place months or years apart. However, this acceleration and transformation of events raises the question of whether attitudes and behavior are adapting to the pace of external evolution. From this point of view, the development of European movements and the formation of a Community based largely on Franco-German entente seem like historical miracles. So, too, are the upheavals in French foreign policy following the Schuman Plan, the replacement of hostile attitudes with bonds of trust, and profound changes of opinion not simply among political and economic leaders but among large sectors of the population. In spite of the EDC shock, the vigor of the union movement, its continuity, and its confidence in the face of sporadic reverses bear witness to the breadth and depth of the union process set in motion by the European movements and the initiatives of European leaders.

Since Messina, the quest for integration has concentrated on the economy and technology, ignoring (with one or two exceptions) problems of political union and its two major components, common external and security policies. Not until the Single European Act did we find acceptance of the idea of political cooperation and the inclusion of security in an official treaty. However, the imbalance between economic union and embryonic political union persisted even in the treaty on European unity.

The Role of European Personalities

The creation of the ECSC and two new Communities is an illustration of the primordial role played by major political personalities in the European union process. Launched by the Schuman-Monnet tandem, the ECSC was, from the start, marked by the strong personality of Jean Monnet and his pragmatic functionalist conception. The EDC crisis led him to abandon the presidency of the High Authority in order to found the Action Committee for the United States of Europe, to promote and create the Common Market and Euratom, and to encourage and deepen European integration.[2] Taking over from the European Movement, whose strength of purpose had been undermined by the trend toward sectoral integration, the Monnet Committee sought to respond to immediate concrete demands with timely declarations and actions. The authority and influence of this committee stemmed mainly from its president's powers of persuasion and from the fifty or so personalities involved in it: pro-European leaders from the Socialist, Christian Democrat, and Liberal Parties as well as from the trade unions.

Later, the Action Committee's approach was very supportive of the work of the European Communities and suggested solutions to obstacles in the way of political union, enlarging the Community and strengthening European-American relations. For example, the Monnet Committee worked very hard for the ratification of the Treaty of Rome, particularly in the French National Assembly and the Bundestag, as Sozialdemokratische Partei Deutschlands (SPD) deputy Mellies, formerly a member of the committee, testified.[3] The Action Committee, closely bound up with the personality of Jean Monnet, was dissolved by its president shortly before he died in 1979. Unlike the Monnet Committee, however, the European Movement forged ahead, despite many vicissitudes.

The part played by particular individuals is illustrated by the powerful influence of Paul-Henri Spaak on European politics. Together with Fernand Dehousse, he was personally responsible for persuading the majority of the Belgian deputies to vote for the ECSC. A fervent supporter of the EDC and a political community, he rejected any concessions of the type put forward by Mendès France, who proposed a transitional period and a weakening of certain powers considered to be too supranational. It was in the name of this principle of supranationality that Spaak rejected de Gaulle's project for a political union eight years later. On the other hand, in the Spaak Report, which laid the basis for the formulation of the Treaty of Rome, he adopted a more flexible attitude in an effort to protect the European Commission from being engulfed by the overwhelming powers of the Council. This prudent strategy, and the support of the Monnet Committee, ensured that the institutional aspect of the two new treaties did not create obstacles to their ratification. At this time, supranationality was a European taboo.

If the watersheds in European integration bear the imprint of great personalities like Adenauer, De Gasperi, Hallstein (first president of the European Commission), de Gaulle, Giscard d'Estaing, Schmidt, Mitterrand, Kohl, Thatcher, and Delors, the integration process as an ongoing movement has involved a multitude of actors, from leaders and political parties to economic and social agents and citizens and public opinion.

Parliamentarians and political parties took responsibility from the start, with the ratification of the treaties setting up the European Communities, by approving the ECSC Treaty and its supranational structure. Later, however, when the French deputies could not find a majority in favor of the EDC, they buried the treaty even though it had been ratified by the parliaments of their partners. Subsequently, the ratification of the Treaty of Rome was rightly regarded as a test of the behavior of political parties in their national parliaments. The votes cast in favor without too many surprises in all six parliaments were characterized, however, by conversion in favor of the European ideal of the German and Italian Socialist Parties, something that was due in part to the Monnet Committee.[4] To a large extent, these conversions were due to pro-European trade union attitudes, which, like the German Deutscher Gewerkschaftsbund (DGB), influenced the parties of the Left. Hence, a few years later Italian trade unions associated with the Communist Party managed to drag the latter into the Euro-Communist way of thinking.

Acceptance of the two Communities by the governments and parliaments of the six member states was won at the price of a new allocation of power; the Council, representing national governments, occupied a central position with the major share of decision-making authority. This slippage toward intergovernmental procedures took place progressively in the ECSC; for lack of solid foundations, its High Authority was led to seek support from the Council of Ministers and member states. The new Community system follows the ECSC experience while reinforcing it under pressure from a historical background that offered little encouragement to the restoration and enlargement of the powers of the supranational institution. The Councils of the two new Communities took the central position that the High Authority had in the ECSC. The Treaty of Rome gave them a key role, even though it was modest in appearance, under the less provocative title of Commissions. The Commissions — or rather the Commission after the fusion of the executives in 1967 — were responsible to the European Parliament and endowed with powers of initiative and proposal. They were also called on to handle the operation and development of the Common Market and nuclear industries. But it was the Council that took the decisions, by unanimous vote and later by qualified majority. The resort to a qualified majority would increase the communitarian nature of the Council. Apart from democratic control, the European Parliament had wide consultative powers, while the Court of Justice acquired broader powers, which gave it jurisdiction over the wide Community domain governing the Common Market. Community acts such as regulations and decisions had an obligatory binding force and took immediate effect with respect of persons and groups. A directive, regarded as a "soft law," was binding as to the objectives it defined but left the choice of means to national authorities.

In the first survey of the Community system, which I drafted in 1961, I observed that in spite of a more markedly intergovernmental structure than that of the ECSC the EEC promised a more significant extension of powers in the area of common external relations and commercial policies, a logical result of customs union, and gave the treaty an unlimited duration. In more than one sector, the Treaty of Rome widened and reinforced the Community character of the European system. My conclusion was as follows.

> The most decisive contribution of the new Communities has been on the practical level. Not only have they broadened the field of common action by increasing the importance of the three Communities, but they (and the Common Market in particular) have launched and extended the integration process.[5] Begun in the ECSC, this process has developed unexpected dimensions in the generalized Common Market.[6] It amounts to a vast chain of actions and reactions; first the economic agents reacted to the *fact* of the Common Market; then they adapted to it; later the planned pace of integration proved too ponderous and it was found necessary to speed up the development of the Common Market.
>
> From this sector, the movement spread to the trade unions, which were no longer content simply to react but strove to participate in what was happening by organizing their common activities at the Community level. Political parties did not remain on the sidelines; they regrouped across national frontiers and sought to give themselves formal structures at the European level in order to rise to their new calling.

This is not all: with the Common Market, Europe "got down to the grass roots" — for the ECSC and Euratom existed on the margins of everyday life and were remote from the immediate interests of the vast majority of the 165 million people who were directly affected by the Common Market. And the fact is that it is only when citizens' concrete interests are at stake that they will begin to take an interest in keeping a check on the administration and then actually to take part in it. From keeping tabs to being actually involved through the constitution of an Assembly elected by direct suffrage — that is the way the European Communities are taking off.

Once they start interacting in any manner, even in competition, transcending national frontiers and working in favor of a more intimate solidarity, these factors come into play in constructing a new social community. Such de facto solidarity, under the control of shared rules and institutions and blessed with the more or less conscious consent of various social agents, foreshadows a political basis for the European Communities. For one element is still lacking in the existing "economic federation": a political dimension.[7]

I tried to isolate one aspect of this complex process and its institutional mechanisms. The fragmented study led me to a limited conclusion; as President Schuman put it, the supranational Communities "mask an uneven reality." Consequently, the term *supranational* may be kept for two reasons: to distinguish the Communities from international organizations, a confederation of states, or a federal state; and to highlight the original features of this new form of international collaboration. However, supranationality is not an aspect of something taken in isolation but reflects the simultaneous operation of a group of fragments and factors.[8]

For all the numerous dangers and tensions that constantly threatened it, this integration process, launched by the ECSC and broadened and deepened by the EEC, was very soon regarded as irreversible. It has not, however, advanced in a straight line; from the start, its trajectory has been interrupted by sudden jerks and U-turns.

The Crises of 1963 and 1965

A series of crises in the European integration process slowed it down without damaging it irreversibly. The failure of the EDC caused political integration to separate from economic integration. Despite the two crises, in the ECSC — which came out greatly weakened — and the ECD, the Messina Conference relaunched economic integration in 1954 only nine months after the debacle earlier in the same year. The work of the Committee of Experts, presided over by Spaak, and the intergovernmental negotiations based on his report quickly led to the signing of the Treaty of Rome on 25 March 1957 (it came into force in 1958). After the worst crisis since the beginning of the European union process, it took a mere three years to put the two European Communities (the Common Market and Euratom) under the same roof. This was the most solid proof of the deep need for European union in spite of disappointments in the areas of defense and external affairs.

The renewed failure of political union plans in 1962 certainly perpetuated the imbalance between economic/technical integration and integration areas that are political par excellence. These repeated efforts showed how necessary yet difficult it was to reach agreement on the form and substance of political union. They also highlight a similarity between the failure of the EDC and the failure of the Fouchet Plan, both of which had aimed to give the Community a global political structure to supplement the sectoral integration embodied in the ECSC and the two new Communities. Moreover, these failures revealed how integration is related to external factors concerning U.S. influence and the problem of U.K. involvement in the European Community. These two factors remained on the European horizon, so much so that General de Gaulle was ready to speak of "an external federator" and call for a "European Europe."[9]

There was a link between the refusal to admit the United Kingdom in January 1963 and the role of the United States. Admittedly, there were other reasons for this decision: the attitude of the British, their insularity, their ambivalence toward the Fouchet Project, and a series of unresolved difficulties. According to Jean-François Deniau,[10] the leading Community negotiator, about half of the problems were still unresolved at the end of 1962. In addition, because of its close relations with the United States, the United Kingdom was often regarded as a Trojan horse that the Americans wanted to introduce into the Community fortress. A whole series of innuendoes and misunderstandings involving De Gaulle and Macmillan — together with the Kennedy-Macmillan Nassau Agreement on Skybolt Missiles — played their part in provoking the general's "non."

A crisis of a different kind arose in 1965: that of the so-called empty chair indicated the deliberate absence of the French from ministerial meetings. This had a protracted effect on the operation of European institutions by causing a delay in the introduction of qualified majority voting and preserving unanimity voting in the Council. However, it did demonstrate — if there was still any doubt — the irresistible force of the integration movement unleashed by the European Communities while revealing the de facto solidarity between countries and socioeconomic actors.

Without reopening the debate about the causes of the crisis, it is worth remembering that the Hallstein Commission proposal had a double objective: to guarantee financing for the agricultural policy and to increase the powers of the European Parliament. In order to put Common Agricultural Policy finances on a sound footing, it proposed the creation of a "common fund" drawn from both customs contributions and agricultural levies. This budgetary autonomy was to be accompanied by parliamentary supervision. The Hallstein Commission proposal satisfied France as regards agricultural financing and planned for an extension of the powers of the European Parliament. There was only one flaw in the logic: the primacy accorded by General de Gaulle to politics over administration.

De Gaulle expressed his refusal by implementing the empty chair policy at the end of June 1965, a move that paralyzed Community initiatives and development. The reasoning behind this attitude became clearer in the light of his September 1965 press conference. The general saw the Commission as becoming a future financial power, a future European government having its own resources and possessed of a broad right of initiative. This seemed to be the ambition of President Hallstein, with his pretensions and his symbolic red carpet, which exacerbated the general's determination to defend the power of the nation-state in the face of the emerging power of a supranational Community. Moreover, any increase in the powers of the European Parliament, even with a substantial financial compensation, could not fail to cut across de Gaulle's logic; he wanted to reinforce the power of the executive in France at the expense of the powers of the National Assembly. How could he accept on the European level what he was stubbornly opposing on the national level?

Behind these various interpretations we can discern a determination to oppose any European or international power potentially able to compete with or threaten the national pride and power of France. This determination fits in with the logic of General de Gaulle's struggle during and after World War II. His empty chair policy triggered a crisis that paralyzed the Community, created uncertainty about its future, and nearly blocked its economic impetus. The threat posed by the empty chair policy to the existence and future of the European Community provoked a series of reactions both on the part of France's fellow governments and on the part of Community and French interest groups.[11] The reactions of these socioeconomic actors highlighted the role they played in the formation of a European social network and in the functioning of the Community. The reaction of farmers, like that of other groups, was not slow to make itself felt. On 8 July, the Committee of Professional Agricultural Organizations in the EC (COPA) gave voice to the deep concern of the agricultural sector about the crisis and called for the six governments to resolve their difficulties while respecting the Treaty of Rome. In the days that followed, consultations took place between COPA, Union of Industries of the EC (UNICE), and the two European trade union secretariats. These consultations led to a common declaration intended to ensure a common line of action, to defend the EEC, and to call for a continuation of its development.

COPA and the General Committee for Agricultural Cooperation (COGECA) repeatedly spoke out in favor of integration. At the same time, it could not be ignored that even within the ranks of COPA traditional diverging opinions had made a more or less discreet appearance. While French professional organizations, in particular the French National Federation of Farmers (FNSEA), threw themselves into the battle to defend the Treaty of Rome, the German smallholders' organization Deutscher Bauernverband took the opportunity to reaffirm its traditional position. However, after the onset of the crisis France's five partners formulated a common position on the financing of agricultural policy. Consequently, the crucial issue, where pressure had to be concentrated if the crisis was to be ended, was the European policy of the French government. This meant that German claims had only a limited effect while the actions of French agricultural organizations, whose views coincided with the positions of other French professional associations and groups formed at community level, were more likely to exercise a direct influence on the turn of events and the resolution of the crisis.

As for industry, UNICE stated its position on 6 July and 7 October 1965. A few days after the crisis blew up it published a communiqué noting that integration was a dynamic phenomenon; accordingly, any stay in its evolution would compromise irredeemably what had already been achieved and indeed the whole future of the Community. UNICE considered that such a situation could not fail to have serious repercussions for all economic and social forces. For this reason, it launched "a pressing appeal to governments and Community institutions to put the higher interests of the Community first and accordingly to find a rapid solution to the crisis."[12]

The second UNICE communiqué, issued on 7 October 1965, was much more explicit. It was the result of a discussion in the Council of Presidents, on this occasion meeting in Paris. After briefly restating that industrialists were committed to the Community, an important factor in economic expansion, and warning that serious consequences could result if its development were blocked, UNICE affirmed its solidarity with the general response of the business community. It argued that economic integration had brought to light a community of interests and had created new links, which were embodied in numerous initiatives for greater cooperation. For several years, business decisions and economic policy options that involved future commitments had been taken on the assumption that the Common Market would be completed. Uncertainty as to the future of this integration would endanger the structural transformations necessary for industry to face ever-increasing global competition. Thus, UNICE thought it necessary for governments to respect the agreed stages in the development of the Community project so that business could stick to its own agendas. Industrialists were ready to put up with some sacrifices provided that they could be sure of growing prosperity as a result of the enlargement of the market. At the same time, industry could not allow such a prospect to be compromised by potentially recurring political incidents.

On 7 July 1965, a declaration by the secretariat of the International Confederation of Free Trade Unions (ICFTU) expressed the deep concern of the trade unions in the face of the European crisis. On the twenty-sixth of the month, in a letter to the president of the Council of Ministers, L. Rosenberg and H. Buiter made an urgent appeal to its members, calling on them to meet within the framework of EEC institutions "in order to undertake negotiations that would allow the work of integration to continue and a strengthening of the Community's democratic institutions." On 30 September, on the occasion of an extraordinary meeting in the course of which the president of the Commission, W. Hallstein, spoke, the Executive Committee of the ICFTU affirmed its hostility to any attempt to return "to the outmoded system of bilateral or multilateral relations between governments" and stated that the trade unions "would at all costs defend respect for the treaty provisions and the preservation of the supranational powers exercised by the organs of the Communities." On 27 October, Buiter expressed his pleasure that the Five had met in council on 25 and 26 October but stressed that a meeting of the Council without the Commission was acceptable only "if the agenda for such a meeting did not compromise fidelity to the Treaties."[13]

In order to maintain its momentum, the secretariat held a further meeting of the Executive Committee in Paris on 19 November to discuss progress. The meeting was followed by a "European demonstration" organized by the CGT-FO. In their declaration at this demonstration, the trade unions first called for "integral respect" for the treaties, then demanded their "resolute application," and finally rejected "any attempt to resolve the economic, social, and political questions of our time by means of the authoritarian nationalist methods of the nineteenth century."

The attitude of the International Confederation of Christian Trade Unions (ICCTU) was no different from that of the ICFTU. In its motion of 15 July 1965, the Executive Bureau affirmed that "integration is an absolute necessity for the peoples of Europe, who are resolutely committed to this way" and that this experiment "must succeed, given its value as an example for the countries of Europe and for other regions of the world."

Likewise, the motion makes it clear that economic and social integration requires the political unification of Europe through democratic procedures. On 4 November, the ruling committee of the organization confirmed the motion adopted by the Executive Bureau and made an appeal to the governments of member countries "to reestablish the unity of the Six without diverging from the Treaties of Rome and Paris." This convergence of positions led the two organizations to take joint action, of which the most significant example was their meeting of 27 January, just before the second extraordinary meeting of the Council of Ministers. In the defense of the Community, contact between the two confederations and COPA and UNICE at the time of this crisis led to a meeting of the four bodies in Brussels on 16 July 1965. The communiqué issued on this occasion expressed the level of concern among the participants, their desire to push forward with European integration, and the determination of all four groups to remain in contact "with the aim of jointly keeping a close watch on developments."

These gestures from within the Community network of central interest groups were vigorously supported by numerous national groupings. Belgian and German industrialists made their position very clear while French industrialists also took vigorous action in defense of the Community. In September, the Belgian Federation of Industry (FIB) made an appeal to the Belgian government to safeguard the future of the EEC in the interest of the economy and to make every possible effort to bring the Community out of the crisis as soon as possible; "the present state of uncertainty — declares their communiqué — is prejudicial to the economic development and social progress of the EEC."

At the same time, the German Bundersverband der Deutschen Industrie (BDI) and its leaders made several declarations about the need to find a solution to the crisis. On 1 October, this federation released a ten-point declaration, asking for negotiations to resume; having studied the main problems, it underlined the importance of European integration from the viewpoint of German industry. The French National Council of Employers (CNPF) announced that a prolonged cessation of Community activities was very undesirable and would lead to "the gravest repercussions for all concerned." But the reaction of the CNPF was not restricted to declarations and press releases. Aware of the threat to the nation's industry, French industrial leaders called on experts to study the effects of the crisis on the French economy and to analyze the likely consequences if implementation of the Common Market were to be blocked. On the question of trade, the experts observed that between 1958 and 1964 French industrial exports to the EEC had risen by 95 percent and those to third nations by 52 percent. These figures gave a very clear idea of the risks to the French economy should the Common Market be compromised. Furthermore, they noted that paralyzing the Common Market could not fail to delay decisions on antidumping measures, levies, and subsidies as well as the formulation of common policies.[14]

Their report suggested that uncertainty over the fate of the Common Market would soon encourage French business leaders to delay or reduce their investment or restructuring programs — the Common Market had exercised a notable influence. By all accounts, this report — intended for the French government — was not a statement of general policy but a detailed position paper comprising an evaluation of the negative forces that could prolong the crisis throughout all sections of the French economy. For the French Business Confederation it was more than a debate on principles; it was of basic interest.

As far as could be seen, the greatest reaction came from the agricultural sector. The strongest opposition to French government policy seems to have come from the president of the Permanent Assembly of Agricultural Chambers. But FNSEA was quickest to take direct action against the authorities, despite an initial caution manifested at the meeting of the Administrative Council on 16 September. FNSEA's opportunity came with the campaign for the presidential elections of 5 December 1965; the call to battle was given at a meeting of the National Council to discuss agricultural prices. On 23 October 1965, *Le Monde* summed up the results of this session with the headline "FNSEA urges farmers not to vote for the incumbent in post of 5th December." The motion of the National Council of FNSEA ended:

> The National Council, aware that the Union's political neutrality prohibits it from backing any particular candidate, nonetheless feels it would be failing in its duty if it did not solemnly warn farmers of the consequences of the way they vote at the next elections, and especially at the presidential election of 5 December. By their vote, farmers will be making their choice as citizens and not on the basis of professional considerations, but in fulfilling their responsibility they must be fully aware that it would be absurd on their part to ask their union leaders to oppose a policy they have apparently approved at the polling booth.[15]

October 1965 saw the opening of the campaign for the first presidential election to be based on direct universal suffrage, the context for the FNSEA motion. In this very concrete way, the presidential election and French domestic politics became enmeshed with European politics. Here was tangible proof that the Community was not a matter of foreign policy but an integral part of French politics, all the more so in that Community decisions and policies produced immediate effects, directly affecting governments, interest groups, economic and social agents, political parties, and public opinion. These consequences transcended national frontiers and the main objectives assigned to them. Thus, a debate on the financing of the Common Agricultural Policy and its institutional embodiment was transformed into a general political debate on the significance and the future of the European Community, a debate in which were involved first the socio-economic groups most directly involved and then, because the presidential election happened to be taking place at the same time, the parties and the candidates. In this context, the candidacy of the third man, Jean Lecanuet, arose from a center-based European and Atlantic movement of those opposed to General de Gaulle's policies. The result is well known: de Gaulle lacked an absolute majority in the first round with François Mitterand and Jean Lecanuet, and de Gaulle's policy on Europe, the subject of a fireside chat on television, began to show more flexibility, thus raising hopes for a positive solution to the crisis.

The Luxembourg Compromise: An "Agreement to Differ" (1966)[16]

Contacts between the partners were renewed in December 1965, and this led to meetings and then a compromise — or rather an "agreement to differ" — in Luxembourg on 30 January 1966. In fact, this agreement blocked progress toward the third stage of the Community, which was to involve a transition from unanimous decision making to decision making by qualified majority voting in several domains, including the Common Agricultural Policy. The text of the "Luxembourg Compromise" was highly revelatory of General de Gaulle's real intentions:

  1. When interests that are very important for one or more partners are at stake in relation to decisions that may be taken by majority vote on a proposal from the Commission, Council members will try within a reasonable timescale to find solutions that can be adopted by all the members of the Council, resolutions that respect their interests and Community interests, in conformity with article 2 of the treaty.
  2. With regard to the preceding paragraph, the French delegation considers that where the interests at stake are very important discussion should continue until unanimous agreement is reached.
  3. The six delegations note that a difference of opinion exists on what should be done if complete agreement cannot be reached.
  4. The six delegations nonetheless consider that this difference of

opinion does not imply any hindrance to the conduct of the normal routine of Community work.

This Community crisis enabled France to delay the introduction of majority voting for several months, even though it could not prevent it completely. Similarly, the new members, especially Great Britain, were in favor of invoking "vital interests," which they saw as an effective way of protecting their national interests through the practice of unanimity voting. On this point, a rather unusual but "practical" convergence of opinion was to be found between French and British positions. The original intention of protecting French interests, especially in agriculture, produced the opposite result. Instead of securing the Common Agricultural Policy, the weapon of unanimity voting was used by Great Britain to block decisions fixing common agricultural prices. A slow return to qualified majority voting did not take place until the early 1980s. More than twenty years after the "the empty chair crisis," the Single European Act made it possible to extend qualified majority decision making.

This prolonged delay ensured that a cumbersome decision-making process in the European Community was maintained for two decades — with the increase to a membership of nine in 1973 making matters worse since unanimity was more difficult to attain for the Nine than it had been for the Six. It is true that in day-to-day Community practice the Council strove as often as possible to take decisions by consensus, so that the difference between unanimity and qualified majority became rather blurred.

In fact, qualified majority voting makes the search for compromise easier in that it puts the majority group in a stronger bargaining position. The minority group is ready to compromise, aware that a decision may be taken without it, and for its part, it is ready to make concessions in hopes of a consensus, reckoning that the most important questions require the approval of the largest number of members if the measures adopted are to be applied. The difference between unanimity and qualified majority voting is thus fundamental: the former slows down the process of decision making and sometimes even paralyzes it while the latter speeds it up and facilitates compromise. With the addition of six more members and the possibility of further enlarging the Community, the difference between these two procedures is likely to increase; with the growth in the number of members, unanimity is likely to become more and more difficult to achieve without unreasonable delay.

At the same time, the financial problem, seemingly technical but in fact pregnant with political consequences, was resolved much more rapidly once the decision on resources was taken in 1970. The new system was transformed and then extended by the Treaty of Brussels of 1975, which granted a (limited but real) power of budgetary codecision to the European Parliament.

The fusion of the Community executives in 1967 came even more quickly, and the integration process continued in spite of all the delays. After an increase in the number of vetoes and blockages, creating successive crises and delays, it showed unexpected continuity and power in the face of repeated prophecies of doom by all kinds of gloom merchants. The forward drive was maintained and even developed in the 1970s, as is shown by the creation of the European Council in 1974 and then the direct election of the European Parliament, which was decreed in 1976 and held in 1979. Integration became deeper and broader, reaching new areas in spite of enlargement and the concurrent economic and monetary crises of the 1980s. Looking back on this jerky progression, one can but regret all the energy wasted on delays and blockages, in spite of which the union movement pushed forward with such unrelenting vigor that more than one observer has seen it as irreversible.

An Embryonic Political System: Decision Making and the Consultative Institutions

Continuously evolving, the European Community eludes all traditional types of classification; it involves a whole mixture of elements and integrates both supranational features that are unique to it and leftovers of intergovernmental practices. Depending on one's viewpoint, it appears to be either federal or confederal, but in reality these two faces coexist or even fuse in the Community structure.

In turn, the Community's character is mirrored in its institutions and their powers. Thus, it is essential to understand the organization of power in the Community and the way it is shared between its principal institutions. Active power is held by two institutions: a Community institution, the Commission; and an intergovernmental institution, the Council. As a general rule, the Commission proposes and the Council decides. But they carry out their tasks and take their decisions in consultation with and under the democratic supervision of the European Parliament as well as under the judicial supervision of the Court of Justice. The initial allocation of powers was modified by the Single European Act, which institutionalized the European Council's practice of formulating overall strategy and acting as the driving force in the Community. It also inaugurated a more direct involvement of the European Parliament in the decision-making process. Since then, the Council of Ministers has taken many decisions "in collaboration with the European Parliament." This institutional group is still evolving and constitutes an embryonic Community power, now endowed with a political dimension by the Maastricht and Amsterdam Treaties.

The nature and reality of Community power is revealed in its institutions and through its decision-making procedures. These are the two most significant indications together with the sociopolitical indications to be found in the structures of the political parties and interest groups and in the extent of their involvement in the Community process.

A Political Portrait of the Commission

A rough sketch of the Commission, a collegial institution and the dynamic foundation of the building of Europe, shows that there are seventeen members (two for each large country) chosen with the agreement of all the governments (but in practice by each government alone), except for the president of the Commission, who is chosen by a consensus of heads of state or government meeting in the European Council. This Community practice tends to bolster the authority of the president of the Commission.

In terms of their political affiliation, the members of the Commission reflect the main political tendencies in the Community, or more precisely the dominant features of the governments and majorities in power. This is the case for the small and medium-sized states, each of which chooses a single member for the Commission. The situation is somewhat different with the larger member states, which generally choose one member from the government majority and one from the opposition (France, Great Britain, Spain) or from another party in the government coalition (Germany and Italy). All in all, and despite the changes of majority or government that can occur during a session, the composition of the Commission is a fairly faithful reflection of the distribution of the principal electoral forces in member states and the Community. The second Delors Commission included six Socialists, of whom the president was one; four Christian Democrats; three Liberals; one from the Portuguese PSD; one from the Irish Fianna Fail, adhering to the progressive democrat grouping alongside the Gaullists; one British Conservative; and a senior civil servant of the state of Luxembourg who has no declared political affiliation. In this way, the composition of the Commission reflected the broad spectrum of the government and opposition parties in the member states. This broad "involvement" of political parties in the Community executive is guaranteed by the present procedure for choosing the members of the Commission. If the choice of the members were to be left to the president-designate and the approval of the European Parliament, it is highly likely that his—or her—choice would be based on criteria similar to those of the governments, that is, membership in a majority political or opposition grouping. This provides a power base and at the same time offers the prospect of future members with the requisite personality and competence. However, although it is highly likely that the European Parliament's choice for the presidency would be a first-rank political individual, what guarantee can there be as to the choice of Commission members? Would the approval of the European Parliament depend on the "grand coalition" of Socialist and Christian Democrats, on alliances reflecting the Left/Right division, or on some temporary compromise?

In terms of training and experience, the members are either lawyers or economists, with one engineer and a doctor of philosophy with extensive experience in management and economics. A dozen members of the Commission have extensive experience in economic affairs. At the same time, a majority of them (fourteen) have previously held European responsibilities as ministers with seats in the Councils, as members of the Committee of Permanent Representatives (Coreper), or as European deputies. In one way or another, they were already involved in European affairs and thus belonged to the European leaders' network (the "Eurosphere").

The importance accorded by governments to the Commission and its political and administrative function is reflected in the personalities of its members. In 1992, nine of its members in fact had high government responsibilities as ministers, including one Bavarian government minister and three who were secretaries of state. In addition, five were Euro MPs, including one party president and one member of the Crocodile Club founded by Altiero Spinelli.

Unlike the Swiss Federal Council, whose presidency lasts one year, the Commission, a collegial institution, has a president whose mandate corresponds in principle to the Commission members' four years, a mandate that was lengthened to five years in the Maastricht Treaty. Hence, the president's role is far from ephemeral, and he has the opportunity to stamp his personality on the Commission's work and policies. Though the presidential powers are obviously important in themselves, it is the officeholder's personality and style that give it a high profile. A detailed analysis of these variables, little studied up to now, would make it possible to comment on the role of the different Commissions in terms of the character of their respective presidents.[17] It is clear that the High Authority under the presidency of Jean Monnet (1952–55) and the Commission presided over by Walter Hallstein (1958–66), comparable despite their institutional differences, are not to be compared with the Rey (1967–70) or Malfatti (1970–72) Commissions. The active, powerful, and creative characters of the first two presidents contrast with Jean Rey's negotiator's style, very much suited to the Kennedy Round, or with Malfatti's more managerial approach. The

1973 enlargement, the problems posed by the assimilation of a large insular nation, and economic difficulties made the task of François Ortoli (1973–77) and Roy Jenkins (1977–81) much tougher. During their mandates, the Commission was much weakened in terms of its role as driving force and helmsman. The difficult transitional phase known as "Europessimism" was well handled by President Gaston Thorn (1981–85) thanks to his talent as a negotiator. In spite of the importance of the president's role, other personalities have left their mark on Commission policy: there is no need to do more than mention the names of the likes of Mansholt, Barre, Spinelli, Davignon, and Brittan.

Following a period of stagnation marked by a consolidation of member states' powers at the expense of the Commission, a resurrection of the Community and the initiatory role of the Commission has taken place under the presidency of Jacques Delors (1985–95), a French Socialist, former collaborator of Jacques Chaban-Delmas, former Euro-MP, former French minister for the economy, finance, and budget, and chief architect of the turnaround in the French economy in 1983. His strong personality and imaginative outlook together with his capacity for hard work and his perseverance, inspired by a profound belief in Europe, have been crucial in reenergizing the Community. The White Book and the preparatory draft for the Single European Act are examples of the significant progress that is attributable to the first Delors Commission, supported by a constellation of pro-European governments often despite very forceful opposition from Mrs. Thatcher. During this period, the Commission took up the reigns of European integration again. The pessimistic forecasts and predictions of numerous observers and specialists in Community affairs have not prevented the Commission from making an unexpected comeback with a variety of highly successful initiatives. Not only has it regained a great deal of lost ground, but it has acquired a political dimension. This is largely due to the participation of the president first in the European Council, of which the Single European Act makes him a member, and second in the various summit meetings of the great Western nations. In this new front-rank political role, the powerful personality of Jacques Delors has helped to guarantee him a high-profile position that could hardly have been foreseen in the days when Community morale was at a very low ebb.

This very positive picture is not without its darker side, which some are happy to emphasize: an exaggerated personalization of Community power that has occasionally been a source of irritation to heads of government; too many demands, too much impatience, and a leadership style that some consider authoritarian; a way of concocting initiatives so secretly that even some members of the Commission are left in the dark (a personal style that in some ways recalls that of General de Gaulle); and a tendency to adopt uncompromising positions that are liable to provoke divisions or clashes within the Commission and put a strain on its cohesion. All these are secondary matters that cannot detract from Jacques Delors's great achievement.

Commentators and observers have been prone to view the role and capacity of the Commission rather pessimistically. According to most commentaries, the Commission has lost its dynamism because of a loss of Community power to national centers. Since the EDC crisis, the creation of the Economic Community, and the empty chair affair, the Commission's authority has been greatly enfeebled. This decline has been seen as leading progressively to a shift of Community power away from the most active representative of the common interest, the only one able to counterbalance the influence of national interests and defend the interests of the small countries during the Community lawmaking process. But as a general conclusion — often asserted without any qualifications — this idea ignores many factors. With the implementation of the Common Market, and then of the internal market and the common policies that go with it, the powers of the Commission have developed commensurately with its new activities. Likewise, the evolution of the Community has seen a progressive development in the Commission's management role, particularly in the management of structural funds, to the point where it has acquired quasi-discretionary powers in certain cases. While the Commission has frequently been an object of envy and criticism among certain governments, it has been given solid support by others. The presence of its president on the European Council is not the least sign of real progress made in the domain of high politics. For all the fluctuations in the degree of the Commission's authority, an overall view of its development, including its successes and failures and enlargements and accumulations of new powers, would in my view show a general upward trend.

As the Community structure develops and evolves, it must find a functional equilibrium between Community institutions and the power of the member states — hence, the periodic adjustments to, and fluctuations in, the Commission's powers. The Commission remains, however, irreplaceable as the chief counterweight to the force of nations and regions.

In comparison with the human and material resources available to national, regional, or local authorities, the Commission is very poorly provided for, considering the job it is called on to do and the responsibilities it carries in a Community whose population reached 370 million in 1995 and 374.6 million in 1998. Its forty-seven meetings in 1990 yielded 726 proposals, recommendations, or bills addressed to the Council together with 237 communications, memoranda, and reports, while at the same time it adopted more than 6,000 of its own acts.[18] Impressive enough in itself, this figure is even more significant when we consider the political dimension and the economic and technical significance of its activity. In this regard, one need only point to its numerous proposals for directives or policies in the framework of the Single European Act or its opinions and reflections on political, economic, and monetary union addressed to the two inter-governmental conferences, not to mention the numerous tasks entrusted to it by the European Council, such as the evaluation of the situation in the Central and Eastern European countries and the former Soviet Union, its proposals for supporting these countries, and its coordination of Western aid to them.

Given this wide range of tasks, the means available to the Commission seem minimal. It has about 17,000 employees, 1,600 of them required purely for linguistic purposes and more than 3,000 for research.[19] Among the other staff, many are working in general services and the secretariat. In all sectors of its activity, it employs 33 director generals, 24 deputy director generals, 140 directors (10 of whom head research institutes), and more than 1,200 planning or executive officials. All this seems negligible given the sheer breadth of the Commission's tasks and responsibilities.[20]

The same applies to the Commission's budget and indeed to the overall resources of the Community. Out of a total budget of 56 billion ecu in 1991, more than half were allocated to agriculture, more than a quarter to structural actions to be carried out by the Commission, about 5 billion for other policies, and 2 billion for research. The way the budget has been allocated over the last decade reflects the evolution of the Commission's political priorities, with a relative decrease in agricultural expenditures, which ten years ago accounted for nearly three-quarters of the Community budget, in favor of structural actions and research and development policies. Finally, overall administrative expenditures amounted to 2.6 billion ecu in 1991, with 1.66 billion allocated to the Commission. According to the *General Report* for 1998, the 1999 budget is 96.9 billion Euro, of which administrative expenditure amounts to 4.5 billion (2.4 for the Commission and 1.6 for other institutions).

In addition to its role as an engine of integration and guardian of the treaties responsible for their application, the Commission is the pole around which gravitate and proliferate multiple networks—of officials, national experts, interest groups, and associations—organized at the Community level. Every year nearly six thousand meetings bring together seventy thousand participants in Brussels for exchange and liaison with senior Community officials. These vast communications networks are responsible for very intense European socialization of national and regional leaders from various administrative, socioeconomic, and scientific milieus who have various tasks in the area of European integration. This particular function of bringing people together and teaching them about Europe is also part of the work of the Council, the European Parliament, and the Economic and Social Committee.

A Portrait of the Council

The Council represents the participation of member governments through their appropriate ministers. The Council has evolved a great deal since the beginnings of the Community. Once it was simply a link between the High Authority and governments, but now it has become the principal place for decision making in the Economic Union. At the same time, negotiations, crises, and fundamental decisions affecting the Community, like General de Gaulle's opposition in 1958 to the British plan to create a great free trade zone, have provided insight into the essential role played by the political leaders of member states. Their role is all the more crucial at turning points in the negotiation or decision-making process. As the Community acquired important powers of a political nature, it is natural that heads of state or government should have intervened to a greater extent. Watersheds in the integration process have been marked by several summits. In 1969, the Hague Conference opened the door of the Community to the United Kingdom. The summit of October 1972 proposed new policies: a policy of regionalism supported by a development fund, an environmental policy, and a program of social action. It was also at this meeting that heads of state and government expressed the political intention of achieving European union before 1980. At the Paris Summit of 1974, the heads of state or government decided to institutionalize their meetings by creating the European Council and to reinforce the Community's democratic dimension by having the European Parliament elected by direct universal suffrage. The Fontainebleau European Council of 1984 put an end to the budgetary quarrel provoked by the United Kingdom and chose a committee of representatives (the Dooge Committee) to bring about European union, an initiative that led to the Single European Act. Subsequently, the decision to implement the Single European Act on the basis of Jacques Delors's report "Réussir l'Acte unique, une nouvelle frontière pour l'Europe," as well as a series of fundamental decisions paving the way for political, economic, and monetary union, were taken in the course of various European Council meetings. The Council also was responsible for formulating Community policy with regard to former communist countries undergoing democratization and in response to the Gulf crisis. When a particular problem was an issue in the wider political arena or had some kind of legitimate importance, the role of the European Council gradually became crucial. Canonized by the Single European Act, the European Council has become de facto as well as de jure the supreme institution of the European Community.

Over the years, the Council acquired a two-level structure: an upper level, the European Council, and an infrastructure formed by Coreper, the Committee of Permanent Representatives in Brussels, and a general secretariat. The Council of Ministers eventually became somewhat fragmented, with several specialized councils for each of the chief sectors of activity, although a general or plenary Council was still maintained. The multiplicity of specialized councils, such as those of agriculture, finance, industry, and research, highlights the very basic problem that the political institution that holds the key position in the European Community decision-making process had fragmented. This fragmentation threatens the cohesion of the Council, and thereby its effectiveness, and it is a serious question whether existing instruments of coordination, notably the guiding role of the Council of Ministers meeting in plenary session, are any sort of compensation. Community experience leads us to doubt whether the plenary session can coordinate such a wide range of decisions. Another question concerns the powers of the specialized councils. Do they have the capacity to impose their political will by dictating their choices and exercising their political oversight over the various administrative mechanisms responsible for making their decisions possible?

By their assiduous attendance, national ministers, who turn up in large numbers — there are about two hundred of them, and the number increases as the questions being dealt with on the Community level increase — clearly show that they attach a great deal of importance to Community affairs. All the same, it is fair to ask whether the eighty-five sessions held in 1990[21] (ninety-four in 1998) by the different councils allowed them to maintain an effective grip on such a complex and diversified decision-making process. Ministers certainly devote a considerable portion of their time to Community affairs in meetings of their own governments, within their own ministries or coordinating bodies, and in the course of their contacts with colleagues and the members of the Commission.

However, in spite of this dense network of communication and action, ministerial interventions in the process are selective and only rarely seem able to ensure that the Council actually exercises the political role — both legislative and executive — that the treaties attribute to it. In carrying out its demanding tasks, the Council relies to a considerable extent on the coordinating role of its presidency as well as on the work of Coreper and its numerous working groups supported logistically by the Council Secretariat with its staff of 2,183 people.[22] On top of this, the 1993 deadline meant that the implementation of the Single European Act required a faster work rate. In a single year (1990), the Council adopted 65 directives, 380 rulings, and 169 decisions.[23] Preparatory work for the Council's decisions is the responsibility of Coreper, under the direction of permanent representatives with ambassadorial rank, and of its numerous specialist working groups of national officials. The permanent delegations in Brussels make up a full-time Eurosphere of Community affairs. These missions include a core of representatives appointed by foreign ministers, while their other representatives come from various ministries involved in Community affairs. The number of specialist members varies according to the importance of the respective Community policies and regulations and the volume of work in each sector. This general observation applies to the activity of the Council and to the number of working groups in each sector as well as to the activity of the Commission and its consultative committees. In fact, the more a sector is subject to Community norms and policies the more it becomes an essential element in Community preoccupations, which influences both the Commissions' administrative structures and the networks around it. The administrative mass and structures of the general directorates quite faithfully reflect this relationship, which extends to all the institutions of the Community as well as to socioeconomic groups. Likewise, the structure and intensity of the activities of Community interest groups only confirm the rather banal observation that there is a close link between Community demands, powers, structures, and decisions. The members of Coreper belong to an intermediate sphere that lies somewhere between the true Community sphere and the different national spheres. They constitute special official channels of communication between the Commission and the member states and their administrations. Their frequent daily contacts with Commission representatives and their colleagues from other countries create a dense network of communication and solidarity that makes them more aware of (if not more receptive to) Community interests. Required to defend national viewpoints in the Community and at the same time to act as spokespersons for the Community viewpoint to their governments, they are caught between European solidarity and their own national allegiances and constitute one of the main cogs in the Community process.

In this complex ensemble of structures and relationships, it is easy to conceive the role of orchestral conductor that has to be played by the presidency with the assistance of the General Secretariat. This raises the question whether the presidents' six-month mandates leave any possibility of continuity in their work of coordination and reconciliation of viewpoints or in their representative roles. Long experience confirmed by extensive variations from one presidency to another suggests a need to renew debate on the rule of six-month rotation. In spite of the practice of collaboration between the "troika" of the outgoing president, the actual president, and his successor, frequent changes at the head of the Council do not leave scope for any guarantee that there will be coherent continuity in the Councils and the numerous organizations with government-level participation in the European Community without any holdups. Moreover, this is a question that will arise even more pressingly as the Community takes on new responsibilities as an economic and monetary union and a political union, too, especially in the spheres of foreign relations and security. The inadequacy of the Secretariat for Political Cooperation and the relatively low-key role of the Commission in these issues, which are political par excellence, seem to call for serious consideration of their functions and in particular of the place of the Commission in a political union.

I would suggest that with its new dimensions the European Community should be given a two-headed executive made up of a collegial presidency — European Council and Council of Ministers — and a Community government — the Commission. I believe this is the only way to reconcile effective participation by government leaders of member states with a sufficient degree of coherence and effectiveness of political vision.

The Court of Justice: A Dynamic Institution

Since passage of the Single European Act, the thirteen judges of the Court of Justice have been assisted by a Court of First Instance.[24] Thanks to this lightening of their burden of responsibility, the judges of the Court will be able to concentrate on their essential task of sifting and interpreting Community legislation. Their dynamic approach to their work has attracted all sorts of comment. Some have been quick to speak of "government by judges." As frequently happens with criticism intended to cut deep, this one is too extreme to be effective. The role of governing the Community is quite clearly shared between the Commission, the Council of Ministers, and the European Council. The highest judicial authority provides these bodies with support and encouragement. The question that should be asked is therefore: has the Court of Justice taken on the mantle of legislator? Instead of sticking to its own mandate, has it taken the liberty of creating Community law? However this question is answered, we have to accept extenuating circumstances where the Court is concerned insofar as it operates in an evolving legal system. Consequently — unlike national legal systems — it has to cope with many gaps and much imprecision, and it has frequently been obliged to use the teleological method to fill in various judicial gaps. In doing so, it is contributing to the development of Community law both by a generous interpretation of the fundamental norms of the treaty and by the creation of a new judicial order.[25]

While basing itself on existing sources of law in the exercise of its contentious, prejudicial, or consultative powers, the Court both clarifies and reinforces the content of the law. It thereby acts as "a backup legislator, which is what the authors of the treaties intended."[26] On the basis of the need to ensure the smooth functioning of the Common Market, the European judge has not simply been interpreting the free circulation of merchandise in a very generous sense but has also been applying this principle to other sectors — individuals, capital, and services — integral to the market. In certain famous cases, the intervention of the European judges has been tantamount to the creation of law. In the notorious AETR case of 1971, the judges ruled that member states could not conclude any agreement that affected Community rules since such agreements fall within the exclusive competence of the Community. Even before the Stuttgart Declaration of 1983, the systematic jurisprudence of the Court confirmed that fundamental laws constituted a part of Community law. In another decree, the Court confirmed the binding force of directives and their direct effects. This innovative interpretation is all the more important in that directives have become the special instruments of the Single European Act. This confirms the fundamentally dynamic role of the remarkable jurisprudence of the Court and its contribution to Community law.[27]

Government by Committee?

The accusation that the Community is subject to "government by judges" is unfounded, then, but others claim that it is actually subject to "government by committee." It is true that there are innumerable networks of committees at all levels of decision making, but here the Community merely reproduces a phenomenon that is becoming the norm in national and regional structures. Organized consultation occurs within a vast network of working groups and consultation procedures. In view of the proliferation of consultative instruments, one might conclude that this function somehow corresponds to the development of knowledge and technology as well as to the complexity of a society characterized by ever more extreme specialization. This society has become too complex for governments to deal with alone, and they are obliged to consult. Because of this, organized groups and experts of all shades of opinion are able to infiltrate the structures of authority. This phenomenon can sometimes lead to technocratic forms of government, but such exceptions do not allow us to conclude that we are governed by technocrats, still less by committees.

The networks of committees at the Commission and Council levels amount to approximately *three hundred* bodies.[28] In addition to mixed and professional consultative committees, this figure includes numerous committees whose members are national or governmental experts, officials, and directors of public bodies like the central banks. The density of these networks varies depending on the respective sectors of Community activity. For example, there are fifteen assisting with the work of the Customs

Union; thirty collaborating in the areas of employment, social affairs, and education; thirty in the areas of the environment, consumers, and security; and just over thirty for the internal market and industrial affairs. As might be expected, the network of committees becomes denser in the agricultural sector, where Community policy is at its most structured. There are 70 committees, 35 of them consultative, 16 assorted, and 20 or so devoted to management.

The consultative committees give opinions on formulating or implementing regulations and decisions on agricultural issues. The management committees are made up of government representatives and are intended to simplify Council procedure by overseeing the implementation of measures that the Commission has to adopt for each category of product or when dealing with the organization of agricultural markets. Draft measures are submitted to the relevant management committee, which gives its opinion on a qualified majority basis. If the Commission passes a measure without taking notice of this opinion, the Council may modify the Commission's decision within the period of one month. Although there is no question that the management committees participate in the decision-making process directly and effectively, it is much harder to assess the influence of the agricultural consultative committees. The significance of their opinions, which are not binding on the Commission, varies according to the representativeness, the importance and competence of their members, and the degree of consensus attained. It is worth noting that, even though they do not ignore these committees, several professional organizations do not consider them a highly effective means of accessing the Commission administration.

The Economic and Social Committee (ESC) fulfills a general institutionalized consultative role similar to that of the economic and social councils of member states. The aim of the ESC is "to guarantee adequate representation for the different categories of economic and social life" (art. 195 of the EEC). Composed of 189 councilors, it is organized in three groups. Group 1 comprises fifty-seven employers' representatives from industry, commerce, transport, and banks. Group 2 comprises sixty-five representatives from workers' organizations, almost without exception (though not the French CGT) members of the European Trade Union Confederation, with the result that this group has a high degree of homogeneity. Group 3 is the least homogeneous, with sixty-seven councilors representing a variety of activities: agriculture, small and medium-sized businesses, skilled workers, commerce, liberal professions, and family and consumers' associations. The support of group 3 is sought by the other two groups, and it is subject to pressure from various sides; its votes are often divided between the industrialists' group and the trade union group when controversial matters are at issue. The variety of interests in this "ragbag" group is reflected in the fact that councilors belong to several Community organizations such as the farmers' COPA. The very cohesion of these sectoral interests explains the divisions within group 3. The homogeneity of groups 1 and 2 is strengthened, however, as their positions and votes are coordinated by UNICE and the European Trade Union Confederation. Where these two groups are concerned, their homogeneity indicates a desire to enjoy parity in consultation, the element of parity being weakened when diverse interests are present.

The relatively small number of councilors in relation to a market of 340 million weakens the representativeness of the ESC and its members. It is doubtful in fact whether the highly diversified categories of activities that are present in the Community and its member states can be faithfully reflected by the allocation of twenty-four members to each of the largest countries, twenty-one to Spain, twelve to the medium-sized countries, and six to nine to the smallest. This numerical insufficiency is all the more obvious when the ESC is compared with the French Economic and Social Council, whose membership is two hundred (representing a population of 58 million) while its functions are similar.[29] Here we are very far from an "adequate representation," and the principal categories of activity are not sufficiently well covered; several important sectors are entirely absent, high technology having only a modest representation, while consumers are overrepresented, predominantly from northern countries and mainly from Germany and the United Kingdom. This imbalance is only partially rectified through the coordination and aggregation carried out by the UNICE and the European Trade Union Confederation at the Commission level and to some extent by their members represented on the Economic and Social Committee. This raises the question of whether an increase in the number of councilors would ensure improved representation.

The influence of the ESC and the effectiveness of its work depend on many other criteria: the quality and competence of the councilors, the proportion of "personalities" and experts, the time available, the extent of influence in the organization of origin — a whole series of factors that determine the ESC's capacity to exercise influence and the scope of its opinions and its work. Notwithstanding the factual or technical quality of a given opinion, its impact is often attenuated by the customary laborious search for compromises that have little chance of influencing Community decisions because of their excessive generality. In such cases, it is far better for the decision maker to have at his or her disposal the much more clear-cut opinions to be found in majority and minority reports. A division of the votes that is too close to fifty-fifty also tends to weaken the significance of an opinion. But the fate of an opinion depends also on the stage at which it enters the decision-making process or the decision-making center in question and which route representatives on the ESC choose to reach most directly the holders of decision-making power. Overall, the significance of these opinions is difficult to assess; they vary from one case to the next, although their influence is definitely more weighty where the matters at issue are specialized and technical.

My research at the ESC in the 1980s left me with the impression that the Committee had neither found its place among the institutions and within the Community consultative network nor succeeded in defining its role in the Community system. In spite of what has been achieved, the ESC does not seem to have succeeded in its efforts to carve out an identity and exert any significant influence.

The European Parliament: Its Composition and Functions

Paradoxically this body, which is the product of an election by direct universal suffrage, represents the peoples of the Community, and embodies in itself the principle of direct democratic legitimacy, has only limited powers in comparison with the European Council, the Council of Ministers, or the Commission. The initial division of powers in the Community is centered on the institutions that represent member governments and the two Community institutions — one having the initiative and administrative oversight of the application of the treaty (the Commission), the other responsible for its legal enforcement (the Court). In this initial schema, the European Parliament occupies only a marginal position and largely has only consultative powers; its power to censure is more fictional than real. However, the powers of the European Parliament have grown progressively, especially with regard to budgetary matters, where it has acquired the power of sharing decisions, and in the context of the internal market, where its role has developed from the merely consultative to the cooperative or sometimes codecisionary.

In the course of three direct elections, the composition of the European Parliament has undergone changes that reflect developments of the Community electorate. The first of these developments concerns the two largest political groupings, the Socialist and the PPE (European People's Party–Christian Democrats). They came out of the 1979 election almost neck and neck, but subsequently the relative size of their vote has diverged. In 1979, only 1.5 percent separated them; in 1984, it was 4.7 percent and in 1989 11.2 percent. The second development is a consequence of the evolution of the relationship between the two largest parties; the decline in the fortunes of the Conservatives, who fell from sixty-one members in 1979 to thirty-two in 1989, and Labor, which increased from eighteen to forty-six members during the same period.

The European Democrat grouping has thus literally fallen apart while the Socialist grouping has gained twenty-eight British members. A third development is the split of the Communist grouping along the lines of the old division between Euro-Communists and orthodox Communists, with the former taking twenty-eight seats against fourteen for the latter. A fourth development is the success of the Greens, who have formed a separate grouping with thirty members, while the Rainbow grouping from which they have separated is principally drawn from regionalist and federalist parties with significant support from the Danish anti-European Community Party. The fifth development concerns the grouping of European right-wing parties; the German Neo-Nazi Republicans have joined forces with the French National Front while the Italian Neo-Fascists have abstained from involvement in Parliament. Two chief tendencies are discernible from this, one toward concentration and the other toward fragmentation: a concentration of European MPs from the two main groupings of Socialists and Christian Democrats (PPE), who hold 300 out of 518 seats. Moreover, the Liberal grouping supported by the Portuguese, Spanish, and French MPs is a significant force. Where the other groupings are concerned, splits among the Communists and on the far right accentuate the fragmentation of seats in spite of the powerful advance of the Greens.

Under such conditions, several strategies for creating a majority seem possible. Clearly, the most logical and reliable coalition would be that of *the two largest groupings,* the Party of European Socialists (PSE) and the European People's Party (PPE) and the Christian Democrats. Despite their ideological differences, these two groups seem destined to form the "great coalition" or "European majority" since both have European convic-

TABLE 1.   Distribution of Seats among Political Groups

	Elections 1979		Elections 1984		Elections 1989	
	N	%	N	%	N	%
Party of European Socialists	113	27.6	130	30.0	180	34.7
European People's Party	107	26.1	110	25.3	122	23.5
Liberal Democratic and Reformist	40	9.8	31	7.1	49	9.5
European Democrats/Conservatives	64	15.6	50	11.5	34	6.6
Greens	—	—	—	—	30	5.8
Communists	44	10.7	43	9.9	—	—
Euroleft (GUE-European United Left)	—	—	—	—	28	5.4
Alliance of European Democrats	22	5.4	29	6.7	20	3.9
The Right	—	—	16	3.7	17	3.3
Coalition of the European Left	—	—	—	—	14	2.7
Rainbow group (Arc-en-ciel)	11	2.7	19	4.4	13	2.5
Nonaffiliated	9	2.1	6	1.4	11	2.1
Total	410	100	434	100	518	100

tions and a European policy. Together they constitute the powerful core of the European family on which Altiero Spinelli relied in 1984 to get the draft European Union Treaty passed. The PPE is dominated, in fact, by pro-European German, Italian, and Benelux MPs, while within the Socialist group the pro-European note is equally dominant under the influence of the Germans, the French, the Italians, and converted Labor supporters. Moreover, it is noteworthy that the ideological distance between the elements that make up these two large formations has tended to diminish with the progressive rapprochement between Christian and Social Democrats — paralleled by that between the Social Democrats and their Socialist partners, due to the evolution of the French, Spanish, and Italian Socialist Parties in particular. Between 1984 and 1989, the two big groups drew even closer when the presidencies of both were held by German MPs (Arndt of the SPD and Klepsch of the Christlich Demokratische Union [CDU]). Since the 1989 elections, the Socialist group has chosen a French MP, Jean-Pierre Cot, for president, but this has not affected the preexisting understanding. It seems that the implementation of the Single European Act and the European Union has prompted a renewal of their entente.

The majority enjoyed by these two groups — comfortable in spite of the occasional hiccup — is frequently bolstered by the votes of Liberal MPs heavily committed to European union. In the face of the entente between the two larger groups, the Liberals have only a modest role and are for the most part reduced to voting with them. It is hardly surprising then that President Giscard d'Estaing made several overtures to the PPE. Nonetheless, an alliance between the Liberals and Christian Democrats was rejected by the Liberal MPs, who refused to fall in with their president's strategy. A move toward such an alliance is, however, far from unthinkable in the case of the European Democrats, who include thirty-two British Conservatives out of a total of thirty-four members. Its isolated position in the European Parliament and its tendency to align itself with the PPE, with which it shares political sympathies if not religious ones, have encouraged the Conservative group to join the PPE bloc. Such a coalition has become all the easier to contemplate with the evolution of the PPE away from its original Christian Democrat position toward one in which its popular European dimension has been reinforced by the advent of new partners — the Greek New Democracy Party and the Spanish People's Alliance. This move by the PPE and the Conservative grouping follows the abortive project to establish one major European Right or Center Right bloc. Conservative leaders expressed anxiety about the fragmentation of the Center and Right — hence, the initiative from the CDU/CSU to establish the European Democratic Union. In June 1977, Mrs. Thatcher spoke in favor of such an idea when she visited the Christian Democrats in Rome. In April 1978, a

TABLE 2. Distribution of Euro-MPs by Political Groups and Countries (1989 elections)

Political Groups	Total	B	DK	G	GR	S	F	IRL	I	L	NL	P	UK
Party of European Socialists	180	8	4	31	9	27	22	1	14	2	8	8	46
European People's Party	122	7	2	32	10	16	7	4	27	3	10	3	1
Liberal Democratic and Reformist	49	4	3	4	–	6	13	2	3	1	4	9	–
European Democrats/Conservatives	34	–	2	–	–	–	–	–	–	–	–	–	32
Greens	30	3	–	8	–	1	8	–	7	–	2	1	–
Communists	28	–	1	–	1	4	–	–	22	–	2	1	–
Euroleft (GUE-European United Left)	20	–	–	–	1	–	13	6	–	–	–	–	–
Alliance of European Democrats	17	1	–	6	1	–	10	–	–	–	–	–	–
Coalition of the European Left	14	–	–	–	3	–	7	1	–	–	–	3	–
Rainbow group (Arc-en-ciel)	13	1	4	–	–	2	1	1	3	–	–	–	1
Nonaffiliated	11	–	–	–	–	4	1	–	5	–	–	0	1
Total	518	24	16	81	24	60	81	15	81	6	25	24	81

Note: B = Belgium; DK = Denmark; G = Germany; GR = Greece; S = Spain; F = France; IRL = Ireland; I = Italy; L = Luxembourg; NL = the Netherlands; P = Portugal; UK = United Kingdom.

meeting in Salzburg of ten parties, including the Christian Democrats, the Conservatives, and the Right, founded the European Democratic Union. The Union came into being in a cloud of ambiguity: the French Rassemblement pour la République (RPR) was actively involved, while the Giscard party was there only as an observer. For their part, the European Democrats were divided: the CDU, urged to join in by the leader of the Christlich Soziale Union (CSU), F. J. Strauss, hesitated, while the Italian Christian Democrats and the Belgian and Dutch Christian Social Parties refused to get involved along with their Luxembourg counterparts and the French CDS.[30] Far from uniting the Christian Democrat and Conservative Parties of the Center Right, this initiative merely brought into the open the divisions within the Christian Democrat family and between the French RPR and Parti républicain (PR). It also revealed how difficult it was to bring together the parties most fervently in favor of a European union with those that were either neutral or opposed. The differences and nuances separating the parties of the Center Right and Right in the Community make it even more unlikely that there will be a wider bloc formed around the PPE. The bipolarization of political groupings along the Left-Right ideological fault line has for the time being given way to the "European interest" around which a "great Socialist/PPE coalition" has been established. However, this coalition obscures differences between the eight other political groups, which remain as strong as ever. Thus, it seems that functional needs are for the present being reconciled with attachment to differences. Interestingly, the three truly European groupings cover the whole range of member states except for the United Kingdom and Greece, which are absent from the Liberal group. Membership in these groups is also more evenly spread among the various countries, taking account of the fact that there is a certain cohesion between Benelux MPs.

Other groupings in the European Parliament are for the most part restricted to two or three countries; leaving aside the extreme case of the European Democrats, with their thirty-two British members out of a total of thirty-four, the Alliance (Rassemblement) of European Democrats is a significant example of binational domination, with thirteen French RPR and six Irish Fianna Fail out of a total of twenty members. Likewise the twenty-two former Italian Euro-Communists—including one who is actually of French nationality[31]—make up the majority of the twenty-eight members of the group promoting a united European Left, while the seven French Communists make up half of the leftist coalition group. There is more balance with the Greens, where eight French, eight Germans, and seven Italians form a troika among a total of thirty members.

The idea of a "progressive majority" reflecting the classic, periodically renewed Left-Right cleavage has not been translated into consistently con-

vergent behavior between potential partners. According to the most optimistic (though far from realistic) hypothesis, the left-wing coalition could
attract a maximum of 265 MPs—a tiny majority in the European Parliament. However, apart from two groups capable of a certain amount of
disciplined voting and close to one another by virtue of their European
convictions—the Socialist group and the United European Left—the elements in this hypothetical majority look less trustworthy, either because,
like the Rainbow group, they are divided or because they are less pro-
European like the Greens or the left-wing coalition under the domination
of the French Communists. As things stand at the moment, this "progressive majority" offers no guarantee that the European Union will make any
progress.

The European Parliament's Functions and
Their Evolution

Parliaments are the keystones of democracy; as elected bodies, they directly secure the foundations of democratic regimes and thereby fulfill the
role of depositories of democratic legitimacy. Since 1979, the European
Parliament has been elected by universal suffrage; it has introduced a new
balance in the Community system even though it lacks the full powers that
national parliaments have. It exercises only a limited *legislative function,*
although the formula introduced by the Single European Act did reinforce
its consultative power, which is more binding in areas related to the internal market, so that they are now regulated by the Council "in cooperation
with the European Parliament." From this point of view, there is less
difference between it and a national parliament; it colegislates with the
Council on proposals put to it by the Commission, though without exercising the same powers as a national parliament. It is true that parliaments
today are more like chambers for registering government proposals, especially when the executive has a parliamentary majority. But even if parliaments no longer embody the legislative function on their own they are still
arenas where proposals put forward by governments—usually in close consultation with external interest groups and experts—are publicly discussed
and sometimes amended before being approved.

The budgetary power of the European Parliament—like that of national parliaments—always guarantees it some influence over legislation
with budgetary consequences, hence the importance accorded by the English Parliament to its budgetary role. Establishing the Community's own
resources in 1970 required parliamentary controls. The 1975 treaty settled
the division of budgetary powers between the European Parliament and
the Council. The Council has the last word on the expenses deemed obliga-

tory that arise from the treaty and from its secondary legislation, especially that relating to agriculture, but Parliament has the last word on expenditures corresponding to credits allocated for new policies. Such expenditures seem likely to grow substantially in the future; initially only about a quarter of the Community budget, they are now rising toward the 50 percent mark. Thus, the European Parliament is strengthening its grip on the budget and making its control over Community activities more effective. Moreover, it has the right to reject the overall budget if it sees important reasons to do so, as was the case in 1985. In addition, the European Parliament has had the exclusive right to approve the Commission's implementation of the budget since 1975. This is the origin of the Court of Auditors, which assists the European Parliament in its operation of financial controls.[32] This Court employs a staff of 380, reports annually on the implementation of the Community budget, and gives opinion on Community management.

In the Community, there is no link between election results and the composition of the Commission, unlike the situation in the parliamentary systems of the member states, whose governments come from majorities or majority coalitions. There is, however, a visible correspondence in the Community between the political profile of the Commission and the principal groupings in the European Parliament. This correspondence is not the result of chance or the influence of Parliament on the choice of Commission members. It is a reflection of the governmental groupings or, in the case of the bigger countries, of a second grouping that is usually part of the opposition. The absence of any direct relationship between parliamentary election results and the composition of the Commission has sometimes been cited as the reason for the fairly high level of abstention in European elections—a parallel being suggested with elections to the Swiss Parliament.[33] This hypothesis seems to be disproved by the level of participation in American presidential elections, which is below the level of participation in the Community and raises the question as to whether sharing government powers and responsibilities at several levels in federal states does not tend to distract electors and reduce the level of their participation. Again, the example of the high level of electoral participation in West Germany makes it impossible to generalize.

Throughout the course of its development, the European Parliament has sought to extend its powers in the area of *political control.* Following the Stuttgart Declaration of 1983, the president of the Council of Europe sounded out the opinion of the extended Bureau of the Parliament on the choice of the next president of the Commission. This *preliminary consultation* was completed with the presentation of the new Commission to Parliament by a *vote of investiture,* like the one to which the Delors Commission was subjected in January 1985. In 1987, the European Parliament approved a renewal of the Commission president's mandate as well as that year's Commission program, and this vote of confidence in the program has since become the norm. What should be the most powerful weapon — the passing of a censure motion — has proved to be the least effective: out of four *censure motions,* two have been put to the vote and rejected. How is this behavior on the part of the European parliamentarians to be explained? In the present-day context, Parliament is the natural ally of the Commission and in this role it has been more concerned with supporting the Commission than with weakening it. To overthrow the Commission under the present system would expose it to the whim of governments by giving them the opportunity to appoint a new one. In addition, a sanction applied to the Commission would not affect the Council, which carries the main responsibility for Community decisions. Furthermore, in the present state of cohesion among the main groups — which are in fact significantly favorable to European integration — it is difficult to obtain the requisite two-thirds majority of the members of the European Parliament. The censure motion seems to be an instrument that is poorly adapted to the structure and mode of functioning of the European Community.

In 1990, other methods of control were devised: more than 3,000 *written questions* were put, 2,732 of them to the Commission, 217 to the Council, and 126 to the foreign ministers, together with nearly 2,000 oral questions essentially addressed to the Council and the foreign ministers.[34] In 1998, the number of questions grew considerably: Parliament addressed 5,573 questions — 4,114 written questions (3,737 to the Commission and 377 to the Council); 204 oral questions with debate (125 to the Commission and 79 to the Council); and 1,255 during question time (788 and 467 respectively). The written or oral replies and the debates to which they give rise cast a realistic and sometimes critical light on the work of Community institutions and member governments. Parliament also has the power to set up *commissions of enquiry* at the request of a quarter of its effective membership, thus following a practice common in several member states' parliaments. Since 1981, commissions of enquiry have studied such issues as drugs, agricultural surpluses, the status of women, and the reemergence of fascism and racism. In the framework of investigations by a commission of enquiry on the storage and transport of nuclear materials, the Belgian government questioned its power to require evidence from civil servants in member states while the German minister for the environment and a certain number of highly placed civil servants agreed to testify. For its part, the Council held that the European Parliament did not have the power to force civil servants from member states to give evidence but that by virtue of the principle of healthy cooperation the latter could give evidence before parliamentary commissions of enquiry. The work of such commissions has had a positive effect and sometimes leads to concrete action by the relevant authorities.[35] In parallel with such enquiries, European Parliament commissions have begun to hold *public hearings,* which widen the scope of parliamentary exchange and debate by involving interested groups and persons with appropriate scientific expertise.

A system of *petitions* and complaints for citizens of the Community has opened up new means of access and appeal to Parliament and through it to the Commission or even, when appropriate, to the Court of Justice. The European Union Treaty added an ombudsman, which gives the European citizen further access to the system. Using the right of recourse possessed by Community institutions, Parliament referred to two decisions handed down by the Court of Justice in the isoglucose affair in 1980 and accused the Council of negligence.

Of course, effective control depends on the relationship between Parliament and the Commission, which has the right of initiative and proposal; it also depends on Parliament's relationship with the European Council and the Council, the main decision-making institutions. The European Council presents reports at the close of its meetings and submits an annual report on *the state of the Union* and the progress achieved since the Stuttgart Declaration. This has established a dialogue, enabling Parliament to give its opinion when there are weighty Community decisions to be taken. In fact, since 1987 its president has regularly addressed the European Council at the beginning of its sessions. This is how the president of the Parliament was able to express to the European Council the opinions of Euro-MPs on intergovernmental negotiations, on the economic and monetary union, and on the political union. Thanks to such consultation, the European Parliament was able to make known its opinion on the future of the Community.

Relations between Parliament and the Council of Ministers have evolved progressively, although an element of tension has made itself felt at times. The declaration of the European Council at Stuttgart codified a number of practices: the Council and its members must reply to questions and requests for observations on the important resolutions of the European Parliament. The president of the Council presents programs and reports on progress achieved. MPs may debate these programs just as they may debate political cooperation; such practices constitute a learning process for Euro-MPs. Their active and diversified involvement in the European Union gives publicity to legislative debates and procedures and helps to remedy the democratic deficit from which the European Community suffers.

The *communication, information, and training functions* of Parliament make it all the more open to the European public. Parliaments occupy a privileged position in democratic societies as centers for communication and meeting places for political forces, where the opposition and members of the government majority have an opportunity for exchanges of opinion and confrontational public debates. The executives, with the Commission at their head, can access an abundance of information and expert advice in coming to their decisions. The information is filtered, assimilated, and then diffused through the governmental circuit. This closed procedure is not the way of Parliament, which fulfills an irreplaceable public function as a source of all kinds of (sometimes contradictory) information transmitted by the parties and the media. Parliament adds a new perspective and a new dimension to the more coherent but also more one-sided information coming from the Commission. Publicly expressed opposition in Parliament and the media is an integral part of the democratic debate. This democratic process certainly slows down and sometimes even blocks decision making, but it is still more effective in the long term by virtue of its contribution to the kind of social dynamism and cohesiveness that emerges from the clash of views and the availability of information from many sides.

The European Parliament also plays an educative role. It is an instrument for an apprenticeship in Europe and for the political socialization of its members. Members of the Commission and governments who have worked at the European Parliament have knowledge and experience of integration that are useful to them in their work. By training its members, the European Parliament thus helps to enlarge the sphere of European leaders and make it more active. As a general rule, leaders who pass through the parliamentary school at the European level are better at handling tasks related to Europe and more dedicated to the pursuit of union.

Finally, the question arises as to whether the European Parliament has the capacity to study, master, and regulate the huge and complex mass of European affairs. In the course of its twelve sessions in 1990, it adopted 600 resolutions and decisions, including 159 consultative opinions and 119 opinions under the heading of "cooperation."[36] On a second reading, it approved the common position of the Council in eighty-one cases without amendments, while amending it in twenty-eight cases. This statement takes no account of all the work of analysis, preparation, and editing of numerous reports, still less of the time taken up by debates, contacts, and exchanges with other institutions, interest groups, and representatives of associate or third countries. Nor does it take account of the debates organized in plenary sessions on such major issues as German reunification and the changes in Central and Eastern Europe. Through its activities, commissions, and infrastructure, Parliament plays a major part in the preparation of reports, opinions, and resolutions. However, the sheer abundance of issues and their complexity and technical nature are reasons for doubting whether the European Parliament has the capacity to make decisions on either overall issues or their minutiae and therefore to exercise effective control over the Community process.

For this reason, there have been proposals for a more selective approach and the introduction of a distinction between *Community law* and *Community rulings*. The laws would establish options and objectives and fix parameters for action, while the rulings would clarify details. In the case of directives that formulate goals, the means and the details would be left to the choice of national parliaments. Community rulings would automatically be binding unless an express request was made by the European Parliament or its commissions to examine them. This new procedure would make it possible to lighten the burdens on Parliament so that it could concentrate on major questions and fundamental options. The problem of overload will become increasingly acute as Parliament's field of action extends to external affairs, defense, and economic and monetary policy. If certain of its activities were delegated to commissions, this would be a partial solution, but the danger is that it will ultimately damage the integrity and uniqueness of Parliament's role. Hence, there is a need to lighten the load on the European Parliament and to provide effective technical and human support in order to increase its political oversight and influence over the Community's action, which will become not simply more transparent but also better known to a wider European public. Parliament has to make these choices, and they have an effect on other Community institutions, especially since the constant growth of the Community and its fields of action have helped to increase the diversity of its constitutive elements and have inevitably raised the problem of the representation of states and regions alongside that of European citizens through the European Parliament.[37]

Chapter 4

From the European Parliament Union Plan (1984) to the Single European Act (1987)

The European Parliament Project (Spinelli Plan), 1981–84

Origins and Protagonists

The draft European Union Treaty, which was approved by the European Parliament in February 1984, belongs to the long tradition of global projects for a European political community and a union of European states on the presidential or confederal model favored by de Gaulle. Although different in nature and structure, these three projects share the common goal of providing a political structure for all of the activities that normally fit into the area of competence of a federation. To differing degrees and in different ways, the European Parliament's plan, known as the Spinelli Plan, also suggested a global approach to existing and future Community arenas and added to them certain typically political issues — external relations and security.

Three principal protagonists were crucially involved in the promotion and elaboration of the European Union Plan: Altiero Spinelli, the Crocodile Club, and the European Parliament with its Commission on Institutions.

The Treaty Project was launched by Altiero Spinelli and a small group formed in 1980 by the nine Euro-MPs. It came to be known as the Crocodile Club, after the Club du Crocodile, a well-known Strasbourg restaurant where the first meeting was held.[1] It is no accident that Spinelli was the inspiration behind this project. As a young Communist, he had been imprisoned by Mussolini on the island of Ventotena just before World War II. There he was converted to federalism, and in 1941 he drew up the Ventotena Manifesto with Ernesto Rossi. Thenceforth, he threw himself into the struggle to create a European federation. His European involvement lasted for more than forty years until his death in 1986. He was the founder of the European Federalist Movement, and as a general delegate of the Congress of the European People he preached the gospel of a European constituent assembly in the 1950s.[2] It seemed to him that the only way to overcome the obstacle of traditional state structures was to appeal directly to the people. In the face of his failure to achieve immediate results, this European revolutionary federalist and democrat turned to research, which he pursued for several years before becoming a member of the European Commission in 1967. Faithful to his own ideas, he sought to encourage closer collaboration in *technological and industrial areas* within the European Community and strove to leave his federalist mark on Community projects.

Spinelli's next move was a return to his roots. He was elected to the Italian Parliament as an independent on the Communist party (PCI) list, which inspired the Euro-Communist movement. He remained faithful to his European vocation and entered the European Parliament after its first elections in 1979. There he pursued his original idea: an in-depth democratic social revolution brought about by a European federation. He was, in fact, one of the small number of MPs convinced from the start that the European Parliament had to become a constituent assembly. He was convinced that it would be possible to transcend party divisions and bring together a European majority in the European Parliament. His foresight was confirmed when the constitution of the draft treaty was adopted four years after he had appealed to MPs and political groups favorable to creating Europe anew. On that occasion, he suggested that a wide debate on the institutional crisis of the European Communities be launched, that a working group charged with drawing up a plan for institutional reform be appointed; that this plan be debated and voted on by the European Parliament, and that national governments and parliaments be asked to adopt it.

Initially made up of nine parliamentarians, the Crocodile Club grew to seventy in a few months. It initiated discussions on the major options and especially on the choice between going back to the Treaties of Paris and Rome and the drafting of a new treaty. As has often been the case in the history of the European Union, a division appeared between pragmatic minimalists and the maximalists, who saw themselves as realists. Most members accepted the idea of adopting a *"treaty-constitution"* instead of revamping existing treaties. Institutional reform should be accompanied by revision of the powers of the European Union so as to preserve what the Community had achieved, finish the work already undertaken, and evolve new common policies.[3]

The Crocodile Club's proposal was discussed by the European Parliament, which in July 1981 decided to set up an Institutional Commission tasked with modifying the existing treaties.[4] This European Parliament resolution is in line with a long tradition of initiatives, manifestos, and projects aimed at building a European federation or, less ambitiously, a union. For example, the first steps in this tradition were taken after the war by the Hague Congress, in the course of which (as Denis de Rougemont recalled in *l'Europe en jeu*) the supporters of federation (the Continentals) confronted supporters of intergovernmental cooperation (the British).[5]

The Commission set about its task by studying the various union and reform projects to be found in the *Recueil des documents de la Communauté de 1950 à 1982*. It thus gave due attention to the range of projects and experiments that were so many milestones on the often tortuous road to building Europe. Indeed, all along the way Commission members have swung to and fro between initiatives sponsored by promotional groups (e.g., the European Movement) or individual personalities (e.g., Jean Monnet), on the one hand, and official government undertakings and actions, often reductionist but generally positive, on the other. The European Communities already contained partial elements of a political structure, partial because they were principally applied to the socioeconomic and technical sectors.

Hence, there was a series of moves to either give the whole enterprise more depth or extend the field of Community activity, in particular into the areas of external relations and security. In this period, the European Community was marked by several innovations: European regional policy (*the Regional Fund*), *the European Monetary System* (EMS), *the ACP association* of sixty-six African, Caribbean, and Pacific countries, partial *budgetary codecision* (attributed to the European Parliament in 1975), and the European Parliament elections. Following suggestions contained in the Tindemans Report (1975)[6] and the Wise Men's Report,[7] the European Parliament decided to complete the Community's work by launching its draft Treaty on European Union.[8] In spite of all the progress in the economic domain following the direct elections to the European Parliament, numerous projects and initiatives in the areas of external relations and security came to nothing.

While the Commission repeatedly expressed anxiety about the weakening of Community institutions, it continued to advance new proposals, most noticeably its 15 October 1981 recommendation to the Council and the Parliament on relations between Community institutions.[9] In May 1984, on the occasion of a lecture at the European University Institute in Florence, the president of the European Commission, Gaston Thorn, expressed views very close to the main lines of the draft Union Treaty in his speech entitled "European Union or Decline: To Be or Not to Be."[10]

General Philosophy and Basic Principles

The draft treaty was characterized by a global approach and its references to a few basic federative principles. Since the 1950 Schuman Declaration, the chosen path to European unity had been the functional-sectoral method proposed by Jean Monnet in contrast to the global method favored by the federalists and constitutionalists. Both approaches aimed to create a United States of Europe, but it is clear from its preface that the 9 May 1950 declaration was a product of the functionalist approach: "Our attempt to create Europe was a failure, and instead we had a war. Europe will not be built at a stroke, nor can it be constructed according to some blueprint. It can only be the result of individual concrete achievements that will lay the foundations of a de facto solidarity."

Accordingly, it seems clear that the Community that was built is the Europe of the ECSC, the EEC, and Euratom, all embodying integration by function and sector. Coal, steel, nuclear energy, and economic activity would all be progressively shared, and thus the substance of national policies would gradually and progressively come under shared sovereignty. So this shared sovereignty would then have to acquire political powers, and a political authority would have to cover all of the sectors already integrated.[11] According to this method, and the integration strategy pursued since the failure of the various political projects, political union would take place gradually and imperceptibly ("painless integration," as Raymond Aron called it) in a series of stages and through cumulative, concrete achievements. However, though this method has indeed led to economic integration, it has failed to create a political community. At the end of his life, Jean Monnet, the founding father of the European Community, seems to have acknowledged the limitations of his method with his praise of Denis de Rougemont, the founding father of cultural Europe: "if I had to start all over again, I would begin with culture." For Denis de Rougemont, what constituted the basis for political union and a European federation was cultural unity and diversity.

All too aware of the limitations in what the Community had achieved, the authors of the draft treaty deliberately chose a global approach, deciding to combine under a single constitutional umbrella the achievements of the Community and the task of relaunching the project of a democratic union of Europe. In place of the three treaties that established the three European Communities and the decisions that made it possible for several important areas outside the scope of the existing treaties to be dealt with on the basis of ad hoc cooperation, the Union Plan contained a single constitutional text. Thus, the three treaties, the European Monetary System, political cooperation, and new areas were brought together in a single, coherent, institutional framework.[12] The Union Plan sought to make a qualitative leap into fresh domains — environment, culture, and information but especially international relations and security. The Union would be based on the following federalist principles.

The first is the *principle of subsidiarity,* according to which what may be done by a smaller unit should never be made the responsibility of a larger one.[13] Under this principle "the Union will only assume tasks that may be accomplished together more effectively than by each state separately or tasks whose solutions require a contribution by the Union" (European Parliamentary Resolution, 6 July 1982). This principle is enshrined in the preamble to the Union Plan: "In conformity with the principle of subsidiarity it is intended to entrust to common institutions only those powers they need to fulfill tasks that they can carry out more effectively than individual states are able to do in isolation."[14]

The second principle relates to *double participation* — by peoples and states — in the operation of the Union. In federal states, such participation takes on the institutional form of a chamber of representatives or elected MPs whose numbers are proportionate to the populations of the member states together with a senate representing member states as such. The Union would include the same institutions as those of the European Communities (Parliament, Council, Commission, and Court of Justice) but also the European Council, bringing together heads of state or government leaders of the member states and the president of the Commission. But the division of the institutions' powers and in certain cases also their composition and the mode of their appointment are modified. Thus, the Union proposes to increase the powers of the European Parliament, which would comprise 518 members elected by direct universal suffrage. Within the framework of the Union, the European Parliament would take on a legislative function that it would share with the Council, and together these two institutions would form the Union's legislative and budgetary authority. Accordingly, the plan proposes a return to the old interpretation of the institutional structures of the European Community according to which the European Parliament corresponds to a chamber of representatives, while the Council represents a senate, and both constitute a form of congress reflecting the principle of double participation.

The Union would be based on the *principle of democracy:* only a democratic European state may be admitted as a member. The Union would protect the dignity of the individual and recognize that every person under its jurisdiction has fundamental freedoms and rights. The plan is, however, quite timid about the involvement of the regions, which, according to Denis de Rougemont, should constitute the foundation of a European federation. With this in mind, he had suggested the creation of a senate of the regions.[15] There is nothing like this in the Union Plan, which does not propose any form of representation for regions. On the other hand, the preamble does contain a reference to regions; the contracting parties declare themselves "convinced of the necessity of allowing local and regional authorities to participate in the appropriate manner in the European construction."

The Strengthening of the Common Institutions and Their Powers

The Union Plan proposed strengthening Community institutions.[16] The European Parliament would be given increased powers. Council procedure would be more flexible and its functional effectiveness improved by *recourse to qualified majority voting*. The Commission really would become an executive authority; its role would be reinforced and its nomination procedure transformed. Thus, instead of Commission members being appointed by the unanimous agreement of member states' governments — in reality each government makes one or more appointments from its own ranks — it was understood that each would accept the nominees of the others. The president of the Commission would now be appointed by the European Council while the president, in turn, would appoint the Commission after consultation with the European Council. This formula is meant to guarantee a greater homogeneity in the team that makes up the Commission while strengthening the president's position. The Commission would then submit its program to the European Parliament and would be invested by Parliament before taking office. Thus, its authority would rest on the approval of the European Council and on investiture by Parliament, an idea that appeared among the proposals in the 1975 Tindemans Report. As for the Commission's functions, they would be those of an executive and would largely correspond to the functions laid down by the Treaty of Rome. The same was true for its responsibility to the European Parliament, although with one fundamental difference — the Union Plan settles the tasks of the executive, which in the European Community are shared between Commission and Council, solely on the Commission. The plan eliminates confusion between the Council's executive and legislative functions by establishing a separation of powers similar to the American model. Under this new division of powers, the Council would take on shared responsibility with the European Parliament for legislative and budgetary matters and as a general rule would decide questions on the basis of majority voting.

The European Council, which would become an institution of the Union, would preserve its role as the driving force of cooperation. It would decide on the issue of increasing the Union's powers and establish a dialogue with the European Parliament. Another innovation concerns the appointment of judges to the *Court of Justice*. Half would be nominated by Parliament and half by the Council; there would also be a wider right of appeal for individuals, greater protection of fundamental rights, and over-all more extensive judicial control. Alongside existing organs like the Economic and Social Committee or the Court of Auditors, the plan proposed creating a European Monetary Fund (EMF) with the task of preserving monetary stability.

Other innovations should be noted. The plan distinguishes between the laws applying to Community action and rulings and decisions.[17] Henceforth, the two latter instruments would come under the power of the Commission, which would use them in accordance with the laws of the Union. Moreover, the project sets out how and when laws are to be voted on by the Council and Parliament. It also generalizes the practice of giving interested parties a hearing before the institutions of the Union.[18] Finally, the plan strengthens the sanctioning powers of Union institutions, which may take a range of measures against member states guilty of persistent and serious violations of democratic rights or other obligations, including suspending the member state from the European Council and the Union Council as the most severe sanction.

Thus, without actually accomplishing a constitutional revolution, the plan sought to consolidate the Union's democratic foundation and increase both the actual powers of its institutions and the effectiveness of their decision-making, executive, and supervisory powers. In fact, the Union Plan represents significant progress on the way to a European federation. In this spirit, its article 3 defines citizenship of the Union as an extension of citizenship of a member state, thus extending the citizen's right of appeal to the Court of Justice. Establishing a European passport follows this idea of a strengthened European citizenship. The reinforcement of common policies is proof of the constructive intent underlying the Union Plan.

The plan distinguishes between joint cooperative actions and the coordination of national actions. At the same time, it distinguishes the exclusive powers attributed to the Union from the concurrent powers it exercises in parallel with the powers of member states. Both sets of powers are exercised in such a way as to enable imbalances between the different regions of the Union along with a balanced expansion of the Union to be eliminated progressively while balancing the expansion of the Union as a whole.

Exclusive powers are attributed to the Union to complete the Common Market and freedom of circulation as well as the competition policy at the Union level. The Union would establish a European company and take the necessary measures to harmonize legislative and administrative provisions relating to companies.

Most Community policies are characterized by concurrent powers exercised by the Union in various areas, including conjoint and economic policies and monetary and credit policies involving the creation of a European Committee on the capital markets, a European supervisory authority for banking, and a European Monetary Fund as an instrument of the European Monetary System. The aim of this monetary policy would be gradually to build a monetary union. A range of policies are also proposed in the following areas: agriculture and fisheries, transport and telecommunications, research and development, and industry and energy. In these sectors, the Union would share powers with member states to carry out such policies at the Union level. Specialized European agencies could be set up in each sector where there is common action. This idea of European agencies followed one of Denis de Rougemont's original proposals, which he revived in his work *L'Avenir est notre affaire,* a project inspired by federal agencies in the United States.[19]

Under the title "Policy for Society," the plan sets out all the policies reflecting different options for, and embodying values common to, Europeans. These are policies in which the Union would exercise concurrent powers regarding social and health issues, consumer protection, regional questions, the environment, education, research, culture, and information. Some, such as cultural policy, were new, while others, such as regional policy, had already been implemented in the European Community. The plan incorporates them in the draft treaty's constitution and proposes that they be developed. In its preface, it asserts (somewhat timidly) a need for local and regional authorities to be allowed, somehow, to participate in the building of Europe. This is, however, still a long way from Denis de Rougemont's "Europe of Regions." He defined *region* as primarily a space for civic participation made up of groups of communities. He thought that a "Europe of Nations" would be difficult, if not impossible, to attain and felt that a European federation could be founded only on the basis of regional and local communities. At present, member states are going all out to keep a grip on their regions as well as on relations between those regions and the Community authorities. Hence, the plan maintains cautious approach, although it does encourage transborder regional collaboration.

Funding is a touchstone for federal institutions. The levy of a federal tax is, of course, an essential element in the autonomy and capacity for action of central authorities. In the history of federations, the question of taxes has often unleashed conflicts between federalists and confederalists; think of the United States, for example. The 1965 crisis developed over resources for financing the agricultural policy and for the growth in the European Parliament's budgetary powers. On this occasion, General de Gaulle attacked the powers of the Commission, especially its power to initiate and finance projects. He tried to turn the Commission with its independent financial powers into a boogeyman. Fortunately, the Commission was able to establish a more solid financial base, and in 1975 the European Parliament gained a partial right to budgetary codecision, thanks to a special treaty. Thus, progress was made in spite of setbacks and crises.

Like the European Communities, the Union would have its own funding. However, the plan indicates that budgetary authority is vested in the European Parliament and the Union Council, the two legislative institutions. There is another double innovation to be noted: the Union may modify the nature or basis of existing revenue or establish new bases by an organic law, and a system of adjustments would be introduced to attenuate excessive economic imbalances between different regions.

External Relations and Security

The plan sets out ambitious objectives in the area of international relations. Union efforts would focus on maintaining peace and security, détente, and a balanced mutual and verifiable reduction in arms and military forces. Its work would also focus on respect for human rights, Third World development, and the improvement of international economic, monetary, and commercial relations. The Union would adopt either the method of common action or that of cooperation to achieve these objectives, and it would be endowed with exclusive powers to pursue common action in the area of external trade. However, after a ten-year transition period its policy of development aid must increasingly be the object of joint action. The Commission would undertake this joint action in the name of the Union, and negotiations would be carried out in accordance with guidelines established by the Union Council. Other matters would stay in the domain of cooperation, responsibility for which would fall on the European Council. In these matters, the Commission would have the power to propose policies and actions to the European Council.

As these policies and powers in the area of international relations demonstrate, the method put forward by the plan is pragmatic and gradual. Delicate issues are covered, but the way they are handled is left to Union institutions. The latter thus would have the scope to extend the field of common actions progressively. Similarly, the European Council may extend the sphere of cooperation, particularly in the areas of weapons, arms sales to third countries, defense policy, and disarmament. The plan also proposes a right of legation: provided the Council agrees, the Commission may establish representation in third countries and national organizations. Such representations would have powers in matters pertaining to joint action and may also take part in the coordination of diplomatic action by member states in areas involving cooperation. While progressively committing member states to cooperation and joint action, the Union Plan stays behind federal states in terms of defense, security, and external policy, which are in the hands of the federal authorities. A united Europe speaking with one voice is an idea that has often been put forward in the course of developing the Union, and it was strongly advocated in the Tindemans Report. With few exceptions, the member states of the European Community seem anxious to preserve their individual sovereignty in these areas even though they are fully aware of how it weakens their role. Their loss of influence results from their isolation and their fragmented actions in external policy and security.

There is, therefore, nothing surprising about the fact that this Union Plan, inspired by federalist ideas, did not find favor with governments. Was it the hint of federalism — even such a comparatively feeble hint — that encouraged the idea that the European Parliament planned to set up an embryonic federal state? Whatever the truth of the matter, governments stuck firmly to tradition, preferring to modify existing treaties rather than absorb the message of the Union Plan.

A Turning Point: The Single European Act (1987)

The Single European Act fits in with the general orientation of the European Parliament's draft treaty, which, inspired by Altiero Spinelli, was adopted by the European Parliament on 14 February 1984 after two years of work. As described earlier, the plan proposed to rewrite the treaties of Paris and Rome that established the European Communities, aiming to strengthen Community institutions and extend their fields of activity. The European Parliament's initiative, more ambitious than the European Council's, served as an inspiration and a reference point for governments, which nonetheless proceeded to sideline it in favor of a partial and more modest reform of the existing treaties. So in the end an exciting visionary leap was reduced to a few limited but concrete steps — not for the first time in the history of the union process.

In 1986, inspired by the initiatives and labors of the European Parliament and under pressure from the crisis in decision making in the European Community, the governments negotiated and adopted the Single European Act (on 17 February in Luxembourg and 28 February in the Hague) under the watchful eye of the European Council.[20] The great work was finally completed in December 1985 under the presidency of the smallest country in the Community, Luxembourg. The ratification process was brought to an end before the close of 1986, and the Single European Act came into force in July 1987.[21]

The European Council and Negotiation by Synergy

Since the early 1960s, there has been a relentless erosion of European Community powers and a gradual slippage from Community to intergovernmental power. Several events have marked this ebb of Community power.
First, there was the weakening of Council decision-making power on account of the requirement for unanimity after the 1966 Luxembourg Agreement (or rather the "agreement to differ"). After this, it was enough for a
member state to invoke its vital interest to impose a unanimous vote, which
put national above Community interest and reinforced the governments'
control over the European Community decision-making process. A parallel
erosion of the Commission's powers of initiative meant that it tended increasingly to consult governments of member states about planned initiatives
before formulating them officially instead of asserting its own responsibility
and autonomy. Dynamism and courage gave way to prudence, which became the essential feature of the Commission's activity. In 1974, an imbalance favoring intergovernmental institutions in the guise of the Community
was confirmed by the institutionalization of the summits of heads of state or
government as the European Council. Although its original intention was to
provide inspiration, promotion, and arbitration, the European Council actually helped reinforce the grip of national governments on the Community
process. The election of the European Parliament by universal direct suffrage did not fulfill the hopes it aroused and contributed only modestly to
rebalancing institutions by increasing Community powers. The European
Parliament remained a prisoner of its mainly consultative power even
though it was strengthened in terms of its legitimacy and its authority due to
its democratic bias. Moreover, the ensuing expansion of the European Community (in 1973, the United Kingdom, Denmark, and Ireland; in 1980,
Greece; in 1986, Spain and Portugal) helped to make decision-making procedures more ponderous. The result has been numerous calls — including those
from the Commission under Jacques Delors — for a deepening and strengthening of the process toward Union.

    The European Council sought to relaunch the European Union pro-
gram on the basis of the 1981 Genscher-Colombo Plan. This plan set out a
more global approach to integration on the basis of a conception that aimed
to bring together Community activities and the activities of member states
already exercised through other subsystems. The latter include political
cooperation, which was to cover external relations, security, cultural activities, the guarantee of fundamental rights, and the measures used against
terrorism and crime. The main institution that was to take up the "political
direction" of this ensemble was the European Council assisted by the Council of Foreign Ministers. Following lengthy discussions, the European Plan

proposed by Ministers Genscher and Colombo took the form of the solemn Declaration on a European Union adopted at the European Council meeting at Stuttgart in June 1983. This declaration set out the main lines for reflection and negotiation that were to lead to the 1986 Single European Act. On the basis of the Genscher-Colombo Plan, the declaration's goal was to reestablish a certain unity while maintaining a distinction between Community policies and political cooperation. The coherence of this two-dimensional "ensemble" was to be guaranteed by the European Council and the Council. Thus, the idea of institutionalizing the European Council was officially admitted. This was the logical conclusion of a process that began with its birth at the 1974 Paris Summit at the instigation of President Giscard d'Estaing and Chancellor Schmidt.[22] There was one difference: the Stuttgart Declaration expanded the membership of the European Council and ratified the participation of the president of the Commission on the basis of practice: "The European Council brings together the heads of state or government of member states and the president of the Commission of the European Communities. They are assisted by foreign ministers and a member of the Commission." Thus, the declaration authorized the full association of the Commission with the activity of political cooperation as recommended by the 1981 London Report on political cooperation. It confirmed the European Council as the principal institution of the European Union and the link between Community affairs and external policy. Finally, the declaration expressed a desire to take a further look at the way the decision-making procedures laid down in the Treaties of Rome and Paris were applied in order to improve the European Communities' capacity for action.

Following this assertion, five member states out of ten declared their adherence to the "Luxembourg compromise." However, while France and Ireland accepted a delay in voting, the other three members thought that discussions should continue until agreement was unanimous whenever a state believed that its own vital interests were at stake. These attitudes are an indication of the shift in opinion between 1983 and 1985, the year qualified majority voting was reintroduced with the Single European Act. After Stuttgart, the December 1983 Athens Session was stymied by Great Britain's budgetary demands; it also raised the problem of the increase in Community resources and the issue of the enlargement of the European Community toward the Iberian Peninsula.

It was not until the European Council meetings in Brussels in March 1984 and in Fontainebleau in June of the same year that these problems were basically solved. A few months later, the Dooge Committee of personal representatives of heads of state or government presented its final report, whose conclusions fell well short of the European Parliament Plan. The

Committee, under the presidency of Dooge and Adonnino, presented reports devoted to the institutions, including one by Maurice Faure, and a report on "Europe of the citizens." The aim of the final report was to make a qualitative leap into the creation of a real political entity. To this end, it proposed a range of priorities: a homogeneous economic space, including, inter alia, a technological Community and a reinforced EMS; the promotion of common values, including the protection of the environment, a European social space, and cultural values and political cooperation based on a permanent secretariat and covering external policy, security, and defense policy; the improvement of the decision-making process by recourse to majority voting; the strengthening of the Commission's autonomy and executive powers; and European Parliament involvement in the legislative process. As for intergovernmental negotiation of a European Union Treaty, it was to be based on the Community as it was, the Stuttgart Declaration, and the draft European Union Treaty adopted by the European Parliament. Thus, the report established a link between the work of the European Council and the work of the European Parliament, the one providing a judicial foundation, the other an elaborate project.

Giulio Andreotti, the Italian foreign minister, remarked: "At the European Council in Milan (June 1985), encouraged by the work of all those who went before us in this effort to set out the main lines of a European Union and especially by the work of the European Parliament, we managed to mark out the route we have to follow."[23] At the Milan European Council meeting, the proposals were met with substantial reservations and only seven of the member states supported the idea of an intergovernmental conference to modify the existing treaties and incorporate the practice of political cooperation in another treaty. Although it is worth noting that the proposal made at this conference was adopted by only seven members at the following session, all member states, including Spain and Portugal, took part in the conference convened by the Luxembourg presidency in spite of opposition or reticence on the part of the United Kingdom, Denmark, and Greece. Two separate groups were involved in the preparatory work: directors of political affairs, tasked with political cooperation, organized the codification of a system to bring it about, while a preparatory commission under the presidency of Secretary-General Dondelinger drew up amendments to the Treaty of Rome on the basis of the Commission's proposals. Following numerous meetings of the Dondelinger Commission and the ministers, negotiations came to a conclusion in December 1985. The European Council decided to bring together the two dimensions of the negotiations — political cooperation and amendments — in a single act: hence, the expression "Single European Act."

The first Delors Commission was responsible for the impact of the

White Book, which gave rise directly to a broad political consensus on the proposal to build a huge internal market within a fixed period, the Europe of 1993. This proposal was approved by the European Council in March 1985 and is reminiscent of Jean Monnet's approach: it acted as a catalyst, defining the objectives capable of bringing together the range of different intentions; it came on the scene at the right moment; and it set precise deadlines. Moreover, thanks to the dynamism it brought, the vision of a technological Europe, a space without frontiers and support policies — essential factors in the context of global competition with the United States and Japan — this proposal produced a series of institutional reforms indispensable to the efficient functioning of the Community economy. According to Emile Noël, this led to the creation of a synergy between economic dynamism and its logical extension, the institutional framework.[24] It seems clear that the dynamism of the internal market was in danger of being bogged down in an institutional system that was often paralyzed by the abuse of unanimity. In contrast with the practice of the "package deal" leading to global accords at the lowest level between often disparate groups, synergy engenders a dynamic process that makes it possible to create a cumulative and progressive movement by an accumulation of positive elements. Unlike the "package," a static operation, synergy engenders a dynamic process and produces a real encouragement to progress. To develop synergy between two or more otherwise entirely separate dossiers will mean that one will help push the other along, which in turn will be a political aid to the success of the first. The "package deal" corresponds to a leveling process; synergy engenders a cumulative process, a process of escalation aimed at obtaining the maximum result in all the sectors.[25]

It was a creative initiative from the Commission that set the wheels in motion again. On the basis of a statement of the obstacles to freedom of circulation, it proposed a deadline of 1993 for the completion of the "internal market, a space without frontiers," which the Milan Council approved in the shape of the White Book. On the basis of the consensus created by this "political invention," a synergy process developed after the Milan Council (1985). The most ardent partisans of the internal market, Great Britain and Denmark, could hardly maintain their opposition to the institutional reforms that the Benelux countries considered necessary for the efficient operation of the area without frontiers. The consensus between the two antagonistic groups unleashed a synergy that provoked France and Germany to commit themselves more resolutely and make the Milan Council meeting a success, with the support and blessing of the Italian presidency.

This movement was then stimulated by new proposals from the Commission in positive areas such as technology and the environment. The Luxembourg presidency showed equal imagination in 1985 when it called on the

Commission to come up with a package of proposals to modify or fill out the treaty in six areas, following the strategy set out by President Delors; these areas were the internal market, economic and social cohesion, research and technological development, the environment, culture, and monetary policy.[26] The Commission was thus able to realize its full potential and become the driving force behind integration thanks to its ability, hard work, global vision, and mobilizing strategy. Accordingly, it moved toward greater cohesion around a set of interactive objectives and interests.

An example of this dynamic spillover was provided by an initially very reticent proposal from Denmark that ultimately led to the addition of a chapter on social policy, endowing the Community with a new dimension and contributing to a renewed involvement of the European Trade Union Confederation in Community activity. Greece meanwhile committed itself to economic and social cohesion, an expression of solidarity between rich and poor regions that was made a condition of its final agreement. Thus, a spiral movement gradually developed that made it possible not merely to authorize policies outside the scope of the treaties, but to create new policies and define new objectives such as economic and monetary union. This constituted a series of interventions, which in turn required a partial reform of decision-making procedures as well as the institutionalization of the European Council.

In order to complete this new construction, the European Council inserted a chapter on political cooperation in the Single European Act. In the preamble, the member states expressed their desire to transform the totality of their relationships into a European Union in accordance with the Stuttgart Declaration of 19 June 1983. They stated their resolve to implement the Union based on the Community's own rules as well as on cooperation in foreign policy. They also decided to endow this Union with the necessary means of action. Similarly, they declared themselves determined to promote democracy and fundamental rights while improving the economic and social situation by deepening common policies and pursuing new objectives and to ensure better functioning of the Communities by allowing institutions to exercise their powers in the manner most in accordance with Community interests.

The Internal Market and Supporting Policies

One of the main aims of the Single European Act was to complete the work of the Common Market by setting up a true internal market without obstacles or frontiers.[27] This global strategy based on the objectives of the Treaty of Rome is both an extension of work undertaken since 1958 and an adaptation to new conditions such as, for example, new technology and environmental policies. This meant adaptation not only within the Community space but outside it in order to increase the competitive capacity of the Community in the face of its two greatest rivals, the United States and Japan.

The Common Market provided the foundation for this new strategy, which intended to achieve complete freedom of movement within an area with 340 million inhabitants and to create the measures with which imbalances that might threaten the competitiveness and growth of the whole could be avoided or corrected. There was implicit acknowledgment that numerous obstacles still hindered the free circulation intended by the Treaty of Rome. Among these obstacles were national administrative regulations embodied in complicated formalities as well as a range of more or less subtle nontariff barriers: technical norms for the production, composition, and presentation of products; and health, security, and ethical norms, controls often essential for the protection of collective goods but easily manipulated in the interest of protecting national markets. Hence, a plethora of measures were included in the Single European Act to guarantee the free circulation of goods, services, capital, and persons.

This attempt at liberalization also affected the traditionally impenetrable domain of public markets. The difficulty of this task may be comprehended if one thinks of the experience of local public markets in other countries, in particular the public markets hedged in by protective ordinances in the German Länder, the Swiss cantons, and the American states. The opening of the public markets together with controls on subsidies provided the conditions for fair competition in the Community space, which has as one of its principal objectives the protection of the conditions for healthy competition. Freed of all obstacles, the single market must make it possible to guarantee the main missions of economic policy as defined in article 2 of the Treaty of Rome:

> The mission of the Community is to promote the harmonious development of economic activity throughout the Community, along with a constant balanced expansion, an increased stability, an accelerated improvement in living standards, and closer relations between member states; this is to be done by the establishment of a common market and by a progressive drawing together of the economic policies of member states.

On the basis of this idea, the Commission set out the three overall functions of its economic policy in 1987:

> The quest for greater stability (the battle against inflation and external imbalances), the optimal allocation of resources to profit from benefits of scale and stimulate innovation and competitiveness, and the balanced distribution of wealth, which is also a function of the merits of each.[28]

This idea shows how the development of the Community was generally conceived. In concept, it was similar to the Spaak Report, but it differed in that it was an extension of the Treaty of Rome, on which it was based. Compared with the Spaak Report, which was an innovation in itself, the White Book and the Single European Act renewed and provided an original adaptation of the existing treaty. Moreover, if we look back over the way projects for union have evolved we can see an exceptional continuity and the influence of certain *key ideas;* the concepts of a "common market" and "perpetual creation" formulated in the Briand Project have traveled a unique road that in many ways, in the context of the dynamics of capitalism,[29] has ultimately led to the Common Market of the European Community and to its renewal by the Single European Act. The latter looks like another step in the momentum of *perpetual creation.*

For this internal market to achieve its greatest potential, freedom of movement and fair and healthy competition are accompanied by a set of policies and programs. In spite of greater economic profits there is a danger that the single market might accentuate disparities between different regions or social groups and thus create imbalances, instability, or even conflict. The *regional policy* implemented under the form of a structural policy is not simply a matter of budgetary transfers or financial adjustments but is meant to have a real impact on regions with inappropriate structures or regions going through conversion. As a complement to national and regional policies, Community instruments are to play an important role in the convergence of economies. Thus, they will be able to help strengthen economic and social *cohesion* within the European Community. This general orientation and these objectives will make it possible to increase harmony and complementarity within community programs and actions and also with policies followed in different sectors by member states. This seems particularly to be the case with the actions undertaken by the Structural Funds, for example, the European Regional Development Fund (ERDF), the European Social Fund (ESF), and the European Agricultural Guidance and Guarantee Fund (EAGGF).

There is evidence of a new approach in the Community's structural measures, which are centered around two basic ideas:

> In the first place, the use of programs will be preponderant. The Community's support for the efforts and initiatives of member states should be given at the right level. Rather than intervention through particular projects, intervention should occur within the framework of programs.
>
> This will make it possible to harmonize effectively the specific interventions made by various instruments for grants and loans, each repre-

senting specific competence and experience in terms of territorial development, employment policy, and agricultural techniques. It will also make it possible to decentralize Community action and give the maximum scope to local or regional initiatives, which are the most effective when it comes to investment and employment. Programs will enable contracts to be made between the Community, member states, and regions. Based on the preparation, follow-up, and common evaluation of actions, they will in fact establish true partnerships.[30]

Other support or development policies follow the same logic: *transport* policy, given a particular stimulus by projects of Community interests, programs for huge infrastructure networks and policies for the development of exchange; and a common *scientific and technological* development policy whose actions, brought together in a quadrennial framework program of research and technological cooperation, concentrate on the essentials (i.e., on actions guaranteed to produce a far-reaching effect). These development policies aim to encourage cooperation between businesses and research institutes in different countries; they ensure that resources are pooled and common norms formulated at the stage of precompetitive research; and they encourage geographical mobility among academics and scientists.

The Single European Act opens up a *social dimension* only marginally touched upon in the EEC treaty, which was centered on economic development. In the latter, the social dimension was a mere appendix to economic growth, which constituted the principal focus of the EEC. This concept can be explained if we think of it in the context of a world dominated, as it was then, by increasing GNP and by the reconstruction of the European economy. There was more of a need for rebuilding and renovating than there was for innovation. Hence, only marginal importance was allotted to research, technological development, and the social aspects of economic activity. As for the environment, it was either ignored or considered a negligible variable. The Single European Act updated the 1957 treaty with the introduction of these three new policies, which extended Community activity and encouraged or intensified participation by social and scientific players in the common task. The result was to enlarge the circle of players and to reinvigorate the activity of the European Trade Union Confederation (ETUC), which previously had exercised no real influence on Community life. Once again the "law," according to which there is a correlation between the level of development of Community powers and the degree of activity of groups and individual players in the domains affected by those powers, is proven true. Dialogue with social partners, problems of employment and the job market, the free circulation of labor, and emigration policy combined with considerations of health, social security, and living conditions were henceforth to be arenas for trade union involvement in modest support of the European Social Fund.

This emphasis on social policy reinforced the "cohesion and solidarity" that formed a new dimension in the Community. By associating social players more directly with Community enterprise, the Single European Act has helped establish harmony between social partners and accordingly has increased the competitive capacity of the Community as a whole. The experience of economic success and the high levels of competitiveness found in countries as diverse as Switzerland and Japan seem to corroborate this conclusion.

In the same spirit, new priorities emerge from Community actions in the sphere of continuing education and higher professional training, with exchanges and collaboration between students, teachers, and scientific researchers. Though quantitatively unimpressive, such activity was a concrete embodiment of a common concern for a future resource of primordial importance, *human resources,* Europe's greatest treasure. Alongside this, there is a determination to preserve *natural treasures,* which is expressed in the environmental dimension that the Single European Act introduced into the sphere of Community activity. This new policy is typical of the innovative style and strategy of Community action. According to the guidelines formulated by the European Council in Dublin, activity undertaken by the Community and its member states is carried out in a coordinated way and with respect for the principles of sustainable development and preferential recourse to preventive measures. In defining its priorities, the European Council set guidelines for Community policy in the area of the environment for years to come. This policy bears the mark of the principle of *subsidiarity* and of the *coordinating* role of the Community. It is above all complementary to national policies, to which it assigns a minimal level of protection, which the states have the power to increase, and coordinates measures taken by member states. It defines common objectives and overall priorities and manages to pull the slower members along without holding up the countries that are in the forefront in environmental matters (witness the stricter controls on automobile emissions in Holland).

Another strategy involves integration of the environmental dimension into other policies, structural actions, and economic and fiscal instruments. There is an obligation to protect natural resources arising from article 130E of the Single European Act. Also, the priority of structural actions is given to a certain number of sensitive regions or zones, coastal or agricultural, which benefit from Community subsidiaries or incentives. For example, 34,000 farmers have benefited from an incentive to adopt production practices compatible with the requirements of the natural environment.[31] The

Community's approach to environmental issues is a model to be followed from another point of view, for the creation of the *European Environmental Agency* represents a turning point in the concept of Community management in certain specific sectors. This new approach makes it possible to unblock certain Community activities by making them the responsibility of specialized agencies, centers, or study units, which are autonomous but act in liaison with Community institutions and in a framework of guidelines and norms defined by these institutions. With the multiplication of Community spheres of action, a new Community approach has emerged progressively and pragmatically, proceeding by means of the federative approach in the general sense of that term.

Economic and monetary union was part of the logical extension of the internal market and common policies. The development of Community monetary capacity is based on experience gained in the framework of the European Monetary System and thanks to the evolution of the European currency unit (ecu).

Initiatives in favor of the creation of economic and monetary union by stages originated well before the Single European Act. They go back to the conference of heads of state or government at the Hague in 1969 following the resignation of General de Gaulle. This relaunched negotiations for the admission of the United Kingdom and at the same time allowed an agreement to be reached on the creation of economic and monetary union. This initiative coincided with the end of the transitional period that led to customs union, the finalization of the Common Agricultural Policy, and a system of specific resources. It also coincided with a period in which the Bretton Woods system showed signs of weakening. This was the beginning of the long trail leading, via several stages, to the Single European Act and the intergovernmental conference inaugurated in December 1990. The cornerstone of the Economic and Monetary Union (EMU) was laid in the 1970 *Werner Report,* which set out the main lines of monetary union and indicated each of its phases. The "political will to establish an economic and monetary union" was expressed by member states after the *Werner Report* gave birth to the "monetary snake" in 1972 and to the European Monetary Cooperation Fund (EMCF) in 1973. In the course of the following year, the Council passed a resolution regarding the convergence of economic policies and issued a directive on stability, growth, and full employment. These efforts came to grief in the oil and dollar crises, which produced divergent reactions among member states; the commitment to convergence gave way before de facto divergence.

Not until 1979 did the monetary integration process show signs of reviving with the creation of the European Monetary System and the ecu. At one and the same time the name of a medieval French coin and the

European currency unit, the ecu is an accounting unit based on a basket of member countries' currencies. The success of the EMS, which made it possible to ensure that currencies within the system were more stable, explains the revival of the monetary union process in the context of the Single European Act. After periods of stagnation and even regression, the process was relaunched in 1987. The long and winding road to monetary union, paralleled by fluctuations in the integration process and economic and political circumstances, was nonetheless remarkably rapid given the member states' traditional reluctance to yield an inch in matters of monetary sovereignty. For centuries, in fact, currency has been the symbol of unity and sovereignty.

In spite of this weight of tradition, which tends to accentuate the obstacles to monetary union and the substitution of a single European currency for the national currencies, the progress that has been made is a definite sign of the immense attractive power of the integration movement, which is increasingly seen as having priority even over anxieties about national sovereignty. In fact, as interdependence grows and as the symbols of national monetary sovereignty gradually lose their substance, the movement toward monetary union is broadening. Resistance is melting away in the face of a determination to achieve common monetary capacity and autonomy. Although she remained stubbornly opposed, even Mrs. Thatcher had to admit defeat when faced with the decisive results of the efforts of Great Britain's partners to acquire a "shared sovereignty." This illustrates the principle of subsidiarity, which makes it possible to strengthen real capacity for action by the common exercise of powers that (at least to some extent) lose their initial potential when exercised separately.

One of the last acts of Mrs. Thatcher's government was its decision in October 1990 to join the European Monetary System. This represented the United Kingdom's first step toward full participation in the conception and implementation of an economic and monetary union. The machinery has been set in motion, but the path to monetary union is tricky and the gateway narrow. The same applies to its necessary complement, a Central Bank and a single currency, especially since what is involved is a partial but substantial transfer of sovereign powers, which amounts to a qualitative leap within the process of economic integration.

The Revival of the Spillover Process and the Readaptation of the Institutions

This brief survey of the progress made by the Single European Act is a typical illustration of the application of Jean Monnet's method: a global strategy that spreads contagiously from one sector to the next on the way to

European integration. Based on interfunctional links built and developed between interdependent sectors, this method makes it possible to respond, sometimes in advance, to the demands and needs of these sectors with an eye to the efficient performance of tasks and with the aim of reinforcing de facto solidarities and overall cohesion. The Single European Act gave a fresh impetus to the *spillover process* on the level of the norms, powers, and operation of Community institutions. By means of amendments and innovations, it reestablished an overall perspective encompassing a multitude of interdependent elements that together form a coherent whole. By their own internal dynamism, these elements produce a force that is gradually communicated by synergy to other parts of the whole. Of necessity, the Single European Act promotes a movement toward greater efficiency and cohesion to reduce costs compared with those of "non-Europe." The results obtained or expected in this way, though partial, are incentives and factors that enable the Community to improve both its competitiveness and its negotiating capacity. In fact, by encouraging greater economic and social cohesion within the Community, the internal market and supporting policies have unleashed a dynamism that has had a significant international impact. This cohesion will be reinforced by the effect of the Economic and Monetary Union and will contribute to the affirmation of a European identity and an increase in Community influence in comparison with its principal rivals on the world market as well as in the General Agreement on Tariffs and Trade (GATT) and the International Monetary Fund (IMF). Hence, the Community will have an increased capacity for external economic relations, particularly within international economic organizations. This relationship between internal integration and cohesion and their extension outside the Community was clearly confirmed by the Court of Justice; the Community's external capacity is exercised within the limits and as a function of its internal powers.

By reinforcing cohesiveness, economic and social integration has had an impact that extends beyond the economic and social spheres. Economic union constitutes not only one of the main elements of the Community's capacity for influence but also one of the essential foundations for security and an effective external policy. Thus, the fabric of an external policy, which includes commercial and economic policy, is gradually woven, converging from several sources, and the foundations of the security of the European Community are laid down progressively. Hence, the Single European Act mandates external and security policies that are coherent with the Community's economic and social policies. Thus, the necessary unity and complementarity between economic and political integration within the European Union are gradually being recognized and implemented.

General de Gaulle was not mistaken when he declared at his 1962 press conference:

> When we negotiate tariffs, that's politics; when we adjust our coal prices, that's politics; when we make wages and social charges the same in the six countries, that's politics; when each state allows workers from the five others to enter its country and settle there, that's politics; when we make the necessary decrees and ask Parliament to vote the necessary laws, credits, and sanctions, that's all politics. It's politics when we bring agriculture into the Common Market, and it was the Six, and they alone, who managed this last January by their political authority. It's politics when we discuss the association of Greece or the African states or the Republic of Madagascar. It's politics when we negotiate with the United Kingdom on the issue of her request to be admitted to the Common Market. It's also politics when we consider requests from other states for admission or association. And it's still politics when we study requests from the United States relating to its economic dealings with the Community.

The general then concluded that the economic development of Europe cannot be guaranteed without a political union. Yet, despite its political significance, the economic integration process has continued to evolve quite independently of the political process, which through its delays was threatening what had been achieved in the social and economic spheres. This artificial separation was made necessary by political conditions and was criticized as *upside-down federalism* by Rector Brugmans. In fact, while federal states involve themselves chiefly in spheres having to do with sovereignty — defense, external relations, currency — the European Community regulates spheres having directly to do with "civil society": agriculture, the steel industry, freedom of movement, the environment, and transport.[32]

This paradoxical situation is easily explained. In the first place, although federal states do have responsibility for high politics, they also exercise powers in the area of economic policy, the environment, and transport. Second, these federal systems involve an advanced degree of political and social integration resulting from a more or less lengthy union process; in comparison to these established states, the Community is still in a formative phase. For all its multinational diversity and technological dimension, its origins and evolution are reminiscent of certain features of the Zollverein that was the basis for German integration. Third, the fact of having begun the integration process backward in relation to these federal states might actually be a positive factor in the sense that this type of integration has helped to build "civil society" — ultimately the foundation of every human community. By creating the conditions that encourage and stimulate interaction, cooperation, and synergy between many social players, the Community is creating a network of solidarity at various levels of society. Nonetheless, as integration progresses, the need for political union grows ever more acute, which is in fact precisely what Jean Monnet hoped for and anticipated.

An adequate institutional capacity is a sine qua non for the operation of the internal market, with the support of a whole panoply of common policies and instruments. Accepted by the member states, this requirement helped to improve Community institutions and decision-making processes, thus confirming the spillover logic and the relation between the objectives fixed by the Single European Act and the institutional resources able to fulfill these objectives. The synergy between the internal market, common policies, and Community institutions gave rise to a series of institutional reforms: the European Council has become accepted as a Community institution, qualified majority voting reappeared in the Council of Ministers, the European Parliament is more closely associated with Community legislative procedure, the Commission's role in the implementation of decisions has been strengthened, directives are becoming the main instrument for the accomplishment of the objectives of the Single European Act, and a tribunal of first instance has been created. In addition to these reforms, the most important innovation is the incorporation of political cooperation into a single treaty called the Single European Act. Rather than being an element in the European Community, political cooperation is juxtaposed and linked to it by a series of bridges: the European Council, the Council of Foreign Ministers, (less obviously but indisputably) the Commission, and of course the European Parliament. The Maastricht Treaty confirms this evolution.

After the shock of the empty chair crisis, qualified majority voting was only used on ten occasions prior to 1974. The first enlargement of the Community, taking its numbers up to nine, made it more difficult to achieve a consensus by weakening the internal cohesion that (for all its sporadic crises) had been characteristic of the Community of the Six. Strangely, despite the presence of the United Kingdom with its attachment to the unanimity rule, or else precisely because of this fact, resort to qualified majority voting then became more frequent. Between 1974 and 1984, approximately 130 decisions were reached on a qualified majority, and they became more frequent after 1980. From then on, member states gradually made more and more use of qualified majorities to ensure the necessary functioning of institutions and to facilitate decision making in the Council. This growing practice helped to demystify qualified majority voting, making it more acceptable to member states, bringing out the advantages of majority rule, and minimizing its weaknesses. Thanks to the use of this procedure, or the possibility of such use, the decision-making process has become both swifter and more efficient and has often led to compromises that did not necessarily reflect the lowest common denominator.

However, the problem of the fragmentation of the Council — between the council for general affairs and the specialized councils — does not seem to have been satisfactorily resolved; the Council does not have any effective coordination system. With new spheres of activity being added and existing policies becoming more entrenched, the Council will have even more work to do and fragmentation will worsen. This growth of responsibilities threatens to accentuate the Council's present weaknesses by depriving it of overall vision and coherent authority. This danger is all the more real in that its future tasks include new responsibilities, not simply in the area of economic and monetary policy but also for political cooperation. The Gulf crisis showed both the inadequacy of the political machinery and the absence of commitment such a situation requires of Community foreign ministers and in particular of the presidency.

Under these conditions, the question is whether the Council, or rather this proliferation of councils, is in a position to have the global vision, that is, the political vision, and to carry out coherent actions. The probability would seem to be that the Council will imperceptibly lose its substance as its power is eroded and its scope for action limited. Divided and not permanent, the Council is subject to growing demands from all sides and no longer seems to be up to its new tasks. The discordance between its many responsibilities, its limited activity, and its lack of an overall vision could lead to the Council being stripped of its functions, which would then be given to other Community institutions and organs. This slippage of powers would no doubt favor Coreper or the Commission, both of them in permanent session and exercising key functions in the decision-making process. Each of these hypotheses raises questions.

On the one hand, in relying too much on Coreper, whose membership is permanent but relatively restricted in number, the Council exposes itself to a reinforcement of technocratic domination. It is in fact highly probable that the limited means available to Coreper with respect to the increased tasks and responsibilities it then would have would inevitably encourage it to farm out work to working groups and experts whose activities would tend to elude its control. Thus, the responsibilities initially entrusted to the ambassadors of permanent missions would end up being fulfilled by bureaucrats and experts. Supervision of the work would then tend to fall to specialist bureaucrats and experts rather than to senior officials. As a result, the global vision and political role of the Council and Coreper would be obscured by the fragmentation resulting from more technical approaches, and in the end this would encourage excessively technological power.

On the other hand, it seems that, although Council powers seem less likely to migrate toward the Commission under the current system, this would have certain advantages, leading in particular to greater control over specific matters, according to the general interest given to them, within a global vision that is shared exclusively by the Commission and the European Council. Such a shift of powers toward centers of activity controlled by the Commission would involve adjustments. In particular, I am thinking of the counterbalance that ought to be set in place by increasing European Parliament control over the Commission. A second adjustment might be to distinguish between Community laws as adopted by a Council/European Parliament codecision and rulings made within the framework of these laws by the Commission. Whatever the solution, measures will have to be taken to avoid the erosion and collapse of political, legislative, and governmental powers or indeed simply a blurring of the lines between them.

In this new configuration, the *European Council* appears on the Community horizon as the supreme political institution in terms of the political weight of its members, its global vision, and the growing role it is called to undertake in the Community. A quick glance at the Commission's twenty-fourth general report tells us that there are hardly any important areas of activity where the European Council has not played a crucial part. It stands as a central institution that directs Community activities, consolidating its key role in the framework of political cooperation.

The European Council, Political Cooperation, and the Support of Public Opinion

Established by the December 1974 Summit Declaration, the European Council was given a legal basis by the Single European Act, which legitimized it as a Community institution. The Single European Act gives official approval to the role of the Council, disregarding the old fear of a supreme intergovernmental institution allowed to dominate the Communities and establishing a form of direction or controlling authority over the Communities and their political cooperation. In point of fact, bringing together the most senior political figures in the member states — like the supreme institutions of regional integration between developing nations — and the president of the Commission twice yearly (art. 2), the European Council continues to do what it did before: provide impetus and direction, fix priorities, and set the agenda for Community institutions. The European Council has not hesitated to act as a referee in major conflicts, preventing them from producing the kind of paralysis that grips the Community decision-making system. The Council has powers enabling it to direct common policies, as is shown by its actions in such new areas as economic and monetary policy, social policy (the Social Charter), and environmental policy. According to article 146 of the EEC Treaty, its members may act as the Council of the Community if a political desire for this is expressed.

Finally, it seems difficult to establish a legal separation when, de facto and de jure, presidents and prime ministers give their ministers sitting on the Council of the Communities directives on crucially important questions. Although political cooperation is chiefly a matter for member states, the Single European Act establishes an organic link with the Council. The foreign ministers and a Commission member meet at least four times a year in the framework of political cooperation. However, they may also deal with foreign policy issues in the context of political cooperation during sessions of the Council of the European Communities (art. 30, sec. 3a). In addition, the Single European Act confirms that the Commission is fully associated with the work of political cooperation (art. 30, sec. 3b). Thus, without setting up an overall structure like the 1984 European Parliament Union Plan, the Single European Act formalizes the existence of the European Council and defines the outlines and organs of political cooperation. So progress (timid but effective) was made toward bringing political cooperation within the Community structure, the two, however, remaining separate even though they are juxtaposed. This rapprochement was confirmed by the requirement that European Community external policies (commercial policy, relations with developing nations and the ACP states, and so on) be coherent with policies agreed upon in the course of European political cooperation.[33] Without laying down sanction, the Single European Act attributes to the presidency and the Commission the responsibility for overseeing the search for, and preservation of, such coherence. In codifying the practice of political cooperation established since 1969, the act introduced innovations relating to security and the institutions of political cooperation. Henceforth, questions of *European security* are to be part of the sphere of activity of political cooperation. Member states took the view that closer cooperation on questions of European security would make an essential contribution to the development of a European identity in the area of external policy (art. 30, sec. 6a). This represents a timid return to security and defense issues, sidelined since the shock of the collapse of the EDC and the rejection of the Fouchet Plan. Without taking on any obligations in this area, member states expressed their readiness to coordinate to a greater extent their positions on political and economic aspects of security. This intent reflected a new conception of security that included not simply a military but a political-economic dimension. This dimension constitutes a fundamental element of security and confirms member states' determination to preserve the technological and industrial conditions necessary for their security (art. 30, sec. 6b). Member states committed themselves to work toward this end both at the national level and in the framework of the appropriate institutions. There is, of course, no reason why certain states should not develop closer cooperation in the area of security in the context of the Western European Union and NATO, although not all of them are members (art. 30, sec. 6c).

As far as institutions and bodies of cooperation are concerned, the Single European Act referred to the contracting parties, who in practice sit with the president of the Commission of the European Council, assisted by foreign ministers and a member of the Commission. The act defined the role of the presidency, institutionalized the Political Committee (the group of correspondents and working groups), and set up a permanent secretariat. The *presidency* of political cooperation (art. 30, secs. 10a and 10b), which coincides with the presidency of the Council of the European Community, is responsible for launching initiatives and coordinating and representing member states to third countries and in international organizations where activities having to do with European political cooperation are at issue. The presidency is also responsible for the management, political cooperation, and functioning of the secretariat. The *Political Committee* (art. 30, secs. 10c and 10d) is made up of the political directors of the foreign ministries, who meet regularly to give the necessary impetus to political cooperation, to ensure its continuity, and to do the preparatory work for the ministers. The *group of European correspondents* (art. 30, sec. 10c) has the job of following up the implementation of political cooperation and studying general organizational problems within the terms of directives from the Political Committee. The *working groups* (art. 30, sec. 10f) meet as dictated by Political Committee directives. Finally, although these institutions and bodies were formally established by the act, its institutional innovation in fact consists chiefly of establishing a *permanent secretariat* in Brussels (art. 30, sec. 10g). The secretariat assists the presidency in the preparation and implementation of actions having to do with political cooperation and on administrative questions. It carries out its functions under the authority of the presidency. Countries that are signatories to the Single European Act committed themselves to considering whether it would be appropriate to revise the provisions relating to political cooperation in the light of experience. The inadequacy of the instruments of political cooperation was visible from the beginning, but it was brutally exposed by the Gulf War. In 1990, the European Council decided to undertake a complete revision of these instruments with the intention of establishing a political union.

As this survey has revealed, the Single European Act effectively improves the decision-making process by applying qualified majority voting generally in the context of the European Communities. Moreover, it incorporates a series of new policies into the EEC Treaty and deepens the Community's mission by putting in place instruments that will make it possible to improve and complete the internal market. Finally, the Single European Act formalized the first institutions of a political union. In this, it reminds us of the Fouchet Plan (although simplified), put forward in 1959 by General de Gaulle, which aimed to cover not just the economic domain but the areas of politics, defense, and culture. Indeed, the Fouchet Plan aimed at a wider field of activity than the Single European Act undertook more than a quarter of a century later. Not only did it tackle defense questions more directly, but it sought to include the cultural domain in its purview. Though not totally excluded from the sphere of Community action, the latter is not formally included in the Single European Act.

From the institutional point of view, the Fouchet Plan looks like a precursor of the new institutions and bodies responsible for political cooperation; indeed, in the plan the highest supreme institution was to be a council of heads of state or government, the equivalent of the present European Council. Furthermore, it contrived to set up a political commission made up of directors of political affairs and a permanent secretariat. Thus, it took more than a quarter of a century to establish a similar structure, which in fact is probably less structured than Fouchet's original concept. What matters nonetheless is that real progress has been made—slow and modest, perhaps, but effective and essential. In the words of Aristide Briand, the Union of Europe is a "perpetual creation," and in its turn the Single European Act has contributed to fresh negotiations on economic and monetary union and on a political union.

This integration process relies on a broad consensus of public opinion. There is a very strong majority in the Community, on average eight persons out of ten, in favor of efforts to unite Western Europe.[34] Against this background of general support, we see a majority of people approving a *European political union* and a largely favorable attitude toward *common action* in the key sectors of activity in a political community. Public opinion understands concrete common actions and supports them readily. It can, therefore, hardly fail to approve the common policies that the Single European Act incorporated into the Community treaties, even though it fell well short of the European Parliament's plan.

Opposition to *majority voting* was certainly not insignificant, but nonetheless six people out of ten were in favor of it. The opposition registered in Portugal, and more especially in Greece and Denmark, did not prevent ratification of the Single European Act, though it had to be put to a referendum for approval in the case of Denmark. As for the institutional dimension, the present and future role of the European Parliament was supported by just over half of those who expressed an opinion. On this point, the Single European Act coincides with public opinion insofar as it did not propose any increase in the powers of the European Parliament but rather associated it more closely with Council decisions.

As with common policies, the central aim of the Single European Act — the creation of a European space without internal frontiers — was approved by a huge majority of 83 percent, with a maximum of 96 percent in Portugal and a minimum of 67 percent in Denmark. Overall, public opinion in the Twelve was very favorable to the substantial innovations introduced by this reform of the Community treaties. Even those member states least inclined to approve the rule of qualified majority voting gave their assent to this reform, which taken as a whole has many advantages. This majority procedure of course aims to improve the operation of the European Community and to facilitate the implementation of common policies as well as the creation of a free space. Although often much less adventurous than public opinion, the governments have adopted reforms that correspond to the wishes of the majority of Europeans.

A Turning Point: The New Federalist Approach

The majority policy change, the federalist approach, inherent in the Single European Act attracted very little comment. This federalist turn had in fact been anticipated by numerous indicators over time. The White Book and the Single European Act gave official confirmation to a movement that went back to the late 1970s. Initially inspired by the French tradition of centralization, the Community had originally sought common norms, preferably uniform, for all member countries. The very concept of harmonization was equated with standardization and encountered vigorous resistance for this very reason. Rulings — acts directly binding in all their parts — clearly dominated Community legislation. But this initial approach aimed at creating a common system became more flexible through experience of the reality of Europe's diversity. Little by little, the notion of union in diversity, federalism's fundamental principle, came to dominate. This recognition of the wealth of Europe's differences completely reversed the initial current, which, once diverted from its original aspirations, came to reflect both a new conception and a more flexible approach closer to the federalist conception and approach. The new priority became a quest to optimize the management of the various states and regions in the Community. The clearest proof of this radical change could be seen when French MPs formulated the concept of *differentiation* at the time of the negotiations over the Single European Act.

There were plenty of pointers to the way things were moving, whether in the shape of regional policy or of policies for the development of research and technology. Regional policy is based on coordination measures and incentives applied to different regions according to their specific needs. A "Europe of Regions" is by definition a Community founded on the diversity of its regions, areas of development, and participation, a diversity that offers broader development within a union, favoring both solidarity and the combination of forces for growth at various levels. This is a concrete illustration of the application of the *principle of subsidiarity,* which has become a major preoccupation in the Community and indeed threatens to become a "Community obsession" or a kind of universal principle of organization and point of reference. In the area of the environment, for example, the principle of subsidiarity has a privileged sphere of application — without even being mentioned: "The Community acts in the area of the environment to the extent that the objectives set out in paragraph 1 may be better achieved at the Community level than at the level of an individual member state" (art. 103R of the Single European Act). These objectives are the following: the preservation, protection, and amelioration of the quality of the environment; the protection of the health of individuals; and the prudent and rational use of natural resources (art. 130R, par. 1).

Other notions and methods confirm this new tendency. Thus, *coordination* and *cooperation* have become central concepts, particularly in the areas of economic, research, technology, transport, regional, and environmental policies. On this issue, the Commission stated quite unambiguously: "There is no question of transferring all the powers of economic and social policy to the European level."[35]

Thus, the Community is becoming a center of coordination that provides guidelines and acts as a driving force, launching various selective actions in the shape of incentive and support measures. It is also leaving more room to maneuver in decentralized actions at the national and regional levels while seeking to limit the proliferation of interventions and rulings that used to be the Community's original sin.

This more realistic approach has been adopted with an eye to an internal market that rehabilitates the initial objective of a liberalization of Europe, including its protected markets, in combination with healthy competition. This liberalization is based on a series of selective actions, control mechanisms, and relevant supporting policies. This revived synergy in economic fields, reinforced by restructuring and readaptation, is boosted by support measures and incentives coming from structural funds, the European Investment Bank, and various Community programs. Through a combination of normative guidelines, selective support, and coordinated programs, the Community aims to increase the efficiency and coherence of policies intended to encourage the expansion of decentralized activity. The initial rigidity of Community rulings and interventions is now giving way to more flexible policies and actions better adapted and more sensitive to the rich diversity of Europe. This new concept, seeking to reconcile the need for effective Community policy with the diversity of its autonomous activities and players, corresponds to an efficient and balanced social market economy within a federal type of democracy and is a fundamental link underlying the progress of the Community—the best guarantee of its competitive capacity and of the fulfillment of its potential.

This approach, which establishes a new model of society, is also embodied in the generalized use of two fundamental measures: the rule of *mutual recognition* and *the directive.* The first rule will have a wide application in the area of homologation and the authorization of products in the Community as well as in the mutual recognition of diplomas and professional training. In the first case, the Community fixes a minimum of common requirements guaranteeing the quality and safety of products, and in the second case the recognition of diplomas is obligatory but the member states or the relevant professions establish the basic criteria. Such are the necessary conditions for the single market to open itself up to products, services, and people.

For the internal market, and the policies that support it, the Single European Act not only set up a return to qualified majority voting but also proposed a general use of directives. The term *regulation,* as opposed to *directive,* does not appear in the Single European Act. However, article 18, which supplements article 100 of the Treaty of Rome, provides that "the Council, passing degrees on the basis of a qualified majority on propositions from the Commission cooperating with the Parliament and after consultation with the economic and social Committee, confirms measures relating to the rapprochement of legislative, regulatory, and administrative provisions of member states, which have as their aim the establishment and functioning of the internal market." The term *measure* does not have a very precise meaning, so that at first sight it could be assimilated in the term *regulation* were it not for a declaration in the final provision, which announces that "in its proposals the Commission will, under article 100A, paragraph 1, favor the use of the instrument of the directive if harmonization in one or several member states involves a modification in legislative provisions." Thus, unlike regulations, such measures should not impose harmonization involving legislative modifications but could modify the regulatory or administrative provisions of member states.

Directives are distinguished from regulations by the greater flexibility and diversity in the means left open to member states for achieving their common objectives (defined by the directives). In fact, directives bind every member state for which they are intended as regards the desired result, but they leave open to national authorities the choice of forms and means. Although they have indisputable advantages, the flexibility of directives has the unfortunate tendency to lead to all sorts of abuses. Thus, numerous delays led the Commission to insert in its directives a clause according to which they become automatically applicable at the end of a period fixed in advance. In 1970, the Court of Justice invoked the *objectives* of the Treaty of Rome in order to recognize the validity of such automatic transformation of directives into regulations directly applicable in member states at the end of a fixed period. This automatic transformation can only take place if the means of attaining the objective specified by the directive are set out with sufficient precision. However, this requirement for precision in the definition of *means* tends to bring directives closer to regulations by reducing their particular elements of flexibility and variety. One can question whether directives will have any practical significance in the future. This significance will largely depend on the determination of the national parliaments to undertake the responsibility of choosing which means are to be used to implement directives.

The passivity of the national parliaments — indeed, their desire to limit the application of certain directives — was merely another justification for the step taken by the Commission with the support of the Court of Justice. In view of the accumulated delays in the application of directives, two-thirds of which have, as provided by the act, been approved by the Council, the position adopted by the Commission looked like the only way to guarantee the realization of an internal market by the end of 1992.

The Community, and the Commission in the name of the Community, takes on a *coordinating* role that is increasingly becoming one of the main areas of Community activity. For example, the coordination of structural policies, the objective and the main thrust of the reform of the Structural Funds, is being carried out by the Commission. This reform has a dual aim: to increase the efficiency of Community actions in this area using available instruments and to make these actions more *coherent* with other Community policies. As part of this strategy, the Commission set up *partnerships* in collaboration with national and regional authorities in the form of *Community support frameworks* (CCA) and the twelve *Community initiatives,* of which eight are regional in scope, three relate to the resources themselves, and one refers to rural development. If we account for programs currently in place, such as STAR, the Community initiative programs for the period 1989–93 represent a sum of approximately 5,500 million ecu, with 3,800 allocated to the twelve initiatives. Thanks to the coordination of the various actions promoted by the Commission and undertaken in cooperation with state and regional authorities, the Community benefits from a multiplier effect, greater efficiency, and increased cohesion. These ensure that its actions are more effective and have a greater impact, although they are ultimately fairly modest in comparison with the resources committed by member states. Considering the limited nature of its resources, Community action produces unhoped-for results on account of its ability to mobilize and provide guidance. This example, like so many others, illustrates the various aspects of the principle of subsidiarity, which expresses an action that is both complementary and provides significant added value.

The movement toward federalism has been indicated by a series of provisions and methods based on the federalist approach. Only their application and development will make it possible to confirm this trend in the future. As the Community continues to function in a manner appropriate to the requirements of the internal market and the achievement of fresh objectives, particularly in the spheres of monetary policy, external relations, and security, a return to centralizing methods is very improbable. In fact, the breadth and complexity of present and future Community activities and the extra burden they represent leave little scope for centralizing policies. The Community will be obliged, however, to rely more on Community bodies and agencies and on the capacities of member states, their administrations, the regions, and local authorities. It will also be obliged to turn to socioeconomic organizations, research institutes, and external experts. A plethora of networks, both public and private, is therefore developing around and in synergy with the Community and its guiding force. If this is the way of the future, the Community will have to concentrate its energies on setting general guidelines, providing impetus, and coordinating and encouraging participation rather than wasting them on frivolous bureaucratic interventions that go against the dynamic of contemporary European society.

PART 2

Integration and Political Innovation

Chapter 5

The Integration Process

European Society in Development

European society is weaving its fabric as national, regional, and local societies do, through communication networks that link men and their organizations. In his thesis on the nation, Karl W. Deutsch defines this community as a dense network of exclusive communications. The same is true of the European Community, as it progressively reshapes itself, with the participation of its member states and regions, as a vast communications network weaving together a dense fabric of human solidarity around its core institutions. De facto, solidarity is a force in society; it is what holds between men and women who perceive, create, and enjoy life based on the facts that come into being through their efforts.

The *vertical relation* is a current flowing from Community institutions to national, regional, or local administrations and associations, and it ends up with those for whom it is chiefly intended — individuals. Another current, in the form of action or retroaction, flows from the base to the decision-making centers. These vertical relationships, which are political by nature, are supplemented by the *horizontal relationship networks* constituted by organizations, associations, and various interorganizational and interpersonal communications.[1] Together, these two kinds of relationship, which form the human and political community, direct the totality of energies and resources by combining and pooling them. This capacity for bringing people together, a fundamental function combining the activities of public institutions and mixed or private associations, was called "political action" by Bertrand de Jouvenel.

In European integration, we can distinguish official or institutional from informal integration without treating them as entirely separate. The traditional distinction between state and society emerges in more complex guise. What is original about the Community is its complex and multiform union (without fusion) of states and societies in a work of political creation. While there is extensive writing on European institutions and *vertical relationships,* there are few studies of the *horizontal relationships* or the emergence of a multiplicity of players and a new societal structure on the European level. It is *a living Europe* that is forming around the central (but not necessarily the only) core formed by the European Community. These two forms of solidarity develop in very close correspondence while maintaining broad areas of autonomy and freedom. It is in this subtle and dynamic equilibrium that the secret and the force of democracy and federalism reside.

At the center of this structure (with its many and various substructures) stand individuals, the main actors and those for whom it is all ultimately intended. Formed by and forming society, they generate a whole spectrum of activities in it, fulfill several functions, and have several affiliations. They are producers, consumers, and intermediaries; they identify with an ethnic group, a nation, or a community; they are part of a community of faith or ideology; they are members of families and of one or several professional organizations such as management associations, trade unions, organizations of the liberal professions, scientific societies, and sporting associations; and they are electors and citizens who may belong to a party or associated organization in which they are militants, sympathizers, or electors. In his book on Switzerland, André Siegfried[2] laid great stress on these multiple affiliations. According to Denis de Rougemont, this "demonstrates the condition of civic liberties in a federalist regime, where there are simultaneous affiliations to several overlapping groups or communities."[3]

Of course, a multiplicity of affiliations is found at the level of activities, interests, and beliefs in pluralist democracies — Robert Dahl calls them polyarchies — but the particular feature of federalist systems is the existence of multiple levels. For example, in Switzerland the homeland can have a local dimension without excluding attachments to wider communities such as cantons or indeed the federation. Allegiances and loyalties are divided at these various levels, each involving a degree of intensity but normally without creating contradictions. Loyalties complement one another and coexist harmoniously, so that at one and the same time one can be Breton, French, and European with affiliations at all of these levels, each one of which involves its own set of values.

Despite a lack of data on the distribution of allegiances, it is possible to tackle the problem via the question of public support for the Community as well as from the point of view of the contradiction or complementarity between European and national identities. *Membership* in the Community was considered a good thing by 69 percent of the public and a bad thing by 7 percent in 1990 as against 60 percent and 11 percent in 1985.[4] One group of seven member countries came in between 73 percent for Germany and Belgium and a maximum of 82 percent for Holland. France was slightly below the average with 66 percent giving positive responses followed by Denmark with 58 percent and the United Kingdom with the smallest proportion in favor at 53 percent. The latter two countries were distinguished by a high level of negative responses, with the highest at 19 percent for Denmark followed by 16 percent for the United Kingdom, as against 7 percent for France. The degree of *attachment* to the Community can also be measured in terms of regret or relief if the Common Market were to be abandoned. Considerable regret would have been felt by 42 percent according to polls in 1985 and 49 percent in 1990, while indifference would have been felt by 38 percent and 34 percent, respectively; 9 percent would have felt great relief in 1985 but only 6 percent in 1990. This increase in support for the Community between 1985 and 1990 confirms its acceptance by the public.

The second dimension relates to the preservation or disappearance of member countries' national identities in a truly united Europe. This raises the problem of diversity in union, of the compatibility of national identity with European unity. Overall, in 1988 a majority of 53 percent considered that the defense of their national, historic, and cultural identities and the national economic interests of the Community in the face of challenges from the great world powers was possible only through union. On the other hand, 23 percent considered that the construction of a European union would sound the death knell for their national, historic, and cultural identities and would imply the sacrifice of their national economic interests. The remaining 15 percent were neutral. In this overall picture, two facts are particularly striking: variations from country to country and oscillations of opinion within most countries over a very short period from spring 1987 to autumn 1988. Recognition of complementarity was expressed by a majority higher than the Community average in France, Italy, Ireland, Spain, Portugal, and Belgium, with a maximum of 69 percent in France and 67 percent in Italy in the autumn of 1988. Responses reflecting a fear of losing national identity were above the Community average in four countries: 47 percent in Denmark, 44 percent in Great Britain, 35 percent in Ireland, and, though with a substantially lower proportion than the others, 28 percent in Germany.

On these questions of complementarity or contradiction, fluctuations that are sometimes quite impressive are an indication both of the instability of opinions and of their sensitivity to external events. Thus, in Great Britain "complementarity" fell from 44 to 32 percent while "contradiction" leaped from 35 to 44 percent. In Luxembourg and Germany, "complementarity" fell from 61 to 44 percent and from 52 to 39 percent. On the other hand, the tendency in Spain and Portugal was in the opposite direction: from 45 to 53 percent and 43 to 52 percent. The most surprising case was France, where opinion showed great stability in favor of complementarity, which may seem odd given the recurring debate among the political classes and intellectuals over the threat of a loss of French identity.

The predominance of such an opinion among the French is all the more surprising in that France has been the very embodiment of the centralized nation-state that has successfully assimilated regional differences. But maybe it is precisely this confidence that explains the positive nature of French public opinion. Whether or not this is so, the real degree of diversity within a European union will depend to a considerable extent on whether the form adopted by the European Community is more or less federal.

It was no accident that Ernst B. Haas focused on this whole area of loyalties in his classic work on Europe, the *Uniting of Europe,* which is still relevant on several counts. With the birth of the Community, loyalties that prior to the construction of the European Communities were mainly directed toward national institutions began to shift toward the European level. Such transfers of loyalties from national to Community institutions being an index of informal integration, the question raised by Haas is how far they will go. This point, which he raised in 1958, is equally relevant today. On one issue, it is close to the position of Denis de Rougemont, who put individuals and their allegiances at the center of his analysis. But there is one essential difference between them: while Haas used the term *transfer,* Rougemont refers to the *sharing* and *allocation* of allegiances at different levels. This latter conception seems less logical on the face of it, corresponding neither to a binary system nor to the "zero sum game," but it actually reflects the reality of a federal community more faithfully.

In today's European Community, whose powers mainly affect economic, social, and technical players, it is the human dimension, regarding individuals as persons and citizens, that will be directly affected, first as producers of goods and providers of services, but more generally as consumers in the internal market and therefore in their various functions as boss, employee, and worker. They will also be affected in their capacity as members of professional associations or of users' or consumers' organizations. As the Community widens its field of action, it covers ever wider spheres of activity and interests. Thus, with direct elections to the European Parliament, Community citizens play fundamental political roles through the choice of their representatives. Significant in themselves, these roles have not yet fulfilled their potential because of the way the European Parliament's powers are restricted. Nonetheless, it is this new dimension of citizenship in Europe that will develop in the Political Union, for which it is instrumental in providing immediate democratic legitimacy.

This is, however, a concept with a very low profile in comparison with other indicators of the reality of the Community and the Europe of citizens in public opinion. The ability to cross frontiers freely (approved by 51 percent), the freedom to buy foreign products without paying customs duties (42 percent), the opportunity for young persons to study in the countries of their choice (44 percent), the mutual recognition of professional qualifications (39 percent), and the existence of Community law (26 percent)[5] are but a few of the visible signs that demonstrate the depth of Community action. Community rules and policies are causing changes — sometimes revolutionary — in numerous sectors, while at the same time they are stimulating economic agents, bringing about the emergence of socioeconomic structures at the European level, and encouraging political parties to create embryonic common organizations in the new context of a developing European public opinion.

**Economic Factors: From the Corporation to the
Small Business**

Incentives to adapt come on the one hand from the establishment of freedoms and the enlargement of the space without frontiers and on the other from common policies that give a general orientation and generate synergy. These rules of competition regulating the great market have helped to encourage rationalization projects, collaborative projects between businesses, cooperative agreements, acquisitions of holdings, and even mergers. The Belgian Société générale affair was a palpable demonstration of the rivalries and alliances between European financial giants. Against a background of competition and interdependence, networks of collaboration and concentration are emerging capable of competing with American and Japanese multinationals. In the 1960s, the challenge and the threat of the United States were often evoked.[6] Today it is clear that not only has a united Europe been able to respond to this successfully by learning from the Americans but European businesses are themselves setting out to conquer America. The lesson has been salutary. The situation with Japan is not comparable because of cultural differences and the barriers raised by Japan against penetration by foreign capital. The "Japanese fortress" has laid siege to the United States and established bridgeheads in the United Kingdom. The tendency toward concentration has found a second wind in Europe, with the number of amalgamations doubling in four years: there were less than five hundred in 1984 but as many as one thousand in 1988. In spite of this leap forward and in spite of success stories such as those of Ariane[7] or Airbus, two of the most important sectors, automobiles and electronics, are in difficulty.

On the other hand, the European chemical industry is a huge global success even though the number of companies is still too large. It represents 27 percent of world production—as against 25 percent for the United States, 17 percent for Eastern Europe, and 14 percent for Japan—and nearly 10 percent of its production is exported. The single market has favored an accelerated rate of amalgamations: in 1988, 240 mergers took place in Europe, involving U.S.$134 billion, with 100 of them within a national context ($60 billion), 101 between Europe and North America ($53 billion), 15 between Europe and Asia ($19 billion), and a mere 24 between European countries ($13 billion). The restructuring of this sector in Italy and France is taking place primarily at the national level but is mainly due to the opening up of the Community market and the prospect of global competition. In this new dimension, companies seem to apply the principle of subsidiarity quite naturally, pooling their resources to ensure a better adaptation of their capacities to an enlarged and highly competitive environment. However, in spite of the restructuring under way in France and the partnerships set up in particular with German chemical companies, as with the industrial cooperation between Rhône-Poulenc and Hoechst, the French chemical industry has not grown to the same extent as those of its partners or rivals. In Germany, the four major groups represent 39 percent of the German chemical industry in comparison with 25 and 12 percent for the five major groups in the United States and United Kingdom, respectively, while the four major groups in France represent only 14 percent of the French chemical industry.[8] Of the world's five largest chemical companies, three are German (BASF, Bayer, and Hoechst) and one is British (ICI). These companies are concentrated in an area of high technology and required huge investments to become established in the world market. In the chemicals sector, as in many others, Community action aims to create the kind of general environment that will encourage industrial operations and industrial regrouping while making human, financial, and technological resources available to companies. Its role is to create the basic conditions and to direct and encourage the activities and initiatives of economic agents. The Community is also active in the important sphere of small and medium-sized businesses. The size of these companies, with a maximum of five hundred employees, means that they have a lower profile, but in no way does that diminish their economic and social importance. Together they comprise more than 95 percent of Community firms and provide more than two-thirds of all jobs, with about 60 percent in industry and more than 75 percent in services.[9] So there is nothing surprising in the fact that the European Council has emphasized the need to develop entrepreneurship and reduce the burdens on such businesses while the Commission, for its part, has a program for the improvement of the environment and the encouragement of small and medium-sized businesses in conformity with the Council decision of July 1989. Its first actions in favor of such businesses date from 1973. The Business Cooperation Center (BCC) helps firms to negotiate agreements while respecting the rules of competition, and subsidies have been granted for numerous projects undertaken by professional organizations. Activity in this domain has grown considerably with the implementation of the Single European Act. Administration has been simplified and levies reduced in member states; access to structural funds — both from the European Investment Bank and the public markets — has been facilitated; and the two chief networks of direct assistance for small and medium-sized businesses — *euroguichets* (Euro Info Centers [EICs]) and the Business Cooperation Network (BC-Net, with 460 members) — have been expanded and tasked with developing cooperation between companies and subcontracting. The availability of information, particularly about Community legislation, has been improved by means of 188 *euroguichets* and 16 regional *sous-guichets*. Europartnership operations have been organized, including one at Cardiff in June 1990 where 2,500 contacts were made. Pump-priming capital has been made available by the European Association of Venture Capital Companies.[10] A new instrument of transnational cooperation has been put at the disposal of small and medium-sized companies, and the European Economic Interest Group allows them to carry out certain of their activities together — research, purchasing, production, sales, computerized data handling, the formation of consortia for public or private tendering, and so on. Another important aspect of Community action concerns the involvement of such companies in technological research and development programs such as Esprit, Brite, and Sprint together with the Comett program, which brings together companies and research institutes from several countries.

Of course, a considerable amount of the promotional and incentive work falls to the member states, public organizations, and professional associations, but by virtue of its subsidiary action the Commission has the task of ensuring the coherence of the whole so as to maintain competition and give substance to the strategy of stimulating growth and employment in the Community. This is a concrete example to add to the dossier of the many flexible applications of the principle of subsidiarity — the Community takes on the tasks of stimulation and coordination while providing overall strategies that member states are not in a position to formulate on their own.

Community Interest Group Networks

In this huge web of companies and economic agents, socioeconomic groups pool their interests and efforts in order to influence the policies and decisions of Community institutions in their favor. Still under development, these new channels of discussion and communication form complex flexible networks linking directors and organizations involved in or affected by the integration process. The emergence of European economic and political power has caused European associations to evolve, and by their constitution and activities these associations testify to the scope and influence of Community institutions. As the Community's field of action expands, new sectors are being created around Community decision-making centers, with networks of associations and lobbyists, lawyers, and consultants serving as intermediaries and defenders of a huge variety of interests. In 1990, there were 525 socioeconomic groups at the Community level, with 50 percent in the industrial sector and more than 40 percent in services (which are in a phase of rapid growth) while the remaining 10 percent were spread between agricultural groups and a variety of associations, including liberal professions and public interest groups. From the point of view of social partnership, the employees' world has a much less varied structure than that of the employers. Industry has the widest network of organizations structured according to the divisions of labor and branches of activity. The whole of the private sector is represented by UNICE, which brings together the directors' institutes of member countries at the highest level. Its homologue in the public sector is the European Center of Public Enterprises (CEEP). Leading market sectors, such as chemicals and textiles, joined forces at Community level as soon as integration began. Numerous subgroups and increasingly specialized activities then created joint bodies covering areas where their interests were directly affected by Community decisions. Hence, there is a parallel between the expansion of Community policies and measures and the emergence of new Community interest groups. From more than one point of view, these organizations reflect the growth and essential features of Community power and constitute a more or less faithful response to it.[11] This relationship merely echoes national experience. Legislation, the state, its administration, and its traditions visibly influence the structures and behavior of associations and interest groups; in turn the latter influence the development of political power.

The prospect of freedom of movement and establishment set out by the Single European Act accelerated the formation of organizations in the service sector. The Committee of Commercial Organizations in the EC Countries (COCCEE), a kind of business confederation, had disappeared by 1978, and a more flexible and varied system, which involved several central organizations, was set up in its place. At the same time, the free circulation of persons, the recognition of diplomas, and the freedom to practice professions abroad have given a new impetus to associations in the liberal professions. Only the agricultural sector, the most integrated since the development and implementation of the agricultural policy, has not undergone much substantial change. In fact, COPA (the Committee of Professional Agricultural Organizations) and the more specialized groups are distinguished by both their high degree of representation and their influence. At the time of the reform of agricultural policy, COPA mobilized agricultural forces in defense of farmers' incomes. As in the past, it is to be expected that pressure will be applied in all sorts of ways ranging from disseminating technical papers to adopting common positions and organizing demonstrations by farmers in Brussels and other capitals.

Trade unions are represented by the European Trade Union Confederation (ETUC), which, in spite of its 40 million members, has played a relatively low-key role because of the traditionally limited importance of social policy in the Community. However, its recent activity shows how new prospects are opening up for the ETUC following the revitalization of social policy, the adoption of the Social Charter, and improved possibilities for collective negotiation at the Community level. The result will be that the confederal structure will be supplemented by further federations and trade union committees, of which there are currently only twenty, including the powerful European Federation of Metalworkers, which was founded in 1971. In addition to sectoral bodies such as the Textile Trade Union Committee, there are trade union committees in the large European companies such as Philips and Airbus. It seems inevitable that the intensification of large-scale transnational activities will encourage various union bodies to expand in line with European multinational companies, a concrete example of the spillover effect generated by European integration in the area of social dialogue. The creation of the European Confederation of Executives in 1989 was a response to both the need for managerial staff to enjoy higher status and executive mobility and the existence of potential openings for participation in social dialogue with employers. With the number of executives on the increase and the impact of the Single European Act, the field of European influence and action is progressively extending to wider and wider spheres.[12] Just as the networks of interest groups in local organizations and regions are integrating into national networks, these networks are integrating into European networks as the field of Community and European activities expands around the main pole of integration, the European Community.

This regrouping process also affects the domain of new public interest groups in which there are two networks of influence in the areas of the protection of the environment (EEB is the European Environmental Bureau) and consumers (BEUC is the European Bureau of Consumers' Unions). Despite its lightweight structure, the EEB is managing to mobilize the most dynamic players in this field and to form coalitions between national organizations and the Greens in the European Parliament.

Differences between national conditions have not prevented successes in the struggle against pollution, especially vehicle pollution. Moreover, the objectives of the EEB largely coincide with the concerns of the public, whose opinions are creating a climate broadly favorable to the adoption of certain environmental measures. As regards the BEUC, it and its members have an even more important task given that in an internal market the application of mutual recognition may lower levels of consumer protection, especially in countries already benefiting from higher levels. Hence, there is a need to establish certain common standards guaranteeing a minimum of protection for the whole of the single market.

Likewise, new forms of promotion are emerging that bear more than a little resemblance to Jean Monnet's Action Committee or the European League for Economic Cooperation. Thus, several leaders of some of the most prestigious European multinationals (Volvo, Fiat, Philips) have created a forum of debate to support the achievement of the great European objectives, including the single market without frontiers.[13] Another action in favor of the ecu and the European Central Bank has been initiated by the Association for a European Monetary Union, which, with its more elaborate structure, is dedicated to furthering an objective that is more precise but quite essential to the future of the Community. The association includes more than 170 large European companies employing about 3.5 million staff in the twelve member states. Its president is the former president of Philips and its vice president is Giovanni Agnelli. This association works in cooperation with the Committee for a European Monetary Union, which, under the copresidency of Valéry Giscard d'Estaing and Helmut Schmidt, is composed of seventeen senior bank chiefs who are nominated in the same way as the members of the Commission. Each applying its own particular methods, these two promotional associations carry out activities that converge in favor of monetary union, encouraging and supporting the actions of governments and Community institutions.

Originally, these networks of influence were organized along traditional lines, but they have evolved in many ways. First, they developed in specialized technical sectors, diversifying as they strove to adapt to the complex realities of individual countries and the Community as well as to the nature of the various activities involved in achieving the particular objectives they set for themselves. Consequently, their modes of organization, their membership and decision-making procedures, and their ability to influence events vary considerably. While consensus was de rigeur to begin with, so as to maintain cohesion between members and interests that were often very dissimilar, this practice proved to be very ineffective insofar as the resulting, often vague, compromises had no more than a feeble impact on Community decisions. Majority decisions or the method of majority and minority reports were therefore used. By better adapting to the requirements of the Commission, these networks of influence have been able to increase their impact on decision-making centers.

At the same time, interest groups are progressively widening their membership as their activities expand and the membership of the Community widens. Interest groups in neighboring countries, in particular those of the European Free Trade Association (EFTA), have in most cases been associated with the work and discussions of Community groups. Another trend that seems to be developing is a tendency to make organizational forms more flexible, thanks to structures that are more lightweight and effective, as they are able to exploit the communications networks and mobilize the resources of their members as the need arises. Communication and mobility emerge as key factors in this new trend because of the need to adjust to the variety of questions handled at Community level and the various forms of intersecting cooperation, more or less durable, that result. The rapidity of technological and economic change requires forms of organization that are more adaptable and dynamic and favor more flexible networks of influence that are able to react quickly. Hence, structures tend to be less rigid and hierarchical, favoring an expansion of horizontal relationships, thanks to the role of coordination, orientation, and support fulfilled by the permanent secretariats in Brussels. Less cumbersome and bureaucratic, these secretariats are also efficient because of their ability to use and consult numerous committees of experts from national organizations and to exploit the various networks of influence and competence by acting together. As relationships grow closer and meetings are multiplied, an excessive concentration in Brussels has been avoided. Meanwhile, these groups are developing their networks of communication with the Community and governments through personal contacts and relationships. The invasion of the fax and microcomputer interconnections are of course speeding up intercommunication and consultation while shortening response times without reducing the role of personal relations, which are now more selective, concentrating on essentials. These improved methods of communication also make it easier to handle the complexities of reality and make it possible to avoid oversimplification or overstandardization. Complexity can be coped with, and cultural diversity is once again becoming a positive element and a trump card in a changing world.

A new generation is bringing radical change to institutions and society, a phenomenon already evident in the network of European groups: a new generation of leaders made up of young, dynamic, and efficient managers has replaced the pioneers. Its arrival at the head of the European network has brought a fresh drive and a new style. Key positions in various organizations are now held by young managers who are helping to remove the traditional distinctions between the leaders of the private sector, the public sector, and employers' and workers' organizations. Frontiers are vanishing not simply between states but between the public and private sectors and between employers and unions to the extent that psychological barriers are disappearing and leadership styles and management forms converge.

The ability of different European groups to exert effective influence varies, as does that of interest groups in general; such variation depends on different factors and their interaction. Influence in general is a function of the importance of the sector or sectors in which the action is being taken. The automobile or chemicals sector clearly does not have the same level of importance as the bicycle sector does. Nonetheless, the relative efficiency of the group of bicycle manufacturers, homogeneous and more united, could be greater within its own domain. Other indicators need to be taken into consideration, in particular the cohesion and organization of the interest group in question together with its level of competence and representation. In addition to these elements, there are the human and material resources available to the group. Wealth is of course a factor in influence, even if it is not the only criterion in a world of high technology where knowledge is also a form of power. For example, groups lobbying for protection of the environment are short on material means but have frequently been able to attract the support of top-ranking scientists. The competence of the leaders is one of the keys to success, but, paradoxically, personality is far from being of merely secondary importance. In addition to those already mentioned, other factors are highly relevant to the degree of influence of an interest group: its means of access to the authorities, its use of its resources, its means of exerting pressure, and its capacity to form alliances with other groups. However, although they are very reliable, these measures enable us to evaluate only the potential influence of interest groups and not their real influence; only empirical analysis can provide the data for assessing the effective influence of an interest group. Such assessment is clearly easier to carry out in a limited sector than in more general areas of activity. One definite result emerges from numerous studies: European institutions, and in particular the Commission, are in continual contact with European groups that provide them with information, studies, and indications as to the division of interests and forces within the Community. In turn, European groups receive information on Community projects and policies, and there is a constant flow of information, creating a sphere around institutions. Through consultation and exchanges, the latter obtain the knowledge they need and at the same time forge consensus and garner support. In negotiating situations or moments of crisis, the Commission will continue to profit from the support of this network of European groups.

In the early days of the European Communities, the Commission gave near-exclusive preference to the channels of consultation offered by the European federations. On some occasions, it even furthered the creation of European groups, as was the case with the consumers' group. But more often the Commission gave financial support to certain groups to ensure a balance in the representation of interests at Community level. For a long time, direct consultation carried out by the Commission was limited almost exclusively to Community groups; recently, however, the growth in Community power and the expansion of Community legislation have led the Commission to consult a wider range of socioeconomic organizations. National and indeed regional organizations are present in numerous consultative committees devoted to agricultural policy, regional or social policy, and the Economic and Social Committee, but they were rarely present when the Commission drew up its proposals. Now this consultation, based on a customary practice that does not have the institutional form of permanent consultative committees, constitutes one of the essential elements of the Community decision-making process. For example, while the European Banking Federation customarily makes its views known to the Commission, the latter also regularly listens to the opinions of the British Bankers' Association. The same applies to Confindustria and other national employers' confederations and the Permanent Assembly of French Chambers of Commerce and Industry (APCCI), which have set up agencies in Brussels. Such direct contacts allow the Commission to obtain a much clearer picture of the positions of national groups within European organizations, which often fail to bring together differing interests or adopt common positions that faithfully and substantially reflect the opinions of their membership. This tendency toward diversifying contacts and widening the circle of interlocutors is mirrored by the propensity of big national and multinational companies to draw closer to Community decision-making centers in Brussels. Large companies like Fiat, Mercedes-Benz, Rhône-Poulenc, Philips, and ICI have been established in Brussels for quite a while and in particular have networks of contacts at all levels with the Commission. Their presence (along with numerous American multinationals) is further proof of the Community's dominant role. Another example is that of Electricité de France, which has its own intervention unit in the Community; it can make its point of view known directly as well as through the normal channels provided by the International Union of Producers and Distributors of Electrical Energy (UNI-PEDE) and the Center for European Public Companies (CEPE). Access is therefore provided not just through these European organizations and the French government but through direct channels.[14]

Regional authorities and certain regional organizations are also being caught up in this process as it develops in line with the extension and strengthening of Community powers. Accordingly, since becoming associated with the action of the Community, the German states have set up their own representative offices in Brussels. Regional organizations from other countries have also tended to develop direct relationships with the Commission in order to make their interests better known to those responsible for regional policy and the ERDF. Such is the case for a dozen French regions, four British local organizations, and five Spanish autonomous regions.[15] As early as 1982, the Generality of Catalonia set up the "Patronat Catala pro Europa," a promotional and research body, which opened an office in Brussels as soon as Spain entered the Community. In the 1980s, especially since the implementation of the Single European Act, there was a sharp rise in the number of lobbyists, financial and juridical counselors, consultants, and specialized bureaus. The resources of these Community affairs specialists enable them to offer a wide range of services from legal and economic consultation to public relations. This network of professionals from various countries in the Community and also from the United States allows firms with problems on account of distance or lack of knowledge, or that are too small to undertake direct action on their own behalf, to draw closer to Community institutions and familiarize themselves with European affairs. Estimates of the number of lobbyists in Brussels vary, but in June 1990 the magazine *Fortune* suggested a figure of three thousand.[16]

In addition to this impressive figure, there are more than 100 diplomatic missions from Third World countries, including the 66 diplomatic representatives of the African, Caribbean, and Pacific states and the general secretariat of the ACP group. The total number of missions accredited to the European Community was 165, and the Commission was accredited to 128 countries and international organizations.[17] Hence, European national and regional groups, companies and their chiefs or spokespersons, and lobbyists and councils of all kinds are gradually building up networks of players and observers in the great game of Europe.

Political Parties, Leaders, and Public Opinion

Political parties have sometimes made innovative contributions to the integration process, particularly when voting to ratify the Treaty of Rome and the Single European Act. For a long time, their activities with regard to European issues were mainly at the national level, where they take part in Community decisions through their presence in government, their interventions in debates on the Community in national parliaments, and their votes on bills to incorporate European directives in national legislative structures. In the course of the run up to the 1979 European elections, the parties had a relatively low-profile role through their representatives in the European Parliament. The political groupings formed with the creation of the ECSC Common Assembly, which became the single European Parliamentary Assembly of the three Communities, did create the beginnings of both the future federations of parties and the instruments for European apprenticeship and socialization, but their involvement in the decision-making process remained limited mainly because the European Parliament possessed limited and purely consultative powers. In principle, their involvement in Community affairs was proportional to the restrictions on the powers of the European Parliament.

The 1979 European elections began a new phase in the strengthening of the powers of the European Parliament, as it became more attractive to the political parties. Organizing this election gave a new breath of life to inter-party collaboration that went beyond mere cooperation within political groupings; the Community had ceased to be the preserve of the narrow circle of parliamentarians who had a special interest in Europe and was attracting the attention of a much wider spectrum within the political parties, including their leadership, to a lesser extent their membership, and even the voters the parties sought to mobilize during the electoral campaign. Direct election encouraged the creation of federations or unions of parties belonging to the same political families on a European scale and present in the majority of member states.

This was the origin of the Union of Socialist Parties, the European People's Party (PPE), and the Federation of Liberal Parties.[18] Their aim is to provide structural support for interparty collaboration, preparing electoral campaigns, and drafting common programs. In the event, their cooperation in pursuit of this objective was to be much more difficult than anticipated. The PPE and the Liberal Federation did formulate pro-European programs inspired by their concept of a European union. The Socialist Union, however, had more difficulty in avoiding the trap of generalities and preferred to restrict itself to a common declaration in 1984. At the same time, apart from certain sporadic instances of collaboration, campaigns have for the most part been conducted by national parties within a national framework. There is nothing surprising in this if we compare the situation with that of federal parties in the United States or Switzerland. American parties only operate on the federal level when the time comes to prepare for presidential and federal elections, while party activities are mainly organized within the states. The situation is not very different in Switzerland, where party activity occurs mainly in the cantons. Moreover, there are differences within federal parties from state to state and from canton to canton even after so many years of the federal state's existence. Party platforms reflect this fact, and campaigns mainly center on electors' concerns in the federated states or cantons.

In these federal states, as in the Community, the closest and most effective collaboration between parties exists within the parliamentary groupings and leadership circles. The process of mobilizing militants and members is painfully slow and uneven in spite of the very high level of public support for a union and the Community. However, it is noteworthy that the European theme is taking on increasing importance in programs and debates within the parties as well as in their dialogue with their allies and in their controversies with their rivals and opponents. To the extent that European problems are tending to become a daily concern in government and management, parties are tempted, and indeed obliged, to include them more or less permanently in their agendas. This is especially true in that since the onset of integration the division between those for and against the Union has run not simply between the parties but also between blocs within the parties, the classic case being the EDC quarrel in France. Even today, the French Socialist Party has to live with the presence in its ranks of more or less pro-European attitudes, although this does not prevent it from actively taking up positions on European matters. Another example is the division in France, whose two large formations, the RPR and the UDF, are distinguished by differences of opinion about the future of the Community. Overall, however, the great majority of political parties in the EC countries are (with a small number of exceptions) massively in favor of a European union; in this, for the most part, they follow the pro-European stance of their electorates. For the time being, however, as we have seen, efforts to mobilize political players and parties remain fairly feeble in comparison with those made in the socioeconomic arena.

European leaders are responsible for managing institutions and businesses at the Community, national, and regional levels.[19] They are European to the extent that they have responsibility for European affairs and devote themselves to activities arising from European, and above all Community, policies and decisions. Descriptions of institutions reveal that there are two sorts of leaders of Community institutions: those who devote themselves full time to these tasks (members of the Commission, European parliamentarians, judges, officials) and those who are involved in decision making in the European Council and the Council of Ministers and in preparation and orientation of Community decisions at the national level. In their European roles, these leaders are assisted by hundreds of officials, members of permanent missions, government experts, and heads of European units in ministries or their coordination. The heads of German states and regions participate in these various processes with varying frequency, for example.

In general, socioeconomic leaders and managers are adapting their operational structures in conformity with governmental institutions. They comprise business leaders involved in the European process; heads of promotional groups with European, national, or local interests; European lobbyists and specialists; professional experts and consultants; professors and researchers; parliamentarians; and the heads of political parties. To the extent that they are involved in the European integration process, they all belong to the Eurosphere. The time devoted to European affairs, the intensity of their activity, and their level of responsibility figure among the main criteria that allow leaders to be found in more or less densely packed European networks, with looser ties the farther they get from the major Community and national centers. Opinion leaders are thus to be found on the periphery of the European networks. These networks contain a huge variety of communications "crossroads," where there are leaders with intersecting affiliations such as professionals or heads of interest groups who are also Euro-MPs or members of the Commission with links to political parties.[20] These multiple and varied networks fit into a vast ensemble of which each element gravitates around different poles at the regional, national, and Community levels. The resulting energies seem to be borne along by new currents that create innovative synergies.

Is there such a thing as *European public opinion?* The truth is that this is more or less the same as asking whether such a thing as "public opinion" exists in a particular country. Public opinion in a given country is in fact made up of sectoral public opinions brought together by category or level and distinguished by a certain coherence of duration. For example, levels of support for the Union of Western Europe among member states are highly homogeneous between the countries of the Twelve. There is a general average of 81 percent in favor, with minimal variations, apart from peaks of 87 and 84 percent for Italy and Spain and lows of 74 and 64 percent for Great Britain and Denmark. The general level of support barely exceeded 60 percent in 1973, but it increased progressively to about 75 percent in 1978 and 81 percent at the end of 1990. The relative stability and convergent tendencies of national opinions in individual countries reveal the outlines of a European, or rather a Community, opinion. The conclusions emerging from an analysis of the support of the public for membership in the Community (69 percent in favor), its appreciation of the benefits of such participation (59 percent), and the regret that would be caused by the disappearance of the Community (49 percent as against 34 percent indifferent) follow the same trend. Similar tendencies are evident with respect to certain fundamental values or attachment to democratic institutions. It seems that collaboration within a stable institutional framework of actors and groups interacting through a web of increasingly dense communications is gradually helping to shape public opinion, drawing the views of different constituencies closer and closer to each other and integrating them into what may for simplicity's sake be referred to as a developing European public opinion.

Chapter 6

The Decision-Making Process and the Spillover Effect

The Decision-Making Process

How do the various institutions and players contribute to the process that leads to the adoption of norms, policies, and decisions within the Community? This process is principally based on the active power of the Commission-Council tandem, which runs the various institutions and the consultation networks. Although fairly faithful to its initial model, it has undergone changes with respect to voting in the Council and the role of the European Parliament as well as modifications of various consultation procedures. While the Luxembourg Compromise maintained the unanimity voting rule, the Single European Act reintroduced qualified majority voting and ushered in a new era of "cooperation" between Parliament and Council. Moreover, by institutionalizing the European Council, the Single European Act gave official sanction to a well-established practice. In the course of this evolution, the Commission widened the circle of groups and parties consulted by increasing the number and diversity of the consultative bodies. It aimed thereby to base its authority on the widest possible range of supporters. The model of a decision-making process as seen in the period prior to the Single European Act is illustrated in figure 1.

General Outline According to the Treaty of Rome (1957)

Figure 1 shows the decision-making process as it has developed since the Treaty of Rome. It deliberately illustrates the longest possible distance from the origins of a decision through the preparation and consultation phases that take place within the Commission and up to the final decision taken by the Council.

In the course of drawing up draft decisions or proposals, the Commission consults widely with European groups. Entrusting the preparation of such drafts to a general directorate, the Commission can carry out studies or use external services of experts or groups of experts. During this *preliminary*

Sources of decisions: Treaty, basic statutes, proposals, and initiatives of the
Commission; initiatives of the Council, governments, or
private organizations

First phase of the Commission

COMMISSION

General orientation

Responsible commissioner: group of three or four commissioners
plus general directorate (GD)

(A) *Preliminary information*

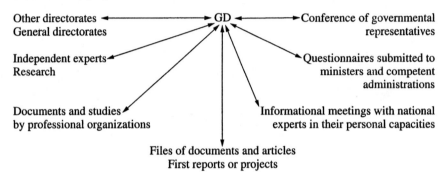

Other directorates ←——————————→ GD ←——————→ Conference of governmental
General directorates   representatives

Independent experts ←   → Questionnaires submitted to
Research   ministers and competent
                                                                                              administrations

Documents and studies ←   Informational meetings with national
by professional organizations   experts in their personal capacities

Files of documents and articles
First reports or projects

(B) *Consultations*

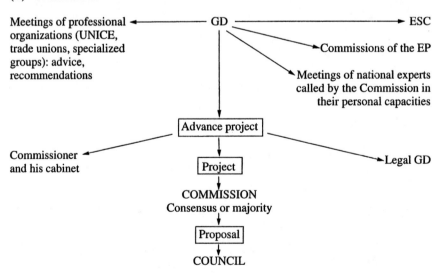

Meetings of professional ←——————— GD ——————————→ ESC
organizations (UNICE,
trade unions, specialized   →Commissions of the EP
groups): advice,
recommendations   → Meetings of national experts
                                                                    called by the Commission in
                                                                    their personal capacities

Advance project

Commissioner ←   →Legal GD
and his cabinet

Project

COMMISSION
Consensus or majority

Proposal

COUNCIL

FIG. 1.   Treaty of Rome (1957): Decision-making process

Second phase: Council and Commission

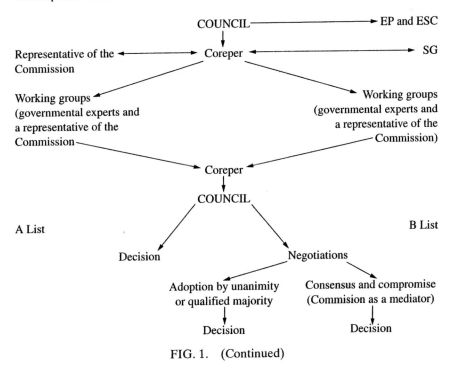

FIG. 1.   (Continued)

phase of information gathering, the Commission may send questionnaires and requests for information to national administrations and representatives of European and national professional bodies as well as carrying out a variety of other inquiries and studies. At the end of this preliminary stage, in which the Commission aims to clarify its position, comes a fairly long period of *consultation.* Many contacts are made and numerous meetings take place with representatives of UNICE, COPA, ETUC, and various professional federations but especially with national experts. Summoned by the Commission as individuals, the latter attend meetings without an official mandate; nonetheless, they express the opinions of national administrations while maintaining enough room for maneuver to allow them to take part in drafting the Commission's preliminary texts.

During this *consultation phase,* groups aim to maximize the resources available to them using their informal contacts as well as their official relations, which do not always provide the most effective means of access. This phase actually favors European groups — as against national groups — with a capacity for direct, almost exclusive, influence.

This process of consulting European groups has advantages and disadvantages. The main advantage lies in the fact that the Commission can allow European groups to act as arbiters between the different positions and interests of the national groups affiliated with them. But this process also has its weaknesses, particularly due to the aggregation of interests, which vary throughout Europe. The structural deficiencies of European confederal organizations mean that this high degree of aggregation does not lead to clear positions and in fact frequently results in compromise. Sometimes the members of a European organization opt for another way by adopting majority and minority reports. Thus, instead of reaching vague compromises, certain organizations elect to vote on issues that allow majority and minority positions to emerge. A united front is sacrificed in favor of clearer and more precise opinions. Under such conditions, the Commission of course can take on the role of arbiter between rival opinions submitted to it, but a European interest group has a better chance of influencing the Commission's choice if it adopts positions that reflect divisions among its members as faithfully as possible. The fact that the Commission consults only European groups has favored their expansion while initially simplifying the Commission's task. If this practice has become the rule, however, it is sometimes at the expense of the possibility of acquiring a wider range of information that could be useful in the Commission's work. That is why the Commission has acquired the habit of seeking further opinions from national groups and key companies, especially in the case of divisions between different national organizations. In these latter cases, it is in the Commission's interest to solicit the opinions of dissenting parties. Another debatable aspect of this process is the choice of the bodies to be consulted, which is sometimes random if not arbitrary. Hence, it is necessary to define a few principles or criteria of selection. Finally, the overall process is far removed from the public eye in an exclusive dialogue between experts and representatives of the Commission and their opposite numbers in professional bodies. The Commission does very occasionally hold hearings of interested parties in sectors that are sensitive or in crisis such as nuclear energy, the metalworking industries, and textiles.

In a *second phase,* the process continues at the level of the Council and Coreper. In the course of this phase, the European Parliament and the Economic and Social Committee contribute in a consultative capacity. Nevertheless, at this stage it is noticeable that European groups play only a marginal role; thus, COPA action is limited to organizing farmers' demonstrations at the time of meetings of the agricultural councils in Brussels or Luxembourg and to sending messages and telegrams to the Council. This second phase is essentially characterized by the crucial role of Coreper and its working groups of official experts. Member states therefore may de-

velop a considerable ability to influence matters in the course of this negotiating process with which a representative of the Commission is associated,
all the more so in that, if an agreement is reached at the level of experts or
permanent representatives, it is put on the "A list" and is normally automatically rubber-stamped by the Council. On account of the primordial
role played by member states, national groups return to their traditional
means of access to the authorities in their countries. In agriculture, for
instance, the similar views of agricultural organizations and the French
government illustrate these organizations' capacity to influence national
decision-making centers which then participate directly in Community decision making. Ultimately, arbitrage occurs at the Council level due to the
compromises sought by member states on Commission proposals. However, even in the case of France the positions of professional organizations,
and especially of FNSEA, are not always identical to those of the government; a divergence of opinion was all too evident in the 1965 crisis.

In the course of the *first phase,* the Commission takes on the role of
initiator and master of ceremonies; it drafts proposals in dialogue with
governments, administrations, and experts and in consultation principally
with socioeconomic groups constituted at the European level. During the
second phase, it is the members of the Council, their representatives, and
their official experts who take the final decisions on the basis of proposals
or compromises worked out by the Commission. In the 1970s, the balance
between the two institutions was modified to the advantage of the Council;
the growing power of the member states helped give it a predominant role
in the Community system. The Commission got its fingers burned in the
crises of 1963 and 1965 and became more cautious, especially in seeking
Council backing before launching its initiatives and in making a variety of
preliminary contacts with member states and their administrations. Its
power of initiative was diluted and its dynamism weakened. The Commission does, of course, enjoy the advantages accruing to it from the high level
of competence and the personal and political prestige of its members, but
in spite of such undeniable qualities its administration is often overbur-
dened as a result of the restructuring imposed on it by the fusion of the
three Communities' executives in 1967 and by Great Britain's entry into
the Community in 1973.

Under the impact of these different factors, the Commission's position
grew weaker, all the more so in that important support for it was lacking: a
number of member states, among those normally solidly behind it, were
showing a certain reticence due to self-interest; the socioeconomic groups
around it held fluctuating positions, and their structures were as yet fragile in
relation to national groups; and its old ally the European Parliament, on the
one hand, did not have sufficient authority and, on the other, occasionally

showed signs of a more critical stance toward it. Lacking a firm base, the Commission did not have enough substance in the face of the powers of the member states. With the support of the Court of Justice, the Commission turned resolutely toward the European Parliament and sought backing from economic and social forces and new political participants to fill the void that handicapped the European Community in its work.

In the complex negotiations accompanying the *second phase,* the Commission acts as guardian of the treaty and mediator between member states who exploit their power to assert their rights. In fact, the Commission bases its capacity for influence on the treaty; its right to make proposals, which can be modified only on a unanimous vote of Council members; and on its competence, its permanent action, and the backing it can expect from certain states and interest groups. There are almost always one or more states with an interest they regard as fundamental and that coincides with the line proposed by the Commission: France and Italy in the agricultural domain, Germany in the industrial sector, and the United Kingdom in regional policy matters. As often as not, decisions are the result of lengthy negotiations and arbitration between Community priorities and the interests of member states in various domains. The "package," or global agreement, is the clearest expression of this.

The process became more cumbersome in the aftermath of the 1965 crisis, since which date unanimity voting has been observed for matters considered by a member state to affect its vital interest. In Community practice, the Council of course has sought as often as possible to reach decisions by consensus, and the difference between unanimity and qualified majority voting has seemed to blur. In reality, qualified majority voting makes the search for a compromise easier, as it gives a moral advantage to the majority group. The minority group is ready to compromise, aware that a decision may be taken without it. On the other hand, the majority group is ready to make concessions to reach a consensus, aware that the most important questions require the agreement of the majority of members if the measures adopted are to be implemented. In the light of Community experience, the difference between unanimity and majority voting becomes fundamental: the former slows down and may even paralyze the decision-making process, while the latter speeds it up and facilitates compromise. With the entry of the three new members and the perspective of a further enlargement, the difference between these two procedures is likely to grow, since unanimity will become more and more difficult to achieve within any reasonable period of time.

These difficulties have been made worse by other factors: first, the requests for admission by the three new members, then the negotiations between 1970 and 1973, and finally the problems raised by their integration into the Community. This period coincided with a deteriorating economic background and the appearance of fresh obstacles. Under these circumstances, the Council lost its vigor and major decisions were often postponed. Governments, therefore, felt the need for more frequent summits of leading figures in the member states.

After 1975, the conference of heads of state or government began to meet regularly two or three times a year in the form of a European Council. These regular meetings meet the need to give a new impetus to the union process and to address jointly those issues vital to member states. Collaboration between national leaders in the common task helps to accentuate the Community's political dimension, for in transcending sectoral limitations they acquire a global role, taking initiatives, formulating guidelines, and making political agreements while leaving the Community's other institutions free to act. Several positive results can be attributed to these meetings: the removal of obstacles to the admission of Great Britain, the expansion of agricultural subsidies, a decision on European elections, and the creation of the European Monetary System.

In this decision-making process, as it was initially conceived and later developed in practice, there was little place for an unelected European Parliament. The Treaty of Rome does lay down about thirty cases of obligatory consultation, but if in practice Parliament has almost always been consulted its opinions have only rarely been heeded by the Council and the Commission. The election of the European Parliament opened a new phase in the functioning of Community institutions by reinforcing the authority and significance of the Parliament in the Community system.

Figure 1 deliberately shows the most drawn out form of decision making possible. Thus, for example, the duration of the preliminary work may be considerably shortened when the Commission has accumulated enough information over a period of time in an area where it is planning to make new proposals. In such a case, it may simply update the data in its records. In fact, on numerous occasions the Commission has presented proposals on the basis of Community knowledge and experience, proposals that fit into a chain of decisions. In addition, the duration of the overall decision-making process may be reduced when the decisions to be made concern the application of general rules or common policies.

The Common Agricultural Policy is an illustration of the possibilities opened up by using auxiliary mechanisms and exercising powers of execution delegated by the Council. Thanks to the system management committees, the Commission is empowered, within a preestablished framework, to take binding decisions, except where they run counter to a suspensive decision made by a management committee, in which case the final decision is made by the Council.

In contrast to decisions that are derived from existing instruments and frequently repeated, the drafting of innovative acts or fundamental decisions in principle follows the path set out in the diagram of the decision-making process. The original model only partially reflects the complexity of the real processes and may be altered in response to needs and conditions. In contrast to rigid models, this decision-making schema is characterized by flexibility and adaptability. In this hypothesis, the diagram is subject to adjustment and is only partially applied. However, for all categories of decision the duration of the process depends largely on the convergence or divergence of member states' interests.

The Single European Act: Improvements in the Decision-Making Process

The Single European Act considerably improved the decision-making process in four essential areas: restoring qualified majority voting in the Council, strengthening the Commission's role in the execution of legal measures, increasing the participation of the European Parliament in adopting Community standards, and obtaining approval by the Parliament of admission and association agreements. The logic of the new system is simple: in order to guarantee that the internal market and the principal policies that support it work properly, unanimity has been replaced by qualified majority voting, a return to the philosophy of the Treaty of Rome, under which development toward qualified majorities was brutally interrupted following the shock of the empty chair crisis and the Luxembourg "agreement to differ." This partial return to the rules and the spirit inspired by the founding fathers is twenty years late, but it is a return that is all the more inevitable in that, with the Community now composed of twelve members, the decision-making system has become more vulnerable to the threat of paralysis. In the flush of the same reforming enthusiasm, the member states accepted the need to associate the European Parliament more closely with the Council in the regulation of the internal market: now directives and decisions are adopted by a qualified majority "in cooperation with the European Parliament." Within the framework of this new procedure, the European Parliament may propose amendments with the agreement of the majority of its members. Just as the Council could not dissent from the Commission's proposals other than by unanimous agreement, so unanimity is required when the Council rejects amendments introduced by the European Parliament; in both cases, this procedure benefits Community institutions.

The *first phase* did not involve any substantial modifications that had not already been progressively introduced in practice. Thus, on account of its more numerous and burdensome tasks the Commission widened the possibility of using external experts. It was already tending to associate such experts more closely with its drafting work by entrusting them with "packages" of tasks. The implementation of the Single European Act, a very burdensome task, encouraged the Commission to develop consultation and even to entrust certain responsibilities to external experts who sometimes carry out their tasks within the Community administration. Moreover, it is not unusual to find that assignments concerning innovation are sometimes given to those experts. This practice is justifiable on a number of grounds but nonetheless raises a fundamental question: will the Commission be able to keep tabs on this network of external experts or will it gradually be invaded by them and become more vulnerable to subtle influences that are all the more powerful in that they act from within? Of course, the advantage lies in much greater transparency, but for the moment it is a transparency that benefits only a few experts and consultants, whose services are for sale to the highest bidder. The point here is not to criticize a method that seems likely to have a great future in various domains but simply to draw attention to the perverse effects it may have for lack of effective controls or the ability to either direct the work of experts or decide between the merits of the various options on offer.

The same need for a variety of data and information is driving the Commission to widen the circle of consultation with professional organizations by intensifying its exchanges with socioeconomic groups in particular. Thus, it has become accustomed to consulting not only Community groups but national groups and large firms. At the same time, it practices a policy of transparency by encouraging exchange: it receives more data, knowledge, and experience and in turn establishes daily and varied contacts that prevent it from creating Community laws from within an ivory tower. It can thereby also remain more in touch with reality and better able to reflect national and regional differences. At the same time, it is more exposed to very direct influence as well as to the danger of confusion since opinions and advice tend, at least in part, to take the place of sustained autonomous thought of any depth. Time and competence become rarer with increasing demands and needs, and the Commission is adopting a variety of pragmatic solutions, depending on the sector of activity concerned, until it is in a position to reexamine the problem thoroughly and find a balanced solution.

This quest also involves internal restructuring, breaking down the barriers between the directorates. Breaking down internal as well as external partitions, creating horizontal networks to overcome administrative barriers, establishing procedures that are more flexible, less hierarchical, and more adaptable to changing realities, these seem to be the Commission's main concerns. From the point of view of effective management, the Commission must imitate "megacorporations" in "turning the pyramid upside down." The upside-down pyramid implies a proliferation of horizontal exchanges and multiple networks but also clear-cut leadership. If at that time no one questioned the leadership of the Commission by its president Jacques Delors, it is nonetheless true that this new approach again raises the problem of how the president is chosen, what exactly his job is, what sort of backing he gets, and indeed what sort of personality he must have. These various factors, together with the networks developing within as well as outside the administration, are exerting convergent pressures in the direction of a European government.

Strengthening of the European Parliament's Role

The *second phase* was changed more radically (fig. 2); the Commission's proposal accompanied by the opinion of the European Parliament (together with opinions and advice from other sources) passes through the mill of the Council, that is to say, of Coreper and its working groups, in which representatives of the Commission are involved. The Council then reaches a *common position,* which it presents and explains to the European Parliament. This also applies to the Commission to the extent that it is led to revise its initial proposal in order to allow the Council to adopt a common position.

At this point, the *second reading* begins, first by the Parliament and then by the Council. In the course of this second reading, the Parliament deliberates on the Council's common position, and if, within three months, it approves this common proposal or does not come to any conclusion the Council definitively adopts its common position on the basis of a qualified majority. But within this period the European Parliament can decide to either amend or reject the common position on the basis of an absolute majority of its members. If the European Parliament rejects the common position, the Council can rule only on the basis of unanimity; on this condition alone can it confirm the common position without modifying it. Once again, unanimity is a shield protecting Community institutions.

If the European Parliament decides by an absolute majority of its members to amend the common position, the Commission has a month to reexamine the proposal and the amendments and formulate a "reexamined proposal." The Commission is free to modify its proposal, thereby following a general rule of the Community, and to allow the amendments it thinks justified. Thus modified, the proposal may be adopted on the basis of a qualified majority by the Council, which may only dissent from it on the basis of unanimity. Similarly, the Council may take up amendments proposed by the Parliament but rejected by the Commission. Thereby, the Commission can filter parliamentary amendments and its choice is protected by the

First phase of the Commission (fig.1)

Second phase: Commission, European Parliament, and Council

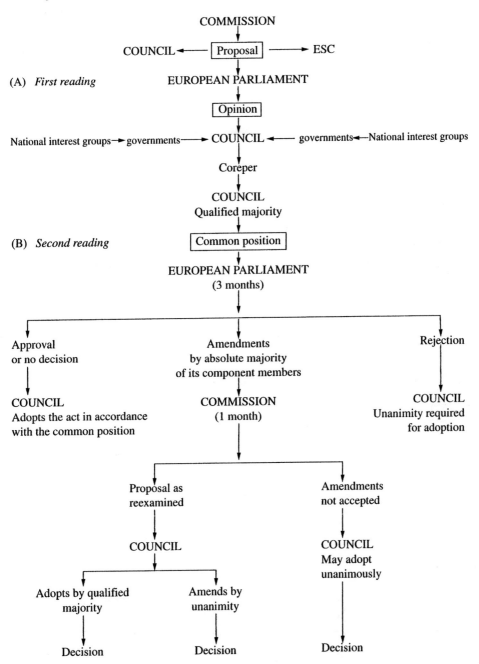

FIG. 2.   Single European Act: Decision-making process

requirement of unanimous vote by the Council. This gives it greater power than the European Parliament in conformity with the initial division of powers in the Community. In spite of its preponderant role, the Commission is open to proposals for amendments from the Parliament; since 1987 it has accepted 1,052 amendments out of 1,724 proposed, while 719 were ultimately adopted by the Council.[1]

This new "cooperation" procedure clearly increases the importance of the European Parliament without giving it a real power of codecision; effectively it has such power only in cases of admission and the association of countries with the Community and to a large extent concerning budgets. Parliament is closely associated with the Commission and the Council in the decision-making process in relation to the internal market. Its influence has certainly grown, but at the same time so has its responsibility and its work load. In fact, the double reading of a growing number of directives, rulings, and decisions represents a heavy load that the European Parliament in its present form, and with the means currently at its disposal, has great difficulty carrying out, all the more so in that, along with the increase in the number of bills and the extension of its fields of activity, its deadlines have been made tighter than ever.

Parliament's capacity for analysis is not up to the demands on it, and the expert help it can draw on is insufficient in relation to the volume and breadth of business with which it has to cope. In fact, the European Parliament has a very weak infrastructure in comparison with what is available to national parliaments and a fortiori with the American Congress. Nonetheless, it sustains an ongoing program of lawmaking and innovation in the interests of twelve countries that, for all they have in common, diverge widely in their legislation, customs, and practice. Can the European Parliament carry out its functions effectively in current conditions? The risk is that it will be defeated by highly technical questions or submerged in regulatory details and thereby lose sight of essentials. The cost, in terms of the fragmentation inherent in all this activity, is the reduction of its capacity to make fundamental choices on fundamental questions. Given the sheer volume of business to be handled, how will Euro-MPs and their assistants manage to control this process, which is still expanding as Parliament takes on the increasing burden of ever more technical rulings?

The European Parliament will sooner or later have to face the following dilemma: either it will become more and more dependent on expert analysts and assistants like the American Congress or it will have to accept the idea that it cannot keep an eye on everything but must concentrate on essentials. Whatever way it chooses, it will surely have to admit in the end that its legislative role must be limited to drafting *laws* and *directives* (framework laws), with the executive having the power to supplement laws with *executive rulings* and national parliaments having the task of transposing directives into national legislation. To prevent rulings being entirely left to the discretion of the Community executive, they could be split into two categories: the first depending in principle exclusively on the Commission, the second having to be subjected to parliamentary examination at the request of the European Parliament, for example, at the request of fifty Euro-MPs, of a group linked to a European political group, or perhaps of a minimum of two other groups. Thus, rather than having their attention dispersed Euro-MPs could concentrate on fundamental questions and formulating major options, reserving the right to intervene in technical matters or questions of detail for occasions when they think it is necessary. By so doing, their democratic supervision could become a reality rather than an illusion while their authority and credibility would be strengthened. If there are no reforms in this area, the danger is that the illusion of democratic participation will be perpetuated in such a way that even the growth in parliamentary powers will not be enough to provide a remedy for the democratic deficit. This growth ought to be accompanied by a reform of methods and instruments if Euro-MPs are not to be overwhelmed by an avalanche of business.

In spite of these difficulties, the European Parliament as an expression of popular legitimacy is designated to take on a share of legislative power and exercise democratic oversight in the Community. The multiplication of issues and domains raises considerable uncertainty with regard to its ability to cope properly, under current conditions, with its responsibilities, which will be further increased in the areas of external relations and security in the context of a political union. The Commission itself, even though it has better resources, has yet to find a lasting solution to the work overload that the internal market and its new fields of activity have brought with them. Hence, there is a need to adapt the functions of Commission and Parliament to this growth in tasks and demands.

It is necessary to endow Community institutions with the means of performing, under the best possible conditions, tasks that are beyond the resources of member states working separately. Like all other public institutions, as long as Community institutions are starved of adequate resources in knowledge, manpower, and means, they become more permeable, vulnerable, and exposed to the influence of interest groups. While institutions do need to develop networks of groups and experts around them, they have to go on asserting their autonomy, and such autonomy exists at a certain cost. Since it acquired more effective powers by virtue of the "cooperation" system, the European Parliament has become a target for interest groups. Previously ignored or neglected by these groups, it began to attract their attention from the moment of its direct election in 1979. This was made easier by the presence in its ranks of numerous Euro-MPs, who, like MPs in the national parliaments, had come from professional organizations or organizations linked to them. Moreover, the European parliamentary commissions, which generally bring together MPs according to their constituency interests, affiliations, or knowledge, constitute favored targets for lobbyists and interest groups. These targets are all the more attractive in that the importance of the preparatory work carried out by parliamentary commissions is well known, to the point that certain parliaments have accepted both in law and in practice that technical bills, or bills deemed secondary, come within the competence of committees. This method may well find its application in the European Parliament, within precise limits, and under the control of parliamentarians who would, when appropriate, have the opportunity to bring before a plenary session a question dealt with in committee. Indeed, certain apparently technical matters often raise problems of principle or political options.

To the extent that interest groups direct their actions toward an institution whose decisions they seek to influence, they may be useful indicators of the role and powers of that institution, especially since these groups are not inclined to waste their own time and generally seek to maximize their efficiency. Thus, a study of interest groups enables us not just to evaluate their influence but to assess the importance they accord to an institution in the political system. Direct election to the European Parliament and the strengthening of its authority have thus helped transform the relationship between the Parliament and interest groups.

In spite of the distance between national parliaments, with their legislative, budgetary, investiture, and political control powers, and the European Parliament, which as yet does not have such extensive powers, interest groups adopt the same approach to both. In addition to the traditional activities they undertake outside institutions, their approach consists in placing their representatives *within* them, securing the election of leaders of groups or of persons close to them. These "spokespersons" of interest groups are in principle members of parliamentary groups of parties with which they maintain special relationships; they obtain seats on commissions whose activity has a direct link to the objectives being pursued by the interest groups. This infiltration strategy is accompanied by a range of actions that aim to influence parliamentary acts from the *outside*. Like the classic means of exerting pressure, these take varied forms: submitting specialized studies and documentation and reports and letters while opinions and positions are being formulated. In other cases, direct contacts are encouraged, followed by a series of indirect means of influence through the mass media and public opinion right up to organizing demonstrations. Exploiting the whole range of pressure as their resources allow, interest groups also use their networks of relationships with political parties and their leaders, parliamentary groups, and MPs. Finally, they also exert influence through European Parliament hearings and the mediation of experts used as consultants, experts who in many cases have more or less close links with interest groups.[2]

The Process of Informal Integration

The European Parliament: A New Target for Interest Groups

From the moment it was elected, the European Parliament began to attract increasing interest from interest groups. The example of agricultural prices is very instructive. Immediately after the budget was rejected in 1979, Parliament used the Delatte Report to declare itself in favor of the control of excess production. It wanted to give this question priority, and when it refused to consider raising prices agricultural organizations reacted vigorously. In 1981, huge demonstrations were organized; farmers began to abandon their farms because their income was falling relentlessly under the impact of price control policies. These policies were, in reality, the only compromise the Council had been able to reach. Mr. Gundelach's efforts to align pricing policy with income and promote a levy on the harvesting of excess produce were completely frustrated by the demonstrators' actions. Frightened by such violent reactions, MPs from the PPE, the Liberals, and the European Democrats for Progress (EDP) Group then agreed to back a general rise in prices.[3]

Another example is the draft directive on informing and consulting workers in companies with complex structures, discussed in 1981–82. Fearing that the Vredeling Directive might be adopted, UNICE and employers exerted strong pressure, especially on the European Parliament. In the course of the debate, and the conflict of influences aroused by the draft directive, interested organizations and factions used all kinds of strategies, from delaying tactics to threats. European and American business interests threatened to review their investment plans if obligations to inform workers of strategic company decisions and take notice of their opinions were imposed in the Community. On the other hand, moderate trade unions on the ESC threatened to withdraw their support from European institutions if there was any retreat on this point. European employers were able to call on the support of a variety of organizations, interest groups, and companies. For example, in a letter addressed to the president of the European Parliament, the French branch of an American multinational drew his attention to the dangers inherent in this draft directive and the obligations it entailed, requirement that could cause their factory in France to lose its autonomy and independence in decision making.

The grouping of savings banks in the European Community thought that it was "imperative to take account of the particular situation of credit establishments." At the close of their opinion, they stated: "The savings banks of the European Community want the Commission of the European Communities to amend its proposal to take account on the one hand of the particular situation of the credit sector and on the other hand of certain inopportune provisions and obligations in the proposal. Certain member organizations are, in fact, opposed in principle to any directive in this area.[4]

The European Parliament Social Affairs and Employment Commission organized a hearing on the Commission's proposal for 21 October 1981. Although agreement had been reached in principle on the importance of informing and consulting workers about questions with a crucial bearing on their activity, this exchange, far from producing a consensus, revealed differences concerning the proposed objectives and solutions. For example, UNICE was confirmed in its conviction that the basic principles on which the Commission's proposals were based needed a thorough examination. Moreover, its secretary-general wrote in a letter to the president of the Social Affairs and Employment Commission, indicating that in view of the unsatisfactory nature of the Commission's draft it was hardly surprising that instead of building a bridge of understanding between social partners the draft was producing the opposite effect.[5] Finally, he expressed the hope that the parliamentary commission and the European Parliament would be in a position to prepare the ground for further serious consultations with the Commission. According to UNICE, such consultations, backed by European Parliament recommendations, offered the opportunity for a close study of the problems and for a solution to be found through a directive. Fundamentally, UNICE was questioning the use and timing of the directive by asking that it be reexamined in new consultations.

In an appendix to this letter, UNICE sought to identify the key problems that seemed to be particularly important for the Social Affairs and Employment Commission. A considerable number of companies, in fact 46,644 firms with more than one hundred employees, would be affected by the directive; instruments already in force at Community and international levels ought to be studied carefully (in particular the OECD code of conduct). The requirement for professional secrecy and the inefficacy of protective measures such as those proposed by the Commission should be considered along with the possibility of bypassing, which seemed to give credence to the notion, in any event incorrect, that major decisions were not taken at the branch level but at the head office. This idea was contradicted, in fact, by the current trend toward decentralization; as for the obligation to consult and come to an agreement, there was a danger that it would lead to a paralysis of the decision-making process in the companies concerned. Whatever the validity of the arguments put forward, UNICE was aiming to use a delaying tactic and attenuate or even neutralize the effects of the directive.

After a long process marked by many consultations, working commissions, hearings, and debates on the basis of three reports, the European Parliament handed down its opinion in December 1982. In July 1983, the Commission submitted to the Council the "modified draft directive on informing and consulting workers" drawn up in the light of the opinions of the Economic and Social Committee (79 votes for, 61 against, and 11 abstentions) and the European Parliament (161 votes for, 61 against, and 84 abstentions) and taking into account the consultations with interested parties in January and February 1983.[6]

In the introductory section, the Commission constantly refers to the amendments proposed by the Parliament, which confirms the impact made on the Commission by Parliament's opinion. On numerous points, in fact, the Commission accepted the Parliament's opinion. An assessment of the importance of access to Community institutions reveals that along with the Commission the European Parliament has become the preferred target of interest groups since it was elected and as its participation in the decision-making process has grown more significant. The frequency and breadth of relationships with an institution are an indication of the importance accorded by groups to that institution. Interest groups clearly concentrate their efforts on institutions whose attitudes and policies they hope to be able to influence with the most likelihood of a beneficial outcome for themselves. This indication does not allow us, however, to determine the real power of Community institutions. The choice made by interest groups is governed by two criteria: the real or estimated importance of decision-making centers and the opportunities interest groups may have to gain access to and influence any given center or centers more or less effectively. The behavior of interest groups toward institutions nonetheless remains a precious guide to the significance of institutions and to their relative power in the European Community.

By strengthening Parliament's powers, the Single European Act has helped develop a network of ties between the Parliament and interest groups. Community or national interest groups that fail to get what they want from the Commission make strenuous efforts to exert pressure on Parliament in hopes of altering the common position or indeed of procuring its rejection.

Early in 1991, the European Parliament was attacked more vigorously than ever by large companies and several associations; what was at stake was the protection of software copyrights for a market thought to be worth

U.S.$11 billion. The common position was a compromise on "reverse engineering" and the commission for legal affairs adopted a series of amendments aimed at widening its use.[7] These amendments were formulated in response to the demands of users and several producers and retailers grouped around IBM. While the latter accepted that the common position, given a limited usage of "reverse engineering," was a reasonable compromise between rival factions and associations, several members of the European Committee for Interfacing Systems and the European Association of Computer Users considered that the proposed directive did not go far enough and seemed likely to prevent various types of software from being profitable.

Caught in the crossfire, Parliament chose the middle way by not adopting any amendments in plenary session. It preferred to rubber-stamp the compromise reached with difficulty by the Commission and the Council. This practice is well known in the Swiss Parliament, which often hesitates to modify the elements of a compromise that has been laboriously achieved by the authorities and the main interest groups. At the same time, the European Parliament is a public forum, where debates are held and disputes can throw fresh light on controversial topics, forcing authorities and interest groups alike to put their cards on the table. In this respect, the European Parliament fulfills a vital function in developing democracy.

Parliament also takes on an important role in promoting such ideas and proposals as environmental measures. Because of European Parliament initiatives launched by Danish and German groups, in concert with the Greens and supported by Socialist, Christian Democrat, and certain Liberal MPs, the way was opened to Community antipollution legislation. By showing interest in the environment, the European Parliament has pulled the Commission along with it, preparing the ground for a suggestion from the president of the Parliament to create a *European Environmental Agency*. In this, the Parliament has faithfully interpreted the aspirations and concerns of European public opinion. Such problems are certainly felt more or less acutely by public opinion in the different member states, but a majority of 66 percent consider that they should be made a matter for Community decisions.[8] The European Parliament acts as a transmission belt enabling particular national problems to be dealt with at the European level by virtue of the principle of subsidiarity without imposing excessively rigid rulings and taking into account the diversity and pluralism of the European Community. Moreover, Parliament has a real power of codecision in the form of an assent, which comes into play in the closing stages of the negotiation process before the Council must pronounce unanimously and before representatives of the governments sign the agreement with the applicant state (art. 237 of the EEC; art. 8 of the SEA). With *association agreements* (art. 238 of the EEC; art. 9 of the EUA), a *favorable opinion* is required from the Parliament before the Council makes its decision and the agreement is signed. In both cases, this necessary approval from the European Parliament, which may also reject the results of negotiations, is akin to a "parliamentary ratification," which can be obtained only by a majority of its members.

To conclude, it is worth noting that the European Parliament fits into the Community decision-making circuit both by virtue of its initiatives and by its participation in decision making. With new mechanisms in place, the cogs interlock and function on the whole in a satisfactory manner. Hence, in spite of the problem of work overload that faces the Commission, the Council, and the European Parliament, Community institutions accepted two-thirds of the directives planned in the Single European Act in 1991. In turn, national authorities, parliaments, and administrations (give or take a few disparities) strive to observe the prescribed periods for the transposition of directives in the course of their duties while the institutions continue to produce an impressive number of rulings, decisions, reports, "white or green books," and recommendations of all kinds. Absorbing the innovations of the Single European Act into the normal operation of Community institutions has made it possible to relaunch the Community ship. The impetus given by the European Council has not only helped implement the Single European Act, but it has cleared new paths by establishing intergovernmental negotiations on a political union, whose main lines it has formulated. The European Council is thus asserting itself both as initiator and master craftsman of the great European enterprise.

Executive powers are not exercised in an autonomous fashion by the Commission, as might logically be concluded from the division of labor between the institutions. The Community executive only has executive powers to the extent that they are conferred on it by the Council in the measures it adopts. While upholding this principle, which grants to the Council most of the executive in addition to legislative and decision-making powers, the Single European Act nonetheless confirms what was already clear in practice and jurisprudence, namely, that the Commission is the Community's natural executive organ. Moreover, the council may only keep for itself the right to exercise powers of execution directly in specified cases. In other words, the Single European Act establishes the executive role of the commission as the general rule.[9]

Official and Informal Institutionalized Consultation

The general practice of consultation committees (official and informal) and European interest groups forms one of the principal focuses of the functioning of the Community. With the implementation of the Single European Act, the Council settled the modalities of the exercise of powers conferred on the Commission and defined the functions of the *consultative committees composed of representatives* of member states and presided over by its Commission representative.[10] The Commission representative submits draft measures to the committees, which formulate their opinions on the basis of a qualified majority within a period that the president is entitled to fix, depending on the urgency of the issue in question. The Commission is expected to pay the greatest attention to these opinions in adopting measures; if the measures taken do not conform with the opinions given by the committees, the Council may take a different decision on a qualified majority vote. Its decision sets out several procedures, but as a general rule the Council reserves the right to intervene when the Commission's measures are not in conformity with the committees' opinions. The functioning of the agricultural management committees is governed by a similar principle; in spite of their name, they are only a form by which the Council is present in the Commission and it is the Commission that really manages the various agricultural sectors and makes decisions. If the management supervisory committee is opposed to the Commission's decision by a qualified majority, the Commission must hand its decision to the Council, which may adopt a different one. If the Council does not make its view known within a set period, the Commission's decision continues to hold. Under this system, the Commission takes responsibility for managing the different agricultural sectors under the supervision of the management committees of the Council and ultimately of the Council itself, whose power limits the Commission's autonomy.

Scores of committees and thousands of experts gravitate around the two main institutions empowered to make decisions, the Commission and the Council. It is likely that here such committees are more important in terms of their number and their role than they are in the member states. There are various reasons for this. First, the many committees made up of national experts, officials of the national administration, or representatives of member governments are supplemented by other committees exercising functions comparable to consultative committees that function at a national level. In a multinational Community, consultation with interest groups in the course of the decision-making process is paralleled by the participation of national administrations, indispensable for preparing dossiers and forming a consensus at various levels. This national participation also exists in federal states and has various forms within the Community, whether in committees and meetings of national experts at Commission level or in Coreper working groups in the framework of the Council.

Second, the Community organization, which has neither a long memory nor a lengthy tradition, has to have the help of a dense network of committees able to provide information, data, and studies on rules and practices that often vary from one country or region to another. Faced with this diversity of traditions, concepts, approaches, and responses, the contribution of national experts, independent experts, or representatives of interest groups is useful to the Commission in its attempt to draft a community line. As for bilateral contacts, working in committees offers the advantage of being able to compare approaches and viewpoints, which allows, thanks to a common effort, the essential components of Community interest to emerge and shows the limits of national or sectoral resistance.

Third, these same reasons encourage state administrations to associate with socioeconomic groups and external experts who were in at the beginning of EC consultation processes. In fact, socioeconomic actors share privileged information with the Community (i.e., in-depth technical knowledge of their spheres of activity). In addition to their knowledge, their opinions and decisions keep Community institutions, and above all the Commission, informed about how opinions are divided on a particular problem and suggest solutions. These different considerations lead to a fundamental question, central to our present concerns: what is the effective role of the committees while the Community is drafting and adopting resolutions and at the time of their implementation?

According to the general schema, the Commission plays an active and preponderant role during the drafting period. It also participates actively in the phase of decision making by the Council when it legislates in cooperation with the European Parliament after having received the opinion of the Economic and Social Committee. Once measures have been formulated, it is the Commission's task to oversee their management and execution. This classic structure, however, shows evidence of one major gap: it ignores the contribution of the socioeconomic committees and actors. It is therefore necessary to clarify the direct roles of interest groups and the European Community committees if their contribution to the Community process is to be assessed.

In drawing up and implementing Community rulings, the Commission relies on three types of committee: consultative committees that are socioeconomic in their membership, mixed committees composed of representatives of social partners and public authorities, and committees of national experts. In addition, there are two mixed management committees, one of which is the Council for the Administration of the European Center for the Development of Professional Training, and two mixed committees, the Permanent Employment Committee and the Tripartite Conference. The Permanent Employment Committee represents an equal mix of Community employers' and workers' organizations, UNICE for industry, COPA for agriculture, CEEP for public industries, and the European Trade Union Confederation. The Tripartite Conference, meeting periodically but not on a formal basis, includes four representatives of the Commission, two vice presidents and two members, the president and secretary-general of the Council, and ministers of member states.

The outline given previously shows the networks of existing committees, made up of about *three hundred* bodies at the Commission and Council levels.[11] In addition to the professional or mixed committees, these include numerous committees whose members are national or governmental experts, officials, and senior chiefs of public bodies like central banks. The density of the networks varies according to the sector of Community activity in question and corresponds to the intensity and importance of Community power and the density of networks of consultative committees has already been noted with respect to the development of networks of interest groups at the Community level.

For all its access to this dense network of committees, which has expanded rapidly again in the framework of the events of 1992, the Commission extends its consultation still further while its proposals are at the drafting stage.[12] This consultation involves both professional organizations established at Community level (UNICE, COPA, ETUC, bodies by sector and by branch) and national experts officially invited by the Commission. This simultaneous consultation complements the more official consultation with committees in which professional Community organizations carry out a supporting and coordinating role. However, whether one is talking about consultative committees, professional Community organizations, or national experts, and whatever the importance of their contributions, they amount only to advice or opinions of a consultative nature. After receiving so much advice from numerous experts, consultative committees, and interest groups, the Commission takes sole responsibility for its proposals and decisions. It is a collegial institution par excellence.

The role of committees at the Council level is characterized by direct and official intervention in the decision-making process. So it comes as no surprise to find that apart from the committees of professional organizations the networks of committees or working groups are as crowded as the web of networks around the Commission, all the more so in that more than one committee operates simultaneously at both levels.

While it does much to institutionalize consultation, the involvement of the *Economic and Social Committee* does not substantially modify the parameters of the decision-making process. Indeed, the Economic and Social Committee is a consultative body that brings together various categories of national socioeconomic actors to draft Community norms and policies in a general institutionalized form. Some might wonder whether, on the one hand, the multiple consultative committees do not exercise a more weighty consultative function, to the detriment of the Economic and Social Committee, and, on the other hand, whether the latter ought not to take on a coordinating or supervisory role within the consultative network. As to the first question, in my opinion, the privilege held by the Economic and Social Committee of general institutionalized consultation is usefully complemented by the limited sectoral tasks entrusted to the numerous consultative committees, especially since the Economic and Social Committee is not in a position to cover the multiplicity of economic and social domains on account of its relatively small size. Its general action is oriented toward major Community decisions, whether general rulings or directives, on which it gives advice officially and publicly. For their part, the various committees, which function virtually in secret, take on particular selective tasks, usually of a very specialized, technical nature. Through them, the Community is associated with professional or administrative circles that are directly concerned and better equipped to aid the Commission. Thus, it is obvious that the one cannot be substituted for the others and vice versa; the Economic and Social Committee and the various consultative committees each fulfill distinct tasks. As to the second question, it seems to me that the Economic and Social Committee is already sufficiently busy with the task of ensuring coordination, which in fact is hardly justified, between committees that are very different in their composition, function, and specialization. Consequently, supervision would only lead to an unfortunate centralization, resulting in an impoverishment of the substantial and various contributions of the committees and experts forming the network. On the contrary, it seems to be crucial to develop good connections between these committees and the Economic and Social Committee.

Socioeconomic consultative committees, whether institutionalized or not, are a special means of access available to Community or national interest groups; the influence of these committees, present on various levels at the Commission, is variable and difficult to access, but it is more important in specialized technical fields than in more general matters.[13] With few exceptions, the different analyses have underlined the influence of committees of national experts or governmental representatives in technical or specialized fields. They seem, in fact, to have increased their grip on technical or routine decisions that are considered to be of lesser importance. Moreover, their contribution to important decisions is far from negligible, as can be seen from Coreper's role in the first stages of decision making and in the search for consensus. Economic and technical fields in the Community tend to strengthen the technocratic trend in developed societies. How can the weight of technocratic structures, whether national or Community in origin, be counterbalanced? The answer to this question is chiefly to be found in an increased stress on democratic legitimacy and political supervision within the Community.

The European Parliament has certainly acquired increased power and authority as a result of its direct election and the Single European Act, but the question remains as to whether it and its commissions have the capacity and the effective means to keep an eye on decisions with an economic or technical content. For the time being, apart from decisions of general significance or those that involve political options, doubt exists as to the efficacy of this oversight. Moreover, it is clear that for lack of time or means the Council has often been led to entrust decisions to its committees and working groups composed of representatives of national administrations, excluding only those touching on sensitive political areas or areas where there are significant divisions. Governmental committees exert a marked influence at this level. There remains the Commission, an institution that is both political and technical, having a right of proposal and ensuring continuity in the decision-making process, especially within the network of committees and working groups in the Council. But at this level also issues considered less important or too technical are left to Commission officials and are put through an accelerated written procedure. On the other hand, global decisions and sensitive questions are dealt with at the highest level within the collegial institution. This sometimes fragile distinction between important decisions and those less so, between political and technical decisions, has consequences throughout the decision-making process. Can we therefore conclude that the Community decision-making process is governed by committees?

What judgment should we pass on the Community system with regard to less important decisions of a technical or sectoral order? Fundamental decisions like the adoption of the Single European Act, the reform of the Common Agricultural Policy, or decisions of global politics are a matter for the senior political authorities in the Commission, the Council, the European Council, and the European Parliament. The same is true of decisions that set a new direction, tackle new areas, or give a push to the European union process. These are just some examples illustrating the decisive role played by Delors, Mitterand, Kohl, Thatcher, and other political leaders who have held the presidency of the Councils and their committees.

In both the adoption and the implementation of the Single European Act, their drive and influence have left their mark on the establishment of the space without frontiers, the development of common policies, and negotiations on economic and monetary union and political union. In a whole range of different domains where impetus and political will are vital committees are the support structures that contribute to the preparation of dossiers and the formation of consensus around clearly defined guidelines.

Their contribution is all the more important as the efficiency of the Community system lies less in its power to coerce than in its power to stimulate, coordinate, and turn existing, underused forces into active synergies. Hence, there is a need to bring these committees into all the different stages of the decision-making process. On this issue, Community action both confirms a general tendency in and foreshadows a new concept of the Community's political power. This evolution was noted a long time ago by Bertrand de Jouvenel in his definition of *politics* as an addition or competition of wills. My conclusion expresses a duality: while I recognize the importance of committees in the Community process, I do not hold to the theory of "government by committee," a theory that is all the less credible in that the Community is entering a new dynamic phase, one that is dependent on political will and political support as well as on the participation of political and social forces.

Informal Participation

The integration process involves active participation by numerous circles and networks of interested parties in various forms at the Community, national, and regional levels. These various levels or "participation areas" correspond to particular institutions around which many and divers socioeconomic participants are clustered: interest groups, businesses, economic agents, lobbyists, experts, researchers, and academics, all participating more or less directly in this process according to the degree and intensity of their interests.

In addition to national governments or regional authorities, national parliaments, and especially national and regional administrations, take an active and continuing part in the Community consultation and decision-making process. All the parliaments have an internal body responsible for European affairs, whether it be a commission, subcommission, or, like the French Parliament, a delegation, but their level of participation and their influence vary from one country to the next. In all of the parliaments, these commissions circulate information in both directions and are the point of contact with European institutions, especially the Commission and the European Parliament, as well as with their governments and administrations. They play a role in implementing directives, studying Community dossiers, and more often than not drafting opinions and positions intended for the Community. In the United Kingdom, the minister representing the government at the Council of the Community will not now give his definitive agreement while Parliament is still studying a Commission proposal and has yet to give its opinion. Collaboration on Community matters between the Danish Parliament and its government follows a long tradition.

The EEC Commission is regularly consulted on all major questions that the government is negotiating within the Council. If the Danish government is obliged to diverge from an original position that has won the approval of the EEC Commission, it must once again consult the Commission before any definitive agreement is reached at its Council of Ministers. A list of Community legislative proposals together with summaries is regularly submitted to the EEC Commission. The government also sends it the dossiers that figure on the Council agenda, discusses them with the EEC Commission, and gives it reports at the end of each Council meeting. These practices have encouraged close collaboration between the government and the Danish Parliamentary EEC Commission, which plays an active role, especially in implementing Community directives.

The German bicameral Parliament has broken new ground in that the Länder are more involved since the ratification of the Single European Act. Transfer of power to the European Community and the division of power in the German federal state means that the Länder have been more closely associated with the formation of European political decisions. It seems that legislative powers that have been so transferred are no longer chiefly a matter for the two chambers but rather concern the federal government representing Germany in the Council of Ministers. The agreement reached on this subject obliges the federal government to consult the Bundesrat on all Community decisions that "come under the exclusive legislative competence of the Länder or affect their particular interests." The government must take into account the opinion of the Bundesrat and should it be obliged to reject that opinion for overriding foreign policy reasons it must communicate the reasons for doing so. Under these conditions, the representatives of the Länder must be associated (if they so request) with the work of consultative committees at the Commission and the Council. It is equally interesting to recall that in its reply to the demands of the Bundesrat the federal government commits itself to preserving and promoting federalist principles and principles of subsidiarity in the European Community. In addition, the agreement shows the particular responsibility of the Länder in the area of measures for stimulating the economy and their principal responsibility in the areas of education and culture while confirming the complementarity of Community powers in the new policies regarding research, development, and the environment. In domains coming under the competence of the Länder, the latter have approved numerous directives. Hence, in the context of the "Erasmus" and "Comett" programs, the Länder have initiated direct action at the Commission in Brussels, where they have opened information and liaison offices. The federal government and the Länder have established a common list of committees and working groups in which the Länder can be represented at the Commission and the Council when matters relating to their exclusive right to legislate or to their essential interests are under discussion.[14] The Länder are thus seeking to compensate by various means for the extension of federal powers following the development of Community powers. The Länder's view is clearly expressed in the Bundesrat resolution of 31 January 1986:

> The European Union must have a federal structure. It must guarantee the constitutional position of the states of federal Germany and the traditional diversity and rights of the regions as a preservative component of a European state order. The right of communes to administer themselves must be respected.
>
> Central decision-making authorities must not receive powers except for the areas in which the transfer to the European level is absolutely indispensable to achieve a political union and for problems that cannot be regulated coherently or effectively except at the level of the Community or of a union. Member states and their regions must retain their powers in areas that concern them in accordance with the principle of subsidiarity. The powers of the European Union and of member states, or indeed of their regions, must be unequivocally delimited. It is essential to take into account the federal structure of certain member states, and above all the fundamental sphere of sovereign state power attributed to the Länder of Federal Germany must be preserved with clearly defined powers. Moreover, it is necessary that they be accorded a broad right of participation in the decisions of the Union in conformity with their importance within the state structure of Federal Germany.

PART 3

Europe's Federal Future

Chapter 7

The Era of Federalism

Globalization versus Differentiation

The Double Tension

The world of technological civilization is subject to two opposing forces, the pull of globalization under the impact of the new technological revolution and the simultaneous pull of national and cultural individuality. Resisting a tendency toward standardization and imitation of a common model, a desire to be different in terms of historical heritage or national or regional identity can be seen. Against gigantic size stand values, quality, and the beauty of detail or the miniature: "small is beautiful." In contrast to the integration of Western Europe, which respects national and regional diversities, Eastern Europe has grown more fragmented under pressure from intolerant nationalism and powerful trends, whether opposed or convergent; some of them support multinational unions and others wreck them. These movements, which are shaking the international order established at the end of World War II, are forcing a choice on us. Either we strengthen developing unions, create new institutions able to serve as pillars of a reinvigorated United Nations, or stand by and watch a return to balkanization, a rebirth of the nation-state, or indeed a proliferation of micro- or ethnic states. These illnesses, though still at an infant stage, threaten to reactivate national rivalries and ethnic tension in Western Europe. Limited for the moment to a few marginal areas such as Northern Ireland, the Basque country, and Corsica, these movements might well reach unanticipated dimensions or reawaken ambitions for national grandeur. Certainly, unlike the process of dissolution and collapse seen in the East, with its political void and contempt for economic exchange, these independence movements and nationalist tendencies fit into a Community structure that unites nations and regions without destroying them. Moreover, these pressures correspond more to a need for reconstruction or a new division of power at various levels within the

European Community than to an unbridled desire for independence. This is all the more true in that nations and regions live in freely agreed-upon association upheld by a whole fabric of economic and social interdependence that cannot be destroyed without provoking grave crises. However, such a positivist and rational reading of the Community reality may not take sufficient account of the hypothesis, marginal perhaps but certainly not to be ignored, that reemergent nationalism, although irrational, is an extremely powerful and menacing force.

In September 1990, President Richard von Weizsäcker of Germany issued an unmistakable warning when inaugurating the forty-first academic year of the College of Europe: the inevitable cosmopolitan and egalitarian development of civilization and technology in conjunction with growing mobility is everywhere giving birth to a desire to protect autochthonous regional cultures and historic national identities. However, according to the West German president this legitimate desire must not take the form of nationalism and power politics. Instead Europe as a whole must become a community governed by normative rules such as those envisaged by Immanuel Kant and the Helsinki Final Act and actually established by the Treaty of Rome; such a community is now within the reach of Europeans for the first time. In the great task that awaits them, Europeans may succeed, but they may also fail. This task requires not only long-term vision but immediate action, for the newly acquired freedom in certain parts of Europe may lead in opposing directions, toward international cooperation and union or toward a new instability. European history has frequently shown how the collapse of stability imposed by a dominant power may produce a fundamental instability. In fact, a heroic liberation movement may open the way to dangerous exclusivity and ultimately to chaos. This is the meaning of the well-known concept of "balkanization." President von Weizsäcker noted that we are faced with a clear choice: to unite Europe or fall back into the old latent divisions between states and national groups.[1]

Faced with upheavals that have shaken the established order, what tactic might be adopted? It obviously has to be flexible, open to the complexity of reality and the values of European societies based on the individual and his or her development in communities of various sizes, progressive, and respectful of fundamental values of diversity. In fact, it has to be the federalist method. Such an approach would seem to make it possible to reconcile the two contradictory trends without destroying them. One involves development based on the division of labor, which is emphasized by the impact of high technology; the other, emerging from the force of attraction of communities that resemble one another, is driven by a determination to assert cultural originality and a national or local sense of belonging.

Factors in Change and Regionalization

According to W. W. Rostow, four principal factors are encouraging or accelerating global change: the new technological revolution, the emergence of newly industrialized countries, the threat to the environment, and the end of the East-West conflict.[2] These factors are contributing to globalization, a concept that covers a range of simultaneous phenomena and shows up in various areas: world financial markets, global business networks, new information and communications technologies, and exchanges of industrial products, services, and raw materials. The integration of electronics and other high-technology sectors is creating transnational movements that tend in many ways to erode the powers of the state. To varying degrees, these global phenomena are weakening the grip of states on the behavior of important parties that theoretically come under their control. They are pushing the frontiers of decision making to the global level. This is the conclusion of a document produced by the OECD.[3]

The developments Rostow considers revolutionary are combining to speed up regional integration movements, all the more so as they coincide with a need to organize a response at the regional level to threats to the environment, to pool the resources of regions in order to strengthen competitive capacity, and to coordinate aid to developing countries and Eastern Europe.

A Multipolar World

Globalization, with the United States as its main engine, has become multipolar since new growth centers arose, like the European Community and Japan, around which networks of cooperation are forming. The interaction of high technology and competition, and the United States and Japan, has speeded up European Community integration. The 1993 objective encouraged economic agents and governments, both within and outside the Community, to adapt their strategies to this new phenomenon of the single market. It also influenced the creation of a continental association uniting the United States, Canada, and Mexico. This process of mutual attraction under the pressure of competition represents an example of the *spillover effect* on a global scale.

While globalization is passing over the nation-state, the internal regionalization movement is undermining it. The emergence of regions within the European Community and in several of its member states is working in favor of greater diversification. This is giving rise to intermediate levels either between states and the international community or between citizens, their local associations, and central authorities. The new socioeconomic and political structures thus are helping to increase the diversity and complexity of the most developed societies. This trend is based both on the efficiency of communications networks and on the propagation of microcomputers. It is also supported by the development of new production technologies that, in contrast with mass production, allow for increased flexibility and rapid adaptation to markets differentiated at regional and local levels. New technologies are therefore both creating a global society and promising an abundant diversity for the future.

In a changing world, the sudden disappearance of the superpower that represented the greatest concentration of power in history bears witness to the fragility of fortresses built on rigid structures in a totalitarian spirit. Moreover, it was a determination to be part of the technological revolution that, inter alia, motivated Gorbachev's reforms, whose unforeseen results led to the collapse of the Soviet Union and the Eastern bloc. This collapse, as swift as it was unexpected, of powers founded on political monopoly and economic dirigism is proof of the insoluble incompatibility between technological revolution and a longing for freedom on the one hand and systems of centralized power on the other. The rejection of totalitarian dirigism has aroused extreme reactions and brought into being nationalist movements that are occasionally violent. So, having lived through the threat of totalitarian domination, the world is now living in fear that conflicts between nations and ethnic groups may spread. This trend toward fragmentation, the reactivation of conflicts between nations, and interethnic violence is in contrast to the trend toward globalization and interdependence.

In the context of the new international disorder, the remaining superpower no longer has the will, much less the capacity, to impose a new order on this morass of 170 UN member states (in the early 1990s; 186 member states in 1998). The fragmentation of power within the international community makes the domination of a single country, even of a superpower, less and less thinkable. Hence, there is an inevitable trend toward cooperation and regionalization. Regional unions and cooperation are becoming the pillars of the international community. The emergence of a variety of different levels of authority is a reminder of a particular application of the principle of subsidiarity. To each level there should correspond the functions and powers that it is the most suited to exercise. This is the way recommended by federalism.

The Relevance of Federalism

From Proudhon's Federalism to Current Trends

We are witnessing the fulfillment of the positive aspect of Proudhon's prophecy: "The twentieth century will open the era of federalism or else humanity will once again embark on a thousand-year purgatory."[4]

After several successful experiments with federalism at the national level — the United States, the Swiss Confederation — the twentieth century has set out on the path to international federalism. A variety of international and regional organizations and the progress that the European Community represents testify to the vigor and breadth of this evolution. Based on freedom and respect for the individual, the autonomy and participation of regional interests, the ability to adapt, and a strategy of openness, federalism is less a system or model than a method and a spirit supported by various institutions. If federalism is necessarily based on democratic principles, a democratic community may nonetheless prefer a centralized nonfederal organization. However, the need for small and medium-sized communities to integrate into bigger groups, the complexity of modern societies, and the expansion of science, technology, and the economy all seem to suggest an unexpected development of federalism.

We are worlds away from Littré's definition of 1865, which Denis de Rougemont liked to cite:

Federalism, noun. Neologism. Federal system or doctrine of government. Federalism was one of the political forms found among savages. Chateaubriand, America, government. During the Revolution, a plan attributed to the Girondins for breaking national unity and transforming France into a federation of small states. The Jacobins had serious discussions about federalism, and there was a furious reaction to the ideas of the Girondins. Thiers, *Histoire de la Révolution,* "Convention Nationale, Ch. I."

Paradoxically, federalism now looks like the government of the future. For a long time, the French have lived in fear of federalism, often seen as threatening the destruction of the "one and indivisible" Republic. They fear a possible weakening of the central power in a country that seems all the more remarkable for its unitary system in that it is strongly diversified geographically and culturally, with nine languages and more than four hundred kinds of cheese.

This centralizing obsession has not prevented France from having its own prophet of federalism. In 1863, two years before Littré produced his definition, Proudhon published *Du principe fédératif,* which, alongside the writings of the American federalists, is one of the key works of federalist thought. According to Proudhon, constitutional science may be summed up in three propositions:

1. Form average-sized groups, each one sovereign, and unite them in a pact of federation.

2. In each federated state, organize government in accordance with the law of the separation of organs; I mean, separate everything

in power that can be separated, define everything that can be defined, distribute all that has been separated and defined among organs and officials; leave nothing undivided; surround public administration with all the conditions of publicity and supervision.

3. Instead of absorbing the federated states or provincial and regional interests into a single central authority, reduce the powers of this latter to a straightforward role of general initiative, mutual guarantees, and supervision, whose decrees are executed only when authorized by the confederate governments and their agents . . .

A few lines further on he explains his idea of the division of powers:

The government of a country is not something to be shared solely among seven or eight persons selected by a majority in Parliament and criticized by an opposition minority; it is to be shared between provinces and communes or else political life flows away from the extremities to the center and the nation is reduced to a hydrocephalous creature living in a fog.

For Proudhon, the federal principle is of universal significance:

The federal system can apply to all nations and all times, for humanity is progressive in all its generations and races, while the politics of a federation, which are, par excellence, the politics of progress, consists in dealing with each population according to a regime involving decreasing authority and centralization depending on the state of people's minds and morals.[5]

His vision of Europe is surprisingly up to date.

Thus, as opposed to what happens in other governments, the idea of a universal confederation contains a contradiction. Once again this shows the moral superiority of a federal over a unitary system, which is subject to all the inconvenience and all the vices of the indefinite, the unlimited, the absolute, and the ideal. Europe is still too big for a single confederation; it could only form a confederation of confederations. This was the idea that led me to say in my last publication that the first step to be taken in the reform of European public law is reestablishing the Italian, Greek, Batavian, Scandinavian, and Danubian confederations, a prelude to decentralizing the larger states, leading to general disarmament. Then all nationalities would return to freedom; then we would achieve the idea of a European equilibrium as put forward by all publicists and statesmen but impossible to attain as long as there are great powers with unitary constitutions.

This is the proclamation of a Europe of regions within a federation of federations. With hindsight and since the collapse of communism, we can see that Proudhon has taken his revenge on Marx.

Proudhon's idea for France was to hold its various nationalities together by a federal bond while respecting their autonomy and originality. Today, even the traditionally centralized French are following the powerful trend toward decentralization, regionalization, and federalism. Internally, the autonomy of the regions, attempted unsuccessfully by de Gaulle in 1969, took off under President Mitterrand in the early 1980s. Externally, the construction of the European Community, begun on the basis of the French Schuman-Monnet initiative and then continued, though not without some ambivalence, by General de Gaulle, was revitalized by President Mitterrand. Paradoxically, it was the country of centralism and "one and indivisible" sovereignty that gave a powerful thrust to launching and developing the European Union! The need for federalism had effectively become a fact of life.

This form of government has proved itself in the organization of great and complex assemblies like the United States and India or of smaller assemblies like the Helvetic Confederation. On the other hand, "centralized federalism," having nothing more federalist about it than its outward appearance, has failed in both the former Soviet Union and Yugoslavia. These multinational Communist states broke up under pressure from virulent nationalism. The process of disintegration of multinational communities, far from having come to an end, is threatening to transform itself into interethnic warfare. This is a frequently violent quest for new multinational forms of cooperation. As in the Soviet Union, the process of transition to effective democracy and real federalism is going to be difficult in countries that have long been in the grip of communism. At the same time, in the middle of an economic crisis in Latin America we are seeing a return to democratic practice and a greater autonomy for member sates in federal countries such as Venezuela, Argentina, and Brazil. The movement toward decentralization and regionalization is part of a vast federal current spreading throughout the world under various forms and different circumstances. The success of long-standing experiments in the United States and the Helvetic Confederation has had an impact here. But it is above all the originality of the experiment under way, its dynamism, and its promise of a federation on a European scale that currently constitute a reference point and pole of attraction. A new federalist current is emerging that goes much further than the mere organization of government; it is bringing with it changes in the organization of social life. The federalist revolution has begun.

Federalism is an integral part of European culture and is based on its unity and diversity. The principles of federalism, postulating that man is free and responsible, are increasingly evident in the construction of a united Europe, in the Europe of regions, in the organization of business, in the programming of research, and in the use of microcomputers. These various trends and signs, different but related and convergent, can be seen in the internal transformation of more than one centralized country, and in particular they are developing within the European Community, the driving force of European union. Together with the process of conversion and transition to democracy of countries with authoritarian regimes, military dictatorships, or socialist regimes that traditionally formed a constellation around the USSR, the movement toward a European union constitutes the most remarkable change since the end of World War II.

Opposition to a European union and the sharing and common exercise of certain powers is nothing new. In 1948, at the Hague Congress supporters of the federalist approach met with resistance from partisans of the "unionist" argument in favor of intergovernmental cooperation, defended by the British, with a few exceptions, against the majority of the Continentals. In this sense Mrs. Thatcher's approach reflected a traditional British attitude, which the United Kingdom's admission to the European Community had seemingly killed off forever. This attitude is hostile to the current majority as expressed by the Franco-German-Community troika of Mitterrand-Kohl-Delors, which aimed to promote a federal European union.

In her defense of the "Europe of Fatherlands" that had been so dear to de Gaulle, Mrs. Thatcher attacked the Economic and Monetary Union, the Social Charter, and the Commission's centralizing bureaucratic power. She did this in the name of British sovereignty and her economically liberal and antistatist conception. Basically, she was opposed to a Community that she thought would tend to develop toward a European federation. Here she repeated the traditional argument of the British government as expressed in its response to the Briand Project (1929) or the view of British participants in the Hague Congress (1948), who were "unionists" opposed to European federalists represented in particular by Denis de Rougemont and Henri Brugmans. There is one fundamental difference, however: today the United Kingdom is a full member of a European Community that, since the Single European Act and the Maastricht Treaty, has quite emphatically been on the road to a European federation. The Single European Act created an area without frontiers, open to competition and structured by a series of corrective policies of aid to less developed regions and promotional policies in the areas of research and industry.

The "four liberties" — the free movement of goods, persons, services, and capital — corresponded to Mrs. Thatcher's dearest wishes and explained her acceptance of the Single European Act, which, however, also fixed additional objectives and obligations: economic and monetary union, a social policy, political cooperation in the area of external relations, and security, all of which are part of an overall conception progressively leading toward European federation. These developments, as is demonstrated by the examples of the United States and Switzerland, require a minimum of central power and administrative means.

To a certain extent, Mrs. Thatcher actually rendered a service by criticizing what are undoubtedly sometimes excessive desires for Community regulation. But she confused the defense of national identity with opposition to a federal union. She put the brakes on the movement toward a European federal community, a dangerous thing to do at the very moment when explosive and promising changes in Eastern Europe called for joint action on the basis of a community of solidarity. Her persistence in "dogmatic opposition" made waves with her Conservative Party and contributed to her departure. Her attitude was not uninfluenced by the European turn taken by the Labour Party Congress. In spite of her resistance and criticism, the strengthening of the European Community seemed, to a growing number of even her own supporters, to be a necessity in the long term if not immediately.

Social and economic demands, international competition, and the sudden transformation of the socialist countries and world power relations all called for a strengthening of the Community's magnetic pole, a solid central core of a union and a new configuration of the whole of Europe. These arguments are all the more powerful in that it is evident that the argument in favor of national identity looks specious. In fact, few today believe, or hide behind the belief, that a European union will sound the death knell of national identity. As with the experience of the Swiss cantons, the principle that animates the process of formation of the European Community is union in diversity. The Union safeguards the national identities of France, Germany, the Netherlands, and Portugal. Even Belgium, whose national identity has been threatened from within by conflict between the Flemish and the Walloons, the European Union has helped to preserve national unity.[6] This is especially true to the extent that the direction of the Single European Act and the future of the European Community show a slow progression toward federal structures. Now the collective management of areas of sovereignty, which member states can no longer exercise on their own, not only does no harm to their national identities but actually seems to stimulate regional development. The regions are tending to assert themselves within the national and European framework, just as national identities show their diversity within the European Community. In spite of a certain fondness for centralization and standardization manifested in the early days of the integration process, decentralization and the roles of the states and the regions are irresistibly becoming the norm in the European Community. By conviction or necessity, the main leaders and actors on the European stage are drawing inspiration from the principles of federalism and looking to its particular methods. In fact, the majority practice federalism just as Moliere's M. Jourdain spoke prose. I am convinced that the principles, spirit, and methods of federalism are the best response to the complexity of European society, indeed, of all human societies, and to their needs for development.

A European Federation: Common Ground for Denis de Rougemont and Jean Monnet[7]

Denis de Rougemont and Jean Monnet are usually regarded as representing opposite points of view: de Rougemont, the federalist for whom the unity of European culture provided the foundation for a European federation, and Monnet, the functionalist who sought to build a union sector by sector, from coal and steel to the entire economy, with the final aim of building a political union. But underneath this artificial contrast can be discerned a similarity in the goals sought, a European federation or a United States of Europe.

In *Les Etats-Unis d'Europe ont commencé,* Jean Monnet makes the point on several occasions. The ECSC "shows the way for Europe of the future toward a pacific *federal Community* that will be wider and more prosperous and within which the European nations will pool their resources and capacities and thus live according to the rhythm of the modern world in *liberty* and *diversity*."[8] One of the fundamental principles of federalism is clearly expressed in this text, not as a concept but as a practical reality. The federal Community secures both an essential pooling of resources and the diversity of free nations. This central idea arises again further on:

> What is ultimately at stake is a reconciliation between the rights held by states and a common market in which their production and exchange take place. This fundamental problem will arise in any European structure that is not constituted as a unitary centralized state: if Europe manages to create the *federation* of which, according to the French government declaration of 9 May 1950, the Coal and Steel Community is to be the first stage, the concrete experiment we have set up will have paved the way for the solutions to the most difficult problems associated with a *federal* structure.

According to Monnet, this problem of a federal balance between shared power and the autonomy of member states was already beginning to be solved: "The birth of the Community has already shown that federal institutions can effectively unite the highly developed states of the twentieth century. . . . A federated Europe is essential for the security and peace of the free world." This goal is also to be found in Robert Schuman's declaration of 9 May 1950:

> The pooling of coal and steel production will immediately ensure the establishment of common foundations for economic development, the first stage of a *European federation,* and it will change the destiny of those areas that have for so many years been dedicated to the manufacturing of weapons of war, weapons of which they have at the same time repeatedly been the victims. By pooling basic production and establishing a new High Authority whose decision will be binding on France, Germany, and the countries who join them, this proposal will actually put in place the first concrete base for the *European federation* that is essential for the preservation of peace.

The difference between the two great Europeans does not relate to their objectives but to the ways they plan to achieve them. De Rougemont wanted to see a qualitative leap into a federal Europe while Monnet, a visionary as well as a federalist but also a man of action, was aware of the real obstacles to this direct global approach. In agreement with Robert Schuman, he proposed a progressive advance in stages and by sectors. This limited experiment was based on key sectors that at the time constituted two of the main levers for rebuilding the European economy. Moreover, these sectors related to the resources available to the two powers formerly at odds, with German coke and French ore, both of which are indispensable for producing steel. Hence, Monnet's initiative aimed to abolish borders and reconstitute the natural economic area in this Franco-German region. Since then, steel production techniques have been modified by the use of oil, but the de facto solidarity built on the two initial sectors has survived.

The success of this first joint experiment was the basis of Monnet's strategy: the demonstration of its effectiveness was to bring in other sectors and thus, by multiplying solidarity and institutional networks, lay the foundations for a European federation. Jean Monnet's approach was really quite close to Denis de Rougemont's and they only differed over the way to achieve their shared goals and the question of timing. Monnet's method was not based on abstract projects but on a concrete assessment of the chances of building a European federation in stages. A second difference between them relates to the content of such a federation. While de Rougemont set down the principles of federalism and formulated its main lines in the light of the

Swiss and American experiences, Monnet was mainly interested in the sort of concrete action that would proceed in the right direction if it took place against a federalist background. The differences between these two generally complementary attitudes are self-explanatory; one man was a writer who lived off his thinking and his writing, while the other was a man of action who lived by tangible concepts put to the test of effectiveness.

In spite of this convergence on their final goal, Jean Monnet was very cautious about *l'Europe des Régions,* one of Denis de Rougemont's most cherished ideas. Perhaps Monnet thought that in a European Community that was still fragile the centrifugal forces of regions and nations might put a brake on progress toward union or even block it. On the other hand, de Rougemont gambled enthusiastically on regions against nation-states. Admittedly, in his anxiety to communicate this message he exaggerated its importance, to the extent that he presented the nation-state as the main obstacle to a European federation. This somewhat Manichean approach was more a reflection of his determination to overcome this obstacle than a fundamental concept, more a means of struggle than a faithful reflection of his complex and creative federalist thought. The region is a living reality, a new area for activities and participation developing within states and fitting into the European complex. Every activity, every function, every reality must be able to find free expression in federal structures and processes. Rather than claiming that the nation-state represents the enemy to be destroyed, de Rougemont was really saying that state and nation each form a tier in the federal building. Indeed, according to his own principles, federalism is constructive, not destructive, and based on existing realities. We have to accept that states and nations exist however reluctant we may be to do so. So in his lectures, writings, and discussions with colleagues in the early 1980s de Rougemont adopted a new attitude; "I do not propose to destroy them; that would be impossible. I propose to go beyond them, above and beneath them, something that has only become possible in the twentieth century. To go above the nation-state means a continental *federation;* to go beneath it means the *regions.*" The Europe of Regions is a federal Europe of which the region is one of the dynamic foundations. His idea of a European senate of the regions is intended to ensure more direct participation by the regions, especially the German states and Spanish provinces, in the federal Community. It was within this federal European Community that the varied and multiple areas of participation were to be structured — region, state, European federation.

Thus, freed from the pressure of political circumstances and tactical considerations about timing, the fundamental ideas of these two great European minds meet and combine like two powerful currents, together creating and inspiring the powerful drive toward a European federation.

"If we could start over again, I would begin with culture." This remark is often quoted as Jean Monnet's, but I have not been able to find the source of it. It seals his reconciliation with Denis de Rougemont, for whom any federal union had to be based on the unity of European culture. They came by different routes to the same essential federalist principle, union in diversity. The inner correspondence between cultural pluralism and federalism is reflected in their ideas. The basis of European unity must be a *pluralist culture,* and such unity can only be embodied in a *federal union.* Such a union ensures that all kinds of different potentials develop against a common cultural background and in a structure built along federal lines.

Principles of Federalism According to Denis de Rougemont

Federalism is at one and the same time a spirit, an attitude toward others and society, a method, an approach to reality, and a style of social organization. It is not a rigid model that can be imposed on different societies but a continual quest for solutions, structures, and adequate processes on the basis of a few fundamental principles. It is a living method that works through progressive adjustments, respecting existing functions and bodies.

Beneath the tortuous paths of history, an underlying tendency toward freedom, increasing recognition of individuals and communities, and the constitution of new and wider unions may be perceived. In my 1954 thesis,[9] I borrowed Hegel's model of the evolution of the idea of right in order to give a simplified image of this federal process. Albeit a very oversimplified schema, this model remains useful for a general reading of the historical foundation of democracy and federalism. The constant element over the years is the degree of recognition of the intrinsic quality of persons. During the period of the Eastern Empire, only the tyrant had the quality of a person endowed with free will. Right emanated from this unique person, others being his objects or instruments, while the community was a notion of possession and typified the narrowest sphere of the quality of individuality or "personhood." In the Greek world, the quality of personhood was conferred on a larger number of individuals; recognition applied exclusively between Greeks; all others belonged to the sphere of objects or instruments. The Stoics opened the first breach by affirming equality between free men and slaves and by spreading the notion of the human being. In practice, the dominant principle retained the distinction between Greeks and all others. The Roman world maintained the subject-object, master-slave relationship while widening the base to include specific barbarians. The community rested on a distinction between *jus civile,* which regulated relations between Romans, and *jus gentium,* which covered relations between Romans and subject peoples. The community was built on the *principle of domination*. It was only with the advent of Christianity that the recognition of all human beings progressively spread until it became a universal fundamental principle. This principle of the recognition of individuals and communities of individuals is the foundation of liberty, democracy, and federalism.

Denis de Rougemont reached the same conclusion by a different route; the new notion of *person* as defined at the Council of Nicaea was the essential contribution of Christianity.[10] The ancient Greeks had established the notion of the individual. The Romans in their turn had forged the concept of the citizen. But the individual, like the Roman citizen, developed in a closed world where he or she was contrasted with barbarians and slaves, who constituted objects. Their relations were characterized by a fundamental inequality. By conversion or individual revolution, Christianity liberated every man, whether noble or slave, from the grip of this restrictive concept. It introduced the full recognition of the person, the "other," as a subject and no longer an object and extended it to any human being considered a fully dignified person. The free and responsible man aiming to achieve his own ends is recognized as such within the community in which he was called to develop. This was also the foundation for constructing the notions of the couple, the family, and federalism as de Rougemont viewed them.

In an attempt to clarify and conceptualize, a procedure alien to Jean Monnet's pragmatic approach, Denis de Rougemont set out the principles and virtues of federalism.[11] In the first place, it involves renouncing hegemony and the *esprit de système*. Federalism means combining heterogeneous elements; it does not recognize minorities as a problem, and safeguarding the particular characteristics of each minority is as much the aim of a federation as is preserving the particular characteristics of federated nations or states or regions. Moreover, federalism is built on a love of complexity; it is the opposite of totalitarian simplification or standardization imposed by a central power. A federation is formed gradually through persons and groups. It is born and grows in a space of liberty, democracy, and pluralism; in the midst of a multiplicity of ideas, cultures, parties, and regions; and in a complex and diversified social fabric. The pattern of federalism is a movement that flows upward; it develops from the base up and is not imposed from above, unlike decentralization, a term de Rougemont did not like to use. Like the region itself, federalism is natural and functional and does not result from artificial constraint.

This picture of the principles of federalism may be completed by referring to its characteristic virtues, like the republican virtues defined in Montesquieu's *The Spirit of Laws*. Among them, we find not only respect for reality, especially for regional realities, but also respect for the small in contrast with the centralized state's veneration for the large. Another virtue is tolerance, the acceptance of the otherness of others, the recognition of the personhood of the other, a virtue that ensures that each can develop in his or her own way. The principles and virtues of federalism are just such key ideas projected onto the level of society under the form of federalism.

Toward the end of his life two elements were at the center of Denis de Rougemont's preoccupations: *the principle of subsidiarity* and *the idea of the regions*. Frequently quoting a remark about the United States made by the American diplomat Daniel Moynihan, he put subsidiarity into European terms: "Never ask a large unit to do what can be done in a smaller one. What the family can do must not be done by the town council. What the town council can do must not be done by states. And what states can do must not be done by the federal government." The same principle is applicable to a federated Europe; it must only take on tasks that exceed the capacities of European states on their own. The powers of a commune, a region, a state, or a European federation must be defined according to the size of the tasks to be done. For each different level, there are corresponding autonomous powers. As the size and fields of the tasks grow — transport, energy, jobs, inflation, defense — the decision-making level rises until it becomes continental or global.

By virtue of the principle of subsidiarity or the notion of *exact adequation* put forward by Guy Héraud, each authority and level must receive or possess the power to resolve questions that either by their very *nature* or their *dimensions* can most efficiently and effectively be resolved at that level.[12] Arguing that the principle of subsidiarity is essentially a way of defending autonomy on the basis of the idea that a federation is built from the base upward, Guy Héraud replaced it with the idea of exact adequation corresponding to the union process, that is, to the case where a federation is to be built. In reality, the European federation is being built simultaneously from the bottom up, through transfers from member states to the Community, and from the top down, from Community institutions to member states, regions, and communes.

The *principle of subsidiarity* applies as much to public regional interests as to private bodies. It leads to the state being freed from its overload of work in favor of the European federation but also in favor of regions, communes, or the private sector (i.e., privatization). It leads to an attempt to discover at what level or by what private or public authority a given function is most efficiently to be fulfilled in terms of available resources and capacities. Consequently, when existing levels do not offer sufficient means there is a place for a *pooling* of resources and capacities, for example, at the European Union level. This process of adaptation and union fits in with the federalist method to the extent that it applies the principle of subsidiarity and abandons any attempt to proceed via undifferentiated centralization. That is why, having been explicitly included in the 1984 European Parliament Union Plan, it was picked up again by the Delors Committee Report on an economic and monetary union, which recommends a federal approach and union. Likewise, the principle of subsidiarity is widely applied both in the Single European Act and in research and development programs. The latter have the peculiarity of applying it within the framework of collaboration between public regional interests and private enterprise. The principle of subsidiarity also underlies European Union directives insofar as they are binding in the common objectives they set out while leaving the choice of adequate means up to member states. Thus, they make it possible for means of execution to be better adapted to the particular conditions of member states.

Overall, this principle guaranteeing adequate autonomy and the responsibility of member states or regions (states, cantons, or provinces) is complemented by the *principle of participation.* The decision-making level rises with the growing importance of tasks corresponding to the various areas of participation. In federations, participation has a double or indeed multiple nature: the participation of all the people through their representation within a *parliament* and the participation of member states or regional interests through a *senate* or chamber of states. As for the regions, they can establish electoral constituencies in a chamber of the people or they can be associated with the decision-making process within the federation through member states or representatives sitting in the senate or with the help of other forms of participation.

Thus regions, areas of civic participation comprising groups of communes (according to Denis de Rougemont), are a level of activity where citizens can take their common affairs in hand. Pillars of the European federation, they form a new level between communes, member states, and the Community. They thus weave a new network of multiple and diverse solidarity. The various formulas and structures already existing or still to be found can ensure that the regions participate in Community processes. Thus, in Germany the Länder are demanding more direct participation in the decision-making process at the national and Community levels; accordingly, they are setting up representation in Brussels.

The federalist method requires that rigid prefabricated formulas or dogmatic prohibitions be avoided and that the ongoing search for adequate and flexible solutions in a federalist spirit be accepted while respecting fundamental principles and the demands of reality.

Federalism in the Age of Upside-Down Pyramids and
Microcomputers: Neofederalism

A dynamic alignment based on the principles of federalism and the flexible and creative formulas that follow from it means that the federalist approach, which looks to the future, has not merely succeeded in adapting to change but has actually stimulated it. There is nothing surprising, then, about the fact that the federalist approach enters the field of economic activity and guides management with the support of microcomputer networks.

In suggesting that the pyramid should be turned on end, Jan Carlzon adopted a federalist approach to the restructuring and reinvigoration of Scandinavian Airlines (SAS).[13] He did not specifically recommend the federalist approach but argued that energies should be liberated within the company he leads by removing the imprisoning vertical or pyramidal structure and replacing it with an organization more in tune with a horizontally structured society and modern man. It is an essential element in the West and in business, and people feel a genuine need to take on responsibilities, to take part in the common enterprise, and to be governed by a legitimate authority. The hierarchical and pyramidal structure of the state and company organization stands in the way of such aspirations. Hence, there is a need to turn the pyramid upside down before it freezes whole areas of Western society. Carlzon claims that by upending the SAS pyramid he managed to reinvigorate the company.

In the firm with a pyramidal structure, even unimportant decisions are referred to the top. This excessive centralization overburdens management and deprives responsibility both to management and to the rank and file. In the horizontal model, the division of roles is different. Top management formulates overall direction, company objectives, and general strategy. Such decisions are guidelines that merely indicate a general policy and do not lay down particular measures with regard to its implementation. On this point, they are surprisingly similar to Community directives and the way they are used to create an economic area without borders.

Thus, the pyramid is flattened and vertical departments stripped of their partitions and reorganized according to a decentralization that is oriented according to objectives. This new organization is led not by someone who imposes his will but by someone who seeks to convince the staff and persuade them of an overall vision and collective project. The aim is to share this overall vision with everyone, so that in taking on the responsibilities with which he or she is entrusted each one works toward common objectives. This assumes a wide diffusion of information about objectives and a balancing *commitment* from the staff. Good communication involving both the provision of information and dialogue is an essential prerequisite if the right balance in the division of powers is to be found. Objectives have to be properly understood so that the overall vision is shared and each person's role in the company clarified, while above all each member of the community or company must be associated with the common determination to achieve these objectives. This is political action as defined by Bertrand de Jouvenel, the sum of combined forces.

Carlzon's argument is not for company democracy that involves popular choice or self-management. In his view, a business strategy is not something that can be chosen by universal suffrage; while each must have the chance to put forward his point of view, all do not take part in fundamental decision making. The "leader" — not the "chief" — sets out a strategy for the company after consultations and creates the conditions for the company's operation. Like a conductor of an orchestra, he or she views the whole apart from the details while leaving employees free to assume responsibility in their own areas of activity, which fits in with a coherent vision. Hence, there is a need for a clear definition of company objectives and strategies.

Although Carlzon is talking about companies, the approach he uses and the guidelines he suggests are strongly reminiscent of the federalist perspective even though he does not use the term. In his last chapter, on "the new man and politics," he concludes: "What we need now is a new strategy, which, starting from contemporary social reality, shows the way to the kind of future that most people can recognize as progress." Then he stresses the lack of vision in political programs: "Politics lacks either a fundamental ideology or a vision of the future."

These reflections anticipate the criticism made by Mr. Darmon, the U.S. budget director, of the main actors in American society as being obsessed with the conditions of the moment and lacking long-term vision. This general criticism is echoed in the interpretation of the power structure of American business put forward by Jan Carlzon: "A lot of people think that the United States is the most democratic country in the world, but in fact the truth is that it is in the U.S. that we find the most authoritarian concept of the role of the leader in the Western world." This remark is a commentary on the rigidity of structures in American companies and on the strange marriage between federal political power and the authoritarian power of business. Power structures in the Swiss business world could be analyzed just as pertinently in the light of Carlzon's commentary.

In his conclusion Carlzon finishes with remarks of a general political significance: "The politician must have the same qualities [as those of the leader in a company]: to be able to lead human beings in an ambitious strategy that develops them, by sharing an ideology that the majority can identify with." In the end, New Man is a social fact that cannot be avoided.

The social pyramid is going to be flattened, and the barriers that were encouraged by corporate attitudes will be removed. A new type of solidarity might well leave the politicians high and dry with their old-fashioned ideas. The political world must take account of the deep aspirations of the New Man, keen to share information and understand the choices that are available. He wants to be actively associated with the life of the city and building the future. The best synthesis I know is to be found in the story of the two stonemasons. Both are cutting a granite block. Asked what they are doing, the first replies in exasperation: "Isn't it obvious? I am making a right-angled cut in a granite block." The other adds enthusiastically: "I'm involved in the construction of a cathedral."

This trend toward a federalism that goes beyond the political domain and into the economy, even extending to the management of companies, is paralleled by developments in information technology. At the start of the computer era came the reign of the giant computers of macrocomputing. The result was a strengthening of huge corporations able to afford such giant machines and pay for their operation. This phase reinforced the centralizing trend by imposing a range of constraints that, according to Joël de Rosnay, reflects a particular form of power.[14] Uniform and specialized language, uniform equipment, and intolerance toward differentiated and decentralized solutions were factors that contributed to a marked centralization of power and control that extended even to marginal activities. This led to a proliferation of vast, centralized, pyramidal organizations.

The emergence of the microcomputer reversed the trend by making it possible to develop horizontal organizations that could to a large extent replace vertical structures. Now, computerization of companies and management offers an opportunity to replace a pyramidal organization with one made up of networks. The expansion of networks is tending to transform company organization. Joël de Rosnay notes that traditionally the diffusion of information took place from the top down in the context of a hierarchical, pyramidal structure. Today, thanks to the constitution of networks, we see the emergence of shared horizontal information, information that begins to flow toward the decision-making centers. We are moving from a logic of energy, exclusive and leading to centralized hierarchical systems, to a logic of information based, like biological systems, on complementarity, synergy, and interdependence. According to de Rosnay, the proliferation of personal computers is accelerating and accentuating this trend. Requiring only limited investment, it gives independent responsibility to the users and allows multiple interfaces with local networks. New forms of organization are appearing that give responsibility to individuals based on their contributions and participation.

The convergence of Jan Carlzon's conclusions with those of Joël de

Rosnay is striking. Both focus on companies, one from the point of view of management and the other from that of microcomputers. Both note that the organization of companies is evolving away from centralized pyramidal forms and toward horizontal participative forms that involve shared responsibility. The assertion that "we must turn the pyramid upside down" is both an observable trend and a recognized necessity within firms and society itself.

These two approaches, the one based on the experience of a manager and the other on the experience of a researcher, a user of microcomputers, converge on a common conclusion: new types of relations are spreading throughout society, and microcomputers are making the formation of multiple communication networks and autonomous interconnected subensembles possible. In this new milieu, New Men, new communities, and a new division of powers are developing. These new forms of organization, communication, and power can be found at different levels within society, local, regional, national, European, and international. Thanks to telematics, various modes of transmission and exchange, and even of continuous dialogue, relationships are both autonomous within various networks, horizontal, and at the same time integrated into wider communities. Autonomy and responsibility are developing at a number of levels and in complex communications networks.

Two of Denis de Rougemont's premonitory intuitions are worth remembering:

"Federalism is based on the love of complexity."
"Federalism equals regional autonomy."

I would add the involvement of regions and computers, in particular, microcomputers.

There are several consequences of this for federalism.

The exercise of autonomous powers at the commune, region, state, and European Community levels and their effective grouping into ensembles whose flexibility and efficacy make them respond the most appropriately to needs and aspirations.

More effective participation by citizens and by different organizations and communities in decision making and in the functioning of the political community. Will microcomputers tend to open the way for a certain form of direct participation or direct democracy? At the present time, we can see that new communication and exchange technologies will enable a flow and a continuous dialogue between the Community center and federated centers whether national or regional.[15]

Protection for complex diversities, a quest for dynamic equilibria between base units and the global community facilitating the two-way flow—bottom up, top down—necessary preconditions for the good operation of a federation using horizontal and vertical communications networks.

A further extension of the federal approach, already spreading in the organization of political societies and tending to penetrate economic organizations, both public and private, as autonomy and general involvement of members and services develop within the framework of overall objectives defined by a leader or management. The definition of the common direction is based on information coming from members and units within the company and on an analysis of the context and a vision of the future. In fact, the present trend seems to come close to Alexandre Marc's idea of integral federalism.

These different signs and this convergence of experiences and technologies are part of an evolution that is creating an explosion of diversities and autonomies, enabling them to integrate more harmoniously and participate more effectively in a complex European Community. At the same time, this evolution creates the possibility of various combinations of integration and cooperation organized around different political and economic focuses of development. A cohesive Europe thus has several concentric circles—or, more exactly, several networks—whose main core and development engine are formed by the European Community. It is not surprising, therefore, that hand in hand with these various new federalist tendencies there is a more marked federal direction in the European Community.

The Federal Stamp on the European Community

Sectoral Federalism

The European Community has started down the road to federalism. Although it is only a partial and incomplete federation, the European Community is strengthening its federative features as it develops, something that the Single European Act makes very clear. However, if the Community is seeking forms of participation for the regions at the Community level, the sometimes rather excessive autonomy of the member states, and their sometimes rather cumbersome participation, currently tend to prevent European union rather than contribute to it. The problem here is the opposite of that which surfaces in certain federal states where autonomy has to be safeguarded from the grasp and encroachment of the central state. The problem is that the institutional embryo of the European Community encounters difficulties when it wants to assert its autonomous power in relation to the member states, several of which are old European nations. When we speak of the centralizing ambitions of Brussels, it is worth remembering that this emerging power is much less solid and powerful than the central power in several federal states, in particular the Helvetic Confederation. In the early days of the European Community, there was a legitimate fear of certain centralizing ambitions, inspired preponderantly by France (standardization, the use of regulations). In the meantime, France and the Community have both evolved toward greater differentiation and regionalization. The new direction of Community action, set out and confirmed by the Single European Act, is proof that the European Community is searching for a new form or structure of powers. Far from moving toward a single federalist model — federalism offers numerous "models" — the Community is looking for an original form of organization that is both adequate and dynamic: adequate in respect to the requirements and trends of reality and the new forms of power, dynamic as it looks forward to the future and in its flexibility and its ability to adapt rapidly through its federative structures and processes. It is true that, although the term *federalism* sometimes crops up in the speeches of the former EU president Jacques Delors, it has not been officially sanctioned in the European Community. Nonetheless, just as Molière's M. Jourdain spoke prose, the European Community practices federalism in many areas of its activity without using the term or even knowing it is doing so.

Unlike a federal state, the European Community is not responsible for a shared defense, nor is there a European army or a European police force. As regards foreign policy, it has only a few embryonic elements, such as a common commercial policy, including certain powers of negotiation or its aid and development policy, which is in any case concurrent with those of member states. The European Council is nonetheless on the way to formulating common positions with respect to global issues or those of Eastern Europe. In the economic sphere before the Maastricht Treaty, the Community's powers were limited, as can be seen by the lack of common economic or monetary policy, of which the European Monetary System was the beginning. In 1990, the Delors Committee set out the stages of economic and monetary union, involving a system of central banks, a European Central Bank, and a single currency. The substance of the committee's proposals was embodied in the Maastricht Treaty.

Even in sectors that are actually a part of its area of action or jurisdiction, European Community powers are often limited, although such restrictions have not prevented certain irritatingly pedantic rulings from being adopted abusively. Overall, we are a long way from a federation like the Helvetic Confederation and even further away from "centralized power."

European Community powers are limited and are exercised primarily in the form of regulations and initiatives and, more rarely, in matters of common policy (e.g., the Common Agricultural Policy [CAP]) or the management of Community funds. Furthermore, in carrying out its regulative tasks the European Community often uses *directives,* which are binding as to the object they define but leave member states free to choose the appropriate means.

The area without borders is being built by means of about three hundred directives. When the European Community imposes general regulations, "Community laws" that are directly executory according to a technique very common in federal systems, it entrusts their execution to the member states, as does the Swiss Confederation. These few examples confirm that the European Community has a hybrid form, with limited though real powers in socioeconomic and technical matters, powers that are incomparably more limited than those of a federal state. But the European Community is still developing: it is getting bigger, having gone from six to nine then from ten to twelve, then twelve to fifteen members in 1995, and is now preparing for further admissions; and it is getting deeper, strengthening its activities and extending them to areas like the environment, regions, and research.

Finally, it has been given an outline of a political union. This evolution was confirmed by the Single European Act and has been crowned by an economic and monetary union and political union as embodied in the Maastricht and Amsterdam Treaties.

A Hybrid Institutional System (ESA)

Classic categories are inadequate to enable us to grasp the reality of the Community system, which, from a traditional perspective, looks like a mixture of heterogeneous elements. Confederal elements stand side by side with federal and international features, while the whole fits into an assembly of combined interlocking powers. While the European Council and the Council of Ministers, institutions as well as Community institutions, are similar to confederal conferences, the Commission itself is a new type of institution that looks like a future executive organ. For the time being, it can exercise only the limited "governmental" power attributed to it by the Council of Ministers and the European Council. In this respect, as in the carrying out of normative tasks, the Commission-Council tandem functions according to the general rule that the Commission proposes and the Council adopts in consultation or cooperation with the European Parliament. Unlike national systems, the Parliament is a long way from exercising full legislative functions in the European Community, and yet since its election in 1979 it has represented the European "people," more precisely, the European peoples of the Community. From this point of view, it is close to a chamber of representatives of the people, while the Council, the main decision-making organ where each member state has a seat, prefigures a chamber of the states. As for the government of the European Community, it is difficult to find an institutional seat for it, as governmental functions, still fragmentary but in the process of developing, are shared between the Commission, the Council, and the European Council. However, it is the European Council that, with the help of the Commission and the Council of Ministers, holds most of the power when it comes to issues with strong political overtones or that are fundamentally political.

In the socioeconomic domain, the European Community may be seen as a complex union whose active power is based on a Commission, a collegial institution with seventeen members, which became twenty in the enlargement of 1995 (reminiscent of the Swiss Federal Council, a stable executive elected by Parliament but not responsible to it), and a Council that is a prototype Council of States, which as an expression of member governments exercises certain executive functions and is the ultimate legislator. It is an open question as to how this institutional complex is going to evolve. Since the Single European Act, the European Community seems to have been moving in the direction of decentralized solutions. Even in the area of legislation, the concept of common uniform rules is tending to give way to a concept of harmonization and decentralization, the objective being to remove the obstacles to free movement and thus create "a European area without borders" while building an environment that allows the activities of economic and social agents to develop favorably.

Alongside the principle of *double participation* by the member states and by the people is the principle of *union in diversity.* Thus, we read in the introduction to the *General Report* of the European Community for 1988 that "Interdependence between the European countries imposes its own logic of cooperation in the face of divergent interests; it leads to an acceptance of diversity while recognizing differences and helps the twelve to live together."

Jacques Delors emphasized this same idea:

> There is no cause for any anxiety that national particularities might disappear any more than that specifically regional features might be eliminated. It is true that to give Europeans a feeling of belonging to a single body governments have decided to establish a number of elements of a Europe of citizens, a European passport, student exchanges, sporting and cultural events. But nothing in all that shows any sign of a desire for standardization. After all, each country is free to cultivate the heritage of its own history, traditions, customs, and peculiarities. Our Europe will be united only in diversity.[16]

Two innovations set out in the Single European Act are a proof of this, the use of *directives* and the rule of *mutual recognition.* In fact, the implementation of the internal market is based on a web of about three hundred directives that are binding as to the objectives they define while leaving the means up to the member states. In the same spirit, while making due allowances for real diversities and difficulties, the goal of harmonizing national legislation and the practice of issuing uniform regulations is giving way in many places to the principle of mutual recognition. Thus, a diploma or regulated product in one member state will be recognized automatically in the others. These different forms of Community instruments and actions move toward a generalized though sometimes imperfect application of a fundamental principle of federalism, the *principle of subsidiarity.* For example, the European Council of June 1989 stated in its final resolution that the Delors Report was completely faithful to its mandate. It held that the building of an economic and monetary union must take account of the correlation between economic and monetary aspects, respect the principle of subsidiarity, and reflect the diversity of specific situations. Similarly, the final stage provides for the full operation of a European System of Central Banks (ESCB) on a *federal basis* and a European Central Bank, a wholly *autonomous* Community institution responsible for the formulation and implementation of the common monetary policy. Furthermore, in this *federative* type of structure the national central banks will be responsible for carrying out operations in conformity with decisions taken by the ESCB Council. As for the ecu (now the Euro), the report announces that it has the necessary potential to become a real common currency after a transition period during which it will act as a parallel currency. This is the final objective put forward by the Delors Report.[17] This project clearly reproduces the structure of the American Federal Reserve (FED) and is inspired by the example of the Bundesbank. Such a step toward autonomous subsystems and institutions is close to Denis de Rougemont's idea of *European agencies.* It was in this spirit, for example, that the Commission recommended creation of an *autonomous environmental agency* within the Community system.

There is also the principle of *differentiation* in the form of the variety of Community sectoral and regional interests. Consultation between socioeconomic groups organized at Community level is one of the main elements of this process, allowing the Commission to gather the opinions of Community groups and assess the level of their support. It is not surprising, therefore, that about six hundred Community organizations form a dense web of communications and relations around the Commission. Likewise, with regard to *regions,* regional policy supported by the work of the Regional Development Fund ensures that the *European regions* are not left out of the overall Community. The recent creation of a Consultative Committee for the Regions brings them into the decision-making process and strengthens regional structures while opening up new opportunities for the expression of regional and minority differences within the European Community.

The principle of the protection of minor communities is more specifically embodied in the overrepresentation of small and medium-sized states in Community institutions and processes. The small and medium-sized states each have one member on the Commission compared to two members for each of the five large nations. In the Council, each member state has one representative, and the small and medium-sized states are highly privileged in the weighting of votes when a qualified majority of 54 votes out of 76 is required (Luxembourg = 2; Denmark and Ireland = 2 times 3; Belgium, Greece, Portugal, and Holland = 4 times 5; Spain = 1 times 8; and France, Italy, Germany, and the United Kingdom = 4 times 10). This weighting prevents excessive dominance by the large nations, which cannot impose their will on the Community even by acting in concert. To obtain a qualified majority, they need the support of several small and medium-sized members. The influence of the small and medium-sized states is strengthened when unanimity is required for certain fundamental decisions (e.g., the Economic and Monetary Union and the harmonization of tax systems).

The European Parliament also includes the strong representation of small and medium-sized states in relation to their population in millions: Luxembourg (0.36) = 6; Ireland (3.5) = 15; Denmark (5.0) = 16; Greece, Portugal, and Belgium (10.0) = 3 times 24; and Holland (14.5) = 25.0; compared with Spain (38.5) = 60; and France, Italy, Germany, and the United Kingdom (55.0 to 61.0 or 80.0) = 4 times 81 (for a total of 518 Euro-MPs). Each member state has a judge on the Court, and both the Economic and Social Committee and the Committee of the Regions contain strong representations of counselors for the small and medium-sized states.

The Community system also involves a remarkable *balance* between the large member states, none of which can hold a dominant position permanently, while their influence is counterbalanced by the small and medium-sized countries that create more or less stable subgroupings like the three Benelux countries. This balance is strengthened all the more in that, despite the Community's dependence on the energetic leadership of France and Germany and on the action of the Commission, of which the small and medium-sized states are the most loyal defenders, there are no permanent coalitions. The Commission preserves a general equilibrium by seeking to identify the Community interest, all the more so in that its proposals cannot be amended other than by a unanimous vote of Council members. Hence, paradoxically, unanimity protects and reinforces its proposals and its negotiating strength.

This handful of federative features in the European Community is reflected by the growth, still insufficient but real nonetheless, of a democratic basis. The European Parliament is increasingly involved for several reasons: its direct election, its increasing grip on the Community budget, its cooperation in the legislative process in the framework of the Single European Act, and its power of codecision as laid down by the Maastricht Treaty, recently reinforced by the Amsterdam Treaty. As its role grows, the political parties are tending to take a more active part in the union process. Initially limited to the activity of their parliamentary groups in the European Parliament, the parties belonging to the three large European political families (Socialist, Christian-Democrat, and Liberal) have formed federations. Although still only embryonic, these federations have several characteristics in common with the Swiss parties, which are established around their members in the cantons, where their main activities are conducted. Whether labeled as Community or federal, what is expressed within unions of parties is actually national or cantonal diversity.

Federalist or Regionalist Evolution in Member States

The countries of the European Community are in general evolving forms of organization that are at least more regional or decentralized if not actually or potentially federative. The general trend is no longer toward a strengthening of national central authority but toward the development of the potential of the regions.

By virtue of its power, structure, and federal experience, Germany has had a central role in the evolution of the European Community. It exerts its influence toward federalism, not only reinforcing the tendencies outlined above and proving (if proof were needed) the effectiveness of the federalist approach and organization but also giving its backing to the implementation of the subsidiarity principle. It also sets an example of the principle's application; when the Single European Act was ratified, the Länder codified their participation in the Community process as an agreement with the federal government. While asserting their powers at the national level, they have established representation at the European Community in Brussels in order to have a direct voice at the Community level. Moreover, regionalization and federation are gradually advancing within the Community member states. In fact, another member state has moved in its own inimitable manner toward a federal structure; having avoided breaking apart, Belgium has given its support to the "federal party" within the European Community. After the 1995 enlargement, a third member state, Austria, joined the "federal party."

The regional policy of the European Community has been supported and supplemented by the regionalization undertaken by several member states. Thus, over the years Italy has seen its regions, particularly its four autonomous regions, grow more independent, to the point of becoming real political and economic powers. More recently, the automous communities in Spain have begun to develop rapidly and are now political powers and centers of economic and cultural development. Other member states have also set out on the road toward regionalization. Even France, the very example of a centralized state, has given in to this trend and is evolving toward a regionalization that is ceasing to be purely economic and is becoming more and more political. Since 1997, devolution has been progressing in the United Kingdom. There are many signs of a slow march toward federalism, a federalism henceforth to be built on member states and regions. Within the European Community, we see Denis de Rougemont's *Europe of the Regions* emerging, including simultaneous parallel movements, the one aiming to create a *European federation* and the other to develop *the potential of the regions* and the wealth of local resources within the European Community and its member states. This is how the principle of subsidiarity is embodied at different levels in the European Union.

The Future Is an Open Door

The application of federalist principles makes it possible to avoid numerous *conflicts* by softening the impact of clashes and preventing antagonisms from concentrating in the center. In centralized political communities, even those with local or regional sources, conflicts, disputes, and coups automatically come back to the central power, the only one with decision-making capacity. Contrast this with a federal system, where stresses and troubles may find local or regional solutions to the extent that different levels of authority have their own power to arbitrate in conflicts or to respond to fresh demands. Hence, in France the events of May 1968 were centered on Paris and it was mainly government spokesmen who dealt with the protesters; violent protest movements in Zurich were handled by the cantonal authorities and therefore only marginally affected the confederation as a whole.

The variety of situations and needs of federalist practices encourages people to search for *consensus,* to compromise or harmonize positions, and also to favor the policies best adapted to particular conditions instead of hankering after uniformly rigid measures. From this point of view, thanks to its flexibility, federalism is better equipped to manage the technological revolution. The current attitude of the European Community is also going in this direction. The rules of differentiation and mutual recognition, like the use of directives and the principle of subsidiarity, confirm this. A growth in tolerance and mutual understanding, a particular concern for small and medium-sized member states, and the involvement of the regions and a large number of groups are all helping to strengthen the same general trends. This is especially so in that as federalism is being built at the highest level of the European edifice it is also penetrating the structures of those member states that are either federal or quasi federal (Germany, Belgium, Austria, and Spain), regionalized (Italy), or on the way to regionalization (France). The federalist approach and principles are spreading through most of the member states, penetrating their economies and businesses and gradually transforming even their societies. Moreover, federalism as an approach, a method, and mode of organization is supported and encouraged by the spread of microcomputers and communications networks. In fact, its flexibility and adaptability make federalism a highly effective response to postindustrial society's multiple requirements and to the needs of modern man in the postnational era.

Federalism does not attempt to impose one fixed model but suggests an ensemble of principles and experience articulated within "a union in diversity." The federal Union brings together interest groups and forces while encouraging local, regional, and national potential to develop, which it then directs toward common objectives. It thus allows autonomous and diversified groups to develop while ensuring that they participate in achieving shared ambitions and goals within dynamic ensembles. This method, generating a variety of synergies with common aims, is also becoming prevalent in business and human resource management. We are witnessing the creation and multiplication of numerous horizontal communication and participation networks that counterbalance the vertical relationships represented by the centralized state. The state, only one stage in a chain of communities and associations, is now striving to rediscover its true role, an important one, of course, which is somewhere between the regions and a community of states like the European Community. The idea of a supreme state, sovereign and independent, is losing ground to the reality and experience of shared powers exercised in common in a Community marked by solidarity, interdependence, and federalism. Groups of states now tend to assume joint responsibility for their security and to coordinate their foreign policies and their economic, social, and democratic development. In this configuration, the state avoids being overloaded by exercising certain functions in partnership within the European Community and by handing over other tasks to the regions. And, yet, at the same time its role as policeman, interventionist, or provider is evolving and broadening as it also provides drive, stimulus, support, and coordination. Lacking public power, the European Community, more than the traditional state, has developed and highlighted this function as a *motor and innovator* in response to the double need for union and innovation. This new function is embodied in exemplary fashion in the scientific and technological research programs in which the Community takes an enabling, supporting, and coordinating role among the various participants: states, public interest groups, universities and research institutes, and public and private sector businesses. Comett, Esprit, and numerous other programs illustrate this point, creating a new triangular synergy between public and private sectors and universities. The same principle of *mutual support* is (at a different level) behind the science and technology parks. Thus, the federalist approach, combining flexibility, autonomy, and participation in the pursuit of common objectives, is finding an increasingly rich and extensive application at many different levels.

A common aim adapted to shared medium- or long-term objectives inspires this process, a process that guarantees the free collaboration of men and communities. This is the strength of the *European project* and its components, as compared to what Richard Darmon calls "cultural now-nowism" or obsession with the present and the conditions of the moment, which currently involve overwhelmingly American values. This abuse of the present at the expense of the future and this lack of longer term vision contain the seeds of decline. Darmon's recommendations are similar to Community programs and the 1993 objectives. The 1993 deadline was Jacques Delors's "Columbus's egg." After a prolonged period of stagnation, this "ardent obligation," which emerged from the consensus of member states and was embodied in the Single European Act, gave a new impulse to the union process, crowned by the European Union created by the Maastricht Treaty and strengthened by the Amsterdam Treaty.

The pace of the union process speeded up as the 1993 deadline approached and under the pressure of external and internal factors. Preparations, restructuring, and regrouping are in full flood in the European Community countries and neighboring states and among its economic partners. Eurobarometers show the extent of the 1993 effect and its echo in public opinion. External pressures are reinforcing this movement by acting as powerful stimulants; in addition to the pressure of American competition, and even more that of the Japanese, there has been significant transformation in Eastern Europe.

Two readings of the phenomenon have been given, one by President Mitterrand and one by Mrs. Thatcher; the former is to be preferred. In President Mitterrand's view, there is only one possible response to the mad dash to reform and democratization in the socialist countries and to the destabilization of communist systems in Europe: to speed up the union process and coordinate common action in favor of socialist countries in the process of democratization. Furthermore, German reunification and more recently the Gulf crisis have demonstrated the urgent need for the European Community to acquire adequate powers in the areas of foreign relations and security. A dynamic and united Community will be required to form the core of a larger, multifaceted Europe under the banner of democracy and federalism.

Chapter 8

The Maastricht Treaty: The Deepening of the European Community (1993)

A Federal Union

Forty years of economic integration have opened the way for political integration. The pooling of resources, the management of the Customs Union, common institutions and policies, the political significance of economic decisions, and the political importance of trade and external economic relations all show that the European Community has acquired a political dimension. As yet, no political union has been created, but the foundations have been progressively laid and structures built for such a union as the practice of working together has gradually become institutionalized. The internal market completed by the Single European Act is now in harness with its natural companion, the Economic and Monetary Union. Similarly, establishing an area without borders has created a need for a minimum of internal policy instruments, and the free movement of persons, for example, has encouraged member states to cooperate more systematically in the domains of justice and internal affairs. New needs have created the need for new tasks, which have in turn brought about institutional innovation.

One aspect of the space without frontiers relates to the issue of the entry and freedom of movement of emigrants from countries outside the European Union, that is, immigration and asylum policy. A second aspect covers judicial cooperation, and a third relates to the fight against terrorism, drugs, and international crime together with the cooperation of police forces and the creation of the European Police Office (Europol).

Some of these issues have implications for the sensitive question of national sovereignty. The supply of visas, conditions of residence, and immigration and asylum policy are elements of the internal politics of member states. They are also questions that concern the public. According to a poll taken in the spring of 1991, there is a widespread feeling that there are too many immigrants — around 50 percent of those questioned were of this opinion.[1] In countries with a high proportion of immigrants (Germany, Belgium,

216

France, and the United Kingdom), over half of those polled felt this way. As regards taking in immigrants and asylum seekers, three people out of five (slightly fewer for asylum seekers) were in favor of restrictions, with a third of those polled wishing them to be extended in the future. Intolerance, outright xenophobia, and racial violence are at the heart of extremist movements and parties, which also arouse and exacerbate such phenomena by their speeches and policies. These internal political problems are now taking on a European dimension and calling for organized cooperation. Such cooperation, to supplement and coordinate the actions of national governments, involves respect for human rights and fundamental liberties.

Political cooperation operates in a predominantly intergovernmental way that differs from the Community approach. On this issue, Community institutions like the Commission and the European Parliament have a back room role, while the main work falls to the Council assisted by a Coordinating Committee. Although for issues of internal politics, the decision-making process is similar to the corresponding mechanisms relating to external policy and common security. It differs from them, however, by the following features: the absence of the European Council (even though the latter will certainly be the guiding inspiration behind major decisions); the role of the Coordinating Committee, which is composed of senior Interior Ministry officials and other ministers as appropriate; and the role of the Commission, which does not have the right to take decisions on judicial cooperation over penal issues, cooperation among police forces, or, surprisingly, customs cooperation (art. 31 (ex K.3 par. 2)), even though it is fully associated with the work of the Coordinating Committee. The effects of this new cooperation on national administrations, which have been kept on the margins of integration up to now, suggest that adaptations, or indeed new structures, within interior and justice ministries will occur along with an enlargement of the Eurosphere.

A Qualitative Leap or Just Another Phase?

At the European Council in Maastricht on 9 and 10 December 1991, the European Community crossed the threshold of political integration. It committed itself to a process involving the shared exercise of the essential attributes of national sovereignty, namely, foreign and security policy, shared defense, economic union, a single currency, European citizenship, and criminal and domestic affairs. These areas of action are considered political par excellence and fall under the exclusive jurisdiction of the federal authority in Switzerland, Germany, and the United States. In line with the approach set out by Jean Monnet, the European Council in Maastricht established objectives, settled deadlines, and parceled out tasks among the institutions of the Community. Like General de Gaulle's Fouchet Project, it included a revision clause calling for an intergovernmental conference to be held in 1996 to consider the consolidation of the Union. In other words, the impetus given by Maastricht and the fundamental decisions taken there are more a beginning than an end, hence the difficulty of assimilating all its implications at the present time. For, although this is a "Pascalian wager," the real significance of it will not be clear until there is a fund of shared experience and the members' cohesion has been put to the test.

It is natural, therefore, that opinions on the importance of Maastricht and its interpretations should fall into two extreme categories; some hold that there has been a significant qualitative leap forward, others that it is just another stage on the road to a political union. Each of these perceptions has some truth. The former holds that since the European Defence Treaty and other abortive initiatives, and following the consecration of the practice of political cooperation by the Single European Act, this is the first common commitment by member states in a range of political domains generally considered sovereign powers. The Community can no longer be accused of building nothing more than a "grocers' common market." In fact, the Treaty on European Union aims to reinforce and extend what the Single European Act briefly outlined. Moreover, it innovates by establishing a binding set of deadlines for an economic and monetary union as well as a common currency, which is to be in place before the year 2002. In this way, the Community has endowed itself with a new political dimension based on four dynamic aspects: two aimed at guaranteeing it a place on the world stage corresponding to its economic weight and two others intended to harmonize member states' judicial and political orders within the open borders area and to increase citizen participation. Now that the decisive step has been taken, the spillover effect of political integration will begin. This is the interpretation inspired by the dynamic concept of the founding fathers.

There has been no lack of more prudent and more skeptical views disputing this optimistic vision. Indeed, some believe that Maastricht represents just one more phase or just another piece of modest progress. They emphasize the weaknesses of the system as it emerged from the Maastricht deliberations: the unforeseeable or even negative consequences of the exception made for Great Britain, the continuing democratic deficit, and above all the inadequacy of the measures provided to cope with the challenges presented by the transition and crisis in Eastern Europe. Such doubts become questions. Will the efforts of the Twelve have any impact on the upheavals currently shaking the world system and its components? Fragmentation of the Soviet Union, the war in Yugoslavia, and the crisis in countries in transition toward democracy, not forgetting the difficulties and growing needs of the Third World, such are the challenges facing the political Europe now developing. These sudden changes, destabilizing political systems, and balances are occurring in the midst of an economic crisis and a state of penury that is making the transition to democracy and a market economy even more difficult. In a profoundly changing world, the Community may be a stable, dynamic, and democratic factor, but does it have the means and instruments to cope with the conflicts subverting the old communist fortress? Does it have sufficient resources to meet the calls for aid addressed to it and the hopes it has aroused? The reply to these questions can only be given when the results of the Community's own actions and those of its members have become clear.

The General Architecture and Objectives of the Union

Like the Project for European Union put forward by the European Parliament in 1984, the treaty establishing a European Union groups together various elements, treaties, instruments, and Community experience in a single institutional framework that is intended to ensure the coherence and continuity of measures taken in pursuit of the Union's objectives. Brought together in a single "constitutional treaty," these various instruments are creating a new division of powers and a variety of decision-making processes. The allocation of powers in the respective domains of the three European Communities gives a stamp of legitimacy to the active power of the Commission-Council tandem acting in cooperation with the European Parliament. Following in the footsteps of the Single European Act of 1987, the 1992 European Union Treaty extends the use of qualified majority voting and strengthens the European Parliament's role. In the economic and social arenas, it seeks to make the Community both more effective and more democratic. On the other hand, it highlights the marked separation between an economic sector dominated by the Community and a political sector firmly in intergovernmental hands. Regarding common foreign and security policies—and here lies the major innovation of the Union—the European Council and the Council of Ministers have assumed a leading role while the Commission has been pushed into the background, despite the fact that its president is a member of the European Council.

In the political sphere, the Commission does not have the exclusive right of initiative that would ensure that Council decisions in the framework of the Economic Community are based on its own ideas. It is, however, fully associated with the work of the presidency and the Council in the domains of common external and security policy, and the same holds for justice and internal affairs. In both of these areas, the Commission has the power to submit proposals to the Council on the same basis as each member state. In this context, the term *proposal* clearly has a general meaning that distinguishes it from the specific meaning given to it by the Treaty of Rome and the European Community section of the Maastricht Treaty. Here there is a right of initiative that the Commission did not have before in the context of European political cooperation. Without having powers comparable to those it possessed in the European Community, the Commission will in the future acquire the role it creates for itself through its competence, abilities, and dynamism and the personalities of its president and members.

The architecture of the European Union is therefore based on three pillars: (1) the European Community; (2) the common foreign and security policy; and (3) cooperation in the fields of justice and home affairs. For the Community, the European Union Treaty deepens and extends it role by taking a decisive step toward a single currency and a European Central Bank. It strengthens existing policies in the fields of the environment, research, and training and extends them to other sectors like those of health, trans-European networks, consumer protection, culture, and education. The Community nature of these policies has been confirmed in several cases by increased recourse to qualified majority voting. Moreover, the decision-making process, as it has developed in the framework of the Treaty of Rome and the Single European Act, has made some progress in encouraging European Parliament involvement. As well as maintaining its original consultative powers, Parliament is now more closely associated with the exercise of the Council's legislative function through "cooperation" according to the Single European Act and "codecision" in the Community sphere of the European Union. Moreover, in its new structure the Community expects to seek the consent of Parliament more frequently.

Procedures involving intergovernmental cooperation, exceptional in the Community context, are the rule in areas covered by the Political Union. Although it has adopted a *single decision-making center,* as previously suggested by the Tindemans Report and the European Parliament's draft Union Treaty, the Maastricht Treaty is endowed with different powers, depending on whether they relate to Community affairs or to foreign and domestic issues. The result is a distinction between, on the one hand, Community decision-making processes regarding the internal market (and supporting policies) and economic and monetary union, and, on the other hand, decision-making processes relating to foreign policy, common security, and internal policy.

While retaining the distinction between Community areas and those of political cooperation, the Maastricht Treaty essentially confirms that the Union has a "federal vocation." Even though the term itself was omitted at the request of the United Kingdom, the truth is that the European Union is generally moving toward federalism. Formally omitted, the idea is nonetheless present in the substance and spirit of the Maastricht Treaty. The European Union, flawed and vulnerable though it may be, constitutes an unprecedented breakthrough to the extent that it enshrines this federalist tendency. Only experience and the behavior of political, Community, and national leaders can confirm or refute this view based on signs of a new Community dynamism. The ratification of the Maastricht Treaty triggered furious debates in Germany and France, while similar debates preceded the no vote in Denmark, providing concrete proof of the political significance of this new European statute, which establishes the joint exercise of important aspects of national sovereignty.

The common provisions comprise principles that define objectives and guide and orient the actions of common institutions and confirm the mission and mode of organization of the European Council. Overall, these provisions define the objectives of the European Union, which "mark a new stage in the process of creating an ever closer union among the peoples of Europe, in which decisions are taken as closely as possible to the citizen" (art. A, par. 2).

This first clause puts the emphasis on the dynamic nature of the concept of union in contrast to the static concept of unity. In fact a union involves a process of association, the bringing together of peoples and men, that is, political action par excellence according to Bertrand de Jouvenel. Moreover, the reference to the beneficiaries of the Union is more than a little reminiscent of one of Jean Monnet's key ideas: "We are not uniting states but men." In this spirit, the introductory provision reflects the concern of member governments to reduce the distance between citizens and decision-making centers, a distance that has increased with the establishment of a European-level power. In seeking to bring citizens closer to decision-making structures, it is intended to create areas for participation and consequently to implement principles of subsidiarity and participatory democracy. Basically, there is a need to avoid an inappropriate centralization and allow for effective participation and to preserve decentralization and the autonomy of decision-making centers at various levels. Thus, the European Union is gradually being built on the basis of two fundamental federalist principles, the principle of the autonomy of member units and the principle of their participation in joint decision making. In its current phase, the European Union is actually far more vulnerable to the centrifugal forces of national powers than to the danger of an excessive concentration of Community power. The emerging Community power cannot really be compared with the powers of the Helvetic Confederation or with U.S. federal powers. Europe needs to follow the general federalist model while it is still embryonic and malleable.

The Principle of Subsidiarity

Based more on the spirit than on the letter of the Union Treaty, this free interpretation has been confirmed again and again by references to the principle of subsidiarity, which the Union Treaty made a fundamental principle. According to the common provisions, the objectives of the Union must be achieved while respecting the principle of subsidiarity as defined in article 15 (ex 3b):

> The Community shall act within the limits of the powers conferred upon it by this treaty and of the objectives assigned to it therein. In areas that do not fall within its exclusive competence, the Community shall take action, in accordance with the principle of subsidiarity, only if and insofar as the objective of the proposed action cannot be sufficiently achieved by the member states and can therefore, by reason of the scale or effects of the proposed action, be better achieved by the Community. Any action by the Community shall not go beyond what is necessary to achieve the objectives of this treaty.

The principle of subsidiarity becomes a general approach and a guiding standard whose initial outlines go back to the philosophies of Aristotle and St. Thomas Aquinas. In the nineteenth century, it was studied (under various names) by Proudhon, and it was put into practice in the Helvetic Confederation. In the encyclical *Quadragesimo Anno* issued by Pope Pius XI on 15 May 1931, subsidiarity was defined as a principle of organization of society: "It would be very unjust and damaging to the social order to deprive lower-order groupings of the functions they are perfectly well equipped to fulfill and hand these functions over to a larger and higher authority."[2]

At the same time, the founders of personalism, Emmanuel Mounier and Denis de Rougemont, working together on the review *Esprit,* gave it a privileged place in their reflection on the role of the human in modern society. The foundation of Denis de Rougemont's federalist thought, subsidiarity also underlies Alexandre Marc's concept of integral federalism.

Unusually in the history of a principle, subsidiarity has succeeded in attracting almost unanimous support. This surprising unanimity can be explained by the general application of a principle that allows each to attribute his own meaning to it. Thus, in the European domain this federalist principle may express two opposing concerns: for some it may constitute a protective barrier for the powers of member states or regions, while for others it may by contrast make it possible to broaden the Union's areas of competence and strengthen its powers, in particular in the name of efficiency

and the common interest. The first interpretation (with a defensive intention) is similar to the meaning given in Switzerland to the actions of federalists: a federalist is someone who defends the prerogatives of the cantons
against the incursions of the central power of the confederation. The fact
remains that there is a fundamental difference between an established federal state and an embryonic European union with a federal vocation.

In Switzerland, Germany, and the United States the federal state exercises the main powers relating to state sovereignty, while in the European
Community these powers pertain essentially to the member states, who, for
reasons of necessity or efficiency, have attributed or propose to attribute
certain portions of them to common institutions. The exercise of some
aspects of their national sovereignty is therefore shared. In federal states,
central authorities are endowed with wide political powers and are tempted
to increase them beyond what is strictly necessary, while in the case of the
European Union Community institutions are far from possessing the minimum of powers needed to achieve common objectives. The European
Union is still far from the position reached by the multinational federal
state in Switzerland or by the institutions of the American federation.
There is really no need to emphasize that the division of powers within the
European Union greatly favors member states that retain most areas of
governmental authority. However, the traditional powers with which member states are endowed are not always sufficient for their current responsibilities or new tasks. Hence, there is a need for unions of states, something
the American states and the Swiss cantons became aware of in the past and
something the European states are becoming aware of today.

Within the European integration process, the principle of subsidiarity
meets the aims of the Community and the developing Union. While making it possible to avoid unnecessary excesses, it seeks to optimize the division of powers within the Community and to facilitate the fulfillment of
new tasks that go beyond the capacity of the individual states. This division
of labor is accomplished according to the objectives that the member states
hope to achieve by means of the European Union. Assigning objectives to
a state or a community of states is a constitutive act, a political act par
excellence. The question then arises as to how to allocate tasks and powers
between various institutions at different levels of authority according to
comparative advantages. This step assumes an evaluation of comparative
advantages, taking account of the spread of values and priorities in a society. From this point of view, the application of the principle of subsidiarity
is based on an evaluation of comparative advantages, offering a more
objective basis for allocating tasks and distributing powers. This is, at this
stage, too, an eminently political act, which (like the choice of objectives)
is reflected in the fundamental law of the state (the constitution). That is

why, particularly in Switzerland, any new definition of objectives or new allocation of tasks (e.g., the protection of the environment) requires constitutional reform by means of a referendum. The same is true for modification of the division of powers and in particular for the attribution of new competencies or new powers. In federal states, where there is a tendency to strengthen the central authority, the chief concern is to put a brake on this slide toward increased centralization. In the European Union, on the other hand, the big question is how to strengthen the authority of Community institutions, for in reality they are much too weak to offer a counterbalance to the weight of the member states. But the support of member states for the Union reflects their leaders' perception of its necessity and their assessment of it in terms of cost-benefit and comparative advantages.

In their efforts toward union, senior political leaders at the Community and national levels rely on the support of public opinion and are sensitive to the way it assesses the effectiveness of the allocation of tasks. *Eurobaromètre* provides extremely useful research; the opinion poll of October 1991 produced a league table of the decisions that public opinion wished either to attribute to Community institutions or to make the preserve of national authorities.[3] With a few minor variations, the preferred allocation confirmed certain general tendencies: cooperation with developing countries (78 percent) and scientific/technical research (73 percent) have long appeared at the top of the list of areas most people feel should be the object of Community decision making, followed by foreign policy (69 percent). Further behind came currency (54 percent), value added tax (VAT) rates (49 percent), and defense and security (49 percent). On the one hand, overall the areas considered by the majority to belong to Community institutions are generally those entrusted to the central power in federal states. As might have been expected, opinions vary from country to country; however, in the four areas attracting a high level of support in favor of Community action the threshold of the absolute majority was crossed in each country, with Italy and Holland in the lead. Opinion was more divided on the question of VAT and security. Where currency was concerned, all countries were in favor of decisions being made the preserve of the Community, leaving aside a certain hesitancy in Luxembourg and a decisive note of preference for national decision making in the United Kingdom. This tendency in British opinion became even stronger on the eve of Maastricht at the moment when monetary union and a single currency were on the point of being accepted by the European Council. On the other hand, on a whole range of areas, including education, health, and social security, opinion was favorable to national action. In all federal states, education is within the competence of the member states, with the action of the central power secondary.

While the structure and division of powers are clearly defined in federal states, which show only small variations, the European Union is marked by a process and structure that are still developing, so that their forms are far from being definitive. The fact is that the search for new forms of Community organization is the most prominent feature of the integration process. This process of "continuous creation" (as the founding fathers put it) cannot be enclosed within a rigid mold. There is, therefore, what is known as the Monnet approach, which defines objectives, guidelines, and deadlines, leaving the tasks of elaborating and implementing the norms to the common institutions. It is hardly surprising that, with its innovations in the domain of relations between states, the Treaty of Rome foresaw the unforeseeable in its article 308 (ex 235): if it proves to be necessary for the accomplishment of treaty objectives, the Community may undertake certain tasks exercised previously by member states. This is the positive application of the principle of subsidiarity. In the same spirit, the Court of Justice has established a parallel between the internal and external powers of the Community.

Since the early 1980s, the principle of subsidiarity has become a key subject of debate within the European Community. Mentioned officially for the first time in the 1975 opinion of the Commission on a European Union, this principle was to enjoy extraordinary success. Placed at the center of the Community system, as proposed by the European Parliament in 1984, it then made a timid appearance in the chapter of the Single European Act devoted to the protection of the environment. Following its appearance in the 1989 social chapter, the Maastricht Treaty gave its official blessing to subsidiarity as a fundamental principle of the European Union, whereby the principle clearly defines a general guideline to the powers that Community institutions exercise jointly with the powers of member states and in certain cases with the regions. But this general principle does not make it possible to determine the precise limits that separate Community and national powers. These limits evolve over time and are the object of a cost-benefit/efficiency-opportunity assessment and an evaluation of comparative advantages or ultimately a political decision by member states. A political decision may be taken on the basis of a unanimous vote under the terms of article 308 (ex 235) when it bears on the adaptation of the powers necessary for the Community to operate properly. However, when the aim is either substantially to increase Community powers or to extend them to new areas, the use of the revision procedure is necessary. This was the procedure followed at the time of the adoption of the Single European Act and for drafting the Maastricht Treaty. On the basis of these fundamental political statutes, and of the division of powers they define, the Court of Justice will have to pronounce on the way these rules are respected and the appropriate use of these powers by Community institutions and national authorities.[4]

Accordingly, the principle of subsidiarity appears as both a criterion for a guiding concept for new powers and a guardrail against too much central authority. In connection with this, Jacques Delors reminded us that "in any system of federal inspiration like the European Community, the principle of subsidiarity brings a permanent counterbalance to spillover mechanisms that tend to overburden the central power in a complex world."[5] At the same time, however, the notion of subsidiarity could be exploited by the Council and the member states as an excuse to reject an innovative project related to Community action or to minimize the importance of a decision taken.

Complex and polyvalent, the principle of subsidiarity has occupied an important and perhaps exaggerated position in the European debate about the federal future of the European Community. A fundamental principle, it takes various forms, implicit or explicit, in aspects of the European Union. Embodied in the Economic and Monetary Union Report, it is the guiding principle of the new elements contained in the Maastricht Treaty, which provide for the creation of a European Central Bank and the establishment of a single currency. Subsidiarity is, above all, reflected in activities in the areas of research and technology, which are based on a close and multiform cooperation, bringing together the Community, states, public interest groups, universities and research institutes, private associations, and companies. Within these cooperative networks, the Commission inspires, encourages, and coordinates. Although the Maastricht Treaty remains generally mute on partial agreements between member states, regions, and other public and private bodies, cooperation as applied in the areas of research and technology has a bright future. Besides, classic federal states have themselves developed various forms of agreement, as certain of their services are entrusted to semigovernmental or private bodies. Wide prospects are open to the creative imagination, provided that it avoids the straitjacket of rigid federal models, or still worse those of the nation-state, and also avoids ideological conflicts that oppose the public and private sectors.

In response to concrete needs, the Community carries out its secondary actions in various forms of cooperation or coordination and also in actions providing encouragement and support that complement the efforts of member states. There are plenty of examples: regional policy, protection of the environment, and a whole range of new Community activities in areas such as public health, consumer protection, education, professional training, culture, and industry. These complementary actions accompany the main activities of the Community and illustrate the spillover effect that began with the birth of the European Community.

Similarly, but in a different context, the Union provides secondary contributions in the areas of common foreign policy and security as well as cooperative actions in the fields of justice and internal affairs. These innovations fit into the dynamic of the integration process and its dual internal and external dimensions. Thus, establishing an area without borders required a new chain of joint actions and sectoral cooperation. Customs cooperation, cooperation in civil and penal matters, common rules and actions relating to the entry and movement of immigrants, police cooperation in the prevention of terrorism, drug abuse, and international crime are all examples that provide evidence that the concept of the spillover process as originally put forward by Ernst B. Haas is being overtaken by events. Elaborated on the basis of an analysis of the internal dynamics of the Community, it did not take sufficient account of external factors. According to P. Soldatos, this analysis overlooks "the externalization of the integration process and its progressively increasing insertion into the international system."[6] And yet history shows that this external dimension has often been a decisive factor in the creation of federal states that (like Switzerland) have come into being as a common response to external threats.

It is true that the role of external factors has sometimes been exaggerated for reasons of political influence rather than with a scientific explanation; on several occasions, General de Gaulle referred to an "external federator" as he sought to underline the excessive influence of the United States in European affairs. Today, however, communication and interaction between external and internal elements are clearly visible in the Maastricht Treaty. Thus, for example, international competition is inciting the Community to increase it competitive capacity while its economic importance obliges it to take on more political responsibility at a global level. At the same time, the political union process has accelerated since the collapse of the communist wing of "Greater Europe" and the consequent insecurity.

In order to account for all the factors that are the basis of federal unions and their operation, three aspects may be put forward: a causal aspect, an objectives aspect, and a substantial dimension.[7] The first includes those factors most often invoked upon the formation and evolution of federal unions such as geographical proximity, cultural similarity, economic and technical interdependence, and external threats. The second relates to objectives, that is, to the goals that certain parties plan to achieve through union, the pooling of resources, and common institutions and policies. Such goals are an expression of the systems of values, key ideas, and aims of the members of federal unions. The substantial aspect covers a range of factors characteristic of a federal community. In my approach to federalism, this dimension is formed by a series of fundamental principles and rules that condition the existence and development of a federal community as set out earlier.

Democratic Principles and European Citizenship

As with subsidiarity, the principle of respect for the national identity of member states, which are supposed without exception to apply democratic principles, is a federalist principle. Only European states that respect human rights and democratic principles may be admitted to membership in the Union. Moreover, by its reference to the Council of Europe and the Human Rights Convention, the European Union Treaty attributes considerable responsibility to the Council of Europe, which is called on to assess the democratic quality of candidate states. When accepting certain Eastern European states into its ranks, it officially acknowledges their democratic credentials and thus ushers them into the antechamber of the European Community. This requirement for democracy is reminiscent of the teachings of Immanuel Kant. In his work *Perpetual Peace,* one sine qua non for the existence of a community of peace is similarity among the political regimes of member states. This condition was reaffirmed at the 1948 Hague Congress in the face of the threat from totalitarian regimes, and today it is fully embodied in the European Union, membership in which is clearly not compatible with the undemocratic nature of certain regimes and societies. More than ever, a strict application of this fundamental requirement is necessary to guarantee the European Union's democratic nature and future. This shows the importance of, first, the recognition of the new states of former Yugoslavia and the former Soviet Union according to criteria set out on 16 December 1991 by the Community's Council of Foreign Affairs, which is the equivalent of a certificate of good democratic conduct, and, second, the importance of the admission of Eastern European states into the Council of Europe.

Among the other principles and objectives of the Union are economic and social cohesion at the internal level and the Union's identity on the international stage. A single institutional system has the task of ensuring the coherence and continuity of common actions both internally and externally while respecting and developing what the Community has achieved. These objectives and the revision planned for 1996 bore witness to member states' determination to push the Union forward and ensure the efficiency of Community mechanisms. The common objectives of the member states must be achieved in conformity with the treaty provisions and in a spirit of respect for the principle of subsidiarity, which, in turn, takes on its full meaning in this progressive perspective of the Union.

Since the creation of the Community, European citizenship has been steadily growing in importance. In setting up its legal order, the Community has helped to make the European citizen a subject and beneficiary of common rights. As a counterweight to the direct or immediate power of Community institutions over citizens, the latter acquired both rights at and access to the Court of Justice. Moreover, their involvement increased, initially indirectly through socioeconomic organizations and consultative committees, then after 1979 directly through elections to the European Parliament. Similarly, the Committee of the Regions will be able to include elected representatives of regions, cities, and local powers.

In turn the Maastricht Treaty has widened the sphere of European citizenship. It guarantees the rights of freedom of movement and residence in the territories of member states to any citizen of the Union. In addition, it grants voting rights and eligibility for elections to the European Parliament and for local elections to any citizen of the Union residing in another country of the Community. These rights are exercised by citizens under the same conditions as the rights of the nationals of the state where they reside. The application of these provisions may allow for derogations when problems specific to a member state justify it. Denmark, Ireland, and Holland have already introduced the practice of voting in local elections. For most of the other countries, the right to vote and eligibility for local elections will require constitutional revisions or, failing that, at least derogations concerning eligibility.

While it does extend the areas of participation, the exercise of these rights does not seem likely to cause a revolution in local political landscapes. In this same perspective, the next stages should open up participation at regional levels to European citizens and in a more distant future participation in other representative institutions of member states. A second innovation concerns the protection of Union citizens in third-party countries where the member state from which they come does not have diplomatic or consular representation. In this case, they will benefit from the protection of any member state under the same conditions as do its nationals. A third innovation bears on rights of petition and recourse to the Community mediator. Following a fairly widespread custom, these rights are not exclusively reserved to citizens of the Union but are accorded to any physical or moral person residing or having a head office in a member state.

These are the main provisions that have created a European citizenship and aim to reduce the distance between citizens and Community institutions. They reinforce measures such as the protection of public health, consumer protection, the participation of citizens in European professional training programs, student and academic exchanges, and numerous Community research programs. Work on professional training and conversion courses, for example, will be the object of programs developed in collaboration with member states, companies, and professional training bodies. Such programs will be organized in the workplace or educational and training establishments.

The introduction of the notion of European citizenship in the Union Treaty, put forward by the Spanish government at the end of 1990, was approved by 60 percent of Community opinion. The Spanish led in terms of favorable opinion, with 78 percent, followed closely by the Greeks, Italians, and Portuguese, and more distantly by the Irish and the French (62 percent). The Belgians, Dutch, and Germans were less favorable, while the British and the Luxemburgers came next to last. Bringing up the rear was Denmark, the only member state where negative opinions were in the majority (54 percent as against 28 percent in favor).[8]

The Deepening of Economic Integration

The Single Currency and Economic Convergence

By channeling the main energies of the Community into establishing an economic and monetary union and strengthening economic and social cohesion, the Maastricht Treaty made substantial progress. In line with the internal market and the policies supporting it, this double innovation is the central axis of the integration process. It is generally agreed that preserving the balance between member units constitutes an essential element in any federation. In the medium or long term, cohesion in a federation is vulnerable to the threat of domination by one or some of its members and to tensions that may arise from a significant disparity between the economies of member states or between developments in different regions. Keen to reduce existing disparities in the Community, the signatory governments sought to reinforce socioeconomic solidarity within the Union. In this way, the Community aims to reduce disparities between regions and promote cohesion between member states, seeking greater integration and economic and social equilibrium.

At the same time, the Maastricht Treaty triggered a theoretically unstoppable move toward a common currency, a move that affects one of the essential attributes of national sovereignty. Currency is a symbol of the sovereign's exclusive power. Devised by the European Council and the governments at the request of the business and financial world, this commitment is an illustration of the spillover effect, which, whether little by little or by qualitative leaps, moves the Community forward. The binding deadlines laid down by the Maastricht Treaty will stimulate in turn the activities of economic operators such as bankers and financiers, who will formulate their strategies and responses in terms of this goal.

This commitment involves the creation of a European Central Bank and a single currency and opens a new phase in European integration with the transfer of member states' monetary authority to the Community. The Monetary Union will be administered by a European system of central banks with an independent European Central Bank as its core. This phase will require national economic policies to converge under a common budgetary discipline. This set of objectives, rules, and institutions provides concrete proof that the European Union has a federal vocation, while the single currency represents the power of sovereignty that is an attribute of the federal state.

The path to economic and monetary union is long and winding; it was outlined in the 1968 "Barre Memorandum" to coordinate economic policies with monetary cooperation, and the establishment of an economic and monetary union was the subject of the *Werner Report* two years later. The Council had made plans to set up such a union, but their timetable was disrupted by the international monetary crisis. The resulting delay in the implementation of the Council decision is a brutal illustration of the connections that in this domain (which is undergoing rapid globalization) there is a close interdependence between inside factors and outside forces. In fact, the integration process is governed by their interaction. In order to avoid a general paralysis, the less ambitious "bypass" system was set up in 1972 in the form of the "monetary snake." Despite the negative effects of stagnation in the world economy and the integration process, the European Monetary System was born in 1979. It inaugurated a fresh stage based on three mechanisms: exchange rates, credit, and a monetary unit, the ecu. The value of the ecu, a "basket of currencies," represents a figure obtained by summing a fixed quantity of each Community currency, calculated as a function of the economic importance of the country in question. Since 21 September 1989, the currencies of the twelve member states have represented the following percentages of the ecu: DM = 30.1, FF = 19, UKL = 13, LIT = 10.15, HFL = 9.40, B/LFR = 7.90, PTA = 5.30, DKR = 2.45, IRL = 1.10, Esc = 0.80, and DRA = 0.80. Although the EMS has not yet succeeded in creating a European monetary fund, it has prepared the way for economic and monetary union. This whole fluctuating pattern of development is typical—in its advances, holdups, and incomplete results—of the integration process, which could fairly be represented in the form of an ascending spiral.

At present, the Economic and Monetary Union is slated to take place in three stages, the first having begun in July 1990 in conformity with a decision of the European Council in Madrid. This first phase involves the participation of all member states in the exchange rate mechanism, as is currently the case with the exception of Greece, the liberalization of movements of capital, and multilateral supervision of national economic policies. The second phase began on 1 January 1994 with the creation of the European Monetary Institute (EMI) and implementation of a range of measures related to the independence of central banks, the definitive composition of the ecu basket, the convergence of economic policies, and the reduction of public debt and deficits. The EMI is headed by a council made up of a president (chosen unanimously by the heads of state or government on the recommendation of the Committee of Governors and after consultation with the European Parliament and the Council) and the governors of the central banks, one of whom takes on the vice presidency. The fact that the president is chosen by the highest national authorities underlines the importance attributed to the Council of the EMI.

The third phase had to begin at the earliest on 1 January 1997 and at the latest on 1 January 1999. The value of the Euro will be fixed irrevocably at the start of this phase. The decision concerning the transition to the third phase is a matter for the Council assembled at the level of heads of state or government. Giving its rulings by a qualified majority on the basis of EMI and Commission reports, European Parliament opinions, and the recommendations of the Council of Ministers, it must decide whether the majority of member states are fulfilling the necessary conditions for the adoption of a single currency. This fundamental decision creating a single currency has three essential features.

First, it is based on the reports and recommendations of the EMI, the Commission, and the Council, this last on the basis of a qualified majority. These are reports and recommendations bearing on the prevailing degree of price stability, on evidence of respect for normal margins of fluctuation within the EMS, and on the durability of economic convergence and budgetary discipline aimed at eliminating excessive public deficits. Second, in the course of this process the Council, assembled both at ministerial level and at the level of heads of state and government, decides on the basis of a qualified majority. It is worth noting that the treaty does not refer to the European Council but to the Council assembled at the level of heads of state or government, which could conceivably be a way of ensuring that the president of the Commission, who is also a member of the European Council, will not take part in this decision. The distinction might also be attributed to the fact that in this case the Council, assembled at the level of the most senior national leaders, takes its decisions by qualified majority according to a precise procedure peculiar to it. One consequence of this distinction is that, while the Council of the Community is composed of representatives of member states at the ministerial level, there is nothing to stop the Council from assembling at the highest level in the future and taking decisions by qualified majority voting. Third, the treaty follows the Monnet approach in setting precise deadlines. In addition, it organizes the Monetary Union within the framework of the European System of Central Banks, a decentralized system in which powers are divided between the European Central Bank and the national central banks. So, while the ECB alone is entitled to authorize the emission of currency in the Community, it shares with the national central banks the power to issue bank notes. Moreover, the governors of the central banks sit on the Council of Governors of the ECB alongside members of its directorate. Like the EMI, the president and members of the directorate are nominated by the governments of member states assembled at the level of heads of state or government on the recommendation of the Council and after consultation with the European Parliament and the Council of Governors of the ECB.

The criteria fixed to test countries' readiness for the transition to a single currency are five in number: price stability; the state of public finances (i.e., budgetary deficits, public debt); participation in the narrow bands of the EMS (at least two years); and long-term interest rates. These criteria set the conditions for a Community-wide discipline.

1. For at least a year, the inflation rate must not have exceeded by more than 1.5 percent that of the three member states with the best showing in the area of price stability. For 1991, the three benchmark countries were Denmark (2.3 percent), Luxembourg (2.6 percent), and Belgium (2.8 percent). The highest inflation rate currently acceptable would have been therefore around 4 percent. This first criterion of relative significance is adjusted according to the performance of the three member states with the greatest price stability.

2. The public deficit must not exceed 3 percent of GNP unless circumstances are exceptional. These requirements establish a precise connection between economic convergence and monetary stability. To a certain extent, this represents the German thesis of the necessity for convergent policies prior to establishing a single currency. However, the treaty does not make this a precondition even though it recognizes that a strong currency must be based on economic foundations that guarantee stability of purchasing power and make it possible to encourage harmonious and balanced development of the overall Community. Once again, the treaty ultimately reflects a variety of conceptions and manages in particular to reconcile French and German viewpoints. In addition, it defines overall objectives and entrusts their implementation to institutions, so that the Council, making decisions by a qualified majority on the recommendation of the Commission, is to draw up a draft proposal for the main lines of the economic

policies of member states. In a later phase, the Council will adopt, by a qualified majority and on the basis of the European Council's conclusion, a recommendation fixing these main lines. Then, with the help of the Commission, it will watch over economic developments and regularly make general assessments. This multilateral review will give rise to recommendations that are not binding in and of themselves but will acquire their full significance in the context of monetary union and the discipline that it imposes. In turn, the common monetary policy will govern the convergence of member states' economic policies. This example highlights the need for coherence and links between economic policies and monetary policy within the Community.

The creation of a European Central Bank within the European system of central banks and the adoption of a single currency constitute a decisive step toward a federal community. This step involves an indispensable minimum of centralization that is still far short of the traditional practice of federal states like Switzerland and Germany. It is a fundamental decision if ever there was one, leading to the abandonment of national currencies. The Community made its choice between the deutschmark and the ecu, a choice that will prevent the deutschmark from becoming the dominant currency in Europe. It is hardly surprising, then, that German public opinion is in the throes of a vigorous debate about abandoning the deutschmark. As for the United Kingdom, it has obtained an exemption that should muffle the shock waves liable to be produced by the disappearance of the symbol of British greatness. The adoption of a single currency is a concrete test of the will of member states to push on with the construction of the European Union.

A study of this complex text raises several questions. Indeed, at the beginning only two members, France and Luxembourg, could meet the criteria imposed. Germany and Denmark were among those admissible, but the German public deficit was just over 3 percent of GNP as a result of reunification, while the Danish public debt, though well above 60 percent of GNP, was gradually drawing closer to the threshold. The United Kingdom, Holland, and Belgium formed another group of serious candidates; the task of the two Benelux countries was to reduce their debt and public deficits, whereas the United Kingdom needed to bring down its inflation rate and the margins of fluctuation of its exchange rates from 6 to 2.5 percent. Ireland and possibly Spain might have been able to join the seven others provided that they accepted a touch of economic stringency, but Portugal, Italy, and Greece were so far behind that they seemed unlikely to be able to make the grade in the foreseeable future.

While there has been skepticism in certain quarters, others have argued more optimistically that the Community's past experience has shown common objectives progressively helping to impose a salutary discipline on member states in the face of repeated delays. In this regard, the battle against inflation in France has been exemplary and demonstrates the effort that governments will have to undertake to create the conditions required for establishing a monetary union. These convergent efforts will be a tangible step forward in themselves.

The monetary union that does not comprise all fifteen member states has to operate at two speeds on the pattern of the EMS. The EMS is in fact a mechanism outside the Community system that, although limited to start with, has proved itself possessed of a magnetic ability to draw all the members of the Community into it one by one with the exception of Portugal and Greece. The hopes of a monetary union are based on this power of attraction, together, of course, with the efforts of its supporters and promoters. The assumption is that there will be a spillover effect and positive responses from financial markets and that businesses, especially small and medium-sized ones, will realize that they will be among the chief beneficiaries of the establishment of fixed exchange rates. Finally, public opinion supports monetary union, with 55 percent in favor of the ECB and 54 percent in favor of the ecu, although attitudes vary considerably from country to country as usual. According to an October 1991 poll, nine countries showed a majority in favor of the ECB, with Luxembourg (a financial haven) the exception (48 percent for and 28 percent against) together with Denmark (47 percent for and 40 percent against). Only British opinion was solidly opposed (41 percent against and 39 percent in favor). As for the ecu, attitudes were divided. Germany took the place of Ireland in the camp of the lukewarm, with 45 percent voting in favor but 32 percent against. This is something to be followed closely, given the pivotal role of the German economy and the deutschmark in the Community and their influence over the countries of Central and Eastern Europe. On the other hand, there are few surprises in the United Kingdom and Denmark, which both had majorities against, except that British opinion proved unexpectedly indecisive, with 40 percent for and 42 percent against, while in Denmark strong opposition was registered by a vote of 54 percent against with only 35 percent in favor. These attitudes suggest the depth of hostility in Denmark, and they also explain certain reserves expressed by the British government on the eve of the April 1992 elections. Once reelected, and therefore having more freedom to maneuver, the Conservative government could have afforded to become more actively committed alongside its European partners.

In July 1992, in the light of future obligations entailed by the Maastricht Treaty, the German Central Bank raised its interest rates unilaterally. This decision provoked widespread reactions from governments and financial centers. There was a domino effect in the stock markets, which fell, anticipating a delay in the recovery of Western economies. In addition, while the Lombard rate for the refinancing of commercial banks at the German Central Bank did not change, this interest rate rise did affect the dollar, which fell to an unprecedented low. Thus, a decision whose purpose had been to put the brake on inflation in Germany provoked a chain reaction on account of the interdependence of the major financial markets. At the same time, it demonstrated the international responsibility of the monetary authorities and raised two questions pertinent to the future of economic and monetary union: what is the significance of the independence of the German Central Bank, which has served as a model in this respect for the European Central Bank, and is this unilateral decision, contrary to the spirit of economic and monetary union, a bad omen for Community discipline?

Surprisingly, the independent decision by the German Central Bank did not meet with the wholehearted approval of the German government. It gave concrete proof of the meaning of the institution's independence from political power. Whether this means that in the future the ECB could be allowed a similar margin of liberty within the Community is an open question. However, it is now clear that the action of the ECB will fall within the general guidelines defined by the European Council. It is within those limits that the ECB will be able to assert its independent authority.

This unilateral decision is definitely not in line with the obligations set out in the Maastricht Treaty, which, it should be remembered, was not in force at the time the decision was taken. It provides proof by default of the need for the kind of Community discipline prescribed by the Maastricht Treaty. In fact, within the framework of the Union such decisions can no longer be adopted except in consultation or agreement with other Community members, so national interests will now have to be in harmony with Community interests.

Cohesion and Regional Policies

The Maastricht Treaty extends and deepens the work done in a range of areas since the Treaty of Rome and the Single European Act, while in other sectors it introduces real innovations. In the sphere of common commercial policy, it adheres to the traditional way of doing things while generalizing the use of qualified majority voting. In research and technological development, the Union has shown improvement by allowing the use of article 2.51 (ex 189B) and giving the Council the task of fixing rules for the participation of businesses, research centers, and universities together with rules applicable to the diffusion of research results. For its part, the Commission is empowered to take initiatives to encourage and ensure coordination and coherence in the actions of the Community and its member states. Similarly, Community policy has the objective of strengthening the scientific and technological bases of Community industry and increasing its international competitiveness, a direct reference to Japanese and American competition. The new section on industry is part of the extension of efforts in the area of research, which is aimed at creating a favorable environment for the development of the competitive capacity of Community industry. Community actions are intended to facilitate adaptation to structural changes, encourage development initiatives (particularly for small and medium-sized companies), and favor cooperation between firms and a better use of research and technological innovations. As well as coordinating research and pooling resources, the aim set by the Community is to shorten the delay between innovation and industrial application since such periods are longer in Europe than in the United States and Japan. Other complementary and supporting actions are planned in areas such as professional training, education, and culture. Environmental action in the Community has been strengthened and extended by the Community's contribution to the protection of public health and consumers. These Community actions fit the overall policies of the Community, whose mission it is to supplement, support, and coordinate the policies of member states.

From the point of view of federalism, two areas of Community policy merit particular consideration: regional policy and the new dimension of social policy/solidarity. In these two fields, the Union Treaty aims to complete the work that was undertaken by Community institutions and given the stamp of legitimacy by the Single European Act. "A Europe of Regions," an idea launched by Denis de Rougemont in the 1960s, is gradually being written into facts and institutions. Regional policy became a reality in the 1970s before being incorporated into the Single European Act in 1987. In the Maastricht Treaty, a whole range of common policies is directed toward better regional equilibrium and the development of the poorest regions. This evolution of regional policy is based on the actions of the Structural Funds and the dynamics of the regions; they are asserting themselves, sometimes applying the principle of subsidiarity without realizing it, by strengthening their internal and cross-border activities. The development of the regions and regional diversity is producing new coordination networks as well as inspiring the emergence of a series of exchange and collaboration agreements between them.

Regional policy and the achievement of economic and social cohesion are based on actions by the Community itself through funds with structural goals: the European Agricultural Guidance and Guarantee Fund, the European Social Fund, the European Regional Development Fund, the European Investment Bank (EIB), and other financial instruments. Structural funds operate on the basis of new principles: priority accorded to the least favored regions, programming, partnership, and synergy. While the Single European Act aimed chiefly at neutralizing or compensating negative effects, the Maastricht Treaty aimed to encourage the regions to develop closer ties, ensuring cohesion and supporting efforts toward a convergence of economic policies.

Disparities between countries go hand in hand with disparities between regions within each country, as within the Community as a whole. The persistence, and even increase, of these disequilibria could be a source of grave difficulties and a factor in political and economic instability in the Community. To the extent that the Community draws nearer to an economic and monetary union, disparities will tend to consolidate or even increase. In order to soften these foreseeable consequences, the Maastricht Treaty intensified preventive action and Community efforts on behalf of the least favored regions and countries. Thus, in accordance with European Council guidelines, the main efforts of the Commission will bear on the undeveloped regions, including the five new German states.[9] To this end, it is proposed that the Commission should increase its resources by two-thirds, compared with an increase of 50 percent in the funds made available for other structural policy objectives. Overall, the credits for structural funds over the period 1984–93 amounted to 60 billion ecu, of which 63 percent was reserved for poorer regions, 12 percent for regions in decline, and 12 percent for retraining and youth employment, with 6.2 percent going for rural development and agricultural adjustments.[10] The new strategy is also based on the principle of connecting various resources and interventions to create synergies between mutually supportive policies. Moreover, it introduces more flexibility and lightens decision making and programming procedures. It also strengthens the partnership between Commission, states, and regions and clarifies responsibilities in accordance with the principle of subsidiarity. Thus, by variously seeking to create the conditions for a better balance between various levels of authority, the Community is putting into practice the principles of federalism.

Proposed by Spain, the Cohesion Fund, which favors countries with a GNP per inhabitant lower than 90 percent of the Community average (Spain, Greece, Ireland, and Portugal), is for those member states what structural policies are for the regions. Since 1994, the Cohesion Fund has supported programs for economic convergence put forward by these least favored states. The actions of the various support and incentive measures available to the Community are to form part of the main economic policy guidelines established by the European Council. Thus, all the multiple, diversified, and decentralized actions will be orchestrated according to general themes proposed by the latter.

This "preestablished harmony" will not come without tensions, which may arise as much from the pressure of internal or external competition as from the effects of research and high technology. For instance, the opening of the Common Market to products from Eastern Europe or the consequences of the Uruguay Round will mainly affect the least developed countries and regions in the Community. Imported agricultural products, steel goods, and textiles often match products from regions situated in the poorest countries of the Community.

In turn, the development of new technologies may become a factor in regional disequilibrium. Competition from the United States and Japan has produced a range of initiatives at both the national and Community levels. But advanced technologies are developing mainly in the ten great "islands of innovation" in Northern Europe, where, according to a study by Le Fast in 1991, 80 percent of science-based innovations are concentrated. Already favored by their wealth and environment, these regions are equally favored by the rush to technological development on account of the advantages they offer in terms of university know-how, highly-qualified manpower, and capital. This concentration in the advanced industrial centers runs counter to regional development. Hence, there is a need to reconcile these antagonistic trends by taking measures to ensure technological development and the regional allocation of benefits.

In this context, results will be dependent largely on the decentralization of centers for research and advanced scientific training and also on communications networks. Progress in advanced technologies in the area of the diffusion of knowledge, communications, and microprocessors is promising for the development of peripheral regions. Thus, paradoxically, the "Europe of Regions" seems likely to enjoy an impressive future thanks to the tools provided by high technology.

To ensure the necessary coherence of Community actions, the missions, priority objectives, and organization of this fund have been established by the Council on the basis of unanimous decisions on proposals from the Commission after the assent of the European Parliament has been received and after consultation with the Economic and Social Committee and the Committee of the Regions (established by the European Union Treaty). Moreover, member states are committed to pursuing and coordinating their economic policies with an eye to encouraging harmonious development and reducing regional disparities. Finally, the new Cohesion Fund aims especially at supplementing Community action by helping to finance projects in the areas of the environment and trans-European networks.

The Europe of Regions is gradually becoming a reality within the European Union, while at the same time it is posing the problem of the regions' involvement in drafting and implementing Community programs and decisions. The judicious application of the principle of subsidiarity will allow for a better division of tasks between the three levels of action: Community, national, and regional. But this application has often been slowed by states jealous of their prerogatives, which, like Italy, Spain, France, and the United Kingdom, are struggling to preserve their role as essential channels of communication in the hope of maintaining a grip on the activities of their regions. In practice, direct contacts between Community institutions and regional groupings are tending to intensify, primarily at the operational level; with few exceptions, participation of the regions in the Community decision-making process continues to be only marginal and consultative.

Naturally, a federal member state is leading the way in this area. In fact, the German states have long been present at various stages in the decision-making process through the inclusion of their "observers" in official delegations and various working groups. The states' involvement at the national level was strengthened at the time of the ratification of the Single European Act. Moreover, they were not slow to establish representation in Brussels, thereby drawing closer to the center of Community decision making. Their example was followed by the regions of several member states. To date, Jose Luis de Castro has counted ten informational and representation offices of the German states in Brussels, including a Hanseatic Bureau shared between three states (Hamburg, Schleswig-Holstein, and Lower Saxony).[11]

By virtue of their more limited autonomy, the offices representing the regions of other member states have more modest functions that concentrate principally on development issues. For example, the French regions have ten offices in Brussels, three of which are shared by several regions: the offices of the Great East (Burgundy, Champagne-Ardennes, and Lorraine), the Great South Association (Aquitaine, Languedoc-Roussillon, Midi-Pyrénées, and Provence–Côte d'Azur), and Eurodom, representing the French overseas territories. The same desire for close contact with the Community's decision-making centers formulating and implementing regional aid policies lies behind the establishment of ten offices by UK regions. The eight Spanish regions' offices have their own distinctive practices, whose true objectives are concealed because of restrictive legal conditions. According to Jose Luis de Castro, they appear in turn as development agencies (Andalucia, Murcia, and Madrid), limited companies (the Canary Islands and the Basque country), or institutions made up of regional authorities and employers (Catalan Pro Europa Employers, the Galicia-Europe Foundation, and the Office of the Valencian Community). Relations between Catalonia, Madrid, and Brussels are a good illustration of the region-state-Community problem in a system in which the external autonomy of the regions still remains under the jealous control of the states.[12] In spite of their utilitarian functions, which are centered on aid and development programs, development agencies and information offices representing French, English, and Spanish regions are the first signs of communications networks gradually forming within the European Union.

The German states and their representatives at the Bundesrat have put forward the idea of setting up a regional chamber with real participation rights. Such initiatives express the will of the German states to seek Community solutions, making it possible to compensate for a possible reduction of their powers in favor of the federal executive as a result of their direct participation at the Community level. The idea of a senate of regions, suggested by Denis de Rougemont, and the proposals put forward by the Assembly of European Regions are along the same lines and are an incentive to institutionalize regional representation within the Community. It is true that the creation of a Committee of the Regions only partially fulfills the aspirations of supporters of a Europe of Regions and the representatives of the German states. This innovation actually goes beyond what the members of the Commission dared to anticipate. This case is an example of negotiation by synergy within the Community, with results that often fall short of more ambitious plans but exceed the expectations of realists.

The *Committee of the Regions* is modeled on the Economic and Social Committee. Its 189 members are chosen according to the same procedure and are allocated on the same basis. The two committees have the same consultative powers and organizational structures. Similar but complementary, they represent two dimensions of Community activity, reflecting sectoral and regional diversity. Even though all its functions are limited, the Committee of the Regions institutionalizes consultation with the regions within the Union. Generalized consultation with the Economic and Social Committee is sometimes supplemented by a parallel consultation with the Committee of the Regions. This two-dimensional consultation is provided for in the areas of education, public health, trans-European networks, and regional policy, based, of course, on economic and social cohesion (arts. 158–62 (ex 130a, b, c, d, e)). As regards culture, however, the Committee of the Regions is the only body that has to be consulted. In contrast, it is absent from the scene in cases in which its presence would seem to be essential. It is not consulted in the course of drawing up framework programs lasting several years or specific research and technological development programs, nor in the area of industrial or social policy. But its absence is most surprising when we come to environment policy, especially since article 174 (ex 130R) stresses "the diversity of conditions in the different regions of the Community" and the need for a balanced development of the regions. Revision of the Maastricht Treaty will make it possible to fill in these gaps and strengthen the contribution of the regions. Moreover, whatever the real value of texts and institutions, the intention behind them is only to provide a framework and create an environment. It is up to the regions to set goals. Often present on an individual basis in Brussels, they have an opportunity to contribute together to the development of a European Union with a double federal and regional vocation.

The Committee of the Regions is certainly a long way from being a senate of the regions. Even with the best will in the world, it would have been difficult to create a second chamber made up of regions alongside the European Parliament given the huge disparity between member countries with respect to the statutes, responsibilities, and autonomy of their regions. All the same, this first opening is very promising for the future role of regions in a European federation, especially in that they are represented by both elected persons and professional categories. Moreover, the regional policy of the Community, strengthened by the activity of the Regional Committee, will not fail to stimulate in its turn the development of regions in member states. By reflecting cultural, economic, and geographical diversity, the regions are helping to shape a federal union within which the characters of the states and the regions can assert themselves. In addition, the regions, as arenas of civic participation, make it possible to reduce the distance between citizens and Community institutions. It is in just such a diverse Europe, complex and yet united, that individuals and their basic communities will find the opportunity to grow, each bringing a personal contribution to the construction of a united Europe.

The great majority of Community opinion considers it essential that there be a Community policy for the most deprived regions. As to the priority objectives for regional policy, 44 percent think that they must be given more equal opportunities, 38 percent that their living standards need to be raised, and 12 percent that their competitiveness should be improved. Where their identity is concerned, citizens of the Community show an attachment to several communities, as opinion polls show.[13] Overall, they identify to a high degree with their countries (88 percent), their regions (87 percent), and their localities, towns, or villages (85 percent). Their attachment to the European Community and Europe as a whole is much weaker, and citizens seem very divided on this point: 48 percent say that they feel an attachment to the Community while 46 percent do not. This feeling toward the Community is highly variable from country to country. As might be expected, it is weak in the United Kingdom (35 percent) but also in Ireland, which is a symptom of that country's geographical and psychological remoteness. Other surprises are Denmark and Holland, with the Danes showing the same attachment as the Germans (42 percent). In contrast, the Dutch, despite their long history of devotion to European unity, show very little attachment to the Community (28 percent). This lack of attachment is in contradiction to other opinions: 88 percent of those polled think that it is "a good thing" for Holland to belong to the Community, 74 percent consider that their country has profited by it, and 53 percent would regret it if the Community collapsed. However, these questions refer only to the utilitarian aspect of the Community, while the question concerning attachment involves an emotional element and a comparison with the feelings held by citizens for their traditional communities. Nonetheless, such a gap certainly exists, even though to a lesser extent, in the opinion of all the countries of the European Community. In spite of these inconsistencies, the replies to the general question give us a clear indication of the way citizens feel about their simultaneous membership in several communities and confirm the emergence in public opinion of a sense of multiple loyalties.

Institutional Innovations

The development of the European Community and the extension of the tasks and responsibilities entrusted to the common institutions have created a need for more effective and efficient institutions. This logic led to improving the operation of Community mechanisms at the time of the Single European Act negotiations by introducing the use of qualified majority voting in the Council and establishing closer cooperation between the Council and the European Parliament. It is no accident that this institutional improvement focused first on the sphere of the internal market and its supporting policies. Accompanying this functional concern was a desire to bring Community institutions closer to the fundamental principles of Western European democracies. This is why the European Parliament was brought into closer association with the exercise of legislative functions, initially attributed to the Council, legislating on proposals from the Commission and after consultation with the European Parliament. Indeed, when the Community was created the institution with a legislative vocation par excellence was given only consultative powers, while the legislative function was attributed to a Council composed of representatives of national executives. The democratic model was deformed at birth. The various provisions of the Maastricht Treaty seek, even if only timidly, to cure the Community of its childhood weaknesses and give it its true political dimension.

The Confirmation of the European Council

From the beginning of the process of European integration, the most senior political leaders, the heads of state or government, have taken an active part in negotiating and implementing the treaties founding the European Communities. Their role as driving force, directors of strategy, and arbiters has sometimes been exercised through summit conferences but more often through consistent intervention at the national government level. When it comes to European issues, decision-making and coordination processes differ from country to country; despite that, the political significance of certain Community decisions has had the effect of involving senior national leaders. From the start of the European integration process, the relationship between the political weight and significance of Community action, on the one hand, and the level of national decision makers, on the other, has become increasingly evident. Two examples, the French and the German, illustrate different modes of organization and coordination, one centralized, the other decentralized, and at the same time confirm this relationship. The more a decision implies a political option or produces political effects, the greater the tendency to leave it to higher political echelons. While general political decisions usually come within the competence of foreign ministers, assisted by other relevant ministers, the most important political choices and decisions are retained by the president and prime minister in France and the chancellor in Germany. With the expansion of the integration process, the participation of heads of state or government increased and became institutionalized with the creation of the European Council in 1974. After this, the European Council's role grew continually, starting with the impetus it gave to negotiations for the Single European Act, followed by dynamic guidance given to the work on economic and monetary union and political union, and concluding with its approval of the new European Union Treaty on 9 December 1991 at Maastricht. This evolution is merely a reflection of the reality of political power in the European Community.

Following on the Single European Act, the European Union Treaty confirms the European Council's eminently dynamic and political role: "The European Council gives the Union the impetus necessary for its development and defines its general political orientation." While not modifying its composition and operating rules, as established in the Single European Act, the new treaty broadens its field of action. For example, on the basis of a Council report adopted by a qualified majority on the Commission's recommendation, the European Council will debate a resolution on the general outlines of the economic policies of member states and the Community (art. 99 (ex 103)). In turn, and on the basis of this resolution, the Council adopts by a qualified majority a recommendation establishing the broader outlines of economic policy. In the areas of common foreign and security policies, the European Council itself takes on the task of determining general principles and guidelines to be implemented by the Council.

On a unanimous basis, the governments of member states at the level of heads of state or government nominate the president of the ECB and members of its directorate and, during the transitional phase, the president of the European Monetary Institute (EMI). In contrast, neither the European Council nor heads of state or government are expressly mentioned in article 214 (ex 158), which defines the nomination procedure for the Commission and its president. Involvement in this important decision is restricted to the governments of member states. However, by long-standing practice, it is plausible to assume that the European Council or its members will take on a predominant role in the course of this nomination procedure. This is all the more likely as governments, at the level of heads of state or government, intervene in the nomination of the president of the ECB, who, in spite of his or her eminent role, does not have a political position comparable to that of the president of the Commission.

Another case is important in this connection; the conclusions on the question of the conditions that the majority of member states must fulfill prior to the adoption of a single currency are transmitted by the Council of Ministers to the Council assembled at the level of heads of state or government. As some writers have suggested in the past, this clause officially confirms that meetings can take place at the highest level in the framework of the Council. Is this explicit reference to the Council intended to prevent involvement of the Commission president in his capacity as a member of the European Council? Or is this distinction between the European Council and the Council assembled at the level of heads of executives intended to allow their decision on the single currency to be taken by a qualified majority, thereby avoiding the need for a consensus, which is generally European Council practice? This second interpretation seems doubtful if we bear in mind that on several occasions the European Council has ruled on the basis of a strong majority of its members or has upheld a view despite strong opposition from one or more of its members. In this particular case, the European Council in Milan gave the green light to negotiations on the Single European Act and the Madrid Council approved monetary union.

Article 121 (ex 109J) (2, 3, and 4) refers three times to the "Council composed of the heads of state or government." Constituted thus, the Council resorts to qualified majority voting. After consulting the European Parliament, the Council decides, based on recommendations from the Council of Ministers, which itself formulates its recommendations on the basis of a qualified majority with reference to recommendations from the Commission. Thus, from recommendation to recommendation, the Council, assembled at the highest level, decides whether a majority of states fulfill the conditions for the adoption of a single currency and the transition of the Community to the third phase. The same procedure will be applied with the automatic transition to the third phase in 1999.

Whatever interpretation is preferred, one distinction between the European Council and the Council retains its importance: the European Council has no definite procedure, while the Council functions on the basis of precise rules. This is only one example among many that throw into sharp relief the great complexity and variety of decision-making processes within the European Union. Even so, through such complexity the reality of European political power emerges at various levels, and as the political importance of the problems at issue grows the authority of the heads of the executives is asserted at both the national and Community levels.

The Investiture of the Commission

The new treaty did not modify the Commission's composition even though this question is on the agenda for study by the Community. In contrast, however, it progressed in the direction of suggestions put forward by the Tindemans Report and the Spinelli Project. As a first step, governments of member states consult with the European Parliament before agreeing on the president of the Commission, so that from the start the Parliament is involved in the choice of the candidate for the presidency. The next step is for governments, this time in consultation with the president designate, to select other people they plan to nominate for membership in the Commission. This new formula is intended to allow the president designate to intervene at the moment when the members of his future team are chosen in order to ensure its cohesiveness. The last stage in the nomination process takes place in two phases: first, the Commission designate is subjected to a vote of approval, a kind of "preliminary investiture" by the European Parliament, which pronounces on the composition of the Commission and its program. Then, *after* this parliamentary approval, the president and members of the Commission are nominated on a unanimous basis by the governments of the member states.

To emphasize the significance of this nomination procedure, the Maastricht Treaty extends the duration of the Commission mandate to five years, beginning in 1995, so that it can be brought into line with the duration of parliamentary tenure. In the future, as requested by the European Parliament, a new Commission will be appointed during the months following each European election, which is traditionally held in June. The positive effect of this new procedure will be twofold: it will broaden the role of the European Parliament and increase the authority of the Commission and its president by ensuring that they acquire a wider democratic base. On the other hand, the Maastricht Treaty did not modify the number of members of the Commission. This question will have to be tackled in the perspective of the forthcoming enlargement of the Community.[14]

The Extension of Recourse to Qualified Majorities

The Single European Act reintroduced the use of qualified majority voting, which had fallen by the wayside after the 1966 Luxembourg Compromise. The return to this procedure, which was contained in the Treaty of Rome but put into cold storage after the empty chair crisis, corresponded above all to a functional need, the need to implement and ensure the sound operation of the internal market. The Maastricht Treaty not only repeated these provisions, but it extended qualified majority voting to several new sectors, including the environment, development policy, commercial policy, consumer protection, education, public health, and trans-European networks. As a general rule, the application of qualified majority voting is limited by the division between the Community dimension, which constitutes its principal field of application, and the political dimension, which is dominated by intergovernmental procedures and unanimity voting. This distinction, corresponding to the two great pillars of the European Union, allows one exception, which became applicable after 1996; it relates to the designation by qualified majority voting of third-party countries whose citizens must be in possession of a visa while within the Union. As to the possibility of recourse to qualified majorities in the areas of foreign policy, justice, and internal affairs, the new treaty makes use of an old expedient; it enables the Council to define by unanimous agreement those foreign policy decisions that may be taken by a qualified majority requiring a favorable vote by at least eight member states (art. 73, par. 2). The corresponding articles on the Consolidated Treaties are as follows: title V, the CFSP, article 23, paragraph 2; and title VI, police and judicial cooperation in criminal matters, article 34, paragraph 3; a favorable vote requires at least ten members out of fifteen. Similarly, the Council may, in the name of cooperation in the areas of justice and internal affairs, decide in principle and on the basis of unanimity measures that are to be adopted by a qualified majority of at least eight member states (art. 3 (ex K3, par. 2C)). A doubt persists concerning the exception to the unanimity rule bearing on "procedural questions" (art. 32 (ex K4, par. 3)). In the event, predicting the outcome of the decision-making process in the area of a common foreign security policy cannot at this stage be anything more than guesswork. Only the actual operation of the measures laid down in the treaty in these purely political domains will make it possible to assess their effectiveness. That is why the Maastricht Treaty provided for calling a revision conference in 1996. In fact, it will only be on the basis of an assessment of the progress made and the experience acquired that revision will be possible "with a view to ensuring the effectiveness of Community mechanisms and institutions" (art. 2 (ex B, par. 5)).

Growth of the European Parliament's Power

Quite justifiably, the European Parliament is not satisfied with the powers attributed to it in the European Union. The lack of democracy, or the "democratic deficit," is the subject of its complaint. While the division of powers in the Community certainly does perpetuate disequilibrium at the expense of the European Parliament and the Commission, it is nonetheless important to note the gains made by the Parliament. The procedure for nominating the Commission establishes a form of codecision, and other powers of codecision ensure a more effective and wider participation by the European Parliament in the legislative process within the Community. Out of fifteen cases for codecision laid down in article 2.51 (ex 189B), seven were regulated by the "cooperation" procedure in the Single European Act. To these seven cases, bearing mainly on the internal market and mutual recognition, the Maastricht Treaty added eight new cases of codecision applying to new sectors.[15] In 1995, the Council pronounced itself by a qualified majority on fifty-four cases (*General Report* [*R.G.*], 1995, no. 1028).

The requirement for parliamentary approval ensures that there is codecision in the strictest sense of the word. According to this procedure, the agreement of the Parliament is an integral part of the decision, and without this agreement the decision cannot be made. Such approval is required in eight cases, six of them relating to new domains.[16] This is required particularly for the admission of new members, for certain international agreements that create a specific institutional framework and have serious budgetary implications for the Community, for the definition of objectives, for the organization and coordination of structural funds, and for the creation of cohesion funds. In two of these cases of codecision, culture (art. 151 (ex 128/5)) and framework programs lasting several years (art. 157 (ex 130/1)), the Council is obliged to take decisions on a unanimous basis, a procedure that seems to contradict the spirit of codecision.

At the same time, the cooperation procedure established by the Single European Act has been extended; out of eighteen cases, only three were taken from the Single European Act, while the other fifteen are innovations.[17] Four cases deal with technological research and development programs, two with (regional and social) funds, four with the Economic and Monetary Union, and two with social policy. The consultation procedure, too, has been extended to more than twenty cases of which ten relate to the

Economic and Monetary Union.[18] Under these three forms, codecision, cooperation, and consultation, parliamentary involvement in the Community legislative process has been greatly developed and diversified.[19]

Now the European Parliament also has a right of legislative initiative. The European Union Treaty introduced a new provision in article 192 (ex 138B) by the terms of which "The European Parliament may, acting by a majority of its members, request the Commission to submit any appropriate proposal on matters which it considers that a Community act is required for the purpose of implementing the treaty." The keystone of the Community system is not touched since the Commission preserves its power of making formal proposals as before, although it no longer enjoys the exclusive right of initiative.

In addition, the new treaty fills out the European Parliament's array of control and intervention powers. For example, budgetary control is strengthened and Parliament's access to information is facilitated with respect to both the Commission and the Court of Auditors, institutions from which it may require any information deemed necessary. Moreover, the Commission must follow up the Parliament's observations, in particular those concerning the handling of expenditures. However, although it does have the right to be consulted on the Community's own resources, more than one claim by the Parliament has failed to evoke a favorable response from governments. It has, however, been endowed with a right of inquiry; like national parliaments, it has the ability to appoint temporary commissions of inquiry to examine alleged infractions or mismanagement, so that its hearings have been supplemented by investigations. Other provisions fill out the array of interventions available, two of which are measures that should allow European citizens to draw nearer to the Parliament: the right of petition and the right to contact an ombudsman authorized to receive complaints. Finally, in article 191 (ex 138A) the treaty sets the stamp of legitimacy on political parties as important expressions of the citizens' political will and as factors of integration. This token of encouragement to the political parties ought to galvanize them into improving their structures and moving beyond the stage of national political parliamentary groupings to a position where they are more focused and organized for operations at a European level. The development and consolidation of federations of parties should help restore the balance between the different interest groups within the Community while progressively forming a European political consciousness. In spite of numerous criticisms about the role of political parties, there is agreement in principle that they are irreplaceable in democratic systems. It is, however, still necessary for them to assume more fully their responsibilities and commit themselves to a greater extent to operating within the Community. It is also necessary for the institution that constitutes their exclusive access to power, the European Parliament, to be given the main characteristics of a representative institution. Despite all the initiatives intended to give it constitutive powers, the European Parliament still has only a consultative function in the essential area of revision of the treaty. According to article N, the initiative for revision is reserved to member states or the Commission. The Council can call an intergovernmental conference "after consulting the European Parliament and, where appropriate, the Commission."

The revision process will probably follow a path similar to those that led to the Single European Act and the Maastricht Treaty. Alongside the Commission, the European Parliament was a prime mover behind the Single European Act because of its adoption of a draft European Union Treaty in 1984. On the other hand, it was the European Council of Milan in June 1985, and not the Council of Ministers, that took the decision to call an intergovernmental conference by a majority of seven of its ten members. During the negotiations for both the Single European Act and the Maastricht Treaty, the Commission fulfilled a discreet but effective role, while the European Parliament was associated with negotiations for the European Union. If in practice the European Parliament takes a more active part in revision than article N might lead one to expect, it is still far from having the role assumed by national parliaments with regard to constitutional reforms.

In contrast, the Maastricht Treaty (art. 190 (ex 138, par. 4)) gave the European Parliament the task of drawing up drafts of a uniform electoral procedure. Its role is confirmed by the requirement for its approval prior to the Council's unanimous recommendation and the adoption of this uniform procedure by member states. In this "constitutional innovation," the European Parliament occupies a leading position in both authorship and codecision.

The Court of Auditors Elevated to the Rank of an Institution

The Court of Auditors was created by the 1975 treaty, and the Maastricht Treaty elevated it to the rank of a Community institution. Like other European Union institutions, the European Parliament, the Council, the Commission, and the Court of Justice, it is charged with carrying out the "tasks entrusted to the Community" (art. 4). This innovation constitutes some progress toward the democratization of the Community system, for according to Daniel Strasser, a French member of the Court of Auditors, it is intended "the better to ensure equal treatment for each member state and greater protection for the European taxpayer."[20]

The Court of Auditors has twelve members, each appointed for six years by the Council, who rule on a unanimous basis after consultation with the European Parliament. All highly qualified, the members carry out their functions in the general interest of the Community and with complete independence. The Court audits all the income and expenditure accounts of the Community and of each body created by it, guaranteeing to the European Parliament and the Council the accuracy of the accounts and of the legality and regularity of related operations. Its task is to ensure the good financial administration of the Community. In addition to the assistance it brings to the European Parliament and the Council when supervising the implementation of the budget, the Court of Auditors produces an annual report that forms the reference document for the European Parliament when it is called on to accept the Commission's annual accounts. The Commission is solely responsible for the implementation of the Community budget. The Court of Auditors may also present at any moment observations in the form of special reports on particular questions and give opinions at the request of a Community institution. Its broader mission is to ensure the regularity and transparency of Community finances, its vocation being that of the "financial conscience" of the Community, as Daniel Strasser puts it.

The New Social Dimension

The social dimension of the Economic Community was for a long time marginal, but it resurfaced discreetly in 1985. Under the impetus given by the internal market, dialogue began between the Union of Industries of the European Community, the European Center for Public Enterprises, and the European Trade Union Confederation. From 1985 to 1991, eight common opinions were adopted, including agreements on the introduction of new technologies (1987), the adaptability of the labor market (1991), and access to professional training (1991). In October 1991, this social dialogue reached an important new stage with the opening of the way to employment relationships governed by collective agreements at the European level. This agreement to a large extent inspired the contractual method set out in the protocol annexed to the Maastricht Treaty.[21] As for the European Council, in Madrid in June 1989 it affirmed that "in the framework of the Europe construction, it is important to give the same importance to the social dimension as to the economic, and therefore there must be balanced parallel development of the two." This new impetus arising from a consensus between social partners led to a doubling of the resources of the Structural Funds and to adopting directives in the area of safety and hygiene in the workplace.

Nonetheless, the draft Social Charter that resulted was blocked by the hostility of the Thatcher government, which was adamantly opposed to a revitalization of trade unions through the action of the Community. Consequently, the Social Charter could not be adopted till December 1989 and then only by the Eleven. Subsequent directives that were to ensure its implementation could not be approved as a consequence of the requirement for unanimity in the Council. In order to avoid such institutional blockages, the Maastricht Treaty contains two protocols relating to social policy, the first approved by the Twelve, the second by the Eleven. The Twelve authorized the Eleven to go further down the path of the Social Charter and use the institutions, procedures, and mechanisms of the European Community to this end. For these deliberations by the Eleven, a qualified majority means forty-four votes out of sixty-six. The decision of the Eleven is not applicable to the United Kingdom.

By means of a second protocol, the Eleven modified certain treaty articles, attributed wider objectives to them, and provided that account must be taken "of the diversity of national practices, in particular in the area of contractual relationships, and of the necessity of maintaining economic competitiveness" when achieving these objectives.

Following the traditional pattern, the protocol distinguishes between three categories of action. First, directives establishing minimal prescriptions can be adopted by a qualified majority and in cooperation with the European Parliament in the following areas: health and safety at work, working conditions, informing and consulting workers, equality between men and women, and the reintegration of persons excluded from the job market. Second, unanimity and consultation with the European Parliament are appropriate in areas such as social security, layoffs, joint management, and the employment of immigrants from outside the Community. Finally, the third category comprises matters explicitly excluded: pay, union rights, the right to strike, and the right to impose a lockout.

These protocols represent several innovations. First of all, they set up a method that makes it possible to proceed without the agreement of members unwilling to commit themselves. This implies a two-speed integration process, but it does not exclude the possibility of slower members catching up. Second, the protocol of the Eleven illustrates the recognition of diversity and the application of the principle of subsidiarity. Thus, this principle is applied both vertically between the Community level and national and regional levels and horizontally between national or regional Community institutions and national or regional European social partners. Third, the role of the social partners is strengthened by a recognition of European collective agreements. These may apply in two ways: according to the practices particular to the relevant social partners and member states or, if the social partners so desire, by a decision expressing their content taken by the Council on a proposal from the Commission. Before taking any Community initiative, however, the Commission must consult the social partners and, if a collective agreement is possible, leave them to engage in negotiations directly. The social partners also may be responsible for implementing European directives by way of agreements. The protocol establishes a flexible method that not only provides for a contractual approach alongside the legislative but also provides for directives to be implemented through agreements between the social partners.

The active role that the social partners propose to play was confirmed in their July 1992 declaration reiterating their intention to be closely associated with the creation of the Community social structure and indeed to be one of its main elements. The representative of the Confederation of British Industry did not oppose the adoption of the declaration but indicated that the text would have to be approved by his organization's highest authorities. With this one reservation, the social partners confirmed their intention to enter fully into the framework of the social protocol, and it should be possible to advance on a contractual basis with the agreement of the Twelve. Nonetheless, negotiations at the Community level raise the problem of representation, mainly in relation to the absence of the French Confédération générale de travail (CGT), which is not a member of the ESC, as well as the question of whether negotiations will be undertaken sector by sector.[22] One thing is quite certain, however: social dialogue has inaugurated a new stage, an innovation in the process of social integration.

The Decision-Making Progress according to Article 251 (ex 189B)

As the integration process deepens and extends its field of action, its effects are felt inside and outside the Community and demand for efficient operations and institutions grows. The Maastricht Treaty sought to satisfy these demands as well as the aspirations toward more democracy. Accordingly, the authors of the treaty sought to improve the abilities and operations of Community institutions. The whole range of provisions mentioned in previous chapters is intended to increase the authority and efficiency of the main institutions responsible for Community decision making and policy formulation. Following the work accomplished by the Single European Act, the Union Treaty seeks in its turn to improve the decision-making process, and article 251 (ex 189B) is the result of these efforts. The "cooperation" procedure is supplemented by a procedure that leans toward "codecision."

The *first phase* of the new process is not substantially different from the decision-making practices that developed following the Treaty of Rome and the Single European Act. Initiatives from various social and institutional players produce a Commission proposal, and among these players we find not only promotional groups, interest groups, and businesses but governmental and Community institutions, including the European Parliament. These initiatives have no legal basis but appertain to unofficial influence and actions. The Maastricht Treaty innovates, insofar as it enables the European Parliament to ask the Commission to draw up proposals on questions it considers important. Unlike informal initiatives that influence but do not create an obligation for the Commission, which alone is entitled to launch the decision-making process, the European Parliament is now endowed with a right of initiative through the Commission. Experience shows how national parliaments are reluctant to use their right of legislative initiative, and in practice it is mainly the executive that takes the initiative by introducing legislation on which parliaments are called to vote. It is, however, essential that parliaments have the power to take initiatives when they think it necessary. Innovation must not be the exclusive domain of the executive, especially in that young parliaments often exhibit a great willingness to take initiatives and show more political imagination. Even parliaments of many years' standing seem to become more involved when dealing with problems untouched or neglected by governments that are more caught up in the daily round of political business; for example, parliaments have been more sensitive and open to environmental problems. The still youthful European Parliament seems on more than one score to wish to launch initiatives expressing the preoccupations of the citizens whom it represents. The weight of these new rights of initiative will nonetheless depend on the actual use the Parliament makes of it in the future.

The *second phase* will follow the procedure set out in the Single European Act and reiterated in article 189C of the European Union Treaty. According to this procedure, the European Parliament is initially involved at the start of the second phase, or for a second time if it was the originator of the Commission proposal. The Commission presents its proposal to the European Parliament for a first reading and to the Council, but the latter does not determine a common position until it has received an opinion from the former. Adopted on the basis of a qualified majority vote, the common position then returns to the European Parliament for a *second reading*. The Council and Commission keep the Parliament fully informed, the former of the reasons that have led it to adopt its position and the latter of its views. Thus, with detailed information from the two institutions the European Parliament may either (a) approve the proposal or let it pass without comment; (b) propose amendments; or (c) reject the common position by a simple majority vote of its members. The difference between the provisions of the Single European Act and those of the European Union lies here, but it increases when the Council fails to come to a decision on the basis of the amendments voted by the Parliament (b) or when faced with rejection from the Parliament (c) (see fig. 3).

In case (a), the Council may finally approve the common position on the basis of a qualified majority since it expresses the convergent positions of the three institutions. In case (b), the Parliament transmits the amendments to the Council and also to the Commission, which then has to submit its opinion. In case (c), if the Parliament does not confirm its rejection by a simple majority of its members, it proposes amendments according to the same majority procedure. In this last case, the procedure follows the line of case (b), which concerns the procedure for proposing amendments.

When the European Parliament proposes amendments to the common position, they are sent to the Commission for an opinion. A favorable opinion from the Commission is the equivalent of a modification in its initial proposal, which allows the Council to confirm its own common position by means of qualified majority. Hence, the Commission is only applying a general rule according to which it may modify its proposals at any moment, while the Council can deviate from that position only on the basis of a unanimity vote. In the logic of the system, therefore, unanimity protects the Commission's proposals and strengthens its influence in the complex negotiations that lead to the adoption of Community decisions. Following the same logic, the Council may take decisions by a qualified majority as laid down in the treaty on the condition that the Commission is in favor and has modified its proposal, accepting the amendments retained by the Council. The result is that the Council may rule only by a unanimous vote on amendments that are the object of a negative opinion from the Commission. There remains the question of amendments that are not accepted by the Commission. In this case, the Parliament may allow itself to be persuaded or resort to the ultimate weapon of rejection.

With time, this seemingly very complex mechanism will probably appear simpler in operation. As with the cooperation procedure in article 252 (ex 189C), practice will help to rectify the complexities of procedure. However, we are able to discuss the essence of this new decision-making structure. First, the European Parliament has formidable powers of rejection, and even when they are not used they increase its influence by enabling it to exert pressure for an agreement. Second, it can propose amendments to the common position. Third, in cases of blockage a new procedure has been set up through a Conciliation Committee. In fact, when the Council does not take a decision its president immediately assembles the Conciliation Committee with the support of the president of the European Parliament.

The mission of the *Conciliation Committee* is to bring about agreement between Council and Parliament with the assistance of the Commission.

First phase of the Commission (fig. 1)

Second phase: Commission, European Parliament, and Council

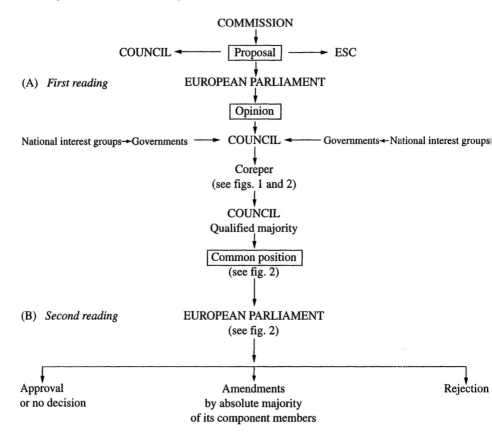

FIG. 3.   Maastricht Treaty: Decision-making process

Thus, it is called on to exercise a key role when the Council is not in a position to ratify an act. The intervention of the Conciliation Committee is an innovation that can be evaluated only in light of experience. But this conciliation or arbitration function rests on agreement between the Council and the European Parliament. This agreement, not requiring the unanimous consent of the Council even if its effect is to modify the Commission's proposal, does raise several questions concerning the role of the Commission and the way that role will be exercised in practice, the frequency and modalities of recourse to this procedure, and the influence that this collaboration between Council and Parliament will have on the future of the legislative function in the European Union.

Third phase: (b) Amendments or (c) Rejection

(C) *Third reading*

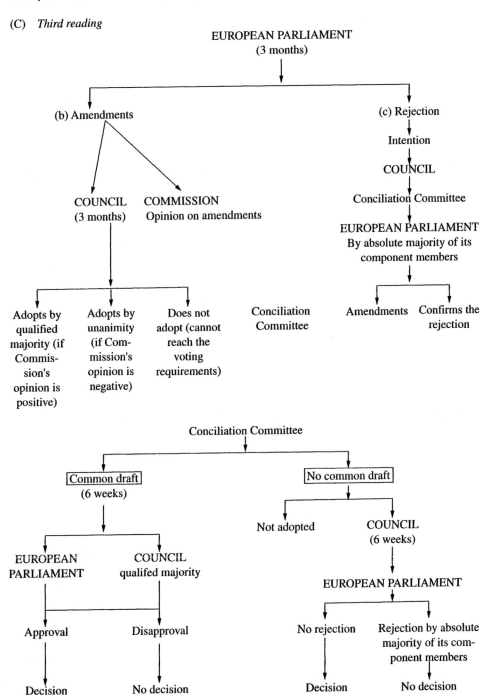

FIG. 3. (Continued)

The Conciliation Committee assembles, on a parity basis, the twelve members of the Council or their representatives and the same number of representatives from the European Parliament. The Commission is fully involved in its work and takes all the initiatives necessary to encourage rapprochement between parliamentary and Council positions. From this point of view, conciliation relates to conflict or misunderstanding between these two institutions in the exercise of their legislative functions. Thus, the Commission's role in this context is similar to that of another broker or mediator, but it is likely that within the Conciliation Committee negotiations will in most cases be much more complex than the text of article 251 (ex 189B) might seem to suggest. The opinions of the participants may change in the course of the discussions, which, far from being limited to bilateral negotiations, will be more like a multidimensional negotiation within the limits set by the two institutions.

In carrying out its mission, the Conciliation Committee aims to draw up a common draft that will win the approval of a qualified majority of the Council representatives and a majority of the European Parliament representatives. There are two possibilities, depending on whether the Conciliation Committee establishes or does not establish a common draft. If the draft is approved, the definitive approval of the two institutions is sought. The probability of obtaining a favorable vote of confirmation from the Council is quite high, given that its representatives have already approved the common draft on the same qualified majority basis; in rare cases, there will be new developments following U-turns by one or more Council members, leading to either approval or disapproval of the draft. For the European Parliament, the situation is more complex in that representatives could have decided not to retain the initial position of the parliamentarians in order to reach a compromise. Moreover, a precise position becomes even more chancy by reason of the number of MPs and a voting discipline that is not consistently respected. The act is definitively passed only if the two institutions approve it. If, in contrast, the Conciliation Committee does not manage to approve a common project, the proposal is considered as not adopted unless the Council decides to confirm its common position by a qualified majority. In this case, if the European Parliament then decides by an absolute majority of its members not to reject the common position, the proposal is definitively adopted. The Council may modify its common position with amendments put forward by the European Parliament in order to avoid incurring opposition from that body.

This very complex procedure will have to be given time to work itself out, but in any event its effectiveness will depend on the conduct of the members and representatives of the two institutions. As for the Commission, there is no doubt that in the conciliation between the institutions with legislative functions the requirement for unanimity will be sidelined by the Council on amendments put forward by the Parliament in the case of a negative opinion from the Commission. Moreover, the conciliation procedure allows Parliament and Council to modify the Commission's initial proposals without its consent and without unanimity on the Council but on the condition that the two institutions approve the common project. It is clear that in this case the Commission's proposal is no longer protected by Council unanimity, and consequently there is a reduction in the Commission's negotiating power. Nonetheless, in the spirit of this legislative co-decision procedure, the initial dialogue between Commission and council is replaced by a dialogue or collaboration between the two institutions called to exercise a legislative function jointly on the basis of proposals from the executive. In this system, which reflects more than a little certain features of the bicameral system in federal states, the fate of the executive's proposal ultimately depends on its approval in its initial or amended form by the two institutions. This innovation modifies the division of powers; what is conceded by the Commission is acquired by the Parliament. In this way, Community interests are expressed from the start by the Commission's proposal and guaranteed in the final phase by the approval of the Parliament. The fact still remains, however, that only lengthy experience after a period of adjustment will enable article 251 (ex 189B) to be understood more precisely through the realities of the actual decision-making process. During 1995, there were fourteen codecision procedures, of which six required the services of the Conciliation Committee. In March 1995, the European Parliament reflected a common project that came from a conciliation committee. The proposition concerned the copyright of biotechnological inventions.

There remains the third case (c), in which the common position is rejected by Parliament. An intention to do this must be communicated to the Council immediately. The Council may then assemble the Conciliation Committee in order to clarify its position, following which the European Parliament has two options: by an absolute majority of its total membership, to either confirm its rejection of the common position or propose amendments. If the proposal is rejected by the Parliament, the decision is not adopted. If it proposes any amendments, the decision-making process follows path (b). According to the use that the Parliament makes of its weapons, and the threat of rejection in particular, the decision-making process, according to article 251 (ex 189B), will tend either to introduce a paralyzing use of the veto or to institute a form of codecision. Only the use of this weapon will make it possible to judge its positive or negative effects. In 1995, in twenty-four cases out of twenty-six, the Parliament proposed amendments, and in eleven cases it got the Council to modify its position. Out of the thirty-five codecision cases, the Parliament proposed amendments to the Commission's proposition in thirty cases and modified the common position in fifteen (*General Report* [*R. G.*], 1995, T.21).

Except in cases of nonadoption, this decision-making process, whose duration in principle ought not to extend beyond nine or ten months, leads to Community instruments, rulings, directives, and decisions signed by the presidents of the Parliament and the Council. This double signature symbolizes codecision by the two institutions that exercise the legislative function in the Community. These decisions may vary with respect to their immediate application, but they are binding and enforceable and are addressed to both member states and physical and moral persons residing in the Community. By virtue of the principle of proportionality or equilibrium of rights and obligations in a democratic system, this legislation may be availed by states or persons for whom it is intended or who are affected by it. Resort to the Court of Justice may also be made by Community institutions, the Council, the Commission, the European Parliament, and the ECB. These two latter institutions were given a right of recourse to the Court by the Maastricht Treaty.

Composed of thirteen members, the Court of Justice normally sits in plenary session; however, it may create within itself chambers with three or five judges either to carry out certain inquiries or to judge certain categories of business (art. 221 (ex 165)). The Court of Justice sits in plenary session at the request of a member state or an institution that is party to a case before the Court. These provisions are intended to lighten the work load of the Court of Justice and accelerate its decision making. The Court of First Instance, set up by the Single European Act, is a response to the same concern for efficiency and speed. This Court of First Instance is charged with hearing certain categories of cases determined on a unanimous basis by the Council at the request of the Court of Justice and after consultation with the European Parliament and the Commission. At the request of the Court of Justice, the Council, ruling on a unanimous basis, may increase the number of judges and make necessary adjustments; these various improvements are based on both experience and functional requirements. Of course, the decisions of the Court of Justice have been binding and enforceable since the creation of the European Communities. But, although they are generally respected by member states, the decisions were made more effective by the Maastricht Treaty, which introduced sanctions with regard to member states that do not respect Community law. From now on, according to article 228 (ex 171), if a member state has not carried out a decision of the Court of Justice the Commission may appeal to the Court and indicate the amount of a fine or penalty. If the Court of Justice in its turn holds that the member state has not respected its ruling, it may inflict a fine or penalty even if the Commission has not proposed that it do so. Thus, the Maastricht Treaty strengthens the legal powers of the Commission with respect to member states, making them liable to sanctions.

In conclusion, the Maastricht Treaty aims to strengthen the European Parliament's role in the Community decision-making process, to make voting procedures at the Council more functional, and to guarantee the application and the enforcement of decisions, in particular those taken jointly by the European Parliament and the Council as well as those of the Court of Justice. These improvements and innovations will help the European Community operate more efficiently.

Several positive features of this new legislative procedure deserve to be emphasized. First, and crucially, the European Parliament can intervene early, in some cases at the very first stage of the decision-making process. In fact, numerous studies of the influence of institutions, pressure groups, or personalities have stressed the fundamental importance of the moment when interventions occur. All other things being equal, the closer an intervention is to the source of a piece of legislation and the moment a decision is drafted, the greater the probability that it will have an effect. On this issue, the development of the European Parliament's position is significant; its right of initiative, though limited, enables it to be a source of Commission proposals. Moreover, since it has to consider the Commission's program, it is kept informed of the Commission's decision-making calendar through its enlarged bureau and therefore has the chance to discuss with the Commission the priorities and the pace of decision making. In fact, on numerous occasions during the drafting of Commission proposals the European Parliament, and especially its various commissions, has had the chance to make its views known.

At a more advanced stage in the decision-making process, the European Parliament delivers its opinion after a first reading of the Commission's proposal. This opinion is taken into account by the Council when it establishes its common position according to "cooperation" or "codecision" procedures. In what is known as the codecision procedure, which estimates suggest will affect between eighty and one hundred acts a year, the influence of the European Parliament is growing both because of its recourse to the Conciliation Committee and because of its formidable power to reject a common position. According to article 189B,[23] by using these powers skillfully the European Parliament will be able to increase its importance not only by means of its amendments but by its continuous involvement throughout the decision-making process. The effect of resorting to the Conciliation Committee or the threat of rejection will certainly make itself felt in the very early stages of that process. However, the real effectiveness of the increased powers of the European Parliament will in the last resort depend chiefly on its ability to use effectively the new instruments available to it.

The main institutional innovations and the increase in European parliamentary powers have met widespread approval from the public. According to the results of an autumn 1991 poll, 65 percent of those questioned were in favor of the European Parliament and the Council having legislative codecision, while only 15 percent were against it.[24] As usual, Italy was in first place with 79 and 6 percent. Then came Holland (70 and 18 percent), Greece (69 and 7 percent), Portugal (67 and 5 percent), and France (67 and 14 percent). At the bottom came Denmark (49 and 38 percent), the United Kingdom (51 and 27 percent), Luxembourg (53 and 20 percent), and Ireland (55 and 11 percent). In spite of these variations, there was a clear majority in favor of legislative codecision. The approval of parliamentary investiture of the Commission was at a slightly lower level, with 59 percent in favor and 17 percent against. The structure of the variations remained similar, with the exception of Danish opinion, which showed a majority against (39 and 42 percent). A similar division emerged on the subject of the European Parliament's legislative initiative: 58 percent were in favor as opposed to 24 percent against, with a slight majority against in the United Kingdom (40 and 43 percent). Judiciously enough, public opinion was more reluctant to approve the European Parliament's being given power to ratify all the Community's accords and conventions (52 and 24 percent), and it does seem pointless to subject all the Community's contractual instruments to parliamentary ratification. As for the power of supervising the management of the Economic and Monetary Union, public opinion seemed to accord it less importance (52 and 24 percent). It remains true, nonetheless, that overall European public opinion provides unhesitating support for the provision of increased powers to the European Parliament. The "excessive democratic deficit" is on the way to being reduced.

Chapter 9

The European Community on the Way to Political Union

The Internal Affairs Dimension

The area without borders, in particular the free movement of people, means that a variety of controls carried out at crossing points between member states have been removed. There is, therefore, a need for controls at the Community's external frontiers as well as within the Community as a whole. Many areas that prior to the implementation of the Maastricht Treaty came within the exclusive competence of national authorities will now be the object of more extensive cooperation and even of common policies and joint actions. In a progressive sequence, similar to the steps between a customs union and a common commercial policy, various forms of cooperation between the governments and administrations of member states will be established, ranging from simple collaboration to common positions and actions. Moreover, certain governments will be able to commit themselves to closer collaboration in the framework of the Schengen Agreement, concluded by the six founding countries of the Community, while inviting the other member states to join them as soon as possible. As with the case of the EMS or the single currency, a certain number of member states will have the opportunity to integrate more rapidly while allowing time for the others to join them. This is a less obvious form of two-speed integration, sector by sector, in which a subgroup of member states takes on the leading role, and, by demonstrating the effectiveness of joint action, those member states will be able to pull the others along behind them. Anticipating such a development, the treaty approves this multi-speed method of integration in article 35 (ex K.7): the provisions of section 6 "shall not prevent the establishment or development of closer cooperation between two or more member states insofar as such cooperation does not conflict with or impede that provided for in this title." The effectiveness of this method will be tested by experience.

As with all negotiations, optimistic goals were set in the area of internal security at the suggestion of Prime Minister Felipe Gonzalez and

Chancellor Helmut Kohl. In 1989, in order to prevent the free movement of persons and capital from taking place in 1993 at the expense of internal security, they proposed creating a Community police force. Its brief would be to fight international crime and terrorism within the area without borders established by the Single European Act. Their idea was that there should be a "supranational police force," like the American Federal Bureau of Investigation (FBI), able to operate within the European space to prevent the creation of a common market in crime. Although the member states already have coordinating groups in the struggle against terrorism and drugs, their police forces have no right to act beyond their own borders. Several countries, with the United Kingdom prominent among them, oppose this solution, arguing that the coordination of police work is sufficiently effective or pointing out the accomplishments of Interpol.[1] As usual, the negotiations resulted in a compromise. For the moment, member states consider several areas of justice and internal affairs to be questions of common interest, while under the proposal police would cooperate in areas of preventing and fighting terrorism, illicit drug dealing, and other serious forms of international crime. Police cooperation will operate in liaison with a system of information exchange organized at the Union level within a European Police Bureau named Europol (art. K.1, par. 9). Thus, the prevention of and fight against terrorism and international crime will be supported at the operational level by police cooperation and the creation of Europol. Conceived in the image of Interpol, Europol will be able to limit itself to its initial function of a system of information exchange or will become an embryonic European federal police force. Member states are still the main authorities responsible for maintaining public order and safeguarding internal security, but the exercise of their responsibilities within an area without borders implies systematic collaboration at every level.

The Maastricht negotiations coincided with the fall of the Berlin Wall and the crisis in the Communist bloc, which aroused great fears about hordes of immigrants from the East. It is not surprising that the list of questions of common interest begins with asylum policy, immigration policy, and policy toward citizens of third countries. These issues include the rules covering crossing the external borders of member states and the way such crossing is controlled, conditions of entry and movement for persons from third countries in the territories of member states, conditions of residence for these people (including the reunion of families), access to employment, and the battle against clandestine immigration, illegal residence, and illegal employment of persons from third countries. In addition to economic and social actions, the creation of a Community space involves a new chain of activities to be carried out increasingly in common. As of now, customs cooperation and the battle against international fraud complete the range of preventive, control, and operational actions made necessary by the existence of the area without borders. It is self-evident that the provisions of section 6 of the treaty do not prejudice the exercise of responsibilities incumbent on member states for the maintenance of public order and the safeguarding of internal security. But the exercise of their responsibilities in the Community area itself requires systematic collaboration at every level. Activities with a European dimension will go hand in hand with corresponding common policies and joint actions. The integration process as it has developed, sector by sector according to needs, is covering new areas and gradually extending into those reserved up to now exclusively to member states. The exercise of various activities and rights within the European space has made judicial cooperation necessary in civil and criminal matters.

In the same vein, several new specialized councils will be established to ensure the participation of the competent authorities, the ministers of justice and the interior. In accordance with long-established practice, the relevant ministers will, depending on areas and needs, be called on to collaborate with other relevant officials such as foreign and finance ministers. This extension of the domains of cooperation and joint action will enlarge the EU's area of influence. In addition to ministers, senior officials will be called on to collaborate within the Coordinating Committee, and many officials and agents will consult with one another, coordinate, and carry out certain activities in common. Such cooperation and common action will be based on collaborative networks composed of the relevant services that member states have agreed to establish (art. 31 (ex K.3, par. 1)). In the shadow of formal cooperation, a new phase of informal European integration, socialization, and apprenticeship will develop.

The Council, with the assistance of the Coordinating Committee, has a central role in the decision-making process in internal affairs and justice, while the Commission is relegated to a more modest function; it is to be "fully associated with the work" in these areas. Within this system, the division of the powers and roles of various institutions under the authority of the Council is distinguished from the Community model; initiative is no longer the quasi-exclusive privilege of the Commission, which, moreover, no longer enjoys its right of formal proposal. The initiative may just as well come from any member state as from the Commission in the areas set out in title VI, with the exception of cooperation in civil, criminal, and police matters, where only states have a right of initiative. The Commission is fully associated with the work, however, as it is in all the other domains covered by title VI. As to the European Council, whose powers remain undefined, it may intervene at any moment to encourage new activities or guide major decisions. As is often the case, it is discreetly but essentially omnipresent when fundamental issues are at stake.

The Council operates in four different ways:

1. It is a place for information exchange and mutual consultation between member states for the purpose of coordinating their actions.

2. Except in the areas of justice and policing it may, on the initiative of any member state or the Commission, encourage cooperation that may serve to achieve Union objectives and settle common positions: member states are committed to common positions in the context of international organizations and at international conferences.

3. It may adopt common actions according to the *principle of subsidiarity,* that is, to the extent that Union objectives may be better realized by a joint action than by member states acting alone on account of the size or consequences of the action envisaged; it may decide that measures for the application of a joint action may be adopted by a qualified majority.

4. It has the ability to establish conventions that it will recommend member states adopt according to their constitutional rules. Except where there are contradictory provisions written into such conventions, measures for their application are adopted in the Council on the basis of a majority of at least two-thirds of the contracting parties.

In the exercise of its functions, the Council is assisted by a Coordinating Committee composed of senior officials. In addition to its coordinating role, this committee formulates opinions for the Council and prepares the work of the Council in the areas of justice and internal affairs. On the basis of this work, with which the Commission is fully associated, the Council decides in principle on a unanimous basis. However, in addition to the exception made for conventions, the Council may decide by a qualified majority on procedural questions. Likewise, it may decide that measures for the implementation of a joint action adopted unanimously may be passed by a qualified majority. In such cases, the treaty imposes a strengthened qualified majority by requiring a vote in favor by at least eight members. This requirement fits into the general logic of the European Community, according to which a strengthened qualified majority is necessary when a Council decision is not based on a Commission proposal. However, the treaty does not contain a right of proposal, which is generally the basis for Community decisions, in areas that are part of the Political Union in the narrow sense of the term. The result is that the treaty gives the Commission a more modest role in this sphere.

In turn, the role of the European Parliament, which has not been given full power of codecision in traditional Community domains, is being reduced in the new areas set out in title VI. Parliament is certainly kept regularly informed by the Council and the Commission presidency, which recovers part of its permanent function on this occasion. Although consulted by the presidency, Parliament is deprived of its ability to give opinions and can only express its views. It is clear that the presidency has the task of making sure that these views are duly taken into consideration. There is no doubt, however, that, in spite of its questions and recommendations to the Council and its annual debate on progress achieved, the European Parliament has come out of the Political Union negotiations with its role reduced. If legislative codecision and democratic oversight by Parliament are at all essential to a democratic system, it is precisely in sensitive domains like immigration policy, visa and judicial cooperation policy, and a fortiori police cooperation and the struggle against international crime. Is there a danger that the powers exercised in these new domains will be partially withdrawn from national democratic oversight without being subjected to compensatory supervision by the European Parliament? Furthermore, in the absence of the Court of Justice, which Community institution will guarantee respect for human rights and fundamental freedoms in these areas, as is required by article 30 (ex K.2)? Ultimately, the question is whether this extension of the European Union's field of action will have perverse consequences by eroding fundamental values and increasing the democratic deficit.

In the decision-making process in the areas of justice and internal affairs, the role of the Council, and therefore of national governments, is increased at the expense of the Parliament. A similar division of responsibilities also applies in the areas of foreign policy and common security, although traditionally in member states this domain is chiefly the concern of the executive. That is not at all the case with justice and internal affairs, which are normally governed by laws that the executive is charged with enforcing under the supervision of the Parliament. Though these two decision-making processes are similar in the European Union, they differ in certain respects; in the domains of justice and internal affairs the Council has the main role, whereas in the area of foreign policy and common security it is the European Council that lays down orientations and the Council of Ministers that formulates common policies and actions. In both cases, the initiative may be taken by either a member state or the Commission. However, in the area of judicial and police cooperation the treaty grants the initiative only to member states and not to the Commission (art. 31 (ex K.3, par. 2)). Finally, there is an important difference in the fact that cooperation in the areas of foreign policy and security, unlike cooperation in justice and internal affairs, enjoys the advantages or suffers the handicaps of a long tradition of intergovernmental political cooperation.

General Reflections on External Policy

Now a large economic power, the European Community can no longer retreat from its political responsibilities. Since its creation and as its functions have developed, the Community has undertaken some external policy actions. The first steps were made at GATT in the shape of a common commercial policy at the time of the Kennedy Round in the early 1960s. This was the moment when the Community, speaking with one voice in the name of the Six, began to become aware of its commercial power. More recently, the Community of the Twelve was the main interlocutor with the United States and Japan in the Uruguay Round negotiations. At the same time, it progressively developed a policy of granting aid to developing nations, especially through the ACP, which now includes sixty-six nations in Africa, the Caribbean, and the Pacific. This policy of aid for development, as a complement to the programs of member states, is supported and assisted by the European Development Fund (EDF).

A vast network of association and assistance agreements of varied importance and at several levels testifies to the Community's intense activity in its external relations with its neighbors and transatlantic or global partners. The substance of these agreements is economic, but they also have a political significance — like the agreement of the European Economic Area (EEA), which inaugurated a new multilateral association. On the global scene, the Community's presence at the G–7 summit meetings is a clear indication of its international dimension; four large member states and the president of the Commission take part. Although they do not necessarily adopt a common policy, member states do seek to coordinate their positions within international organizations and especially in the United Nations, where two of these members, France and the United Kingdom, hold permanent seats on the Security Council. There are many elements in place that can form the basis for a common external policy. Over the years, the Community has sought to bring these together and coordinate them, although it has not been helped by the attitude of those member states who wish to continue to behave like the great powers they once were. A common external policy has developed gradually, sector by sector, often haphazardly and mostly without any global vision or concern for coherence. The European Union's task is to ensure the coherence of external actions and policies in the area of external relations, security, economics, technology, and development.

In the movement toward union, the European Coal and Steel Community should have been followed by a European Defence Community, which in turn would have contained the seeds of a European political community. The essential mission of the political community would have been to establish and carry out common foreign and economic policies and to provide a coherent framework for all the actions carried out together by the Six. The process launched by the 1950 Schuman Plan was intended to lay the foundations and sketch out the structures for a European federation. All the pieces were in place for launching a European union in the mid-1950s. However, under the pressure of internal policy conflicts the French National Assembly decided otherwise and refused to launch the boat. Forty years were to elapse before the governments of the Twelve finally took the decision to found the European Union.

Those who, for differing and sometimes incompatible reasons, are opposed to a European union never fail to refer to the post-EDC experience as proof that European integration did not come to a halt with the failure of the Defence Community. But they studiously ignore the circumstances and realities that made that experience different from the situation today. At that time, the economic reconstruction of Western Europe with U.S. help had hardly begun and security was being guaranteed by U.S. protection in the face of the Soviet threat. Then a divided Germany, only just beginning to rebuild, was struggling to reconstruct its economy and recover its sovereignty. Now a reunified Germany, the third-ranking economic power in the world, is beginning to assert itself on the political level. On the other hand, the impressive economic potential of the Western European states means that the United States has less and less reason to continue to bear the burden of European security, especially with the Soviet Union in a state of collapse amid resurgent ethnic conflict. Who, then, is to take on the main responsibility for European security? Will it be France, the United Kingdom, or Germany individually, each following its own ambitions, or the European Union and its allies, which alone have both the potential to rise to the demands of the situation and the requisite common objectives? The reply to this question is self-evident. It is enough to consider a few of the obvious consequences that would result if the European Union were to be stymied again: the risk of renewed domination by an America that is less willing to use its economic power at the very moment when its lack of rivals means that it occupies a dominant position on the military level; the danger of a fresh relapse into the threadbare traditional policies of the great and medium-sized European powers; and the danger of a European economic crisis, and perhaps incipient disintegration, on the Eastern European "model."

In 1970, after the failure of the draft Union of States put forward by President de Gaulle, member states began to practice intergovernmental political cooperation in a discreet way on the margins of the European Community. Basing themselves on the "Davignon Report," which laid down information-sharing and consultation procedures, foreign ministers and their political directors held periodical meetings at which they worked on the harmonization of member states' positions in the sphere of international policy. In its turn, the European Council, created in 1974, was to contribute to a strengthening of political cooperation. But it was not until 1987 that the instruments of political cooperation were incorporated into the Single European Act (which remained distinct from Community structures and procedures). This was a very modest advance, for it did not permit external policy actions, numerous and sometimes uncoordinated as they were, of sufficient scope to meet demands and expectations from the outside since whole sectors of external policy were left unaddressed. The timorous prudence of member states in these political domains, traditionally considered as their won back gardens, is to be explained by earlier setbacks and the repugnance of governments to concede or even share the exercise of what they see as their right to govern par excellence.

Another reason for a certain inertia is the marked differences distinguishing the responsibilities and roles assumed by the major states of the Community in comparison with the low-profile role of the small and medium-sized member states. Across the Twelve, degrees of responsibility and areas of interest are variable, means are disparate, and influence is very uneven. The result is that the small and medium-sized states have more limited ambitions and more sectoral interests than the responsibilities and regional roles of the major states and the global responsibility assumed by two member states in the UN Security Council. This disparity of objectives, approaches, and policies, as well as of ambitions and means, renders the elaboration and conduct of a common external policy very awkward.

On a very much more limited scale, the Swiss cantons, with equally divergent external policies and interests, have had a similar experience. The unequal positions of the cantons used to mean that they canceled each other out, and this contributed to the adoption by the confederation of a statute of neutrality. This might seem to provide a model for the European Union, but it could equally well be a temptation. In practice, this option is to be excluded by reason of the European Community's much greater dimensions and importance and therefore its inescapable responsibility. No doubt simple solutions that work for a small country like Switzerland are out of the question for the European Community with its global role to play.

The definition and implementation of a common foreign and security policy raise numerous questions concerning the conduct and management of such a policy, the capacity of the institutions, the competence of the various administrations, and the weakness of a rotating presidency. In the future, the Community will no longer be able to evade its regional and global responsibilities. It is becoming more and more obvious that the spillover process is at work and indeed developing under the impetus of endogenous and exogenous factors and under the impact of their interaction. From the start of European integration, international circumstances and U.S. actions in particular exerted a direct influence on the birth and growth of the European Community, so much so that General de Gaulle did not hesitate to speak of an "external federator" with reference to the role of the United States. If today the Community enjoys an increased autonomy in decision making, it is nonetheless as exposed as ever to external pressures and demands requiring a response. The collapse of communism and the fall of the Eastern fortress, the disintegration of the Soviet Union, and the violent explosion of Yugoslavia constitute a major challenge and a traumatic test for the European Union. At the same time, although cooperation in the development of the southern countries has for the moment lost its apparent priority under the shock of events in the East, the Community's responsibility to the developing world remains as pressing as ever. Likewise, at different levels the Community and its member states are facing the tasks involved in the quest for global equilibrium and the construction of a new world order. Global and regional security requires a heavy contribution from the Community, and the current global upheavals and degradation of the world situation mean that the Community and member states must take on growing responsibilities that will place a strain on their capacities and resources. The Soviet Union and the Communist bloc, previously the greatest threats to Western Europe, have been transformed overnight into a new zone of political and economic development with an acute need for aid and assistance; in certain parts of this zone, societies are even in a state of acute distress, for example, the former Yugoslavia.

The "new revolution" in the East and the disintegration of the Communist bloc have brought unprecedented political responsibility to the Community in the new configuration of greater Europe without leaving it the time to formulate new policies and mobilize the instruments provided by the Maastricht Treaty. It is, however, obvious that in the destabilization and reconstruction of the postwar order, an upheaval as profound as it was unexpected, the Community is becoming the only reference point in a fluid and highly unstable situation, the only federative focus in a changing Europe. Hence, the task of coordinating Western aid has been entrusted to it and it has taken actions to support the efforts of countries in the East while trying to avoid destroying the web of cooperation and exchange built up by them over four decades.

For all these positive signs, the continuing uncertainty of its global strategy underlines the Community's weakness in the political arena. This situation is all the more paradoxical in that the Community provides a benchmark and pole of attraction for countries undergoing democratic restructuring at the very moment when its own institutional system is so deeply flawed. However, in spite of its degree of incompleteness, the Community provides an invaluable example of economic integration and especially of the way conflicts between nations formerly at odds can be superseded through their commitment to a common task. In this area, it has some obligation to participate actively in the search for ways to master renascent nationalism in the countries of Eastern Europe. Here a political and economic approach seems to be evident in the conclusions of the Rome I European Council, which held that "the Community has an obligation to contribute to the search for means to consolidate and develop the general reform process under way in these countries and especially by taking its part in the stabilization of their financial situation."

So, while taking account of the differences of degree in their transition to democracy and the market economy, the European Council seems committed, even if still only timidly, to a less sectoral/bilateral and more coherent/multilateral policy toward the countries of Central and Eastern Europe. Consequently, the European Council and the Council of Foreign Ministers have been at pains to put greater stress on respect for democratic principles and human rights as well as the principles of the market economy. For example, the Council of General Affairs on 11 May 1992 adopted a declaration on the respect for these principles, which "constitute essential elements of cooperation or association accords between the Community and its CSCE partners."

Moreover, the Council invited the Commission to include an appropriate operational provision in the accords to be negotiated by the Community. For their part, the Community and its member states have been called on to inform the five countries of Central and Eastern Europe of the importance they attach to respect for these principles. The essential question remains, nonetheless, to discover by what means Community institutions will be able to ensure effective respect for these fundamental principles.

The invasion of Kuwait and the Gulf crisis confirmed the main European leaders in their resolve to endow the Community with instruments able to ensure a common political action that is both speedy and effective. In fact, while inspiring renewed solidarity and strengthening their sense of community, the Gulf crisis provided a brutal revelation of the inadequacies of political cooperation between European Community member states. In spite of the progress made with the Single European Act, the European Community remains the marriage of an economic giant and a political dwarf. After 1948, great Europeans like Denis de Rougemont and Maurice Allais were forever emphasizing the necessity for a parallel development of economic integration and political union. In light of the delay in political integration, it is fair to ask whether the Maastricht Treaty, whatever its merits, will allow Europe to make up for lost time and meet the pressing challenges of the times.

The Gulf War created a new awareness, not only among leaders but among the public, of the need to accelerate progress toward a political union. According to a poll taken in spring 1991, two-thirds of those questioned wanted the Community to speed up its political, economic, and monetary integration in order to cope with such crises.[2] In addition, the direct impact of the Gulf War on public opinion was expressed as the desire of a great majority of the European Community for a common military intervention force (61 percent) and a common foreign policy (75 percent). A common foreign policy won the largest majority in the United Kingdom, with 80 percent, while the common intervention force was backed by 72 percent. For the first time to my knowledge, British positive opinion outdistanced the Italians' and took first place in the classification. The question is whether this stemmed from some misunderstanding or a British premonition.

In other countries, opinions were differently divided depending on whether the question related to foreign policy or the intervention force. Nonetheless, while a common foreign policy attracted large majorities in big, medium-sized, and small states alike, it was less popular in Denmark (58 percent), Ireland (64 percent), and Portugal (66 percent). The correlation with replies on the subject of the intervention force applied overall, but there were a few significant exceptions. Thus, for example, Luxembourg showed surprising division, with only 49 percent in favor of the intervention force while 77 percent favored a common foreign policy. We may doubt whether this division had great significance given the modest size of the country, but the discrepancy of opinion in Germany is another matter. There 77 percent of those polled favored a common foreign policy, but on the intervention force German opinion was split down the middle, with only 46 percent in favor. One sector remained faithful to the line defined by the Fundamental Law, which prohibits Germany from taking part in international or European intervention forces. This provision was the reason why Germany did not take direct part in the Allied action against Iraq, but it did not prevent it from supporting the proposal for a European intervention force in Yugoslavia. Paradoxically, the German government was in favor of interventions in conflicts while fully aware that Germany could not take part in them. Its ambitions in foreign policy were limited by the Fundamental Law, opposition from the Social Democrats, and public opinion. However, the constitutional restrictions, which the government was then seeking to remove, are not an obstacle to the pursuit of political objectives by economic means. At the same time, reunification, which in the long term will strengthen German power, is a reminder of the urgent need for the country to be unshakably anchored in the European

Community. Although the formation of this power in the center of Europe has caused considerable disquiet, it fortunately has taken place within the containing structures of the Community. The fulfillment of the great European ambition will be all the more assured if this immense potential can be channeled, in accordance with the clearly expressed wishes of the main German leaders, into a European Community with political institutions.

So it is very understandable that in 1990 member states decided to commit themselves more resolutely to a political union. They could not fail to be confirmed in their resolution by the lesson of the Gulf crisis, which highlighted the changes under way on the international scene as well as the deficiencies in European political cooperation. At the same time, this crisis brought out the significance of the gap between the European Community's economic power and its political capacity.

In his work on the emergence and decadence of great powers, Paul Kennedy stresses precisely this relation between military/political and economic power. The military and political domination of the two superpowers is no longer supported by their economies, while the revival of the Community economy has no complement in the area of external and security policy. By restoring the original role of the UN, the current crisis has to a certain extent given a renewed importance to the United Kingdom and France by virtue of the permanent seats they have on the Security Council and also on account of their military and political freedom of maneuver. But there is a stark contrast between the growing economic power of Germany and its limited role in the Gulf crisis. Paul Kennedy's point highlights a complementarity between France and the United Kingdom on the one side, as nuclear powers with Security Council seats, and Germany on the other side, a rising economic power that has yet to find a corresponding position in the political order. Given this complementarity, the pooling of economic and political resources would allow a united Europe to give an immediate direction to global politics and to take responsibility for its own security in cooperation with the United States. The progressive but foreseeable withdrawal of American troops from Europe in the long term and the withdrawal of Soviet forces call for the more or less long-term establishment of a system of Community defense and a pan-European security system in cooperation with America and Russia. A certain European identity under the form of cooperation was close, despite its inadequacies, and it seemed to be a feature of the presence and action of Community member state forces in the gulf.

Greater cohesion in the area of external policy would allow the Community to assert its influence by speaking with one voice on the Security Council and providing the example of regional participation in the construction and operation of the new international order. The creation of this order is too vital to be left to the discretion of the United States; in the future, it will be indispensable for the success and credibility of international security and cooperation for a united Europe (and other great regions of the world) to be involved. The orientations formulated by the Rome I European Council fit into such a perspective. In fact, "in the area of external policy, the European Council has arrived at a consensus on the objective of a common foreign and security policy: to strengthen the Community's identity and the coherence of its action on the international stage. New challenges and new responsibilities must be met. The Community's international action will be open to world needs but strongly orientated toward development policy."

With this in mind, the Community will also be tightening its links with other European countries whose situation requires ever closer structures of cooperation. Concerned to provide itself with the means for its common policy, the European Council has noted the need to review procedures and mechanisms for the preparation, adoption, and implementation of decisions in the area of external policy so as to increase the coherence, rapidity, and effectiveness of the Community's international actions. The European Council has stated that no aspect of the Union's external relations will be excluded in principle from the common external policy, and it noted that there is a consensus to go beyond current limits in the field of security.

In order to avoid the inextricable difficulties raised by any enumeration of the domains or zones considered as being of essential common interest, the Commission proposed that the European Council should decide which areas will pass from the arena of political cooperation to that of Community policy. The Maastricht Treaty sought to translate its intentions into obligations.

An assessment of the European Union, even if only provisional, will require an experience of sufficiently long duration, for the institutions need to be shaped by contact with reality. Events have moved more swiftly than the union process, and the Community had to face its first grave crisis, in Yugoslavia, before it was able to exploit the Maastricht Treaty instruments. What lesson will it draw from this crisis, one that is showing signs of lasting a long time?

Toward a Common Foreign and Security Policy

General Objectives and Fields of Activity

Following in the footsteps of the Single European Act, the Maastricht Treaty deliberately marked the way to a political union. The Single European Act incorporated political cooperation and had only a marginal place for common security, yet it has the merit of having made some place for it, considering that security was for so long considered a taboo subject in Community discussions. With this first opening, the European Union took a decisive step by uniting in one common policy two areas artificially kept apart by history. However, the treaty did not provide for the inclusion of the third area, that of a shared defense, except in the long term. These three areas of action, together with external economic relations and aid and development policy, create the identity of a political community in the global arena. This identity of the European Community, which is being progressively built on the basis of economic integration and political co-operation, is finding a coherent expression in the European Union. The commitment is clearly expressed in article B of the common provisions:

> The Union shall have the following objectives . . . to assert its identity on the international scene, in particular through the implementation of a common foreign and security policy, which shall in time lead to establishing a common defense policy.

The Union has the particular task of ensuring that all of its external actions are coherent within the framework of its external relations, security, economic, and development policies, while the Council and the Commission are responsible for enforcing such coherence. From now on, the Union will house common institutions, policies, and actions under one roof and create new synergies in domains that are by their very nature political. In providing for a common foreign and security policy, the Maastricht Treaty assigns to it the following objectives in article J.1: safeguarding common values, fundamental interests, and the independence of the Union; strengthening the security of the Union and its member states; preserving peace and strengthening international security in accordance with the principles of the UN Charter as well as the principles of the Helsinki Final Act and the objectives of the Paris Charter; promoting international cooperation; and developing and consolidating democracy, the rule of law, and respect for human rights and fundamental freedoms. The Union shall pursue these objectives by establishing systematic cooperation between member states in the conduct of their policies, gradually implementing joint action in areas in which member states have important interests in common. In order to ensure the efficiency of this systematic cooperation, member states have committed themselves to support "the Union's external and security policy actively and unreservedly in a spirit of loyalty and mutual solidarity. They shall refrain from any action which is contrary to the interests of the Union or likely to impair its effectiveness as a cohesive force in international relations" (art. J.1). These are the principles that now guide the behavior of member states. The treaty gives the Council the task of ensuring that they are respected.

If the general objectives and principles do not of themselves raise any problems, their realization and implementation are fraught with difficulties. Thus, the formulation of common guidelines and actions in matters in which member states have important interests in common will be a difficult task for the European Council and the Council of Foreign Ministers. The difficulty of their task may be measured by the complexity of the structure established by the Maastricht Treaty negotiators. This structure of authority reflects the variety of member states' objectives and interests and highlights the problems of bringing them together in an arena that touches the heart of national sovereignty. Member states are therefore concerned to control and manage matters by using a predominantly intergovernmental procedure in which they not only assume the bulk of responsibility but ensure that they will be effectively protected by a requirement for unanimity. On the other hand, the Commission no longer provides the main thrust in this area, although it remains fully associated with the European Council's work, thanks to the presence of its president, as it is also with the work of the Council and the Political Committee. The Commission is only entrusted with a back seat role, but it will have to make itself useful and even indispensable. In the meantime, the treaty maintains a clear distinction between the way power and responsibilities are divided in the Community and the Union. As a pillar of the Community, the Commission-Council tandem is at the center of the decision-making process, while within the political union the Council holds this key position. It is the Council that is mainly responsible for carrying out a common foreign and security policy according to the general guidelines set by the European Council.

The logic behind this system dictates that the common foreign and security policy be based on principles and general guidelines laid down by the European Council. Thus, the European Council has the ultimate responsibility for the Union's external policy, and its general guidelines provide the basis for decisions taken by the Council of Foreign Ministers in formulating and implementing this common policy. Likewise, the Council oversees the unity, coherence, and effectiveness of the Union's actions (art. 18 (ex J.8)). As for the Commission, it is fully associated at different stages with work on the common foreign and security policy. The Maastricht Treaty creates two levels of responsibility. One deals with the overall conception and general guidelines, the responsibility for which lies with the European Council, with the president of the Commission as an ex officio member. The other level deals with formulating and implementing concrete policies through the adoption of common positions and joint actions, a task entrusted to the Council aided by the Commission. According to article 14 (ex J.4): "The common foreign and security policy shall cover all questions related to the security of the Union, including the eventual framing of a common defense policy, which might in time lead to a common defense."

This same article goes on to establish a distinction between security in the broad sense and defense properly so called. Consequently, questions with defense implications are not subject to the procedures in article J.3 relative to the adoption of joint actions but are regulated by particular provision in article J.4. The inclusion of defense alongside joint action constitutes the main innovation of the European Union, which furthermore structures and integrates the elements and the practice of a common foreign and security policy.

A Common External Policy

For the formulation and implementation of its common foreign and security policy, the Union has three instruments: common positions, joint actions, and joint representation.

In the framework of systematic cooperation and according to long-established tradition, member states keep each other informed and consult one another in the Council on every matter of external policy that is of general interest. In this way, they aim to consolidate their influence on the international scene by carrying out actions that are convergent, even though not necessarily joint. A higher level of cohesion may be reached when the Council establishes a common position, when it thinks it necessary. Hence, convergent actions are undertaken jointly or according to common positions initiated by a member state, the Commission, or the presidency of the Council. In light of the experience of political cooperation, even systematic cooperation remains a flexible and only partially binding instrument. It is member states that have the duty to see to the conformity of their national policies with common positions. The example of the responses of member states to the Yugoslav crisis and the recognition of Slovenia and Croatia is certainly far from providing a model with respect to common positions, but the pre-Maastricht experience does allow us to cherish some hope with regard to the concerted or convergent approach prescribed by the European Union Treaty. In fact, member states commit themselves to coordinate their actions and defend common positions in the international arena even when some are absent. The treaty does tie member states down more regarding the conduct of their national policies and their positions within international organizations and meetings, but, with a display of possibly excessive confidence, it also leaves the implementation of these policies mainly to them.

Aware of the uncertainties of this approach, the member states decided to strengthen their common identity by establishing a new procedure for adopting and implementing *joint actions* (art. 13 (ex J.3)). This procedure makes it possible to undertake joint actions that are more narrowly defined and binding. In adopting a joint action, the Council has a particular concern to settle its scope, objectives, and means. In turn, member states are bound by the terms of the joint action when taking positions and carrying out their own actions. Following up the joint action is the task of the presidency, which as a general rule is constituted by the "troika" and, according to article J.5, par. 2, is "responsible for the implementation of common measures."

The Commission is fully associated with these tasks, which also involve the Political Committee made up of the political directors of foreign ministries. According to the terms of article J.8, par. 5, the Political Committee "shall also monitor the implementation of agreed policies, without prejudice to the responsibility of the presidency and the Commission."

If we bring together the elements of this complex system, we begin to grasp the intention of the member states to give themselves a common external policy that is more effective than mere political cooperation. Joint action demonstrates a higher degree of coherence, unity, and effectiveness on the part of the Union. Joint actions can now be carried out within the Security and Cooperation Conference on Europe (CSCE), now the Organization for Security and Cooperation in Europe (OSCE), as well as in the areas of disarmament, nuclear nonproliferation, arms control in Europe, the export of arms to third countries, and the transfer of military technologies.

The presidency's role in representing the Union needs to be seen in this context.[3] In accordance with its responsibility for representing and implementing joint actions, in principle the presidency presents the Union position within international organizations and at international conferences. As a general rule, the Commission is fully associated with tasks in the areas of foreign policy and common security, but with regard to international economic organizations and conferences it is actually the Community's representative. It speaks, therefore, in the name of the Community in the area of commercial policy and carries out negotiations on commercial agreements by mandate from the Council. Representation, cohesion, and hence the Community's role in international organizations and conferences depend to a large extent on its powers and development. As a consequence of the Commission's exclusive competence in the field of commercial policy, the Community is able to speak with one voice through the Commission at the World Trade Organization (WTO) talks. In 1991, it acquired special status at the United Nations' Food and Agriculture Organization (FAO), that of a regional organization for economic integration, by virtue of its common agricultural and fisheries policy.

In the United Nations, the Community has asserted its identity in economic and social areas. In these sectors, the tradition has been to prepare for UN Conferences in the Council and set common guidelines on the basis of Commission proposals. Although the Community has more limited powers in the political arena, political cooperation resulting from the provisions of the Single European Act has made it possible to achieve a high level of coordination in recent years. Joint declarations have become much more frequent at the General Assembly (82 in 1989, 113 in 1990, and 128 in 1991), and the assertion of purely national positions has become the exception.[4] Thanks to the information and cooperation network, and the work of the group of permanent representatives at the UN, the Community has gradually been able to assert its political personality. It is, however, quite natural to wonder whether the high degree of cohesion shown at the General Assembly, and especially at the Economic and Social Council (ECOSOC), does not owe a great deal to the generally low level of obligation associated with those institutions' powers. The real test of cohesion would seem to be provided by important questions or crises in institutions having the power to make binding decisions. In any event, the Maastricht Treaty aims to strengthen the presence of the Union in the various UN institutions, commissions, and conferences. Witness the presidency's representative role as spokesman for the Community and member states and also its concern to ensure that member states that are not represented in particular international organizations or conferences are kept informed. The presidency, moreover, or those member states that are present, is under an obligation to defend common positions.

Where the Security Council is concerned, the issue is different, especially with respect to the permanent seats. Should the number of permanent members and other members be enlarged? The economic power and growing political influence of Germany and Japan seem to fit them naturally for positions of great responsibility. But can these two economic powers become permanent members of the Security Council, which decides on sanctions and collective actions to preserve peace, when they are not in a position to make their contribution to peacekeeping on account of constitutional hindrance or customary reticence? It is no accident that the German government intends to try again to reform its Fundamental Law when it returns with a renewed request for a permanent seat. Moreover, does the presence of a third member of the Community not threaten to raise the question of overrepresentation of the Community and Western powers? Suppose that Italy, too, a member of G-7, were to make an official request for a seat? In contrast, it would seem to be opportune to make an effort to reestablish a global equilibrium within the Security Council by opening it up to a Third World country such as India, Brazil, or Nigeria. This has recently been suggested by the UN secretary-general. Or would it perhaps be wiser to adopt a regional approach? The representation of large regions or regional organizations would be all the more appropriate in that they will be called on in the future to bear a greater share of responsibilities and burdens as a function of the local dimensions of so-called peripheral conflicts. For the time being, the Maastricht Treaty adopts a solution that includes an obligation to share, inform, and act together on matters that come before the Security Council. As for France and the United Kingdom, which are permanent members, it is up to them in the exercise of their functions to ensure that they defend the positions and the interests of the European Union. It may be doubted whether this representation formula can satisfy the ambitions of a unified Germany, which is striving to assert itself more effectively on the global and European stages.[5]

As regards bilateral representation, ambitious projects for the creation of Community embassies have been abandoned in favor of a consultation and cooperation formula. To this end, article J.6 declares that "The diplomatic and consular missions of the member states and the Commission delegations in third-party countries and international conferences and their representations to international organizations shall cooperate in ensuring that the common positions and common measures adopted by the Council are complied with and implemented." This is a long way from the right of joint legation set out in the draft European Union Treaty adopted by the European Parliament in 1984. On the other hand, a more precise obligation of the Maastricht Treaty codifies the customary cooperation between the representations of member states and the Commission. In doing so, it introduces the practice of joint assessment together with a closer collaboration for the protection of European Union citizens outside the Union.

Following a step-by-step approach that fits existing needs or codifies customary practices, the European Union is progressively asserting its international personality. Sometimes, indeed, it introduces innovations and strengthens its cohesion outside by acquiring new instruments and means. The question is whether these means, considered adequate or even advanced in earlier days, have been adapted or are adaptable to the changes and challenges of today, let alone tomorrow. Before this question is answered it will be necessary to obtain a clearer grasp of the way this complex system functions by setting out the various twists and turns of its decision-making process.

Toward a European Defense Policy: The End of a Taboo?

"The common foreign and security policy shall include all questions related to the security of the Union, including the eventual framing of a common defense policy, which might in time lead to a common defense" (art. J.4). This is the first time since the shocks of the EDC and the Fouchet Project that defense has figured explicitly in an official text. It is true that a European approach to security resurfaced discreetly in the early 1980s in European Parliament reports and drafts,[6] but it was the Single European Act that, after so many years of silence, introduced the concept of European security in its provisions for political cooperation: "The high contracting parties consider that closer cooperation on questions of European security would contribute in an essential way to the development of a European identity in external policy matters. They are ready to coordinate their positions more closely on the political and economic aspects of security" (title III, art. 30, par. 6a).

This provision shows that security is now officially part of the European Community's external policy and political personality. The test prudently restricts itself to the political and economic aspects of security, but in reality defense remains the exclusive domain of the Western European Union and especially of NATO.

Behind this compromise one can discern the old conflict going back to the end of the war and setting the supporters of an Atlantic defense under American leadership against partisans of a more autonomous European defense within NATO.[7] This division became all too apparent when President de Gaulle proposed that defense be included in the draft treaty for the Union of European States. Fears that de Gaulle wanted to get control of European defense and that American protection might be weakened were among the powerful arguments used to block the Fouchet Project. The conclusion of the Elysée Treaty and France's withdrawal from NATO were signs of de Gaulle's persistence in promoting European defense. Was this a way of filling the void left by the failure of the EDC?

General de Gaulle resigned and many governments of different political hues came after him in France and her partners, but the division has not disappeared. Hostility between partisans of an Atlantic defense and those of a European defense has left its mark on strategies and outlooks. Thirty years after the failure of the Fouchet Project, at the time of the Maastricht Treaty negotiations and while France and Germany were arguing for a more European approach within the Atlantic Alliance, the British government, supported by the Italian government, pleaded for an Atlantic defense. The treaty opted for a compromise between these two strategies, affirming that in the long term European security involved the formulation of a common defense policy. Thirty years later, the Maastricht Treaty exorcised the European taboo by including common defense in the concept of European security. This painfully slow progress is a testimony to the prevailing rigidity of concepts and ideas that ignore changes in reality. In fact, since the fall of the Berlin Wall, the Gulf War, and the explosion of nationalism in Eastern Europe, the underlying conditions have been turned upside down. The Soviet threat has been replaced by the danger of the spread of ethnic conflict in Europe. At the same time, the United States, the only superpower left since the collapse of the Soviet Union, is tending to take a more distant attitude toward Europe. In a state of relative economic decline and burdened with deficits and public debt, America no longer has the economic muscle to match its military domination. Reluctant to go on carrying the excessively burdensome expense of defending others, it is tending to slim down its global military presence, especially in Western Europe. Reduced to about 150,000 troops, its presence now has more of a symbolic significance. In spite of these limitations, the United States is not resigned to abandoning its leading role. The debate over the new roles of NATO and the Western European Union, and over the creation of a European or Atlantic multinational rapid intervention force, is a clear sign that both Atlantic and European misunderstandings are still very much alive. In a morass of ambiguities, the Maastricht Treaty performs a masterful balancing act.

The concept of European defense has been asserted without any dates being set for its realization. Article 14 (ex J.4), however, sets out a range of concrete measures indicating a determination on the part of member states to forge a European defense identity. Its secular arm is "the Western European Union, which is an integral part of the development of the Union." Without being integrated into the European Union as of now, the WEU is to "elaborate and implement decisions and actions of the Union which have defense implications. The Council shall, in agreement with the institutions of the WEU, adopt the necessary practical arrangements."

The nine states that are members both of the WEU and the European Union set out the role of the WEU and the scope of the provisions of the European Union Treaty in a declaration adopted at Maastricht. The Nine agree on the necessity of creating a European identity in terms of security and defense and for Europe to assume increased responsibilities in the area of defense. This identity is to be elaborated little by little and in successive stages. As of now, the WEU is an integral part of the development of the European Union and aims to strengthen its contribution to solidarity within the Atlantic Alliance. Thus, the WEU has a current role to play and a future role within the European Union. At the same time, it is becoming clear that one of the goals and consequences of this European identity will be to lighten the burden of American responsibility, while at the same time it will increase the share of Europeans in the Atlantic Alliance. To this end, the WEU will be developed as an integral part of the European Union's defense and as a means of buttressing the European pillar of the Atlantic Alliance.

While waiting for the integration of the WEU in the European Union, the Nine have invited Denmark, Ireland, and Greece to join the WEU or become observers. They have also decided to take a range of measures to consolidate cooperation between the two organizations. These include synchronization of meetings and harmonization of working methods; informing and consulting the Commission; and cooperation between the European Parliament and the WEU Parliamentary Assembly. These measures, creating closer links, will be facilitated by the transfer of the seat of the WEU to Brussels. The Atlantic debt is respected, relations between WEU, the European Union, and the Atlantic Alliance being clearly established; the policy of the Union respects obligations arising for certain member states from the North Atlantic Treaty, and it is compatible with the common security and defense policy set out in this context. The WEU, whose role is to buttress the European pillar of the Atlantic Alliance, acts in perfect conformity with positions adopted in the Atlantic Alliance. Its members are committed to increased coordination on questions that represent an "important common interest" within the Alliance, which remains "the essential forum for consultation between the allies and the arena in which they agree on policies concerning their security and defense commitments under the North Atlantic Treaty."

The experience of the Gulf War and the Yugoslav conflict has encouraged members of the WEU to increase its operational role by discussing and planning the appropriate missions, structures, and means; instituting a planning cell; calling meetings of chiefs of staff; and encouraging closer military cooperation. Members are also going to consider the creation of a European armaments agency and the transformation of the WEU Institute into a European security and defense academy. Anticipating the development of a security and defense policy, the members of the European Union have accepted, according to a principle applied in other sectors, that closer cooperation may take place between two or more member states at a bilateral level in the framework of the WEU and/or the Atlantic Alliance to the extent that this cooperation does not contradict or hinder the cooperation planned for in the Maastricht Treaty. The coproduction of weapons and the creation of a Franco-German army corps are examples of cooperation between two or more member states. Flexibility and a determination to protect each other's interests are characteristic of the pragmatism shown in this particularly sensitive area. As an example, article 14 (ex J.4) stipulates that Union policy in this sector shall not prejudice the specific character of the security and defense policy of certain member states. The treaty seems to have sought to preserve both the special Anglo-American links and French commitments to certain African countries.

The formation of a European security and defense identity is a gradually evolving process, which is why the treaty stipulates that in order to further its objectives security and defense provisions may be revised on the basis of an assessment of progress achieved and experience gained. This assessment will be the object of a report to be submitted in 1996 by the Council of Foreign Ministers to the European Council in anticipation of the definitive integration of the WEU into the European Union, which might happen in 1998, the year when the treaty of Brussels expires.[8] Thus, the Maastricht Treaty has indicated the steps to be taken to achieve a common security and defense policy; the future of this common policy is entirely in the hands of the member states.

The Decision-Making Process

The decision-making process in the area of a common foreign and security policy is evolving within the Community system and is based on its institutional and administrative network. This process, with its complex and cumbersome mechanisms, is markedly different from the normal Community decision-making model and is much closer to the practices of inter-governmental political cooperation. In a sector considered to be truly political and the preserve of the highest levels of government, it is more difficult to persuade national governments to adopt Community methods. If, at most, they are accepting a certain sharing and joint exercise of powers, they have not decided yet on any sort of transfer of powers. Foreign and security policy being part of the preserve of heads of state or government and their foreign ministers at the national level, logic dictates that at the Community level the essential roles must be given to the European Council and the Council of Foreign Ministers. As the supreme political authority of the Twelve, the European Council is made up of the highest political leaders, all elected by universal suffrage, together with the Commission's president, who is chosen by this same group and invested by the European Parliament. In the new division of responsibilities in the European Union, a key function is attributed to the Council of Foreign Minsters assisted by a Political Committee made up of their political directors. This mechanism is somewhat similar to the institutional structure of the draft Treaty of the Union of European States proposed by General de Gaulle in 1959. In fact, that draft provided for a council of heads of state or government, a council of ministers, and a political commission. A feature that increases the similarity was that managing institutions reported to the European Parliament and could receive opinions from it. That the current setup, in the changed world of today, should have such a resemblance to this thirty-year-old project is extraordinary; it seems that the institutional evolution simply has not matched the pace of change. Only one concession has been made to the irreplaceable experience of the European Community: the Commission is to be associated with the work of intergovernmental institutions throughout the decision-making process. More than thirty years on, this is the essential point that distinguishes the European Union from de Gaulle's project.

The first phase of the decision-making process is initially devoted to establishing general principles and directions, then to formulating common positions and, where appropriate, joint actions. The European Council is first and foremost responsible for defining these general principles and directions. It is in this general framework that common positions and joint actions are adopted. The initiatives that set the process in motion may come either from the European Council and the Council of Foreign Ministers or from the Commission, the member states, or the Political Committee. While the particular area in which a proposal is drawn up or a project launched is easy to localize, it is very difficult to see how and where the ideas originate and the various routes that lead up to initiatives. Ideas and opinions in fact are carried down the formal or informal national and European channels of the European Community, a vast communications and exchange network. The result is that at any given moment a European government or institution can launch a proposal or take an initiative that sets the mechanism of the European Union in motion.

As a general rule, and apart from urgent cases, the European Council mandates the Council to prepare reports that will serve as working documents for establishing the principles and general directions of foreign and common security policies. Supported by the Political Committee, the Council associates the Commission with this work, allowing it to exert its influence from the start of the process, all the more so in that its president can support its action from within the European Council. His seat on the Council obviously secures him a privileged position, the importance of which has yet to be fully appreciated, especially in the context of political union. It will be remembered that on certain occasions the Commission president has been able to call on the support of the European Council in the face of overly timid ministerial attitudes. These examples cannot be extrapolated, and in the new political context it is dangerous to predict what use the Commission president will be able to make of his privileged position as a member of the European Council. However, there is little doubt that his influence will depend to a large extent on his personality, competence, and political judgment.

On the basis of its general directions, the Council takes the decisions necessary to formulate a common foreign and security policy. Following the traditional lines of political cooperation, it establishes a common position whenever it thinks this is necessary. The common position guides and provides a context for the actions of member states, who have an obligation to ensure that their national policies conform with the common position. It also determines their conduct in international arenas where they are committed to defend the common position. Even when it is not thought essential to establish a common position, member states keep one another informed and consulted on any question of general interest. The aim of such cooperation is to ensure that their combined influence is exercised as effectively as possible through the convergence of their actions. In the past, experience has shown that it was easier to achieve agreement on a resolution than to ensure that the subsequent actions of member states converged.

The next stage, the adoption of joint actions, was the principle innovation in external policy. First, the Council decides on a unanimous basis which area or issue will form the object of a joint action. It then determines to carry out a joint action and precisely fixes its scope, objectives, and means, the requisite procedures, and the conditions applicable for its implementation. Although unanimity is the rule, the Council may also decide to use a qualified majority voting procedure: "The Council shall, when adopting the joint action and at any stage during its development, define those matters on which decisions are to be taken by a qualified majority" (art. 13, par. 2 (ex J.3, par. 2)).

The requirement is for a strengthened qualified majority of fifty-four votes, reflecting a favorable vote by at least eight members. Thus, while offering a maximum guarantee to each member state, the Maastricht Treaty opens the way to qualified majority decisions for reasons of efficiency. Moreover, it provides an exception for procedural issues. In an appendix to the treaty, the declaration on votes in the area of foreign policy and common security tries, in the same spirit, to make the unanimity rule more flexible: "The conference agrees that, with regard to Council decisions requiring unanimity, member states will, to the extent possible, avoid preventing a unanimous decision where a qualified majority exists in favor of that decision."

These are just a few timid openings in an area that has suffered from the application of the unanimity rule. It is true that unanimity is a guarantee for member states, but it can also be a way of paralyzing the European Union. However, unanimity is fully applicable when taking decisions and actions that have implications for defense. These decisions are not subject to the procedures set out in article 13 (ex J.3). Such decisions and actions are worked out by the WEU at the request of the European Union. In principle, their adoption requires a conjoint decision by the Council and the WEU. The practical aspects of implementation are adopted by the Council. At the implementation stage, joint actions and decisions commit member states when they take certain positions and in the conduct of their actions. These may be convergent actions undertaken individually by member states following the objectives and modalities of a joint action or actions effectively undertaken in common such as sending European observers, providing humanitarian aid and assistance, and in the long term dispatching European blue helmets. All such actions are watched over by the Council, which "shall ensure the unity, consistency, and effectiveness of action by the Union" (art. 18 (ex J.8)).

Responsibility for the implementation of joint actions belongs to the presidence of the Council, which associates the Commission fully with its tasks. Without prejudice to the rights and obligations of the presidency and the Commission, the Political Committee also oversees the implementation of agreed-upon policies. The division of labor ought not to present too much difficulty inasmuch as the presidency exercises general supervision with the help of the Commission while the Political Committee with its fifteen groups of experts takes on oversight. Nonetheless, several problems could crop up in the future due to the frequency and intensity of joint actions. We should bear in mind the fact that the Political Committee meets only periodically and that the continuity of Community activity is ensured by the Council secretariat and especially the Commission and its administration. For this reason, too, the Commission will have a crucial role to play in the area of foreign and common security policy, particularly so in that this policy is difficult to separate from external economic policy.

The treaty attributes a modest role in this process to the European Parliament. According to article J.7, the Parliament must be kept constantly informed by the presidency and the Commission. In addition, the presidency should consult it and ensure that its views are given due consideration. This formula seems to both attenuate the consultative power manifested by Parliament's opinions and ensure that its "views" will have an impact. As in other domains, the European Parliament can address questions and recommendations to the Council. Moreover, it is able to debate annually on the progress made in common foreign and security policy. By making use of these various means, the Parliament will be able to influence to some extent the Union's external policy. Unlike national parliaments, it has no means of keeping a check on the Council of Foreign Ministers, the central cog that is not responsible to the European Parliament.

Reflections on Decision-Making Powers

Figure 3 offers a simplified view of the decision-making process in order to make it easier to understand: we shall only be able to assess the effectiveness of this mechanism when we have seen it in action. Some, in particular Jacques Delors, have strongly criticized how cumbersome and complex it is. The European Movement and the federalists have also made their views known. And yet when we consider the positions, the claims, and the reticence of governments, it has to be admitted that in spite of its weaknesses the procedure, established in one year, shows some definite progress. It reflects what is currently possible for Europe, that is, an occasionally clumsy compromise between national interests that are often divergent and the universally accepted necessity of pursuing and consolidating the construction of a united Europe. Ultimately, the effectiveness of this mechanism, which reflects the preoccupations of the moment, will depend chiefly on the determination of member governments, on the capacity of institutions to translate that determination into decisions and actions, and on their skill at adapting to change and to new conditions.

While the Commission, a permanent Community institution, ensures continuity for the economic and social enterprise, the question is who will take on this task within the political union. The Council of Foreign Ministers will have its hands full ensuring the coherence of decisions taken in various domains by Community institutions. In the exercise of this global policy function, it of course will act on the basis of the principles and general guidelines established by the European Council, but the range of these multiple tasks and its infrequent meetings will not allow it to oversee the coherent application of its decisions or joint actions, all the more so in that at any moment it may be confronted with serious problems or crises.

In fact, continuity and representation are the responsibility of the presidency, which relies both on the Commission and on the Political Committee. Although supported by the latter, the troika will be put to a hard test; confronted with the crises and difficulties in Eastern Europe, it has shown its limitations in its ability to handle the Community's external policy. A brief study of its role in the Yugoslav crisis will enable us to gain a better understanding of the different aspects of the problem of the government of the Community and to learn some lessons for the future. However, we should note right away that a presidency that changes every six months is heavily overloaded. In the course of the last few years, it has taken on, in addition to its normal work, a major portion of the responsibility in the intergovernmental negotiations for the European Union and European Economic Area (EEA) Treaties in the midst of the Gulf War and the crises arising from changes in Eastern Europe. This new dimension in the Community's external political activities requires the Commission to make a more active contribution and adopt new mechanisms in the light of experience. It was no accident that the members of the European Union planned a general review in 1996 and anticipated a partial revision of the common security and defense provisions. In fact, when article 4 is revised, other amendments can be made to provisions relating to foreign policy and common security (art. J.10). In other words, governments have paid special attention to the problem of the efficiency and adaptability of the Union system, hence the importance accorded to the evolution of the European Union.

This asymmetrical structure, based on two pillars, has for a long time posed a crucial problem of cohesion and coherence. Each member state acts in terms of its own interests and priorities in its internal and external policies. The latter are the result of both its structure and its history, of perceptions of its interests and objectives as well as of multiple pressures to which its government and its decision-making authorities are subject. The judgments handed down by its political institutions, balancing on the one hand external factors and party influences, interest groups, and media and opinion groups and, on the other, choices made according to defined priorities and available resources, are reflected in political decisions if not always in consistent behavior. In the field of interaction between internal and external factors and in the exercise of this role of sifting and decision making, governments and parliaments are required to make political choices and ensure their coherence while overseeing the implementation of policies. This task is difficult enough in the context of the Community's competencies but critically so in the Political Union, hence the treaty's almost obsessional emphasis on cohesion and coherence.

From the beginning of the Community, "packages" have been the best illustration of these complex decision-making processes. Packages have involved compromises between the principles and provisions of the treaty, the Commission's proposals, and the interplay of national policies. In 1961, the transition to the second stage was accompanied by the simultaneous adoption of basic regulations in three sectors: common agricultural policy, competition, and equality of men and women's salaries. These three processes evolved in parallel in three specialized councils before a global decision was reached by the Council for General Affairs. The "package" looks like the result of a series of concessions and arbitrages made according to rules fixed by the treaty and overseen by the Commission. Coherence is ensured by the Commission's proposals and its active participation. However, such coherence, difficult enough to achieve on the national level by means of effective interministerial coordination, is even harder to attain in a place meant for debating and formulating policies common to several member states. This is all the more so in that over the years we have seen a process of specialization at the level of the councils, which has contributed to a certain fragmentation of Community methods and power in spite of its undoubted advantages. Specialized authority structures have emerged in this way. These structures are often compartmentalized and seem like "subgovernments" based on a close and continued collaboration between institutions and interest groups, and they have developed behind the facade of the consultation process. However, the more that collaboration with interest groups intensifies and extends, the more necessary it is to assert the autonomy of Community power. Therefore, it might be asked whether specialization within the Commission, the compartmentalization of its administrative apparatus, and the fragmentation of the Council's responsibilities are really helping to consolidate the cohesion and abilities of Community power.

Far from representing the global approach sought by national governments, the Council, already handicapped by its internal tensions and the intermittent nature of its meetings, tends to break up into specialized councils in spite of the role of the Council for General Affairs. As an example, the Agricultural Council, on which ministers of agriculture sit, is more inclined to lend an ear to its constituency than to pursue general objectives and take decisions in the framework of the Common Agricultural Policy. This fragmentation of power further strengthens the influence of particular interests and vested privilege, making sectoral innovation and reform more difficult. Whatever the real or hoped-for advantage of this specialization, it would seem that the time is ripe to stop the fragmentation of Community authority and to try to rebuild the coherence of the Community's political vision in the perspective of the European Union.

Problems of cohesion and coherence have grown. Increasing levels of integration; the internal market and its natural extension into the Economic and Monetary Union; and the extension of cooperation and Community action to new sectors such as the environment, health, and education are all factors that by their diversity make coherent policies more difficult to establish and implement. Problems are made even worse, if that were possible, by the addition of further internal and external areas of activity falling under a predominantly intergovernmental decision-making process. In the new political subsystem, the coherence that proposals emanating from the Commission initially ensured is lacking. Based on national approaches and the lack of a permanent institution with the task of identifying the common interest, the process is exposed to sporadic contradictions between various polices reflecting national interests. The European Council does, of course, set out the general orientations that serve as a framework for common decisions and joint actions for which the Council has responsibility, but one cannot help but feel very doubtful about the Council's capacity to guarantee any sort of coherence, continuity, or follow-through in common policies.

As the field of action grows, difficulties tend to increase. How does one ensure compatibility between technological development and regional development? How does one manage the variety of objectives and interests of the different member states coherently or successfully link the various segments of external policy?

The Community is simultaneously facing the problems of its deepening and enlargement and grappling with those of aid and security. This cluster of problems cannot be resolved by a leadership blinkered by "short-termism"; it requires a long-term global vision capable of taking into account the interaction between internal and external factors. At the heart of the negotiations on the European Economic Area was the question of the participation of EFTA members in the Community decision-making process. While preserving the indispensable autonomy of its decision-making capacity, the Community accepted a formula for information and consultation prior to any Community decision relative to EEA domains. The example of the Uruguay Round negotiations illustrates very clearly the close relationship between international competition and national agricultural subsidies. In the case of the Community, external pressure has spurred the process of reforming the Common Agricultural Policy long but unsuccessfully called for by several member states. It was this conjunction of internal demand and external pressures that finally made it possible to carry out a reform of the Common Agricultural Policy in 1992.

The complexity of so many interactions is further increased by intervention of the security factor in this process. The WTO negotiations influence both general external policy and relations between American and European allies in NATO. Vice versa, security concerns in relation to the Eastern European countries are an incitement to give them increased support while modifying the division of responsibilities between Americans and Europeans. In turn, these factors of change, which are putting the capacity of the Community to the test, seem to be threatening to divert its attention and resources away from the southern countries that are being deprived of part of the European aid they need. The Community, faced with the crisis of the Eastern European countries, may not have the will or the means to persist with and increase its contribution to the development of the Maghreb, Africa and the ACP, or the Latin American countries. It is true that the largest commercial power, in which one job in four is dependent on external trade, cannot withdraw from its international and regional responsibilities. But how does one manage limited resources in the context of European and global responsibilities? How does one obtain the required level of coherence and optimize the Union's abilities in the absence of a European government? Faced with such problems, as well as the upheavals in Eastern Europe and the violent conflicts in the former Yugoslavia, the European Union seems to have been left high and dry by events. Apparently overwhelmed by the violence of contemporary change, it does not seem to have found the time or the means to produce an adequate response.

The Community Facing External Crises

Two serious crises overwhelmed the Community at the very moment when it was struggling to make an adequate response to changes in Eastern Europe, grappling with negotiations over GATT and the European Economic Area, and trying to cope with the implementation of its internal market and the drafting of the European Union Treaty. These two crises were the Gulf War and the violent disintegration of Yugoslavia. They were crises that called for powers and instruments that the Community did not and does not possess but that were, in fact, the subject of negotiations on political union at that time. In the confusion of these sudden events, the Community has been forced to improvise and take on tasks for which it was not prepared.

The Gulf War

The Gulf War put the European Community as well as the political cooperation outlined in the Single European Act brutally to the test. It emphasized the inadequacy of the powers and means available to the Community in the areas of external policy and security. The relatively modest role played by the Community and its member states served to highlight the resurgence of American power and a recovery of vitality by the UN, in particular, by the Security Council. Under resolute pressure from the United States and its chief allies, including France and the United Kingdom, which are permanent members, the Security Council agreed to sanctions and then to intervention against Iraq. In the face of aggression against Kuwait, the Security Council had to condemn this invasion and authorize the members of the UN to reestablish, if necessary by force, the situation as it existed previously in this region, as it was considered to be of vital importance to the industrialized world. In this case, the issue was not the defense of democracy and human rights, for the whole ethos of the states in this region is at the opposite pole from Western values, but rather the preservation of the stability of states that represent the main source of the world's oil.

That "the Gulf War showed, if ever there was a need to do so, the limits of the influence and action of the European Community" was the opinion of President Delors. The United Kingdom and France of course committed significant military resources to the conflict, while the other WEU countries coordinated their own interventions, particularly in the naval sphere. Overall, however, European collective action was not, according to François Heisbourg, director of the International Institute for Strategic Studies in London, on a level with the ambitions of the European Union as expressed in the intergovernmental conference, nor did it have much to do with the way the Gulf crisis was resolved. While acknowledging the importance of the British and French commitment at the Security Council and on the ground, he had to admit that "Europe remains an idea and not a reality in the area of international security, and the Europeans neither can nor know how to take the initiative effectively and establish the agenda in terms of the management and resolution of a great crisis that is geographically close to them."[9] He concluded that only the United States was able to take on the leadership of the international community in the face of the challenge from Iraq. Leaving aside the issues of military success and the political management of this crisis, it is surely exaggerating to speak of Europe's "failure" since the Community does not have the weapons to cope with such crises. Neither the objectives nor the means or resources of political cooperation allowed anything more to be achieved than was actually done. In fact, political cooperation was overtaken by the extent of the crisis, and the Community was not able to preserve a consensus in a situation that involved the areas of security and military intervention, the preserve of member states.

Professor Closa's analysis can help us understand better the difficulties and ambiguities of Community action in the Gulf crisis.[10] This action had two distinct phases. The first, which lasted until October 1990, was characterized by a high level of consensus expressed in declarations or by the use of collective sanctions despite certain divergences in viewpoints between member state governments. The Twelve decided to keep their embassies in Kuwait, guarantee the protection of their citizens, condemn hostage taking, and demand the liberation of hostages. They also acted together in expelling the military attachés of the Iraqi embassies and limiting the freedom of movement of Iraqi personnel. It is certain that the experience of protecting European citizens on the spot had a direct influence on the adoption of the Maastricht Treaty provisions on this subject. These are just a few examples of joint actions that illustrate the adoption of positions condemning the aggression against Kuwait. An interesting case is provided by the Council decision prohibiting Community trade with Iraq and Kuwait, which illustrates an effort to adapt Community policy to a range of mainly national initiatives. On this occasion, the Commission's role was confirmed by the mandate given to it by the Council to oversee both

Community and non-Community measures. The Commission was authorized to supervise national policies and mandated to coordinate matters relating to energy, finance, and economics. The Council also approved the Commission's proposals on aid to refugees and support for countries penalized by the embargo. Here is a demonstration of the function the Commission can perform under the heading of the economic aspects of political cooperation.

But these examples of collective action must not blind us to the individual, often uncoordinated, and even divergent initiatives taken by member states. There is no need to mention the semi-official humanitarian peace missions undertaken by political personalities, in particular, visits to Baghdad by former German chancellor Willy Brandt and former British prime minister Edward Heath. Ignoring these unilateral initiatives, including some from Paris, the Twelve unanimously reaffirmed their intention to stick to the European Council declaration. At the same time, the Community was concerned to maintain its traditional dialogue with Arab countries and reaffirmed traditional Euro-Arab friendship.

The second phase was marked by a deepening of the crisis and increased military intervention but also by the emergence of more pronounced disagreements between Community members. These disagreements in turn affected its ability to adopt common positions and coordinate national policies. Traditional attitudes were embodied by two European leaders. On the one hand, the United Kingdom, supported by Holland, recommended an alignment with the policy of the United States, while on the other hand France, with the support of Spain and Italy, called for a more autonomous policy. Traditional differences of opinion were reflected in these attitudes, echoing traditional preferences and options on the part of political leaders and public opinion. Ultimately, the military and political commitment of both sides showed Europe's solidarity with the United States, although with differences in emphasis. Faithful to tradition, France proposed two peace plans. The first envisioned two international conferences, one on the Near East and the other on Mediterranean security. The second, which was presented to the Security Council without preliminary consultation with France's partners, clearly showed the differences between member states. The British delegation rejected this plan for the same reason that the American delegation did, namely, on account of the link it established between the Gulf crisis and the Palestinian question.

Carlos Costa's analysis highlights cases of convergence and divergence as well as the Western European Union's role in the sphere of military coordination. While noting that the real leadership was exercised by the United States, he does not underestimate the contribution of the two main European leaders, Mrs. Thatcher and President Mitterrand, nor does he overlook the more discreet part played by Germany in the form of substantial financial support. The last part of his article is based on an analysis of the three internal policy considerations that influenced the decisions of governments and therefore of the Community: the role of the national leaders, the degree of political cohesion within parliaments and political parties, and the influence of the media and public opinion. These are certainly the main factors underlying the national constraints that influence Community policy, whose effects were all the more powerful in that the Community area was made up of a number of intercommunicating networks. "Linkages," well known in international relations, are more numerous, complex, and effective between actors and factors in the European Community.

Although the Single European Act contains a commitment to speak with one voice, a commitment that cannot fail to narrow the field of action of national policies, the facts do not bear this out in reality. Rapprochement of national policies remains possible in areas where procedures and mechanisms are established for the purpose of political cooperation and where decision-making powers and executive measures are attributed to the Community. It is true nonetheless that, for all the evidence of increasing coordination, political cooperation still seems to be basically a means for the pursuit of national policies. This certainly seems to be the approach of the larger European states, which have the greatest share of responsibility in the domain of international politics. Another conclusion confirms that mechanisms for the handling of crises are absent. When responsibilities and demands go beyond the fields of action of political cooperation, constraints exerted by national policies on the formulation of joint actions become stronger. These national constraints are, however, one of the main obstacles to the adoption of common policies. Lacking more binding rules and mechanisms of cooperation, member states are tempted to pursue independent and often divergent policies. The Gulf War highlighted the gaps and weaknesses in political cooperation; established to deal with normal situations, it does not provide the means for the joint handling of serious crises.

This analysis of the way countries behaved during the Gulf crisis raises several questions about the effectiveness of political cooperation. Even during the phase of economic sanctions, action depended on the mandates that the Council was willing to entrust to the Commission. On the other hand, the Commission's role remained blurred and uncertain in the second phase, and this raises a question about the role attributed to it within the European Union. Will its association with the work of the Council and its presence on the European Council be enough to ensure the continuity and effectiveness of joint action by counterbalancing national constraints? Has it really been granted sufficient means to cope with heavy tasks in the area of common external and security policies? Reactions at the time of such a serious crisis develop mainly from the policies of the member states with the appropriate political and military means. In the Gulf crisis, the United Kingdom and France were undeniably the leaders in Europe, and this raises two questions about the European Union and its future. How is the Union to reconcile this de facto situation, that is, the leadership of the members who carry the essential weight of any joint action, with the unanimity rule? In the future, should the weighting of votes not take account of the real division of influence and responsibility at the international level? How is the Union to reconcile leadership and the need for a political line with a rotating presidency limited to six months, whose changing composition does not always correspond to the situation and the need for joint action? As for the Community vis-à-vis the UN, experience shows that short-term presidencies and the need for long-term policies and objectives are to a certain extent incompatible. The rotating presidency could adversely affect political cooperation and deprive the Community of a positive and innovative capacity for action. In fact, it has been noted that at the UN in particular the Community often tends to react rather than act.[11] In addition, the cumbersome nature of the cooperative mechanism can only encourage the principal leaders to take initiatives and action on an individual basis, as was the case in the Gulf crisis. In the future, do we need to think of a presidential "troika" reinforced by the presence of the main protagonists or of ad hoc forms of presidency? Whatever the solution chosen, it is essential to ask this question in light of Community experience in the face of current challenges, including the convulsions in Eastern Europe and in particular the Yugoslav conflict.

The Community and the Yugoslav Crisis

The Yugoslav crisis is at the very heart of Europe; in it, the future of Europeans is at stake. It is a conflict that is part of a wider process of disintegration among multiethnic states in Eastern Europe in the name of anticommunism, democracy, the people's will, and self-determination, as if totalitarian regimes could magically transform themselves into democracies overnight. It is true that these explosive and disintegrative nationalist movements manifest varying degrees of violence, from the complete collapse of Yugoslavia and the USSR to the more peaceful divorce that occurred in Czechoslovakia. All these movements carry within them the seeds of destruction, intolerance, and authoritarian regimes and emphasize the defense of the nation and the building of nation-states. The danger is that the threat of the atomic bomb is being replaced with that of the nationalist bomb. The European

Community managed to disarm the latter for a while after the war, but nothing is permanent where human beings are concerned; both democracy and federalism are ceaseless actions of creation and conquest. The fascination with war and destruction is so great, especially when they bear the seal of national legitimacy, that integration, peace, and constructive action are fragile achievements; hence, no individuals and no people are definitively free of the danger of their seductive and contaminating power. The future of Europe depends on Europeans and their Union, but these violent nationalist crises are pulling them in the opposite direction.

Under cover of popular nationalist legitimacy, the resurgence of nationalism and the reconstruction of the nation-state by means of psychological and physical violence are taking over the instruments, methods, and leaders of the old communist regimes. The party state is giving way to the nation-state, and the latter is slipping into the mold of the former. The national identity of the "new state" is being asserted with intolerance and discrimination and in a spirit of confrontation. This is a new form of nationalist racism, one of whose outcomes is "ethnic cleansing," the forced transfer or even the destruction of populations considered "alien" to the nation. Cloaked in a new sort of legitimacy, it is a return to the archetypes of racism that even the inhuman experience of World War II, with its Nazi and Stalinist camps, has apparently failed to eradicate. This resurgence of the nation-state and the revival of coercive assimilation and "cleansing" policies is intolerable. It is also absurd in the extreme, given that all states without exception, whether old or new, contain multinational elements, numerous minorities, and mixtures of populations and families. It is vital for Western Europe to avoid becoming involved in these chain reactions so destructive of its values and ideals. As a matter of urgency, the rest of Europe must open its eyes to the reality of the changes taking place in its central and eastern territories and oppose those movements which, disguised as nationalism and democracy, are busily building a counter-Europe openly contemptuous of fundamental values. It is a matter of extreme urgency that the chain reaction of violence and intolerance be halted, the trend reversed, and peace reestablished so that a truly democratic society can be re-created and progressively integrated into a united Europe.

The European Community has been caught off guard by the sheer speed of the disintegration process sweeping Eastern Europe, especially its multinational states, with the former Soviet Union and the former Yugoslavia at the forefront. The two models, the Soviet model of original communism and the Yugoslav national model of self-management, have been overwhelmed by the torrent of nationalism unleashed since the fall of the Berlin Wall. Whereas the problems raised by the dissolution of one superpower have become the responsibility of the other, and indeed of the whole international community, the dimensions of the Yugoslav crisis seem to come more within the scope of the European Community's abilities. That is why the Community has committed itself to helping to find a solution to the conflict. Lacking effective external and security policy instruments, however, the Community could only set up a Yugoslav Peace Conference and appeal to the UN Security Council.

With the unleashing of a chain reaction of belligerent verbal violence, the Yugoslav Republics, hell bent on independence at any price, were swept by an explosion of physical violence. Accordingly, the first priority was to keep the peace and then look for a lasting solution. This double action was all the more urgent in that the crisis constitutes a test for the pacific solution of the numerous open or latent conflicts of nationality that hang over Eastern Europe like the sword of Damocles and also casting their shadow over Western Europe. The fact is that the solution ultimately adopted in this case will constitute a precedent for the future of the whole of Europe. Hence, there is a need to set this conflict in a European context and tackle it from the perspective of the process of creating a union of European states and regions.

Does the creation of independent states and their recognition by the international community offer a lasting solution to the problems of nationalities and minorities in Yugoslavia and Europe and an appropriate response to the problems of the transition to democracy and development? To me, this seems to be the fundamental question here. The truth is that the creation of states can actually precipitate crises in certain cases without doing anything to resolve the problem of the cohabitation of peoples and minorities within these new states and without automatic guarantees for them of democracy, development, or economic well-being. The existence of a state is not a solution in itself, for a Croatian or Serbian state is perfectly capable of oppressing its own minorities. The case of Slovenia, of course, does not raise the same difficulties as Croatia, Serbia, Bosnia-Herzegovina, or Macedonia on account of its national homogeneity. But if we accept self-determination for Slovenia, following its unilateral declaration of independence, can we deny this right to the Serbian minority in Croatia, the Albanian minority in Serbia, the Serbian and Croatian communities in Bosnia-Herzegovina, and so on? In the name of what principle can we justify a denial of this same right to the Hungarian minorities living in neighboring countries, to the Polish and Romanian minorities in the Soviet Union, to the Turkish minorities in Bulgaria and Greece, to the Kurdish minority in Turkey, to the Northern Irish, to the Basques, or to the Corsicans? In short, can we deny such a right to any independent people who may, now or in the future, demand the establishment of their own independent state, either by the ballot box or by force? Where does the right of any people or minority to live in its own state begin and where does that right end? Once this process is unleashed, how is the proliferation of nation-states, ethnic states, and microstates to be limited? Surely, the moment has come to stop sacrificing everything to the sacrosanct principle of the state and its independence, more fictional than real, and to start showing more imagination in developing the new architecture of Europe. At a time when Western Europe is moving toward union and the Eastern European countries are seeking an identity, it seems a matter of some urgency to begin thinking and acting in terms of communities and regions that derive solidarity from their membership in one multinational European entity, proliferating in religions and languages, with a flexible structure based on federal lines.

The Serbo-Croat conflict is at the heart of the problem. Slovenia's homogeneous population makes it an exception; it is Croatia that illustrates the inextricable interlinking of peoples and minorities in Yugoslavia. A declaration of independence or a unilateral remodeling of frontiers cannot fail to unleash a wave of violence sweeping from one republic to the next and threatening to overflow the frontiers of the former Yugoslavia. The key to the problem is to be found principally in the relation between Croatia and Serbia, especially as Croatia was inhabited by a significant Serbian minority that settled there long before Yugoslavia was created. This minority represents 12 percent of the population of Croatia (4.7 million people) and is deeply rooted in the Krajina and Slavonia regions. Thousands of Serbs are spread through other regions of Croatia and live together with the Croat majority: Serbian and Croatian villages are neighbors, and indeed many villages are mixed; the town of Zagreb alone contains more than 100,000 Serbs. What is to be the fate of these Serbs in an independent Croatian state? The Croatian government has offered guarantees of Serbian rights, but nationalist fever, the explosion of intolerance and hatred, and daily acts of violence have revived memories of the genocide of Croatian and Bosnian Serbs perpetrated by the Ustashis of the fascist Croatian regime installed by the Third Reich on the ruins of the Yugoslav state in 1941.[12] The violence suffered by a minority enclave reawakened an instinct for self-defense supported and indeed encouraged by Serbia.

Appealing in their turn to the principle of self-determination, the Krajina Serbs voted massively in favor of the maintenance of a Yugoslav state, the best guarantee of their survival and autonomy. Refusing to live in an independent Croatian state, they are determined to become part of Serbia. This popular choice, embodied in a vote and supported by weapons, coincides with the proclaimed intention of the president of Serbia to unite all Serbs in a greater Serbia. But a revision of frontiers cannot provide a lasting solution; it does nothing for the many thousands of Serbs in different parts of Croatia. The Serbo-Croat conflict is a perfect example of the zero-sum game in which what one of the parties gains the other loses. From this point of view, it resembles the Franco-German wars and the changing destiny of Alsace-Lorraine. The situation is constantly aggravated by the fact that every conquest provokes revenge while the question of Serbs dispersed throughout Croatia remains unresolved.

Such being the case, only one outcome is possible, the negotiation of some kind of formula of cooperation between Serbs and Croats. Yet this is only a representative sample of the population mixtures and minority problems typical of all the republics of the former Yugoslavia except for Slovenia. Under such conditions how can homogeneous nation-states be formed without further disrupting populations and their traditional religious and linguistic divisions or provoking fratricidal wars and perhaps even a total conflagration?

There is a vicious circle; collapse threatens Bosnia-Herzegovina, a buffer state between Serbia and Croatia, which is coveted by its two neighbors, which might well agree to share the spoils one day. This republic is composed of one-third Serbs, one-fifth Croats, and a majority of Muslims of Slav descent (44 percent). Rumors of separation were confirmed in a declaration by the Croatian president to the British press on the weekend of 14 July 1991, and such a partition would be welcomed by him as one of the best ways of resolving the Serbo-Croat conflict. The president of Serbia could hardly fail to agree with this, given his idea of collecting the Serbs into one state. Only the president of Bosnia-Herzegovina believes that such a partition would be the worst of solutions, bound to result in a bloody war, and he is fighting for the integrity of a Bosnia that he, too, wishes to organize on the model of the unitary state. Such contradictions between the objectives of the chief antagonists in the conflict demonstrate the impossibility of finding any sort of lasting solution without turning to federalist values and methods in a multinational and multireligious community.

The process of destabilization and disintegration that is liable to be unleashed by these nationalist explosions could spread like wildfire from one republic to the next, from one province to the next, and from one country to the next in Central and Eastern Europe. More than one of Yugoslavia's neighbors has been fondly indulging its dreams, desires, or nostalgia for a past long gone by toying with the vision of a Mittel-Europa. The World Congress of Hungarians was held in Budapest on 19–22 August 1992, and it brought together representatives of Magyar minorities in Central Europe, giving new life to the specter of a "greater Hungary." Prime Minister Josef Antall, a historian, was careful to keep away from this, but he still asserted that "all Hungarians belong to one and the same spiritual fatherland, 'Magna Hungaria.'"[13] It is difficult to assess what impact such a pronouncement had on Hungarian minorities in Romania, Serbia, and

Slovakia, but it looks like a portent of that vicious circle of claims, counter-claims, and conflicts created by the unbridled nationalism that threatens to wreak havoc throughout the Balkans. Hence, there is an urgent need to contain the nationalists and foster peaceful conditions that will allow a real dialogue to be conducted between all parties and begin a search for a lasting solution based on consensus. The future of Eastern Europe, and indeed the whole of Europe, is at stake.

The danger is all the greater in that the Yugoslav conflict has deep roots and wide ramifications. It revives a history that leaders on all sides manipulate in their own way and for their own ends. Interpretations of history by leaders and media alike are mainly intended to arouse national-ist feelings. After forty-five years of official history, the whole gamut of his-torical fantasy has reappeared to emphasize everything that separates while ignoring everything that unites. The supposedly Western culture of the Slovenes and Croats contrasts with the allegedly oriental culture of the Serbs and the southern republics, Rome against Byzantium, Catholicism against Orthodoxy, as if European culture were not based on the old traditions of ancient Greece, Christianity, Rome, and Byzantium as well as Latin, German, Slav, and other extra-European contributions. As Denis de Rougemont used to say, European culture, the foundation of European federalism, is a mixture of various cultures, a union in diversity. In the Yugoslav conflict, it is the diversity that is stressed while the common basis is forgotten.

In the same spirit, Yugoslavia, an "artificial state" that was a product of World War I, is regarded as bearing the mark of two hostile empires, the Austro-Hungarian and the Ottoman, which reigned for a long time over the southern Slavs. But there are two glaring omissions in this historical perception: after many fits and starts, the Serbian national revolution fi-nally achieved an independent Serbian state in the late nineteenth century, while the dissociation of Slovenia and Croatia from the Austro-Hungarian Empire was the result of the Allied victory in 1918.

The Kingdom of the Serbs, Croats, and Slovenians was created (founded) in 1919 under King Peter I Karadjordjevic (1919–21). His son Alexander I ruled as a constitutional parliamentary monarch until 1929, when an authoritarian regime was imposed. The tensions between Serbs and Croats culminated in the assassination of the King Alexander I in 1934 by a Croatian extremist (ustashi). The regency was assumed by his brother Prince Paul, who signed the Tripartite Pact with the Axis, provoking a large popular reaction and the overthrow of the regime by the army, which put on the throne the young king Peter II on 27 March 1941. On 6 April, Hitler bombed Belgrade, and Yugoslavia invaded and occupied the country in two weeks. Under German Nazi protection, the ustashi government of

Ante Pavelitch was established in Croatia. This was a major dramatic split between Croats and Serbs that, despite the unifying role of Tito's Communist party, left profound marks as confirmed in recent years.

The idea of a common state for all the southern Slavs, Serbs, Croats and Slovenians is really the creation of leading Slovenian and Croatian intellectuals. The Yugoslav state was founded on an association that was widely welcomed to begin with, despite the fact that it owed its creation to the victors in World War I. In many respects, this multinational and multi-ethnic collection may seem artificial, but the common origins and languages of the southern Slavs and strong Muslim minorities make Yugoslavia a much less artificial entity than the European Community. Besides, the example of Switzerland furnishes additional proof that linguistic, ethnic, or religious criteria alone are not sufficient to allow us to assess the viability of a community that ultimately rests on a common destiny. What constitutes the principal motivation and goal of the European Community is a common future built on the new demands of economics and technology, global competition and security. Who knows whether, at some time in the more or less distant future, the independent republics may not be called on to cohabit again in the context of a common membership in the Community?

Each republic in turn has presented itself as democratic, and each has staged its first free election since the end of World War II. But an election does not create a democracy. The construction of a democracy requires a series of free elections, democratic institutions, and behavior in a pluralist environment, two or more competing parties, and an independent media ensuring that a wide range of information is made available. These are what Robert Dahl calls the criteria for polyarchy. Societies emerging from forty-five years of communist rule naturally find it very difficult to create such conditions. The platform on which both the parties in power and the opposition parties have been elected is that of national independence, and whole republics, provinces, and regions have been swept by nationalist enthusiasms. This powerful theme has enabled numerous communist leaders to find a *new legitimacy*. In reality, it is hardly realistic to expect a whole generation of new politicians to appear at once. Whole swathes of the ruling class, as described by Djilas in the 1950s, and their successors, are perpetuating their grip on power, with all the more success in that they have managed to convert from Marxism to an often virulent variety of nationalism.

The governments in Slovenia and Croatia resorted to referenda to give their power a solid base. But the referendum in Croatia had nothing in common with such events as we know them in the West. Carried out with only a few weeks' preparation, preceded by a "campaign with one voice," and accompanied by strong social pressure, in practice it could have had only one result. No Western democracy would proceed in this way. Likewise, the Serbian communist leaders, who converted to populist nationalist socialism and held elections in late 1990, failed to allow time for opposition parties to organize or conduct an electoral campaign under the normal conditions of democracy. These elections and those that followed merely resulted in the strengthening of authoritarian power, leaving the transition to democracy handicapped by rigid structures left over from the old regime. The current mentality and behavior, not just of the leaders but of many citizens, bear all the hallmarks of communism. In spite of the new freedom allowed or promised by self-government and decentralization, great effort and much patience will be required for "democratic virtues" and the sense of individual responsibility to be assimilated into these societies.

Although certain changes are occurring, the ruling class and the infrastructure inherited from the old regime are still there. The administration and the police have changed very little, while the media, particularly television and radio, are governmental instruments and censorship is still in evidence. Finally, for all the slogans and the handful of laws on privatization, governments remain in charge of important sectors of the economy and are in fact strengthening the state's grip on the levers of power. While the current regimes in the republics continue to be prisoners of old structures and vulnerable to the appeal of various forms of authoritarian nationalism, or indeed totalitarian nationalism, it is doubtful whether they may be called democracies.

Slovenia and Croatia's Declaration of Independence of 26 June 1991 took the conflict a stage further. Resolutely asserting their desire for independence, these two republics unleashed a series of unexpected reactions. This obsession with the nation-state, in the teeth of the movement toward a union of Europe, results from a nineteenth-century dream, a dream frequently made very real in the shape of war. Moreover, there remains the problem of how to achieve a match between state and nation in this human jigsaw puzzle without arousing or exacerbating cultural, religious, and ethnic quarrels.

Here two experiences are particularly instructive, although different: one, with a long history but small dimensions, is that of Switzerland, while the other, with a brief history but a scope adequate for today's problems, is that of the European Community. The former provides the example of fruitful coexistence between different cultures, languages, ethnic groups, and religions within a federation that possesses nothing more of a confederation than the name. The latter, on the basis of a lasting peace established between traditional enemies, aims to provide a response to the world's economic and political challenges by pooling the resources of the states and nations of Western Europe and by creating a vast market and political area without frontiers while respecting national and regional diversity. These two experiences are distinct in terms of their histories, but they are close to one another in terms of their federalist orientations, and each in its own way is highly attractive to the Eastern countries. But the special attractions of the European Community will ensure that it has an essential role in the Eastern European countries' journey to democracy and the economy of the free market.

Accordingly, questions have to be answered about the Community's involvement in the search for a solution to the Yugoslav crisis. Lacking a coherent policy and consistent action and subjected to a variety of national pressures, the Community chose to partially offload its responsibility by organizing a Conference for Peace in Yugoslavia in September 1991. After a series of intermittent and abortive attempts at making a succession of cease-fire agreements stick, the Community launched its own appeal for a cease-fire and made preparations for drawing up a peace plan. At the same time, it created an Arbitration Commission under the presidency of Robert Badinter, president of the Constitutional Council in France. Faced with an escalation of violence in the Krajina and Slavonia regions (Vukovar, Osijek, and Vinkovci) and the blockade imposed on several ports (including Dubrovnik), the Council of Foreign Ministers adopted sanctions against Serbia in particular and prepared to send an intervention force. The WEU meeting on 19 September 1991 closed with an admission of impotence due to the United Kingdom's opposition to the commitment of European blue helmets.

This was the start of a new phase of parallel complementary actions by the Community and the UN, with the Community striving for a global solution and imposing economic sanctions, corresponding to its current capacity, while trying to coordinate the positions of member states on the recognition of Slovenia and Croatia. On this point, Germany and Italy, which favored recognition, differed from France and the United Kingdom, which opposed it. The United States and the UN secretary-general also opposed recognition, probably because of reports from European observers and Cyrus Vance, the former secretary of state under President Carter and defense secretary under President Kennedy, who had been entrusted with a peace mission by the UN secretary-general. However, under pressure from Germany, Community member states gave official recognition to Slovenia and Croatia on 15 January 1992.

In October 1991, the Peace Conference drew up a plan for a global solution to the Yugoslav conflict, proposing that those republics wishing to become sovereign and independent could do so. At the same time, the plan included guarantees of human rights and similar guarantees for national and ethnic groups while allowing for a free association between independent

republics on the Community model and in the perspective of a rapprochement with the European Community. For all its defects and omissions, this
was a truly remarkable effort. Unfortunately, the plan was not accepted by
Serbia and was not implemented. In any case, it appeared too late, given
that the disintegration process was already far advanced and difficult to
control. Moreover, it allowed for the recognition of independent states
without adding precise obligations and effective guarantees. Hence, it was
easy to foresee that once recognition was a fait accompli, the new sovereign
states would not be too concerned about the other conditions and proposals
in the plan. In fact, the plan legitimized dissolution without putting any form
of cooperation in its place. In spite of these defects, it could have provided a
basis for negotiations if it had been put forward in an initial phase of the
conflict. It was a positive effort to the extent that it aimed to ensure protection for individual persons and peoples as well as establishing a common
economic area managed by common institutions.

Human rights and the rights of ethnic and national groups are based
on the Paris Charter of November 1990 and on the statute and instruments
of the Council of Europe, the Conference for Security and Cooperation in
Europe (CSCE), and the United Nations. The plan contained two categories of protection. Those belonging to ethnic and national groups not forming the majority in zones where they lived were to enjoy cultural and
religious rights, freedom of association, and the right to participate in
public affairs without discrimination. These principles were also to be applied to ethnic and national groups constituting minorities in the zones
where they were settled. The other category of protection concerned national or ethnic groups constituting the majority in any particular region,
which were to be granted a special status guaranteeing them wider autonomy. This status included, in particular, the right to dual nationality, to the
national symbols of the group, and to an autonomous educational system
respecting the values and needs of the group. The region, moreover, was to
possess autonomous institutions comprising a legislative body, a regional
executive with an administrative structure, a regional police force, and a
legal system. It was also stated that this status would be placed under
appropriate international supervision. Moreover, the republics would commit themselves to applying a special constitutional status to the autonomous provinces, enforcing full respect for the rights of ethnic or national
groups and subscribing to all international agreements, including measures
for redress.

Economic cooperation was to be based on the principles of the market
economy as practiced in the European Community, involving a customs
union, an internal market (the four freedoms — movement of goods, persons, capital, and services), and an array of common norms, particularly in

the area of competition. Compared to its level in the economic area, co-operation looked much more blurred and less binding in other sectors. The range of cooperation and protection guarantees was to be managed by institutions comprising a court of human rights, a council of ministers for economic cooperation, an executive committee headed by a secretary-general, a council of foreign ministers, and a parliament. In fact, the global solution that the plan was intended to put forward was only a pale reflection of the Community system, implemented and aided by the Community without any credible guarantees. Moreover, the democratic expression of popular wishes was taken for granted when in fact there were no grounds for this in these postcommunist systems with their nationalist tendencies. Electoral processes and referenda, together with respect for political pluralism, the freedom of the media, and respect for opposition, needed to be closely watched from the start by the European Community and the Council of Europe. Likewise, the protection of human rights and the rights of national and ethnic groups needed to be scrupulously observed. To be effective, such protection needed to be guaranteed by means of the direct participation of European institutions and accompanied by speedy and effective means of redress so that an atmosphere of trust could be reestablished. The legal and institutional guarantees envisaged did not seem adequate to ensure peace and security in this region. On the other hand, provisions relating to cooperation in foreign policy, security, and legal matters seemed both unclear and insufficiently binding.

Finally, excessive freedom in the military domain threatened to perpetuate border conflicts between different nationalities by allowing all sides to retain their weapons instead of forcing them to submit to controlled disarmament. For all its modicum of positive aspects, the peace plan failed to create a binding chain linking independence, peace, and the maintenance of a "Yugoslav community." On the other hand, it gave a green light to the recognition of Slovenia and Croatia and other republics that were an integral part of Yugoslavia.

In the last months of 1991, a public debate began on the question of the recognition of the Yugoslav republics and of Slovenia and Croatia in particular. This problem of recognition had three main aspects. First, the Community procedure that led to the recognition of Slovenia and Croatia was a test of the cohesion of the post-Maastricht Community and highlighted the influence of Germany within the European Community. Second, recognition had a direct effect on the search for a peaceful solution; it is an open question whether it contributed to peace and the consolidation of democracy in the states that became independent. Finally, this Community recognition based on several criteria created a significant precedent that raised additional questions as to how criteria defined by consensus were to be respected. In defiance of France, the United Kingdom, the United States, and the UN secretary-general, Germany and Italy pronounced themselves in favor of recognition in late November 1991. Without being a member of the Security Council, Germany used its influence to water down the terms of the invitation addressed by the Security Council to member states calling on them to postpone recognition. Under pressure from public opinion at home and then from his foreign minister, Chancellor Kohl promised to recognize Slovenia and Croatia before Christmas of 1991. This unilateral promise, motivated by the violence of the fighting in Croatia and by violations of the cease-fire, cut right across the desire to establish a common external policy, as set out by the Maastricht Treaty, which was approved by the European Council on 9 December 1991. It is noteworthy that this European Council did not tackle the Yugoslav crisis. The deliberate silence was probably due to the fact that the heads of state and government were not keen to display their differences, which could have hindered approval of the Treaty for European Union.

The fact remains that the Yugoslav question was postponed until the meeting of the Council of Foreign Ministers on 16 December 1991. In the course of this meeting, the ministers adopted France's proposal, defined the criteria that were to govern recognition decisions, and decided to ask the opinion of the Arbitration Commission in order to take a decision on 15 January 1992. In this perspective, ministers adopted guidelines for the formal recognition of new states in Eastern Europe and the Soviet Union. The following criteria were to guide their decision on the recognition of the Yugoslav republics:

1. Respect for the provisions of the United Nations Charter and for the pledges signed in the Helsinki Final Act and the Paris Charter, especially with respect to the rule of law, democracy, and human rights.

2. A guarantee of the rights of ethnic and national groups and minorities in accord with the pledges signed in the CSCE.

3. Respect for the inviolability of territorial boundaries, which cannot be modified other than by peaceful means and common agreement.

4. A renewal of all the relevant pledges relating to disarmament, nuclear nonproliferation, security, and regional stability.

5. A commitment to settle all questions relating to the succession of states and regional differences by agreement and, failing that, by arbitration. The Community and its member states will not recognize entities that result from acts of aggression. They will take into consideration the effects of recognition on neighboring states. Commitment to

these principles opens the way to recognition by the Community and its member states and to the establishment of diplomatic relations. It may be included in accords.

These criteria, adopted at France's suggestion, imposed a series of conditions to be met before any republic was to be recognized. These demands were submitted by the presidency of the Conference for Peace in Yugoslavia to the Arbitration Commission so that the latter could give an opinion before the date of implementation. However, without waiting for the date of 15 January 1992 and the opinion of the Arbitration Commission, Germany alone recognized Slovenia and Croatia on 23 December 1991. In doing so, Germany prejudiced the common decision of the Council of Ministers; it imposed its will by presenting its partners with a fait accompli and rode roughshod over the decisions of 16 December as well as the fundamental rules on common external policy embodied in the Maastricht Treaty, which Germany had just approved. This first post-Maastricht experience underlines the lack of external cohesion in the Community and its inability to control its members' desire to pursue their own policies. It seems more urgent than ever for a reunified Germany to be firmly anchored in a united Europe if a balance is to be maintained within the developing European federation.

A second point relates to the consequences of this recognition and in particular to the question of knowing whether it is helping to restore and preserve peace. The tragic facts and the escalation of violence speak for themselves. It is perfectly clear that the creation of an independent state is not of itself going to guarantee respect for democracy, human rights, and the rights of national groups, that is, respect for the criteria laid down by the Community. Unconditional recognition might actually aggravate border problems, which is why, following Cyrus Vance's plan, peacekeeping forces were deployed in conflict zones but not on any of the disputed borders. Unfortunately, this precaution was not enough, since recognition did not lead to disarmament but allowed massive rearmament in Croatia.

Recognition of Slovenia and Croatia by the Community and its member states naturally led to recognition by the United States, which made an unexpected U-turn, as did the international community. Instead of encouraging the Community and the United States to greater prudence, this first step actually speeded up the recognition of the Republic of Bosnia-Herzegovina and thereby the outbreak of civil war there. This consequence was foreseeable since the decision was taken by the Muslim majority with the support of the Croats, despite opposition from the Serbian population. The recognition was all the more surprising in that it was not preceded by any form of proposed solution for the inevitable problems or followed by any guarantees for constitutive minority populations. How could the dire past of this region, rivalry between three religions, the shadow of the Serb-Croat conflict, and the role of the militias (supported by armies but acting independently) have all been overlooked? Not one of the criteria set out by the Community for the recognition of new states seems to have been taken into consideration, neither democratic conditions nor respect for human rights and the rights of the peoples having to cohabit in this new state. This was recognition of a state that the Muslim president wanted to be unitary, ignoring the desires of Croatian and Serbian leaders seeking "cantonization" or indeed a confederation.[14] If there is a proposal to maintain the integrity of Bosnia-Herzegovina in spite of the centrifugal forces pulling the Croats toward Zagreb and the Serbs toward Belgrade, a politically viable solution can be sought only in a form of federal union based on self-determination for the three peoples and on real democratization. Under conditions such as these, the voice of the citizens may have a chance of being heard.

The London Conference of 26–27 August 1992, presided over jointly by the UN secretary-general and the president of the Council of Ministers of the European Community, hoped to open the way to a lasting solution. It put forward immediate measures such as the dismantling of detention camps, the dispensing of humanitarian aid, the return of refugees, supervision of the progressive reduction of weapons, the control of all forces (in particular, irregulars and paramilitary forces), the stationing of observers on the border between Bosnia and Serbia, and the dispatch of supervisory missions to the territory of the former Yugoslavia. At the same time, it proposed to establish a permanent structure for negotiation and supervision in Geneva. The basic conditions seemed to be in place to allow the vicious chain reaction to be thrown into reverse and to gradually create an environment favorable to a global political solution. The implementation of such a solution would largely depend on real respect for the principles of the European Union and on a true and profound democratization of life in this region.

Two aspects of this crisis are significant from the point of view of the European Union, namely, the lessons the European Community can derive from it, and which general conditions are liable to ensure lasting solutions. The fragility and vulnerability of political cooperation seemed even more obvious than in the more remote Gulf crisis. The European Community showed the whole world how impotent it was in its present form to cope with grave political crises. More so than in the Gulf crisis, national constraints and the pressure of public opinion and the media created divergent tensions. The policies of member governments showed how they responded more to the requirements of internal policy than to a desire to seek a solution to the crisis appropriate to conditions in the region. The desire to preserve a consensus among member states proved to be more important than the responsibility to face the challenges of a conflict whose essential elements have been in place for a long time and whose consequences for neighboring countries were to a large extent foreseeable.[15] Several considerations stem from this. National constraints, such as pressures from parties, media, or public opinion, particularly in Germany, or negative experiences like the United Kingdom's being bogged down in the Northern Ireland conflict or the ambivalence of the French government, with its simultaneous desire to preserve Franco-German unity and to define the criteria for the recognition of the new states of Eastern Europe, were particularly influential. Consensus was preserved despite many differences, but it merely served to mask the fact that this decision was foisted on the others by Germany, and at the lowest going rate for the Community, namely, unconditional formal recognition, a decision that proved to be very costly for Europe's credibility as well as for the peoples of Yugoslavia. This consensus raises a general problem in that it looks like a compromise between external requirements and internal interests. What part was played in this Community decision by factors internal to the Community such as the need to reach an agreement on the new treaty on European Union, obtain German support in the GATT negotiations, or satisfy the concerns of the media and public opinion? Is it in terms of these factors that the Community must decide common policies and actions in such grave crises? These ambiguities made it difficult to follow a consistent line in foreign and security policy in the framework of political cooperation as set out in the Single European Act. It may be argued, of course, that without such cooperation the member states would have acted in an even more uncoordinated manner, simply reflecting geopolitical archetypes. Nonetheless, the inadequacy of these instruments of political cooperation is clearly proven. The Maastricht Treaty tried to provide a remedy by committing the Community more forcefully to common policies. But by showing up the gaps in political cooperation the Yugoslav crisis will force leaders to reflect on the inadequacies of current political cooperation and on the requirements of a European Union that can truly measure up to the responsibilities of a great economic power. When shall we see the establishment of instruments for political planning and analysis? When shall we see the adoption of a real common policy? These questions the Maastricht Treaty leaves unanswered.

It is true that many major events and changes were not anticipated by anyone: the rise of the republic of the ayatollahs in Iran, the fall of the Berlin Wall, the speed of German reunification, and the collapse of the Soviet empire. In certain cases, predictions were not taken seriously, sometimes because no one really understood them. Foresight is hardly the forte of governments nor of the European Community, where many are blinded by partial vision, short-term interests, or prejudices or are swept along by the prevailing manner of thinking or dulled by routine. To anticipate what is coming, and then to instigate the necessary preventive action, is a task beyond the current capacities of most governments and international organizations. This is why it has been suggested that instruments be created for observation and analysis in different regions so as to facilitate preventive action, arbitration, and mediation at an acceptable cost. Such urgently needed multidisciplinary analysis and forward planning centers and agencies would be invaluable for political leaders as an aid to external policy decision making.

For lack of a truly European policy with any continuity or consistency, most of the European Community's efforts have been purely reactive and often inappropriate, lagging behind events and lacking effective support measures. Irregular conferences and consultation meetings have been quite inadequate in the face of the complexity or gravity of situations and hopelessly unable to prevent the escalation of violence. The classic formal approach has helped restrict negotiations to an official circle that excludes representative elements of society such as leaders of the opposition, the economy, the trade unions, or indeed the churches and intellectuals. All that has resulted is a false dialogue of the deaf between the official protagonists in the crisis. Far from enabling it to get to grips with basic data or to analyze their evolution, the Community's intermittent interventions have frequently had a permissive or lax effect, with the result that antagonistic leaders have been left complete freedom of action. The consequence has been a weakening in the Community's credibility, making its mediation and arbitration mission more difficult.

In addition, the crisis has highlighted the problem of the presidency and the role of the Commission. The presidency orchestrates the management of the Community's economic affairs in collaboration with the Commission, but it has shown itself impotent in the face of a major political crisis. Admittedly, management of the crisis has been made more difficult by the fact that it has coincided with presidencies of small or medium-sized member countries. Lacking effective backup, the rotating presidency has been significantly overworked in the aftermath of the Gulf War, the Maastricht Treaty negotiations, and above all the Yugoslav crisis. Under such circumstances, it is hardly fair to complain about ignorance of local situations, lack of continuity, or the ease with which the big member states can influence it.

The insufficiency or inadequacy of the presidency raises the problem of how political power in the European Union should be exercised. In the absence of a European government with the task of establishing a policy that conforms with the general interest of the Community and implementing that policy, this double governmental function could be entrusted to the European Council, assisted by the Council of Foreign Ministers, and to the Commission. It is the Commission that would have the task of producing a proposal for a common policy on the basis of sound knowledge of the relevant data and circumstances, a proposal in keeping with Community interests and the interests of the region in crisis itself. Once the European Council has defined a common policy and common actions, their implementation would be ensured by the Commission and the presidency of the Council. Other formulas could be suggested, but the main point is that the role must be effectively filled by Community institutions capable of formulating a common policy in conformity with the Union's basic principles and general interests.

To conclude this provisional analysis, a few key points stand out that may help us find a lasting solution to this serious crisis, which threatens the peace of the European Union, not to mention its future. The preconditions for such a solution were set out in the London Agreement of 26 August 1992: eliminate the camps, condemn those responsible for ethnic cleansing and acts against humanity, install control posts on borders and throughout the territory, and impose disarmament and arms control on all parties, in particular on the irregular forces. Supervision, observation, and aid tasks to be carried out by the UN and the European Community ought to apply without discrimination to the whole region. In addition, the UN and the Community should put in place effective measures to guarantee and protect human rights and the rights of peoples and minorities, while supervising the application of democratic rights and the principles of mutual recognition of the diversity of persons, nationalities, religions, opinions, and parties. Respect for these foundations of democratic federal regimes is a prerequisite for survival and cohabitation in multinational communities. From this point of view, once peace is reestablished an in-depth action will be required to help bring democracy to the states and regions of the former Yugoslavia. The best guarantees of lasting peace will lie in training new elites and managers in a democratic spirit, freely disseminating information, respecting electoral and voting practices, and education. With the restoration of peace and security, the economic and social needs of everyday life will soon become more important than evanescent nationalist passions. People cannot live on nationalism or ideology alone. The return to normality and the daily search for well-being will, with the Community's help, contribute to rebuilding gradually a web of solidarity and exchanges.

These states and peoples will be obliged to coexist as associates one day, and in a more distant future, they will live together as fellow members of the European Community, something they all desire.

Only determined negotiation under the joint presidency of the UN and the European Community stands any chance of achieving a pacific conclusion to this ethnic-religious conflict, which could all too easily set the Balkans alight and even split the European Community. For this fratricidal war poses a very serious threat to the foundations and goals of the European Union, a union that respects the identities and diversities of European states, regions, and peoples. The creation of nation-states in an area where peoples, families, cultures, and religions are so interlocked does nothing to encourage people to accept Community principles and solutions, all the more so in that for the time being these nation-states guarantee neither truly democratic values nor human rights nor the rights of peoples, basing their legitimacy on the glorification of national feelings with its corresponding self-assertiveness. The consequences of nationalist passion are tragic, finding their extreme expression in intolerance and the assimilation or even elimination of others. Neither the defense of a nation or minority nor any concept of the nation-state can justify such a negation of the fundamental values of the European Union.

But how do we explain the role of Germany, a federal democratic state, in the recognition of nation-states and the support it is giving them? It is a well-known fact that of itself the independence of a state does not automatically lead to the existence of a *democratic state.* This is shown all too clearly by the long history of the emergence of independent states after World War II as well as by the more immediate history of Croatia. Nation-states are not by nature democratic and peaceful; on the contrary, according to Denis de Rougemont, they are the worst warmongers. One explanation for Germany's behavior might be the desire of the German government and people to see democracy and the market economy established as soon as possible in the East. Another reason would be its intention to transform a civil war into an international war, thereby allowing the UN to intervene. The experience of reunification on the basis of the right to self-determination supports this interpretation. But another interpretation invokes historical continuity and views Germany as revisiting history, with its geopolitical millstones, and this time undertaking a peaceful expansion to the east and south, using the weapons of economic and technological penetration. The collapse of Eastern Europe will ultimately strengthen the power of a reunited Germany.

Certain American analysts already view Germany as the great global superpower of the future and advocate a U.S.-German partnership. Still others are predicting a transformation of the G-7 into the G-3, a troika made up of the United States, Germany, and Japan.[16] In any event, Germany's intoxicating sense of its own power, the aid it is giving the East, and its influence there, together with its role as the lone warrior in certain movements of the Yugoslav crisis, can only strengthen the hand of those among the Germans and their European partners who are calling for it to be as solidly anchored as possible in the European Union. The Yugoslav crisis is proof that any weakening of the European Community is liable to cause a chain reaction in France, the United Kingdom, and other member states. The integration process is far from being irreversible, and, even while it is overshadowed by economics, politics remains the predominant factor. A lengthy domination by one member state or incipient disintegration could signal a return to power politics and the balance of powers, which could again transform Central and Eastern Europe and the Balkans into an area of rivalry and conflict into which Russian could eventually be drawn. Lurking in the background is the ghost of the "wars of religion" and the power of the Serbian and Russian armies. Negotiation for a political solution is preferable to any interventionist adventure. The logic of peace must replace the logic of war, for only this can offer these peoples the hope of escaping from the vicious circle of violence and repression. The trail blazed by the European Community is the only one that has anything to offer them.

The crisis tearing at the states and peoples of the former Yugoslavia provides proof by its very absurdity that nationalism and its organized form, the nation-state, are a grave threat to Europe. In the remnants of the wrecked Soviet empire, wars are pitting nations, republics, ethnic groups, and religions against each other. Nationalism and racism are a common peril, though they come under different guises; they all pander to intolerance and urge the rejection of the others, calling for communities to be based on resemblance. They foster ethnic and religious movements, assertions of identity and difference, quests for origins, and recourse to the myths of history, all of which are potentially violent reactions to the global uniformity of industrialized civilization. The melting pot and standardization inspired the growth of religious sects and communities of ethnic groups and races in America. The American model is beginning to show cracks, while its communist rival has broken into pieces. Imposed by the force of a totalitarian state, the original communist model has been engulfed by a wave of obsession with national identity, and the desire for autonomy and independence has shown signs of being on the brink of spreading from Eastern Europe to the West. But tensions in Canada and the Belgium language debate have been handled much more effectively in their democratic environments. Within the European Community, there is plenty of evidence, showing various degrees of violence and intensity, of a prevailing temptation to fall back on the nation, of the desire for national grandeur, unfettered regionalism, and extremism of varying types. Their impact, however, is somewhat blunter or better absorbed in a pluralist society organized at several levels of power and integrated into a community on a European scale. The process of integration is developing progressively, in spite of the occasional delay or retreat, through a strategy that is both pragmatic and well conceived; a community is being built as a "union in diversity."

As long as the world was settled in the comfort of the tense East-West balance, the European Union continued to progress under the pressure of the universal search for well-being. Today the Community is a large economic power facing the challenge of a destabilized world and coping with the shock of a new revolution in Eastern Europe. A growing radicalization of nationalist and ethnic-religious movements is visible on every side, taking on epidemic proportions. Linguistic and cultural claims are being transformed into demands for autonomy and independence or indeed into a desire to create a national territory or homogeneous nation-state whose inevitable consequences will always be war and ethnic cleansing. The former Yugoslavia, the Caucasus, and Central Asia have been swept by this fever, which now threatens to spread to other countries. Worrying signs are appearing in Hungary and Slovakia, while ethnic discrimination is affecting the Baltic states, too. Talk of a greater Hungary, calls for cultural space, the specter of "living space," and appeals for a gathering of all Hungarians into a nation-state echo claims and conflicts in neighboring countries. The right wing of the Democratic Forum goes even further with its claim to be the "sole representative of the historic Hungarian identity," and through the mouthpiece of its leader it is calling for the creation of a "Magyar *lebensraum.*" On the other hand, the new Slovakian constitution (1992) ignores demands for cultural autonomy from the Hungarian minority, declares Slovakian the "national" instead of the "official," and begins with the words "We, the Slovakian People" instead of "We, citizens of the Slovakian Republic." For all the claims to a European and democratic nature, the constitutions of more than one republic of the former Yugoslavia contain similar references and sentiments.

The truth is that simply adopting democratic institutions and holding elections does not establish democracy. The weight of the old political and administrative structures and the accompanying mentalities are blocking the way to democracy. What is needed for this form of society are values, virtues, and behavior that are in harmony with the requirements of democracy, along with a political culture that is the opposite of what these peoples have been forced to practice for the past fifty or so years. In fact, life in a democracy requires a set of instruments and behavior supported by a pluralist society and articulated by political partes under the eyes of an independent media.

In a society bankrupted by its totalitarian past and lacking a sense of responsibility, the apprenticeship of democracy is a long one. Leaders who pander to explosive nationalist feelings are using authoritarian methods in the name of the defense of the nation. Violent or latent conflicts, pressures, or external support are threatening to force these new states into becoming authoritarian nationalist regimes. This process of transition from communism to nationalism and from a totalitarian to authoritarian national system is exposed with all its nefarious consequences by the conflicts and civil wars in the former Yugoslavia. It also threatens, though currently under a more benign appearance, most of the erstwhile popular republics of Eastern Europe.

What can be done to put the peoples of Central and Eastern Europe on the real path to democracy and peaceful cohabitation? Only a common commitment and unrelenting dedication can guarantee that human rights and the rights of peoples are respected. In situ observation agencies are required as well as the supervision of democratic procedures during elections (technical assistance, aid to political parties, neutral observers, and so on); massive training programs for political, economic, and social leaders and their immersion in democratic societies; exchanges of leaders, students, and professionals; training for journalists and the maintenance of pluralist media; the revision of history books and civic education (values, institutions and how they really operate); apprenticeship in negotiation; and community experience. Moreover, the conditions for acceptance into the Council of Europe or closer association with the European Community will have to be strictly observed and proofs required. The initially lax approach inspired by enthusiasm at the liberation of the Communist bloc exposed the Council of Europe and the European Community alike to the loss of democratic credibility.

Help in democratization clearly also involves a parallel policy of support for economic development: rebuilding cross-border economic areas and regions, reviving networks of exchanges of persons and goods, giving preference to joint or regional projects and multinational collaboration, training staff at the regional level, and gradually transferring Community experience and management methods. This kind of support program toward a market economy presupposes a general framework, a kind of Marshal Plan, with a series of measures designed to unite the Eastern European states instead of dividing them. The strategy employed with regard to the EFTA countries at the time of the EEA negotiations can be adapted to Eastern Europe to initiate the rapprochement of Eastern European states with the European Community by encouraging them to reconstitute their collaborative links and form areas of cooperation and regional common markets.

The Monnet method began by creating natural economic areas like the Ruhr before going on to create a larger internal market, and this kind of approach can be used to guide the process of renovation in Eastern Europe. It is all the more necessary in that in recovering their freedom the countries of that region have regained their desire for identity and sovereignty. Yesterday they were oppressed while today they are calling for absolute independence, and in doing so they are laying bare the contradiction between sovereign identity and vital interdependence, a contradiction that will only be resolved within federal structures.

Chapter 10

New Steps Forward and
New Challenges

From Maastricht to Amsterdam

Events have been taking place at high speed since the European Union Treaty came into force on 1 November 1993. The delay in ratification that was caused by the rejection of the treaty in a referendum in Denmark on 2 June 1992, with 49.3 percent in favor and 50.7 percent against, revealed the gap between public opinion and political representatives; while parliaments approved the treaty with large majorities, the voters themselves were much more hesitant. It took a second referendum, following a few adjustments to the treaty, for the Danes finally to approve it on 19 May 1993, with a majority of 56.7 percent in favor (43.4 percent against). This "unblocked" the treaty but showed, and even created, doubts in people's confidence in the idea of a unified Europe. Finally, the German Constitutional Court declared the treaty compatible with its constitution on 12 October 1993.

The ratification crises point first to the need for more transparency in Community institutions and for greater public information. Second, in order to ensure that delays, or rejection, by one or several members do not stop the others from proceeding, a mechanism is needed enabling treaties to come into force when two-thirds of the member states have ratified them. The idea of this new procedure has been supported by some senior officials and political leaders at both the national and European levels. The system would enable states that wish to do so to proceed toward unification instead of waiting while the pace is set by the slowest. It is in this spirit that the Union Treaty provides for monetary union in stages, while on issues of social policy the Eleven went ahead without the United Kingdom until the new Labour government decided to join them. Some common actions, such as those of the common foreign and security policy or the Schengen Agreements, are motivated by these same intentions.

If the structures and basic orientations of the Union have only been modified to a small degree, several noteworthy events have taken place that have tested the system. On the one hand, there have been events tied to the normal functioning of the institutions such as the election of the European Parliament in June 1994 and the appointment of the new Commission. On the other hand, in a difficult context of economic crises and wars in the former Yugoslavia, other events in the areas of economic and monetary union and common foreign and security policy have tested the commitment of member states and their capacity for a common response.

The 1994 European Parliament

Since the Treaty on European Union came into force, the role of Parliament has become more and more important. Two indicators show the importance that Parliament is acquiring in Community processes: first, the fact that its proposals for amendments, whether in the cooperation or the codecision procedure, are now taken into account and that it has assumed a role in the nomination procedure of the Commission; and, second, the greater attention given it by the Council and the Commission as well as pressure groups and lobbyists.

The June 1994 elections revealed a few new phenomena. The newly elected Parliament was composed of 567 deputies. The reunification of Germany caused seats to be redistributed following the enlargement of its population, so that the demography of the member states is now better represented, even if smaller states still have proportionally more seats than they are entitled to given their demographic weights.[1]

There have also been a few political changes. The large pro-European coalition of Socialists and Christian Democrats was strengthened, but it now includes only a few Italian Christian Democrats, who used to be the backbone of the PPE, and there are fewer French Socialists than before in the Socialist group. Whereas German, British, and Spanish MPs are mainly divided between two main groups, the French have scattered into groups such as the Alliance radicale européenne, the Rassemblement des démocrates européens, and the Europe des nations, which are all dominated by the French. Political changes in Italy led to the creation of a new group, "Forza Europa," which includes exclusively members of the "Forza Italia" movement. Together with the Greens, whose numbers have risen, Forza Europa's position on many issues remains unknown, although both parties are acting pragmatically and on the whole constructively compared with the actions of the seventy anti-Europeans of the extreme left and right wings. When united, these extremists can form a strong opposition to the pro-European majority supported by forty-three liberal and eleven radical groups. This opposition controls more than four hundred seats in the Parliament, and it can sometimes count on Forza Italia, the European Democrats, and even the Greens to join. A large consensus has not stopped very critical opinions from being expressed as well as major splits over some issues. In general, the "grand coalition" will grow in importance as the importance of the Parliament grows.

The Nomination and Profile of the Santer Commission

In its first sitting, the new Parliament immediately displayed its colegislative powers by blocking a decision of the Council intended to liberalize the telecommunications market before 1998. This was the first use of this power within the framework of the Maastricht Treaty. It was followed shortly afterward by its first major political-institutional test with the nomination of the new Commission. Jacques Delors was leaving office in 1993, and three candidates were "possibles." Two were former prime ministers and the third a brilliant vice president of the Commission: respectively, Jean-Luc Dehaene (Belgium), Rund Lubbers (the Netherlands), and Sir Leon Brittan (United Kingdom). The high political profile of the candidates and the presidency's new position in the European Council, which is nearly that of a head of state, showed the importance the Commission had gained under Delors.

Well before the first European Council meeting on 24 June 1994 in Corfu, Presidents Mitterand and Kohl had made their choice of Dehaene clear. This initiative was curtailed by a veto from John Major, then the British prime minister, who saw Dehaene as too federalist; to avoid an untimely crisis, the Eleven gave in to the British veto. As president of the European Council at the time, Kohl again had a chance to display his negotiation skills in leading the Twelve to choose Jacques Santer (Luxembourg) in an extraordinary meeting of heads of states. The European Parliament approved this choice with 260 votes in favor, 238 votes against, and 23 abstentions, including that of the new German Socialist president Klaus Hänsch. The "grand coalition" in the Parliament did not stand up to this test; the nomination was secured on the one hand by the support of the PPE, some Socialist and Liberal dissidents, Forza Europa, and the Alliance Nationale as well as several votes from the RDE, the EDN, and the ARE and by pressure from Kohl and Gonzales, who had to discipline their troops. Several of the no votes were a protest against the requirement for unanimity in the Council, a mandatory procedure for the nomination of the president of the Commission.

During the assent given by Parliament, its president stressed its right to interrogate members of the Commission. The members, chosen by agreement between Santer and the heads of state, would then be questioned by committees of the Parliament. All new members were accepted with a good or average level of approval, although some were nearly rejected, such as

Padraig Flynn of Ireland, who was criticized for antifeminism, and Yves-Thibault de Silguy, who was held to be too cautious. All in all, after two days of debate the European Parliament gave its assent to the Santer Commission with a large majority of 416 in favor, 103 against, and 59 abstentions. The pro-Europe grand coalition confirmed its existence and gave democratic legitimacy to the new Commission. On the whole, the Santer Commission reflects the political distribution both in Parliament and within the member states. Holding eight seats, the Socialists are strong compared to the PPE, but the PPE has the presidency. Liberals kept two seats, with the rest going to various governmental parties except for two members who are politically nonaffiliated. The Commission has gained politically in that thirteen of its members have held ministerial positions, two of whom, Santer and Cresson, were prime ministers. All but four have held elective positions, thirteen nationally and eight in the European Parliament. Many have been in contact with European politics and policies, ensuring they are informed and experienced. Their background is generally economic or legal, and, breaking with the past, five out of twenty are women. Significantly, the average age is around fifty-two; the youngest member is forty-two and the oldest sixty-two. Continuity between the Delors Commission and the Santer Commission is ensured by the renomination of eight members. Combining a high level of technical knowledge with political authority, the new Commission seems all the more ready to take on the responsibilities that await it between 1995 and 2000. It will certainly need all its skills regarding monetary union and even more so in the areas of foreign and security policy and justice and home affairs, in which it only has a participatory role in the Council. In such an intergovernmental system, the Commission will have to prove itself to be capable, authoritative, strong, and knowledgeable as well as a visionary partner.

An Ambitious Aim: The Euro

Economic and monetary union (EMU) appears to be a fundamental objective of economic integration, which by unifying a dedicated core of countries will create the monetary stability essential for a common market. EMU is facing a tough time, however, as member states fight against giving up any share of sovereignty involved in this union and against the closer politics the union will require. What is more, EMU is subject to collective economic fluctuations. The economic crisis has proved the need for monetary union and since 1992 has been an obstacle to the introduction of common measures. In 1992, the lira left the exchange rate mechanism of the EMS, and in the April 1993 crisis the fluctuation margins had to be taken from 2.25 to 15 percent. In early 1995, the peseta crisis and devaluation of the lira, the escudo, and the Swedish crown increased the difficulties and doubts about monetary cohesion and stability and the convergence of monetary policies. It has become evident, however, that there can be no common market without monetary discipline, as imports and exports rock the stability of the market at every devaluation.

The essential question is whether the leading countries that support EMU are able to satisfy the criteria established by the Maastricht Treaty. As regards public deficits in 1994–95, only three countries met the criterion of less than 3 percent of GNP: Germany, Luxembourg, and Ireland. Four countries (Germany, France, the United Kingdom, and Luxembourg) were below the 60 percent of GNP level set for public debt. In the area of inflation, better results have been achieved; eight countries met the criteria. France had the lowest inflation of 1.7 percent per annum, whereas Germany and Ireland show 2.8 percent. In 1995, the conclusion was that only two countries, Germany and Luxembourg, met all three criteria, followed by France, Ireland, Denmark, Holland, and Belgium (even though it has a large public debt at 140 percent of GNP); the United Kingdom benefits from an exemption clause. Spain, Portugal, Italy, and Greece, in last position, lagged behind in a group of southern European countries. The differences between this group and Northern Europe may lead to a future increase if there is no economic convergence. Structural funds, in particular economic development and cohesion funds, are all the more relevant in this context. The large gap indicated how much needed to be done to create EMU, avoiding a north-south divide that would sow the seeds of instability in the Union.

On 19 June 1995, the ministers of finance declared that the deadline of 1997 was not realistic given the monetary situation. This point of view, expressed by the French minister of finance, was challenged by the commissioner responsible for the matter, Yves-Thibault de Silguy, who spoke against such a cavalier attitude toward the treaty. To avoid giving a negative impression, the European Council, which convened in Cannes on 26–27 June 1996, did not sustain the position held by their ministers of finance but reaffirmed the objectives of the treaty. The Commission and the European Monetary Institute reported at the end of 1996 on the situation of each member state with respect to the convergence criteria. According to the Treaty of Maastricht, however, if the third stage of EMU, fixing the exchange rates, establishing a central European bank, and issuing common currency in 1997, could not be undertaken in 1997, it would take place automatically in 1999. The establishment of the Euro will mark an important step on the road to a federal union.

Despite the bumps, therefore, the European Council was still on the road to a common currency. Since the European Council has confirmed the treaty objective of a monetary union, the minsters of finance have sent a warning to Greece, Spain, and Portugal to reiterate their wishes to meet the objectives established by the treaty. For the moment, the Commission is responsible for supervising efforts toward convergence, most of all those aimed at reducing budgetary deficits. In case a country should stray from the limits established, the Council may apply sanctions by retaining structural funds.

Meanwhile, in 1997 extraordinary and somewhat unexpected progress was made toward achieving the convergence. In relation to the budget deficit as a percentage of GDP, almost all the member countries meet, according to Eurostat, the entrance criteria to the Euro, including Germany, France, and Britain. A special effort was made by the southern countries: the deficit was reduced from 6 percent in 1995 to 3 percent in 1997 by Portugal, from 7 to 3 percent by Spain, from 9 percent in 1993 to 3 percent in 1997 by Italy, and from about 13 percent in 1993 to approximately 4 percent in 1997 by Greece. A similar result was obtained in Britain, Belgium, and France. From about 6 percent and even 7 percent in Britain during 1993, the deficit diminished to 3 percent or less in 1997. The most surprising example was afforded by Sweden, where the deficit dropped from 12 percent in 1994 to 2 percent in 1997. Due to these remarkable efforts by all member countries, practically all of them, with the exception of Greece, meet the deficit criterion for the Euro, though three of them, Britain, Denmark, and Sweden, are not willing to engage in the first phase.

Nevertheless, in spite of their resolution not to take part from the beginning, they made efforts to achieve the common goal of a maximum 3 percent budget deficit. It is still highly probable that the British government, under strong pressure from the city, the Confederation of British Industries, and many trade unions, and after a period of "wait and see," will adopt the Euro after the year 2000. This will be followed by the three remaining countries, including Greece, in the absence of some major crisis. Similar positive results have been achieved by almost all countries regarding the inflation rate, and at the same time interest rates have been drawing ever closer with the single currency. There will be only one monetary policy led by the European Central Bank in cooperation with national central banks and in accordance with the general guidelines defined by the European Council. Everything points to the importance of the dynamic core of the Community and of the role of common long-term objectives combined with the mutual stimulation.

According to the European Commission's *General Report* for 1997 and 1998 (no. 41), inflation has continued to fall in the European Union from 2.6 percent in 1996 to 2.1 percent in 1997 and 1.6 percent in 1998. The consolidation of member states' public finances has also continued: the average budget deficit has been cut from 4.2 percent of GDP in 1996 to 2.3 percent in 1997 and 1.8 percent in 1998, with most member states registering a deficit of 3 percent or less, while public debt, which declined in most member states, has come down from an average of 73 percent of GDP in 1996 to 71.9 percent in 1997 and 70.3 percent in 1998. While the macro-economics environment is particularly favorable to growth, there has been only a modest fall from 11 percent of the European Union labor force to 10.7 percent in the continuing high level of unemployment in 1997[2] and 10.0 percent in 1998. For the same period, the GDP growth was 2.7 percent and 2.9 percent respectively.

The Dynamic Federal Core

In a study of integration and disintegration based on successful American and Swiss examples, Karl Deutsch concluded that when several states formed a durable union this union was built around a dynamic federal core of states. Since World War II, one can clearly identify three "Europes": a divided geographical Europe, a Europe of freedom and human rights incarnated in the Council of Europe, and a committed Europe with common aims represented by the European Community. Today, the latter has become the European Union at the heart of greater Europe. In turn, the Union is led by its own dynamic core, the Franco-German tandem.

The Schengen Agreement, signed in 1985 by the five founding members of the Community and added to in 1990, is an outstanding example of how gradual integration takes place under the guidance of a dynamic core. Italy joined the agreement in 1990, followed by Spain and Portugal in 1991, Greece in 1992, and Austria in 1995. The initial three-month trial period had elapsed, and the Schengen free movement zone, with no border controls, came into being on 1 July 1995. Until 1996, France used a safety clause to delay implementation and has even increased its border controls for counterterrorist reasons. The creation of a political area, complementing the economic area, shows both how compelling as well as difficult it can be to apply. The Schengen zone is integrated into the European Union by the Treaty of Amsterdam. It is composed of a dynamic core, joined by Portugal, Spain, and Greece, where border controls still exist. Later, Denmark, Sweden, and Finland joined. Whereas the United Kingdom and Ireland have stayed out, other countries such as Norway, Switzerland, and Poland benefit from a special status. The Schengen example shows how limited special agreements expand within the Union and may create synergies that attract countries outside the Union. In this sense, the agreements anticipate concretely the future enlargement of the European

Union. The Schengen Agreement was incorporated into the European Union by the Treaty of Amsterdam.

The Union of Fifteen

Austria, Finland, and Sweden joined the Union on 1 January 1995 with no major problems. Several modifications were made to accommodate the new members. Their membership was ratified by national referenda, while Norway said no a second time.[3] If economic and institutional adjustments took place without any obstacles, difficulties are foreseeable in the areas of foreign policy, security, and defense due to these countries' neutrality.

For the moment, the European Parliament has increased by 59 members to 626. The distribution of seats among the political groups of the European Parliament on 31 December 1998 was as follows:[4]

Party of European Socialists (PSE), chaired by Pauline Green (United Kingdom)	214
European People's Party (PPE), chaired by Wilfried Martens (Belgium)	202
European Liberal Democrat and Reform Party (ELDR), chaired by Patrick Cox (IRL)	42
	458
Union for Europe (UPE), chaired by Jean-Claude Pasty (France)	35
Confederal Group of the European United Left/ Nordic Green Left (GUE-NGL), chaired by Alonso José Puerta Gutiérrez (Spain)	34
Green Group in the European Parliament (V), chaired by Magda Aelvoet (Belgium)	27
European Radical Alliance (ARE), chaired by Catherine Lalumière (France)	20
Group of Independents for a Europe of Nations (I-EDN), chaired by Jens-Peter Bonde (Denmark)	15
Nonaffiliated (NI)	37
	168
Total	626

(General Report, 1997, 423)

On this occasion, the national parliaments delegated twenty-two Swedish, twenty-one Austrian, and sixteen Finnish MPs. These new members spread across the existing political groups as follows: PSE, twenty-three members of whom eleven are Swedish Social Democrats; PPE, sixteen, with six Austrians and six Swedes; and the ELDR, ten, of whom six are Finns. To this pro-Europe "grand coalition," one has to add four non-registered anti-Union Austrians, three Greens, and two members from the Gauche unitaire. These new members do not modify the general balance of the grand coalition but have strengthened the liberals.

If one takes into account that a parliament is not functional if it has more than 650 members, the number of representatives will have to be reduced in the event of any further enlargement. In the Union of Fifteen, the 626 members of the European Parliament represent a population of 370 million Europeans. As new members enter the Union, constituencies will become larger and larger, increasing the distance between citizens and Union institutions. Already a need for access to the institutions is felt by different sociopolitical actors — the regions, cities, communes, and communities that have been trying to make themselves heard. A Committee of Regions, with elected representatives of regions and cities, accordingly has a promising future. As a new institution, it will have to learn to fulfill its representative role and make itself felt instead of getting lost in technical details. Recently, it has offered an interpretation of subsidiarity that ought to be a contribution to Community action, as many of these representatives have greater experience in this area than in other institutions. This is a promising moment for the Committee of Regions, in particular at a time when the Union's institutions need to open up to their citizens.

The number of commissioners has risen from seventeen to twenty. This raises the question what will happen when future members join. To ensure that this collegiate executive works well, several proposals have been made. However, before any major changes are made, member states, their administrations, other economic and social actors, and even the public have to accept the Commission as an independent institution representing the common interests of the member states. Its members are independent, as the recent difference of opinion over EMU between the French minister of finance and a French member of the Commission showed. Once this is clearly accepted, it will be possible to find different ways of modifying the Commission to meet new situations. Some have suggested that there should only be one member per country, but with the entry of smaller countries this is likely to weaken the institution. Others propose reducing the number of members to twelve, following a proposal made by the French government. If the five large member states are to have a seat each, how should the other ten be shared? The European Court of Justice may offer the answer, following its system for advocate generals. Smaller member states may have assistant commissioners, who would become full members of the Commission in rotation for a period of two and a half years. The twelve would constitute a sort of "ministerial cabinet" or restricted Commission. Any similar solution would require a large degree of mutual confidence between member states and a recognition of the real autonomy of the Commission.

As for the Council of fifteen ministers, the new weighting for a qualified majority is sixty-two votes out of eighty-seven (Sweden and Austria have four votes each, Finland three) when decisions are to be made on proposals from the Commission. If decisions are to be adopted on proposals that are not made by the Commission, then a second requirement is added to the sixty-two-vote qualified majority: the proposal needs the support of ten member states. Treaty revision projects propose that qualified majority voting be extended, which will be necessary in the event of any further enlargement. This is the price of the Union working well. On the whole, when using qualified majority voting, ministers have preferred to look for consensus so as to avoid a minority state feeling that its vital interests are in danger. With enlargement, many new small and medium-sized states will join the Union (Cyprus, the Baltic States, Central and Eastern European States), and the idea that such states may come to dominate the Council worries the larger ones. Accordingly, there has been a proposal to adjust voting to take into account demographic, political, and economic factors. The double majority voting requirement reflects this concern, and, in the case of the codecision procedure, one is tempted to think that the participation of the European Parliament brings these factors into play, particularly in demographics. Within this framework, the Council in its legislative function looks like a Swiss Council of States, a U.S. Senate, or a German Bundesrat.

The Tragedy and Ordeal of the Former Yugoslavia

The war in the former Yugoslavia is violent proof of the gap that separates the Union and the Western world from some of the former communist states. The interests at stake in this fratricidal conflict were present at the beginning of the process that led to the disintegration of Yugoslavia.

The repression and exclusivity of the communist ideology that lasted fifty years as well as long-term economic crises were among the main causes of the explosion of extreme nationalism. Seen as antidotes to communism, nationalist movements benefited from Western support. Ignorance of the real situations and motives, media fog, and prejudices made the conflict worse, freeing, as Freud says, the savage and destructive impulses of war. The recognition of independent states, without guarantees for minorities, exacerbated the war, especially in Bosnia, and fueled the drive for military reconquest. War prospered as conflicts divided the "Contact Group" of the United States, France, the United Kingdom, Germany, Russia, and other Western countries, even within the European Union.

Three significant events marked the period between 1992 and 1995. The first was President Milosevic's change of attitude toward the Serbs in Bosnia when he failed to get an agreement on peace plan 49/51, which had been proposed by the Contact Group. Consequently, his main objective was to keep himself in power and get the embargo lifted.[5] The embargo, under which the civilian population suffered badly, has been a justification for maintaining an authoritarian government and a paradise for black marketeers.

The second event was the arrival at center stage of the United States, following realpolitik at the expense of high principles and long-term vision. Under pressure from a Republican-dominated Congress and public opinion, the U.S. government's discrete embargo-breaking assistance to Croatia and Bosnia found favor with those advocating military assistance and the lifting of the embargo, while President Clinton's energetic relaunching of peace negotiations protected him from the opposition and assisted his electoral ambitions. Two events caused the U.S. intervention: French president Chirac's pressure after the fall of the two UN security zones, Srebenica and Zepa, and the humiliating exhibition of French and British hostages, which led to the creation of the Franco-British Rapid Reaction Force. These initiatives and local political issues propelled President Clinton to the forefront and led him to assume the leadership of the United Nations and of the West.

Besides, the killings that took place in the Sarajevo marketplace prompted massive bombing of Serb positions around the protected zones before even the Franco-British investigators expressed their doubts about the responsibility of the Serbs. The intervention of the air force revealed the U.S. strategy, which entailed balancing, by force if necessary, the warring factions and forcing them to conclude a peace based on a "balance of powers," a concept that has caused Europe a lot of problems in the past. This strategy was implemented in February 1994. Under U.S. pressure, a Croat-Muslim federation in Bosnia was established, conveniently avoiding the creation of the independent Muslim state that had been the dream of President Izetbegovic, as described in 1971 in his Islamic Declaration.

This U.S. strategy, with the support of Germany and in infraction of the UN embargo, included rearming the Croatian army, which was seen as a counterweight to the Serbs, thereby balancing the two key actors. This unilateral strategy entailed major risks, as it supported an authoritarian government in Croatia and indirectly tended to give U.S. approval to discrete discrimination against Croatian Serbs, which has been put into practice since the proclamation of independence in Croatia. Following the same logic, the May 1995 conquest of Krajina by the Croatian army was the first step down the road to an ethnically "homogeneous" state in Croatia.[6] Zagreb announced that "Krajina doesn't exist any more," and Professor Zarko Puhovski described it as a "brilliant" ethnic-cleansing operation.[7] After throwing out the 150,000 Serbs who had lived there for more than four hundred years, the expulsion and destruction led, most probably, to a situation of no-return in Krajina for an indeterminate period. This third event raises substantial questions as to whether support should be given to ethnic cleansing in the name of military balance. Of the 600,000 Serbs living in Croatia, only 130,000 remain. In the name of realpolitik, can the West give up defending multinational cultural and religious pluralism, which forms the fundamental values of the European Union?

In any case, U.S. direct involvement had an important positive consequence: the main achievement was a peace agreement negotiated in Dayton in November and signed in Paris in December 1995, which saved the Bosnian Serbs from being defeated by a Croat-Muslim coalition. The Dayton Agreement maintains a Bosnian state as a whole under the guarantee of a peacekeeping force, SFOR.[8] The constitution contained in the agreement establishes a central government empowered to sign treaties, print money, confer citizenship, represent the state, and guarantee free circulation of goods, services, and people. Despite the fact that any member of the three-man joint presidency can block a decision, as can any national group in its Parliament, this power of veto has not been misused. The Muslim-Croat Federation, whose cohesion seems to be precarious, and the Serb Republic each have their one presidency and a House of the People or National Assembly.

The Serb Republic, long dominated by Karadzic, was exposed to the tension between Banja Luka, governed by Mrs. Plavsic with the support of the West, and Pale and its Serbian Democratic Party (SDS)–Parliament. Once President Plavsic dissolved the Assembly and called for new elections, the SDS lost its majority but remained the biggest party.[9] The result was the establishment of a new government more committed to implementing the Dayton Agreement. Nevertheless, the core problem is the culture of fear and intolerance that makes the cohabitation of Muslims, Croats, and Serbs more difficult. "The divisions are created by power elites to preserve their power" says Carlos Westendorp, the European Union chief representative in Bosnia, who succeeded in making the Bosnians agree to a long-postponed passport and citizenship law.[10] According to him,

> Bosnia suffers from the same phenomena we experienced in Spain. The church bears a large responsibility for the war. The Bosnians are the same people. They are all Slavs. Religious identity is simply the

raison d'être for these nationalist leaders to hold on to power, like animals who cling to their turf. We need to build a new set of values, new traditions, new political parties to present competing ideas and culture to overcome these nationalist movements.[11]

Despite his efforts to promote multinational political parties, the main parties correspond to national cleavages. The Croatian Democratic Union (HDZ) runs from Mostar the "Community of Herceg-Bosna." It distributes Croatian textbooks and pays pensions, and Bosnian Croats elect several deputies to the Parliament in Zagreb who form the most nationalist fraction of the Croatian HDZ. This special relationship threatens the solidarity of the Muslim-Croat Federation, which is largely dominated by Muslims.

The consolidation of peace in Bosnia faces many obstacles and difficulties: resettlement of refugees, the repair of transport and communications networks, free movement and establishment, security, more equal distribution of assistance, and establishment of a "train and equip program" leading to growing military superiority for the federation.[12] But the most fundamental question remains how to change the mentality of leaders and people. "The immediate risk to Balkan peace is not so much aggression but secession by minorities big enough to contemplate statehood, which in turn could trigger war. This survey will argue, therefore, that peace depends on how Balkan countries treat their minorities."[13] In a different context, the conflict in Kosovo shows the same fundamental pattern, that is, the will to establish a homogenous national or ethnic state, the lack of respect for persons and minorities, and the absence of a real democratic process. Notwithstanding this common pattern, the durable solution can only be guaranteed by a political compromise, a multicultural and multinational society, and a real autonomy inside a broader political community and in a framework of regional integration in close association with the European Community.

The Yugoslav conflict is a real test of European solidarity. From the start, cracks appeared in the Union: a lack of preparation of common positions, common strategies, and coherent and sustained policies. The lack of common positions created tensions between the partners, as unilateral decisions were taken by one state or another. But more fundamentally these conflicts constitute a frontal attack against the principal values of federalism that are at the heart of the Union, and they may have perverse secondary effects that become a sword of Damocles over the future of European federalism. The worst is not improbable. The main obstacle to union, in the eyes of Denis de Rougemont, was the nation-state, which may reemerge in its most extreme form: exultant nationalism in praise of antidemocratic and antifederal attitudes and behavior. It imposes the "tyranny of the majority" on minorities;[14] it calls for an ethnically homogeneous nation, and while omnipotently centralizing at home it is aggressive and conquering abroad. By opposing the aims and fundamental values of the European Union with authoritarian or totalitarian values, it embodies one's worst predictions. The Yugoslav conflicts constitute a lasting and threatening challenge that has revealed the weak points of the Union. Their pattern reproduces the paradigm of the "tyranny of the majority" based on nationalistic or ethnic and religious intolerance as well as on the failure to recognize and respect the fundamental rights. In spite of all this, it is obvious that the future for the peoples of Southeastern Europe lies in some form of regional integration, fully attached to the Union.

Enlargement and Partnership

The European Union is asserting itself as a powerful force in the process of transformation of the European scene. It exerts considerable economic influence at both the regional and world levels, while its identity is being reinforced by its common policies and positions. Accounting for about 20 percent of world trade, the European Union is the foremost trading power, and its common policy in this field is the logical extension of its Customs Union. Its share in the budgets and operation of international organizations is substantial: it contributes more than half the budget of the United Nations. Within the World Bank, the IMF, and, even more visibly, the European Bank for Reconstruction and Development (EBRD) and the World Trade Organization (WTO), its influence is tending to increase. It also provides more aid than any other donor for the developing countries and, since 1990, for the countries of Eastern Europe.

The European Union is the main trading and economic partner of most of the countries in transition. It is also in first place as a provider of assistance for these countries, including the countries of the Commonwealth of Independent States (CIS), with total aid estimated at 75 billion ecus between 1990 and 1996. Having subscribed 51 percent of the capital of the EBRD, the member states of the Union occupy a central position within that institution. This has led the G-4 and the G-7 to entrust the European Commission with the coordination of all Western aid for Eastern Europe. It has thus been called upon to assume, with the assistance of the EBRD and the UN Economic Commission for Europe (ECE), a major role in providing support for these countries and in the construction of greater Europe.

In general, it is possible to distinguish three categories of European countries with which the Union is developing relations: the first consists of the applicant countries belonging to the Western sphere of influence (Cyprus, Malta, and Turkey);[15] the second is made up of the countries of Central and Eastern Europe and the Baltic States, which, under the enlargement strategy, are expected to join in the near future; and the third is composed of the CIS countries, whose accession, at least for the time being, is not envisaged. All these countries, whatever their situation and the type of agreement they have concluded with the European Union, are full and equal members of the Economic Commission for Europe.[16] The European preaccession agreements, like the partnership and cooperation agreements with the countries of the CIS, are intended to promote collaboration in the fields of democratic reform, economic development, internal affairs, and foreign and security policy. The establishment of exchange and cooperation networks, together with the aid and assistance measures, serves an important objective of the European Union and Europe as a whole, namely, to preserve and strengthen the stability of these regions. Despite differences between the accession and partnership strategies, both are directed toward the same goal. These few remarks simply underline the obvious importance of the role the Union is playing in European integration and cooperation.

For implementing its support strategy, the European Union has two main instruments at its disposal: association and partnership agreements. Association agreements — so-called European agreements — have been concluded with the countries applying to join. They provide for free trade, assistance programs, and regular consultation within common institutions (the Association Council and Committee and the Parliamentary Association Committee). Cooperation and the preaccession strategies are supported by the Programme of Community Aid for Central and Eastern European Countries (PHARE) with a budget amounting to 1.31 billion ecus for 1998 and 1.53 billion ecus for 1999.[17] The national operations financed (in millions of ecus) were: Albania, 30.5 in 1998 and 46 in 1999; Bulgaria, 68 and 51; Czech Republic, 127 and 21; Estonia, 21 and 8; Hungary, 77 and 103; Latvia, 21 and 16; Lithuania, 37 and 30; Poland, 125 and 231; Romania, 117 and 167; Slovakia, 50 and 78; and Slovenia, 10 and 31. The financing of national programs was extended in 1999 to Cyprus (14.5 million ecus) and Malta (7 million ecus). In addition, 180 million ecus were committed for cross-border cooperation; 461 million for regional and horizontal programs; 42 million for rehabilitation of the former Yugoslavia, excluding Kosovo reconstruction aid; and 62 million for other purposes.[18] These institutional and financial instruments are administered by a Community department with a staff of three hundred officials, compared to only ten in 1990. This illustrates the importance the European Union attaches to these countries, which are destined to join it in the near future.

The PHARE program helps the associate countries to restructure their economies and adapt their legislation to the Community patrimony. The multiyear assistance programs incorporated in the national strategies relate mainly to investment aid, particularly in the areas of infrastructure, the environment, and private sector development. To supplement the bilateral aid and agreements, the Commission is supporting intraregional cooperation and neighborliness between associate countries by financing several multinational programs and a transborder cooperation program. This support is strengthening the cooperative institutions, encouraging the development of civil society, facilitating the movement of persons and goods, and promoting trade in the region.[19] Thus, the associate countries are in the process of restoring cooperation networks and renewing their interdependence. For its part, the ECE is contributing to this effort by deploying all the good-neighbor and integration instruments it has developed as well as through its analyses that emphasize the importance of subregional trade.

New guidelines for PHARE were adopted by the Commission in March and approved in June 1997 by the Council, with the aim of gearing the program to preparing the applicant countries for membership by helping them implement *acquis communautaire* and upgrade their enterprises and major infrastructures to Community standards. The Commission proposed that PHARE should focus on two main priorities: institution building and financing investment. Special attention will be paid to justice and home affairs (fraud, illegal immigration, and organized crime). Overall, 30 percent of PHARE funding will be devoted to these matters. The second priority (70 percent) concerns areas where adoption of Community rules will require substantial resources (environment, transport, product quality, working conditions, reducing economic imbalances, and so on) and major infrastructure projects connected with the trans-European networks.[20]

In accordance with the provisions of article 49 (ex art. O) of the Treaty on European Union, in July 1997 the European Commission presented its opinions on the membership applications of ten associated countries of Central Europe.[21] In its opinions the Commission applied objective economic and political criteria, which were defined by the European Council in Copenhagen in 1993: An applicant country had to have:

1. Stable institutions guaranteeing democracy, the rule of law, human rights, and respect for and protection of minorities;
2. A functioning market economy and the capacity to cope with competitive pressure and market forces within the Union;
3. The ability to take on the obligations of membership, including adherence to the aims of political, economic, and monetary union.

The Commission sought to evaluate the progress each applicant might reasonably be expected to make in the years ahead, bearing in mind that *acquis communautaire* (established Community law and practice) would continue to evolve.

Hungary, Poland, Estonia, the Czech Republic, and Slovenia were evaluated positively, and therefore the Commission recommended that accession negotiations should begin with those five countries.[22] The accession negotiations with Cyprus began after the conclusion of the Intergovernmental Conference in accordance with a resolution adopted by the European Council in Florence in June 1996 and a favorable opinion issued by the Commission as long ago as July 1993.

According to the Commission, the five Central European countries previously mentioned fulfill the political criteria and should be able to participate fully in the single market provided they maintain the effort to transpose and implement Community law. But a further special effort, and investment, will be needed on the environment (for all applicants), customs, energy, transport, and agriculture (differing accordingly to various economies), as will further administrative reforms to provide the countries with the structures required for effective application and enforcement of Community rules. In March 1999 the process of accession negotiations was opened with Hungary, Poland, Estonia, the Czech Republic, and Slovenia.

Regarding the remaining five applicants, Romania, Slovakia, Latvia, Lithuania, and Bulgaria, the Commission considered that negotiations between them and the European Union should begin once the countries had made sufficient progress toward meeting the accession criteria set out by the Copenhagen European Council. Slovakia is the only country that does not meet the political conditions satisfactorily because its institutions are unstable and there are shortcomings in the functioning of its democracy. The Commission considers this situation all the more regrettable as Slovakia would be capable of meeting the economic criteria in the medium term and is firmly committed to adopting Community law and practice.

Following the installation of new governments in Romania and Bulgaria, the current improvements indicate that those two countries are on their way to meeting the political criteria. They also have made considerable progress toward establishing a market economy, but they would still have difficulties in the medium term in coping with competitive pressure and market forces in the Union. Both Latvia and Lithuania present the characteristics of a democracy and meet the general political conditions, but steps need to be taken by Latvia as well as Estonia to speed up the naturalization of Russian-speaking noncitizens to enable them to integrate more fully into their societies. Contrary to Estonia, Latvia, and Lithuania would still have, despite their progress, serious difficulties within the single market of the Union.

The analyses and warnings of the Commission of the European Union and the ECE are material for political reflection and decision. They propose an economic angle of approach and democratic criteria. However, from a more global viewpoint a more original political course of action might be envisaged: the preaccession strategy could be directly incorporated with the existing agreements and institutions in a framework treaty intended to enter into force rapidly while allowing for periods of adjustment. This procedure, which involves reversing the sequence adjustment first and then accession, would have the advantage of immediately creating a security area while ensuring the progressive integration of the countries of Central and Eastern Europe. The latter thus would become members of the European Union, within which they would continue their development in order to achieve cohesion. In fact, closer association with the Union, which is, moreover, their principal market and major source of aid and capital, has become their priority. Though moving at different speeds, all the countries of the region have set out along the twin paths of economic and democratic transition, with the aim of fulfilling the conditions of membership in the European Union.

The path of economic transition, which leads in the opposite direction to the authoritarian state economics practiced for half a century, is strewn with numerous obstacles. Despite the growing importance of private ownership, in most of these countries the state remains the principal owner alongside the workers' collectives and foreign investors. According to the official statistics, the privatized sector's share of GDP is usually in excess of 50 percent, which confirms the distance traveled since 1989, when it was generally less than 5 percent (with the exception of 30 percent in Poland). Direct foreign investment is flowing mainly into three countries of the Visegrad group: first, Hungary, with 11,394 million dollars in 1995, followed by the Czech Republic (5,881) and Poland (2,751).[23] Everywhere the decline in GDP has been considerable, least so in Poland, where GDP fell by about 1.5 percent between 1989 and 1995, but around 15 percent in Hungary and the Czech Republic during the same period. Everywhere inflation has been more or less brought under control, although it remains high by Western European standards. On the other hand, the economic and social disparities have become more pronounced, giving rise to greater inequality and a feeling of insecurity. This general situation largely explains the return to power or progress of the socialist (ex-communist) parties in some of these countries. On the other hand, it is also true that, conversely, in other countries serious economic crises under socialist governments have led to the opposition coming to power. This shows that, by and large, the *transition to democracy* is on the right track.

In addition to the PHARE program of aid for the countries of Central and Eastern Europe there is the Programme for Technical Assistance to the Independent States of the Former Soviet Union and Mongolia (TACIS) aimed at the countries of the Commonwealth of Independent States (CIS), cooperation with which takes the form of "partnership agreements." Relations between the European Union and Russia entered a new phase in 1997 with the entry into force of the partnership and cooperation agreement. The agreement in force since 1 December 1997 governs all political economic and trade relations between the parties and will lay the foundations for cooperation in social, human, scientific, technological, and cultural matters. As stated in the *General Report* for 1997, relations with the other independent states of the former Soviet Union also progressed substantially, except in the case of Belarus, whose political and human rights situation has prevented closer relations with the European Union.[24] Among the measures adopted under the TACIS program were a cross-border cooperation program (30 million) concentrating on the environment and developing the trans-European networks and a "democracy program" (11 million). New projects concern such sensitive areas as the conversion of chemical weapons plants in Russia and combating the drug problem. In 1997, the total value of contracts drawn up was 691 million ecus, while payments totaled 397 million.

The contributions of the West, and the European Union in particular, are far from being negligible, but are they sufficient and appropriate? Indeed, at the time of the dismemberment of the Soviet Union, the worst was avoided. Although tensions persist between Russia and Ukraine, fears of a conflict were not realized. On the other hand, several peripheral conflicts broke out on the fringes of Russia and within its borders, which illustrate the instability of this region. Though weakened, Russia continues to play a leading role in this region, which still bears the mark of the system of structural and economic interdependence inherited from the Soviet Union. The states of the region are seeking to open up new channels of cooperation with the outside world but at the same time are renewing their links with Russia.

Because of its role as the once dominant power in the Eastern European region and its status of former superpower, the transition in Russia has affected both security and economic cooperation at the European and world levels. At the same time, it has given rise to positive trends by rousing society and triggering revivals in the fields of culture, education, and the arts. It has liberated social creativity and dynamism and made possible a flowering of pluralism of expression and association. This pluralism of ideas and opinions has its counterpart in the multiparty system, political competition, and the regular organization of elections. The other advantages of transition include freedom of movement, both inside Russia and for those wishing to travel abroad.

The new transparency has revealed the role of both governments and institutional and legal structures in providing guidance, coordination, and certainty of the law for the economies in transition, but it has also revealed the complexity and weaknesses of the political system of the Russian

Federation. Although progress has been made—notably in separating the powers of the executive and the judiciary and in affirming democratic principles and respect for human rights—the balance between the Duma and the presidency has tilted sharply in favor of the latter. The problems that divide the center and the provinces and the resulting tensions have been accentuated by the disparity between the rich regions and the poor. This disparity seems likely to increase because of differences in industrial structures, natural resources, and the agricultural situation. The economic divisions are compounded by ethnic, cultural, and religious divisions, which are creating minority community problems both between republics and regions of the federation and within these various entities. The coexistence of populations of different origins and speaking different languages in the countries that border Russia is another source of tension. Furthermore, at the social level a middle class has not yet succeeded in emerging in Russia, and a rift has developed between the new rich and the rest of the population, which includes a high proportion of the socially excluded. Rather than the egalitarian society that it aimed to become, Russia is a country of extreme inequalities. Thus, the gap between the 10 percent with the highest incomes and the 10 percent with the lowest widened from 4.5 percent in 1991 to 13.5 percent in 1995 (after reaching 15 percent in 1994).[25]

Under these circumstances, it is not surprising that the reforms should be running up against numerous obstacles. Privatization has been broadly achieved among small businesses and in services, but it is making only slow progress in the large and medium-sized business sector. Admittedly, prices (except for oil and gas prices), trade, and the foreign exchange regime have been liberalized and inflation was brought under control in 1996. These achievements have earned Russia the approval of the IMF, of which it has been a member since 1992, and the allocation of a 20 billion dollar credit. However, the reforms and the revival of production have been held back by the structure of the productive system, impaired by the hypertrophy of the military complex;[26] by the inability of the central government to collect taxes from the republics and regions; and by the cessation of payments, which is threatening to paralyze the economy. These difficulties are compounded by the persistence of attitudes left over from the previous system, which is tending to discourage the assumption of responsibility and the risk taking inherent in any market economy. It is hardly surprising, then, that growth should still be proving elusive or that, according to estimates, GDP should have fallen by 40 percent between 1989 and 1995. In 1996, GDP declined even more sharply, recording a fall of 6 percent over the first nine months of the year.[27]

The problems of transition in Russia and their repercussions are having an impact on the Commonwealth of Independent States and affecting Russia's relations with the states of Central and Eastern Europe as well as its relations with the West and the world at large. In short, they are causing a geopolitical upheaval. To halt the process of fragmentation and to limit the damage it is doing, the political leadership has tried to contain these movements within a flexible system of cooperation based on the common need for security and on economic interdependence.

Established in 1991, the aim of the CIS is to provide a framework for cooperation and coordination between twelve independent states and to preserve, by a variety of means, the zone of the former Soviet Union, excluding the Baltic States. Grouped around Russia, Belarus, Kazakhstan, and Kyrgyzstan form a nucleus with which, in varying degrees, Armenia, Georgia, and Tajikistan, together with Azerbaijan, Moldova, Turkmenistan, and Ukraine, have all established links. Russia and Belarus have, for their part, committed themselves to forming a closer union. Thus, the CIS appears to represent a multitrack integration process. All the member states are facing problems of transition and integration into the world economy. They are also seeking to reconcile their recently acquired political independence with interdependence in the economic, energy, and, in some cases, security fields. The result has been a range of solutions and modes of cooperation. This fluidity of the situation in the CIS is having repercussions on foreign relations as well. Thus, the development of peaceful relations within the CIS and CIS relations with the European Union, in particular, constitute an important element of European and world security.

The Europe of Small Steps or the Treaty of Amsterdam

One Small Step?

By all accounts, the Treaty of Amsterdam, which entered into force on 1 May 1999, did not take into account the expectations raised by the planned revision of the Maastricht Treaty. Previously, the negotiations that led to the treaties of the European Single Act and Maastricht were marked by the determination to further the process of integration. Political will was manifested in the form of a "negotiation by synergy," as opposed to the "package deal" method, which is a sectoral compromise. As Emile Noël put it, negotiation by synergy does not proceed by reducing proposals but rather by a cumulative process in the course of which each member state makes its own contribution, which, enhanced by joint efforts, serves to enrich the final result.[28]

According to eyewitnesses, the Amsterdam negotiations were particularly arduous. First of all, and rightly so, most of the efforts focused on the Euro, the social dimension, and employment. In spite of economic difficulties and unemployment, which affect the majority of the member states of the Union, they undertook, at great sacrifice, to meet the Maastricht criteria for monetary integration. The European Council has definitely given the green light to launching the single currency on 1 January 1999, at the same time strengthening coordination between economic policies in favor of employment. At France's request, the Pact on Stability and Growth, which was adopted in its entirety, was accompanied by two resolutions that firmly set employment at the heart of the Union's priorities. Following these preoccupations, a new chapter was written on employment, strengthening the provisions for the social dimension and aiming to establish a better balance between economic considerations and social aspects with a view toward a "European social model." Furthermore, these negotiations took place within a general climate less favorable to speeding up European integration. The indications were all there: varying support from the general public, cracks in Franco-German unity in the engine room of the Union, and splits between large and medium-sized member states on the composition of the Commission and the new weighting of votes in the Council. Moreover, several proposals, fortunately avoided, were aimed at weakening the role of the Commission, reflecting certain countries' intention of taking advantage of divergences that go beyond the mere lack of political will. Hence, there is a concern to safeguard the institutional *acquis* and proceed by small steps, leaving until later fundamental issues such as the deepening and strengthening of the Union's institutions. As Commissioner Marcelino Oreja remarked, the goal of preparing the EU's institutions for enlargement was not attained, even though it was one of the essential goals of the Intergovernmental Conference.[29] Unlike earlier negotiations, this time the European Council, instead of giving political impetus to achieving qualitative progress regarding the challenges facing the Union, had to minimize its losses and make do with sectoral progress and institutional modifications. From the viewpoint of this unfavorable context — marked, according to President Jacques Santer, by a lack of political resolve and a worrying tendency to give greater importance to purely national views — attempts must be made to redress the imbalance in the Intergovernmental Conference and the European Council of Amsterdam. In his address to the plenary session of the European Parliament, he stated:

> In my view, the text of the presidency brought ambition and realism together. I hoped that further effort would be made by the heads of state and government to reinforce and improve it. The fears that I expressed to you last June, Mr. President, to a certain extent proved to be accurate. One way or another, ground has been lost. And what can be said of the plethora of protocols and declarations: fourteen protocols, forty-six declarations. It is a record that does not make the treaty more readable.[30]

The stage thus set, I propose to emphasize the positive results that stand out from this exercise, which, in spite of good intentions, did not result in an account that is intelligible, consistent, or accessible to European citizens. An abstruse and complicated treaty accompanied by a host of protocols and declarations, it does have the merit of having safeguarded the essential experience and accomplished a measure of progress, undoubtedly inadequate and partial but proceeding in the right direction by pragmatically adding a few stones to the edifice of the future European federation.

Some Substantial Progress

The widespread disillusionment generated by the Treaty of Amsterdam has overshadowed to a large extent the more discreet but no less important steps regarding fundamental rights, integration of employment, the social dimension, and the Schengen Agreement. The same is true of the integration into the Community of the third pillar and improvements in the field of the environment.[31] On the whole, this progress is in answer to the demands of citizens concerning their rights, their work, and their security.

The fundamental rights held in common by the member states are the foundation of the Union: the principles of liberty and democracy, respect for human rights and basic freedoms, and government based on the rule of law.[32] Thirteen years after the draft Treaty on European Union was adopted by the European Parliament under the aegis of Altiero Spinelli, the Treaty of Amsterdam instituted a sanctions mechanism in the event that a member state breached these principles.[33] The Council may confirm a "serious and persistent breach," meeting at the level of heads of state or government and ruling unanimously on a proposal by one-third of the member states or by the Commission after obtaining the assent of the European Parliament. While taking its decision, the Council shall act without taking account of the vote of the representative of the member state concerned or the abstentions by members present or represented. Furthermore, its decision cannot be taken without obtaining the assent of the European Parliament, acting by a two-thirds majority of the votes cast, representing a majority of its members. Thus, the participation of the European Parliament is a decisive factor. Where a breach has been determined, the Council, acting by a qualified majority, may decide to suspend certain rights derived from the application of the treaty to the state in question, including its voting rights in the Council (art. 7 (ex F.a) of the Treaty of Amsterdam). These innovative provisions not only reinforce fundamental rights and democratic principles but provide for *sanctions* should they not be respected. They apply to member states, while at the same time constituting clearly and explicitly a sine qua non condition for any European state applying to become a member of the Union. In fact, any European state that respects the principles set out in article 7.1 (ex F.1) may apply for admission into the European Union (art. 237, EEC Treaty, and art. 48 (ex O) of the Treaty on European Union).

The rights of persons and citizens have been reinforced and the procedures to promote and apply them have been institutionalized. The progressive establishment of an area of freedom, security, and justice has become a concrete obligation.[34] On account of the obvious failure of the third pillar, a discreet but strong demand has been taken into consideration by the new treaty. The "transfer to the Community pillar" of this sector covers internal and external borders, policies on visas, asylum and immigration,[35] and judicial cooperation in civil matters. In these various fields, results exceeded expectations. Despite minor resistance, intergovernmental cooperation, which turned out to be ineffective, gave way to Community methods and procedures: using directives or regulations instead of conventions, instituting judicial control by the Court of Justice, and introducing the Commission's right to propose. These innovations will enter into force after a five-year period, replacing the initiative powers of member states and the Commission. At the same time, the Council's process of decision making continues unchanged within Coreper and its working groups, thus ensuring greater consistency and effectiveness.

Another innovation consisted in a new article 13 (ex 6a) inserted in the Treaty of the European Community, which provides for measures that the Council may adopt by unanimity on a proposal from the Commission to combat discrimination based on sex,[36] racial or ethnic origin, religion or belief, disability, age, or sexual orientation. These guarantees against discrimination aim at learning from certain national or ethnic conflicts as well as satisfying the demands of citizens. More than one such demand is echoed in other provisions of the treaty, namely, those relating to fighting against social exclusion or in favor of equal opportunity and equal treatment for men and women contained in the chapter on social policy. The foregoing are a number of elements, which, besides acknowledging the role of services of general interest such as public service broadcasting and strengthening aspects of social policy, indicate, even if incompletely, the existence of a European model of society distinct from that in the United States.

These are several examples, certainly of the highest importance, chosen from substantial improvements accomplished by the Treaty of Amsterdam. Other innovations already mentioned, such as social and employment policies, reinforced and widespread rules concerning the environment, and regulations determining the importance of the principle of subsidiarity or introducing the notion of *transparency,*[37] can also be noted.

The latter opens better access to citizens and their associations to the institutions' documents. This has confirmed the right of access to the European Parliament. As for the Council's and Commission's documents, the principle of openness has also been taken into consideration. For the majority of member states, with the exception of some Nordic countries, the distinction between open legislative and closed executive decisions has been accepted in principle, taking into account the fact that the Council performs both legislative and executive functions at the same time. The former, which it shares most often with the European Parliament, will be open to citizens in general. Both of these measures aim at reducing the distance between European institutions on one side and citizens and their associations on the other.

The same intention appeared in the protocol aimed at the implementation of the *principle of subsidiarity*.[38] It is one of the fundamental principles of federalism whose general application has often been implied at different levels. That principle consists of the allocation of powers to different echelons, which is a distinctive feature of federal systems. Precisely, the protocol gives this principle legality and provides guidance, particularly for member states that are not used to federal practices. In reality, it deals with the learning process of both the attribution and the exercise of powers on the level of the Union and member states as well as the regions, cities, and local communities. This same principle of subsidiarity can be useful in the distribution of functions between the public and private sectors. For instance, certain, almost unnoticed innovations in the Treaty of Amsterdam contributed to the enrichment of more than one substantial aspect of the European Union.

The same is true of the idea of *closer cooperation*.[39] The Chirac-Kohl letter of December 1995 officially renewed this reinforced cooperation, which had already been present in the transition periods and EMU as well as in the CDU/CSU parliamentary group's proposition intended to form a federalist core. The long debate that followed made it possible to introduce two slightly different articles into the Treaty on European Union and another into the Treaty of the European Community. The general rules prescribe a series of conditions: closer cooperation is aimed at furthering the objectives and the interests of the Union, at least by the majority of the member states. Closer cooperation between member states also means that all of them can take part in Council deliberations but only those representing participating member states shall take part in adopting decisions. The Treaty of the European Community stated that reinforced cooperation can neither interfere with the Community's exclusive competence nor affect its policies, actions, or programs; and that closer cooperation cannot touch upon citizenship in the Union nor discriminate between nationals of member states. These general conditions mean that one group of member states can play an avant-garde role without harming the solidarity of the whole. Their real importance will be evaluated in light of experience and by their future implementation by member states. However, one hopes that closer cooperation will be organized around the same federal core to avoid excessive dispersion and preserve a certain degree of coherence within the Union.

Institutional Reforms

The key questions being postponed for the later period, I propose to present a brief analysis of the most relevant institutional reforms.[40] According to EU president Jacques Santer, two areas of high interest to the European Parliament caused significant innovations.[41] The first concerns a codecision procedure, which was extended and replaces the "process of cooperation" with the exception of some cases concerning the EMU. In particular, the codecision procedure now consists of about fifteen supplementary articles. The majority concern measures for, and decisions on, their application: the European Social Fund, European Regional Development Fund (ERDF), transport policy, a ban on discrimination, free circulation, and settlement. The process of codecision has been adopted apart from the series of new dispositions. These dispositions deal with equality of opportunity, social policy, measures encouraging employment, the fight against crime, and frontier cooperation.[42] Instead, the Intergovernmental Conference has not followed the European Commission's recommendations, particularly in the following areas: voting rights and eligibility, general acts on the common agriculture policy and fishing, free services, antidumping legislation, actions concerning the environment, and financial regulations.[43] The consequence of the extension of the codecision-making process is the suppression of cooperation procedures as well as the elimination of the third reading. Gradually, the power of the European Parliament has grown, allowing it to become a real colegislator with the Council.

Overall, the European Parliament's powers to legislate and supervise have been reinforced, together with its political power to intervene in a growing number of areas of interest to the European Union. Besides extending the codecision procedure, the European Parliament's assent is needed to apply sanctions in the case of serious and persistent violations of human rights.[44] This progress is accompanied by three types of simplified parliamentary procedures: consultation, codecision, and assent. In addition, the third reading was abandoned; it brought the European Parliament face to face with the Council and excluded the Commission, reducing it to the secondary role of executive, disproportionately in favor of the Council. Since then, the European Parliament seems to have shared equality with the Council. This trend confirms the bicameral structure of the legislative power by assuring representation of both member states and the peoples of the Union. This is a significant step on the path toward European federalism. Finally, the Treaty of Amsterdam ratifies the practice of the European Parliament by which it was customary for it to approve the choice of president designated by the European Council. In the Treaty of Amsterdam, the custom became a formal rule and obligation: the role of the European Parliament in nominating the president and members of the Commission was confirmed as the power of investiture. This innovation, which allows the European Parliament to intervene from the beginning of the process of nominating the president, is significant in that it reinforces the role of the president of the Commission as a political leader.

If the European Parliament seems to hold the advantage following those changes, the Council's decision-making procedures seem to be a disillusion. The discussion on adopting the qualified majority as a general rule raised many hopes. This question, however, received only a partial answer. In the EU, the qualified majority of fifteen member states implies the following weighted votes: Germany, France, Italy, and the United Kingdom have ten votes each; Spain has eight; Belgium, Greece, the Netherlands, and Portugal hold five each; Austria and Sweden dispose of four each; Denmark, Ireland, and Finland have three each; and Luxembourg has two. The qualified majority is sixty-two out of eighty-seven votes when the decisions are adopted on a proposal from the Commission. In other cases and in sensitive situations, this qualified majority is reinforced by requiring ten positive votes out of fifteen member states. Qualified majority voting applies to many new measures in the treaty such as incentives for employment and social policy, public health, and measures against crime. Two important areas concern substituting majority voting for unanimity, that is, the outermost regions considered as far distant areas and the adoption of the research framework program and its adaptations or complements.[45] In principle, qualified majority cases are associated with the codecision procedure when they concern legislation. Instead of and in contrast to the Intergovernmental Conference's (IGC) preparatory work and its results, a large number of areas did not get the extension. The areas in question are social security and previous social measures, professions, indirect taxation and financial regulation, culture, industry, and environment inter alia.

In the face of opposition by small and medium-sized member states, the question of new weighted votes in the Council has been postponed. This question can be approached as concerning either simple weighted votes or a system of the double majority of member states and their populations. The postponement has been justified particularly by the close connection between the revision of the weighted votes and the number of members of the

Commission. Governments seem to rely on the immediate pressure of future enlargement negotiations, which will tend to adopt an effective solution. Obviously, the decision-making process of the fifteen members will become even more difficult with the growth of the number of the member states. Consequently, the presence of new members will not only increase the spectrum of interests and vision, but the differences in structures and thinking could well hinder the effectiveness of the decision-making process. As for the Council, the essentials remain to be determined.

The European Council is emerging both in practice and legally as a key institution in coordinating economic policies in highly sensitive and political areas and in defining the external policy's strategic orientation. Nonetheless, a major reform concerning its decisional capacity and working methods has to be undertaken in the future.

The Commission, in its turn, sees its authority strengthened owing to the approval of the European Parliament in monitoring the Commission's future president.[46] Its cohesion and capacity for action will increase since its nominated president will be associated with the selection process for Commission members from now on. It is important that the members of the Commission be appointed by the governments of the member states by common agreement with the presidential nominee, who enjoys power to negotiate and even to oppose. This method resembles national nominating procedures for government members in the member states. At the same time, it guarantees the best cohesion within this collegiate institution.

Contrary to the current situation, in which the leadership of the president of the Commission depends basically on his or her personality, the new provisions consolidate his or her position as a leader. This has been achieved by emphasizing that the Commission works under the political guidance of its president. According to the declaration of the IGC, the president must enjoy broad discretion in the allocation of tasks within the college as well as in any reshuffling of those tasks. The conference also noted the Commission's intention to undertake in parallel a corresponding reorganization of its departments and to bring external relations under the responsibility of a vice president. These intentions were previously announced by the Santer Commission.[47] This increase in the president's legal power becomes very important in light of his participation at the highest instance in the European Council. Furthermore, the Commission's field of competence and its exclusive right to make formal proposals have been gradually extended to some of the traditional areas of intergovernmental cooperation. Like the member states, the Commission can take the initiative in police and criminal cooperation, the area that so far has been out of reach of its activity.

These innovations confirm the authority enjoyed by the Commission among the majority of member states. Throughout its many years of activity, the Commission has managed to strengthen its power by means of its objective interpretation of common European interests and to consolidate its authority through its competence and efficiency.

Notwithstanding its independence and objectivity, the Commission suffers from misconceptions that reflect an image of an institution consisting of government representatives. This tendency has often been mentioned in the press. In this respect, differences among member states explain why adopting an efficient solution is impossible considering its twenty members. Far from the French proposition to reduce the number to ten, and not being able to put together the divergent positions of the fifteen member states, the IGC could do nothing but sketch a few guidelines. This question will be put on the agenda of another conference planned at least one year prior to the date of the next enlargement of the Union to more than twenty member states.[48] This obligation, already scheduled, imposes close interdependence on solutions for both the composition of the Commission and the weighted votes in the Council in particular. The reliable functioning of the enlarged Union's institutions will mainly depend on an appropriate solution to these problems. This double method, consisting of obligatory deadlines and *acquis communitaire,* has avoided a complete standstill and allowed step-by-step progress.

Provided that the Community tends to replace intergovernmental co-operation and those decisions of the Union with a more direct impact on people, enterprises, and groups, one could logically expect democratic equilibrium to be preserved between obligations and rights. It also could be anticipated that the guarantees agreed upon under the supervision of the Court of Justice, as well as the direct appeal of individuals and groups directly affected by Community decisions, will nevertheless have a spillover effect. In the future, the Court of Justice will exercise competence in fields relevant to internal and legal affairs, but its competence will be limited. In the area of free movement of people, asylum, and immigration, a new title in the Treaty on European Union provides that the competencies of the Court of Justice, according to article 234 (ex 177) are applicable under the following restrictive conditions:[49] where a question of interpretation of this title or of acts of the institutions is raised, the Council, the Commission, or a member state may then request a Court hearing; the ruling given by the Court shall not apply to judgments of member states' tribunals, which have become res judicata. In any event, the Court of Justice shall not have jurisdiction to rule on any measure or decision relating to the maintenance of law and order and safeguarding of internal security (art. H, which was not reproduced). In title VI of the Treaty on European Union, on police and judicial cooperation in criminal matters,[50] the Court of Justice shall have jurisdiction only if member states have deliberately accepted it.[51] However, citizens do not have the right of direct access to the Court; only member states or the Commission have the right to apply to it. As for the interpretation and application of conventions established under this title, the Court has jurisdiction to rule on any dispute between member states and the Commission. In the logic of the system, acts by Union institutions have in many cases directly impacted on citizens; consequently, in order to preserve a balance between rights and obligations, citizens and associations should have the right to apply to the Court directly. In the future, one could expect that it would be granted to citizens. This particular characteristic of the European Community distinguishes it from traditional international organizations and ties it closer to federal systems.

Among other institutional reforms, one should mention extending the areas of consultation on social matters, particularly by the Economic and Social Committee and the Committee of the Regions. The Committee of the Regions has just been given an autonomous administrative infrastructure as well as the power to consult in the following areas: environment, social funds, professional formation, and transport. In spite of their obvious regional dimension, all these areas were forgotten in the Maastricht Treaty. The Treaty of Amsterdam intentionally enables the European Parliament to consult the committees. Finally, one can rightly question the significance of the new disposition concerning the incompatibility between membership in the Committee of the Regions and membership in the European Parliament.[52] It is possible that this incompatibility in some way emphasizes the political dimension of the Committee of the Regions. In this connection, more than one observer sees the Committee as a future chamber of regions and cities as well as other local public bodies. The senate of the regions was a dream of Denis de Rougemont, and it was proposed by the Länder as well. It shows an evolution aiming at reducing the distance between the regions and different local bodies, on one hand, and the institutions of the Union on the other. It is one more indication that the search for the original European federalism is under way.

A Political Sector Par Excellence: The Union's
External Relations

External threat holds an important place in the classical theory of federation, yet this threat has hardly been mentioned in the theory of integration.[53] It is only recently that authors such as P. Soldatos have begun to study the external dimension of the European Community.[54] Among the factors most influencing the formation, development, and functioning of the federation, common dangers and feelings of solidarity are often mentioned to explain the origins of federal unions.[55] The role of external factors can be seen in the very birth of the Swiss Confederation. Generally speaking, the need to assure external security is one of the motives that makes people unite in political communities. Their most important function is to defend themselves against external danger and to jointly guarantee their security. Certainly, this initial motivation is sufficient in creating a federation. However, it often represents the initiating factor for integration. This integration can take the form of the federal union corresponding to prefederal conditions, which seems to be the case in the European Union today.

Basically, for years the integration process has referred to the economic sector and its external growth: association agreements, the ACP, and commercial negotiations—GATT and the WTO, for example. Since the upheavals of 1989, the external political dimension and security became its priority for the following reasons: exterior political events, the importance of the European Union in the world economy, and its political potential. Under the influence of these factors, the European Union was supposed to refurbish the parallels between economic and political integration, whose discord threatened the continuation of the integration process. In truth, the incoherent external policy, tensions, and insecurity caused by integration can have consequences for economic and monetary union as well as cohesion and common solidarity. There is an urgent need to recreate the global political cohesion of the Union, characterized at present by fragmented sectorial policies, vision, and powers and by different and even incompatible decision-making processes.

Reinforcement of the Union's capacity is intended to meet pressing external and internal demands, which include the following:

Supporting the peaceful transition to democracy and economic and social development of the countries of Central and Eastern Europe, especially those intending to join the Union.

Contributing to the stabilization of the CIS countries, particularly Russia, which is still the second military and nuclear power.

Enabling the Union to face crises and conflicts by learning from the Yugoslav conflict in particular.

Guaranteeing political equilibrium within the Union following German reunification. This has to be done in order to avoid either the hegemony or geopolitics of the past (see the memorandum by the German government party, "The CDU: A Report Issued by the CDU Parliamentary Group"). It will also assure effective representation of the Union within the Security Council by two permanent members, France and the United Kingdom.

Covering up inadequacies in intergovernmental processes such as insufficient real involvement of the European Council, the dominant role of the Council of Ministers in foreign affairs, the overloaded presidency (troika), and the overly "diplomatic" character of the Political Committee, which is reminiscent of the "political commission" suggested by General de Gaulle in Fouchet's Project and the modest if not marginal role of the Commission.

Reinforcing the European pillar in NATO, assuring the autonomy of defense and intervention throughout the Western European Union, and establishing equilibrium with the quasi monopoly of American power.

In view of the new situation, revision is necessary. Besides, from time to time the United States seems to face the dilemma of isolation followed by disengagement in Europe or continuation of its leadership in NATO. Shifts in American policy often contrast with the European stance, on the one side, and the incoherence of European member states' policies on the other, which are destabilizing factors in Europe. Recent changes in the U.S. government's attitude toward Cuba and Iran may bring changes. Nevertheless, assuring stability and security in Europe through common external and defense policies remains an urgent issue. More than anything else, recent events in Kosovo and the ongoing Yugoslav conflict emphasize the shortcomings of the system and the need for fundamental revision.

It is interesting to recall that in the member states public opinion (79 percent as opposed to 15 percent) considers maintaining peace by intervening more freely in potential conflicts to be an essential priority (*Eurobaromètre*, no. 45:54, table 3.11). This attitude coincides with its most important goal and responsibility, which 88 percent of the public has attributed to the European Union for the last ten years in order to encourage the establishment and the maintenance of peace in Europe (3.10). At present, between 67 and 70 percent estimate that the European Union's foreign policy decision toward other countries should be made jointly in the Union, although 23 and 22 percent prefer them to be made by national governments (*Eurobaromètre*, no. 44: table 5.5; 45:59).

Has the Treaty of Amsterdam's answer to its external challenges lived up to expectations? In the first place, it has reinforced the responsibility of the European Council. Also, it has reformulated the roles of the Council and the Commission, which are more closely associated. Apart from that, the treaty has introduced constructive abstention and extended the use of qualified majority voting when adopting joint actions and common positions, taking any other decision on the basis of a common strategy, or implementing a joint action or a common position. By defining the objectives of the external policy, the new treaty endeavors to give more coherence to global action for the Union in general external relations, security, the economy, and development. In this respect, the Council and the Commission are given the responsibility of assuring this coherence, based on the general guidelines and strategy defined by the European Council.

Among the principal objectives of the external policy are the following:

Safeguarding common values, particularly the independence and integrity of the Union.

Strengthening the security of the Union, preserving peace, and strengthening international security as well as promoting international cooperation and developing and consolidating democracy, the rule of law, and respect for human rights and fundamental freedoms.[56]

On the whole, some progress has been made in this very sensitive area in which the Union's efficiency depends on the political will of member states more than anything else. For example, according to article 19.2 (ex J.9.2) member states that are also members of the Security Council of the UN will act in concert and keep the other members fully informed. At the same time, they will execute their functions and ensure the defense of the positions and interests of the Union. This was not the case during the Gulf War nor concerning the Yugoslav conflict. In the case of Iraq, the United Kingdom supports the American policy (threat and strikes) in opposition to the French diplomatic approach. Practice will test the willingness and mutual solidarity of the member states, which are supposed to act in accordance with common principles.

The European Council defines the principles and general guidelines for the common foreign and security policy, including matters with defense implications. But in addition it is going to decide common strategies to be implemented by the Union in areas where member states have important interests in common.[57] The distinction between common interests and the individual policies of member states was suggested by the Tindemans Report of 1975. According to the Treaty of Amsterdam, common strategies shall set out their objectives, duration, and means to be made available by the Union and the member states. Within the framework and according to the general guidelines, the Council of Foreign Ministers makes the necessary decisions on the definition and application of the common exterior policy. It adopts joint actions and common positions. Further, the Council may ask the Commission to submit to it proposals appropriate to ensuring the implementation of joint actions.[58]

Several other innovations hold our attention. The first refers to the constructive abstention contained in article 23 (ex J.13), which provides that abstentions shall not prevent the adoption of common decisions. The abstaining countries are not obliged to apply the decision but shall accept that the decision commits the Union. Also, in a spirit of mutual solidarity, they shall refrain from any action likely to conflict with or impede Union action. If member states qualifying their abstention represent more than one-third of the votes of the qualified majority, the decision cannot be adopted. In accordance with the rules of the qualified majority, this is a logical consequence that eliminates the possibility that a minority of member states could make common decisions in the name of the Union.

The second important innovation concerns the functioning of the qualified majority[59] when adopting joint actions and common positions or taking any other decision on the basis of a common strategy. Similarly, the qualified majority is used when adopting any decision implementing a joint action or a common position. However, a restriction is imposed in the case of a member state opposing the adoption of a decision for important reasons of national policy. This notion resembles that contained in the Luxembourg Agreement of 1966. Opposing this kind of veto, the Council, acting by the qualified majority, may ask that the matter be referred to the European Council for a unanimous decision. One can hope that general paralysis will be avoided by turning to the highest political instance.

The third innovation results from a compromise on the French proposition for appointing a high-ranking politician as the high representative of the Union.[60] That idea was accepted but emasculated. The secretary-general of the Council was nominated as the high representative of Union, granting him a new political dimension. As high representative, he assists the Council and the presidency in matters concerning common foreign and security policy, in particular by contributing to the formulation, preparation, and implementation of policy decisions. He may conduct political dialogue with third parties at the request of the presidency.[61] It is also stated in article 27 (J.17) that the Commission shall be fully associated with the work carried out in the field of common foreign and security policy. Taking into account this structure and interinstitutional collaboration, President Santer considers it possible to speak about a "new troika." This would consist of the president, the secretary-general, and the Commission being mutually responsible, while bearing in mind that the president of the Commission is a full member of the European Council.

This interpretation seems to have been confirmed by the establishment of a Policy Planning and Early Warning Unit. Responsible to the secretary-general of the Council, the unit consists of personnel drawn from the general secretariat, the member states, the Commission, and the Western European Union.[62] In addition, appropriate cooperation with the Commission has been foreseen in order to ensure full agreement with the Union's external economic and development policies. This appears to provide a solution to previous disparities that were of great concern. In the future, the organic link between different aspects of external policy will be strongly established, while the planning unit will support it.

This unit has the following tasks: monitoring and analyzing developments in areas relevant to the CFSP, identifying future fields of common interest, providing early assessments, and warning of threatening situations and potential political crises. From this perspective, it is suggested that the unit should send its own observers to different regions besides using information obtained from member states and the Commission. Further, it will be asked to cooperate with member states' diplomatic missions and consulates, Commission delegations, and special representatives nominated by the Council. These provisions are designed to form a strong network of institutions and organizations involved in preparing, defining, and implementing the common foreign policy. This new institutional structure has been granted a solid financial foundation; expenses of the Common Foreign and Security Policy (CFSP) will be charged to the European Community budget and treated as expenditures not necessarily resulting from the treaty. Without being revolutionary, this structure offers a framework and support for a more coherent foreign policy. However, it will be conditional upon effective support and full political engagement by the majority of member states. Previous conflicts in Yugoslavia, particularly in Bosnia, showed that new, more efficient institutional structures came too late.

Progress on the chapter on commercial policy has been more modest. While the commission intended to insert into article 133 (ex 113) services, intellectual property rights, and foreign direct investments in order to face up to changes in the structure of the world economy, participants at the Intergovernmental Conference preferred to add a new provision to paragraph 5 of the same article. The Council, acting unanimously on a proposal from the Commission and after consulting the European Parliament, may extend the application of article 133 to international negotiations and agreements on services and intellectual property insofar as they are not already covered by this article. Hence, the Treaty of Amsterdam will not consider these new domains. Instead, it will authorize the Council to include them in the future if necessary.

The EU's single currency and consequent unique monetary policy will introduce a new dimension into external relations, bringing a series of direct and indirect results. In addition, it is going to reinvigorate spillover effects that will have a multiplier effect both within and outside the Union. The Euro will be a powerful European social and political force, and its influence on the world market, where it should have the most prestigious place next to the dollar, will be on the Union's external trade, its economic and political power, external banking, and other financial services. From now on, the European Union will have to take great international responsibility for monetary policy, which will be added to the other dimensions and instruments of its foreign policy. This foreign and common security policy refers to economic and trade transactions, financial and monetary dealings, and different partnerships and associations with Eastern, Southern, and Western countries. Creating an interdependent system, this accord between several sectors is gradually going to require the globalization of the European Union's external relations. Obviously, carrying out such a policy will require a minimum of coordination together with a coherent external policy for common interests.

In the near future, these areas should include a common defense policy, but in this field the innovations were extremely modest. Defense is a particularly sensitive subject and one of the main attributes of national sovereignty. Since the French National Assembly rejected the European Defence Community in 1954, defense has given rise to tension between partisans of European defense, on the one side, and Atlantic defense under the leadership of the Americans on the other. Concerning this issue, President Chirac reminded us of General de Gaulle's words: "Europe cannot have political personality unless Europe has its own vision of defense." Chirac added that the European Union has the task of creating such a personality. Despite these positive statements, the IGC has been particularly timid regarding the defense chapter. It has not even provided the European Union with a legal international personality, and at the same time, paradoxically, the Union is invested by the treaty with powers corresponding to its internal competencies and rules, so that the Union acquires a partially international personality and the power to sign and conclude international treaties and agreements.[63] As expected, the Union's international personality is limited where defense is concerned. Nevertheless, a careful reading of article 7, which is dedicated to the security of the Union and the progressive framing of a common defense policy, may infer some progress. This depends on the willingness of the European Council, which is mostly responsible for developing common defense.

The same method is applicable to integrating the WEU into the European Union. The new treaty confirms in its article 17.2 (ex J.7.2) that the WEU plays an integral part in Union development, providing it with access to an operational capability. The WEU supports the European Union in framing defense aspects of the Common Foreign and Security Policy. Within the extension of these competencies and increasing institutional collaboration, the Union will avail itself of the WEU in order to elaborate and implement Union decisions and actions with defense implications, for example, through its participation in the Policy Planning and Early Warning Unit. Accordingly, the WEU will be in charge of the tasks agreed upon in Petersberg in which all member states are entitled to participate. The tasks in question are the following: humanitarian and rescue operations, peacekeeping operations, and the tasks of combat forces in crisis management, including peacekeeping (art. 17.2). At this highly political level, the European Council is testing its authority and its supreme institutional role. Because the highest political figures participate — heads of state or government — the new treaty confirms the competence of the European Council to establish guidelines and decide on common strategies. Member states of the Union that are not members of the WEU are entitled to participate fully in the Petersberg tasks. In order to allow all the states contributing to the Petersberg tasks to participate on an equal footing in planning and decision making in the WEU (art. 17.3 (ex J.7.3)), the Council shall adopt practical arrangements. By these multiple interconnections, the Union encourages the reinforcement of institutional relations with the WEU with a view to the possibility of integrating the WEU into the Union should the European Council so decide. It seems that this decision might be taken without the new IGC, but its adoption should be made in accordance with the constitutional requirements of the member states. The process of integration of the WEU into the Union is under way. It can be stimulated by developing much closer cooperation between two or more member states at a bilateral level in the framework of the WEU and the Atlantic Alliance. At the same time, the WEU intends to become the European pillar within the Atlantic Alliance. Once more, the real importance of these small steps for common defense depends on the political will and behavior of the European partners.

The Union's Federal Vocation

Undoubtedly, the progress made in Amsterdam has not brought about a qualitative change. However, reviewing those small steps already accomplished, one could rightly conclude that on the whole they have allowed some progress to be made. Although slow, that progress is based on the federalist method and approach. Its objective is to create a unique European federation, taking into consideration the new problems of governance and overload and applying modern communications as well as a new approach to organizing society. As a conclusion, and after reflecting on the next phase, some suggestions follow concerning the general structure of the European Union.

In order to enhance the Commission's efficiency and its autonomy prior to its enlargement, different methods have been suggested. Their goals are to reduce the number of members and reinforce both its collegial ties and its democratic legitimacy. The proposal to reduce the number of members coincides with the resistance of many member states; in general, public opinion tends to consider Commission members as their "official representatives." The current perception is based on the principle that each country should have one member. If that reduction proves insufficient, it would be advisable to find a solution whereby there is one member for each large state with a rotation among the others like the existing system in the Court of Justice.[64] While waiting their turn, the other future full members would be able to take over the functions of associate or deputy commissioners. This method would be beneficial in reaffirming the communitarian character of the Commission. In some member states, this type of arrangement is part of the tradition of the "ministerial cabinet" composed of principal ministers.

The European Council, with its increasing competencies, is expected to provide the structures and means to enable it to take over its important responsibilities. If necessary, it could delegate some of these functions to the ad hoc committees for limited periods or to the operational task forces with the participation of the representatives of the Commission. The ad hoc arrangements would ease its work load by avoiding the heavy procedures of plenary meetings. This type of arrangement will work within the general guidelines and common strategies adopted by the European Council with the full participation of all member states.

Following developments inherent in the codecision procedure, the Council of Ministers should be restructured so that it can perform either governmental (foreign and security policy) or legislative functions. This division of labor or separation of powers could give rise to distinctive institutions such as a council of ministers or a council of states. In the near future, the council of states could have one-half of the delegates designated by the member states for five years and another half elected by national parliaments, so that national parliaments would be fully and closely associated in legislation, with the backing of the great majority of governments and members of parliaments, together with the European Parliament. In addition, such a structure would assure transparency in the legislative function without interfering with the council of ministers' governmental procedures.

As for the Council of Foreign Ministers, which can be enlarged when this is deemed necessary by the ministers of defense, it would assume its role within the CFSP together with the Commission and representatives of the Council of the WEU after its integration into the European Union. In turn, the council of states and the European Parliament will have the authority, as proposed in the Maastricht Treaty, to express opinions on the CFSP. At the request of the European Council, they might also be asked to approve the general guidelines for foreign policy, security, and common defense. In my opinion, these are not generalizations that determine the efficiency and functioning of the European Union. This is one outline, inter alia, that would enable the European Union to obtain the resources and the ability to face present and future challenges and to progress more firmly toward European federalism.

Achieving this goal will require careful preparation, which implies a constant effort to influence governments, political parties, socioeconomic groups, and public opinion. Such systematic efforts will be essential if the Union is to assume its responsibilities when faced with future enlargement. Besides developing the Economic and Monetary Union, the indispensable attributes of the future European federation are a single currency and common social policy as well as reinforcing the common external policy, security, and defense.

The suggested method is similar to the ECSC negotiations under Jean Monnet's presidency and the Spaak Commission Report, which served as a basic proposal for the European Economic Community and Euratom. Later, the same method was on the agenda for negotiating the Single European Act and then the European Union, both conducted under the leadership of the president of the Commission and the Mitterrand-Kohl tandem. From now on, it will be essential to entrust such a stimulating task to a highly qualified and dynamic European leader.

The best choice for such a task is undoubtedly Jacques Delors. Apart from his unique experience, he has the general trust of political and socioeconomic leaders as well as authority and an exceptional reputation with the European public, which should be more closely associated with this new step toward a federal Union. The second important step is to adopt a new role concerning the treaty revision. The new treaty would come into force after ratification by two-thirds of the member states. In the spirit of reinforced cooperation, the new rule will avoid the risk of some kind of veto or delay by one or more member states.

A final proposal aims to simplify the treaty's constitution where it defines general principles and main objectives as well as an institutional framework and distribution of power. The constitution will be completed by a framework of laws that should simplify the *acquis communautaire* and make it more coherent. The overriding aim is to make good, clear sense of the European Union's constitution for its citizens.

Europe and Beyond

Trends in the European Union

Ernst B. Haas was right not to stick rigidly to traditional concepts of intergovernmental or international relations but to propose a dynamic spillover approach. Certainly, this process is not growing continuously and is to an even lesser extent linear. It is subject to different rhythms, dictated as much by internal as external changes, and it sometimes halts, becomes bogged down, or even reverses direction. *Spillover* does not exclude *spilldown;* integration and disintegration are twinned, moving in opposite directions with opposite effects. This is the conclusion reached by Karl W. Deutsch and the Princeton team in their historical study of the formation and disintegration of political communities. It is corroborated by the integration process within the Union and the breakdown of multinational communist states. The difference between these two European areas is marked by basic values, the role of individuals and groups within society, political and economic organizations, the degree of freedom or constraint, and the effective respect for people and communities that underlies basic human rights. The enlargement process and cooperation, driven by the European Union via European or partnership agreements, means internalizing fundamental values and norms and also greater compatibility between political and economic structures and conduct. Hence, the traditional process and institutional approach is being substantially enriched by the key role of basic values set in context by the gap between the two European areas as they draw closer together. In turn, the Maastricht and Amsterdam Treaties reinforce the role of basic human rights and emphasize the Union's evolution toward a more democratic and federative system.

Spillover, which is both a chain reaction and an overflow, shows itself as a sequential effect from one sector to another, provoking an interaction between the three pillars of the European Union, and thereby setting active interdependence in place between these artificially compartmentalized pillars. Thus, not only is the Union tending to expand its influence, particularly in home and legal affairs, but it is exerting a growing influence in the sphere of the Common Foreign and Security Policy, where the intergovernmental approach still predominates. This political sector is a prime example of one of the last bastions of national sovereignty in member states, where executives play a preponderant role.

One instance of spillover can be seen in the sensitive area of unemployment, precisely on account of the high rate of unemployment in most European Union countries. Since its inception, the EU's social dimension has been little more than the poor relation of what has been essentially economic integration. Nevertheless, the concern of governments and the pressure of public opinion have led to social policy being incorporated into the Maastricht and Amsterdam Treaties. The problem materialized when Renault decided to close its factory at Vilvorde in Belgium in July 1997 and to terminate some three thousand jobs in France. The Renault trade unions called upon all European production plants to stop work for an hour in protest against this decision. The shock of Vilvorde and the Euro-strike sparked debate throughout Europe on employment, economic efficiency, monetary discipline, and the fight against unemployment. This triggered a dynamic that, supported by the socialist government in France and by trade union agitation, led to an extraordinary meeting of the European Council on 21 November 1997 in Luxembourg, preceded and accompanied by massive demonstrations by European trade unions. Long considered as a matter for national authorities, unemployment has now become a Community concern and responsibility.

In response, the Fifteen launched a concerted employment policy, giving the Union a social dimension. After setting guideline targets for national employment plans, they agreed on a method to be followed and a timetable for joint actions. Foremost among these guidelines is job placement and training for the young and the long-term unemployed. A maximum of five years has been set aside for accomplishing these goals, with provision for regular monitoring. Employment action plans were examined at European Council meetings in December 1998 and their implementation assessed. While it has no power of sanction, the European Council may adopt recommendations designed to exert pressure on those lagging behind. This approach combines setting common goals with member states' autonomy in attaining them. It acts as an incentive and has the further advantage of recognizing that monetary and economic policies and the European fight against joblessness are interconnected. Despite its initial reluctance, the Spanish government was ultimately pressured by the trade unions into recognizing the validity of this approach, which is inspired by global solidarity within the European Union.

The dynamics and the federal effect of the single currency illustrate the driving force of this common objective and the predominant role of political will as formally set down in the Maastricht Treaty and specifically endorsed by successive resolutions of the European Council and by converging economic policies in member states in general. The self-discipline imposed by governments in complying with criteria, the ground covered despite criticism and resistance, and the phase of resignation followed by an extensive adjustment process are all signs of impressive progress toward the Euro. It is hardly wrong to predict a profound impact with countless ramifications following the creation and introduction of the Euro. Institutional changes such as the creation of an independent European central bank and the reinforcement of the role of the European Council will provide a decision-making framework that will in turn facilitate the convergence of economic policies, interest rates, and, in the longer term, fiscal policies. This will have a ripple effect on restructuring, mergers, and cooperation in banking and finance, bringing a change of attitude among economic and social players and ultimately the population at large. The fact is that money has a general, day-to-day impact; it pervades public and private life. The Euro and Europe will become part of everyday life. After all, in domestic German politics the Euro was one of the main planks of Chancellor Kohl's 1998 election campaign, representing the meeting point between national and European politics.

At the institutional level, the question has been raised regarding the place and power of a European central bank not integrated into the economic and political system, as are central banks in the countries of the Union. The absence of an institutional framework and a political authority has spawned the suggestion that a kind of "economic government" should be set up, an ambiguous concept that, despite the intentions of its authors, would risk concentrating economic power. At the European Council meeting of 12–13 December 1997, the Fifteen agreed on a transitional formula for the creation of a "Euro Council" within which the single currency countries may consult within the Management Committee for the Euro. With due notification, countries outside the first Euro circle may request the Ecofin Council to deal with "questions of common interest." This is an early institutional impact of the Euro not foreseen in the Maastricht Treaty, another illustration of a spillover effect at the institutional level.

In the process toward the single currency, the European Union is following a pace opposite traditional nation-building sequences. In the history of nation-states, the establishment of the political structure provides a framework for the creation of a central bank and a single currency. The logic of power is inverted in the case of the European Union in the way that the Euro and the central banking system, which are the natural consequences of the single market, will induce fresh progress toward a kind of political authority within the European Union. At present, the European Monetary Union already constitutes an essential federal pillar of the future European federation.

On 2 May 1998, the Council of the European Union, meeting with the heads of state or government, adopted a fundamental decision regarding the third stage of economic and monetary union, which, in accordance with article 109.J, par. 4, shall commence on 1 January 1999. On the basis of reports presented by the Commission and the European Monetary Institute, the Council decided, after having made an overall evaluation for each member state, that Belgium, Germany, Spain, France, Ireland, Italy, Luxembourg, the Netherlands, Austria, Portugal, and Finland fulfill the necessary conditions for the adoption of the single currency on 1 January 1999. At present, Greece and Sweden do not fulfill the necessary conditions and will have a derogation as defined in article 109.K of the treaty. In contrast,

the United Kingdom and Denmark have stated that they will not participate in the third stage of EMU. Finally, after much skepticism, criticism,
and hesitation, the political will and convergent efforts toward a common
goal prevailed when eleven member states succeeded in respecting criteria
imposed by the Maastricht Treaty. This is an extraordinary example of
what can be performed despite many obstacles and difficulties, by means of
a common political will.

The Euro's identity will not only leave a strong imprint on its users
within the Union but it will have powerful repercussions further afield,
increasing the EU's global economic and commercial influence by giving it a
monetary device and presenting itself anew. The common symbol as well as
the Euro's place in world trade will confirm the identity of the Union. By
eliminating exchange rate fluctuations within the Union and contributing to
world market stability and security, the Euro will be in a position to counterbalance the dollar and American monetary policy and mitigate some of the
deleterious consequences of globalization. Because of its weight in world
economics and finance, the influence and the responsibility of the Union in
the world community will grow. It is hardly conceivable that such a monetary

TABLE 3.   European Monetary Union: A State of Convergence

Annual Average Convergence	Public (government) Deficit	Public debt (% of GDP)	Average Inflation Rate	Long-Term (% for interest rate, 12 months)	Member of the Exchange Rate Mechanism (ERM)
Objectives	minus 3% of GDP	60%	2.7%	7.8%	last two years
Belgium[b]	2.1	122.2	1.4	5.7	yes
Denmark	−0.7	65.1	1.9	6.2	yes
Germany[b]	2.7	61.1	1.4	5.6	yes
Greece	4.0	108.7	5.2	9.8	no[a]
Spain[b]	2.6	68.8	1.8	6.3	yes
France[b]	3.0	58.0	1.2	5.5	yes
Ireland	−0.9	66.3	1.2	6.2	yes
Italy[b]	2.7	121.6	1.8	6.7	yes
Luxembourg[b]	−1.7	6.7	1.4	5.6	yes
The Netherlands[b]	1.4	72.1	1.8	5.5	yes
Austria[b]	2.5	66.1	1.1	5.6	yes
Portugal[b]	2.5	62.0	1.8	6.2	yes
Finland[b]	0.9	55.8	1.3	5.9	yes
Sweden	0.8	76.6	1.9	6.5	no
United Kingdom	71.9	53.4	1.8	7.0	no

Source: Eurostat and national statistical offices.
[a]Member since March 1998.
[b]Member of the European Monetary Union—Euroland.

revolution allied to the commercial power and economic potential of the Union could fail to have an impact on external relations in general and on European or even world security.

Now that the Euro has made its world debut, the Union's economic weight is already boosting its political influence in international organizations and contact networks, including the ACP, the CCEE, the CIS countries, and numerous trade networks and economic and humanitarian assistance programs. The influence of the Union's economic aid within its foreign and security policy was highlighted in the Commission's communication on the Middle East peace process. Its statement that the Union does not wish to disengage is an affirmation that its assistance to the Palestinians is the best guarantee of Israel's short- and long-term security. For lack of tangible results and because of the blockage of the peace process, largely owing to the Israeli attitude, a four-year, 1.7 billion ecu aid package was reconsidered. This was an indirect warning to the government of Israel and the United States, which was neglecting support from Europe even though peace remained elusive. Despite American interventions (by Carter, Nixon, Kissinger, Albright et al.), progress has been slow and peace remains fragile. U.S. room for maneuver would seem to be limited mainly by domestic policy constraints and Israeli influence. Having supplied more than half the funding for the peace process, the Union has acquired direct experience, extensive links, and considerable political capital. The constructive role of the Union would be much improved if the parties and the United States acknowledge the need for the European Union, both at the ministerial level and through its special envoy, to participate alongside the United States.

The insistence on a political role clearly points to the linkage between the Union's financial contribution and its foreign policy. More generally, the rule implying that responsibility or power within the Union will extend outside its borders is engendering a series of "natural" effects on foreign policy. Thus, for example, at the Kyoto Conference on greenhouse gas emissions held in December 1997, the Fifteen presented a united front to the United States, with the result that it signed, albeit reluctantly, an agreement envisaging a 6 to 9 percent reduction of toxic gas emissions. This unity, forged by consensus around an international problem, is cogent testimony to the Union's political influence in the world arena.

It is becoming increasingly clear that good relations between the United States and the European Union, the two pillars of the Western world, will preclude any hegemonic and unilateral U.S. policy and will only be possible if based upon broad agreement and cooperation between equals. Admittedly, this partnership of equals is somewhat skewed in favor of the United States. But, as David C. Gompert said, the Atlantic partnership can become the "leading force" in the world only if the United States challenges Europe to expand its interests, take on more responsibility, and fulfill its stated aspiration to be a global actor. However, such a challenge ought not to be issued unless the United States is genuinely prepared to accept a partner with which it will share not only the burdens but also the prerogatives of leadership.[65]

This opinion is shared by Zbigniew Brzezinski:

> As Europe gradually and hesitantly unifies, the internal structure and processes of NATO will have to adjust. On this issue, the French have a point. One cannot someday have a truly united Europe and yet have an alliance that remains integrated on the basis of one superpower plus fifteen dependent powers. Once Europe begins to assume a genuine political identity of its own, with the EU increasingly taking on some of the functions of a supranational government, NATO will have to be altered on the basis of a 1 + 1 (US + EU) formula.[66]

NATO's revision appears to be urgently necessary in view of new challenges and conflicts. Its present capacity to resolve conflicts is limited (witness the conflict in Cyprus and the Aegean between Greece and Turkey, both members of NATO). This example shows that without undertaking profound changes and a thorough revision, the North Atlantic Treaty Organization cannot guarantee peaceful relations among its members, which is one of the arguments in favor of NATO enlargement in Central and Eastern Europe. At present, NATO and the EU, when confronted with new internal and international conflicts, do not seem to be able to react appropriately. This explains the demand for a new regional and international order.

Even so, the European Union is itself gradually emerging as a future great power looking for influence proportional to its economic weight and financial contributions. Like Germany at another point in time, the European Union is striving to shrug off the ambivalent status of economic giant and political dwarf. By asserting its place and influence in world affairs, it will be able to contribute to stability and security in the world. Indeed, it has already taken the lead in some instances. A case in point was the initiative to reestablish ambassadorial relations with Iran, which paved the way for normalization with the United States. It has also helped Iran to reemerge from its isolation and resume its international role in a peaceful manner. Nevertheless, in the sphere of conflict prevention and peacekeeping, the Union has fallen far short of the hopes it has aroused. It intends to strengthen its capabilities and accordingly shoulder greater responsibilities within NATO, especially through the Western European Union.[67] The creation of the Planning and Early Warning Unit within the Union, with WEU participation, was a promising step. More significant is the intent to prepare the Eurocorps to carry out crisis management missions: WEU humanitarian actions and peace-making operations. Broadly speaking, the European Union is already contributing to security in Europe by supporting economic reforms and the transition to democracy in Eastern Europe. Accordingly, the European Council meeting of 12–13 December 1997 took a momentous decision pertaining simultaneously to foreign and domestic policy. While preparing to increase the list of candidates for EU membership in Central and Eastern Europe to ten and confirming Turkey's eligibility for membership in the Union, the Council decided to launch membership talks in the spring of 1998 with six countries: Poland, Hungary, the Czech Republic, Estonia, Slovenia, and Cyprus.

In the complex and vast networks that comprise the European Union's foreign relations, each member country is called upon to contribute according to its financial resources and know-how. Thanks to its characteristic diversity, the European Union has the advantage of being able to vary its strategies toward Eastern Europe, Africa, Latin America, or other regions that cooperate and at times compete with the United States. By its presence and actions both common and divers, the Union preserves, indeed affirms, the national and regional identities that are its strength in the face of the swelling tide of globalization engulfing the world. By increasing collective capacity through shared European sovereignty, the Union is in a position to influence the course of globalization, reduce the negative impact of regional crises, and reap maximum benefit from global interdependence.

European integration is a step-by-step process of development at the heart of the European Union. I am firmly convinced that what is often a trial and error approach is leading toward a new federalism, the hazy outlines of which are only beginning to take shape. In pursuing this novel form of federalism, the Union and leading political players are turning to the federal method, more specifically to the principle of subsidiarity. As a unique experience in the history of the peaceful formation of communities of states based on the principle of free association, the Union seems to represent an original example of the harmonious management of the identities and particularities within a totality comprised of interconnected states, regions, and communes.

From this experience, a strong tendency is leading to democratization in the Union in parallel with increasing decentralization of democratic systems in member states such as France and the United Kingdom. There are even moves toward federation in Belgium and Spain. This massive restructuring inspired by democratic and federative principles depends upon the development of communications and trade networks. It indicates a significant alliance between trends in high technology and the search for fresh expression of federal awareness both within the European Union and throughout the continent. Europe's common culture is open to the world, rich in its diversity, and at the same time forms the basis and driving force of Europe's federalist adventure.

The European Union's trade and economic policy, integral to its foreign policy, is helping to affirm its global identity, all the more so since the European Union is the only entity capable of counterbalancing the weight and excesses of the United States. It has thus been able to challenge the United States in a series of disputes brought before the WTO's arbitration tribunal (e.g., Boeing versus Airbus). It has also had to contest American extraterritorial trade laws such as the Helms-Burton Act, which is aimed at foreign companies and their investments in Cuba and designed to stiffen the embargo against that country, and the D'Amato Act, which penalizes any foreign company investing more than 40 million dollars per year in the oil and gas sectors of Iran or Libya. European companies present in these three countries have been affected by the threat to their activities posed by these laws. In more general terms, however, Europeans are opposed to the "principle of extraterritoriality" of national laws, which, moreover, infringes on international trade rules. Part of politically motivated sanctions and embargoes, these laws in turn provoke political, economic, and trade reactions.[68] They are further evidence of the political and economic components of international relations. Globalization also pertains to horizontal links between politics and economics; the complete separation of these two factors, which characterized the beginnings of European integration, created a burden that the Union is still trying to shed.

Reflections on the European Union and Beyond

With respect to greater Europe, Russia and the Community of Independent States will form one of the two main hubs of the Europe of the future. This raises many questions, and two American authors have set out contrasting and extreme scenarios: Lester Thurow in his book *Head to Head* (1992) and Samuel Huntington in *The Clash of Civilizations and the Remaking of World Order* (1996).

Huntington's contribution rests on the importance of content, civilization, and culture, which he links to the overall way of life of a population. For him, civilization and culture mean "values, norms, institutions and modes of thinking to which successive generations in a given society have attached primary importance."[69] He borrows from Durkheim and Mauss the notion of a kind of moral environment, embracing some nations, where each national culture is only a particular aspect of the whole.[70] This definition is somewhat reminiscent of Denis de Rougemont's formula, according to which European culture is both common and diversified, as if the cultures referred to as national, regional, or local were but variations on a common theme. To de Rougemont, cultural heritage

> represents first and foremost the sum total of all the "products" of culture down the ages: religions and philosophies, arts and literature, science and technology, political ideals, and practices, laws and city ordinances, moral, aesthetic and critical judgments, learned reflexes and proverbial wisdom, and, first and last, languages and all that they touch upon, ways of feeling, judging, thinking. To this can be added, because these component elements are many and often contrasting, their combination into ever more complex systems, successive or simultaneous, and the interactions among these systems.[71]

Huntington's starting point is not essentially different. He begins by taking account of several parameters: language, religion, and modernization (separation of church and state, representative institutions, lifestyles). While recognizing the role played by these factors, he concludes that to a great extent major civilizations have historically been closely identified with the world's great religions.[72] Accordingly, while disregarding other works and aspects of civilization, Huntington mainly uses religious criteria, which leads him to reestablish the dividing line between those who belong to Western Christendom (Catholics and Protestants) and those espousing Islam and Orthodox Christendom (Muslims and practitioners of the Orthodox rite).[73] This dividing line runs through Europe between Finland and Russia, the Baltic States and Russia, and through western Belarus and Ukraine (separating the Uniate West from the Orthodox East), through Romania between Transylvania (with its Hungarian Catholic population) and the rest of the country, and through the former Yugoslavia along the border separating Slovenia and Croatia from the other republics. It should be recalled that in the Balkans, this line coincides with the historical division between the Austro-Hungarian and the Ottoman Empires.

He goes on to affirm that the cultural border of Europe also constituted the political and economic border of Europe and the West in the era following the Cold War. For him, the paradigm of civilization thus provides a clear division and a compelling answer to the question confronting Western Europeans as to where Europe ends: Europe ends where Western Christianity ends and Islam and Orthodoxy begin. By the same token, he excludes Greece, the birthplace of European civilization, and refuses to consider Orthodox Christians as European. He emphasizes the religious criterion by overstating and attributing to it an effect of separation if not antagonism. Under these extreme conditions, all other factors are overshadowed, whether cooperation based on economic interdependence, geographical proximity, or linguistic affinity. By definition, religion, which he identifies with civilization, is viewed as a factor of separation rather than a force for reconciliation and solidarity. His thesis is opposed to the idea of an ecumenical Christendom and a fortiori to concord between religions, particularly between Catholicism and Orthodoxy, two sister faiths with a common source.

As early as the nineteenth century, the Russian philosopher Soloviev launched a major campaign in Russia and among the southern Slavs to bring these two major currents of Christianity closer together.[74] Yet Huntington separates, even opposes, Catholics and Protestants from Muslims and the Orthodox; more surprisingly, he interposes Muslims between the Orthodox and the other Christian groups, accentuating this divide. This approach indicates a misunderstanding of the real and extremely complex situation in the Balkans. It is a well-known fact that during centuries of occupation under the Ottoman Empire, the Greek, Serbian, and Bulgarian Orthodox peoples preserved and even strengthened their identities. Some consequences of these rifts can still be detected, especially in Bosnia, Serbia, and Macedonia and in relations between Greece and Turkey. Is this a reason to attempt to attribute to them today a role similar to that played by them in the past?

The dangers of this for European security were made manifest by the conflict in the former Yugoslavia, a conflict that is a test for Europe and for all of us. Human rights and dignity have been trampled underfoot, and instead of a multinational Yugoslavia, nation-states have arisen that aspire to become homogenous, that is, ethnically and nationally pure as opposed to the principles of tolerance and respect for minority communities. Some historians and political scholars see the origin of this conflict in the cultural fault line between the West and the Orthodox East, with an epicenter in Bosnia. This interpretation applies equally to the antagonism between Croats and Serbs. It does, however, have one flaw: it overlooks the fundamental importance of European culture, which sprang from ancient Greece, Jerusalem, and Christianity, and the contributions of many other cultures. This is to forget European values, which, though little respected in this region, should be reimplanted there, starting with respect for and tolerance of others.

Huntington predicates a Europe divided in two: the Catholic and Protestant West and the Orthodox and Islamic East. Based on these religious criteria, the implication is that Western Europe should strengthen its partnership with the United States within the North Atlantic community.

The Yugoslav tragedy in the heart of Europe is a warning. The fact is that it could spread, the more so since violent demands in the Basque country, Corsica, and Northern Ireland, within the European Union itself, are not unrelated to the outburst of extreme nationalist sentiment in the former Yugoslavia. Other latent or full-blown tensions exist not only within the CIS countries but in Bulgaria, with its Turkish community, and between Hungary and Romania or Slovakia, with the resident Hungarian communities. Should we therefore resign ourselves to the clash of cultures and civilizations predicted by Samuel Huntington? Should we set Byzantium against Rome, Athens against Jerusalem, Western European culture against Russian culture, on all of which, to different extents, European culture is based and which continue to enrich it? I believe that we should reject such an approach, as it seeks to divide rather than unite and it is re-creating cultural boundaries to justify or explain current conflicts.

And what can be made of his exclusion of Eastern and Southeastern European countries, particularly Russia? Is European culture conceivable without Russian input? This European exclusiveness is not just an abstract judgment but has concrete effects on the development of the Western world and on which countries are chosen for inclusion in the European Union or NATO. Calls for the observance of democratic principles, human rights, and the rule of law expressly affirmed in the Amsterdam Treaty, as well as of economic demands, do not seem to have been taken into account by the author.[75] He concludes that in EU enlargement preference should be accorded to states that are Western in culture and tend to be economically advanced. If this criterion were to be applied, the Visegrad states (Poland, the Czech Republic, Slovakia, and Hungary), the Baltic Republics, Slovenia, and Croatia would become EU members, making the European Union conform to Western civilization as it has historically existed in Europe. It should be recognized, however, that Huntington then attempts to promote a dialogue between civilizations for the sake of peace. Despite the criticism leveled at Huntington's book, it has the merit of having stimulated an intense discussion and underlined the key role of cultures and values, of which religions are a major, although not the only, source.

In his book on the "House of Europe," published well before that on the "clash of civilizations," Lester Thurow takes an opposing view to Huntington by highlighting the preeminent role to be played by the *norms* that will govern world economic relations. For him, the question is who (among the United States, Europe, and Japan) will be responsible for writing the world trading rules for the twenty-first century. He concludes that the United States will be the military superpower of the twenty-first century, but that will be its main handicap if it also wishes to remain an economic superpower. Paul Kennedy has discussed the divorce between U.S. military and economic might, with the latter having a lesser capacity or willingness to support the former,[76] and the Gulf War provided an illustration of the split between military and economic dominance. In Thurow's view, while maintaining impressive economic potential and unrivaled scientific dynamism and technological innovation, the United States has squandered much of this advantage by allowing its basic educational system to atrophy, even though it has significant cultural strengths. American culture makes it possible for foreigners to be assimilated very rapidly, an advantage that would seem to be jeopardized by calls for ethnic-national cultures, and it lends itself to the efficient management of multinational corporations: "The American problem is not winning but forcing itself to notice that the game has changed, that it will have to play a new game with new rules, with new strategies."[77] This holds all the more, for having become the single dominant superpower in 1989, the United States has been tempted to impose its solutions and rules unilaterally on a diversity of world economies. Yet, in a world subject to competition from the United States, Japan, and Europe, the three main economic powers, and subject to tension between globalization and fragmentation, it is becoming less and less possible to impose lasting solutions by force. Such solutions in fact demand a cooperative approach based on the consent if not the participation of the leading economic players.

In Thurow's view, Europe holds the strongest strategic position on the world economic chessboard. It will have a chance of becoming the economic leader of the twenty-first century. It has numerous strong points: it is the only group of 800 million inhabitants who are both well educated and not poor. More than ever before, human resources and education constitute the main factor in development. As well as Germany, number one in production and trade, there is the scientific potential of Russia, the design flair of Italy and France, and London's world-class financial market. Together, these potentials, combining both group and individualistic strains of capitalism, represent an exceptional opportunity. Moreover, due to Europe's position in the world of economics and trade it will have the advantage of being responsible for writing the world trading regulations in the twenty-first century. At present, it is not clear which of the two, Europe, the United States, or both, will become the economic leader and main world "legislator" through the WTO and various UN institutions.

For that, Europe would first have to meet several conditions; it must truly integrate the economies of Western, then Central and Eastern, Europe and forge a close association with Russia and the CIS countries; it must succeed in the transition of former communist countries to market economies with substantial aid from Western Europe; it must rise above the ethnic and border rivalries that have resurfaced in the East and could spread to the West; and it must understand that national identities will not be suppressed but will be preserved within a diversified Union. Once these obstacles have been overcome, Europe will be in a position to make the most of its assets, whose rich diversity should predispose it toward better acceptance of differences and the search for common solutions in compromise and cooperation.

These are two interpretations of the EU's evolution, one from the perspective of civilizations closely associated with the major religions and the other from that of trade and human resources. Their basic concepts may be at odds, but in view of their consequences they are brought closer together by a shared concern with norms, whether religious or moral, economic or technological, as well as the importance they attribute to culture and education. Yet, according to Denis de Rougemont's central thesis, Europe's new and embryonic federalism is based on the shared essentials of European culture, rich in its diversity, an integral part of which is the highly creative Orthodox and Russian world. Based on this deeply rooted community of culture, the two Europes can pull closer together and gradually build a larger Europe that unites two dynamic hubs under a common roof: one around the European Union, the other comprising the CIS countries around Russia. But such a new architecture, rising above national, cultural, or political boundaries, can only be founded on common values and principles: freedom of association, democracy, human rights, and respect for individuals and minority groups. These principles underlie the European Union and are codified by the Amsterdam Treaty in its revised version, signed on 2 October 1997. The Union's enlargement process and the construction of Europe are proceeding on this basis, and the latter process could thrive within a confederal entity underpinned by two federative centers. Such are the challenges and prospects of a new European federalism seeking a dynamic balance between unity and diversity wherein the two centers can preserve their own identities and those of their components while maximizing their potential in the context of a United Europe.

The newly emerging European federalism is trying to place itself at the meeting point between cultures and values, economics and high technology, via a global, multifarious, and varied political approach. This means that, while benefiting from the contribution of federal unions, the federalist vision of the founding fathers, and the neofunctionalist, system-, and communications-based approaches, the new European federalism is not limited to decision-making players and processes but is enriched by the significant dimension of values and norms and by the far-reaching impact of communications networks. Groundbreaking trends are emerging around the focal points of a multiplicity of networks in a highly diversified environment as cultural, political, national, regional, and local identities as well as linked networks that are constantly adapting to new needs and aspirations. This framework, with its shifting elements, is instrumental in creating and removing groupings around federalist cores, based on closeness of interests, security, and affinities of culture and values. Europe's federalist future is being forged, step by step, in a worthwhile direction, generating the hopes of the coming generation.

A Conclusion Open to the Future

The Union treaties open a new stage in European integration that strengthens the Community and innovates by fixing new objectives for the year 2000 and beyond. In this way, it opens long-term perspectives for business and socioeconomic agents, imposing discipline on member states as well as defining objectives and the framework for future development. These objectives and obligations are accompanied by the promise of increased prosperity inside the Union and increased competitive capacity to challenge Japan, the United States, and other newcomers to the world of high technology. In their race for prosperity, the member states have made some institutional improvements and agreed to strengthen their solidarity toward lesser developed states and regions. Moreover, cohesion and coherence within the Union contribute to a better and more stable political and economic balance, a necessary condition for the survival of a federal community. Indeed, it is not enough to reject all forms of hegemony; the Union has to avoid the formation of dominant positions by stimulating and supporting the efforts to catch up of lesser developed regions and member states. At the same time, it is following the old objective within a new context, aiming to tie the reunified Germany closer than ever to the European Union.

The Union treaties keep Europe on course for a democratic Union. Since the direct elections to the European Parliament in 1979, its authority and participation in legislative and budgetary procedures have been growing. The requests for its opinion, codecision procedures with the Council, and the procedure for nominating the Commission are evidence of a continuing search for democratic balance within an innovative and flexible system. This system is based on member states but also on regions and growing ties between socioeconomic groups and agents, leaders, and public opinion. New participants — the citizens and national parliaments — are now due to play increasingly important roles in the integration process. Moreover, the European Parliament has set out to tighten its links with national parliaments regarding its legislation and oversight functions. The democratic deficit is diminishing.

At the same time, deepening integration is bringing the economic sphere of the Union closer to the political spheres, and as decisions become more important the level of political involvement rises. This is why the European Council, whose members are the highest representatives of legitimate national power (except for the president of the Commission, who is a European Council member), has a central role to play in the future. At present, the European Council does not meet on a permanent basis but only a few times a year, so its decisions, despite its powerful members, are taking the form of guidelines that give impetus to Community actions. They are relayed by the Council of Ministers, assisted by the continuous activity of the Commission. The fundamental character of the Commission's work in the Community is confirmed by the nomination procedure for its members. This process strengthens its authority and the role of president, received from the European Council, and its democratic legitimacy, which is based on the European Parliament, as well as its role as a collegiate and Community institution. However, in spite of the development of its political authority, the Commission still plays a marginal role in matters of foreign and security policy and in home affairs.

The distinction between economic integration and political cooperation comes from the past failure of the EDC and the projects for a political community. The great ideological divide that preceded the French rejection of the EDC Project shows the weakness of the arguments of those, including General de Gaulle, who fought it. By refusing to integrate the German army into a common institution that would have given legitimacy to its rebirth, these opponents gave way, in fact, to the solution least wanted by all, the rebirth of an independent German army. The Fouchet Project for a European Union, which explicitly included authority in matters of foreign policy and defense, was probably an idea of General de Gaulle intended to enable politics to catch up with economics. But the rejection of this project by France's partners, in the name of supranationality and in defense of NATO, widened the artificial gap between economic and political union. In the end, the de Gaulle-Adenauer treaty replaced the failed Fouchet Project and gave birth to the current Franco-German tandem.

Since then, neither political cooperation nor the Union treaties have managed to bridge this gap, the "original sin" constituted by the imbalance between the Union's economic power and its political capacity. The commitment to common positions and actions in foreign policy, the beginnings of common policies in matters of defense and security, are signs of progress, but, due to an irony of history, they reflect a more complicated form of ideas contained in older projects, closer to the Gaullists' proposals than those of the federalists.

Despite the great distance between the Union's economic pillar and that of cooperation in foreign and security affairs, for many years the

Community has emphasized its federal aspects. The Single European Act and the Treaties on European Union entrenched this position and strengthened this vocation. In the beginning, especially under the influence of the French, Community institutions sometimes were tempted to set uniform rules. These errors of youth have not lasted in the face of the diversity of conditions and traditions in the Union. Inspired by the jurisprudence of the Court of Justice, the Single European Act generalized the principle of mutual recognition and provided increased scope for the greater use of directives, thereby establishing more autonomy and flexibility. Besides, the return to qualified majority voting makes the decision process more functional. At the same time, however, the voting system puts into the limelight small and medium-sized states, which have proportionally more weight in both the Commission and Parliament than the size of those countries or their populations warrant. In this, the Union shares a few characteristics with the Swiss Confederation, and the Maastricht and Amsterdam Treaties are positive steps toward the federalization of Europe.

The Community has shown an ability to create synergy and a favorable environment for further development. But resting on the laurels of its economic success, it has been unable to face the crises in Eastern and Central Europe and the conflict that has torn Yugoslavia apart. The awaking was rude: the Yugoslav crisis revealed a lack of political backbone in the Community and its inability to conduct foreign policy in line with its responsibility or to manage major political crises.

The conclusion is that the spillover process that lies at the heart of economic integration has not led inevitably to political union in spite of the optimism of the founding fathers. Experience has shown, moreover, that politics has kept its primacy; phenomena such as nationalism are quite capable of reversing progress and setting off a process of disintegration. The Union, therefore, urgently needs a political framework capable not only of living up to the expectations of Eastern and Central Europe and developing countries but capable of facing the technological challenge set by the United States and Japan. In short, this would be a more ambitious European Union for which the Maastricht and Amsterdam Treaties are temporary boundary measures.

1999: A Political Turning Point?

Collective Resignation of the Santer Commission and Appointment of the Prodi Commission

The severest crisis in the history of the European Commission, which resulted in its collective resignation on 17 March 1999, cast a spotlight on certain institutional and administrative aspects of the European Union. The European Parliament proved to be efficient in exercising control and using the motion of censure as its main weapon. Collective resignation is a new and concrete approach to the responsibilities of the members of the Commission and to the observance of the basic rules of public conduct and political behavior in the European Union.

The primary task of the committee of five independent experts required by the European Parliament was to establish to what extent the Commission as a body or as individual commissioners bears specific responsibility for the recent examples of fraud, mismanagement, or nepotism arising in parliamentary discussions. Throughout a series of hearings the committee has observed that commissioners sometimes argued that they were not aware of what was happening in their services. Undoubted instances of fraud and corruption in the Commission have thus passed "unnoticed" at the level of the commissioners themselves. For the committee, such protestations of ignorance by the commissioners regarding problems that were often common knowledge in their services, even at the highest official level, are tantamount to an admission by the political authorities that they lost control over the very administration that they are supposedly running. This loss of control implies a heavy responsibility for the commissioners individually and the Commission as a whole.

It is clear that fundamentally the Commission and its members have seen a substantial increase in their direct management responsibility. Does this mean that the Commission has been transformed from an institution that devises and proposes policies into one that implements policy? In fact, management tasks have relied primarily on the administrative staff while the senior hierarchy, particularly at commissioner level, remains more concerned with the political aspects of its work than with management. Nevertheless, in the context of its general responsibility it is highly important that the Commission not only continues and develops its fundamental political functions but also acquires the means of extending its control of the administration. Faced with many new challenges, such as preparing for successive enlargements and humanitarian crises, the Commission invoked the shortage of human and financial resources. In this regard, the committee felt that these reasons were at odds with decisions taken by the Commission itself to continue the policy of austerity budgets since 1995. It is obvious that the committee did not take into account the general situation and the financial discipline imposed by member states in view of the Euro's arrival.

Significantly, the committee did not encounter cases where a commissioner was directly and personally involved in fraudulent activities. It found, however, instances where commissioners or the Commission as a whole bears responsibility for instances of fraud, irregularities, or mismanagement in their services or areas of special responsibility. Furthermore, the committee found no proof that a commissioner had gained financially from any such fraud, irregularity, or mismanagement.

Over a lengthy period the Commission and successive commissioners bear responsibility for failing to react to clear warning signals that serious problems had arisen and for failure to ensure appropriate disciplinary sanctions. In the Mediterranean program (MED) the commissioner Mr. Marian acted swiftly and correctly in response to the discovery of irregularities, conflicts of interest, and a lack of control. All the same he allowed too long a period to elapse between detection and the launch of an administrative inquiry.

The Leonardo vocational training program and the commissioner responsible, Mrs. Edith Cresson, were subject to severe criticisms by members of the European Parliament who observed that she failed to act in response to serious and continuing irregularities known for several years. Among other irregularities, she bears responsibility for one instance of favoritism, having appointed an old friend as her special adviser. More generally, the commissioner had to assume wider responsibility for lax control over the Technical Assistance Office.

A leitmotiv is that the Commission and the commissioners bear joint responsibility for formulating and attempting to implement a policy for which resources are not available and over which it is exceedingly difficult to exert effective control. Major policy initiatives and new, politically important, and highly expensive programs are launched without appropriate resources. This is a general criticism formulated by the committee. At this point it raises a key question about the type of policy that the Commission should follow: either a prudent approach as suggested in the committee's report or a dynamic and more risky policy. It is clear that the latter approach corresponds better to the philosophy of the Commission, to its dynamic role, and to its innovative action.

Moreover the main programs launched by the Commission were in response to needs and demands expressed or suggested by governments and other axial actors. They were decided and in many cases required by the Council. This is, in fact, the Commission's and the Council's joint responsibility. In general there is a marginal comparison between the accomplishments and major tasks fulfilled by the Commission and the cases of fraud, mismanagement, irregularities, and favoritism. It is almost certain that similar cases could never result in the collective resignation of a government of member states or even in the resignation of a single minister considered personally responsible, especially if no proof could be produced that a minister had gained financially from any such fraud or mismanagement.

It is possible that the resignation of the Commission not only confirms its global and collective responsibility but also reveals some weaknesses of the Santer Commission. Some students of the European Union as well as many official and informal actors have reached the conclusion that the Commission lacked strong leadership capable of reinforcing its cohesion and its dynamism. Among other examples, they refer to the limited time dedicated to plenary meetings of the Commission. In contrast to collective thinking and acting under presidential leadership, the main responsibilities for important affairs were in fact in the hands of individual commissioners. The quality of initiatives and proposals led to much criticism of the dual responsibility at the political and administrative level. For these various reasons, the Santer Commission suffered from loss of authority while the European Parliament was gaining in influence. Consequently, the major task of the president, Mr. Romano Prodi, will be to strengthen the authority and the collective capacity of the Commission, as well as to adopt new reforms in order to improve its operation, its efficiency, and its authority.

During the crisis, the Santer Commission has adopted a code of good behavior. Commissioners are not permitted to have any professional activity, and, if they have the right to accept positions on the executive bodies of political parties, they cannot accept any elected position. They have to avoid any conflict of interests, even those related to their honorary functions. To demonstrate greater transparency, they must declare all their financial interests as well as those of their partners. This was the first lesson from the crises. For its part, the committee has defined the standard of proper behavior. The Commission and commissioners must act in complete independence in the general interest of the Community and with integrity and discretion, based on certain rules of conduct. The appointment of any individual numbered among the close friends or the entourage of a commissioner to a well-remunerated position in the Commission, or the granting of an equally well-remunerated consultancy contract, is in contravention of existing rules. This has occurred where the person concerned was recruited into a staff category for which he or she lacked the required qualifications. However, even where no such irregularity occurs and no rules are infringed, commissioners should abstain from appointing spouses, close relatives, or friends, even those with appropriate qualifications, to positions for which an open competition or bidding procedure has not been held. In such instances there should be at the very least an obligation of disclosure during the appointment.

The principles of openness, transparency, and accountability are at the heart of democracy and are the very instruments ensuring its proper function. Openness and transparency imply that the decision-making process at all levels is as accessible and accountable as possible to the general public.

This means that the reasons for decisions taken or not taken are known and that those making decisions assume responsibility for them and are ready to accept the personal consequences when such decisions are subsequently shown to have been wrong. For instance, calls for bids should be much more open and transparent; any bidder should be in a position to know why his or her bid was not chosen and why another one found favor.

The committee found that the relationship between commissioners and general directors did not always meet this standard. The separation between the political responsibility of commissioners for policy decisions and the administrative responsibility of the directors general and the services for the implementation of policy should not be stretched too far. The requirement of mutual information implies that commissioners must know what is going on in their services, at least at the general directors' level, and should bear responsibility for it.

Generally, no information may be withheld from other institutions, such as Parliament, or other officials, especially commissioners, when they are called upon to play a role in the decision-making process. This applies equally to information that has not yet been entirely subjected to what are often lengthy contradictory procedures, as in the case of audit reports. Such information must be shared at an early stage, of course under cover of confidentiality, with the officials, services, directorates, or commissioners who need to have full knowledge of the facts in light of the decisions to be made or to be prepared.

Prodi Commission: Toward a "European Government"?

The preceding are the principal guidelines that Romano Prodi, president of the European Commission, took into account when he launched a first reorganization of the Commission. In his speech to the European Parliament on 21 July 1999, he mentioned among others the following changes.

The Commission bureaucracy is being streamlined and rationalized and the number of departments cut.

Commissioners will be housed in the same building as their departments.

Commissioners' offices (*cabinets*) will be smaller and more multinational: the head or deputy head of each cabinet will be a nonnational, and each cabinet will include at least three nationalities.

The rules on senior appointments will be tightened and made more transparent.

There will be greater internal mobility for senior Commission staff.

A new reinforced media and communications service has been created to ensure that the Commission's policies are communicated professionally to reach all European citizens.

President Prodi stressed that the Commission, which provides a fair balance between the political complexion of the national governments and the European Parliament, does not function along party lines. The Prodi Commission is, in his view, a college, and commissioners are no more an extension of political groups than they are representatives of national governments. In fact, the European People's Party (EPP) criticized President Prodi for forming a Commission that does not reflect the gains EPP made in June elections. The present rules of procedure for the nomination of the Commission do not guarantee correspondence between commissioners' political affiliations and the importance of political groups in the European Parliament. The commissioners are chosen by national governments subject to approval by the president-designate. Practically, the new selection procedure involved intensive consultations over several weeks with the governments to general satisfaction with one exception: instead of agreeing to nominate a member of his own party and a member of the opposition as suggested by President Prodi, the German chancellor Gerhard Schröder persisted in appointing a member of the Green Party as second commissioner despite the suggestion by President Prodi. This example indicates the influence of the governments and the limits of the influence of the president-designate. Finally, the result of the negotiations has to be approved by the European Parliament.

The new Commission headed by Romano Prodi, former prime minister of Italy and leader of the center left coalition "olive tree," is composed of highly qualified personalities, virtually all of whom have been members of national parliaments or of the European Parliament. Three-quarters have been ministers, and several have been leaders of political parties. Twelve are from the left and two do not have clear political affiliation. The majority of the members have had training in economics, law, and political science or simultaneously in two disciplines; four have philosophy, humanities, or history degrees; one has a degree in civil engineering and regional development; one in management; and one in accounting. The average age of the male members is fifty-two, while the five women members have an average age of forty-six.

The main innovation is new ground rules: each commissioner, at all times, will perform his or her duties according to the common European interest. If, at any stage, President Prodi is not satisfied he will exercise the powers given to him under the treaty, even to the extent of reshuffling portfolios or asking individual commissioners to resign as agreed by each of them. This is, as outlined by the president, a prime ministerial approach of his governmental "top quality team," in which jobs were allocated "to match the proven abilities and experience of each commissioner."[78]

In this respect, the striking example is the case of Dr. Michaele Schreyer, author of the thesis on the policy of transfers and budgetary federalism problems of distribution of powers, who has been relieved of the responsibility for the budget of the European Union. President Prodi also stressed that his "government" must meet the very highest standards of public life and become a world-class administration the watchwords of which will be transparency, accountability, and efficiency. In his speech on 15 September 1999, in the European Parliament, he pledged that the Commission's principle of collegiality "will not become a shield for the individual accountability which all of us have to assume as politicians, before this house and before the European public." He added that relations between the European Commission, which has the main responsibility for initiating European Union legislation, and the European Parliament will mark a new culture of openness and mutual cooperation. On the same day 426 deputies of 626 voted to give President Prodi a full five-year term, while 134 voted against this and 32 abstained. A lesser number, 404, voted to give the entire Commission a full term, with 153 voting against this and 37 abstaining. After the resignation of the Santer Commission, the new Prodi Commission won by a large majority. As in many other circumstances, the outcome of a crisis is a new step toward the progress and consolidation of the integration process and its democratization.

A Changing Profile of the European Parliament: Elections
June 1999

On 13 June the election of 626 Euro members of the European Parliament took place. The two most striking features of the elections were a shift to the right and a huge abstention. The general turnout of voters was 49 percent compared with 57 in 1994, 59 in 1989, 61 in 1984, and 63 in 1979. For the first time, the rate of abstention passed the 50 percent threshold: the "Kosovo effect"; the forced resignation of the Commission, which could have had the opposite effect as a result of the growing powers of the European Parliament; the increased trust; and the distance between European citizens and the European institutions were some of the main factors behind it. The difference between the intentions to vote expressed in the *Eurobaromètre* March–April 1999 (69 percent) and the actual turnout rates (49 percent) became as large as 20 percent.

The Kosovo effect is difficult to evaluate. One fact is evident: the crisis and the war have coincided with the EU electoral campaign and have almost monopolized the attention of political leaders, the media, and the general public. In these circumstances, the election of the members of the European Parliament could not possibly compete with the concern arising from NATO's war against Yugoslavia. Compared to the vital problems faced by NATO and EU countries, the electoral campaign appeared rather marginal and dull.

Public confidence in the European institutions was declining, while dissatisfaction was on the increase. Comparing the *Eurobaromètre* figures for 1997 and 1995, we find that public confidence has diminished by about 6 percentage points at both the national and the European levels. The decrease in citizens' professed confidence in their respective governments (40 percent compared to 45 percent in 1995) and national parliaments (40 percent against 48 percent) has been matched by a slight increase in the proportion of respondents who "have no confidence" or "don't know."

Similarly, the average level of confidence in the European institutions has dropped from 42 percent in 1995 to 36 percent in 1997. Notably, public confidence in the European Commission has declined from 41 to 36 percent, in the European Parliament from 45 to 38 percent, and in the Council of Ministers from 40 to 34 percent. The parallel between the downward trends at national and European levels is predictable, considering that European issues are increasingly becoming domestic issues. However, it is striking that the degrees of confidence in national and European institutions should be so similar, despite the fact that the levels of information and the distance between institutions and citizens are different.

In many aspects the results from the *Eurobaromètre* March–April 1999 regarding the European institutions are striking in contrast with the stability of the trust in national institutions. Forty-one percent still have trust in national parliaments and 40 percent in national governments, while confidence in the European institutions increased significantly: the trust in the European Parliament reached 50 percent (+12 percent), while the confidence in the European Commission again reached the previous level (1995), but, due to the Santer Commission's resignation, the level of mistrust also increased (33 percent highest level). The trust in the Council of Ministers remains fragile despite slight progress that is largely counterbalanced by the high record of mistrust (30 percent).

A survey done by the Louis-Harris Institute in May 1999 confirms the same tendency. Thirty-eight percent still trust the Commission. The most spectacular decline of trust was −51 points in Greece, where it closely reflects strong disapproval of NATO military intervention in Serbia (more than 90 percent and even 97 percent in this Louis-Harris survey). The European Parliament has a slightly better record with 40 percent average level of confidence. All these features combined with the high complexity and low transparency of the Union's institutions contribute to the high rate of abstention compared with the previous turnout.

Nevertheless these figures, disappointing as they are compared to traditional voting patterns in member countries, appear rather normal in comparison with the turnout in American and Swiss elections, where the main activities of political parties, as in the European Union, take place at member state or cantonal levels. From this point of view, the general turnout does not appear so disastrous, but what is worrying is the decline of the overall turnout and the rates of abstention country by country. As expected, exceptions are the four countries where voting is *obligatory:* Belgium with turnout of 90.7 percent, Luxembourg 90 percent, Italy 80.7 percent, and Greece 70.1 percent. The latter two, especially Greece, had lower than usual turnout, partially due to disapproval of the Union's stand on the crisis in the former Yugoslavia. The second group is composed of six countries with percentages close to the *general average:* 64.4 percent for Spain, 50.5 and 50.4 for Ireland and Denmark, 49 for Austria, 46.8 for France, and 45.2 for Germany. The third group includes five countries with exceptionally low turnout: Portugal with 40.4 percent, followed by Sweden with 38.3 percent. Surprise results came from Finland (30.1) and in particular from the Netherlands (29.9); finally the United Kingdom scored the lowest with 23 percent. This high level of abstention accentuated some probably unexpected results.

New 1999 Political Groups in the European Parliament

Table 4 shows the breakdown of political groups in the European Parliament in 1999. The EPP/ED (European Popular Party/European Democrats) became the largest group (233) in the European Parliament, followed by PES (180), reversing the previous distribution where Socialists held 214 seats and PEP 202. The huge shift in favor of EPP is due principally to 19 supplementary seats obtained by Conservatives in the United Kingdom, where Labour lost half of its 61 seats, and to the affiliation of nine French Gaullists. The severe losses suffered by Labour were partially the result of adopting a new voting system of proportional representation and also because of the low electoral mobilization, as well as a vigorous Conservative campaign against the Euro. On a smaller scale, the CDU/CSU win of 6 seats corresponded to the losses suffered by the Social Democrats. The new orientation of their leaders, Tony Blair and Gerhard Schröder, was marked by social-liberal thinking and contributed to the alienation of the left wing of their parties and electorates. The French Gaullist Party of President Chirac also suffered a severe defeat. As stated by the *Economist,* the war against Serbia was supposed to have been a good

TABLE 4. Distribution of Euro-MPs by Political Groups and by Countries (1999 Elections)

	B	DK	G	GR	S	F	IRL	I	L	NL	A	P	FIN	SW	UK	Total
EPP/ED	6	1	53	9	28	21	5	34	2	9	7	9	5	7	37	233
PES	5	3	33	9	24	22	1	17	2	6	7	12	3	6	30	180
ELDR	5	6			3		1	7	1	8			5	4	10	50
GREENS/EFA	7		7		4	9	2	2	1	4	2		2	2	6	48
EUL/NGL		1	6	7	4	11		6		1		2	1	3		42
UEN		1				13	6	9				2				31
TGI	2					5		11								18
EDD		4				6				3					3	16
IND					1			1			5				1	8
Total	25	16	99	25	64	87	15	87	6	31	21	25	16	22	87	626

Note: B = Belgium; DK = Denmark; G = Germany; GR = Greece; S = Spain; F = France; IRL = Ireland; I = Italy; L = Luxembourg; NL = the Netherlands; A = Austria; P = Portugal; FIN = Finland; SW = Sweden; UK = United Kingdom.

war for Europe's leaders and specifically for the leaders of the three biggest European powers, yet almost no party running a major NATO government was thanked for it.[79] Indifference and lassitude if not silent protest in countries like Italy and Germany and vigorous opposition expressed in Greece seemed to follow the chaos and confusion intensively reported by the media during the war against Yugoslavia. The governing Socialist Party in Greece obtained fewer votes than New Democracy (35.9 to 40.5 percent), partly because of its controversial support for NATO's bombing.

As in previous EU elections, national issues dominated the campaign. In Germany, the poor performance of the economy, the tax imposed on energy, and low salaries as well as the declaration proposing a more liberal model for European economic policy probably contributed to a mixture of different factors influencing voters. The surprise came from Italy: the center left governing coalition witnessed success for Forza Italia of the center right, which scored 25 percent; simultaneously, two political groupings won substantial votes: the Radical Party led by Emma Bonino, an outgoing European Commissioner, got 8.5 percent and the New Democrats of Romano Prodi, the incoming president of the European Commission, 7.7 percent. Both were pro-European federalists in the Italian highly pro-European environment.

In France, the former majority UDF-RPR scored 26 percent of votes and 28 seats in the 1994 Euro election. It is now split into three formations, each defending a different position on the future of the European Union. François Bayrou, leader of UDF, took a clear stance for a federal union and obtained 9.3 percent of votes and 9 seats. The RPR, which remained loyal to President Chirac and defended a soft pro-European program, suffered from a new movement, "Rally for France and the Independence of Europe," created by the Gaullist Charles Pasqua and Philippe de Villiers, leader of the former "Europe of Nations" political group. They defend the sovereignty of France and an independent Europe against Maastricht's Europe and the dominance of the United States and NATO. In their campaign, they accused governing parties as well as the opposition of being federalist. The result was an amalgam of conflicts on main European issues with direct consequences for the internal distribution of political forces. From the beginning of European integration, the divisions between pros and cons have troubled the cohesion of most political parties, but this time they produced deep division among Gaullists. The RPR obtained 12.8 percent of votes and 12 seats, while "Rally for France" (RPF) had some slight success with 13 percent of votes and 13 seats. The split in the Gaullist Party weakened President Chirac. The Green Party led by Daniel Cohn-Bendit, the former student leader in 1968 with dual nationality, French and German, had a great success with 9.7 percent of votes and 9 seats.

The surprise came from Hunters-Fishermen-Nature, a new rally defending traditional values against Community prohibition, which won 6.8 percent of votes and 6 seats. The main losers were the National Front (5.7 percent and 5 seats) and the Communists (6.8 percent and 6 seats), while the extreme left "Workers Struggle" succeeded for the first time in achieving more than 5 percent and 5 seats.

Besides these surprises, the main feature is, no doubt, a general shift to the right in the new political complexion of the European Parliament, while Socialist parties compose all but two governments. This new situation raises the question of the internal cohesion of the EPP, which appears to be more heterogeneous than the outgoing Assembly. The role of the fifty-three German Euro-MPs, supported by thirty-four Italians and twenty-eight Spaniards, will be crucial in the group, which includes thirty-seven British Eurosceptics. In any case, as before, the coalition of two main political groups, EPP and PES, totaling more than four hundred deputies and supported in principle by Liberal and Green groups, will form a central core, assuring the smooth running of the newly elected European Parliament.

The left-right opposition marked the election of the president of the newly elected Parliament: Nicole Fontaine (UDF France/EPP) was elected by 306 votes against 200 votes for Mario Soares (PES, Portugal) and 49 for Heidi Hautala (Greens, Finland). For the second half of the Parliament term, Pat Cox (ELDR, Irish) should take over the presidency. That overturned the previous arrangement between EPP and PES. Despite this polarization, the legislative process, which requires a majority of 314 MEPs, can only function normally as previously, based on the grand coalition, EPP-PES, supported by other pro-European MEPs and particularly by Liberals and Greens.

The War against Yugoslavia

Kosovo, Epicenter of Two Nationalisms

The conflict in Kosovo between ethnic Albanians and Serbs reveals many fundamental problems related to the aims and values of the European Union, for example, concerning the link between ends and means, a sense of proportion and moderation, and having to find an appropriate response. It also raises other questions about the sovereignty of the state, about humanitarian intervention in defense of human rights, and about justice and law as well as vindicating the use of force in the face of moral principles. There are many conflicting issues that make decisions both necessary and difficult with unpredictable consequences.

The conflict in Kosovo, which has deep historical roots, nevertheless has the same basic pattern as other conflicts in the former Yugoslavia:

contempt for other citizens, groups, and communities; intolerance; and the attempt to create ethnically homogeneous regions or states. But there are also specific features. It is situated at the epicenter of two virulent strains of nationalism. The two main populations are ethnically distinct and have different cultures, languages, and religions, yet Orthodox Christianity and Islam have frequently coexisted in harmony for many centuries.

Kosovo is the birthplace and heartland of Serbia, the nation and its faith, the latter possessing rich monasteries and churches.[80] Serbia reached its high point during the reign of Tsar Dusan in the fourteenth century and collapsed after the defeat by Turks in 1389 at Kosovo Polje, provoking, according to Freud, a deep national trauma. Under the Ottoman Empire a long period began when the influx of Albanians, loyal servants to the Turks, matched the exodus of wave upon wave of Serbs. The continuing predominance of Albanians was closely linked to their Islamization. After the Balkan wars (1912–13), the Serbs again became masters of Kosovo, and the kingdom of Yugoslavia tried to reverse the migration flow. During the occupation, Kosovo formed part of greater Albania under the protection of Italy; more Albanians came, and violence, harassment, and ethnic cleansing against Serbs grew. Under Tito and after frequent mass protests, Kosovo obtained the status of a province with self-government and a distinct nationality. The process of national self-consciousness passed from demands for autonomy to demands for a republic within the Yugoslav Federation, ending in claims for independence. Through the ages, with few exceptions, the prospect of cohabitation was thwarted by the master-servant relationship, mutual intolerance, and poor communication.

As a result, an intensely nationalistic heritage exploded after the death of Tito in 1980, opening a new cycle of violence. In 1981, major Albanian mass riots were followed by the imposition of martial law, which in turn escalated into the expulsion of Albanians from official institutions, closure of their schools, and violation of their human rights. The spillover process of provocation and attacks followed by repression was at work. Albanian claims that "Kosovo is ours" triggered the awakening of a strong nationalist movement in Serbia that, for the pragmatic and ambitious Communist leader Milosevic, became a springboard. A mass gathering in 1989 to commemorate the battle of Kosovo drew together an estimated one million Serbs of all political tendencies and represented a new wave of nationalism, upon which Milosevic founded his power base. At the same time, he abolished the province's autonomy by integrating it in the new unitary Constitution of Serbia.

According to Chris Hedges, between 1966 and 1989 an estimated 130,000 Serbs left the province because of frequent harassment and discrimination by the Kosovar Albanian majority.[81] But as a result of its inclusion in the Republic of Serbia, this majority in Kosovo became a minority within Serbia. Meanwhile, the gap between the two main communities in Kosovo was deepening, and instead of taking part in Serbia's political life and elections, the Albanian people and their leaders chose to create parallel, usually underground, institutions and networks. The dissolution of the former Yugoslav Federation led the Democratic League of Kosovo (LDK) in 1992 to organize a referendum and to elect its own parliament with Ibrahim Rugova, a moderate leader, as its president. After that, peaceful resistance alternated with violent protests, both aiming by different means to establish an independent Kosovo and abandoning any claim for the restoration of Kosovo's autonomy.

Outbreak of Violence and Civil War

The Kosovo Liberation Army (KLA), comprising two main factions, one tinged with fascism and the other with communism, emerged in reaction to repression.[82] In 1993 it claimed the first armed attack against the Serb police, followed by a series of acts of aggression in 1996 that asserted the KLA's emergence as a potentially significant actor and a rival to President Rugova. Earlier in 1996, having signed the Dayton Agreement and contributed to peace in Bosnia, Milosevic reached an agreement with Rugova reestablishing cultural autonomy; he did not respect this agreement. As a consequence extremists from both sides who tried to impose their solutions by force grew in influence, as confirmed by intensified attacks by the KLA and violent reaction from the Serbian army as well as by the entry of the ultranationalist Seselj into the Serbian government in 1998.

Diverse factors converged, accelerating outbreaks of violence, which led to a civil war in Kosovo with the help of the Kosovar diaspora; the KLA obtained weapons and recruited volunteers who were trained in camps in neighboring Albania. Their aim was not only an independent Kosovo but also a greater Albania uniting all ethnic Albanians in one state, including those living in Macedonia. This objective was certainly not compatible with concerns about regional stability expressed by the U.S. secretary of state, as well as by many European governments. In search of a peaceful solution France and Germany urged Belgrade to negotiate a special statute for Kosovo, but Belgrade rejected their demands. A new level of conflict was reached in spring 1998; attacks against Serbian targets incited disproportionately destructive armed action against a KLA stronghold in Drenica, provoking several thousands to flee to the neighboring hills. While Mrs. Albright was urging action against the Belgrade regime, the six-nation Contact group (France, Germany, Italy, the United Kingdom, the United States, and Russia) issued a statement in line with the European Union and adopted a policy condemning both the "use of excessive force" by Serb paramilitary forces and "terrorist actions by the Kosovo Liberation Army." In fact, on many occasions the European Union expressed deep concern at the violent incidents in Kosovo in early March and urged the "authorities in Belgrade and the leaders of the Kosovar Albanian community to resolve the situation peacefully through a full and constructive dialogue." In May 1998, Milosevic and Rugova held talks, but the Albanian side boycotted further meetings.

Under threat of direct action against Serbia, a short-notice air exercise by NATO, a ban on new investments in Serbia, and the freezing of all Serb foreign assets, a number of Yugoslav troops were withdrawn from Kosovo, and in summer 1998 the KLA seized control of 40 percent of Kosovo before being routed in a large Serb offensive. The spiral of violence was at work. In September Serb forces attacked central Kosovo, where twenty-two Albanians were killed. The Security Council adopted resolution 1199, demanding the cessation of all action by security forces affecting the civilian population and effective international monitoring by the European Community and other organizations facilitating the return of displaced population. A day later NATO decided to increase its level of readiness and to allow the identification of assets for ensuing operations. The escalation continued; the Security Council, after a series of resolutions and warnings, affirmed that the unresolved situation in Kosovo, FRY (the Federal Republic of Yugoslavia), constituted a threat to the peace and security of the region and demanded, under Chapter VII of the UN Charter, that FRY comply fully with resolutions 1160 and 1199, which later constituted a controversial legal basis for NATO air strikes.[83] In October, the European Union issued a declaration on a comprehensive approach to Kosovo supporting the OSCE monitoring mission and envisaging various peaceful means of building confidence and a civil society. This approach endorsed the preference of the European Union for preventive action. This declaration is one proof among others that during 1998 the European Union tried to resist the American drive for the use of force. Under threat of imminent air strikes, the Serb forces were reduced following the Milosevic-Holbrooke agreement; the OSCE verification mission of two thousand monitors was put in place; and the NATO "extraction force" arrived in Macedonia. Notwithstanding these positive signs, on 8 December the General Affairs Council of the European Union expressed concern at the intensification of military action in Kosovo, noting that "increased activity by the KLA has prompted an increased presence of Serbian security forces in the region." In January 1999, the British and French governments aligned their position with U.S. policy. All the ingredients for an armed conflict were present, and a war machine was gaining momentum despite some efforts to preserve peace, which culminated with negotiations in

Rambouillet. The two warring sides were convened to the conference under the threat of air strikes.

The end of 1998 and the beginning of 1999 were a highly troubled period. Many violations of human rights were committed by Serb forces, in particular by parallel military forces. Some observers like Chris Hedges think that "Serbian ethnic cleansing is to a large degree tactical, designed to deny the rebels succor from civilians and therefore aimed primarily at the inhabitants of KLA strongholds."[84] In October 1998, Yugoslav forces launched an offensive against the KLA that provoked a flight of many thousands of Albanians. On the other side there is no doubt that the KLA used well-known guerrilla strategies, consisting of attacks, provocation, and harassment, designed to intensify violent responses and to create "events" that in turn would attract the attention of international media. Given the composition of its leadership and its antecedents it is plausible to admit that all means were used to secure power by armed force in an independent Kosovo and to create a Greater Albania. At the very least, the KLA's aims and means were in complete opposition to the objectives of the EU and NATO. Considered first as a "terrorist group" according to U.S. special representative Robert Gelbard, the KLA became an instrument against Serbs and as such was supplied by weapons. This American tactic, recalling the way in which the United States turned the Mafia into its fifth column before the invasion of Sicily in 1943, should have been a warning sign in view of the negative consequences for both the United States and Italy. Without assimilating the KLA into the Kosovar Mafia, it is possible that there was some collusion, since not only were taxes paid by the diaspora (especially in Switzerland and Germany) but money from drug trafficking served to purchase arms and to develop a lobby. It was clear from the beginning that the KLA was committed neither to a democratic future nor to a multiethnic structure for Kosovo. Useful during the war against Serbia, the KLA is becoming dubious and a nuisance in peacetime.

The violence escalated dangerously. Yugoslav troops killed thirty-six KLA rebels in December 1998, while six young Serbs were killed in a café, prompting widespread Serb protest. In January 1999, the bodies of forty-five ethnic Albanians discovered outside Racak produced a shock. Several raids by Serb police occurred, and rebel attacks were launched. The precarious cease-fire was violated by both sides. While thousands of NATO forces were gathering in Macedonia for a possible peacekeeping mission and inconclusive roundtable talks were held in Rambouillet, the fighting between Yugoslav and rebel forces did not cease. On 20 March Yugoslav forces launched huge offensives against rebels, and international peace monitors evacuated Kosovo as NATO aircraft and warships made ready for bombardment.

The Rambouillet Conference: Negotiation or Ultimatum?
The Rambouillet conference was a turning point in the Kosovo crisis. The negotiation, based on the document elaborated by U.S. ambassador Christopher Hill, was headed by the foreign ministers of France and the United Kingdom but came largely under the influence of the U.S. secretary of state.

The main conditions for an agreement were:

Withdrawal of Yugoslav forces, which were to be replaced by a 28,000-strong NATO force to guarantee peace and security;

Respect for human rights and the return of an estimated 200,000–300,000 refugees;

The reestablishment of autonomy of Kosovo inside FRY.

In principle, this side of the agreement was acceptable to the Yugoslav authorities, who rejected two further requirements, that is, a type of referendum on the future of Kosovo after three years and especially the right of free movement for NATO troops throughout Yugoslavia. According to Henry Kissinger, the alliance abandoned its historic definition as a strictly defensive coalition and insisted on the right to occupy a province of the state with which it was not at war. He noted that NATO reinforced this unprecedented ultimatum by coupling it with a demand for the right of free movement of its troops throughout Yugoslavia. In his view, several fateful decisions were taken in February 1999 when other options were still open and other combinations of diplomacy and force were available. One fateful decision was to use the foreseeable Serb refusal as justification for starting the bombing on 24 March.[85]

At this point, the question arises as to what extent it was possible to avoid war. It seems that the main aspects of the political agreement relating to the organization of the province of Kosovo and its autonomy, as proposed in the Rambouillet Accords, were agreed to by the Yugoslav delegation. During the second round, Kosovo Albanians, including the KLA representatives, unilaterally signed the peace deal despite their divisions, under pressure from Mrs. Albright. As for the Yugoslav representatives, they refused the condition included in the annex imposing free movement of NATO forces throughout all Yugoslav territory. On 23 March the Yugoslav Parliament called on the United Nations to negotiate a diplomatic solution leading "toward the reaching of a political agreement on a wide-ranging autonomy for Kosovo." At the same time, after Milosevic finally refused to allow NATO troops in Yugoslavia, the U.S. special envoy Richard Holbrooke declared in Belgrade that the talks had failed. NATO's first air strikes began on 24 March.

In his statement issued by the Berlin European Council, 24–25 March, after the beginning of bombardments, the head of state and governments concluded:

> In the final analysis, we are responsible for securing peace and cooperation in the region. This is the way to guarantee our fundamental European values, i.e., respect for human rights and the rights of minorities, international law, democratic institutions and the inviolability of borders. Our policy is neither directed against the Yugoslav or Serb population nor against the Federal Republic of Yugoslavia or the Republic of Serbia. It is directed against the irresponsible Yugoslav leadership under President Milosevic. It is directed against security forces cynically and brutally fighting a part of their own population. We want to put an end to these outrages. President Milosevic must stop Serb aggression in Kosovo and sign the Rambouillet Accords, which include a NATO-led implementation force to provide stability.
>
> The Kosovo Albanians showed their commitment to a peaceful solution by signing the Rambouillet Accords. It is vital that they now show maximum restraint. We underline that it is not our aim to keep the Federal Republic of Yugoslavia in its self-imposed isolation in Europe and the World. On the contrary, we would like to end the isolation of the Federal Republic of Yugoslavia in Europe. But for this to happen, Milosevic must choose the path of peace in Kosovo and the path of reform and democratisation, including freedom of the media in the whole of Yugoslavia.
>
> Now the North Atlantic Alliance is taking action against military targets in the Federal Republic of Yugoslavia in order to put an end to the humanitarian catastrophe in Kosovo. The Federal Republic of Yugoslavia is now facing the severest consequences, about which it was repeatedly warned, of its failure to work with the international community for a peaceful settlement of the Kosovo crisis. President Milosevic must now take full responsibility for what is happening. It is up to him to stop the military action by immediately stopping his aggression in Kosovo and by accepting the Rambouillet Accords.

Under the pressure of three leading countries, the United Kingdom, Germany, and France, the European Council approved the military strategy adopted by NATO despite some reservations about this alignment expressed by some members, such as Sweden and Greece. At least two questions arise regarding the role of a sort of directoire of big countries and their predominant influence in security matters. Have some countries resorted to the procedure of "constructive abstention"? The second question is related to the frequent use of the symbolic concept of international community: is it legitimate for NATO or the European Union to speak in the name of the whole international community while some major members of this community, such as Russia, China, and India, voiced opposition to the strikes?

Independent of the NATO campaign's military aspects, which demonstrated the overwhelming superiority of U.S. forces but also reminded onlookers of their limits imposed by "zero deaths strategy," any evaluation of the war against Yugoslavia has to take into account its short- and long-term consequences in relation to the objectives of the whole operation. The campaign was undertaken by NATO on a controversial legal basis, but a consensus among NATO allies was obtained by the United States, despite tacit reservations from countries such as Denmark, Italy, Spain, and Greece. Even if the motives were generally considered just, such an operation was not in conformity with the notion of a defensive alliance and was not approved by the Security Council. For evident reasons NATO took the initiative, disregarding the opposition of Russia in the Contact group and avoiding the foreseeable veto of both Russia and China in the Security Council. Regardless of the United Nations and international law, NATO launched its operations against a sovereign state, with which it was not at war, legitimizing its air intervention by invoking the moral reasons expressed in the proposed Rambouillet agreement.[86] It was consequently labeled NATO's "just war," intended to protect human rights in Kosovo, to hit the Milosevic regime but not the people of Yugoslavia. The notion of just war is ambiguous. "Justum est bellum quibus est necessarium" (War is just for those for whom it is necessary), according to Livy, quoted by Machiavelli.[87]

A Pyrrhic Victory?

More recently, Joseph Nye wrote that "when we do use force, it is worth remembering some principles of the 'just war' doctrine: having a just cause in the eyes of the others; discrimination in means so as to not unduly punish innocent; proportionality of means to ends; and a high probability of good consequences (rather than wishful thinking)."[88]

It is argued that the general perception was that this war of NATO was, in fact, essentially a U.S. war since American forces committed most of the bombing. It is difficult to give an accurate picture of the opinions of others; there were some doubts and protests even among allies, and the final consensus in the European Union was reached under pressure from the major powers (within the European Council) and in reaction to public repugnance at television footage of the suffering of the people in Kosovo. Generally, the world outside of NATO, such as Russia, China, and India, was either opposed to this intervention or suspicious of the allies' real motives and more specifically of the motives of the United States, the only global superpower. According to Samuel Huntington,[89] there is probably some correlation between resistance to the unipolar world as expressed by political and intellectual leaders in most countries. In his article "The Lonely Superpower," written before the war, he reminded us that "at a 1997 Harvard conference, scholars reported that the elites of countries comprising at least two-thirds of the world's people, Chinese, Russians, Indians, Arabs, Muslims and Africans see the United States as the single greatest threat to their societies."[90] From this general observation supported by several facts, it is possible to infer that this war was mainly perceived as a demonstration of the hegemonic power and intention of the United States, in defiance of the international order.

Many effects produced by the bombing cannot be assumed to be proportional to its goals; moreover they violate the 1949 Geneva Convention, intended to protect civil populations and civil infrastructures. In particular, the strikes violated article 14 of the 1977 Protocol to the Geneva Convention, which bars attacks on "objects indispensable to the survival of the civilian population." This opinion was expressed by Michael Mandelbaum, fellow of the Council on Foreign Relations, in his article "A Perfect Failure: NATO's War against Yugoslavia," as well as by Luc Hafner, Swiss colonel and president of the Tribunal of Division 1, in his article "Kosovo: Just War — Criminal Strategy."[91] He argues that this strategy was pursued through the programmed destruction of bridges, water pipes, electric power stations, civil buildings, and transport and communication networks, as well as damage caused to the environment, factories and civil plants, hospitals and schools, the television station, and some embassies, in particular, the Chinese Embassy. In his article "As a Peacemaker, America Is Blundering Badly," former president Jimmy Carter wrote: "As the American-led force has expanded targets to inhabited areas and resorted to the use of anti-personnel cluster bombs, the result has been damage to hospitals, offices and residences of a half-dozen ambassadors, and the killing of hundreds of innocent civilians and an untold number of conscripted troops. Instead of focusing on Serbian military forces, missiles and bombs are now concentrating on the destruction of bridges, railways, roads, electric power, and fuel and fresh water supplies. Serbian citizens report that they are living like cavemen, and their torment increases daily." The main victim, even if considered as collateral damage, is the civil population, not the individuals responsible, not their bosses. This strategy and behavior are in fundamental contradiction to the lengthy progress toward the definition of individual responsibility and culpability established by international law. They correspond, as do all sanctions, to some kind of collective and indiscriminate punishment.

In addition, the bombing did great damage to the very people whom it was supposed to protect. The flood of refugees, which began before the air attacks and which followed the outbreak of the civil war, repression, and violence, quickly grew larger and intensified. The correlation between the beginning of the bombing and a massive flight of Albanian refugees is obvious and was confirmed by independent personalities such as Henry Kissinger and Lord Carrington, the former secretary-general of NATO and previously a British foreign secretary, who said, "I think what NATO did by bombing Serbia actually precipitated the exodus of the Kosovo Albanians into Macedonia and Montenegro." In his view the bombing prompted ethnic cleansing rather then prevented it and made things very much worse. During the bombing, violence reached its highest level: extortion and crimes predominantly by parallel military forces and attacks and killings by uncontrolled Serb, Albanian, and foreign-armed groups. Bombing and violence caused a massive flow of refugees, and this human catastrophe was used in turn as the main argument to continuing indiscriminate bombing. The war aggravated wounds already open.[92]

After being almost ignored at the beginning of the air strikes, which it always opposed, Russia again was integrated into the peace process. President Ahtisaari, mandated by the European Union, and Mr. Chernomyrdin, special envoy of the president of the Russian Federation, interceded in Belgrade and finally reached an agreement; the UN and Russia were again participating in the peacemaking process. NATO's KFOR forces, in cooperation with Russian troops, in total about fifty thousand, were charged with maintaining law and order and peace and with protecting Serbs and the Rom minorities. They were supposed to be assisted by an expected detachment of three thousand UN police, about seven hundred of whom arrived in Kosovo in August 1999. Dr. Kouchner, a former French health minister now designated as the UN high representative by the secretary-general, received a mandate to reconstruct the legal, administrative, and physical infrastructure. But it will be much more difficult to rebuild, after all the psychological damage caused by violence and death to the people, to the multiethnic society, and even to the social structure of Albanian society. Many, many years must pass before trust and peaceful cohabitation between ethnic Albanians and Serbs are restored. In general, bad consequences will prevail before any good outcome ensues, although a favorable outcome has often been confidently predicted. The atrocities and exactions committed particularly by Serb parallel forces (such as those of indicted criminal Arkan), which reached a climax during NATO bombing, were the justification for the intervention by armed forces. But do they justify the use of disproportionate and overwhelming military power and indiscriminate weapons?

What criterion, what concept of humanitarian intervention, helps to distinguish between diverse cases of ethnic cleansing and violations of human rights? In response to this fundamental question, Henry Kissinger wrote:

> And what kind of humanism expresses its reluctance to suffer military casualties by devastating the civilian economy of its adversary for decades to come? Moral principles are expressed in absolutes. But foreign policy must forever be concerned with reconciling ends and means. The fact that ethnic cleansing is repugnant does not obviate the need to devise the most appropriate response. A strategy that vindicates its moral convictions only from an altitude above 15,000 feet, and in the process devastates Serbia and makes Kosovo unlivable, has already produced more refugees and casualties than any conceivable alternative mix of force and diplomacy would have. It deserves to be questioned on both political and moral grounds.[93]

In substance, NATO's just war does not meet the criteria defined by Joseph Nye.

Destabilizing Consequences of War

What are the main short-term consequences in Kosovo and in Serbia, and what are the prospects for a durable solution in the long run, ensuring stability and security in southeast Europe? Seventy-seven days of bombing brought about huge destruction and many victims, mostly civilian, in Kosovo as well as in Serbia and Montenegro. They undoubtedly intensified the atrocities committed by Serbian parallel forces as well as the clashes between the Yugoslav army and the KLA. Besides the great number of mines planted by both parties, more alarming was the inordinate number of cluster bombs, around 1,500, dropped on Kosovo, each releasing 150 to 200 dangerous bomblets that are spread through all parts of the province. Depleted uranium ammunition was also used against Serbian tanks, a fact that was confirmed by NATO warnings to those clearing mines to avoid crawling over tank wrecks.[94] In Serbia's case, the cost of the destruction is even higher: about three thousand dead, half of them civilians, and approximately fifteen thousand wounded. The destruction of the infrastructure, economic and civil targets, is estimated to be 4 billion dollars, while the global effect on the economy as a whole amounts to more than 20 billion dollars, assuming that the negative effects will be confronted during the next decade. The GDP per capita dropped below 1,000 dollars per year, confirming the dramatic picture of most of the population living in extreme poverty.[95] In contrast, a small proportion of those in control have a luxurious life, and they are becoming even richer in this lawless society where the parallel economy flourishes. Abuses and arbitrary behavior by groups allied to the ruling class are tolerated if not supported. However, in addition to physical injury and material damage there is profound psychological and moral disruption, individual and collective. Ethical or simply normal everyday life, regulated by law and judicial power, is an exception in the destroyed social fabric. And obviously this most perverse and lasting damage is impossible to evaluate. The result is an increasing gap between social classes and a general impoverishment of the nation. Actually, after ten years of civil wars, sanctions, and bombing Yugoslavia has become the poorest country in Europe. After World War II the general belief in America was that economic development favors the establishment of a democratic and stable society. The corresponding policy led to the Marshall Plan for Europe and aid programs for developing countries. This policy seems to be giving way to new tendencies wherein budgets for aid and international organizations are cut at the same time as military expenditure is increased, attributing preference to "realpolitik" or power politics in international relations. In the future, presumably this new direction could lead to a parting of ways, if not to divorce, between the United States and the European Union.

Is it possible to explain to the Serbian people and to convince them that the war was not against them but against the regime? All agreed that NATO did not discriminate between cities governed by the Socialist Party of Serbia and its allies and those governed by opposition parties. Indiscriminately, both were targets for NATO bombs. This kind of war from the skies, sparing those who wage and direct it, is dehumanizing and a form of oppression for those who have to suffer it helplessly. Paradoxically, intervention was dehumanized, albeit motivated by humanitarian aims; it did harm even to those civilians it was meant to protect. As William Pfaff noted, for the millions or billions who directly or indirectly witnessed the Kosovo campaign, this so-called antiheroic war provided a terrifying display of what seemed to be unaccountable power in the service not of humanity but merely of the United States and its allies. Thus the precedent has not inspired hope but apprehension. It forces small countries to look for deterrence by means of their own weapons of mass destruction[96] (be the weapons nuclear, chemical, or biological).

At the end of June 1999, Emma Bonino, then a member of the European Commission, urged a strong initiative and action on behalf of the European Union in order to prevent a total Serb exodus from Kosovo. A power vacuum followed the withdrawal of the Yugoslav army; chaos resulted from threats either from the KLA or from groups of ethnic Albanians seeking revenge. Two months later, Kosovo experienced a new ethnic cleansing. In mid-August, the UNHCR (the High Commission for Refugees) estimated that at least 170,000 Serbs out of a population of 180,000–200,000 had fled Kosovo since KFOR and the UN arrived in mid-June. The same source believed that the Serb population of Kosovo's capital, Pristina, had shrunk to less than 2,000 from an estimated 40,000 a few months earlier.

The UN High Commission was alarmed by the situation of Serbs in Kosovo, forced to flee by ethnic Albanian gangs using tactics similar to those used by Serbs in the beginning of 1999. Dennis McNamara, UNHCR's top official in the Balkans and deputy to Bernard Kouchner, the UN mission chief in Kosovo, said Serbia was now home to nearly 700,000 refugees who had fled regional conflicts in this decade. This was a reference to the sequences of waves of Serb refugees from Croatia, Krajina, Bosnia, and Kosovo. Yugoslavia has more refugees and displaced people than any other country in Europe. According to Dennis McNamara, "perpetuating the refugee cycle is going to destabilize the region."[97]

Every Western government that was involved knows that it has won a war but that it is losing the peace. As Prime Minister Tony Blair and President Clinton repeated throughout the conflict, this was a war fought to end *ethnic cleansing* in Europe. This was not to be; instead, there was a reversal of ethnic cleansing, aiming to create a monoethnic Kosovo. The Human Rights Watch stated in its report that the murders, abductions, threats, and beatings of Serbs and Roms have largely been the work of members of the KLA. The report says that peacekeepers have failed to prevent violence against them. The Romany population who sided with Serbs during the war has been openly victimized by the Albanians. Up to 100,000 Roms may ultimately be evicted; in mid-July the UN estimated the number of refugees at roughly 46,000. Since the peace was reestablished, more than forty Orthodox churches or chapels and monasteries have been vandalized or destroyed, according to sources from the Decani Monastery.[98] In his article "Victims of the Victims" Veton Surroi, publisher of *Koha Ditore*, warned fellow ethnic Albanians against fascism in Kosovo and viciously organized systematic violence against Serbs. Serb violence has left a great desire for vengeance in a large part of the Albanian population. Surroi is of the opinion, however, that this is not an excuse. The victims of the greatest persecution at the end of the century will be accused of persecuting others in turn in Kosovo and of allowing fascism to be repeated. "And those who think these actions will end once the last Serbs have left Kosovo will be wrong. It will be the Albanians' turn once more, only this time at the hands of other Albanians. We fought for this?"[99] To have a lasting peace in a democratic Kosovo, we need to ensure the return to a multiethnic society.

There are many obstacles in the way of an equitable and lasting solution, which cannot be imposed by force but needs a firm commitment to fundamental principles and options by the principal actors. In this complex and confused situation many questions go unanswered. What will be the role of the KLA, and what will be the consequences of its conversion from guerrillas to some kind of police force or to a political party? And how will Rugova and his party fit into the various solutions, as well as the Serbs who fled Kosovo? And finally, if the reality of Kosovo, with both its majority of ethnic Albanians and its monuments of profound significance for Serbs, demands some form of cohabitation, would it be in the framework of an autonomous region or an independent state closely integrated into a larger community of southeast Europe?

The KLA is a key actor trying to create a fait accompli and to seize power in Kosovo. Gradually, it is taking sweeping political control, establishing a network of self-proclaimed ministries and local councils; seizing businesses, houses, and apartments; collecting taxes; and preparing its transformation. It is taking advantage of the weakness of the UN administration and the moderate opposition. In addition, some U.S. and UN officials tend to favor the KLA representatives at the expense of President Rugova. Even if the future of Kosovo is highly uncertain, it is obvious that the KLA is an important variable. The agreement reached in June 1999 between NATO, UN officials, and the KLA provided for disarming the guerrilla force under UN supervision. Beginning in September, the two parties agreed to the formation of a civil emergency force consisting of three thousand members from the core of the KLA. It will retain its military command structure and will receive training and equipment, including helicopters. The duties of the Kosovo corps remain a sensitive issue, having direct implications for aspirations to independence and for Yugoslavia's sovereignty over Kosovo. The KLA's leaders see the Kosovo corps as the core of the future army of independent Kosovo.[100] On the other side, shadows subsist in the KLA as a whole. The KLA is composed of several factions and clans, some of which pursue the objective of monoethnic Kosovo, authoritarian government, and others stand accused of having links with the Kosovar Albanian mafia. According to the International Narcotics Enforcement Officers' Association, the Kosovo conflict has turned the province into a magnet for many of the world's notorious drug barons. As reported by the *International Herald Tribune* on 26–27 June 1999, there were also suspicions that the core of the leadership under Hashim Thaci was getting rid of rivals or dissidents. In view of the antecedents of many leaders and various facets of the KLA, this assumption of intolerance has to be taken seriously in the effort to build a democratic and secure community in Kosovo, which implies a number of preconditions.

The Future of Kosovo and FRY in Southeast Europe
What are the prospects for a democratic and multiethnic Kosovo? During his visit to Kosovo at the end of August, Richard Holbrooke, the American

ambassador to the United Nations, met both Thaci and Rugova. He urged the latter to stay the course, remarking that "the war was over but forging a democracy here is a difficult process. NATO has to provide security but it's up to the political leaders to provide the political democracy, and that is the message we hope to convey."[101] He pressed the Albanian leaders (Hashim Thaci, Ibrahim Rugova, Agim Ceku) to live up to their rhetoric about democracy and the rule of the law and to stop using violence and corruption as political tactics.[102] It is surprising that no meeting with Serbian representatives was reported and that he did insist on democracy but did not mention the return of refugees and a multiethnic Kosovo.

The lessons from previous conflicts in the Balkans were drawn by Sergio Vieira de Mello, the UN undersecretary-general for humanitarian affairs and interim administrator of the province: "Maintaining multiethnicity is a moral end in itself, but it is also a matter of pragmatism. Any ideology that accepts the notion of ethnic purity where many cultures in the past have coexisted, as in the case of Kosovo, will lead to exclusion and thus inevitably perpetuate a violent cycle of revenge. . . . What in short term appears expedient in the long term can prove catastrophic." And he concluded that "patient and persistent promotion of multiethnicity in the Balkans may seem anachronistic, but it is the only hope for breaking the cycle of violence."[103]

From the beginning of the Yugoslav crisis, the EU and the U.S. policies have been a case by case approach and reactive conflict management. Instead of preventive action the EU and U.S. intervention was a late response to the explosion of violence. Peace having been imposed by force, the most urgent needs concern security and economic, administrative, and political reconstruction. But the most difficult tasks are the rebuilding of trust and the tackling of a basic problem: overcoming extreme nationalism and fundamentalism, which are rife not only in Kosovo but in the region. The logical conclusion is that what is needed is a new and comprehensive vision for all of southeast Europe, including Serbia.[104] The return of refugees in Kosovo as well in Croatia or Bosnia, the reestablishment of trade relations and free movement, the effective guarantees of minorities' rights and autonomies, the nondiscriminatory indictment of all war criminals, and the reinforcement of law and justice in the region are examples of conditions necessary to ensure peaceful development. The Extraordinary Liechtenstein Colloquium on Peace and the Future in South-Eastern Europe, organized by Dr. Wolfgang Danspeckgruber (of Princeton University) in Vaduz on 17–20 June 1999 reached similar conclusions. Participants, including Prince Alexander of Yugoslavia, Carl Bildt, Hannes Androsch, Albert Rohan, Muhamed Sacirbey, and George Soros, agreed that it is urgent to restore cooperation and to create a common space in the Balkans. References to the experiences of the Marshall Plan and the European Community as well as to the Stability Pact, adopted at the summit conference in Sarajevo, 30 July 1999, designed to build stability, prosperity, and democracy in the Balkans, are pointing in the direction of regional cooperation. The question is, can or should Serbia be excluded as envisaged at the Sarajevo summit? This strategy of sanctions and collective punishment of an entire nation is not the most effective way to maintain pressure on the regime and to help the opposition. A more open approach with positive incentives in favor of the people, the free media, and opposition parties and movements would probably accelerate the change of regime in Yugoslavia. This seems to be the concern of many neighboring countries for which Serbia, situated in the center of the regions, is an important economic partner. Thus the main objective of the programs for reconstruction of the region is to heal and reform the whole region, including Serbia, to restore and reinforce the links between nations, ethnic groups, and citizens. Carl Bildt, former prime minister of Sweden and Secretary-General Kofi Annan's leading envoy in the Balkans, expresses a similar opinion in an interview with Barbara Crossette. He thinks that Europe and the United States need to turn their attention to long-term political as well as economic change, especially in Serbia. Success in Kosovo "is very much dependent on what is going to happen in Serbia," which according to Carl Bildt "is the core nation of the region." And he believes that if Serbia does not reform itself, it will be very difficult to do anything substantial with the rest. "There is need for reconstruction needless to say, but there is a far greater need for reform." He added that inefficient use or diversion of aid is a major impediment all over the region. He does not advocate waiting for Milosevic's trial to begin dealing with the fundamental problems of the country, "which is going rapidly downhill with the economy contracting this year by either 30 or 40 percent. That has to do a very large extent with the bombing, but not only."[105] In this perspective, the contribution of the European Union should consist, as proposed by President Prodi, in a long-term strategy based on reconstruction, reconciliation, and rapprochement within the Balkans but also on rapprochement to the European Union, including the prospect of future EU membership for all countries in the region, as and when they qualify politically and economically.[106] For this purpose, multilateral aid, which is primarily supplied by the European Union, should give priority to regional and multinational projects, and particular attention should be paid to interethnic and cross-border programs and collaboration. All undertakings should contribute to the development of cooperative networks inside the region and with the European Union.

In order to win peace, it is not sufficient to help reconstruct the economic and political community. It is at least as important to cope with the mind-sets of the citizens, which bear the stamps of nationalistic memory and the half century of Communist inheritance, as well as to establish the pluralism of political parties and economic and social organizations and especially of the media, which in many cases are still a monopoly of governments or are under their strict control. As a first step, the OSCE created an independent TV station in Kosovo. However one of the most indispensable initiatives should deal with education, focusing on teaching history and geography in a comparative and European perspective, free of any nationalistic manipulations. The impact on youth of those two disciplines, on the formation of their concepts of nation and homeland as well as of their basic principles and attitudes, is generally recognized. Thus there is an urgent need to revise manuals of history and geography but also to develop the teaching of science through experimental reasoning.[107] Arts and music, languages, all cultural works and creations should be approached with an open spirit and in connection with common and diversified aspects of European culture. On these foundations, the youth of the region, in cooperation with others, can participate in the building of their common future in Europe.

Kosovo's Long-Term Consequences

In a long-term perspective, NATO's war against Yugoslavia raises a number of fundamental questions. During the Cold War period, NATO was guaranteeing Western European security against the Soviet threat, and the defense of Western democracies was under the U.S. umbrella and command. Rejecting the integrated chain of command, General de Gaulle withdrew France from the organization in 1965 but remained in the Alliance. He refused to subordinate the French army to an American commander and to the strategy imposed by the Untied States. Nevertheless he remained loyal to the Allies. For several reasons, the other members were satisfied with the arrangement that ensured their security, allowing them to concentrate on their reconstruction and development.

The disappearance of the Soviet threat (as a consequence of the collapse of the Soviet Union) created a new environment, substituting for the bipolar equilibrium a lonely superpower in a multipolar world economy. This quasi-monopolistic situation has affected many aspects of American foreign policy, leading to the use of unilateral measures and frequent resort to sanctions, coercion, and military interventions. In his article "The Lonely Superpower"[108] Samuel Huntington gave a list of unilateral actions undertaken by the United States and driven by beliefs that American foreign policy is consciously intended to advance universal values, as Deputy Secretary of State Strobe Talbott reminded us. Furthermore, Deputy Secretary of the Treasury Lawrence H. Summers (who became Secretary of the Treasury in May 1999) made the most concise statement on the "benign hegemon" syndrome when he called the United States the "first nonimperialist superpower" — a claim that manages in three words to exalt American uniqueness, American virtue, and American power.

According to Samuel Huntington

in the past few years the United States has, among other things, attempted or been perceived as attempting more or less unilaterally to do the following: pressure other countries to adopt American values and practices regarding human rights and democracy; prevent other countries from acquiring military capabilities that could counter American conventional superiority; enforce American extraterritorial law in other societies; grade countries according to their adherence to American standards on human rights, drugs, terrorism, nuclear proliferation, missile proliferation, and now religious freedom; apply sanctions against countries that do not meet American standards on these issues; promote American corporate interests under the slogan of free trade and open markets; shape World Bank and International Monetary Fund policies to serve those same corporate interests; intervene in local conflicts in which it has relatively little direct interests; bludgeon other countries to adopt economic policies and social policies that will benefit American economic interests; promote American arms sales abroad while attempting to prevent comparable sales by other countries; force out one U.N. secretary-general and dictate the appointment of his successor; expand NATO initially to include Poland, Hungary and the Czech Republic and no one else; undertake military action against Iraq and later maintain harsh economic sanctions against the regime; and categorize certain countries as 'rogue states,' excluding them from global institutions because they refuse to kowtow to American wishes.

In the case of Kosovo, the United States took the lead in the negotiations as well as in the definition of the strategy of NATO and dominated the campaign against Yugoslavia. Its European allies assumed a secondary role despite some theatrical gestures, declarations, and initiatives. The feeling of close dependence on the United States, which was proclaimed "indispensable nation," provoked the aspiration for greater European independence and resulted in the Cologne declaration affirming the urgency of creating a separate military force capable of acting without the United States and without the approval of NATO and having an autonomous European chain of command. The Kosovo campaign produced some cracks in NATO's chain of command. During the phase when peacekeepers were entering Kosovo, British general Michael Jackson, who was in charge of the operation, balked at carrying out an order from NATO's supreme commander,

American general Wesley Clark, to send a force to seize the airport of Pristina ahead of the Russians, who sent two hundred paratroopers. The response of General Jackson was that he was not going to do that because it was not worth starting World War III. This episode was recounted to a Senate committee in September by General Henry Shelton, who emphasized numerous differences in judgment not only between the two generals but also between Washington and London, between European officials and the Pentagon, and even between the Pentagon and the Clinton security team,[109] as well as between General Wesley Clark and his top U.S. Air Force officer, Lieutenant General Michael Short.[110]

Besides the question of relations between Americans and Europeans, their climate of confidence, and their perceptions of future reforms of NATO, the decision-making process during the campaign and the operations in Kosovo reopened a more general question about the relation between main powers in a democratic setting, more precisely between the military and the political powers, as well as the influence of media on both of them. Actually, the military power in NATO was predominant in the definition of strategy and in the extension of targets from military to civilian. Even at an operational stage the question of war and peace is too vital to be left in the hands of the generals. The priority of political authority as confirmed in General Douglas McArthur's case seemed not to be respected during the campaign against Yugoslavia. The NATO strategy and operations were vigorously supported by a highly centralized information service focused on military actions and strategy that, as observed by Henry Kissinger, perversely magnified the suffering of the populations on whose behalf the war was ostensibly being fought.[111]

While the Yugoslav propaganda machine worked in an almost closed space in Yugoslavia, NATO directives were spread through a global network of media. The efficiency of NATO's spokesmen and information service, the passivity of journalists, and a lack of critical opinions caused, a posteriori, some worries about the pluralism of information in Western democracies when they are confronted with such conflictual situations. What is the real impact of the media, which appeared powerful but was easily influenced and fragile at the same time? What is the media's actual role in high-tech information societies?

The war has had some far-reaching consequences at the international level and more specifically regarding the relations with major powers such as China and Russia. The unilateral decision of NATO bypassed the United Nations and humiliated Russia, permanent member of the Security Council and full member of the Contact Group. By re-creating an atmosphere of distrust, it caused Russia's relations with NATO and Western countries to deteriorate, provoking a shift of Russian foreign policy in a nationalistic direction and a new rapprochement with China. It could be, according to some experts, a start of a Eurasian anti-NATO coalition that could include India, bringing together about 2.5 billion people, formidable military might, and a vast stock of nuclear weapons. Their common goal is countering America's global dominance and they already manifested their convergent attitudes when opposing the bombing campaign. Besides, there are concrete signs of growing Russian exports of sophisticated armaments to China and India.[112]

Alarmed at these disruptive trends, the Cologne European Council paid special attention to strengthening the partnership with Russia. For its part, Germany has shifted its focus eastward, striving to create a more stable and secure environment by sponsoring early membership in the European Union for Poland, Hungary, and the Czech Republic; by envisaging an aid package for the Balkans that could amount to 30 billion dollars; and by laying the foundations of a new policy toward Russia. These convergent efforts deployed by both the European Union and Germany aim to restore confidence and to develop a close partnership with Russia in the direction of the "European common house." This strategy tends to avoid the return of the United States–Russia exclusive dialogue and to create a new European peace order of which Russia is an indispensable member. The enlargement of the European Union to Eastern European countries and their natural complement in forms of partnership with countries of the Commonwealth of Independent States pave the way for a greater Europe. This cooperative strategy by means of economic and political integration and partnership appears to be in competition with Washington's idea that NATO expansion requires the alliance to sponsor the democratization and the modernization of Central and East European armies. In this context, NATO is viewed by Washington as an instrument designed to integrate Europe on a military basis. According to William Pfaff, "The plan envisaged the EU as a subordinate regional grouping of West European members of an expanded, Washington-led NATO."[113] This approach is based essentially on military logic, implying relaunching the arms race.

The war revealed the sharp difference between the two approaches and some negative aspects of NATO, which does not have the legal capacity and appropriate means to deal with internal conflicts or civil wars. NATO does not have legitimacy on its own to define universal values and rules or to take unilateral actions, facing the opposition of the major powers and most of the rest of the world. Perceived as a threat, this policy could encourage smaller powers to develop nuclear capacity or biological weapons and to become involved in the new arms race. NATO's war has not helped to reverse this tendency. The policy is opposed to European strategy and a broad concept of security based on cooperation, which is the logical extension of the policy of the European Union and the best guarantee for peace. Thus our conclusion is that NATO, which is the only organizational link between the United States and the EU, is not an adequate institution for the promotion and development of close political and economic cooperation among equals.

Finally, the issue of moral motivation of the humanitarian interventions by military means is a fundamental one. Are the results reached a justification for the actions undertaken? Have they ameliorated the situation and prevented ethnic cleansing? The moral end and intentions do not justify physical and human damage. Proclaiming a civilizing and humanitarian mission but carrying out that mission by a most inhuman means of high-tech war causes many human catastrophes in the name of justice. At this critical stage, it is indispensable to determine what the criteria and the limits of humanitarian military interventions are. From experience, it appears that these interventions are not contemplated against major powers, against members of the alliance, or against allies of major powers. It seems to be more a question of power and geographical distance than of justice or humanitarian action. In the already mentioned article, Henry Kissinger asks: "Then what is left? It would be an odd revolution that proclaimed new universal maxims but could find no concrete application except against a single Balkan thug. Thus more narrowly defined the rhetorical distinction between humanitarian and national interests erodes. But the task of NATO's leaders is to be even more concrete and to supply answers to questions such as these: where and for what humanitarian causes will NATO project its military power?; what risks is it prepared to run?; what price is it prepared to pay?"

Actually, the global responsibilities of the United States appear to have been considerably constricted in the face of the East Timor humanitarian tragedy. Sandy Berger, the president's national security adviser, stressed that this humanitarian problem is not comparable with the "strong security and strategic consequences" that were at stake in Kosovo. This statement contradicts the official rhetoric about humanitarian motivations justifying the bombing in Yugoslavia and raises the question of U.S. strategic interests. The second explanation of the United States regarding direct involvement is that East Timor is a remote, small, and impoverished land of far less strategic importance than Indonesia, which is the fourth largest country in the world, rich in oil, and situated at the crossroads of some strategically crucial sea communications.[114] The East Timor challenge, followed by the conflict in Chechnya, confirmed that the international community has an urgent task for defining criteria for humanitarian interventions.

Toward a European Security Policy:
Cologne European Council

Is Further Development of Europe
and the Union on the Federal Track?
With the exception of the Common Security and Defense Policy the presidency's conclusions at the Cologne European Council (3–4 June 1999) were not a significant breakthrough toward a federal objective. In accordance with the Amsterdam Protocol on the Institutions with the prospect of enlargement, the brief of the Intergovernmental Conference will cover the size and composition of the Commission; the weighting of votes in the Council, that is, reweighting; introduction of a dual majority; the introduction of a threshold for qualified-majority decision making; and extension of qualified-majority voting in the Council. Other necessary amendments could be also foreseen. The preceding example shows a timid and rather restrictive approach adopted by the European Council and a traditional and close intergovernmental procedure in contrast with the more open approach regarding the elaboration of the Charter of Fundamental Rights. As in previous revisions, progress will occur step by step.

As a consequence of the long crisis in the former Yugoslavia, the acknowledgment of the limited role and capacity of the European Union, a new British attitude, and a growing German determination to play an active role, the members of the European Council took a courageous initiative to strengthen the Common European Policy on Security and Defense. In December 1998, at the meeting in Saint-Malo, Tony Blair and Jacques Chirac adopted a plan for the European Union to develop the capacity to conduct military operations independently of NATO. In March 1999, the German presidency presented a discussion paper arguing that the European Union may need its own military staff and policy institutions if it is to make decisions on military action without NATO resources. During the informal weekend meeting of foreign ministers the discussion reflected a widespread desire to escape what one diplomat called "US unilateralism and domination on defense issues."[115]

But the future of Common Security and Defense raised difficult points for many member states, particularly for four neutral countries (Austria, Finland, Ireland, and Sweden) that neither support nor oppose this development. Also other countries such as the Netherlands, Denmark, and Portugal are rather in favor of the status quo under NATO's protection. France and Germany, with their Eurocorps partners, Belgium, Luxembourg, and Spain, support a more autonomous European defense, that is, the nucleus of a future European army. Finally, the development of a European security and defense identity within NATO was backed by the

United Kingdom and approved by the United States and nineteen members of NATO at a meeting in Washington on 24 April 1999.

In its Declaration on Strengthening the Common European Policy on Security and Defense, the Cologne European Council confirmed its intention of giving the European Union the necessary means and capabilities to play its full role in assuming its responsibilities for and in taking decisions on conflict prevention and crisis management. These tasks were defined as "Petersburg tasks" (humanitarian, rescue, and peacekeeping tasks with tasks for combat forces in crisis management, including peacemaking).

The European Union must have the capacity for autonomous action backed by credible military capabilities and appropriate decision-making bodies.

The members of the European Council approved and adopted the report prepared by the German presidency. They committed themselves to developing military capabilities in the areas of intelligence, strategy, transport, and command and control and to undertaking sustained efforts to strengthen the industrial and technological defense base. As for the European Union's decision making regarding security and defense policy, necessary arrangements must be made in order to ensure political control and strategic direction of EU-led Petersburg operations so that the EU can decide on and conduct such operations effectively. Furthermore, the EU will need to acquire the capacity to analyze situations and sources of intelligence and a capability for the relevant strategic planning.

This may require in particular:

regular (or ad hoc) meetings of the General Affairs Council, as appropriate, including defense ministers;

a permanent body in Brussels (Political and Security Committee) consisting of representatives with political/military expertise;

an EU military committee consisting of military representatives making recommendations to the Political and Security Committee;

an EU military staff including a situation center;

other resources such as a satellite center and an institute for security studies.

According to Richard Medley, large standing armies are not only ill suited to Europe's current military needs as emerged after 1989 but economically counterproductive. To remedy this, European countries are committed to reforming their armies and have decided in Cologne that the first goal of their push toward military union will be to develop a European rapid response force, requiring smaller and professional units. As an important step, they also decided to reinforce their capabilities in the fields of intelligence, strategic transport, and command and control, the areas where major economies of scale and investment are feasible. Richard Medley thinks that if the European Union were to match British and American spending proportions for these categories, it would be able to spend nearly 70 billion buying equipment from European manufacturers and directing research toward European laboratories. Equivalent to about 1 percent of European GDP, this would give a significant boost to economies supported by a policy of "Europe first" procurement and improve their technological capacities in broader fields.[116]

Decisions relating to crisis management tasks, in particular decisions having military or defense implications, will be made in accordance with article 23 of the Treaty on European Union. Member states will retain in all circumstances the right to decide if and when their national forces are deployed.

As regards military capabilities, member states need additionally to develop forces (including headquarters) that are also suited to implementing crisis management. The main characteristics include deployability, sustainability, interoperability, flexibility, and mobility. For EU-led operations, the European Union will have to determine whether it will conduct them with or without recourse to NATO assets and capabilities. If operating without NATO is the option, the European Union could use national or multinational European measures previously identified by member states. To lead operations with recourse to NATO, the EU should have assured access to NATO planning capabilities and NATO capabilities and common assets preidentified for just such use. It is stated that in all cases and without prejudice to the principle of the EU's decision-making autonomy the Atlantic Alliance remains the foundation of its members' collective defense. Consequently, the successful creation of a European policy on security and defense will require the development of effective mutual consultation, cooperation, and transparency between NATO and the EU as well as the possibility for all EU member states, including nonallied members, to participate fully and on an equal footing in EU operations. Nevertheless, in practice major member states, among others, will usually take part in these operations, except for those covered by constructive abstention. Their aim is to strengthen the CFSP by developing a policy on security and defense based on a capacity for autonomous action backed by credible military capacity and appropriate decision-making bodies. The first step was the designation of the former secretary-general of NATO, Javier Solana, as "Monsieur PESC" (CFSP).

Changes in the international and European environment mean that the European Union is exposed to new challenges, which imply an innovative approach and require institutional adaptations. This new situation gives rise to an old question: is it possible to have a lasting and solid union based primarily on economic integration but lacking an effective common policy in foreign affairs and security and without even an embryo of common defense? This imbalance is a constant threat, a present-day sword of Damocles. A federal Europe cannot be created without an independent capacity for defense and for prevention of conflict. The Alliance and NATO, which were the best guarantee and protection against the former Soviet Union, nowadays appear to many observers and decision makers to be instruments of American domination rather than an alliance between equals. As noted by Norman Birnbaum, "what is no longer a matter of faith is the idea that NATO is an alliance of equals. The military and political command of the Alliance is not predominantly American; it is exclusively American. . . . It is very unclear why, the cold war ended, the Europeans are now more and not less submissive to American will."[117] Putting it in different terms, Henry Kissinger observes that "the allies share our motives but are beginning to question our judgement." There then follow some critical remarks on American foreign policy and the formative experiences of the Clinton administration. "Obsessively driven by public polls, they are ever tempted to treat foreign policy as an extension of domestic politics. Their diplomacy is quite skillful in dealing with short term tactical issues but obtuse with respect to strategy."[118] In dealing with major world and European crises, the European Union is heavily dependent on America and has a secondary role, despite its economic power.

In his article "From Amsterdam to Kosovo: Lessons for the Future of CFSP," Simon Duke argues that

> Kosovo will have one of two effects: either it will rejuvenate the Common Foreign and Security Policy (CFSP) and give practical effect to a common defense policy and common defense, or it will leave the security of the region largely in the hands of the US with all of the benefits and risks that this applies. The former will involve a change in approach to CFSP and a willingness to invest in appropriate military assets to address the causes and effects of primarily intra state conflict. The latter will continue the patterns established during the cold war whereby the West Europeans rely heavily upon the US for initiative leadership and key military hardware. Kosovo marks a watershed in the sense that its effects may well make or break the CFSP.[119]

Even if the distinction is not so sharp in practice, it is clear that the European Union will have to face some fundamental choices in the near future. The Cologne European Council has marked the new orientation toward a common security and defense policy.

During his visit to NATO in Brussels as secretary of state, Henry Kissinger drew a line between America and the European Community: America was defined as a global power and the reemerging European power as a regional one. Even in the changed environment this difference remains significant and is a key feature in the analysis of transatlantic relations. It is obvious that when America intervenes in a conflict, as in the former Yugoslavia, it takes into account its interests in other parts of the world where it plays an important or preponderant role. As stated, that global approach can be in contradiction to a more limited European approach, with local interests and solutions. When America is invited to intervene, it assumes a predominant military and political role.[120] Its support of the Bosnian Muslim leadership was related to the developing alliance with Islamic countries, and its policy extended the geographical scope of Europe.[121] Another example of America's predominant role is the imposed peace agreement in Dayton, where the European Union made a marginal contribution. Once a military campaign is over or suspended, the European Union regains its importance, when economic and social reconstruction becomes a priority. Is such a division of responsibility an appropriate response to regional and internal conflicts in the European area? Would it not be more efficient in the long run to give the European Union responsibility for conflict management in cooperation with America and Russia? By raising this inquiry, we are questioning NATO's mission and its limits, the future role of the Security Council, and also the network of Atlantic and European organizations. By definition, NATO is condemned to using military means for conflict resolution, which is not necessarily the best way to ensure lasting peace in Europe.[122] During the war against the former Yugoslavia, it was evident that military decision makers overrode political leaders who were supposed to be in command. With the end of the threat from the former Soviet Union, in the future it will be appropriate to substitute a general concept of security for the limited concept of defense and to adopt a more positive and constructive approach based on prevention, association, and partnership rather than on coercion and domination. In fact, even America does not have the capacity to be an effective world police officer, a role contested by Russia and China as well as by a majority of emerging countries. As leading democracies, America and the European Union have a major interest in a stable international order, with all regions and countries freely participating.

This constructive approach corresponds much better to the objective accomplishment and capacity of the European Union, which, having eliminated the old realpolitik relation between France and Germany, has promoted a concept of gradual integration in the main areas of interest, thereby contributing to the creation of a political and security community. A lasting peace is better guaranteed by a close association within a new multinational community than by a collective security system based on domination by a more powerful partner. From this perspective, the Treaty of Amsterdam and the Cologne European Council have set the pace for independent European defense and a system to prevent internal and interstate conflicts in Europe. Recent experiences have shown the urgent need to develop and activate a conflict prevention system instead of a reactive policy applied too late and under pressure of a lingering stage of armed conflict. For these reasons, the CFSP tried to ensure that the Policy Planning and Early Warning Unit was more efficient at decision making, under the responsibility of the high representative, Javier Solana. In so doing, the European Union should be capable of developing a conflict prevention strategy. The question remains whether there will be efficient coordination of those instruments and the political will to make quick decisions. Finally, prevention is heavily dependent on a follow-up policy, attempting to create conditions of peace via multinational common development. In fact, sustained political and socioeconomic development in a larger regional setting seems to be the best available guarantee for lasting peace and security. And it need not be a risk if this positive approach coincides with the mission and the capacity of the European Union.

Consequently, European Union enlargement and close partnership with Russia and Ukraine appear to be the best response to new challenges in Europe. It is doubtful if the rapid extension of NATO under America's hegemonic leadership helps to reinforce security and peace in Europe; on the contrary, it may recreate an atmosphere of mistrust reminiscent of some aspects of the Cold War. Simultaneously, expanding NATO will induce the development of more modern armament in its new member states, which presupposes more investment in defense.[123]

Faced with European Union enlargement and the rapid enlargement of NATO, the choice seems to be between two different options and methods. Less expensive but more hazardous for the future, NATO's further expansion should be preceded by fundamental reform of the organization. More costly but much more positive and constructive, European Union enlargement, with all its difficulties, is, in the long run, the best guarantee of a peaceful future for Europe. It also represents the richest contribution from Europe to America and to the construction of the new world order.

To conclude, we believe, with Joseph Nye, that "In today's world the United States [and Europe, we may add] has a general interest in developing and maintaining the international laws and institutions that deal not just with trade and the environment but with arms proliferation, peacekeeping, human rights and other concerns."[124] What are the best means to realize this objective: coercion or association? Our choice is clear.

Toward a New European Federal Model

In order to bring the EU into sharper focus, an important first step would be to adopt a basic charter or a constitution defining the EU's fundamental objectives and principles as well as establishing the division of powers, responsibilities, and competencies among the national authorities and the European institutions. It would also be necessary to determine how to implement the common regulations and decisions. Nothing but the most essential guidelines should be included in this charter, which should be concise, clear, and accessible. James M. Buchanan, a Nobel Prize winner for economics, did not hesitate to support the idea of a "constitutional opportunity" for Europe. Referring to the lessons learned by the United States, he asserts that the principles of federalism, the diversity of cooperating communities, shared sovereignty, and the effective division of political power and its limits, such principles being codified by constitutional guarantees, offer Europe a prosperous twenty-first century.[125] To Buchanan's reference to the United States we could add the example of Switzerland, a small multinational federation with an outstanding quality of life. These two situations show the adaptability, efficiency, and actuality of federalism. Indeed, these characteristics are inherent in the drive to regionalization currently developing in member states and even in France, which traditionally has been considered a model unitary state.

The constitution must outline the basic principles of democracy and civil liberty and prohibit any form of discrimination on grounds of gender, race or ethnic origin, religion or beliefs, handicaps, age, or sexual orientation. These principles are already enshrined in the Treaty of Amsterdam together with laws concerning the right of asylum, immigration, and social exclusion issues at the top of the priority list of European citizens. Taken together, they form the foundation for a *social model* that rests on a broad consensus and gives substance to the European identity.

The obligation of the Union to respect fundamental rights has been confirmed and defined by the jurisprudence of the European Court of Justice. As stated by the Cologne European Council (3–4 June 1999), "Protection of fundamental rights is a founding principle of the Union and an indispensable perquisite for her legitimacy." In order to make its overriding relevance more visible to the Union's citizens, the European Council made a decision on the drawing up of a charter on fundamental rights and freedoms that should contain the rights guaranteed by the European Convention of the Council of Europe and should be derived from the constitutional traditions common to the member states as general principles of Community law. It should furthermore contain economic and social rights (European Social Charter and Community Charter of the

Fundamental Social Rights of Workers, art. 136 of the Treaty of the European Community).

It is worth noting that the elaboration of this new charter will not be entrusted as usual to an intergovernmental conference but rather should be elaborated by a larger body. Besides the representatives of the heads of state and government and of the president of the Commission, it will be made up of members of the European Parliament and national parliaments. The representatives of the Court of Justice should participate as observers, and representatives of the Economic and Social Committee, the Committee of the Regions, and social groups as well as experts should be invited to give their views. The procedure for adoption of the charter is also innovative as defined by the Cologne European Council: "This body should present a draft document in advance of the European Council in December 2000. The European Council will propose to the European Parliament and the Commission that, together with the Council, they should solemnly proclaim on the basis of the draft document a European Charter of fundamental rights. It will then have to be considered whether and if so how the Charter should be integrated into the treaties." In our view, the constitution should include the essentials of fundamental rights, while the special charter would provide more detailed rules.

Having crossed the threshold into the political dimension, the Union can no longer do without the support of European citizens. This increases the need to put forward clear choices, as was the case during the consultation process leading to the Single Market and the Euro. With these two exceptions, most European issues that have received media coverage and public attention have projected a confusing image of the Union. As a result, the Commission has often been the scapegoat for decisions taken by the Council of Ministers. This also underscores how urgent it is to clarify the roles and responsibilities of the EU's institutions.

To this end, the adoption of subsidiarity is a good beginning, even though its scope needs to be clarified. The basic idea is not to assign to the EU or the state any competences that can best be carried out at the regional or municipal level or by the private sector and, conversely, to entrust the state or the EU with the tasks only they can perform most efficiently. This principle, which lies at the heart of any federal community, can be invoked either to increase or restrict the powers of central institutions. However, it is necessary to define the conditions for choosing one option over another.

Other principles inherent in the majority of European political traditions, such as the separation of powers, accountability, and democratic control, do not appear to have been taken sufficiently into account in the Union's present makeup. There is a persistent confusion between executive power and legislative power within the Council of Ministers. It is damaging and against the true nature of the Union to maintain both legislative and executive functions in the hands of an institution composed of representatives of national executives. Alongside the principle of subsidiarity, two age-old principles inspire the thoughts that follow: on the one hand the principle of the separation and balance of powers and on the other the principle of autonomy and participation. The Commission also presents an ambiguous image: is it a political institution, or is it an administrative and technical body? Are its members independent, or are they some sort of "representatives" of their governments, as perceived frequently by media and some sectors of public opinion. This confused image must be clarified. To clarify the Union's institutional situation and widen its democratic foundations it would be advisable to apply jointly, with certain adaptations, fundamental principles of democracy and federalism. One of the consequences of this approach is the necessity to resort more to free association and participation in common undertakings than to implementation by coercion.

The division of powers should be based to a greater extent on the federal principles of autonomy and participation, which would provide a more solid foundation for the EU's legitimacy. The first ambiguity to be resolved concerns the Council—it should retain only its governing functions, which would continue to be exercised on the basis of the Commission's proposals. The Council would not become a senate, as is often suggested, but would subdivide into a *Council of Ministers* and a *Council of States,* the latter exercising legislative functions together with the European Parliament. In this way, legislative power would be entrusted to a double-chambered institution composed of a Council of States and the European Parliament. The former would ensure the participation of the representatives of the various states—whose autonomy is in no way called into question—while the latter would guarantee the direct representation of the people.

While the election of the members of the European Parliament raises the question of the type of voting procedure, which must be harmonized or even standardized in the near future,[126] the appointment or election of members of Council of States could be carried out in several ways: through nomination by the national governments (similar to the German Bundesrat), election by the national parliaments, or direct election by the citizens of the member states as in the Swiss Council of States. A mixed solution—including national representation, half by ministers and half by national MPs—is also a possibility. Whatever formula is finally chosen, the two chambers should be responsible for adopting EU legislation proposed by the Commission, thereby enhancing their authority and visibility.

In this concept, executive power would rest on two pillars, one representing member states and the other expressing interests common to the Union as a whole. The European Council, representing the top executive powers of member states, could take on the role of a collegiate EU presidency. Its existing role in defining the broad guidelines of economic and foreign policy would be strengthened, and its activities, backed by the Council of Ministers and the Commission, would be more continuous. To ensure this continuity and improve the European Council's visibility, its president would have to be elected by the colleges of heads of government for a term of at least two and a half years.

More revolutionary proposals have been advanced in favor of a single president heading simultaneously the European Council and the Commission. In this case, this official preferably should be directly elected and then would have the task of selecting his or her commissioners. Another choice could be the election of the Commission, which, in the opinion of John Bruton, former prime minister of Ireland, would encourage each political bloc to campaign in each country. "This would force the creation of European political parties as distinct from coalitions of national parties."[127] In substance, "An elected Commission would have as much democratic legitimacy as the European Parliament." This optimum solution being still a remote objective, John Bruton's preferred model for the time being is the European Parliament electing the Commission president, who then selects its members, the president being some sort of an EU prime minister. The general purpose and underlying philosophy behind all these proposals are to establish a direct link between the election of the European Parliament and the choice of the president or even of the members of the European Commission. The result could be more influence from the voters and consequently more motivation to take part in the European elections.

Within this proposed structure, the European Commission would become a fully fledged executive body or *government of the European Union,* with its authority resting on the European Council, the European Parliament, and the Council of States. The procedure already used for the appointment of Jacques Santer as president of the Commission and subsequently strengthened by the Treaty of Amsterdam through increasing the involvement of the European Parliament paves the way for the future European government to acquire full democratic legitimacy while strengthening its president's leadership.

The Commission would share governmental and executive responsibilities and would continue drafting proposals for regulations and decisions and assume its role as guardian of the treaties. Its mission, which would only be slightly modified in economic and social areas, should be strengthened in areas of foreign policy following the lessons learned during the Gulf War and the conflicts in the former Yugoslavia. They showed up the weakness of the Council of Foreign Ministers, which meets infrequently, leading to incoherent action that is more the result of national pressure and constraints than of considered strategies. The preparation, execution, and oversight of Union decisions in matters of foreign policy should, therefore, be carried out by an autonomous and permanent institution such as the Commission, which should be responsible to the European Parliament, the Council of States, and the European Council.

Its origin and composition already give the Commission a political dimension, yet for the moment it possesses neither the competence nor the means to assume any responsibility for foreign policy. Its important role in trade negotiations and the World Trade Organization, as well as in coordinating assistance to Eastern and Central Europe, has not necessarily prepared it for tasks relating to foreign policy. The "European civil war" taking place in the former Yugoslavia has provided irrefutable evidence of the necessity of continuous analysis of crisis situations, within Europe and outside it, so that the Union may properly fulfill its tasks. The Union must be able to define its policies on the basis of a good knowledge of the field, to take appropriate preventative measures throughout crisis situations, and to intervene, if necessary, before situations explode. It must have adequate means for the task. It has been shown that these demands lie beyond the capacities of existing institutions and intergovernmental procedures. It would fall to the Commission, taking into account the different positions of member states, to propose the grand rules of foreign policy, to establish the bases for joint action, and, once it has obtained European Council approval, to oversee it.

The Commission should also have the task of drawing up long-term guidelines and objectives in a global and creative framework. It would be necessary, therefore, for the Commission to withdraw from technical tasks and day-to-day routines and ensure that it can assist the European Council in the conduct of foreign and economic policies. For this, the Commission should be able to delegate certain functions to European agencies and use the potential of consultative organizations and academic and scientific circles. In this respect, one can imagine the Commission surrounded by "interdisciplinary workshops," which would independently oversee and develop possible ideas for the future of the Union. One could also imagine a "council of the wise" as well as a "European council for ethics." Integration is an ongoing creative process and an opportunity for political innovation. The suggestions contained in these guidelines are designed to consolidate the Union as well as ensure a more democratic balance.

The question of the size of the Commission remains: how can its collegiate nature and effectiveness be maintained in an enlarged Union? This is already proving difficult to ensure in today's twenty-member Commission. Reducing participation to only one member per country seems insufficient and reinforces the notion of a Commission composed of "officious national representatives." However, the idea of a Commission with twelve members forming a sort of cabinet — one from each of the larger countries — does not appeal to the small and medium-sized member states. Perhaps a rota system for these countries, similar to that of the Court of Justice's advocates-general, could be devised. While waiting their turn, they could participate in the activities of the Commission as associate or deputy commissioners. This arrangement would strengthen the collegiate character and effectiveness of the European executive for the present and in view of future enlargement.

More direct access to the decision-making centers could be achieved either by creating a third *chamber of the regions* or by *referenda and initiatives at the European level*. When the Maastricht Treaty was being drafted, the German Länder proposed setting up a senate of the regions. Since then a Committee of the Regions has been created, but the original power of codecision envisaged for it has been replaced by a consultative role. The political vocation of the Committee of the Regions has been apparent right from the start through the presence of the elected representatives of the regions, cities, and other collective groupings that adopt positions on European issues. However, the disparity of its members prevents it from being transformed into a senate of the regions. Despite this, it is developing into a sort of intermediate cogwheel, a voice of regional, urban, and local diversity.

All these innovations would have to be submitted to ratification by the member states. Ratifying the Treaty on European Union was more difficult than expected and showed the strength of both the European idea and nationalism. Using a referendum to place the European question at the heart of a public debate reduces the distance between citizens and the Union and leads to a general increase in awareness of the European issue. It also brings out the divisions between and within political parties and reveals resistance to change in the name of national sovereignty, the nation-state, or even outright and violent nationalism. At the same time, it allows support for and opposition to the Union to be measured. The use of referenda by new member states strengthens the legitimacy of their fundamental decisions.

In spite of these advantages, the Danish and French referenda raised more general questions: is it justifiable for the 50.7 percent no vote of a country representing less than 2 percent of the European population effectively to be able to veto the Maastricht Treaty? In France a slim 51 percent voted in favor, but a result similar to Denmark's could have occurred, exposing the Union to paralysis on the basis of one-thirteenth of all the EU's voters. The treaty's provisions need to be modified, and procedures must be established so that a small minority may not block them. A more equitable and less paralyzing procedure should be devised. For example, revision of new treaties could be adopted following *ratification by two-thirds* of the member states. A referendum on a system conceived along the lines of the Swiss federation, requiring the majority vote of both the states and the federal electorate, may be a premature suggestion. Yet a European referendum, as proposed in the past by de Gaulle, would give a stronger democratic foundation and legitimacy to the Union.

Within the EU, exchanges, contacts, and the means of participation are established in many different ways and at different levels. Thanks to fresh advances in information technology, instant communication and horizontal networks are being created. It is in this dynamic context that the European Union is emerging and that more and more cross-border networks are being formed. The EU's growing influence means the question of its future will have to be tackled head-on. Hence the need for clarity as to its objectives, structures, and powers.

To further the federalist cause, a more open and participatory approach will have to be adopted. The Union and its member states are undergoing a process of regionalization, and European private enterprises, whether they are aware of it or not, are also increasingly practicing federalism. Because of this, and because it lacks strong public power and political clout, the EU has no choice but to adopt an innovative strategy. Its power rests more on encouragement, coordination, stimulation, and the ability to convince than on coercion. The involvement of its citizens and their free allegiance to the construction of Europe are indispensable if this political innovation we call the European Union is to succeed.

Federalism Today and in the Future

Scientists, philosophers, and men of action from different backgrounds are currently conceiving flexible and decentralized social organizations that are marked by the spirit and methods of federalism. Professor Bernard observes that the most advanced research in biology recognizes each human being as unique and points toward respect for human rights and fundamental values. Federalism itself draws its roots from the recognition of the person and his or her autonomy, on the one hand, and participation in the common task on the other. This dual principle of autonomy and participation guarantees the achievement of personal fulfillment in a favorable social milieu and is at the basis of new forms of business and human communities. By turning the pyramid upside down, Jan Carlzon emphasizes staff participation and decentralized decision networks, horizontal networks inspired and supervised by managers and leaders with substantial responsibilities. Everything is discussed, but the leaders should offer overall vision and collective projects. These new forms of organization, both complex and efficient, find support in the use of microcomputers, the bases of large networks of decentralized computer systems. At the heart of these forms of organization and communication, which aim at liberating synergy, is Denis de Rougemont's prediction: federalism is a model for the autonomous and participatory organization of communities and regions, with communication networks and microcomputers as the bases for development.

Federalism seems to me to be the form of organization of multinational communities most suited to uniting member states by creating vast economic spaces while safeguarding local, regional, and national identities and respecting the diversity of nations. It allows these sometimes opposing currents to be managed, enriching each other in a complex and adaptable Union. The Union itself reconciles the tendency toward globalization with the assertion of individual and cultural identities at the levels of state, region, and commune. This federalist approach, while taking advantage of computer networks, is vindicating Proudhon and de Rougemont's forecast and confirming the idea that federalism is our future.

These federalist forms of organization and of power evolve at different levels of society in cooperation with multiple networks of social agents. In this sense, new functions, added to the traditional functions of political authority, are more closely connected to those of promotion, guidance, inspiration, supervision, and coordination than to coercion and force, even though the latter may still be legitimate. By breaking down rigid structures and promoting autonomous participation, the European Union foreshadows new forms of political government, which becomes a center of coordination and multidimensional collaboration between public and private agents.

In this developing community, the Union, member states, regions, and communes, as well as companies producing goods and services and cultural research and education centers, will form new, multifaceted networks. While carrying out their own functions and asserting their personalities, together they will tend to create new forms of collective synergy. These new trends are part of the recent evolution of the United States and the Union and its institutions, norms, and practices. European reality and culture, which are at the basis of a "union in diversity," can only flourish in a federation that, while safeguarding national identity and regional diversity, is capable of creating a community and uniting Europeans around a common project and destiny. This is the best way for the European Union to contribute to the security and prosperity of Europe and America as well as that of humanity.

Appendix

TABLE A.1. Institutions and Organs of the European Union Permanent and Temporary Posts, 1997 and 1998[a]

	Permanent		Temporary	
European Parliament	3,491	(3,489)	602	(603)
Council	2,417	(2,441)	18	(18)
Commission	20,178[b]	(17,524)	964	
Administrative duties	16,014	(16,344)	810	(750)
Language services — linguists	1,903		113	
Research duties	3,558	(1,518)	154	(114)
Publications office	525	(525)		
European Centre of Vocational Training	29	(54)		
European Foundation for Improvement of				
Learning and Working Conditions		(83)		
Court of Justice	727	(727)	226	(226)
Court of Auditors	413	(412)	92	(91)
Economic and Social Committee (ESC)	135	(135)		
Committee of the Regions		(88)		
ESC and Committee of the Regions	519	(516 [108 CR])[c]		
Total posts in the European Union	27,880	(25,332)	2,866	(1,802)

Source: General Report (R.G.), 1997, nos. 1136, 1142, 1147, 1151, 1157, 1165; *General Report (R.G.)*, 1998, nos. 1079, 1085, 1091, 1097, 1102, 1107, 1112.

[a]1998 figures in parentheses.

[b]Plus national experts working for Commission equivalent to 582 persons/year paid from the administrative budget.

[c]CR = Committee of the Regions.

TABLE A.2.   Meetings Held by Principal Institutions and Organs, 1997 and 1998[a]

Institutions	Meetings	
European Parliament	19	(16)
Plenary sessions	12	(11)
Part sessions	7	(5)
Council		
European Council	3	(3)
Council of Ministers (general and special)	83	(94)
Commission (weekly meetings)	48	(4)
Economic and Social Committee		
Plenary sessions	9	(9)
Committee of the Regions	9	(6)

Source: General Report (R.G.), 1997, nos. 1126, 1146, 1158; *General Report (R.G.)*, 1998, nos. 1072, 1083–84, 1090, 1103, 1110.

Note: In addition, there is a large number of meetings of permanent committees, working groups, and consultative or official committees.

[a]1998 figures in parentheses.

TABLE A.3. General Activities of the Institutions and Organs, 1997 and 1998[a]

European Parliament	154 (215) consultations, 19 (38) first and 15 (24) second reading cooperation, codecision procedure: 34 (41) first reading, 27 (43) second, and 21 (11) third; 15 (4) assents: 134 (135) other opinions; 24 (16) budget questions; 2 recommendations CFSP and international agreements; own initiatives: 36 (55) reports, 59 (51) resolutions, 93 (107) urgent subjects; 7 (10) miscellaneous. EP addressed 5,440 (5,573) questions: 4,231 (4,114) written questions (3,838 [3,737] to the Commission and 393 [377] to the Council), 185 (204) questions with debate (140 [125] and 45 [79], respectively), and 1,024 (1,255) during question time (689 [708] and 335 [467], respectively).
Council	see table A.4.
Commission	555 (576) proposals, recommendations, or draft instruments, of which there were 52 (63) directives, 238 (230) regulations, 245 (271) decisions, and 14 (5) recommendations; 283 (293) communications, memorandums, and reports.
Court of Justice	341 (253) judgments: 231 (264) preliminary rulings, 32 (70) appeals, and 23 (147) other cases; 444 (485) new cases.
Court of First Instance	149 (129) judgments and 636 (238) new cases. 1998: Cases dealt with, 279; pending procedures, 569; orders, 150.
Court of Auditors	15 specific reports relating to 1996 and 6 opinions; 25 special reports and 14 specific annual reports relating to 1997 and 12 opinions.
Economic and Social Committee	179 (192) opinions and 3 (2) informational reports (63 [71] compulsory and 89 [89] optional consultations; 27 [32] own-initiative opinions).
Committee of the Regions	66 (46) opinions in plenary session, 9 compulsory and 22 optional consultations, and 10 own-initiative opinions; 5 resolutions on the results of the ICG; European Summit of regions and cities and forums on specific topics during plenary sessions.

Source: General Report (R.G.), 1997, nos. 1126, 1134, 1146, 1150, 1155–56, 1158, 1170–73, and table 27. *General Report (R.G.),* 1998, nos. 1078, 1090, 1099, 1100–1101, 1103, 1110, and table 27.
[a]1998 figures in parentheses following 1997 figures.

TABLE A.4. **Legislative Activities of the Institutions, 1997 and 1998**[a]

Enacting Institution	Number of Instruments	Legislative Instruments Enacted, Repealed, or Expiring in 1997[b] and 1998			
		Regulations	Directives	Decisions	Recommendations
European Parliament and Council (codecision)	enacted in 1997	1 (0)	20 (26)	7 (7)	0 (0)
	repealed or expiring in 1997	0 (0)	1 (2)	1 (5)	0 (0)
Council alone	enacted in 1997	208 (202)	14 (27)	157 (189)	3
	repealed or expiring in 1997	271 (146)	38 (44)	82 (187)	0
Commission	enacted in 1997	760 (773)	35 (44)	635 (537)	5 (13)
	repealed or expiring in 1997	503 (551)	27 (13)	199 (260)	2 (1)

Source: General Report (R.G.), 1997 and 1998, table 28.
[a]1998 figures in parentheses.
[b]Data retrieved from CEDEX, the interinstitutional computerized documentation system on Community law (→ points 1121 to 1123) on 15 January, excluding instruments not published in the Official Journal and instruments listed in light type (routine management instruments valid for a limited period).

TABLE A.5. Budget, 1997 and 1998 (provisional figures; in millions of ecus)

	1997	1998
Agriculture	40,805	40,437
Structural operations	31,477	33,461
Internal policies	5,594	5,755
(Research subtotal)	(3,500)	(3,491)
External action	5,607	5,730
Administrative expenditure	4,283	4,353
(Commission subtotal)	(2,797)	(2,843)
Total appropriations for commitments	89,136	91,012
Total appropriations for payments	82,365	83,529

Source: General Report (*R.G.*), 1997, table 19.
Note: Ecu = $1.16.

Notes

Chapter 1

1. See Denis de Rougemont and Dusan Sidjanski, "Généalogie des grands desseins européens de 1306–1961," in *Bulletin du Centre Européen de la Culture* 8, no. 6 (1960–61), Geneva.

2. Henri Saint-Simon, *De la réorganisation de la société européenne, ou de la nécessité de rassembler les peuples de l'Europe en un seul corps politique, en conservant à chacun son indépendance nationale.* Quoted in Denis de Rougemont, *Vingt-huit siècles d'Europe* (Paris: Payot, 1961). Denis de Rougemont's work is a comprehensive presentation of the history of the ideas and projects of the United Europe.

3. Quoted in Hubert Halin, *L'Europe unie objectif majeur de la résistance,* preface by Paul-Henri Spaak (Paris and Brussels: Editions de l'Union des résistants pour une Europe unie [URPEU], 1967), 19.

4. Ibid.

5. Ibid., 22–23.

6. Ibid., 33.

7. Ibid., 47–48.

8. Ibid., 49.

9. *L'Europe de demain, Centre de l'action pour la fédération européenne* (Neuchâtel: La Baconnière, 1945), 73–75.

10. Jean Meynaud and Dusan Sidjanski, *Verso l'Europa Unita, strutture e compiti dei gruppi di promozione,* Collection "Europa una" (Milan: Ferro Edizioni, 1968), 42–45.

11. Centre Européen de la Culture, "*Méthodes et mouvements pour unir l'Europe,*" May 1958, 47, 99.

12. Union européene des fédéralistes, Rapport du Premier Congrès Annuel de l'UEF, 27–31 August 1947, Montreux, Switzerland, 8–16, 33–57.

13. Ibid., 13 (second principle).

14. Ibid., 56.

15. Denis de Rougemont, *L'Europe en jeu* (Neuchâtel: La Baconnière, 1948).

16. Ibid., 134–35.

17. Oliver Philip, *Le problème de l'union européenne* (Paris and Neuchâtel: La Baconnière, 1950), 205.

18. Ibid., 139.

19. Congrès de l'Europe, the Hague, *Résolutions* (London and Paris: Comité international de coordination des mouvements pour l'unité européenne, 1948).

20. *Eurobaromètre,* March–April 1988. The poll was undertaken at the request of the interfederalist group of the European Parliament.

Chapter 2

1. Michel Debré, *Projet de Pacte pour une Union d'Etats européens* (Paris: Nagel, 1950), 61ff.
2. Ibid., 34, 35.
3. "I do not see myself as special—I am a European, just like all the others."
4. Ibid., 18.
5. Ibid., 28.
6. Ibid., 29.
7. Ibid., 40.
8. Ibid., 48, 49.
9. Ibid., 41, 42.
10. Ibid., 49, 50.
11. Ibid., 53, 54.
12. Ibid., 53.
13. Ibid., 41.
14. Ibid., 34, art. 3.
15. Ibid., 22.
16. Robert Schuman, *Pour l'Europe* (Paris: Nagel, 1963), 202, 203.
17. Jean Monnet, *Les Etats-Unis d'Europe ont commencé* (Paris: Robert Laffont, 1955), 17, 110.
18. Ad Hoc Assembly, Rapport de la Commission constitutionnelle, Paris, 20 December 1952, 7 (my italics).
19. Ad Hoc Assembly, "Projet de Traité portant statut de la Communauté Européenne," Paris, Secrétariat de la Commission constitutionnelle, March–April 1953, 119.
20. *La Querelle de la CED* (Paris: A. Colin, 1956), 13.
21. Ibid., 57.
22. Ad Hoc Assembly, "Projet de Traité," 21–22 (my italics).
23. D. Sidjanski, "Auditions au Parlement européen: expérience et avenir," *Res Publica,* no. 1 (1976): 5–32. See also the inquiries into the Mirages Affair and the Kopp Affair, Conseil National et Conseil des Etats en Suisse.
24. D. Sidjanski, "Actualité et dynamique du fédéralisme européen," *Revue du Marché commun* (Paris), November 1990.
25. D. Sidjanski, "Objectif 1993: une communauté fédérale européenne," *Revue du Marché commun* (Paris), December 1990.
26. Cf. my articles "Vers l'Union politique," *Revue politique des idées et des institutions* (Paris), November 1962; and "l'Europe du possible," *Revue générale belge,* December 1963. The purpose of these articles was to relaunch negotiations on a political union.
27. European Parliament, *Le dossier de l'union politique* (Luxembourg, 1964).
28. Ibid.
29. Ibid., 19–23.
30. Ibid.
31. Speech of General de Gaulle delivered at a press conference held on 15 May 1962.
32. Initiatives by the Italian government and Ambassador Cattani to revive the Fouchet Plan through a quest for a general consensus had very little chance of

success, given that they coincided with negotiations for the admission of the United Kingdom, negotiations that were close to stalling.

33. "L'Union européenne," report by Léo Tindemans, prime minister of Belgium, to the European Council, Brussels, 1976.

34. At one of the consultative meetings in Brussels, under Léo Tindemans's presidency, among other suggestions I mentioned recourse to a European referendum, an idea once put forward by General de Gaulle; the point would be to provide the European Union with broad popular legitimacy.

35. Observations made by Léo Tindemans, prime minister of Belgium, as reported in D. Sidjanski, *Journal de Genève,* 7–8 December 1976.

36. "L'Union européenne," 37, 38.

37. D. P. Spierenburg, "Het Rapport Tindemans, een Kritische beschonroing," *International Spectator,* March 1976, quoted in Ch. Frank, "La capacité européenne d'une politique extérieure commune," in *Autour du Rapport Tindemans* (Geneva: Association des Instituts d'études européennes, 1976), 40.

38. S. Hoffmann, "Douze paradoxes pour une absence," *Esprit,* November 1975, 620.

Chapter 3

1. Rapport des Chefs de Délégation aux Ministres des Affaires étrangères (intergovernmental committee created at the Conference of Messina), Brussels, 21 April 1956.

2. Jean Meynaud and Dusan Sidjanski, "Le Comité d'Action pour les Etats-Unis d'Europe," *Annuaire européen* 13 (1965): 1–27.

3. *Verhandlung des Deutschen Bundestages,* 1953–57, 13348.

4. For further details, see my article "Partis politiques face à l'intégration européenne," *Res Publica* (Brussels), no. 1 (1961): 47, 54–57.

5. Cf. my article "Un tabou européen: la supranationalite," *Bulletin du Centre européen de la Culture* 8, no. 3 (1960–61): 38–56.

6. Cf. my study *Les aspects matériels des Communautés européennes* (Paris: Librairie générale de Droit et de Jurisprudence, 1961).

7. See my article "L'Originalité des Communautés européennes et la répartition de leurs pouvoirs," *Revue générale de droit international public,* January–March 1961, 56, 57.

8. Cf. my article "L'Originalité des Communautés."

9. Speech of General de Gaulle, press conference, 15 May 1962.

10. I overheard these observations made by Valéry Giscard d'Estaing and Jean-François Deniau in Verbier at the Christmas and New Year's festivities of 1962–63.

11. Cf. D. Sidjanski and T. Ballmer-Cao, "Les syndicats et les groups de pression français face à l'intégration européenne," in Joël Rideau et al., eds., *La France et les Communauté Européennes* (Paris, LGDJ, 1975), 125–232.

12. Ibid., 222.

13. Ibid., 226–27.

14. Ibid., 224.

15. Ibid., 220.

16. *General Report (R.G.),* 1967.

17. An example of this kind of analysis may be found in the classic work by

James David Barber, *The Presidential Character: Predicting Performance in the White House* (Brunswick, NJ: Prentice-Hall, 1972).

18. These figures did not change in 1995. Forty-six meetings were held, six hundred propositions and projects presented, and 275 communications read (*General Report* [*R.G.*], 1995, no. 1057).

19. These figures did not change in 1995 (ibid., no. 1058).

20. There were 75 billion for 1995 and 82 for 1996, of which 37 and 42 were for agriculture, 23 for structural funds, and 2.8 and 3.2 for research (ibid., nos. 980 and following).

21. There were seventy-six meetings in 1995 (ibid., no. 1050).

22. There were 2,500 in 1995 (ibid., no. 1051).

23. This has reached a stable level. In 1995, thirty-nine directives, 242 rulings, and 175 decisions were handed down (ibid., no. 1050).

24. In 1995, the Court of Justice was composed of fifteen judges, assisted by nine advocates general.

25. Mario Bettati, "Le 'law-making power' de la Cour," *Pouvoirs*, 1989, 59ff.

26. R.-M. Chevallier, "Le juge et la liberté de circulation des personnes et des services," *Droit-Economic*, 1979, 19.

27. The Court employed around a thousand people in 1995. It was asked to decide 409 cases and made 225 rulings, of which 140 were at a prejudicial instance. The Court of First Instance was asked to decide 260 cases and made 165 decisions (*General Report* [*R.G.*], 1995, nos. 1063, 1064).

28. Comités, Luxembourg, Office des Publications officielles de la Communauté.

29. The economic councils of most of the other countries have more limited roles and consequently involve smaller numbers. This is the case for the British and Danish economic councils in particular, in contrast with those in the Benelux countries and France. Cf. my article "Le Comité économique et social et les acteurs sociaux," *Revista Relaçoes Internationais* (Lisbon), no. 2 (1982): 54–57.

30. D. Sidjanski, *De la Démocratie européenne* (Paris: Stanké, 1979), 267–71.

31. This is Prof. Maurice Duverger, an independent, who was elected in 1989 on the Partito Communista Italiano (PCI) ticket.

32. The secretariat of the Parliament employs around four thousand people, of whom one-third are employed in logistic services (*General Report* [*R.G.*], 1995, no. 1047).

33. Abstentions run above 40 percent in the European Community, while they run nearly 50 percent in Swiss federal elections and U.S. presidential elections.

34. Out of 4,971 questions raised in 1995, 3,669 were written (3,217 to the Commission and 444 to the Council). Ninety-seven questions were posed orally. Respectively, 188, 109, and 1,013 were debated publicly (*General Report,* [*R.G.*], 1995, no. 1046).

35. *Les pouvoirs du Parlement européen* (Luxembourg: European Parliament, 1989), 11.

36. Parliament's activities in 1995 included 164 consultations (of which 26 were in a first reading and 12 in a second reading within the cooperation procedure; and 35 in a first reading, 19 in a second, and 7 in a third within the decision procedure). It handed down seventeen assent procedures, fifty-seven other opinions, twenty-five answers on budgetary matters, 253 own-initiative reports and resolutions, and twenty-one miscellaneous decisions and resolutions.

37. In May 1992, the EPP was reinforced when President Valéry Giscard

d'Estaing and a few PR MPs, along with the 32 British Conservatives, joined the ERP. In turn, the Socialist group was preparing to take in the 28 members of the Unitary European Left in January 1993. This means that the two dominant groups account for 207 and 162 members, respectively, or a total of 369.

Chapter 4

1. Several numbers of the *Lettre aux membres du Parlement européen (Crocodile)* were published by Altiero Spinelli and Felice Ippolito beginning in 1980.

2. *Méthodes et mouvements pour unir l'Europe* (Geneva: Centre européen de la Culture, 1958), 55, 56.

3. A. Spinelli, *Vers l'Union européenne,* Sixth Jean Monnet Lecture, 13 June 1983 (Florence: European University Institute, 1983).

4. The proposed resolution from the Institutional Commission on European Parliament policy on the reform of the treaties and the creation of a European Union was presented by its reporter-coordinator, Altiero Spinelli (European Parliament, "Documents de séances," 1982–83, 21 June 1982), and was approved in July 1982 by a vote of 258 to 37 with 21 abstentions.

5. Denis de Rougemont, *L'Europe en jeu* (Neuchâtel: La Baconnière, 1948).

6. Rapport présenté au Conseil sur l'Union européenne (1975). This was followed a decade later by the Dooge Commission Report (1984).

7. Rapport sur les Institutions européennes, presented to the Council by the Committee of the Three (B. Bieshenvel, E. Dell, and R. Marjolin).

8. Rapport fait au nom de la Commission institutionnelle sur l'avant-projet de traité instituant l'Union européenne, reporter-coordinator Altiero Spinelli, European Parliament, "Documents de séance," 1983–84, 19 December 1984.

9. "Le système institutionnel de la Communauté: un équilibre à établir," *Bulletin des Communautés européennes,* supplement, March 1982.

10. Seventh Jean Monnet Lecture, Florence, 24 May 1984.

11. *Méthodes et mouvements pour unir l'Europe,* 4.

12. In February 1984, the European Parliament approved the draft Union Treaty by a vote of 237 to 31 with 43 abstentions.

13. D. Sidjanski, "Penser avec les mains," in *Denis de Rougemont, Cadmos,* no. 33 (Geneva: Centre Européen de la Culture, 1986), 51.

14. Fr. Capotori, M. Hill, Fr. Jacobs, and J.-P Jaqué, *Le Traité de l'Union européenne* (Commentaire de projet adopté par le Parlement européen) (Brussels: L'Université de Bruxelles, Collection dirigée par l'Institut d'études européens, 1985), 25–66, 76–129; *Le Projet,* preamble and arts. 1–11, 14–33.

15. Denis de Rougemont, *L'Avenir est notre affaire* (Paris: Stock, 1977), 352–55.

16. Capotori et al., *Traité de l'Union,* 76–129, arts. 15 to 33. See the analysis of the functioning of Community institutions by E. Noël, former secretary-general of the Commission, in *Les Institutions de la Communauté européenne* (Luxembourg: Office des publications des Communautés européennes, 1985).

17. *Projet,* arts. 34–44; Capotori et al., *Traité de l'Union,* 130–74.

18. *Projet,* art. 41. See also my study "Auditions au Parlement européen: expérience et avenir," *Res Publica,* no. 1 (1976): 29, where I suggest that such hearings should be institutionalized.

19. De Rougemont, *L'Avenir est notre affaire,* 353.

20. Single European Act, *Bulletin des C.E.,* Suppl. /86; H.-J. Glaesner, "L'Acte unique européen," *Revue du Marché Commun,* no. 298 (June 1986).

21. In fact, following an appeal by an individual, the Irish Supreme Court concluded that the ratification of the Single European Act by the Dublin Parliament was not in conformity with its Constitution. According to the Court, title III on political cooperation does not constitute a mere adjustment to the Treaty of Rome but in fact a change in its very nature. To overcome this opposition from the Supreme Court, the Irish had to approve the Single European Act by a means of referendum (in 1972, the Irish had voted in favor of their country joining the European Community by a majority of more than 75 percent).

22. At the Paris Summit, the heads of state or government of the Nine decided "to meet along with their foreign ministers three times a year and whenever necessary as the Council of the Community for the purposes of political cooperation" (*Declaration of the Paris Summit,* 1974).

23. *L'Union européenne: un personnage en quête d'auteur,* Eighth Jean Monnet Lecture (Florence: European University Institute, 1985), 23.

24. Emile Noël, president of the University Institute in Florence, was at the time secretary-general of the Commission and its representative at the Intergovernmental Conference presided over by Jean Dondelinger, then secretary-general of the Luxembourg Foreign Ministry and then member of the Commission (after a long stint on Coreper).

25. Emile Noël, "L'Acte unique européen et le développement de la Communauté européenne," report presented to the International Association for Political Science Congress, Washington, DC, 1988, 4.

26. Ibid., 6ff.

27. "Acte unique européen," *Bulletin des Communautés européennes,* supplement, February 1986, arts. 13–19.

28. "Réussir l'Acte unique: une nouvelle frontière pour l'Europe," *Bulletin des Communautés européennes,* supplement, January 1987.

29. Fernand Braudel, *La dynamique du capitalisme* (Paris: Arthaud, 1985).

30. "Réussir l'Acte unique," 14.

31. *General Report (R.G.),* 1990, 244, 245.

32. Jean-Louis Quermonne, "Existe-t-il un modèle politique européen?" *Revue française de science politique,* April 1990, 197.

33. Ibid., art. 30, sec. 5. Section 4 of article 30 anticipates (among other things) close involvement of the European Parliament in European political cooperation; the Parliament must be kept informed and its views considered.

34. *Eurobaromètre,* no. 24 (December 1985): 5–9.

35. "Réussir l'Acte unique," 7.

Chapter 5

1. Cf. Alexis de Tocqueville, *Democracy in America* (Paris, 1840, 1845).

2. André Siegfried, *La Suisse, démocratie témoin,* 4th ed. (Neuchâtel: La Baconnière, 1969).

3. Denis de Rougemont, *La Suisse ou l'histoire d'un peuple heureux* (Paris: Hachette, 1965), 109.

4. *Eurobaromètre,* no. 34 (December 1990): 10–15; no. 30 (December 1988): B67, B89.

5. *Eurobaromètre*, no. 31 (June 1989): 41, 42.

6. J. Meynaud and D. Sidjanski, *L'Europe des affaires* (Paris: Payot, 1968).

7. As an example, the Commission is collaborating with the European Space Agency in five working groups handling research and technology and also in the framework of its research programs—Brite, Esprit, and Bridge. The Airbus has been one of the causes of contention between the European Community and the United States at the GATT talks and in the WTO.

8. "La chimie européenne doit se concentrer," by A. Dessot, offers a synthesis of work done by the European section of the Society for the Chemical Industry (SCI), Venice Congress (*Le Monde,* 4 October 1989).

9. *La Communauté et les entreprises: le programme d'action pour les PME,* Commission, 1988, 3ff.

10. *General Report (R.G.),* 1990, 124–29.

11. D. Sidjanski and U. Ayberk, "Le nouveau visage des groupes d'intérêt communautaire," in *L'Europe du Sud dans la Communauté européenne* (Paris: PUF, 1990), 43ff.; J. Meynaud and D. Sidjanski, *Les groupes de pression dans la Communauté européenne* (Brussels: ULB, 1971); B. Kohler-Koch, *West German Lobbying in Brussels* (Mannheim: University of Mannheim, 1992); D. Sidjanski, *Networks of European Pressure Groups* (Geneva: Institut européen de l'Université de Genève, 1997).

12. Although the European Confederation of Executives claims only around 800,000 members, the number of executives is very much on the increase. There are nearly 2 million in Great Britain and about 1.5 million in Germany and France according to figures issued by the Association for Executive Employment (APEC) (*Le Monde,* 13 July 1989).

13. Philips estimates that the costs it incurs because of the existence of frontiers are equivalent to 3 percent of its turnover (M. Petite, "Les lobbies européens," *Pouvoirs,* 1989, 98).

14. Ibid., 99.

15. A. Melich, "Problématique centre-périphérie en Espagne: intégration des groupes catalans à la CE," in Sidjanski and Ayberk, *L'Europe du Sud dans la Communauté européenne,* 169ff.

16. S. Mazey and J. Richardson, "Lobbying Styles and European Integration,' European Consortium for Political Research, 1991, 5–7 (manuscript).

17. *General Report (R.G.),* 1998, 331.

18. D. Sidjanski, *De la démocratie européenne* (Paris: Stanke, 1979), 324–47.

19. Cf. Jean Meynaud and Dusan Sidjanski, "Présentation des dirigeants européens," *Il Politico,* no. 4 (1963): 722–24, 750–55 (English summary, 755–56); and my contribution "Eurospère: Dirigeants et Groupes Européens," in *De La Republique à L'Europe. Hommage à Jean-Louis Guermonive,* ed. E. d'Arcy, L. Rouban (Paris: Presses de Science Po, 1996).

20. D. Sidjanski, "Les groupes d'intérêt au Parlement européen," in *Parlement européen: Bilan-Perspectives, 1979–1984,* ed. R. Herbek, J. Jamar, and W. Wessels (Bruges: De Tempel, 1984) 527–32.

Chapter 6

1. *Economist,* 10 November 1990, cited in Mazey and Richardson, "Lobbying Styles," 10.

2. Cf. my "Le Parlement européen et les groupes d'intérêt," in Herbek et al., *Parlement européen: Bilan-Perspectives, 520–53.*

3. Extracts from a speech by M. Woltjer, spokesperson for the Socialist group and member of the Agricultural Commission, reprinted in *Débats du Parlement européen,* no. L295, 7 March (Luxembourg: European Parliament, 1983), 17.

4. EC Association of Saving Banks, Avis sur l'information et la consultation des travailleurs dans les enterprises à structure complexe," Brussels, 29 April 1982, 2.

5. Secretary-general of UNICE to the Social Affairs and Employment Commission, 6 November 1981.

6. Sidjanski, "Le Parlement européen," 552.

7. B. James, "Software Protection Is Lobbied Hard at EC Parliament," *International Herald Tribune,* 16 April 1991, 13.

8. *Eurobaromètre,* no. 33 (June 1990): table A.15.

9. De Ruyt, *L'Acte unique européen,* 139.

10. Decision of the Council, 13 July 1987.

11. *Comités* (Luxembourg: Office des Publications officielles de la Communauté, 1988).

12. D. Sidjanski, "Les groupes de pression dans la CE," *Il Politico,* 47, no. 3 (1982): 539–60.

13. Sidjanski, "Le Comité économique et social," 54–57.

14. Agreement between the federal government and the state governments of Germany in implementation of article 2 of the law of 19 December 1986 relative to the Single European Act.

Chapter 7

1. Inaugural speech delivered by President Richard von Weizsäcker of Germany at the ceremony marking the opening of the forty-first academic year of the Collège d'Europe on 24 September 1990, Collège d'Europe (*Information,* December 1990, 9–10).

2. W. W. Rostow, "The Coming Age of Regionalism," *Encounter,* June 1990, 3–7.

3. OECD Development Center, *Programme de recherche, 1990–1992* (Paris: OECD), 27.

4. P.-J. Proudhon, *Du principe fédératif* (Paris: Bossard, 1921), 155–56.

5. Ibid., 121–23. The following passage is quoted from pages 129–30.

6. Jacques Zeegers, "Mais l'Europe ça peut être naturel sans douleur . . . et fortifiant! Demandez aux Belges," *Le Temps stratégique,* November 1989, 73–80. "In certain countries there are citizens who are afraid of losing their identity in Europe. Belgians, on the other hand, think that in pushing them beyond their frontiers Europe has encouraged them to go beyond an all too limited regionalism and helped them to define their own identity better. The internal political evolution of the country has certainly reinforced specific issues, and many people now feel more Flemish or Walloon than Belgian. Nonetheless, in the great European melting pot they are all becoming aware of their originality and above all of the resources offered by their situation" (78).

7. Cf. my "Actualité et dynamique du fédéralisme européen," *Revue du Marché Commun,* no. 341 (November 1990).

8. Jean Monnet, *Les Etats-Unis d'Europe ont commencé* (Paris: Robert Laffont, 1955), 17. The italics are mine. The passages quoted subsequently may be found on pages 110, 127–29, and 148–49.

9. Dusan Sidjanski, *Fédéralisme amphictyonique* (Lausanne: F. Rouge, Librairie de l'Université, 1956), 5–6.

10. Denis de Rougemont, *L'Aventure occidentale de l'homme* (Paris: Albin Michel, 1957), 60ff. Looking back through Proudhon, I have found a reference to the "Greek Amphictyony" on page 124 of *Du Principe Fédératif.*

11. Jean Monnet, *L'Europe en jeu* (Neuchâtel: La Baconnière, 1948), 70–78; "Notes pour une éthique du fédéralisme," in *Werner Kägi, Menschenrechte, Foederalismes, Demokratie. Festschrift zum F. O. Geburtstag,* ed. U. Häeflin, W. Haller, and D. Schindler (von Lubick, 1979), 259–63; reprinted in *Oeuvres completes de Denis de Rougemont, Ecrits sur l'Europe,* vol. 2. *1962–1968* (Paris: Editions de la Différence, 1994), 679–83.

12. Guy Héraud, *Les principes du fédéralisme et la fédération européenne* (Paris: Presses d'Europe, 1968), 49–50.

13. Jan Carlzon, *Renversons la pyramide* (Paris: InterEditions, 1986). For the passages quoted see pages 134, 161, and 221. Carlzon is the former managing director of SAS.

14. Joël de Rosnay, *Cerveau planétaire* (Paris: Olivier Orban, 1986), 24, 139.

15. According to Professor D. Tsichritzis, the high technology currently being developed is intended to ensure uninterrupted links between government centers in Bonn and Berlin. This experiment may serve as a model for relations between community centers and national or regional centers.

16. Jacques Delors, "Europe: les embarras de la souveraineté," *Politique internationale,* no. 41 (autumn 1988): 295.

17. Comité pour l'étude de l'Union économique et monétaire, Rapport sur l'Union économique et monétaire dans la Communauté européenne, June 1989.

Chapter 8

1. *Eurobaromètre,* no. 35 (June 1991): 40–41, tables 38–42.

2. *Quadragesimo Anno,* Actae Apostolicae Sedis, 23, 1931, p. 203, pars. 126–27, cited in Jean-Marie Pontier, "La subsidiarité en droit administratif," *Revue du Droit Public et de la Science Politique,* 1986, 1515–37.

3. *Eurobaromètre,* no. 36 (December 1991): 28–31.

4. Valéry Giscard d'Estaing, Rapport sur le principe de subsidiarité, European Parliament, 1990–91.

5. Cited by V. Monte in his thesis "La dynamique intégrationniste des Communautés européennes à travers la Coopération politique européenne (CPE) et l'Acte unique," Université de Lausanne, Dorigny, 1992, 447. Cf. Jacques Delors, *Le nouveau concept européen* (Paris: Odile Jacob, 1992), 169.

6. *Le système institutionnel et politique des Communautés européennes dans un monde en mutation: Théorie et pratique* (Brussels: Bruylant, 1989), 198.

7. Cf. Sidjanski, *Fédéralisme amphictyonique,* 2–3.

8. *Eurobaromètre,* no. 35 (June 1991): 19–20.

9. European Commission, *De l'Acte unique à l'après Maastricht: Les moyens de nos ambitions* (European Commission, Brussels: February 1992), 13.

10. Ibid.

11. Jose Luis de Castro, "La Emergente participación de las regiones en el proceso de construcción de la unión europea: Fundamento para la formación de una Europa de los ciudadanos," chap. 3, thesis in preparation for the Department of Political Science, Basque Country University, Bilbao.

12. D. Sidjanski and U. Ayberk, eds., *L'Europe du Sud dans la Communauté européenne: Analyse comparative des groupes d'intérêt et de leur insertion dans le réseau communautaire* (Paris: PUF, 1990).

13. *Eurobaromètre,* no. 36 (December 1991): tables 7, 8, 9, 63.

14. "Déclaration relative au nombre des membres de la Commission et du Parlement européen," Final Act of the Conference, Maastricht, 7 February 1992.

15. The seven cases relate to the following articles: 40 (ex 49), 44 (ex 54), 46 (ex 56), 47.1 (ex 57.1), 47.2 (ex 57.2), 95 (ex 100a), and 96 (ex 101). The other eight cases are contained in articles 149.4 (ex 126.4), 150 (ex 127), 151.5 (ex 128.5), 152 (ex 129.4), 153 (ex 129a), 156 (ex 129d), 166 (ex 130i), and 175.1 (ex 130s).

16. Articles 18 (ex 8a), 16.1 (ex 130d), 190 (ex 138), 300.3 (ex 228.3), final provisions 49 (ex 0), 107.5 (ex 106.5), 110 (ex 108a), and 272 (ex 203).

17. Articles 12 (ex 6), 71 (ex 75), 99.5 (ex 103.5), 103 (ex 104.6), 102.2 (ex 104a), 110.1 and 3 (ex 108.3), 148 (ex 125), 150.4 (ex 127.4), 156 (ex 129d), 162 (ex 130e), 166.1 and 4 (ex 130i), 175 (ex 130s), 179 (ex 130w), 137.2 (ex 118.2), protocol (2), and agreement on social policy article 283 (ex 212).

18. Articles 19.1 (ex 86.1), 19.2 (ex 8b.2), 22 (ex 8e), 70 (ex 75), 89 (ex 94), 94 (ex 100), 95 (ex 100c, c1, c2), 151 (ex 128), 159 (ex 130b), 166.4 (ex 130i.4), 157.3 (ex 130.3), 214 (ex 158), 17 (ex J.7), 34 (ex K.6), 107.6 (ex 106.6), 111.1 (ex 109.1), 112 (ex 109a), 116 (ex 109e), 120.2.3.4 (ex 109i.2.3.4), and 121.2 (ex 109j.2).

19. Supra, 134, 139.

20. Marcel Scotto, "La Cour des comptes rehaussée," *Le Monde,* 14 July 1992.

21. *L'Union européenne, le traité de Maastricht* (Brussels and Luxembourg: European Commission, 1992), 25–27.

22. Philippe Lemaître, "Patrons et syndicats des Douze préparent la mise en oeuvre de la Charte sociale," *Le Monde,* 4 July 1992.

23. According to figures made available in June 1992, out of 3,037 amendments voted on by the European Parliament by virtue of the Single European Act, the Commission gave a positive opinion on 1,577 and the Council accepted 1,300. The European Parliament's role will grow even larger in the framework of the European Union.

24. *Eurobaromètre,* no. 36 (December 1991): 58, 59, table 58.

Chapter 9

1. Barry James, "An EC Police Force When Frontiers Fall: The Big Barrier Is Politics," *International Herald Tribune,* 10 February 1989.

2. *Eurobaromètre,* no. 35 (June 1991): 27, 28, table.

3. The presidency lasts for a period of six months and falls to each member state in rotation. It goes with the presidency of the Union's intergovernmental institutions and organizations functioning under their responsibility. Thus, the presidency of the Union also implies the presidency of the European Council, the Council, Coreper, the Political Committee, and the Coordination Committee as

well as their working groups. The term *troika* designates the current president assisted by the outgoing one and his or her designated successor.

4. Luigi Boselli, *The European Community as a New Actor on the UN Scene* (Rome: SIOI, 1992). An analysis of voting shows that the level of cohesion was as high as 86 percent.

5. See my *Le processus de décision au Conseil de Sécurité* (Rome: SIOI, 1992).

6. European Parliament: the Lady Elles, 1981; Haagerup, 1983; Galluzi, 1986; and Penders, 1989 (reports and the draft European Union Treaty, 1984; WEU, "Les intérêts européens en matière de sécurité").

7. Michèle Bacot-Décriaud and Marie-Claude Plantin, *La Communauté, la défense, et la sécurité européenne: Une identité européenne en matière de défense et de sécurité est-elle possible?* (Lyons: CERIEP, 1991).

8. European Commission, *L'Union européenne. Le traité de Maastricht*, 14–17.

9. François Heisbourg, "Quelles leçons stratégiques de la guerre du Golfe?" *Politique étrangère* 56, no. 2 (summer 1991): 411–22. The quotation is from p. 415.

10. Carlos Closa, "The Gulf Crisis: A Case Study of National Constraints on Community Action," *Revue d'intégration européenne*, autumn 1991, 47–67.

11. Boselli, *European Community*, 10.

12. The chain reaction of violence continued under cover of the resistance and the creation of a communist Yugoslavia.

13. Quoted by D. Rochebin in *Journal de Genéve*, 24 August 1992.

14. It is customary to attribute a pejorative sense to the word *cantonization*, but this overlooks the fact that the system of the Helvetic Confederation is built on cantons. However, the cantons do not constitute homogeneous ethnic states but are most often formed of mixtures of populations and regions and in certain cases languages.

15. See, for instance, my analysis of the crisis in the summer of 1991, *Union ou désunion de l'Europe? La Communauté européenne à l'epreuve de la crise yougo-slave et des mutations en Europe de l'Est* (Geneva: Institut universitaire d'études européennes, 1991), 7–52.

16. J. T. Bergner, *The New Superpowers: Germany, Japan, the U.S., and the New World Order* (New York: St. Martin's, 1991).

Chapter 10

1. Germany now has 99 (instead of 81). France, the United Kingdom, and Italy have increased from 81 to 87; Spain from 60 to 64; Holland from 25 to 31; and Belgium, Greece, and Portugal from 24 to 25. Denmark (16), Ireland (15), and Luxembourg (6) will keep the same number of seats.

2. *General Report* (*R.G.*), 1997 (Brussels and Luxembourg: European Commission, 1998), 41.

3. The results of the referendum were: Austria, 12 June 1994, 66.4 percent in favor, 81 percent participation; Finland, 16 October 1994, 57 percent in favor, 74 percent participation; and Sweden, 13 November 1994, 52.2 percent in favor, 82.4 percent participation. In Norway, the proposition was defeated on 27–28 November 1994 by 52.2 percent (compared to 53 percent in 1972).

4. *General Report (R.G.)*, 1998.

5. The sanctions against Serbia implied the collective responsibility of the whole nation, thus creating a sense of solidarity in the face of the external world. Uses and misuses of the terms *Serbs, Croats,* and *Muslims* contributed to the general confusion.

6. Strangely enough, Serbia will be the only state with more than 30 percent of its population non-Serbian, and except for Macedonia it remains the only multinational state. But after the Kosovo conflict this proportion declined seriously with the likely loss of about two million ethnic Albanians.

7. "Cleansing Krajina," *War Report,* July–August 1995.

8. This is the 35,000 man, thirty-six nation, NATO-led force keeping the peace in Bosnia with the participation of U.S. ground forces.

9. In the November 1997 elections, the Serb Democratic Party (SDS) garnered 33 percent of the vote. The Serb National Party (SNS) of Biljana Plavsic came second, with 20 percent, slightly ahead of the Serbian radicals, with more than 19 percent, followed by the Socialists, with 12 percent of the votes.

10. "A Ghost of a Chance: A Survey of the Balkans," *Economist,* 24 January 1998.

11. Reported by C. Hedges in the *International Herald Tribune,* 11–12 April 1998.

12. Charles G. Boyd, "Making Bosnia Work," *Foreign Affairs,* January–February 1998, 52ff.

13. "Ghost of a Chance," 5.

14. This threat was thoroughly analyzed one and a half centuries ago by de Tocqueville in *Democracy in America.*

15. Malta's application was withdrawn following the elections of 1996 but reactivated in September 1998 after the general election of 5 September. For the time being that of Turkey has not been included in the European Commission's proposal.

16. D. Sidjanski, *The ECE in the Age of Change* (New York and Geneva: United Nations Economic Commission for Europe, 1998), chap. 5.

17. European agreements are in effect with Poland, Hungary, the Czech Republic, Slovakia, Romania, Bulgaria, the three Baltic States, and Slovenia. There are ten Central European countries applying to join the Union (European Commission, *General Report [R.G.],* 1996, no. 785). The participation of Croatia in the PHARE program was suspended following its intervention in Krajina in August 1995, and this situation continued in 1996 (ibid., no. 826). As for the eligibility of other republics of the former Yugoslavia, the European Council has confirmed its agreement for Bosnia and Herzegovina and the former Yugoslav Republic of Macedonia (FYROM).

18. Ibid., 1998, point 814; 1999, point 607.

19. Ibid., 1995, nos. 824–926.

20. Ibid., 1997, point 882.

21. *Bulletin* 7/8, 1997.

22. *General Report (R.G.)*, 1993, point 646; 1997, point 851. I am presenting a summary of the opinions expressed by the Commission (see *General Report [R.G.],* 1997, points 851–62).

23. ECE, 1996.

24. *General Report (R.G.)*, 1997, points 929–34.

25. Thierry de Montbrial and Pierre Jacquet, eds., *Synthèse annuelle de l'évolution du monde* (Paris: Dunod, collection IFRI, 1996), 100.

26. Because of their importance to the Russian economy, the armaments and nuclear industries are seeking outlets for their products on the world market.

27. *Economic Survey of Europe in 1995–1996* (New York and Geneva: United Nations Economic Commission for Europe, 1996); *Economic Bulletin for Europe* 48 (December 1996).

28. The expression "negotiation by synergy" belongs to Emile Noël, then the secretary-general of the Commission and mainstay of the negotiations. See his report "The European Single Act and the Development of the European Community," presented to the Conference of the International Association of Political Science, Washington, D.C., 1988, 4 (of the French version).

29. Circular from Marcelino Oreja, member of the European Commission, Brussels, 18 June 1997.

30. Address by Jacques Santer concerning the Treaty of Amsterdam, Brussels, 26 June 1997, 3 (of the French version; author's translation).

31. Common efforts in favor of environmental protection have been highly valued as priority aims of the European Union (83 percent). In this area, 69 percent prefer common decisions to be made at the Union, rather than national, level (26 percent) (*Eurobaromètre*, no. 45 [spring 1996]: 54, 59).

32. The results of a poll conducted by *Eurobaromètre* (ibid., 54, table 3.11) confirm the high priority that public opinion in member states attributes to basic rights: encouraging human rights (81 percent), equal opportunity for all, regardless of gender or nationality (87 and 86 percent), respect for law and justice (86 percent).

33. This is article F, modified as a new article 6, of the Treaty on European Union and a new article 7 (ex F.1) on measures to be taken in the event of a serious and persistent breach by a member state of the principles on which the Union is founded.

34. A new subtitle was inserted in the Treaty of the European Community (Free Movement of Persons, Asylum, and Immigration), and articles A and B contained therein render this area operational.

35. For example, 76 percent of those questioned consider the problem to be of high priority. They also think that the European Union should be more active with respect to this problem (*Eurobaromètre*, no. 45 [spring 1996]: 54, table 3.11). Also, 59 percent prefer confiding those politics to the Union, as opposed to 34 percent whose preference is the national government (59).

36. Action against discrimination is considered to be very important: the fight to prevent social exclusion (73 percent), equal opportunity and equal treatment for men and women (68 percent), and equal treatment for minorities (66 percent).

37. A new article, 191A, Treaty of the European Community.

38. This is the protocol on the application of the principles of subsidiarity and proportionality. According to the principle of proportionality, the actions of the Community do not exceed the steps needed to fulfill the aims of the treaty. The application of the principle of subsidiarity is perceived as one of the important priorities (64%) (*Eurobaromètre*, no. 45 [spring 1996]: 58).

39. Different terms have been proposed: *reinforced cooperation, flexibility, differentiation* (federal core), and *avant-garde*. The last two, which I prefer, are more positive. See Françoise de la Serre and Helen Wallace, *Les coopérations*

renforcées: une fausse bonne idée? Série études et recherches, no. 2 (Paris: Groupement d'études et recherches, Notre Europe, 1997).

40. See the study of the task force for the intergovernmental conference of the European Parliament, Luxembourg, 12 May 1997; and the study of task force for intergovernmental conference of the European Commission, Brussels, 7 July 1997.

41. Seventy-one percent of the public believes that if the European Parliament has confidence in the Commission, the balance between the Parliament and the Council concerning EU legislation, taxation, and expenses is expected to be only 51 percent (versus 20 percent) (*Eurobaromètre,* no. 45 [spring 1996]: table 3.13).

42. Articles 12 (ex 6), 18 (ex 8a.2), 42 (ex 51), 46.2 (ex 56.2), 47.2 (ex 57.2), 80 (ex 84), 137 (ex 118), 148 (ex 125), 150.4 (ex 127.4), 152 (ex 129), 156 (ex 129d), 162 (130e), 172 (ex 130o), 175.1 (ex 130s.1), and 179.1 (ex 130w.1). The new dispositions are articles 141 (ex 119), 254 (ex 191), 280 (ex 209a), 285 (ex 213a), and 286 (ex 213b). The new title on employment and social policy is Title XI (ex Title VIII), and the customs cooperation article is article 137.2 (ex 118.2) ("Note d'analyse du traité d'Amsterdam," Task force of the European Commission, 7 July 1997, comparative table, p. 2).

43. Articles 19.1 (ex 8b.1), 37 (ex 43), 45 (ex 55), 49 (ex 59), 57 (ex 73c), 93 (ex 99), 94 (ex 100), 133 (ex 113), 137 (ex 118), 159 (ex 130b), 161 (ex 130d), 202 (ex 145), 279 (ex 209), and 283 (ex 212) (ibid., 1, 2).

44. This conforms to a similar opinion contained in article 7.1 (ex F1.1) concerning the implementation of democratic principles and human rights, as well as in article 49 (ex o) relative to applications for new membership; it is also the case in article 161 (ex 130d) regarding structural funds in relation to propositions of the European Parliament for uniform electoral procedure (art. 190.4 (ex 138.4)) and conclusions of specific international agreements (art. 300.3 (ex 228.3)).

45. The extension of the qualified majority is expressed in the following titles and articles: 7 (ex 4), 10 (ex 5), 137.2 (ex 118.2), 141.3 (ex 119.3), 152.4 (ex 129.4), 255 (ex 191a), 280 (ex 209a), 285 (ex 213a), 286 (ex 213b), 299.2 (ex 227.2), 46.2 (ex 56.2), 166.1 and 2 (ex 130i, 1 and 2), and 172 (ex 130o) and new articles on cross-border cooperation 45 (19) 214.2 (ex 158.2), 46 (20) 219 (ex 163), and 48 (22) 7 (ex 4) ("Note d'analyse," 4).

46. Modification of article 158, par. 2, al. 2.

47. Insertion of a new line in article 219 (ex 163) of the Treaty of the European Community.

48. Protocol on institutions with the prospect of enlargement of the European Union.

49. Cf. article 4.

50. This applies to combating racism, xenophobia, international crime and terrorism, trafficking in persons, offenses against children, illicit drug or arms trafficking, corruption, and fraud.

51. Cf. new article, 35 (ex K.7), in the Treaty on European Union.

52. Cf. articles 263 (ex 198a), 264 (ex 198b), and 265 (ex 198c), in the Treaty of the European Community.

53. Cf. Karl W. Deutsch et al., *Political Community and the North Atlantic Area* (Princeton: Princeton University Press, 1957); and Ernst B. Haas, *The Uniting of Europe: Political, Social, and Economic Forces, 1950–1957* (London: Stevens and Sons, 1958).

54. U. Ayberk, *Le mécanisme de la prise de décisions communautaires en*

matière des relations internationales (Brussels: Bruylant, 1978); P. Soldatos, *Le système international et politique des Communautés européennes dans un monde en mutation* (Brussels: Bruylant, 1989), 75–79.

55. D. Sidjanski, *Fédéralisme amphyonique* (Lausanne: F, Rouge et Cie, 1956), 2; *Dimensions européennes de la science politique* (Paris: LGDJ, 1963), 119–22.

56. Cf. title V, article 11 (ex J.1).

57. Cf. article 13 (ex J.3).

58. Cf. article 14 (ex J.4).

59. For their adoption, decisions shall require at least sixty-two votes in favor, cast by at least ten members in conformity with article 23.2 and 3 (ex 13.2 and 3).

60. Cf. article 26 (ex J.16).

61. Cf. ibid.

62. See the declaration of the Final Act on the establishment of a Policy Planning and Early Warning Unit.

63. Cf. new article J.14.

64. The Swiss Federal Council, composed of only seven members, is overloaded, and there are many proposals to improve it. A reform adding seven secretaries of state was rejected by referendum. Fresh proposals to extend Council membership are highly controversial. The latest suggestions recommend extending the presidential term beyond one year's duration and would reinforce the presidency with a strong cabinet—hitherto unknown in Swiss federal politics.

65. Gompert's comments are in David C. Gompert and F. Stephen Larrabee, eds., *America and Europe: A Partnership for a New Era* (Cambridge: Cambridge University Press, 1997), 2.

66. Zbigniew Brzezinski, *The Grand Chessboard: American Primacy and Its Geostrategic Imperatives* (New York: Basic Books, 1997), 76.

67. Ibid. 14: In this case, NATO's forces, plans, command structure, and decision-making procedures must be adapted for the joint defense of distant interests. Also, EU members need to find a way to speak and act in unison within NATO. As NATO comes to resemble a partnership of equals, as opposed to a dominant power leading a band of followers, Europeans will have little incentive for creating a separate EU alliance.

68. Samuel P. Huntington, "The Lonely Superpower," in *The Clash of Civilizations and the Remaking of World Order* (New York: Simon and Schuster, 1996), 42, 43.

69. Quoted by Huntington from Adda B. Bozeman, "Civilization under Stress," *Virginia Quarterly Review* 51 (1975): 1.

70. Emile Durkheim and Marcel Mauss, "Note sur la notion de civilisation," *Recherches sociales* 38 (1978): 811.

71. Denis de Rougemont, "L'Héritage culturel de l'Europe," in *Ecrits sur L'Europe*, vol. 2, ed. Christophe Calame (Paris: Editions de la Différence, 1994), 368.

72. Samuel P. Huntington, *Clash of Civilizations*, 42.

73. Ibid., 158–62.

74. Vladimir Soloviev (1853–1900), Russian philosopher who believed in a universal church. In 1889 he published in French *La Russie et l'Eglise universelle*.

75. Ibid., 160, 161: "The identification of Europe with Western Christendom provides a clear criterion for the admission of new members to Western organizations."

76. Paul Kennedy, *The Rise and Fall of the Great Powers: Economic Change and Military Conflict from 1500 to 2000* (New York: Random House, 1987).

77. Lester Thurow, *Head to Head: La maison Europe, superpuissance du XXIe siècle* (Paris: Calmann-Lévy, 1992), 257.

78. *Financial Times,* 10–11 July 1999.

79. *Economist,* 19 June 1999.

80. Among the most beautiful monasteries are Detchani and Gratchanitsa and churches in Petch, which was the center of the Serbian Patriarchy, well known for their frescoes and icons.

81. Chris Hedges, "Kosovo's Next Masters?" *Foreign Affairs,* May–June 1999, 38. Chris Hedges is currently a Nieman Fellow at Harvard University,

82. Ibid., 26.

83. Simon Duke, "From Amsterdam to Kosovo: Lessons for the Future of CFSP," *Eipascope,* European Institute of Public Administration (EIPA), 4, 5. Simon Duke is an associate professor at the EIPA.

84. Hedges, "Kosovo's Next Masters?" 25.

85. Henry A. Kissinger, "New World Disorder," *Newsweek,* 31 May 1999. This is a profound and objective analysis of the Kosovo crisis and its more global consequences, summarized in the subtitle: "The Ill-Considered War in Kosovo Has Undermined Relations with China and Russia and Put NATO at Risk."

86. Ibid.

87. Niccolo Machiavelli, *The Prince,* trans. P. Bondanella and M. Musk (Oxford: Oxford University Press, 1984), sec. 26, 85. "Titus Livius: Justum est bellum quibus necessarium et pia arma quibus nulla nisi in armis relinquitur specs" (sec. 9, 1). The English translation proposed is: "Only those wars that are necessary are just, and arms are sacred when there is no hope except through arms." I choose the French translation: "La guerre est juste pour ceux à qui elle est nécessaire et les armes sont saintes dès qu'il n'est plus d'espoir qu'en elles" (*Oeuvres complètes de Machiavel* [Paris: NRF, La Pléiade, 1952], 368, 1503).

88. Nye, "Redefining National Interest," 32.

89. Huntington, *Clash of Civilizations,* 42, 43.

90. Ibid.

91. *Foreign Affairs,* September–October 1999, 6; *Le Temps,* 31 May 1999.

92. Charles Méla, Georges Nivat, and Dusan Sidjanski, "La guerre aggrave les blessures," *Le Monde,* 7 May 1999, 1, 18.

93. Kissinger, "New World Disorder," 43.

94. Carlotta Gall, "Mine Death Rising in Kosovo," *International Herald Tribune,* 7–8 August 1999.

95. Group 17, Ed. Mladjan Dinkic, *Final Assessment, Economic Consequences of NATO Bombardment: Evaluation of the Damage and the Needs for Economic Reconstruction of Yugoslavia* (Belgrade: Stubovi Kulture Editing House, 1999) (my translation).

96. William Pfaff, "Luck Enabled NATO to Win Its Anti-heroic War," *International Herald Tribune,* 8 July 1999.

97. *Guardian* Web sites, 12 August 1999.

98. <http://www.decani.yunet.com/destroyedchurch.html>.

99. *Guardian* Web sites, 21 August; *Le Temps,* 30 August 1999, 11.

100. Carlotta Gall, "Kosovo Rebels to Join Civil Emergency Force," *International Herald Tribune,* 4–5 September 1999.

101. Steven Erlanger, "Holbrooke Holds Talks with Kosovar Leaders," *International Herald Tribune*, 30 August 1999.

102. Steven Erlanger, "Holbrooke's Message to Kosovo: It Won't be Easy," *International Herald Tribune*, 31 August 1999.

103. *International Herald Tribune*, 25 August 1999.

104. Anthony Borden and Christopher Bennett, "Heal the Whole Balkan Region, Serbia Included," *International Herald Tribune*, 15 June 1999. Anthony Borden and Christopher Bennett are, respectively, executive director and senior editor at the London-based Institute for War and Peace Reporting.

105. Barbara Crossette, "Reforms Crucial, Bildt Says," *International Herald Tribune*, 30 August 1999.

106. Speech by President Prodi, European Parliament, Strasbourg, 21 July 1999.

107. Professors Leon M. Lederman (United States) and Georges Charpak (France), Nobel Prize winners in physics, promoted the new approach to scientific education.

108. *Foreign Affairs*, March–April 1999, 38.

109. Joseph Fitchett, "Disobeying Orders: NATO Veil Lifted, Top U.S. General Calls Command Stand in Kosovo Troubling," *International Herald Tribune*, 11–12 September 1999. General Henry Shelton is the chairman of the U.S. Joint Chiefs of Staff.

110. Dana Priest, "Strikes Divided NATO Chiefs," *International Herald Tribune*, 22 September 1999, 111–12. The disagreement between two main U.S. commanders of NATO was on bombing targets.

111. Henry Kissinger, "Why Europe Must Not Divorce Itself from NATO," *Electronic Telegraph* <www.telegraph.co.uk>.

112. Tyler Marshall, "Russia, China, and India: Do Closer Ties Bode U.S. Ill?" *International Herald Tribune*, 28 September 1999.

113. William Pfaff, "While Europe Dithers, NATO Advances Eastward," *International Herald Tribune*, 24 June 1999.

114. Some military experts question the efficiency of U.S. power when faced with cases like East Timor where there is no concentration of urban centers and economic targets. The strategy of bombing and "zero deaths" could reveal the weakness of otherwise overwhelming military capacity of the only superpower.

115. Meeting in Bremen on 11 May, defense and foreign ministers of the Western European Union issued a statement declaring they were committed to the development of an effective European defense and security policy. Simultaneously, several European governments have concluded that the WEU must be merged with the European Union as soon as possible (*International Herald Tribune*, 12 May 1999).

116. Richard Medley, "Europe's Next Big Idea. Strategy and Economies Point to a European Military," *Foreign Affairs*, September–October 1999, 21–22.

117. The original English manuscript was published in France as "De Pristina à Pékin," *Le Monde*, 17 June 1999.

118. Kissinger, "New World Disorder."

119. Duke, "From Amsterdam to Kosovo," 2.

120. Boutros Boutros-Ghali, former secretary-general of the UN, confirmed that the United States had made it known publicly in August 1993 that it would use air strikes against Bosnian Serbs on its own. This was soon translated into an

ultimatum, with the United States citing authority under previous UN Security Council resolutions. See his book *Unvanquished: A U.S.-U.N. Saga* (New York: Random House, 1999).

121. Susan L. Woodward, *Balkan Tragedy: Chaos and Dissolution after the Cold War* (Washington, D.C.: Brookings Institution, 1995), 397. Susan L. Woodward is senior fellow at the Brookings Institution and former senior advisor to Yasushi Akashi, top UN official in Bosnia in 1994.

122. NATO was not able to impose a durable solution to the difficulties of its two members Greece and Turkey, which are periodically in crisis, Cyprus remaining a serious problem.

123. According to some analysts, the Visegrad states would be expected to pay 70 percent of the costs of modernization. "The belief that the new members should be able to absorb costs of close to 42 billion between 1996 and 2010 overlooks the International Monetary Fund's rules and the Maastricht Treaty's expectations. The IMF requires former Warsaw Pact states to invest in economic infrastructure, and the Maastricht Treaty will accept members only on the basis of their conformity to its rigorous fiscal standards. Where, then, will the money come from to expand their military budgets?" (Amos Perlmutter and Ted Galen Carpenter, "NATO's Expensive Trip East. The Folly of Enlargement," *Foreign Affairs,* January–February 1998, 5).

124. Joseph S. Nye, "The New National Interest," *Foreign Affairs,* July–August 1999, 30. Many other American academic leaders favor cooperation, with coercion to be used only as a secondary option. Only when there is a consensus among the major powers on fundamental rules and issues will a significant degree of order exist. Such cooperation between great powers can diminish if not abolish the dangers of war in the future. (See Richard N. Haass, "What to Do with American Primacy," *Foreign Affairs,* September–October 1999, 39). Nevertheless, the peripheral conflicts and civil wars have to be borne in mind, and cooperation must occur globally and regionally.

125. James M. Buchanan, Victoria Curzon Price, et al., *Europe's Constitutional Future* (London: Institute of Economic Affairs, 1990), 14–18.

126. According to John Bruton, former prime minister of Ireland, "If you opt for a directly elected Commission President, then you would have to have the same electoral system in each country" ("The Case of an Elected EU Government," in *Should the EU Be Redesigned?* [Brussels: Philip Morris Institute for Public Policy Research, 1999], 33–36).

127. Ibid.

Selected Bibliography

General Works

Allais, M. *L'Europe face à son avenir: Que faire?* Paris: R. Laffont, 1991.

Andersen, S. S., and K. Eliassen, eds. *The European Union: How Democratic Is It?* Sage: London, 1996.

Bassan, M. *Culture et régions d'Europe.* Lausanne: Presses polytechniques et universitaires romandes, 1990.

Bekemans, L., ed., *Culture, Building Stone for Europe 2002: Reflections and Perspectives.* Brussels: Pie, 1994.

Bekemans, L., and R. Picht. *European Societies between Diversity and Convergence.* Vol. 2. Brussels: Pie, 1993.

Boutros-Ghali, B. *Unvanquished: A U.S.-U.N. Saga.* New York: Random House, 1999.

Braudel, F. *La dynamique du capitalisme.* Paris: Arthaud, 1985.

Compagnon, A., and J. Seebacher. *L'esprit de l'Europe.* 3 vols. Paris: Flammarion, 1993.

Cosgrove-Sacks, C., ed. *The European Union and Developing Countries: The Challenges of Globalization.* London and New York: MacMillan and St. Martin's Press, 1999.

Delcourt, J., and R. Papini. *Pour une politique européenne de la culture.* Paris: Economica, 1987.

Delors, J. *Le nouveau concept européen.* Paris: Odile Jacob, 1992.

——. *L'Unité d'un homme.* Paris: Odile Jacob, 1994.

——. *Combats pour l'Europe.* Paris: Economica, 1996.

Deutsch, K. W., et al. *Political Community and the North Atlantic Area.* Princeton: Princeton University Press, 1967.

Deutsch, K. W., J. I. Dominguez, and H. Heclo. *Comparative Government: Politics of Industrialized and Developing Nations.* Boston: Houghton Mifflin, 1981.

Dimitrijevic, V. *The Insecurity of Human Rights after Communism.* Oslo: Norwegian Institute of Human Rights, 1993.

Duchacek, I. D. *Comparative Federalism: The Territorial Dimension of Politics.* New York: Holt, Rinehart, and Winston, 1970.

Duverger, M. *L'Europe dans tous ses Etats.* Paris: PUF, 1995.

Foucher, M., and J. I. Oyarzabal, eds. *Visions of Europe.* Bilbao: Fundación BBV, 1996.

Friedrich, C. J. *Europe: An Emergent Nation?* New York: Harper and Row, 1969.

Groom, A. J. R., and P. Taylor. *Functionalism: Theory and Practice in International Relations.* London: University of London, 1975.

Haas, E. B. *The Uniting of Europe: Political, Social, and Economic Forces, 1950–1957.* London: Stevens and Sons, 1958.

———. *Beyond the Nation-State.* Stanford: Stanford University Press, 1964.

———. *When Knowledge Is Power: Three Models of Change in International Organizations.* Berkeley: University of California Press, 1990.

Hallstein, W. *United Europe: Challenge and Opportunity.* Cambridge: Harvard University Press, 1962.

———. *Europe in the Making.* London: Allen and Unwin, 1972.

Henig, S. *The Uniting of Europe: From Discord to Concord.* London: Routledge, 1997.

Heseltine, M. *The Challenge of Europe: Can Britain Win?* London: Weidenfeld and Nicolson, 1989.

Hocking, B., and M. Smith. *Beyond Foreign Economic Policy: The United States, the Single European Market, and the Changing World Economy.* London: Cassell/Pinter, 1997.

Holland, M. *European Integration: From Community to Union.* London: Pinter, 1994.

Huntington, S. P. *The Clash of Civilizations and the Remaking of World Order.* New York: Simon and Schuster, 1996.

Inglehart, R. *Culture Shift in Advanced Industrial Society.* Princeton: Princeton University Press, 1990.

Jacobson, H. K. *Networks of Interdependence: International Organizations and the Global Political System.* New York: Knopf, 1979.

Jacobson, H. K., and D. Sidjanski, eds. *The Emerging International Economic Order: Dynamic Processes, Constraints, and Opportunities.* London and Beverly Hills: Sage, 1982.

Jacquemin, A., and D. Wright, eds. *The European Challenges Post-1992: Shaping Factors, Shaping Actors.* Aldershot: E. Elgar, 1993.

Jovanovic, M. *European Economic Integration: Limits and Prospects.* London: Routledge, 1997.

———. *International Economic Integration.* Vol. 4: *Critical Perspectives on the World Economy.* London: Routledge, 1998.

Kapteyn, P. *The Stateless Market: The European Dilemma of Integration and Civilization.* London: Routledge, 1996.

Kissinger, H. *White House Years.* Boston: Little, Brown, 1979.

———. *Years of Upheaval.* Boston: Little, Brown, 1982.

Labori, M., and D. Bourdelin. *L'Europe des Douze: Une puissance mondiale en devenir?* Paris: Marketing, 1986.

Lewis, D. *The Road to Europe: History, Institutions, and Prospects of European Integration.* Bern: Peter Lang, 1993.

Lodge, J., ed., *The European Community and the Challenge of the Future.* London: Pinter, 1989.

Marc, A. *Révolution américaine, révolution européenne.* Lausanne: Centre de recherches européennes, 1977.

Michelmann, H., and P. Soldatos. *European Integration: Theories and Approaches.* London: University Press of America, 1994.

Mitrany, D. *The Functional Theory of Politics.* New York: St. Martin's, 1976.

Morin, E. *Penser l'Europe.* Paris: Gallimard, 1987.

Pelassy, D. *Qui gouverne en Europe?* Paris: Fayard, 1992.

Petit, M., et al., *L'Europe interculturelle: Mythe ou réalité?* Paris: Éd. d'organisation, 1991.

Pinder, J. *Rebuilding of the European Union.* 3d ed. Oxford: Oxford University Press, 1998.

Plicht, R., et al. *L'identité européenne.* Brussels: Presses interuniversitaires Européennes, 1993.

Rose, R. *What Is Europe?* New York: HarperCollins, 1996.

Sbragia, A. *Euro-Politics.* Washington, DC: Brookings Institution, 1992.

Scardigli, V. *L'Europe des diversités: La dynamique des identités régionales.* Paris: CNRS, 1993.

Telo, M., ed. *Vers une nouvelle Europe.* Brussels: l'Université de Bruxelles, 1992.

Thurow, L. *Head to Head: La maison Europe, Superpuissance du XXIe siècle.* Paris: Calmann-Lévy, 1992.

Todd, E. *L'invention de l'Europe.* Paris: Seuil, 1990.

Tsoukalis, L., and L. Bekemans, eds. *Europe and Global Economic Interdependence.* Brussels: European Interuniversity Press, 1993.

Wallace, W., ed. *The Dynamics of European Integration.* London: Pinter, 1992.

Wolton, D. *La dernière utopie: Naissance de l'Europe démocratique.* Paris: Flammarion, 1993.

Chapter 1. The Roots of the European Union

Brugmans, H. *L'idée européenne, 1920–1970.* Bruges: Collège d'Europe, De Tempel, 1970.

———. *A travers le siècle.* Brussels: Presses Interuniversitaires Européennes, 1993.

Brugmans, H., and P. Duclos. *Le fédéralisme contemporain.* Leyden: A. W. Sylhoff, 1963.

Commission. *Actes du colloque organisé par la Commission des CE à l'occasion du centenaire de la naissance de Jean Monnet.* Luxembourg: Office des publications officielles des CE, 1989.

Congres de l'Europe. *Résolutions.* Paris and London: Comité International de coordination des mouvements pour l'unité européenne, 1948.

Coudenhove-Kalergi, R. *Pan-Europe.* Paris: PUF, 1988.

European Movement and Council of Europe. Forewords by Winston S. Churchill and Paul-Henri Spaak. London: Hutchinson, 1950.

Gilpin, R. *War and Change in World Politics.* Princeton: Princeton University Press, 1981.

Gouzy, J.-P. *Les pionniers de l'Europe communautaire.* Lausanne: Centre de recherches européennes, 1968.

Halin, H. *L'Europe unie objectif majeur de la résistance.* Paris and Brussels: L'Union des résistants pour une Europe unie, 1967.

Heater, D. *The Idea of European Unity.* Leicester: Leicester University Press, 1992.

Monnet, J. *Mémoires.* Paris: Fayard, 1976.

Union Européenne des Federalistes. *Rapport du premier congrès annuel de l'UEF.* Montreux: Union Européenne des Federalistes, 1947.

Chapter 2. Political Initiatives and Missed Opportunities

Association des Instituts d'Etudes Européennes (colloque d'Athènes) (AIEE). "Autour du rapport Tindemans," *Bulletin du Centre Européen de la Culture,* nos. 1–2 (1976).
Assemblée Ad Hoc. *Rapport de la Commission constitutionnelle.* Paris: Secretariat de la Commission constitutionelle, 1952.
———. *Projet de traité portant statut de la Communauté européenne.* Paris: Secrétariat de la Commission constitutionnelle, 1953.
Centre de Recherches Européennes. *Recueil des communiqués et déclarations du Comité d'Action pour les Etats-Unis d'Europe, 1955–1965.* Lausanne: Centre de Recherches-Européennes, 1965.
Debré, M. *Projet de pacte pour une union d'Etats européens.* Paris: Nagel, 1950.
Melchionni, M. G. *Altiero Spinelli et Jean Monnet.* Lausanne: Centre de recherches européennes, 1993.
Monnet, J. *Les Etats-Unis d'Europe ont commencé.* Paris: R. Lafont, 1955.
Musolesi, D. *Progetti federativi europei.* Rome: Istituto di Studi Europei and A. De Gasperi, 1985.
Saint-Ouen, F. *Les grandes figures de la construction européenne.* Geneva: Georg, 1997.
Schuman, R. *Pour l'Europe.* Paris: Nagel, 1963.
Tindemans, L. *L'Union européenne.* Brussels: Ministère des Affaires Etrangères, 1976.

Chapter 3. The Dynamics of Community Institutions

Abeles, M. *La vie quotidienne au Parlement européen.* Paris: Hachette, 1992.
Bardi, L. *Il Parlamento della Communità Europea.* Bologna: Mulino, 1989.
Bourrinet, J., ed. *Le comité des régions de l'union européenne.* Paris: Economica, 1997.
Capotorti, F., et al. *Le Traité d'union européenne (commentaires du projet adopté par le Parlement européen).* Brussels: L'Université de Bruxelles, 1985.
Cecchini, P. *La sfida del 1992.* Sperling and Kupfer: 1988.
De Ruyt, J. *L'Acte unique européen: Commentaire.* Brussels: ULB, 1987.
Emiliou, N. *Constitutional and Institutional Law of the European Union.* London: University of London, 1995.
Hayes-Renshow, F., and H. Wallace. *The Council of Ministers.* London: Macmillan, 1997.
Hayward, J., and E. Page, eds. *Governing the New Europe.* Durham: Duke University Press, 1995.
Herbek, R., J. Jamar, and W. Wessels. *Parlement européen: Bilan-Perspectives.* Bruges: Collège d'Europe, De Tempel, [1979] 1984.
Herman, V., and J. Lodge. *Direct Elections to the European Parliament.* London: Macmillan, 1982.
Kirchner, E. *The European Parliament: Performance and Prospects.* Aldershot: Gower, 1984.
Louis, J.-V., and D. Waelbroeck. *Le Parlement européen dans l'évolution institutionnelle.* Brussels: ULB, 1988.

———. *La Commission au coeur du système institutionnel des CE.* Brussels: ULB, 1989.

Milesi, G. *Jacques Delors: L'homme qui dit non.* Paris: Edition 1, 1995.

Noel, E. *Les institutions de la Communauté européenne.* Luxembourg: Office des publications des CE, 1991.

Nuallain, C. O. *The Presidency of the European Council of Ministers.* Crom Helm: European Institute of Public Administration, 1985.

Nugent, N., ed. *At the Heart of the Union: Studies of the European Commission.* London: Macmillan, 1997.

Philip, C. *Les institutions européennes.* Paris: Masson, 1981.

Pijpers, A., ed. *European Political Cooperation in the 80's.* Dordrecht: Martinus Nijhoff, 1988.

Pouvoirs. *Europe 1993.* Paris: Pouvoirs, PUF, 1989.

Quermonne, J.-L. *Le système politique de l'Union européenne.* Paris: Montchrestien, 1994.

Sidjanski, D. *Les aspects matériels des Communautés européennes.* Paris: Librairie générale de droit et de jurisprudence, 1961.

———. *Europe élections, de la démocratie européenne.* Paris: Stanké, 1979.

Smith, E., ed. *National Parliaments as Cornerstones of European Integration.* London: Kluwer Law International, 1996.

Soldatos, P. *Le système institutionnel et politique des CE dans un monde en mutation: Théorie et pratique.* Brussels: Bruylant, 1989.

Spinelli, A. *Vers l'Union européenne.* Florence: Institut universitaire européen, 1983.

Stephanou, C. *The Institutional Reform of the EU.* Athens: Papazissis, 1996.

Taulegne, B. *Le Conseil européen.* Paris: PUF, 1993.

Westlake, M. *A Modern Guide to the European Parliament.* London: Pinter, 1994.

Chapter 4. From the European Parliament Union Plan (1984) to the Single European Act (1987)

Andersen, S. S., and K. A. Eliassen. *The Explosion of European Community Lobbying: The Emergence of a Political System.* Norwegian School of Management, 1990.

d'Arcy, F., and L. Rouban, eds. *De la Vème République à l'Europe: Hommage à Jean-Louis Quermonne.* Paris: Presses de Science Po, 1996.

Armstrong, L., and A. Dauvergne. *L'Europe 93: Tout ce qui va changer pour les consommateurs.* Paris: Balland, 1989.

Bell, D., and E. Shaw, eds. *Conflicts and Cohesion in West European Social Democratic Parties.* London: Pinter, 1994.

Bossuat, G., and R. Girault, eds. *Europe brisée, Europe retrouvée: Nouvelles réflexions sur l'unité européenne au Xxème siècle.* Paris: Publications de la Sorbonne, 1994.

Bourrinet, J., ed. *Le Comité des régions de l'Union européenne.* Paris: Economica, 1997.

Brigouleix, B. *CEE: Voyage en Eurocratie.* Paris: A. Moreau, 1986.

Caire, G. *L'Europe sociale: Faits, problèmes, enjeux.* Paris: Masson, 1992.

Debbasch, C., ed. *Administrations nationales et intégration européenne.* Paris: CNRS, 1987.

Featherstone, K. *Socialist Parties and European Integration: A Comparative History.* Manchester: Manchester University Press, 1988.

George, S. *An Awkward Partner: Britain in the European Community.* Oxford: Oxford University Press, 1990.

Gorge, M. J., *Euro-Corporatism? Interest Intermediation in the European Community.* Lanham, MD: University Press of America, 1996.

Guiliani, J.-D. *Marchands d'influence.* Paris: Seuil, 1991.

Johansson, K. M. *Transnational Party Alliances: Analysing the Hard-Won Alliance between Conservatives and Christian Democrats in the European Parliament.* Lund: Lund University Press, 1997.

Johnson, S., and G. Corcelle. *L'autre Europe "verte": La politique communautaire de l'environnement.* Paris: Labor-Nathan, 1987.

Juiliani, J.-D. *Marchands d'influence.* Paris: Seuil, 1991.

Irving, R. E. *The Christian Democratic Parties of Western Europe.* London: Allen and Unwin, 1979.

Kelstrup, M., ed. *European Integration and Denmark's Participation.* Copenhagen: Copenhagen Political Studies Press, 1992.

Kirchner, E., ed. *Liberal Parties in Western Europe.* Cambridge: Cambridge University Press, 1988.

Kirchner, E., and K. Schwarger. *The Role of Interest Groups in the European Community.* Aldershot: Gower, 1981.

Kohler-Koch, B. *West German Lobbying in Brussels.* Mannheim: Universität Mannheim, 1992.

La Serre, F. de. *La Grande-Bretagne et la Communauté européenne.* Paris: PUF, 1987.

Marxs, G., F. W. Scharpf, P. C. Schmitter, and W. Streeck, eds. *Governance in the European Union.* Thousand Oaks, CA: Sage, 1996.

Meynaud, J., and D. Sidjanski. *L'Europe des affaires.* Paris: Payot, 1968.

———. *Les groupes de pression dans la Communauté européenne.* Brussels: ULB, 1971.

Nonon, J., and M. Clamen. *L'Europe et ses couloirs.* Paris: Dunod, 1991.

Papini, R. *L'internationale démocrate-chrétienne, 1925–1986.* Paris: Cerf, 1988.

Parkin, S. *Green Parties: An International Guide.* London: Heretic Books, 1989.

Paterson, W., and A. Thomas, eds. *The Future of Social Democracy: Problems and Prospects of Social Democratic Parties in Western Europe.* Oxford: Clarendon Press, 1986.

Pridham, G., and P. Pridham. *Transnational Party Cooperation and European Integration.* London: Allen and Unwin, 1981.

Reif, K., and R. Inglehart, eds. *Eurobarometer: The Dynamics of European Public Opinion.* London: MacMillan, 1991.

Rideau, J., ed. *Les Etats membres de l'Union européenne: Adaptations, mutations, résistances.* Paris: LGDJ, 1997.

Rollat, A. *Delors.* Paris: Flammarion, 1993.

Saint-Ouen, F. *Les partis politiques et l'Europe, une approche comparative.* Paris: PUF, 1990.

Sidjanski, D. *Networks of European Pressure Groups.* Geneva: Institut européen de l'Université de Genève, 1997.

Sidjanski, D., and U. Ayberk, eds. *L'Europe du Sud dans la CE*. Paris: PUF, 1990.
Spyropoulos, G., and G. Fragniere, eds. *Work and Social Policies in the New Europe*. Brussels: European Interuniversity Press, 1991.
Vogel-Polski, E., and J. Vogel. *L'Europe sociale 1993: Illusion, alibi, ou réalité?* Brussels: L'Université de Bruxelles, 1991.

Chapter 6. The Decision-Making Process and the Spillover Effect

Archer, C., and F. Butler. *The European Community: Structure and Process*. London: Pinter, 1992.
Bulmer, S., and W. Wessels. *The European Council: Decision-Making in European Politics*. London: MacMillan, 1987.
Ciavarini-Azzi, G., ed. *L'application du droit communautaire par les Etats membres*. Maastricht: Institut européen d'administration publique, 1985.
George, S. *Politics and Policy in the European Community*. Oxford: Oxford University Press, 1985.
Kirchner, E. *Decision-Making in the European Community: The Council Presidency and European Integration*. Manchester: Manchester University Press, 1992.
Pedler and Schäfer, eds. *Shaping European Law and Policy: The Role of Committees and Comitology in the Political Process*. Maastricht: EIPA, 1996.
Richardson, J., ed. *European Union: Power and Policy-Making*. London: Routledge, 1996.
Siedentopf, H., and J. Ziller. *L'Europe des Administrations? La mise en oeuvre de la législation communautaire dans les Etats membres*. Institut européen d'administration publique, Synthèses comparatives, no. 1. Brussels: Bruylant, 1988.
Wallace, H., and W. Wallace, eds. *Policy-Making in the European Union*. Oxford: Oxford University Press, 1996.

Chapter 7. The Era of Federalism

Annales de la Faculté Clermont. *Expérience suisse et construction européenne*. Paris: LGDJ, 1989.
Burgess, M. *Federalism and European Union*. London: ABP, 1989.
Cadmos. *Denis de Rougemont*. Geneva: Centre Européen de la Culture, 1986.
———. *La Suisse, l'Europe, et le fédéralisme*. Geneva: Centre Européen de la Culture, 1991.
Carlzon, J. *Renversons la pyramide*. Paris: InterEditions, 1986.
Centre Européen de la Culture. *Fédéralisme, Denis de Rougemont, Europe*. Geneva: Centre Européen de la Culture, 1988.
De Rougemont, D. *L'Europe en jeu*. Neuchâtel: La Baconnière, 1948.
———. *L'aventure occidentale de l'homme*. Paris: Albin Michel, 1957.
———. *Fédéralisme culturel*. Neuchâtel: La Baconnière, 1965.
———. *L'avenir est notre affaire*. Paris: Stock, 1977.
———. *Vingt-huit siècles d'Europe*. Paris: C. de Bartillat, 1990.
———. *Dictionnaire international du fédéralisme*. Brussels: Bruylant, 1994.

Duff, A., ed. *Subsidiarity within the European Community.* London: Federal Trust, 1993.

Giscard D'Estaing, V. *Rapport sur le principe de subsidiarité.* Luxembourg: Parlement européen, 1990–91.

Golub, J., U. Collier, and A. Kreher. *Subsidiarity and Shared Responsibility: New Challenges for EU Environmental Policy.* Baden-Baden: Nomos Verlag, 1997.

Heraud, G. *Les principes du fédéralisme et la fédération européenne.* Paris: Presses d'Europe, 1968.

Herr, R., and S. Weber, eds. *European Integration and American Federalism: A Comparative Perspective.* Berkeley: Center for European Studies, 1996.

Hesse, J. J., and V. Wright, eds. *Federalizing Europe? The Costs, Benefits, and Preconditions of Federal Political Systems.* Oxford: Oxford University Press, 1996.

IEAP. *Subsidiarité: Défi du changement (Actes du colloque Jacques Delors).* Maastricht: L'Institut européen d'administration publique, 1991.

Jeffery, C. *The Regional Dimension of the European Union: Towards a Third Level in Europe?* London: Frank Cass, 1997.

Jeffery, C., and P. Saviegear. eds. *German Federalism Today.* London: Leicester University Press, 1991.

Jeffery, C., and R. Sturm. *Federalism, Unification, and European Integration.* London: Frank Cass, 1993.

Keating, M., and B. Jones, eds. *The European Union and the Regions.* Oxford: Clarendon Press, 1995.

Keating, M., and J. Loughlin, eds. *The Political Economy of Regionalism.* London: Frank Cass, 1997.

Michelmann, H. J., and P. Soldatos, eds. *Federalism and International Relations.* Oxford: Clarendon Press, 1990.

Ohmae, K. *The End of the Nation State.* New York: Free Press, 1995.

Proudhon, P.-J. *Du principe fédératif.* Paris: Bossard, 1921.

Rhodes, M., ed. *The Regions and the New Europe: Patterns in Core and Periphery Development.* Manchester: Manchester University Press, 1995.

Rosnay, J. de. *Cerveau planétaire.* Paris: O. Orban, 1986.

Sidjanski, D. *Fédéralisme amphictyonique.* Lausanne: R. Rouge and Librairie de l'Université, 1956.

———. "Federative Aspects of the European Community." In *Futuribles,* ed. Bertrand de Jouvenel. Geneva: Droz, 1965.

Chapter 8. The Maastricht Treaty: The Deepening of the European Community (1993)

Andersen, S. S., and K. Eliassen, eds. *The European Union: How Democratic Is It?* London: Sage, 1996.

Bigo, D., ed. *L'Europe des polices et de la sécurité intérieure.* Brussels: Complexes, 1992.

Cafruny, A., and C. Lankowski, eds. *Europe's Ambiguous Unity: Conflict and Consensus in the Post-Maastricht Era.* Boulder: Westview, 1997.

Clesse, A., and R. Tokes, eds. *Preventing a New East-West Divide: The Economic and Social Imperatives of the Future Europe*. Baden-Baden: Nomos and Institute for European and International Studies, 1992.

Cloos, J., G. Reinesch, D. Vignes, and J. Weyland. *Le traité de Maastricht: Genèse, analyse, commentaires*. Brussels: Bruylant, 1993.

Collignon, S., et al. *Europe's Monetary Future*. London: Pinter, 1994.

De Schouetheete, P. *La coopération politique européenne*. Paris: Nathan-Labor, 1986.

Doutriaux, Y. *Le Traité sur l'Union européenne*. Paris: A. Colin, 1992.

Follesdal, A., and P. Koslowski, eds. *Democracy and the EU*. Munich: Springer-Verlag, 1997.

Hix, Simon. *The Political System of the European Union*. New York: St. Martin's Press, 1999.

Hooghe, L., ed. *Cohesion Policy and European Intregration: Building Multilevel Governance*. Oxford: Oxford University Press, 1996.

Johnson, C., and S. Collignon, eds. *The Monetary Economics of Europe*. London: Pinter, 1994.

Keohane, R., and S. Hoffman, eds. *The New European Community*. Boulder: Westview, 1991.

Monar, J., et al. *The Maastricht Treaty on European Union Legal Complexity and Political Dynamic*. Brussels: European Interuniversity Press, 1993.

Moravcsik, A. *Why the European Community Strengthens the State: Domestic Politics and International*. Cooperation Center for European Studies, Working Papers, no. 52. Cambridge, MA, 1994.

————. *The Choice for Europe*. London: UCL Press, 1998.

Neunreither, Karlheinz, and Antje Weiner. *European Integration after Amsterdam*. Oxford: Oxford University Press, 2000.

Nonneman, G., ed. *The Middle East and Europe: The Search for Stability and Integration*. London: Federal Trust, 1993.

Norgaard, O., et al., eds. *European Community in World Politics*. London: Pinter, 1993.

Pedersen, T. *European Union and the EFTA Countries: Enlargement and Integration*. London: Pinter, 1994.

Philip Morris Institute for Public Policy Research. *What Will EMU Add up To?* by O. Fanjul, N. Hama, P. Hartmann, J. Hegarty, G. Quaden, and T. Ruhe. Philip Morris Institute for Public Policy Research, Discussion Papers, no. 15, 1998.

Pijpers, A., ed. *The European Community at the Crossroads*. Dordrecht: Martinus Nijhoff, 1992.

Rhodes, C., and S. Maze, eds. *The State of the European Union*. Vol. 3. Boston: L. Rienner, 1995.

Sandholtz, W., and A. Stone Sweet. *European Integration and Supra-national Governance*. Oxford: Oxford University Press, 1998.

Schwok, R. *US-CE Relations in the Post–Cold War Era: Conflict or Partnership?* Boulder: Westview, 1991.

Sharp, J. M. O. *Europe after an American Withdrawal: Economic and Military Issues*. Sipri and Stockholm: Oxford University Press, 1990.

Sidjanski, D. "Come sopravvivere in una economia di guerra." *Revista della fon dazione IBM Italia* 111, no. 1 (1995): 22–28.

Soldatos, P., and C. Philip, eds. *Au delà et en deçà de l'Etat-nation.* Brussels: Bruylant, 1996.

Tamares, R. *La Union Europea.* Madrid: Alianza Editorial Textos, 1994.

Veremis, T., and E. Kofos. *Kosovo: Avoiding Another Balkan War.* Athens: Eliamep, University of Athens, 1998.

Wessels, W., and C. Engel. *From Luxembourg to Maastricht.* Bonn: Europa Union Verlag, 1992.

Chapter 9. The European Community on the Way to Political Union

Aligisakis, M., M. De Bellet, and F. Saint-Ouen, eds. *Europe centrale et orientale: Conflits ou nouvelles cohabitations?* Geneva: Georg, 1997.

Allcock, J. B., J. J. Horton, and M. Milivojevic, eds. *Yugoslavia in Transition: Choices and Constraints.* New York and Oxford: Berg, 1992.

Batakovic, D. T. *Kosovo: La spirale de la Haine.* Lausanne: L'Age d'Homme, 1993.

Bergner, J. T. *The New Superpowers: Germany, Japan, US, and the New World Order.* New York: St. Martin's Press, 1991.

Bodansky, Y. *Offensive in the Balkans: The Potential for a Wider War as a Result of Foreign Intervention in Bosnia-Herzegovina.* London: International Media, 1995.

Brzezinski, Z. *The Grand Chessboard: American Primacy and Its Geostrategic Imperatives.* New York: Basic Books, 1997.

Cohen, L. J. *Broken Bonds: The Disintegration of Yugoslavia.* Boulder: Westview, 1993.

Croft, S., and P. Williams. *European Security without the Soviet Union.* London: Frank Cass, 1992.

Cviic, C. *Remaking the Balkans.* London: Chatan House, Royal Institute of International Affairs, 1991.

Danspeckgruber, F., ed. *Emerging Dimensions of European Security Policy.* Boulder: Westview, 1991.

De Vree, J.-K., et al. *Towards a European Foreign Policy.* Dordrecht, 1987.

Delperee, F., and Y. Lejeune. *La collaboration de l'Etat des Communautés et des régions dans le domaine de la politique extérieure.* Brussels: Bruylant, 1988.

Gautron, J. C., ed. *Les relations CE/Europe de l'Est.* Paris: Economica, 1991.

Gellner, E. *Nations and Nationalism.* Oxford: Blackwell, 1993.

Glenny, M. *The Fall of Yugoslavia.* London: Penguin, 1992.

Gompert, D. C., and S. Larrabee, eds. *America and Europe: A Partnership for a New Era.* Cambridge: Cambridge University Press, 1997.

Ham, P. Van. *The EC, Eastern Europe, and European Unity.* London: Pinter, 1993.

Heraud, G. *L'Europe des Ethnies.* Paris: Presses d'Europe, 1963.

Holbrooke, R. *To End a War.* New York: Random House, 1998.

Janjic, D. *Democracy and Minority Communities.* Belgrade and Subotica: Bosko Kovacevic, 1993.

Kissinger, H. *Diplomacy.* New York and London: Simon and Schuster, 1994.

Laursen, F., and S. Vanhoonacker. *The Intergovernmental Conference on Political Union.* Dordrecht: Martinus Nijhoff and the European Institute of Public Administration, 1992.

Lucarelli, S. *Geopolitics of the Yugoslav Crisis.* Florence: European University Institute, 1993.

Maresceau, M., ed. *Enlarging the European Union: Relations between the European Union and Eastern and Central Europe.* London: Longman, 1997.

Merlino, J. *Les vérités yougoslaves ne sont pas toutes bonnes à dire.* Paris: Albin Michel, 1993.

Mironesco, C. *Un enjeu démocratique: Le "Technology Assessment" Maitrise de la technologie aux Etats-Unis et en Europe.* Geneva: Georg, 1997.

Owen, D. *Balkan Odyssey.* London: Victor Gollancz, 1995.

Pavlovitch, S. K., et al. "La Yougoslavie maillon faible de l'Europe." *Cadmos,* spring 1988.

Peterson, J. *Europe and America: The Prospects for Partnership.* 2d ed. New York: Routledge, 1996.

Pinder, J. *The European Community and Eastern Europe.* New York: Royal Institute of International Affairs, 1991.

Ramet, S. P. *Balkan Babel: Politics, Culture, and Religion in Yugoslavia.* Boulder: Westview, 1992.

Reif, K., ed. *Ten European Elections.* Aldershot and Hampshire: Gower, 1985.

Roessingh, M. A. *Ethnonationalism and Political Systems in Europe: A State of Tension.* Amsterdam: Amsterdam University Press, 1996.

Sidjanski, D. *Union ou désunion de l'Europe: La CE à l'épreuve de la crise yougoslave et des mutations en Europe de l'Est.* Geneva: Dossiers de l'Institut universitaire d'études européennes, 1991.

———. *The ECE in the Age of Change.* New York and Geneva: United Nations Economic Commission for Europe, 1998.

Szporluk, R. *Communism and Nationalism: Karl Marx versus Friedrich List.* New York: Oxford University Press, 1988.

Tchossitch, D. *L'effondrement de la Yougoslavie.* Lausanne: L'Age d'Homme, 1994.

Thomson, M. *Forging War: The Media in Serbia, Croatia, and Bosnia-Hercegovina.* London: International Centre against Censorship, 1994.

Woodward, S. L. *Balkan Tragedy: Chaos and Dissolution after the Cold War.* Washington, DC: Brookings Institution, 1995.

Wynaendts, H. *L'engrenage: Chroniques yougoslaves juillet 1991–août 1992.* Paris: Denoel, 1992.

Zametica, J. *The Yugoslav Conflict.* Adelphi Papers, no. 270. London: Adelphi, 1992.

Zimmermann, W. "Origins of a Catastrophe: Memoirs of the Last American Ambassador to Yugoslavia." *Foreign Affairs,* March–April 1995.

Official Documents and Publications of the European Community and the European Union, Luxembourg

Treaty of Rome, Luxembourg, Office for Official Publications of the European Communities, 1973.

Treaty on European Union (Maastricht Treaty), Luxembourg, 1992.

European Commission. *Acte unique européen.* Luxembourg: Office des publications des CE, Bulletin des CE, Suppl. 2/86, 1986.

Parlement Européen. *Les partis politiques dans la CEE et l'unification européenne.* Direction générale des études, Série politique, no. 10, 1988.

European Union. *Treaty of Amsterdam.* Luxembourg: Office for Official Publications of the European Communities, 1997.

Official Journal of the European Communities. *Treaty of Amsterdam amending the Treaty on European Union, the Treaties establishing the European Communities, and certain related acts signed in Amsterdam, 2 October 1997 (entered into force on 1st May 1999); Consolidated Version of the Treaty on European Union: Consolidated Version of the Treaty establishing the European Community.* C 340, vol. 40, 10 November 1997.

Secretariat General du Conseil et Commission. *Treaty on European Union* (Traité sur l'Union européenne). Luxembourg: European Community, 1992.

European Parliament
  List of Members
  (Bureaus, Parliament, political groups, committees, and interparliamentary delegations)
  Official acts, reports, proceedings, etc.
European Council
  Presidential conclusions
  Annual reports
  Documents of intergovernmental conferences
European Commission
  General Report on the Activities of the European Union (annual 1997, 1998)
  Bulletin of the European Commission (monthly)
  White papers, reports, and studies
  Commission Report for the Reflection Group, Intergovernmental Conference, 1996. Brussels and Luxembourg: European Commission, 1995.
Court of Justice and Court of First Instance
  Cases and jurisprudence
Court of Auditors
  Reports and opinions
Economic and Social Committee and Committee of the Regions
  Annual reports
  Documents and reports
  Opinions

Index

Commission of the European Community (*continued*)
decision-making, 159–60; and European Council, 84–85, 125; and foreign policy making, 313; and interest groups, 149; and investiture, 246; and number of commissioners, 327–28; and Prodi Commission, 377–79; and Santer Commission, 321–22, 373–77
Committee of Permanent Representatives (Coreper), 78, 83–84, 177; and European Council, 124, 158
Committee of Professional Agricultural Organizations in the EC (COPA), 69–70, 72, 88, 145, 175
Committee of the Regions, 209–10, 241–42, 327, 348, 416. *See also* Regions
Common Agricultural Policy (CAP), 74, 116, 291–92; and Empty Chair Crisis, 70, 74
Common Foreign and Security Policy (CFSP), 54, 57, 275–318, 348–55, 362–64, 404–10; and decision-making, 270–71, 285–88; and defense policy, 282–85, 354–55; and European Commission, 290–91; and European Council, 277–78; instruments of, 278–80; and post-communist era, 269–75, 409; and Yugoslav crisis, 307–11
Common Market, 66–67, 106. *See also* European Economic Community
Commonwealth of Independent States (CIS). *See* Russia
Community Support Framework (CSF), 132
Conciliation Committee, 255–59. *See also* Decision making
Confederation of British Industry, 253, 324
Congress of Hague. *See* European movements
Congress of Montreux. *See* European movements
Consultation procedures, 157–58; and committees, 86–89, 173–79; and European Parliament, 94

Convention on Human Rights (Council of Europe), 61, 411
Coordinating Committee, 265–66
Coreper. *See* Committee of Permanent Representatives
Costa, Carlos, 295
Coudenhove-Kalergi, Richard. *See* Pan-European Union
Council of Europe, 20, 21, 39, 60, 228, 306, 317; and European Parliamentary Assembly, 22, 61
Council of Ministers. *See* European Council
Court of Auditors, 95, 250–51
Court of Human Rights, 20
Court of Justice, 36, 105, 260–61, 347–48, 373
Crocodile Club, 78, 100–101. *See also* Spinelli, Altiero
Culture, 197; and cultural heritage, 366; and cultural resolution of the Hague Congress, 22

Darmon, Richard, 214
Davignon, Etienne, 55, 79
Debré, Michel, and *Project of a Fundamental Pact between European States,* 10, 25–30, 45
Decision-making, 54, 155–69; and Maastricht Treaty, 253–62, 277; and national parliaments, 179–80. *See also* European Council; Interest groups
Defense. *See* Common Foreign and Security Policy; European Defense Community
De Gasperi, Alcido, 22, 65
De Gaulle, Charles, 43, 45, 48–51, 65, 68, 74, 107, 227, 372; and political union, 122. *See also* Empty Chair Crisis
Dehousse, Fernand, 34, 64
De Jouvenel, Bertrand, 137, 179, 221
Delors, Jacques, 24, 65, 77, 79–80, 95, 112, 178, 289, 357; and Delors Report, 209; and Gulf crisis, 293; and diversity, 208; and subsidiarity, 226
Democracy (principle of), 104, 228, 303, 341, 371; and nationalism, 315–